Minority Voting
in the United States

Minority Voting in the United States

Native American, Jewish American, Arab and Muslim American, Asian American, and LGBT Voters

Volume 2

Kyle L. Kreider and
Thomas J. Baldino, Editors

An Imprint of ABC-CLIO, LLC
Santa Barbara, California • Denver, Colorado

Copyright © 2016 by Kyle L. Kreider and Thomas J. Baldino

All rights reserved. No part of this publication may be reproduced, stored in a retrieval system, or transmitted, in any form or by any means, electronic, mechanical, photocopying, recording, or otherwise, except for the inclusion of brief quotations in a review, without prior permission in writing from the publisher.

Library of Congress Cataloging-in-Publication Data

Names: Kreider, Kyle L. editor. | Baldino, Thomas J. (Thomas Joseph) editor.
Title: Minority voting in the United States : African American voters, women voters, and Latino / Latina Americans / Kyle L. Kreider and Thomas J. Baldino, editors.
Description: Santa Barbara, California : Praeger, an Imprint of ABC-CLIO, LLC, [2016] | Includes bibliographical references and index.
Identifiers: LCCN 2015024853 | ISBN 9781440830235 (alk. paper) | ISBN 9781440830242 (EISBN)
Subjects: LCSH: Elections—United States. | Voting—United States. | Minorities—Political activity—United States. | Immigrants—Political activity—United States. | Political participation—United States. | African Americans—Political activity. | Women—Political activity—United States. | Hispanic Americans—Political activity.
Classification: LCC JK1967 .M57 2016 | DDC 324.973008—dc23 LC record available at http://lccn.loc.gov/2015024853

ISBN: 978-1-4408-3023-5
EISBN: 978-1-4408-3024-2

20 19 18 17 16   1 2 3 4 5

This book is also available on the World Wide Web as an eBook.
Visit www.abc-clio.com for details.

Praeger
An Imprint of ABC-CLIO, LLC

ABC-CLIO, LLC
130 Cremona Drive, P.O. Box 1911
Santa Barbara, California 93116-1911

This book is printed on acid-free paper ∞

Manufactured in the United States of America

Contents

PART IV: NATIVE AMERICAN VOTERS

1. The Right to Vote: A History of Voting Rights and American Indians 3
   Jennifer L. Robinson

2. Native Americans: Voting for Sovereignty and Treaty Rights 26
   Bruce E. Johansen

3. Issues and American Indian Voting 41
   Richard C. Witmer

PART V: JEWISH AMERICAN VOTERS

4. An Introduction to the American Jewish Voter 61
   Ira M. Sheskin

5. The Persisting Liberalism of (Most) American Jews: The Pew Survey of 2013 in Historical Context 95
   Samuel J. Abrams and Steven M. Cohen

PART VI: ARAB AND MUSLIM AMERICAN VOTERS

6. Arab American Voters: The Ballot Box as a
   Vehicle for Community Empowerment   127
   Maya Berry

7. The Political Incorporation and Mobilization
   of American Muslims   155
   Farid Senzai

8. Political Participation of American Muslims in Detroit   179
   Juris Pupcenoks and Farid Senzai

PART VII: ASIAN AMERICAN VOTERS

9. Asian American Voting Rights   205
   Glenn D. Magpantay

10. South Asian Americans: New American Voters
    in a Changing Nation   236
    Deepa Iyer

11. Voting Patterns among Pacific Islanders   247
    Peggy Spitzer Christoff

12. Filipino American Voting   264
    Joaquin Jay Gonzalez III

13. Minority Voting in the United States: East Asian Americans   283
    Jeanette Yih Harvie and Pei-te Lien

14. From Central Cities to Ethnoburbs: Asian American Political
    Incorporation in the San Francisco Bay Area   304
    James S. Lai

15. Korean American Voting Behavior   326
    Yoon M. Lee

16. Electoral Turnout among Vietnamese Americans   349
    Loan K. Le and Phi Hong Su

PART VIII: LESBIAN, GAY, BISEXUAL, AND TRANSGENDER AMERICAN VOTERS

17. The Voting Behavior of Lesbian, Gay, Bisexual, and
    Transgender People in the United States   371
    Barry L. Tadlock

18. From Freedom to Equality: Marriage and the Shifted Priorities
    of Lesbians, Gay Men, Bisexuals, and Transgender People   390
    Andrew R. Flores and Kenneth Sherrill

19. Transgender Voters   408
    Patrick A. Paschall

Conclusion: Minority Voters—Present and Future   431

About the Editors and Contributors   439

Index   447

Part IV

Native American Voters

Chapter 1

The Right to Vote: A History of Voting Rights and American Indians

Jennifer L. Robinson

The establishment of the U.S. government more than 200 years ago placed American Indians in a complex legal position that often resulted in the denial of their voting rights well into the 20th century. Even after passage of the Indian Citizenship Act in 1924, which granted Indians U.S. citizenship, new barriers were constructed by state and local governments to bar Indians' participation in the electoral process. The Voting Rights Act of 1965 and subsequent litigation forced change in electoral systems throughout the nation that have helped ensure American Indians' rights to participate fully in elections. This chapter explores these changes as they relate to the right to vote for American Indians.

HISTORY OF VOTING RIGHTS FOR AMERICAN INDIANS

The history of voting rights for American Indians is complex, primarily due to the unique legal status of this minority group that dates to the nation's founding. The U.S. Constitution references American Indians in two articles, but neither clarifies their relationship with the federal government. In Article 1, Section 2, "Indians not taxed," excludes Native Americans for purposes of congressional district apportionment.[1] Article

1, Section 8, assigns Congress the power "to regulate commerce with foreign nations, and among the several states, and with the Indian tribes."[2] The Constitution's Framers struggled with the exact legal status of American Indians, a struggle that continues well into the 21st century.

Between 1790 and 1834, Congress passed the Trade and Intercourse Acts, a series of laws that consolidated the federal government's control over Indian affairs. "The central policy embodied in the Acts was one of separating Indian and non-Indians and subjecting nearly all interaction between the two groups to federal control" rather than to state control.[3] Congressional action was only one factor in establishing federal control over Indian affairs, as the Supreme Court soon weighed in on the issue, and solidified federal power over Indian affairs.

The Marshall Trilogy

The Supreme Court first engaged in defining the relationship between American Indians and the United States during the 1800s. Three cases, known as the "Marshall Trilogy," illustrate the difficulty in establishing the legal status of American Indians.[4] The central issue in the first Marshall case, *Johnson v. M'Intosh* (1823) was the Doctrine of Discovery: the agreement among European nations that once a European power claimed "discovery" of a particular tract of land, the Indians' rights to transfer their land were limited to a transfer to the "discovering Nation."[5]

The agreement served a dual purpose. It prevented Europe's nations from warring with each other over the right to possess the lands of the various Indian tribes while also restricting the rights of the Indians themselves to sell their lands freely. The issue before the Court then was whether land transfers from a tribe to a non-Indian were superior to land transfers made by a foreign power laying claim to the same property under the Doctrine of Discovery. The Supreme Court determined that Indians retain the right of occupancy that was extinguishable only by discovering European sovereigns.[6]

The second case, *Cherokee Nation v. Georgia* (1831), involved two important questions. Constitutionally speaking, the primary question was whether the Cherokee Nation was a foreign nation that could file suit under the Supreme Court's original jurisdiction. The second issue revolved around the sovereignty of Indian nations and the role of state governments in relation to tribes.

Georgia had divided the Cherokee territory, invalidated all Cherokee laws, and made criminal any attempts of the Cherokee to act as a government.[7] The Cherokee nation sought an injunction to prevent Georgia from enforcing state laws on the Cherokee tribal territory.

At the time of the case, the Supreme Court had original jurisdiction over cases filed against the United States by a foreign nation;[8] thus, in *Cherokee*

Nation v. Georgia, the Court initially had to determine whether the Cherokee nation was a foreign state in the sense of the U.S. Constitution. The Court ultimately determined that Indian tribes are not foreign nations, but rather, the Court described them as domestic dependent nations and wards of the government.

> Though the Indians are acknowledged to have an unquestionable, and, heretofore unquestioned right to the lands they occupy, until that right shall be extinguished by a voluntary cession to our government, yet it may well be doubted whether those tribes which reside within the acknowledged boundaries of the United States can, with strict accuracy, be denominated foreign nations. They may, more correctly, perhaps, be denominated domestic dependent nations. They occupy a territory to which we assert a title independent of their will, which must take effect in point of possession when their right of possession ceases. Meanwhile they are in a state of pupilage. Their relation to the United States resembles that of a ward to his guardian.[9]

In ruling that it lacked jurisdiction, the Court never reached the question of its own power over the state of Georgia.

The following term, the Court again addressed the issue of state jurisdiction over a tribe in *Worcester v. Georgia* (1832). Samuel Worcester, along with others, all of whom were residents of the state of Vermont, had been arrested for preaching among the Cherokee without a state license and in violation of Georgia state law. Georgia law required non-Indians residing on Indian territory to obtain a license from the state government.

The Court ruled that it did have jurisdiction in the case. Further, the Marshall Court established the limitation of the power of states to interfere with the activities of a tribe within the tribes' own lands.

The Marshall Trilogy established tribes as distinct, independent communities and are "the foundation of jurisdictional law excluding the states from power over Indian affairs."[10] The trilogy also solidified congressional power over Indian tribes exclusive of the States.

Citizenship for American Indians

In 1866, Congress was intent on establishing civil rights for freed slaves while simultaneously struggling with the status of American Indians. Two pieces of legislation are noteworthy: the Civil Rights Act of 1866 and the Fourteenth Amendment. Passed over President Andrew Johnson's veto, the Civil Rights Act states:

> That all persons born in the United States and not subject to any foreign power, excluding Indians not taxed, are hereby declared to be

citizens of the United States; and such citizens, of every race and color, without regard to any previous condition of slavery or involuntary servitude, except as a punishment for crime whereof the party shall have been duly convicted, shall have the same right, in every State and Territory in the United States, to make and enforce contracts, to sue, be parties, and give evidence, to inherit, purchase, lease, sell, hold, and convey real and personal property, and to full and equal benefit of all laws and proceedings for the security of person and property, as is enjoyed by white citizens, and shall be subject to like punishment, pains, and penalties, and to none other, any law, statute, ordinance, regulation, or custom, to the contrary notwithstanding.[11]

While the Civil Rights Act of 1866 provided citizenship to all persons born in the United States and afforded them all the benefits and rights of citizenship, it excluded American Indians "not taxed" from these benefits. The Fourteenth Amendment's language further guaranteed and protected the rights of freed slaves as citizens of the United States but excluded Indians not taxed. "In large part the Amendment was designed to ensure the constitutionality of the [Civil Rights] Act."[12] It reads:

Section 1. All persons born or naturalized in the United States and subject to the jurisdiction thereof, are citizens of the United States and of the State wherein they reside. No State shall make or enforce any law which shall abridge the privileges or immunities of citizens of the United States; nor shall any State deprive any person of life, liberty, or property, without due process of law; nor deny to any person within its jurisdiction the equal protection of the laws.
Section 2. Representatives shall be apportioned among the several States according to their respective numbers, counting the whole number of persons in each State, excluding Indians not taxed.

The debate within Congress to include "Indians not taxed" was part of a larger argument over the nation's Indian policy. Senator Doolittle argued for the inclusion of the phrase "Indians not taxed" in the Fourteenth Amendment on two grounds. First, Indians were an inferior race; and second, if Indians gained the right to vote, they would be the political majority in many areas of the country.[13] The Doolittle argument persevered, and the phrase "Indians not taxed" was included in the Fourteenth Amendment, deliberately denying citizenship and the rights and privileges it affords to American Indians.

The Supreme Court decision in *Elk v. Wilkins* (1894), addressed not only the Indian citizenship issue but also the application of the Fourteenth Amendment to American Indians. John Elk, an Indian living in Omaha, Nebraska, was denied the right to vote in the state although he was subject

Amendment."[41] The prior method of addressing voting discrimination, litigation on a case-by-case basis, was not an effective remedy for ending discrimination.[42] "Even those judges who sought to eliminate discriminatory barriers found that every time the courts struck down one procedure, Southern local officials or state legislators devised newer, more subtle ways of minimizing Black voter registration."[43]

The congressional hearings revealed that the efforts of the U.S. Department of Justice to eliminate discriminatory election practices by litigation on a case-by-case basis had been unsuccessful in opening up the registration process. "As soon as one discriminatory practice or procedure was proven to be unconstitutional and enjoined, a new one would be substituted in its place and litigation would have to commence anew."[44] President Johnson and members of Congress intentionally designed the Voting Rights Act to increase the power of the U.S. Department of Justice and to force states and local jurisdictions with a history of voting discrimination to justify changes to their voting laws, thus ending the case-by-case approach.

The 1965 law initially suspended literacy tests and other voter qualifying devices in certain covered jurisdictions, authorized federal supervision of voter registration and new voting laws in covered jurisdictions, and created a triggering formula to bring states and local jurisdictions under the law. Under the original trigger formula, if a state or local jurisdiction had a literacy test or similar voter qualification device in effect on November 1, 1964, and if less than 50 percent of the voting-age residents were registered to vote on November 1, 1964, or actually voted in the 1964 presidential election, then the jurisdiction would be under federal supervision.

Several components of the Voting Rights Act deserve special attention. Section 2 is a key provision that prohibits voting practices or procedures that discriminate on the basis of race, color, or membership in one of the language minority groups protected by the Act.[45] Section 2, unlike some provisions of the Voting Rights Act, is permanent and does not have an expiration date nor does it require renewal. Most cases under Section 2 involve challenges to at-large election systems. Of the 74 American Indian voting rights cases identified by McCool, Olson, and Robinson (2007), 26 of the cases are challenges to at-large election systems, more than any other type of voting rights case.[46] Section 3 of the Voting Rights Act details remedies the courts can impose if they find a jurisdiction in violation of Section 2.

Of particular importance to Indian voting rights is Section 5 under which any change with respect to voting in certain states and subdivisions of states must receive approval either from the U.S. District Court for the District of Columbia or from the attorney general,[47] a requirement contained in the 1965 Act. The covered jurisdictions were identified by a formula in Section 4 of the Voting Rights Act. The jurisdictions originally covered by Section 5 were: Alabama, Alaska, Georgia, Louisiana, Mississippi, South Carolina, Virginia, and political subdivisions (mostly counties) in Arizona, Hawaii, Idaho, and North Carolina.[48]

Section 5 was renewed in 1970, 1975, 1982, and 2006. In 1975, in addition to renewing Section 5, Congress changed the coverage formula in Section 4 to include language minority groups. In 2006, Congress extended Section 5 for an additional 25 years.[49] Nine states were covered in their entirety under Section 5: Alabama, Alaska, Arizona, Georgia, Louisiana, Mississippi, South Carolina, Texas, and Virginia. Seven additional states had counties, cities, or towns covered: California, Florida, New York, North Carolina, South Dakota, Michigan, and New Hampshire. Jurisdictions covered under Section 5 were required to preclear any change in voting practice or procedure and prove that the change does not have a discriminatory purpose or effect. In 2013, the Supreme Court's decision in *Shelby County v. Holder* (2013) had a significant impact on Section 5. The court found Section 4 of the Voting Rights Act, the formula for determining coverage, unconstitutional.[50] Although the Court did not rule on Section 5 specifically, the decision effectively renders the section powerless.

Sections 6, 7, and 8 authorize the U.S. attorney general to appoint federal examiners and observers in covered jurisdictions. Section 10 authorizes the U.S. attorney general to bring litigation challenging a voting practice or procedure that violates the Voting Rights Act. Section 11 provides criminal penalties for those who intimidate voters or impede the vote counting in federal elections. Section 12 authorizes the U.S. attorney general to bring civil actions; it also provides penalties to protect ballots and voting records for one year after an election. Section 13 provides the conditions for terminating federal oversight. Section 14 establishes a broad definition of vote and voting.

THE VOTING RIGHTS ACT AND SUPREME COURT RULINGS

The Voting Rights Act's constitutionality was challenged shortly after its passage. In *South Carolina v. Katzenbach* (383 U.S. 301, 1966) the Supreme Court upheld it, ruling that "Congress had found that case-by-case litigation was inadequate to combat widespread and persistent discrimination in voting because of the inordinate amount of time and energy required to overcome the obstructionist tactics invariably encountered in these lawsuits."

Although the constitutionality of its basic provisions were upheld in *South Carolina v. Katzenbach*, specific issues with the Act arose, particularly with Section 2 as it relates to minority vote dilution. In *White v. Regester* (412 U.S. 755, 1973), an early Supreme Court case addressing minority vote dilution, "The Court revisited the issue of vote dilution and, for the first time, invalidated a multimember legislative redistricting plan on the grounds that it discriminated against minorities in violation of the Fourteenth Amendment."[51] At issue in the case was a multimember district in Texas. Plaintiffs claimed that the system resulted in the defeat of minority candidates. The plaintiffs provided evidence of the history of discrimination, cultural and language barriers, depressed voter registration, racial slating process, and racial campaign tactics. The Court focused not on the motivation behind the law but on its consequences, depriving minorities of equal access to the election process and the totality of circumstances.[52]

In *Zimmer v. McKeithen* (485 F.2d 1297, 1973) the Fifth Court of Appeals, comprising at that time the states of Alabama, Florida, Georgia, Louisiana, Mississippi, and Texas, formalized the totality of circumstances approach.[53] At issue was an at-large voting system in Louisiana. The Court found that a constitutional violation could be shown either by a racially motivated gerrymander or by a plan that "designedly or otherwise ... would operate to minimize or cancel out" minority voting strength.[54]

> The court of appeals identified four primary factors probative of vote dilution: 1) lack of access to candidate slating; 2) unresponsiveness; 3) a tenuous state policy underlying the challenged practice; and 4) the existence of past discrimination that precluded effective minority political participation. Vote dilution could be shown by proof of an aggregate of Zimmer factors, but no particular factor or number of factors had to be proven.[55]

In both *White* and *Zimmer*, the Court found that at-large systems were not per se unconstitutional, but at-large systems were struck down when based on the totality of the circumstances. It could be proven that minority voters were denied an equal opportunity to participate in the electoral process.[56] The effects standard established in *White* and *Zimmer* became the applicable standard in vote dilution cases. However, the Court abruptly shifted position in 1980 in *Mobile v. Bolden*, addressed later.

In 1975, Congress extended for an additional seven years the Act's temporary provisions. In addition to the seven-year extension, two critical elements were added. The law made permanent the temporary ban on literacy tests, and it extended new coverage for language minority voters. Language minorities are defined as persons of Spanish heritage, American Indians, Asian Americans, and Alaskan Natives who live in jurisdictions where (1) the U.S. Census Bureau determined that more than 5 percent of voting-age citizens were of a single-language minority, (2) election materials had been printed only in English for the 1972 presidential election, and (3) less than 50 percent of voting-age citizens had registered or voted in the 1972 presidential election.

The 1975 amendment also added Section 203, which was designed to increase election turnout among language minorities by requiring certain jurisdictions to provide voting materials and oral assistance to language minority voters. Covered language minorities were limited to American Indians, Asian Americans, Alaskan Natives, and Spanish-heritage citizens—the minority groups Congress found to have faced barriers in the political process. A jurisdiction is covered under Section 203 in which the number of U.S. citizens of voting age is a single-language group within the jurisdiction. The number of U.S. citizens of voting age (1) is more than 10,000; or (2) is more than 5 percent of all voting-age citizens; or (3) is on an Indian reservation and exceeds 5 percent of all reservation residents; or (4) has a illiteracy rate as a group higher than the national illiteracy rate.

If a jurisdiction is subject to Section 203, it must provide "any registration or voting notices, forms, instructions, assistance, or other materials or information relating to the electoral process, including ballots, [and] it shall provide them in the language of the applicable language minority group as well as in English," or if the language is unwritten, as for some American Indians and Alaskan natives, oral assistance and publicity are required.[57] Currently, 80 local jurisdictions, in 17 states, are required to provide minority language assistance to American Indian voters under Section 203. Additional jurisdictions are covered under the law for minority language voters other than American Indians.

In 1980, the Supreme Court "dramatically altered the legal standard for proving unlawful dilution of minority voting strength" in *Mobile v. Bolden*.[58] In *Mobile*, the Court required that plaintiffs must show that the voting system or procedure was established or was being maintained with a racially discriminatory purpose.[59] The *Zimmer* factors, as earlier established by the Court as a standard for examining vote discrimination claims, were deemed insufficient by the Court in its ruling. The earlier standard established in *White v. Regester* (412 U.S. 755, 1973), that vote dilution be judged on an effects standard, that is, the system or procedure has the effect of discrimination, was superseded by the *Mobile* decision. The new *Mobile* standard required that any claim of vote dilution was to include proof of racially discriminatory purpose or intent.

In response to the Supreme Court's decision in *Mobile v. Bolden* (446 U.S. 55, 1980), Congress amended Section 2 in 1982 to prohibit vote dilution without requiring proof of discriminatory purpose. According to McCrary, "In the view of many observers, the *Mobile* decision was inconsistent with the intent of Congress when it adopted and expanded the Voting Rights Act in 1965, 1970, and 1975," which, therefore, led Congress to cite "the 'totality of circumstances' test of *White* and *Zimmer* as the evidentiary standard to be used in applying the Section 2 results test."[60]

Parker also concluded that "Both the House and Senate reports indicate that a purpose of the Section 2 amendment incorporating the 'results' test was to restate the original legislative intent of Congress that a Section 2 violation could be made out by showing a discriminatory effect or result." In particular, a compelling piece of evidence for this position was a comment made by then Attorney General Nicholas Katzenbach that Section 2's prohibitions included "any kind of practice . . . if its purpose or effect was to deny or abridge the right to vote on account of race or color."[61] The amendment passed by "huge veto-proof majorities in both houses of Congress."[62]

The first review of the amended Voting Rights Act by the Supreme Court was *Thornburg v. Gingles* (478 U.S. 30, 1986). The Supreme Court's ruling brought "both simplicity and predictability to vote dilution challenges."[63] The majority of the Court majority held that in order for a Section 2 violation to be established in a challenge to multimember districts, the following three criteria must be met: (1) The minority population must be "sufficiently large and geographically compact" to constitute a majority in one or more districts; (2) the minority population must be "politically cohesive"; and (3) the majority population must vote as a bloc usually to defeat the minority's preferred candidate.[64]

If the minority population is not large enough and compact, they are unable to claim that at-large electoral structures or practices dilute their ability to elect a candidate of their choice. "Unless minority voters possess the potential to elect representatives in the absence of the challenged structure or practice, they cannot claim to have been injured by the structure or practice."[65] If the minority group is not politically cohesive, it "cannot be said that the selection of a multimember electoral structure thwarts distinctive minority group interest."[66] Once these three preconditions are met, the Court then determines on the "totality of circumstances" whether the minority population has been denied an equal opportunity to elect representatives of their choice. The courts have relied upon the legislative history of the 1982 Amendment to assist in this determination.[67] As stated in the Senate Judiciary Committee majority report,[68] the factors are:

1. The extent of any history of official discrimination in the state or political subdivision that touched the right of the members of the minority group to register, to vote, or otherwise to participate in the democratic process.
2. The extent to which voting in the elections of the state or political subdivision is racially polarized.
3. The extent to which the state or political subdivision has used unusually large election districts, majority vote requirements, antisingle shot provisions, or other voting practices or procedures that may enhance the opportunity for discrimination against the minority group.

4. If there is a candidate's slating process, whether the members of the minority group have been denied access to that process.
5. The extent to which the members of the minority group in the state or political subdivision bear the effects of discrimination in such areas as education, employment, and health, which hinders their ability to participate effectively in the political process.
6. Whether the political campaigns have been characterized by overt or subtle racial appeals.
7. The extent to which members of a minority group have been elected to public office in the jurisdiction.
8. Whether there is a significant lack of responsiveness on the part of election officials to the particularized needs of the member of the minority group.
9. Whether the policy underlying the state or political subdivisions' use of such voting qualifications, prerequisites to voting, standards, practice or procedure is tenuous.[69]

These factors are a clear standard for states and local jurisdictions to follow in redistricting processes and act as a simplified standard for the courts in determining vote dilution.

In 1992, Congress passed the Voting Rights Language Assistance Act, an amendment to the Voting Rights Act, which requires election information in the language of any language minority group in a county if 10,000 or more such speakers are also of limited English proficiency, which is defined as those who do not speak or understand English adequately enough to participate in the electoral process. In addition, the Amendment requires counties to provide minority language assistance if 5 percent of a reservation's population is eligible for assistance regardless of its proportion of the county population.[70]

More recently, in 2006, Congress amended the Act in response to its findings that although much progress had been made to ensure minority voting rights, "Vestiges of discrimination in voting continue to exist."[71]

> The record compiled by Congress demonstrates that, without the continuation of the Voting Rights Act of 1965 protections, racial and language minority citizens will be deprived of the opportunity to exercise their right to vote, or will have their votes diluted, undermining the significant gains made by minorities in the last 40 years.[72]

The Act extended the temporary provisions for an additional 25 years in. In addition to the extension, Congress restored the broader definition of purposeful discrimination and the emphasis on a minority community's

32. Allen, "Denial of Voting Rights to Reservation Indians."
33. Allen, "Denial of Voting Rights to Reservation Indians"; *Allen v. Merrell*, 1956.
34. *Allen v. Merrell*, 1956, 492.
35. Ibid.
36. Peterson 1956, 121.
37. An earlier case challenging guardianship is *Porter v. Hall* (1928).
38. Cohen, *Handbook of Federal Indian Law*, 158; Council of State Governments, "Voting in the United States." According to the Council of State Governments (1940), Rhode Island law stated that "Narragansett Indians are excluded from suffrage."
39. See, for example, *Trujillo v. Garley* (1948), *Harrison v. Laveen* (1948), *Shirley v. Superior Court* (1973), and *Prince v. Board of Education* (1975).
40. Wolfley, "Jim Crow, Indian Style," 167.
41. U.S. Department of Justice, 2002.
42. Davidson, "Voting Rights Act: A Brief History"; McCrary, "Bringing Equality to Power"; McDonald, Quiet Revolution in Minority Voting Rights."
43. McCrary, "Bringing Equality to Power," 685.
44. U.S. Department of Justice, 2002.
45. Section 203 of the Voting Rights Act targets those language minorities who have suffered a history of exclusion from the political process (i.e., Spanish, Asian, Native American, and Alaskan Native). The Census Bureau identifies specific language groups for specific jurisdictions. In some jurisdictions, two or more language minority groups are present in numbers sufficient to trigger the Section 203 requirements (http://www.usdoj.gov/crt/voting/sec_203/203_brochure.php).
46. McCool, Olson, and Robinson, *Native Vote*.
47. Section 5 is a temporary provision of the Voting Rights Act, and it was included in the original legislation passed in 1965. It was renewed several times. In 1970, it was renewed for 5 more years, with a new coverage formula; in 1975, it was renewed for 7 more years, with an additional formula to protect language minorities; in 1982, it was renewed for 25 years, and it did not include a new formula; and in 2006, it was renewed again for an additional 25 years.
48. Davidson, "Voting Rights Act: A Brief History," 118; U.S. Department of Justice, 2008.
49. The title of the 2006 voting rights bill is the Fannie Lou Hamer, Rosa Parks, and Coretta Scott King Voting Rights Act Reauthorization and Amendments Act.
50. *Shelby County v. Holder*, 2013.
51. The Court had previously ruled on vote dilution in *Reynolds v. Sims* (1964), *Fortson v. Dorsey* (1965), and *Whitcomb v. Chavis* (1971). In *Reynolds*, the Court ruled that the right to vote can be abridged unconstitutionally by a dilution of one's voting strength as well as by outright denial of the ballot. In *Fortson*, the Court recognized that particular apportionment schemes may undervalue the votes of disfavored groups but declined to hold multimember districts as unconstitutional. In *Whitcomb*, the Court held that the fact the minorities were disproportionately underrepresented did not prove a constitutional violation unless they had been denied equal access to the political process by the electoral system (Parker 1983); McDonald, "Counterrevolution in Minority Voting Rights," 276.

52. Parker, 1983.
53. McDonald, "Counterrevolution in Minority Voting Rights," 277.
54. *Zimmer v. McKeithen*, 1973.
55. McDonald, "Counterrevolution in Minority Voting Rights," 277.
56. Parker, "Racial Gerrymandering and Legislative Reapportionment."
57. Voting Rights Act.
58. Parker 1983, 729.
59. McDonald, "Counterrevolution in Minority Voting Rights," 278–279.
60. McCrary, Bringing Equality to Power," 698.
61. Parker 1983, 726.
62. Davidson, "Voting Rights Act: A Brief History," 40.
63. McDonald, "Counterrevolution in Minority Voting Rights," 282.
64. *Thornburg v. Gingles*, 1986.
65. Ibid., 50.
66. Ibid.
67. *Buckanaga v. Sisseton School District*, 1986; *Windy Boy v. Big Horn County, Montana*, 1986; *Cuthair v. Montezuma-Cortez, Colorado School District*, 1998.
68. U.S. Congress, 1982. Report of the Committee on the Judiciary of S. 1992 with Additionally Minority and Supplemental Views.
69. Ibid., 206–207.
70. Voting Rights Language Assistance Act.
71. Fannie Lou Hamer, Rosa Parks, and Coretta Scott King Voting Rights and Reauthorization and Amendments Act of 2006.
72. Ibid.
73. Ibid.
74. American Civil Liberties Union 2009, 11.
75. *Northwest Austin Municipal Utility District v. Holder* (2009). 557 U.S. 193.
76. *Shelby County, Alabama v. Holder* (2013) 570 U.S.
77. Ibid.
78. Robinson, "Empowerment of American Indians."
79. McDonald, "Quiet Revolution in Minority Voting Rights."
80. McCool, Olson, and Robinson, *Native Vote*, 155–158.
81. Robinson, "Empowerment of American Indians."
82. Davidson and Korbel, "At-Large Elections and Minority Group Representation"; Engstrom and McDonald, "Election of Blacks to City Councils"; Grofman and Davidson, The Effects of Municipal Election Structure on Black Representation"; Karnig, Black Representation on City Councils"; McCool, Olson, and Robinson, *Native Vote*; Robinson and Dye, "Reformism and Black representation"; Taebel, "Minority representation on City Councils." A handful of studies have failed to show the detrimental effects of at-large elections on minority candidates (e.g., Cole, "*Blacks in Power*"; Cole, "Electing Blacks to Municipal Office"; MacManus, City council Election Procedures and Minority Representation"; and Welch and Karnig, "Representation of Blacks on Big City School Boards").
83. McCool, Olson, and Robinson, *Native Vote*.
84. Ibid.
85. McDonald, "Quiet Revolution in Minority Voting Rights," 1277.
86. McCool, Olson, and Robinson, *Native Vote*.

REFERENCES

Allen, John H. "Denial of Voting Rights to Reservation Indians." *Utah Law Review* 5.2 (1956): 247–256.
Allen v. Merrell.1956. 305 P.2d 490 (Utah); 6 Utah 2d 32; 1956. cert granted, 352 U.S. 889; 1957. vacated as moot 353 U.S. 932.
American Civil Liberties Union. *Voting Rights in Indian Country: A Special Report of the Voting Rights Project of the American Civil Liberties Union*. Atlanta: GA: ACLU. 2009.
Buckanaga v. Sisseton School District. 1986. 804 F. 2d 469 (8th Cir.)
Canby, William C., Jr. *American Indian Law in a Nut Shell*. 5th ed. St. Paul, MN: West Publishing Company, 2009.
Cherokee Nation v. Georgia. 1831. 30 U.S. (5 Pet) I.
Civil Rights Act of 1866. 1866. Statutes at Large of the USA 14:27.
Cohen, Felix. *Handbook of Federal Indian Law*. Washington, DC: U.S. Government Printing Office, 1942.
Cohen, William, and Jonathan D. Varat. *Constitutional Law: Cases and Materials*. 10th ed. Westbury, NY: The Foundation Press, Inc., 1997.
Cole, Leonard. *Blacks in Power: A Comparative Study of Black and White Elected Officials*. Princeton, NJ: Princeton University Press, 1976.
Cole, Leonard. "Electing Blacks to Municipal Office." *Urban Affairs Quarterly* 10.1 (1974): 17–39.
Consent decree. 1988. Indian L. Rep. 3119 (D. S.D.).
Council of State Governments. *Voting in the United States: Qualifications and Disqualifications, Absentee Voting, Voting Rights of Persons in Military Service*. Washington, D.C.: Council of State Governments, 1940.
Cuthair v. Montezuma-Cortez, Colorado School District. 1998. 7 F. Supp. 2d 1152 (D. Colo.).
Davidson, Chandler. "The Voting Rights Act: A Brief History." *Controversies in Minority Voting: The Voting Rights Act in Perspective*. Ed. Bernard Grofman and Chandler Davidson. Washington, D.C.: The Brookings Institution, 1992. 7–51.
Davidson, Chandler, and George Korbel. "At-Large Elections and Minority Group Representation." *Minority Vote Dilution*. Ed. Chandler Davidson. Washington, D.C.: Howard University Press, 1984. 65–81.
Deloria, Vine, Jr. *The Nations Within*. New York: Pantheon Books, 1984.
Elk v. Wilkins. 1894. 112 U.S. 94.
Engstrom, Richard L., and Michael E. McDonald. "The Election of Blacks to City Councils: Clarifying the Impact of Electoral Arrangements on the Seats/Population Relationship." *American Political Science Review* 75.2 (1981): 344–354.
Fannie Lou Hamer, Rosa Parks, and Coretta Scott King Voting Rights Act Reauthorization and Amendments Act of 2006. 2006. U.S. Statutes at Large 120: 577.
Fortson v. Dorsey. 1965. 379 U.S. 433.
General Allotment Act (Dawes Act). 1887. U.S. Statutes at Large 24: 388
Georgia v. Ashcroft. 2003. 539 U.S. 461.
Grofman, Bernard, and Chandler Davidson. "The Effects of Municipal Election Structure on Black Representation in Eight Southern States." *Quiet*

Revolution in the South: The Impact of the Voting Rights Act, 1965–1990. Ed. Chandler Davidson and Bernard Grofman. Princeton, NJ: Princeton University Press, 1994. 301–334.

Harrison v. Laveen. 1948. 196 P.2d 456 (Ariz.), 67 Ariz. 337.

Indian Citizenship Act. 1924. 42 Stat. 253, codified as 8 U.S.C. Sec 1401(a)(2).

Johnson v. McIntosh. 1832. 21 U.S. 543.

Karnig, Albert K. "Black Representation on City Councils: The Impact of District Elections and Socioeconomic Factors." *Urban Affairs Quarterly* 12.2 (1976): 223–242.

MacManus, Susan A. "City Council Election Procedures and Minority Representation: Are They Related?" *Social Science Quarterly* 59.1 (1978): 153–161.

McCool, Daniel C., Susan M. Olson, and Jennifer L. Robinson. *Native Vote: American Indians, the Voting Rights Act, and the Right to Vote.* New York: Cambridge University Press, 2007.

McCrary, Peyton. "Bringing Equality to Power: How the Federal Courts Transformed the Electoral Structure of Southern Politics, 1960–1990." *University of Pennsylvania Journal of Constitutional La*w 5.4 (2003): 665–708.

McDonald, Laughlin. "The Counterrevolution in Minority Voting Rights." *Mississippi Law Journal* 65 (1995): 271–313.

McDonald, Laughlin. "The Quiet Revolution in Minority Voting Rights." *Vanderbilt Law Review* 42 (1989): 1249–1297.

Mobile v. Bolden. 1980. 446 U.S. 55.

Montoya v. Bolack. 1962. 70 N.M. 196, 372 P2d. 387 (N.M.).

Northwest Austin Municipal Utility District v. Holder. 2009. 557 U.S. 193.

Opinion of the Attorney General, State of Utah. 1940. Oct. 25.

Opinion of the Attorney General, State of Utah. 1956. Mar. 23.

Opsahl v. Johnson. 1917. 138 Minn. 42, 163 NW 988 (Minn.).

Parker, Frank. "The Results of Test of Section 2 of the Voting Rights Act: Abandoning the Intent Standard." *Virginia Law Review* 69 (4) (1983): 715–764.

Parker, Frank R. "Racial Gerrymandering and Legislative Reapportionment." *Minority Vote Dilution.* Ed. Chandler Davidson. Washington, D.C.: Howard University Press, 1984. 85–117.

Peterson, Helen L. "American Indian Political Participation." *Annals of the American Academy of Political and Social Science* 311 (May 1956): 116–126.

Porter v. Hall. 1928. 271 Pac. 411, 34 Ariz. Nov. 1928, 308.

*Prince v. Board of Education.*1975. 88 N.M. 548, 543 P.2d. 1176 (N.M.).

Reno v. Bossier Parish School Board. 2000.528 U.S. 320.

Reynolds v. Sims. 1964. 377 U.S. 533.

Robinson, Jennifer. "Empowerment of American Indians and the Effect on Political Participation." PhD Dissertation. Salt Lake City: The University of Utah.

Robinson, Theodore P., and Thomas Dye. Reformism and Black Representation on City Councils. *Social Science Quarterly* 59.1 (1978): 133–141.

Shelby County v. Holder. 2013. 570 U.S. ___.

Shirley v. Superior Court. 1973. 109 Ariz. 510, 513 P. 2d 939 (Ariz.).

South Carolina v. Katzenbach. 1966. 383 U.S. 301.

Swift v. Leach. 1920. 45 N.D. 437, 178 N.W.

Taebel, Delbert. "Minority Representation on City Councils: The Impact of Structure on Blacks and Hispanics." *Social Science Quarterly* 59.1 (1978): 142–152.

Thornburg v. Gingles. 1986. 478 U.S. 30.

Trujillo v. Garley. 1948. Complaint 1353, filed August 11, 1948.
U.S. Congress House. Senator Snyder of New York speaking on HR 6335. Record 65, 68th Cong., 1st session, Congressional Record 65, P. 9303, 9304. 23 May 1924.
U.S. Congress, 1982. Report of the Committee on the Judiciary of S. 1992 with Additionally Minority and Supplemental Views. Report No. 97-417. Washington, D.C.: U.S. Government Printing Office.
U.S. Department of Justice. 2008. http://www.usdoj.gov/crt/voting/sec_5/about.php accessed 4/16/2008.
U.S. Department of Justice. Accessed 25 March 2002. www.usdoj.gov/crt/voting/intro/intro_b.htm.
Voting Rights Act of 1965. 1965. 42 U.S.C. § 1973.
Voting Rights Act of 1965, Amendments of 1970. 1970. U.S. Statutes at Large 84: 314.
Voting Rights Act of 1965, Amendments of 1975. 1975. U.S. Statutes at Large 89: 400.
Voting Rights Act of 1965, Amendments of 1982. 1982. U.S. Statutes at Large 96: 131.
Voting Rights Language Assistance Act of 1992. 1992. U.S. Statutes at Large 106: 921.
Welch, Susan, and Albert K. Karnig. "Representation of Blacks on Big City School Boards." *Social Science Quarterly* 59.1 (1978): 162–172.
Whitcomb v. Chavis. 1971. 403 U.S. 125.
White v. Regester. 1973. 412 U.S. 755.
Windy Boy v. Big Horn County, Montana. 1986. 647 F. Supp 1002 (D. Mont.).
Wolfley, Jeanette. "Jim Crow, Indian Style: The Disenfranchisement of Native Americans." *American Indian Law Review* 16.1 (1991): 167–202.
Worcester v. Georgia. 1832. 31 U.S. 515.
Zimmer v. McKeithen. 1973. 485 F.2d 1297.

Chapter 2

Native Americans: Voting for Sovereignty and Treaty Rights

Bruce E. Johansen

Knowledge of and respect for Native American sovereignty and its economic implications are a unifying political issue among the only minority group in the United States that has treaty rights retained in compensation for much of the United States' territory. These treaties, 371 of which were ratified by the U.S. Senate before 1871, guarantee land base and, in many cases, rights to several resources, such as timber, coal, oil, uranium, fish, which are quite substantial. Treaties, as legal agreements between nations, also protect Native American sovereignty, including the right to engage in certain potentially lucrative activities, such as commercial gaming. Treaty rights are crucial to economic revival among Native American tribes and nations. Native identity is closely tied to nationality, and thus to treaty rights.

Since their first sustained contact with Europeans, Native Americans have faced competition for lands and resources that once were exclusively theirs. With America's founding, these lands and resources have most often been apportioned by negotiating treaties. Protection of treaty rights is the central political issue that Native Americans share across a wide variety of distinct cultures. Respect for treaty rights becomes an umbrella under which historical and contemporary issues are viewed, providing ideological frames that determine how and why Native Americans decide to vote as well as, in some cases, *not* to vote. Historically, Republicans have more frequently led attempts to terminate treaty rights than Democrats. In Washington State, for example, Republican senator Slade Gorton took the lead as the state's attorney general during conflicts over fishing rights in the 1960s and 1970s. Native peoples in that state later allied with Democratic interests and ended his career in the U.S. Senate.

Native America—"Indian Country"—has never been a single entity. It is an aggregation of several hundred peoples with their own homelands and local issues. What binds everyone, however, is a common heritage of conflict forcing them to cope with the colonial apparatus of the U.S. government. Treaties are the lockboxes of historical rights, the subject of several hundred legal struggles, and the animus that unites Native peoples while also providing agendas for such pan-Indian organizations as the National Congress of American Indians. Most Native people are members and citizens of their tribes or nations, which confers on them a dual citizenship that is unique among U.S. minority groups.

Treaty rights are a key issue that helps to explain how and why Native Americans decide their votes for candidates and parties. Voting rights were not widely offered to Native Americans at the federal level until 1924; some states delayed voting rights till decades later, for example, New Mexico in 1962 and Arizona in 1964. Native Americans' influence on national elections is marginal, comprising only 1.7 percent of the population in 2010. However, in some states, for example, Alaska, North Dakota, South Dakota, Montana, New Mexico, and Oklahoma, Native Americans are sufficiently numerous to sometimes play a pivotal role in individual election outcomes. In other states, such as Washington, their influence has increased when they formed broad, interethnic alliances.

PRIDE IN HISTORICAL PRECEDENTS

Many Native peoples' pre-Columbian political systems utilized forms of counselor democracy. All along the Atlantic Seaboard, Native American nations had formed confederacies by the time they encountered European immigrants, from the Creeks, which Hector Saint John de Crevecouer called a "federated republic"[1] to the Cherokees and Choctaws, to the Iroquois and the Wyandots (Hurons) in the Saint Lawrence Valley, as well as the Penacook federation of New England, among many others. The Illinois Confederacy, the Three Fires of the Chippewa, Ottawa and Pottawatomi, the Wapenaki Confederacy, the Powhatan Confederacies, and the tripartate Miami were also members of confederations.[2]

These traditional councils are democratic, operating on consensus, usually without formal voting. The Northern Cheyenne maintain a traditional council of 44. The Mohawks of Akwesasne have a traditional council, the

Mohawk Nation Council of Chiefs, as well as governments sanctioned by Canada and the United States. The Akwesasne reservation is split between those two countries, as well as New York State, Ontario, and Quebec, making Akwesasne politics uniquely complex.

Clan mothers often choose leaders for traditional councils following informal polls of their relations. Some of these councils are very ancient, as many as a thousand years old, and many of them still operate today, ironically, often without official recognition from the United States. The Interior Department's Bureau of Indian Affairs recognizes councils formed under the Indian Reorganization Act of 1934 that hold elections. The government-sponsored councils are regarded as representative on some reservations, but have been widely boycotted on others.

In the context of participatory democracy, Native peoples in America take pride in their heritage of council-based government that predate European colonization. Native societies in America came to serve the transplanted Europeans, including some of the United States' most influential founders, as a counterpoint to the European order. They found in the Native polities the values that the seminal documents of the time celebrated—life, liberty, happiness, a model of government by consensus, with citizens enjoying rights due them as human beings. The fact that native peoples in America were able to govern themselves in this way provided advocates of alternatives to monarchy with practical ammunition for a philosophy of government based on individual rights, which they believed had worked, did work, and would work for them, in America.

Lewis Henry Morgan (1818–1881) observed during the mid-19th century that the Iroquois Confederacy's government "was an aristocracy liberalized, until it stood on the verge of democracy."[3] Before Morgan, James Adair (ca.1709–1783) had noted that "the Indian method of government" generally consisted of "a federal union of the whole society for mutual safety." Chiefs, he said, exercised only influence, not power, in that they could "only persuade or dissuade the people . . . [by] force of good-nature and clear reasoning." Indians' political behavior, wrote Adair, "is highly worthy of imitation by some of our British senators and lawyers."[4] The Haudenosaunee (Iroquois) Confederacy, which formed about 1142 CE has been cited as one inspiration, among several, for Benjamin Franklin's Albany Plan and early versions of the Articles of Confederation.

Using Iroquois examples of unity, Benjamin Franklin sought to shame the reluctant colonists into some form of union in 1751:

> It would be a strange thing . . . if Six Nations of ignorant savages should be capable of forming such an union and be able to execute it in such a manner that it has subsisted for ages and appears indissoluble, and yet that a like union should be impractical for ten or a dozen English colonies, to whom it is more necessary and must be

more advantageous, and who cannot be supposed to want an equal understanding of their interest.[5]

Franklin put a backward spin on the phrase "ignorant savages." This statement was among several by Franklin asserting that the first peoples of America had much to teach European American immigrants.

Thomas Jefferson wrote that "Societies . . . as among our Indians . . . [may be] . . . best. But I believe [them] . . . inconsistent with any great degree of population."[6] While Jefferson, Franklin, and Tom Paine were too pragmatic to believe they could copy the "natural state," ideas based on their observations of native societies were woven into the fabric of the American Revolution early, and prominently. Jefferson wrote: "The only condition on earth to be compared with ours, in my opinion, is that of the Indian, where they have still less law than we."[7] When Paine wrote that "government, like dress, is the badge of lost innocence"[8] and Jefferson said that the best government governs least, they were recapitulating their observations of Native American societies, either directly, or through the eyes of European philosophers such as Locke and Rousseau. Franklin used his image of Indians and their societies to critique European society: "The Care and Labour of providing for Artificial and fashionable Wants, the sight of so many Rich wallowing in superfluous plenty, while so many are kept poor and distress'd for want; the Insolence of Office . . . [and] restraints of Custom, all contrive to disgust them [Indians] with what we call civil Society."[9]

A COMMON CONTEXT OF COLONIALISM

Given their enduring experience with counselor democracy, many Native Americans characterize the U.S. electoral system as a colonial imposition. The legal context of U.S. relations stems from John Marshall's doctrine of "domestic dependent nations," and "nations within a nation," developed during the 1830s. While Marshall's seminal opinions, like the treaties themselves, are evidence of colonialism, they also frame legal doctrines that guarantee Native rights and provide a sense of common political consciousness. Marshall's opinions were written in an unsuccessful attempt to prevent the Cherokees' removal from their homelands by the Andrew Jackson administration, which committed contempt of the Supreme Court by ignoring them.

On the basis of a clause in the Constitution that denied voting rights to "Indians not taxed," American Indians did not take part in U.S. electoral politics in any numbers until the last years of the 19th century. In what became a prescient case in a negative way, John Elk, an American Indian living in Omaha, Nebraska, sought to vote in a city council election on April 6, 1880, but was denied by a registrar because he was an

Indian. Elk asserted that the denial was discriminatory under the recently enacted Fifteenth Amendment to the U.S. Constitution, which says that "The right of citizens of the United States to vote shall not be abridged by the United States or by any state on account of race, color, or previous condition of servitude." The U.S. Supreme Court denied Elk's claim because the amendment applied only to U.S. citizens.[10]

Within a decade after Elk's exercise of the franchise was denied, however, American Indians were offered citizenship and voting rights, if they took part in allotment of their lands, which was actually a device to break up Native American land base and annul treaty rights. Citizenship was generally extended to American Indians by an act of Congress in 1924. Subsequently, the right to vote was sometimes restricted by literacy tests, most notably in Arizona, a practice made illegal by Congress in 1975.

Attempts to register Native Americans to vote were met by seizure of lands, threats of relocation from reservations to urban areas, and forced enrollment of children in boarding schools. "Such historical events created a sense of disenfranchisement and distrust, which must be overcome to engage Native voters," according to a report by the National Education Association.[11] Historical efforts to suppress voting by Native Americans have been described in detail by Jeanette Wolfley.[12]

POLITICAL PARTICIPATION AND TREATY RIGHTS

During the 1950s and 1960s, black Americans took part in a civil rights movement that was focused on political participation, including the right to vote. Shortly after that, in the 1960s and 1970s, Native Americans also mounted a national movement to assert civil rights, also involving the right to vote, but centered on enforcement of their treaty rights. In Washington State, for example, this movement focused on fishing rights under treaties signed in the 1850s. Native people took to the rivers to fish in a form of civil disobedience they called "fish-ins," a conscious allusion to the "sit-ins" by blacks in the South. As with the black movement, which produced federal legislation on civil and voting rights, the Native American protests reached the federal courts in the form of *United States v. Washington*, the "Boldt decision," which, in 1974, guaranteed them a share of the fish harvest based on earlier treaties. This is one case of many in which protests evolved into a wide range of political participation, including voter registration drives, which continue today. The efforts of the American Indian Movement and other groups, such as the Coalition for Navajo Liberation, resulted in many civil rights initiatives.

Conversely, treaties sometimes have been associated with Native Americans' refusal to vote in state and federal elections. One example is provided by Chief Oren Lyons (Joagquisho) of the Haudenosaunee (Iroquois) confederacy:

On June 2, 1924, Congress passed legislation that granted citizenship to Indians and for other purposes. All of a sudden, the United States said it's about time all these Indians would be citizens. . . . Well, the Haudenosaunee, being ever vigilant, sent a letter . . . to the United States government saying. Thank you, but no thanks. We never were, we are not now, nor do we ever intend to be citizens of the United States. This was the gist of the letter from the Chiefs:

> Knowing that we had a treaty, we understood that when you have an agreement between nations and you obfuscate your national identity, there's going to come a point in time when you're not going to be sure what side of the line you *are* on. If you were an American citizen, it just seemed elementary to us that you could not have a treaty with yourself. So it was extremely important to keep the definition between our nations, because the treaties really are our last bastion to protect our lands.[13]

Jerry Stubben, an Iowa State University political scientist, who also is Ponca, explains that while many traditional Iroquois "consider the act of voting in a non-Indian election of any kind almost an act of treason, a betrayal of one's own indigenous nationality," many other Native American leaders "do not feel that their tribal sovereignty is negatively affected by active participation in local, state, and federal elections [and that] voting may be the best and possibly only remaining way to protect their remaining [treaty-related] land rights, economic rights to conduct gaming operations, and cultural rights, such as bilingual education."[14]

The system as a whole routinely cheated Native peoples on the terms of treaties, a major reason they have had to spend so much time and money hiring attorneys to defend their rights in federal courts. Along the way, many Native Americans have come to view the entire U.S. political system with a jaundiced eye. The "Great White Father" has been a target of Native humorists for many years, right up to the present, as illustrated by the following joke distributed over the Internet early in 2005:

> In a 2004 campaign trip through Wisconsin, President George W. Bush visited the City of Green Bay and met with the elders of the Oneida Nation. He said he had a plan to improve the income of every Native American by $40,000 a year. Details of the plan were not presented, despite frequent requests to do so. Bush also informed the elders that, during his gubernatorial career, he had supported every Native American issue to cross his desk. George W. Bush was adopted as a member of the Oneida Nation and given the name Walking Eagle. After the President left, one of the elders was asked the significance of the name Walking Eagle. His response—"The bird is so full of shit it can't fly."[15]

The same joke has been told on Democrats by Republicans. For example, "One version begins: Senator Hilary Clinton was invited to address a major gathering of the American Indians in upstate New York. She spoke for almost an hour on her plans to increase every Native American's present standard of living, should she one day become the first female president" (Native American, 2005).

Despite their cynicism, Native Americans' electoral participation has increased in recent years, as Russ Lehman wrote:

In most places within "Indian Country," as Russ Lehman wrote, both reservations and other lands that are populated and governed by Native Americans, Native voting has greatly increased. The legal, cultural, and economic conditions of many Native Americans have changed significantly in the last decade, creating an environment more conducive to participation in the electoral process.[16]

In 2008 and 2012, however, Barack Obama's presidential campaign was very active in registering Native Americans. Obama met with Native American leaders as campaign workers organized registration drives reservation by reservation, event by event, stressing Obama's understanding of treaty rights and sovereignty. Indian tribes donated more than $2.5 million to Obama's 2012 campaign.

Obama's campaign also was trying to address many historical transgressions that have soured many Native Americans on the U.S. political system. In 2012, a million Native Americans were not registered to vote.[17] A First Americans Caucus convened at the Democratic Convention in 2004 with 86 delegates. By 2008, this number had risen to 143, and by 2012, it was 161, a measure of the Obama campaign's efforts over time.

During the 2008 campaign, Obama spoke on the Crow Reservation in Montana and was given the name *Awe Kooda Bilaxpak Kuuxshish* ("One Who Helps People Throughout the Land"). Obama spoke as he faced east, the symbolic source of new life. Afterward, according to an Associated Press report, "His adopted Crow father, Hartford Black Eagle, prayed over him. [They then] walked arm-in-arm with Black Eagle's wife, Mary, to a podium, where Obama promised to live up to the meaning of his new name."[18]

Most Native Americans register as Democrats, but accurate statistics on voting behavior are difficult to find. The U.S. Census at least until 2010 estimated voting-age populations for blacks and Hispanics, but no such numbers were kept for Native Americans.[19] "The single largest barrier to studying Native American voting patterns is the lack of accurate and available data," wrote Geoff Peterson in a study of Native American turnout in the 1990 and 1992 elections. "While many of the national political behavior surveys include Native Americans, the number is always so small (often fewer than 10) that statistical analysis is impossible."[20]

Reservation vote totals should not be confused with Native American vote tallies. Reservation populations often are mixed, as is land ownership. Native peoples themselves are racially mixed, from 1/64th, implying 63/64th something else, to full-blooded. More than half of Native Americans now live in cities.

We do know that Native Americans, when they vote, are overwhelmingly Democratic. The county on the Great Plains with the lowest proportion of Republican support between 1980 and 2000 was Shannon in South Dakota on the Pine Ridge Indian Reservation, which averaged 20 percent.[21] There have been crosscurrents, however. Richard Nixon, a Republican, was relatively progressive on some treaty rights issues, although he also regarded the American Indian Movement as irredeemable renegades. He signed several laws establishing Native treaty rights and self-determination.

SMALL NUMBERS, LARGE IMPACT

While Native populations in most U.S. states are small, Montana, North Dakota, South Dakota, New Mexico, Oklahoma, and Arizona contain 4.9 to 9.5 percent Native American population. Alaska's Native population is between 15 and 16 percent. Hawaii includes about 7 percent full-blooded Native, and nearly a quarter Hawaiian, Pacific Islander, full or mixed blooded.

Even small numbers, buttressed by alliances with other voting blocs, can have an impact, however. In late 1999, Native tribes and nations created the First American Education Project (FAEP), which is a Native-owned and operated, nonpartisan, nonprofit corporation. This effort was begun in Washington State, with about 2 percent Native population, before spreading to its neighbors, then nationwide. Voter registration was a priority for FAEP, whose canvassers had to combat deep resistance. Even in 2002, many Native people refused to register because identification by government agents had preceded forcible removal of their parents and grandparents to boarding schools. This was true throughout Indian Country.

According to Lehman, FAEP "was created to assure that politicians understood there would be a political price to pay—organized opposition—for such strident hostility toward Native Americans and their tribes, and eventually, to assist the efforts of those candidates who have a particularly strong record of support on native issues."[22]

A similar effort was undertaken in Shannon County, South Dakota, the poorest county in the United States, where 90 percent of the people are Native American, mainly Oglala Lakota on the Pine Ridge Indian Reservation. In 2002, Tim Johnson beat John Thune for the U.S. Senate by 528 votes. Roughly 2,000 new voters had registered in Shannon County, which Johnson eventually won 90.4 percent to Thune's 7 percent. As a testament to Shannon County's Democratic record in 2000, George W. Bush beat Al Gore by 23 percent statewide in South Dakota, but in Shannon County Gore won 85 percent of the votes cast.

At a time when the U.S. Senate was split nearly equally between Republicans and Democrats, Senators Cantwell's and Johnson's victories following Native registration drives drew some attention on Capitol Hill.

ANTE UP AGAINST SENATOR SLADE GORTON

Senator Gorton jumped into a debate over an Amphitheatre on the Muckleshoot reservation, located south of Seattle, with a proposal to abrogate sovereign immunity, which Native reservation governments share with many other governmental bodies. Senator Gorton had begun pursuing white votes by staking anti-Indian positions as state attorney general during the 1970s with his vociferous opposition to Indian fishing rights. On April 7, 1998, he brought the Senate Indian Affairs Committee to the Doubletree Suites in Tukwila, a suburb of Seattle, where 500 people packed a hearing room so tightly that many people had to stand outside despite the probability that Gorton's proposal, swimming uphill against more than a century-and-a-half of legal precedent, had the proverbial snowball's chance in hell of being enacted. This was Gorton's home ground, where Native rights have been a hot issue for decades, with two very well-defined sides. The controversy over the Amphitheatre lit the fuse on a bomb that eventually blew up in Gorton's face.

The hearing took place in a rancorous atmosphere, "Amidst a din of drumbeats on one side and hoots from a flag-waving crowd on the other," filling the hearing room and spilling into a parking lot.[23] Hundreds of non-Indians rode in on buses from locations around the Northwest, organized by property rights groups. "In a bit of political theater," wrote Tim Egan of the *New York Times*, "they sang *The Star-Spangled Banner*, recited the Pledge of Allegiance, and waved placards such as, "White Man's Rights—Pay Taxes, Die."[24] American Indians converged on the hearing from throughout the western United States, drawn by a chance to express their opposition to Gorton. At the hearing, Gorton confronted former Washington U.S. Senator Dan Evans, a strong supporter of Native sovereignty and economic development, who testified that Gorton's bill to terminate Native nations' sovereign immunity was a "blunt instrument to ravage tribal independence," and "a solution seeking a problem."[25]

When Gorton waded into the Amphitheatre fight and tried to use it as a political kindling in his long-time campaign against Native sovereignty, he seemed not to have realized that Native people in Washington State had acquired quite a bit of political savvy along with the casino-generated cash to make political use of it. Several Native peoples in the state joined in a get-out-the-vote drive that contributed to Maria Cantwell's upset victory over Gorton.

Washington State's Native governments spent more than $700,000 in 2002 on lobbying, roughly equal to the $684,000 spent by the Boeing Company, and far more than the $481,538 spent by forest products multinational Weyerhaeuser. "Campaign contributions is only a part of it," said Allen. "Over time, we have become more astute at playing the political game."[26] Senator Gorton was in FAEP's crosshairs from the beginning. By its own count, FAEP registered about 10,000 new Native voters in Washington, and in 2000 nearly all of them voted for Democrat Maria Cantwell as she defeated Gorton by 2,229 votes, a fraction of 1 percent. In the same election, FAEP also coordinated a $100,000 television advertising campaign against Gorton. In 1994 during Gorton's previous Senate campaign, the Native tribes and nations in Washington had little money and no political clout. By 2000, they could afford to place bets on politics; reports were that roughly $2 to $3 million worth of Native American money went into the campaign against Gorton, about half a million dollars of which may have been contributed by the Muckleshoots. In 1998, the Muckleshoots gave $100,000 to 112 candidates in federal and state political races, and 104 were elected.[27]

Belatedly realizing that Native people had become formidable adversaries, Senator Gorton quickly used the specter of Native influence to frighten his Republican base. A Gorton fund-raising message in 1999 described "Indian tribes flush with gambling dollars . . . spend[ing] whatever it takes to defeat him." Gorton's advertising mentioned Indian tribes along with other groups: "the trial lawyers, the bosses of big labor, [and] the radical environmental groups."[28] "That the chronically poor tribes are being mentioned alongside some of the top powers of politics suggests how much has changed since some of the tribes began making money," noted *Seattle Times* writer Danny Westneat.[29]

The mere mention of Gorton's name raised blood pressures across Indian Country because of his long record in opposition to every Native economic initiative in the recent past, beginning with the Boldt fishing-rights decision. As state attorney general, he had been point man for commercial and sports fishing interests in opposition to Native treaty rights all the way to the U.S. Supreme Court, where he lost. "Slade Gorton's name is known on reservations from Alaska to Florida," said Ron Allen, head of the Jamestown S'Klallam Tribe and president of the National Congress of American Indians in 1999. "If we say we have a chance to beat the dean of the anti-Indian movement, I think tribes everywhere will scramble for money."[30] "This is a very, very American way to spend your money," said Cate Stetson, who owns Albuquerque-based tribal lobbying firm Legi/X.

"It's what Americans have taught tribes to do." Native peoples' loathing for Senator Gorton galvanized the opposition, and Stetson's lobbying firm celebrated Cantwell's win in 2000. In 2000, wherever Native Americans gathered across the United States, Stetson said, "There were [anti-] Slade Gorton buttons everywhere. The hatred for Slade Gorton was comprehensive, profound and activating, and there was no greater enemy in the eyes of most tribes than Slade Gorton."[31]

After he left the U.S. Senate in 2003, state records indicate that the opponents of the Amphitheatre, Citizens for Safety and Environment, hired Gorton as a lobbyist. "People are paying me for what I used to do for free" as a $145,000-a-year senator," Gorton quipped.[32] With several clients, Gorton was earning more than $1 million a year pitching the same established interests he had represented in the Senate, doing it with a smile, and no apologies. Gorton was not able to reverse the legal tide in favor of the Muckleshoots' Amphitheatre, however.

CONCLUSION: THE FUTURE OF NATIVE POLITICAL PARTICIPATION

Look for increasing political participation, including voting, by Native Americans. This is partially due to the increasing affluence in some areas brought on by rising educational levels, as well as tribal enterprises, such as casino gaming. Native Americans are finding new ways to mesh political participation with tradition, treaty rights, and sovereignty. As described in this chapter, Native Americans may comprise a small proportion of the electorate, but they can be quite influential in alliances, in part because of their unity vis-à-vis treaty issues, focused in an organized tribal council, can multiply their impact.

Lobbying is a form of political participation that is also being used more often by Native American governments. During the Washington State Legislature's 2013 regular January–April session, for example, Indian tribes spent $490,779 on lobbying, according to the State Public Disclosure Commission. Nearly all of this spending is related in some way to treaty-related issues that affect economic development. The amount spent by Indian tribes was about half the amount spent by cities ($860, 052), and more than was spent by counties ($334,623). The Puyallups spent $86,400 and the Muckleshoots $77,555. In addition, the Washington Indian Gaming Association spent $79,319. Both tribes outspent the city of Tacoma (about $65,000), with more than 50 times the tribes' populations. Private businesses and business associations spent about $2.1 million, unions $1.9 million, and the insurance industry nearly $950,000.[33]

These tribes are small groups of people, 2,000 to 3,000, so lobbying expenses per person are quite substantial. The rewards of lobbying are many. The exercise of treaty rights spurs business development, known in Indian Country as "nation-building."

The National Education Association reported that "American Indians and Alaska Natives increasingly are becoming more engaged in local, state, and national elections, as voters and candidates. In 2007, 64 American Indians and Alaska Natives served in state legislatures in 14 states, a record. A survey of eight states' American Indian and Alaska Native voters showed increases from 50 percent to 150 percent in voter participation from 2000 to 2004."[34] According to this report, Native American leaders' primary concern, as stated by the National Congress of American Indians in 2008, is:

> *Sovereignty and Government-to-Government Relations:* Indian tribes and Alaska Native governments are sovereigns recognized in the U.S. Constitution and acknowledged in numerous executive actions, federal legislation, and U.S. Supreme Court decisions. This unique government-to-government relationship creates a legal and moral responsibility on the part of the United States. Tribal communities remain vigilant for groups and campaigns promoting the legal termination of tribal status. American Indian and Alaska Native voters seek candidates who support and respect tribal sovereignty.[35]

The National Congress of American Indians (NCAI) operates Native Vote, a nonpartisan campaign to encourage Native voter registration and participation in national, state, and local elections in cooperation with other organizations, including reservation governments and urban Indian centers. The Native Vote campaign worked closely with regional organizations, tribal governments, and urban Indian centers, "to create a strong and permanent infrastructure . . . creating Public Service Announcements (PSAs), and hosting telephone conferences, webinars, and trainings."[36]

The project also appointed election protection coordinators to ensure that every qualified voter had an opportunity to cast a ballot on Election Day. These coordinators worked with lawyers to prevent harassment that might prevent voters from exercising their franchise, including uneven enforcement of voter identification laws. The project also distributed information about candidates and ballot issues, and encouraged Native Americans to run for office. The same program also sought to improve data collection on voter turnout for American Indian and Alaska Native people that "has historically been complex and incomplete."[37]

As the efforts of NCAI and others indicate, and if the recent past is prologue, Native Americans' participation in U.S. electoral politics will continue to trend upward in the years to come as increasing affluence helps create greater knowledge of their stake in off-reservation political activity.

NOTES

1. Crevecouer, *Journey into Northern Pennsylvania and the State of New York*, 461.
2. Johansen, "Chapter 19: Native Americans," 233–244.
3. Morgan, *League of the Iroquois*, 126; Bowden, "River of Inter-civilizational Relations: The Ebb and Flow of Peoples, Ideas, and Innovations," 1359–1374.
4. Adair, *Adair's History of the American Indians*, 459–460.
5. Smyth, *Writings of Benjamin Franklin*, 42.
6. Boyd, *Papers of Thomas Jefferson*, 92–93.
7. Commager, *Jefferson, Nationalism and the Enlightenment*, 119.
8. Paine, *Political Writings of Thomas Paine*, 1.
9. Labaree, *Papers of Benjamin Franklin*, 381.
10. *Elk v. Wilkins* 112 U.S. 94, 99 (1884).
11. "Focus on Tomorrow."
12. Wolfley, "Jim Crow, Indian Style," 167–202.
13. Jemison and Schein, *Canandaigua Treaty*, 72.
14. Stubben, *Native Americans and Political Participation*, 183.
15. John Fadden, personal communication, February 6, 2005.
16. Lehman, "Emerging Role of Native Americans."
17. "Focus on Tomorrow."
18. Brown and Jalonick, "Obama, Clinton Woo American Indian Voters."
19. McCool, "Voting Behavior of American Indians in Arizona," 101–113; Ritt, "Some Social and Political Views of American Indians," 45–72; Peterson, "American Indian Political Participation," 116–126; Rendon, *Voting Behavior in a Tri-ethnic Community*.
20. Trahant, "Elections 2012."
21. Archer, "Voting Patterns, United States."
22. Lehman, "Emerging Role of Native Americans."
23. Egan, "Debate about Tribal Rights Turns Rancorous."
24. Ibid.
25. Ibid.
26. Heffter, "Tribes Becoming Political Players with Casino Cash."
27. Westneat, "Tribes Target Gorton with Casino Money."
28. Ibid.
29. Ibid.
30. Ibid.
31. Ibid.
32. Anderson, "Slade's Slate."
33. Rosenthal, "Local Governments Spend Big to Lobby Legislature."
34. "Focus on Tomorrow."
35. *National Congress of American Indians 2008 Political Platform*. www.nativevote.org.
36. Booth, "2012 Election: Alaska Native and Native American History in the Making."
37. Ibid.

vote extend beyond the many typically discussed during a campaign and include those specific to a single tribe or set of Indian nations, which may include treaty-based rights like hunting and fishing, relations with state governments regarding the provision of federally funded services like temporary assistance to needy families, or some means of economic development, like agriculture, timber operations or gaming. In the next section, issues important to Native Americans as reported in recent surveys of tribal leaders are examined, and their diverse nature is related to Native Americans' political concerns.

The chapter's second part focuses on the role that gaming plays as a political issue. Importantly, gaming is much more than building an Indian casino. It is a means of economic development that extends far beyond a casino, as gaming revenue is an important element in funding services on a number of reservations. Gaming is also a battle for tribal sovereignty and self-determination that has played out at federal and state levels in recent years. At the state level, for example, the establishment of casino-style gaming in western Iowa by Nebraska tribes is the result of state limits on gaming in Nebraska and more expansive gaming laws in Iowa. For these two tribes that are proximate to the Nebraska-Iowa border, gaming policy in two states is an important issue. Gaming has also assisted tribes that engage in the political and policy process, as Indian nations seek representation in Congress and at the state level by employing the financial resources generated by gaming. Yet gaming as a means of economic development has not been embraced by all Indian nations and remains of limited interest for a majority of tribes. Finally, the perception that non-Indians have of Indian gaming often reminds both native and non-Native voters of the contentious politics surrounding tribal casinos and other Indian issues.

Importantly, the diversity of issues important to American Indians reflect the diversity of Native people in the United States, namely, the 566 Indian nations in the United States and 5.2 million individuals who identify themselves as American Indian and Alaska Native.[5] Notably, many of these issues are important to non-Indians, for example, unemployment, education, social services, national defense, and foreign policy. The concern for Native-specific issues may also reflect the on-reservation or off-reservation status of individual Native Americans. Here the tribal government, its duties to tribal citizens, and rights as an Indian nation may reflect the issue concerns of tribal leaders and individual Indians living on or near the reservation. For Indians more removed from their reservation, tribal issues may be less proximate and their concerns more closely resemble those of non-Indians.

Native issues are also a concern at the federal level where Congress has a fiduciary responsibility to act in the best interest of Native Americans. To help assure the trust responsibility is upheld, Indian nations engage with federal officials to make and oversee policy when issues pertinent to their interests appear on the federal agenda. As a result, tribal governments, pan-tribal and pan-Indian organizations, like the National Congress of American Indians, as well as individual American Indians, mobilize around issues of importance to American Indians. For example, tribes, tribal groups, and individuals with timber and logging interests, like many in the Pacific Northwest, seek to influence federal policy decisions about timber harvests on and around tribal land including National Parks and monuments proximate to Indian reservations.

More broadly, tribes have become concerned with issues related to tribal self-determination in the years since the Indian Self-Determination and Educational Assistance Act of 1975.[6] Self-determination includes the ability of Indian nations to carryout federal policy on Indian land as well as the opportunity to make and implement policy required and funded by the federal government. Importantly, tribal governments and Native people have embraced the idea of formulating and implementing policies that are consistent with local needs and cultures.[7] Policy areas covered by self-determination are numerous and include health care, temporary assistance to needy families, housing, and tribal law enforcement among others.[8] For tribal leaders, voters, and office seekers, support for tribal self-determination is a key issue that must be addressed when considering the needs of Indian Country.

In the end, the diversity of the more than 560 Native nations makes it impossible to consider American Indians as a single homogenous group, which makes a coherent overview of Native issues difficult. For example, while tribal governments and Natives may agree that self-determination is an important issue, decisions to engage in policy that furthers tribal self-determination and self-governance vary from tribe to tribe. For information on specific tribes, an examination of individual tribes and Native groups is essential to identify their significant issues. It is possible, however, to consider the wide range of issues that Native leaders themselves have identified as critical to their communities.

Surveys and Native Issues in American Politics

When identifying issues that drive individual vote choice, surveys like the American National Elections Survey are often used, but for individual racial or ethnic groups, more specifically targeted surveys are required. While the Asian, Latino, and African American populations have been surveyed, American Indian voters have not because the Native population represents about 1 percent of the U.S. population. Consequently, large, general population surveys fail to include enough Native respondents to allow for meaningful examination of Native issues, except when aggregating over long time periods.[9] Alternatively, researchers often rely on surveys of tribal leaders to identify issues of concern in Indian Country.

Elite surveys identifying issues important to American Indians are fitting for a number of reasons. First, Native leaders are elected by tribal members to represent their interests. Thus tribal leaders aggregate individual Indian interests as they represent their constituencies. Furthermore, tribal leaders also advance tribal interests off-reservations with non-Indians by considering the issue positions of non-Indian office seekers and rallying tribal support for favorable candidates.[10] Thus tribal leaders must remain abreast of tribal issues as well as those important to Native voters.

Fortunately there are surveys of tribal leaders that identify issues salient to American Indians. For example, Stubben[11] conducted a 1994 survey of tribal council members via mail from Indian nations across the United States. The author surveyed 480 randomly selected past or present members of tribal councils in the continental United States and Alaska. Using 118 completed, valid returned surveys, he identified two key sets of issues. The first focused on issues identified by the respondents as demanding the attention of tribal officials. The 11 issues included the elderly, business, employment, family services, environment, civil rights, tribal jurisdiction, substance abuse, education, tribal traditions, and gambling. Tribal governments are expected to address each of these pressing issues. For example, tribal governments may provide family support services to disadvantaged parents and their children. For the White Earth Band of Chippewa, located in White Earth Minnesota, this included the creation of a White Earth Healthy Families Healthy Community Project. Federal funds were provided to the tribe to create programs that included a child care/early childhood program to provide culturally based child development support and services for children, families, and child care providers.[12] Others, like the Ysleta del Sur Pueblo of Texas, developed an environmental code to protect the tribe's natural and cultural resources, including regulations for hazardous waste and tribal hunting practices on and around the reservation.[13] Again, not all Indian nations will address each issue, nor will each tribe address each issue in the same way.

Stubben also included a question regarding the most important issues that tribal governments and Indian people face, which differed slightly from the earlier question, because the most important problem may not be a problem that tribal governments can directly address. The nine issues identified as key issues by 10 or more respondents on the survey included, ranked from most to least important, the protection of tribal sovereignty, gambling and state compacts, economic development, health care and facilities, each other/individual greed, alcohol and drug abuse, education, lack of federal funding, and tribal self-sufficiency.[14] While there is some crossover with the issues that tribal officials should address, for example, education and gambling, others are not easily addressed by tribal leaders. Many of the important issues identified by tribal leaders were the same as those mentioned by candidate Heidi Heitkamp during her 2012 Senate campaign in North Dakota, including the sovereign rights of Indian nations, health care, education, and economic development on the reservation.

In sum, Stubben identified many issues at the tribal level that confronted Native Americans. Importantly, the issues were well known to office seekers who actively solicit support from Indian communities. As Corntassel and Witmer noted, many of these issues drive the behavior of tribal leaders in the electoral process.[15]

A second set of surveys by Corntassel and Witmer reported findings from questionnaires completed by elected tribal leaders in 1994, 1996, 1998, and 2000. For Corntassel and Witmer, this included the elected heads of the tribal governments at the time of the survey.[16] Like Stubben, the authors relied on elite surveys of elected officials. Two important findings emerged from this research. First, tribal leaders consistently indicated that the reason their Indigenous nations supported any candidate for office was the candidate's issue positions (61%). The other alternatives for tribal support included political party (26%), Indigenous nation membership (16%), and other (17%). While these findings were not surprising considering that the survey allowed for more than one answer, the importance of issues in candidate support was pronounced. For example, the authors noted a recent election in Arizona where an incumbent Republican, who consistently supported Native issues in the state legislature, received far more funding from Indian nations than his opponent, a Democratic member of the Navajo Nation. In this case, a consistent record of support for Native issues trumped membership in two significant groups, the Navajo Nation and the Democratic Party.[17]

The second major finding concerned the issues important to Native leaders. Corntassel and Witmer identified gaming, sovereignty/treaty rights/self-determination, natural resources/environmental protection, taxation, health care, law enforcement, economic development, cultural integrity/cultural preservation, education, and agricultural issues as important to Indigenous leaders. Importantly, their surveys found that tribal leaders encouraged tribal members to support candidates for office based on these issues. Indeed, tribes, tribal leaders, and tribal members used these issue positions to mobilize voters through "get out the vote" efforts supported by the tribes. Additionally, tribes, tribal leaders, and Native voters relied on issue positions to formally endorse candidates and provided financial contributions to office seekers.

Table 3.1 provides an overview of the major issues identified by both Stubben and Corntassel and Witmer.[18]

Table 3.1
Issues Important to Indigenous Leaders

Corntassel and Witmer	Stubben—Tribal leaders	Stubben—MIP*
Agricultural Issues	Business	Alcohol and Drug Abuse
Cultural Integrity/ Cultural Preservation	Civil Rights	Each Other/Individual
	Education	Greed
Economic Development	Elderly	Economic Development
Education	Employment	Education
Gaming	Environment	Gambling and State Compacts
Health Care	Family Services	
Law Enforcement	Gambling	Health Care and Facilities
Natural Resources/ Environmental Protection	Substance Abuse	Lack of Federal Funding
	Tribal Jurisdiction	Tribal Self-Sufficiency
	Tribal Traditions	Tribal Sovereignty
Sovereignty/ TreatyRights/ Self-Determination		
Taxation		

Note: Issues are listed alphabetically in each column.
*MIP is most important problem identified.

The link between issues, American Indian voters and tribal leaders, and support for candidates is also evident in the efforts of "Native Vote," a non-partisan voter information and mobilization campaign supported by the National Congress of American Indians.[19] During the 2012 election, for example, Native Vote actively sought to educate voters, elected officials and office seekers on issues important to American Indian communities. In addition, Native Vote worked to register American Indian voters, mobilize Native voters, and protect Indian access to participation in light of recent efforts to disenfranchise minority (including Indian) voters.[20] These efforts are likely to continue in future elections as well.

A number of issues central to the efforts of Native Vote, such as economic concerns, women's issues, and health care, were also significant issues in the 2012 presidential election as well as numerous Senate races. Economic issues important to Indian Country and highlighted by Native Vote were increasing tribal budgets to meet the needs of Native peoples and tribal governments, increasing and consolidating tribal lands to facilitate economic development, and tax reform to streamline sales tax collection on Indian reservations. Discussions of women's issues included Native support for the Violence Against Women Act and extending the law's coverage to include Indian Nations. Finally, health care incorporated the Affordable Care Act and its impact on the provision of health care services through the Indian Health Service.[21]

Following the 2012 election, Native Vote identified a series of issues that they addressed with federal officeholders they helped elect. Some among them were securing a farm bill to protect the needs of Native farmers both on and off of Indian reservations; assuring that the Affordable Care Act and Medicaid implementation applied to American Indians; trust reform, including better oversight and accounting of federal programs for American Indians; land consolidation to make tribal lands contiguous, thereby reducing checker-boarding and its harsh effect on tribal economies; the implementation of the Helping Expedite and Advance Responsible Tribal Home Ownership Act of 2012 (HEARTH Act)[22] and the Tribal Law and Order Act of 2010 (TLOA).[23] It is clear that many of the same issues remain important to Indian nations and Native people, although a few new approaches that address tribal concerns have emerged.

The HEARTH Act, for example, increased tribal ability to lease restricted lands for business, agricultural, public, religious, educational, recreational, or residential purposes without the approval of the secretary of the interior as currently required, while maintaining the approval of the secretary of the interior for mining, oil lease, and right-of-way leases. The act improved tribal flexibility in deciding what to do with tribal land without needing to seek the approval of the secretary of the interior. The anticipated outcome was greater economic growth, a persistent tribal concern, through tribally appropriated development, an approach advocated by Indian nations seeking local solutions to ongoing policy concerns.

Similarly, Indigenous nations' implementation of the TLOA was a pressing issue. TLOA's purpose was to reduce crime in Indian Country by empowering tribal governments to increase their law enforcement and prosecution abilities, including additional powers to punish criminals, more and larger detention centers on reservations, and grants and other aid to establish and administer domestic violence and sexual violence programs. TLOA will also increase coordination among federal, state, tribal, and local law enforcement agencies. Like the HEARTH Act, TLOA increases tribes' ability to oversee activities within Indigenous nations, thereby strengthening tribal sovereignty while addressing local domestic violence and criminal problems in a way appropriate for the local population. Importantly, HEARTH and TLOA represent specific examples of legislation that support self-determination and sovereignty of Native nations that Stubben and Corntassel and Witmer identified as important to tribal leaders.

INDIAN ISSUES IN STATE LEGISLATURES

As demonstrated by Corntassel and Witmer, tribal leaders rely on issues as the single most important factor determining support for or opposition to all candidates seeking election. In addition, tribal members are less likely to be elected or appointed to positions of power off their reservations.[24] Instead, Native leaders work to elect candidates to office who share their issue positions. Tribal leaders also seek to identify and work with current office holders who are friendly to Native interests and support their efforts within legislative bodies. As a result, although tribal governments are not traditional interest groups, they do employ interest group strategies, such as lobbying by tribal leaders and tribal representatives, to advance their political agenda.[25] Tribal leaders then communicate the response they receive from the elected officials to their members. In this way issues drive support for and opposition to incumbents and their challengers in future elections. Importantly, tribal leaders assist tribal members in linking policy issues in state capitals to voting for candidates. As a result, if Indian issues on legislative agendas across the country can be identified, a greater understanding can be achieved on the range of policy issues that impact Indian nations.

There are several ways to view the issues that influence tribal support for state office seekers. Witmer, Johnson and Boehmke identified legislation that was proposed and passed in state legislatures from 1998 to 2007. Among the legislation passed were laws dealing with recognition of native identities, issues, and cultures; health and human services; environment, natural resources, and land; boards, committees, and commissions; tax issues; education; gaming; cooperative agreements; tribal jurisdiction; economic development; law enforcement; allocation of funds; government-to-government relations; and voting issues.[26] As it is impractical to examine each of the 930 laws passed by state legislatures during this time, these issue categories capture more generally those that have made their way on to the Native issue agenda.

A second approach to identifying issues important to American Indians is to note those on which tribal governments lobby their state legislatures. Research by Boehmke and Witmer provide that information for California, home to more than 100 American Indian nations. The authors identified 26 subject categories for bills that Indian nations lobbied on for 2000–2004.[27] These are general issue categories that are on the issue agenda of tribal nations. Table 3.2 presents the results with number of bills lobbied.

One additional source of information on issues important to American Indians issues is contained in federal legislation. Carlson provided a general overview of the issues that emerged on the federal agenda. She divided legislation into whether Indians were included in broad government programs or whether they focused on Indians and Indian policy specifically. Examples of broad legislation that included Native Americans were health care, education, welfare, housing, employment, federal tax policy, law enforcement (including border security and immigration), military issues, violence against women, environmental policies, and public lands.[29]

Table 3.2
Bills Lobbied on by California Tribes, 2000–2004[28]

Category	Number
Gaming	61
Horse Racing	21
Education	11
Health	11
Tribal Cultural/Historical	10
State and Local Government	8
Human/Social Services	8
Law and Legal	8
Budget	5
Transportation	4
Economy/Development/Business	3
Energy	3
Public Utilities	3
Taxes	3
Waste	3
Workers Compensation/Benefits	3
Environment	2
Food and Agriculture	2
Mining	2
Police and Fire	2
Elections	1
Housing	1
Land and Natural Resources	1
Privacy	1
Tribal Sovereignty	1

In contrast, Carlson identified tribe-specific or pan-tribal legislation that focused more directly on a particular tribe or groups of Indian nations and Indian policy. She identified three general categories: enrollment issues, land acquisition, and claims distributions. However, she found additional subcategories within these larger categories, such as federal recognition requests, water rights settlements, claims settlements, natural resource issues, Alaska Native issues, area-specific conservation, Native Hawaiian issues, tribal courts, health care, economic development, gaming, cultural preservation, child welfare, education, and self-governance.[30]

Importantly, many of the issues, or at least issue categories, that are present at the state level are also present at the federal level, possibly due to the emergence of forced federalism.[31] The authors suggested that many American Indian policy issues that were typically addressed by the federal government are now shared between federal and state governments, like gaming, or have been moving to the state level. This compels tribal governments to work with federal and state governments to meet the needs of Indigenous people. This transition of policy issues to state governments by federal officials may also explain why many of the issues on state policy agendas on which tribal governments lobbied are similar to the issues that Carlson identified at the federal level.

Many of the issues that interest and mobilize non-Native voters are also important to American Indians. But clearly, there are also many issues that mainly affect the Indigenous population and Indigenous governments. Consequently, Native voters must often make electoral decisions based on a host of issues that extend beyond what the typical American voter must consider.

In the following section, one of the issues that has come to dominate the discussion of Native Americans in the last three decades, Indian gaming, is considered. Importantly, gaming is multifaceted, and more than just running a tribal casino.

Indian Gaming

Since the passage of the Indian Gaming Regulatory Act (IGRA) in 1988,[32] no Native issue has likely garnered more attention than Indian gaming. Yet Indian gaming is about much more than table games, slot machines, and Indian bingo. Gaming encompasses a series of political, economic, and legal issues that Indian nations face in the contemporary era, and it highlights the complexity of issues facing Indian nations and Indian voters, particularly the differences within and between Native nations, and between Native Nations and federal, state, and local governments. Furthermore, Indian gaming is a major issue given the number of Indian gaming operations in the United States. The National Indian Gaming Commission reported that in 2013 there were 449 gaming operations associated with 235 tribes in 28 states. These gaming operations generated $28 billion for Indian Country.[33] While the amount of money generated by gaming is impressive, a few caveats are in order. With over 560 tribal nations in the United States, fewer than half of all Indian nations have a casino-style gaming operation, thus any discussion of Indian gaming as an issue directly impacts less than half of all Indian nations, not a majority or most Indian nations as is commonly assumed.

The emergence of Indian gaming in the contemporary era began as an economic issue that rooted in the decisions of the Penobscot Tribe of Maine and the Seminole Tribe of Florida to engage in high-stakes bingo operations in the 1970s. While small-stakes bingo and other games of chance were common, the goal of the Penobscot and Seminoles was to create sufficient revenue to fund needed social and economic programs on their reservations.[34] By the 1980s, budget cuts at the Bureau of Indian Affairs were acutely felt by Indian nations, thus encouraging tribes to embrace self-determination and develop local solutions to assist underdeveloped tribal economies.[35] Bingo was one strategy appropriate for many nations, as existing on-reservation operations could be expanded in size with additional stakes used to entice additional players. Bingo also spread to tribes that did not yet have a gaming operation in an effort to offset lost federal funds. Bingo thus became a viable means of economic development for many, although not all, Indian nations. By 1987, it was estimated that $225 million was made by 113 Indian nations with bingo operations.[36]

Yet bingo did not remain an economic issue for long. As the operations became more prosperous, local and state officials sought authority over Native bingo operations. From inception, state and local governments sought to exert influence over tribal economic policy through the regulation of Indian gaming. As expected, Tribal governments reacted by countersuing non-Indian governments citing tribal sovereignty, or the right to make and implement policy on Indian land free of state interference. A series of legal decisions culminated in 1987 with *California v. Cabazon Band of Mission Indians*, 480 U.S. 202, a seminal decision that limited the rights of states to interfere with gambling activity on Indian reservations. Critical to the decision was the distinction between civil and regulatory laws and criminal and prohibitory laws. In reaffirming the limits on state and local governments over Indian nations, the Court effectively allowed tribes to engage in gaming that was not prohibited in the states where a reservation was located. For example, *Cabazon* noted that California had a lottery, thus making gaming a regulatory and not prohibitory endeavor as some form of gambling was allowed in the state. As a result, the state was not permitted to stop gaming on a reservation given the sovereign status of Indian nations.

Cabazon did not settle the Indian gaming issue, however, as the Court's ruling was not a complete victory for Indian nations. Instead, the Court suggested that regulation was possible as long as the rules that covered Indian gaming came from Congress. States soon engaged in an effort to secure the right to regulate Indian gaming through an act of Congress. Tribes resisted, and sought to secure the right from Congress to engage in gaming as a form of economic development unhindered by state government regulation.[37]

The result was the Indian Gaming Regulatory Act of 1988, which sought to balance the interests of Indian nations with the interests of state governments. Among the interests addressed were types of gaming, with casino-style or type III gaming requiring an agreement between tribes and states. Thus IGRA provided a mechanism, through the compacting process, where Indian nations and states would negotiate in good faith to secure a gaming agreement that allowed Indian gaming. The agreed-upon compact included the interests of tribes to use gaming as a form of economic development while allowing states to engage in some oversight through shared regulatory authority.

From the beginning, the many facets of gaming as a significant issue to Indian nations and Native people are evident. Gaming is an economic issue that provides Indian nations with income that may be used to provide services, including health, education, and a myriad of other social services, to Native people. The Puyallup Tribe, for example, uses revenue from its Emerald Queen Casino to provide elder care services, fund a youth center, and provide educational opportunities, like tribal schools and funding for members to attend college.[38] The National Indian Gaming Association chronicled the impact of gaming revenue in its 2009 Economic Impact of Gaming Report where it highlighted the social services, health care services, and educational benefits that Indian gaming provided for Indian nations.[39]

Indian gaming is also an important economic issue for individual Indians living on and near reservations with gaming operations. Individual Native citizens are given preferential hiring status, and tribes have engaged in training programs for tribal members that prepare them to work in tribal casinos. Individual Indians may also have a financial interest when their tribe distributes per capita payments. In some Indian nations, per capita payments are drawn from funds generated by gaming operations and distributed to tribal members. These may take the form of a yearly payment, like the Oneida Nation of Wisconsin's 2014 one-time payment of $1,000,[40] quarterly, like the Prairie Band of Potawatomi Nation's payment that fluctuates as a function of casino income,[41] or monthly, like the aforementioned Puyallup tribe's $2000 distribution to tribal members.[42]

The requirements set forth in IGRA that require a tribal-state compact also make Indian gaming a tribal-state political issue. Initially, states and tribes were to negotiate in good faith, with tribes having the opportunity to sue states in federal court. When tribes sought redress in federal court claiming states failed to negotiate in good faith by refusing to enter into a gaming compact, states asserted their sovereign immunity, or the right not to be sued. The end result was the 1996 Supreme Court ruling in *Seminole Tribe of Florida v. Florida* 517 U.S. 44. The Court agreed with the states, ruling that the Eleventh Amendment protects the states from lawsuits to which they have not consented. While the Department of Interior responded to the ruling and put in place rules that allowed tribes to engage in casino-style gaming when a state refused to negotiate, *Seminole* tipped the balance in favor of states.[43]

From the beginning, Tribal nations and Indian voters were not content to allow individual states to dictate gaming operations on tribal land. As a result of state efforts to expand their role in tribal economic and political decisions, tribes reacted in several ways. On the one hand, tribes, tribal leaders, and individual Indians passed legislation, through the initiative process, to allow Indian gaming in a number of states. In California, for example, tribal governments passed a constitutional amendment that included Indian gaming in the state's governing document.[44] Tribal leaders and voters were also active in supporting candidates for office who supported Indian gaming and Native rights in their state legislature.[45] Tribes also used gaming funds to lobby members of Congress[46] and elected officials at the state level.[47] Importantly, issues that mobilize voting and lobbying extend beyond gaming and include a wide range of issues important to Native people; yet without Indian gaming, it is unlikely that tribal nations would have had the funds necessary to support their issue advocacy.

In the end, Indian gaming has helped many Native nations and individual Indians through increased economic development and the services that additional funding allowed tribal governments to provide for its citizens. Yet gaming also increased tribal interactions with state governments over compacting and regulatory issues, which resulted in a net negative for Indian nations as they navigate the political process at the state and local levels.[48]

CONCLUSION

Recent success in U.S. Senate elections in states like North Dakota with the election of Democrat Heidi Heitkamp in 2012, Alaska with Republican Lisa Murkowski in 2010, and Montana with Democrat John Tester in 2006 and 2012, point to the strength of Native voters and the importance of American Indian issues in campaigns. Looking forward, the importance of American Indian voters and the issues important to Native voters will continue to grow, especially in the states with sizable American Indian populations. This includes, in addition to the aforementioned states, New Mexico, Arizona, Oklahoma, Oregon, Washington, South Dakota, and Wyoming, where the Native vote will likely represent the margin of victory in close elections. With a number of these states in the toss-up category during presidential elections, we should also expect to see Native issues discussed on the campaign trail in 2016, 2020, and beyond.

These close elections will also make Native issues more important on the campaign trail and among policy-makers. The issues identified by Native Vote that bring Indian voters to the polls, and that we should look for in future elections include tribal government sovereignty, Indian child welfare, education, water, energy, gaming, environmental impact issues, and federal budget and spending. While a number of these issues are ongoing concerns to Indian Country, a few, like energy, water, and environmental impact, are relatively new. Finally, it is worth watching to see whether both parties embrace Native issues. Currently, the range of policy issues would seem to favor Democratic candidates over their Republican opponents, but in close elections we can expect to see all candidates embrace the importance of Native issues.

NOTES

1. "Arizona Indians Gather for Voter Convention," *Tucson Citizen*.
2. Kelley, "Tribes' Top Target in 2000."
3. Jenkinson, "2012 Election in North Dakota."
4. Trahant, "Elections 2012."
5. http://www.ncai.org/about-tribes.
6. Public Law 93–639.
7. Johnson and Hamilton, "Self-Governance for Indian Tribes."
8. Witmer, "American Indian Self-Governance."
9. Peterson, "Native American Turnout in the 1990 and 1992 Elections."
10. Corntassel and Witmer. "American Indian Tribal Government Support of Office-Seekers."
11. Stubben, *Native Americans and Political Participation*.
12. http://www.whiteearthchildcare.com/pdf links/Parent Mentor Program.pdf.
13. http://www.ysletadelsurpueblo.org/environmental.sstg?id=1&sub1=59.
14. Stubben, *Native Americans and Political Participation*, 149.
15. Corntassel and Witmer, *Forced Federalism*.; Corntassel and Witmer, "American Indian Tribal Government Support of Office-Seekers," 519.
16. Corntassel and Witmer, *Forced Federalism*; Corntassel and Witmer, "American Indian Tribal Government Support of Office-Seekers"; Witmer, "High Stakes of Indian Gaming."
17. Corntassel and Witmer, *Forced Federalism*.
18. Corntassel and Witmer, *Forced Federalism*; Corntassel and Witmer, "American Indian Tribal Government Support of Office-Seekers"; Stubben, *Native Americans and Political Participation*.
19. www.Nativevote.org.
20. Ibid.
21. Ibid.
22. Public Law 112–151.
23. Tribal Law and Order Act, Title II of Public Law 111–211.
24. Witmer and Frederick. "American Indian Political Incorporation," 127–145.
25. Evans, "Expertise and Scale of Conflict," 663–682; Boehmke and Witmer, "Indian Nations as Interest Groups," 179–191.
26. Witmer, Johnson, and Boehmke, "American Indian Policy in the States."
27. Boehmke and Witmer, "Attention to State Legislation by Indian Nations in California."
28. Boehmke and Witmer, "Attention to State Legislation by Native Nations in California."
29. Carlson, "Congress and Indians," 41–51.
30. Ibid.
31. Corntassel and Witmer, *Forced Federalism*.
32. Public Law 100–497.

33. http://www.nigc.gov/.
34. Cornell, "Political Economy of American Indian Gaming," 63–82.
35. Cook, "Ronald Reagan's Indian Policy in Retrospect," 11–26.
36. Cordeiro, "Economics of Bingo," 205–238.
37. Mason, *Indian Gaming*.
38. http://www.puyallup-tribe.com/.
39. http://www.africanafrican.com/folder12/african%20african%20american2/Jim%20Crow/NIGA_2009_Economic_Impact_Report.pdf.
40. http://www.oneidanation.org/enrollment/svcpercapinfo.aspx.
41. http://www.pbpindiantribe.com/per-capita.aspx.
42. http://www.jumapili.com/wp-content/uploads/2013/09/www.puyallup-tribe.com_assets_puyallup-tribe_documents_puyallupcommunityreport_2012_web.pdf.
43. Cornell, "Political Economy."
44. Boehmke, et al., "Close Enough for Comfort?," 827–841.
45. Corntassel and Witmer, *Forced Federalism*.
46. Boehmke and Witmer, "Indian Nations as Interest Groups."
47. Mason, *Indian Gaming*.
48. Cortassel and Witmer, *Forced Federalism*.

REFERENCES

"Arizona Indians Gather for Voter Convention." *Tucson Citizen*, 23 September 1996. Accessed 2 August 2014. http://tucsoncitizen.com/morgue2/1996/09/23/229785-arizona-indians-gather-for-voter-convention/.

Boehmke, Frederick J., and Richard Witmer. "Attention to State Legislation by Indian Nations in California: Is All Tribal Lobbying about Gaming?" Presentation at Midwest Political Science Association Meeting. Chicago, IL. 20–23 April 2006.

Boehmke, Frederick J., and Richard Witmer. "Indian Nations as Interest Groups: Tribal Motivations for Contributions to U.S. Senators." *Political Research Quarterly* 65 (2012): 179–191.

Boehmke, Frederick J., et al. "Close Enough for Comfort? The Spatial Structure of Interest and Information in Ballot Measure Elections." *Journal of Politics* 74 (2012): 827–841.

Carlson, Kirsten Matoy. "Congress and Indians." *University of Colorado Law Review* (Forthcoming) (Winter 2015): 41–51. Available at Social Science Research Network. http://ssrn.com/abstract=2275497.

Cook, Samuel. "Ronald Reagan's Indian Policy in Retrospect: Economic Crisis and Political Irony." *Policy Studies Journal* 24 (1996): 11–26.

Cordeiro, Eduardo. "The Economics of Bingo: Factors Influencing the Success of Bingo Operations on American Indian Reservations." *What Can Tribes Do? Strategies and Institutions in American Indian Economic Development*. Ed. Stephen Cornell and James Kalt. Cambridge, MA: Harvard University Press, 1992. 205–238.

Cornell, Stephen. "The Political Economy of American Indian Gaming." *Annual Review of Law and Social Science* 4 (2008): 63–82.

Corntassel, Jeff, and Richard Witmer. "American Indian Tribal Government Support of Office-Seekers: Findings from the 1994 Election." *The Social Science Journal* 34 (1997): 511–525.

Corntassel, Jeff, and Richard Witmer. *Forced Federalism: Contemporary Challenges to Indigenous Nationhood*. Norman: University of Oklahoma Press, 2008.

Evans, Laura. "Expertise and Scale of Conflict: Governments as Advocates in American Indian Politics." *American Political Science Review* 105 (2011): 663–682.

indiangaming.org/info/NIGA_2009_Economic_Impact_Report.pdf. http://www.africanafrican.com/folder12/african%20african%20american2/Jim%20Crow/NIGA_2009_Economic_Impact_Report.pdf. Accessed 15 July 2015.

Jenkinson, Clay. "The 2012 Election in North Dakota: A Resounding Endorsement of Oil Development." *(ND) Bismarck Tribune*. 18 November 2012. Available at http://bismarcktribune.com/news/columnists/clay-jenkinson/the-election-in-nd-a-resounding-endorsement-of-oil-development/article_b8c8aace-2e89-11e2-b9e6-001a4bcf887a.html. Accessed 30 July2015

Johnson, Tadd M., and James Hamilton. "Self-Governance for Indian Tribes: From Paternalism to Empowerment." *Connecticut Law Review* 27 (1994–1995): 1251–1377.

Kelley, Matt. "Tribes' Top Target in 2000: Sen. Slade Gorton." *Los Angeles Times* 30 April 2000. Accessed 30 July 2014. http://articles.latimes.com/2000/apr/30/local/me-24924.

Mason, W. Dale. *Indian Gaming*. Norman: University of Oklahoma Press, 2000.

Peterson, Geoff. "Native American Turnout in the 1990 and 1992 Elections." *American Indian Quarterly* 21 (1997): 321–331.

Public Law. 100–497.

Stubben, Jerry. *Native Americans and Political Participation*. Santa Barbara: ABC-CLIO, 2006. 139–165.

Trahant, Mark. "Elections 2012: North Dakota Candidate Reaches Out to Native American Voters." *Indian Country Today* 18 September 2012. Accessed 30 July 2014. http://indiancountrytodaymedianetwork.com/2012/09/18/elections-2012-north-dakota-candidate-reaches-out-native-american-voters-134658.

Tribal Law and Order Act. Title II of Public Law. 111–211.

Witmer, Richard. "American Indian Self-Governance: Tribal Agreements with the Indian Health Service." Paper presented at the Midwest Political Science Association. Chicago, IL. 2–6 April 2014.

Witmer, Richard. "The High Stakes of Indian Gaming: Economic Development and the Political Behavior of Indian Tribal Governments." *Red Ink: An American Indian Journal* 5 (1996): 26–31.

Witmer, Richard, and Frederick Boehmke. "American Indian Political Incorporation in the Post-Indian Gaming Regulatory Act Era." *Social Science Journal* 44 (2007): 127–145.

Witmer, Richard, Joshua Johnson, and Frederick Boehmke. "American Indian Policy in the States." *Social Science Quarterly* 95 (2014): 1043–1063. DOI: 10.1111/ssqu.12086.

Part V
Jewish American Voters

Chapter 4

An Introduction to the American Jewish Voter

Ira M. Sheskin

Data on the number of American Jews are not available from the U.S. Census. This is due to restrictions caused by the separation of church and state and the treatment of Jews by the U.S. Census Bureau as a religious group, rather than as the ethnic group that they also constitute. As a result, the organized American Jewish community has collected its own data via national and local telephone surveys on the demography, geography, and religiosity of American Jews.[1]

Various estimates of the number of American Jews are available, ranging from about 5.7 million to about 7.1 million.[2] The reasons for these differences are discussed in the academic literature in Sheskin and Dashefsky[3] and DellaPergola[4] and have been widely discussed in the Jewish press,[5] but they hardly matter in the current context. Why? Because, even if the 5.7 million estimate on the low end is correct, in which case Jews represent 1.7 percent of Americans; or if the 7.18 million estimate is correct on the high end, in which case Jews represent 2.2 percent, it is difficult to imagine that the ability of the American Jewish community to influence public policy and elections is significantly impacted by the difference between these two percentages. For example, compare this approximately 2 percent with the population percentages for Hispanics (17%), for Blacks (13%), and for Asians (5%).[6] Even when viewed as a religious group, the 2 percent is dramatically smaller than evangelical Protestants at 26 percent, Catholics at 24 percent, mainline Protestants at 18 percent, and historically Black churches at 7 percent.[7] Jews are also a tiny minority compared to other assorted groups mentioned during elections, such as "soccer moms," suburbanites, the elderly, and baby boomers.

After discussing the relative merits of the various data sources employed in this chapter, three main purposes are addressed. First, considering that Jews are such a minimal percentage of the American population, this study examines the reasons Jews play such a significant role in the American political system.[8] Second, issues related to political parties and American Jews' political ideology are discussed. Third, the reasons most Jews continue to vote Democratic, when other groups who have "made it" in American society have tended to become Republican, are addressed.

DATA SOURCES

Much of this chapter relies on data from (1) the Pew Research Center Survey of Jewish Americans,[9] (2) the 2000–01 National Jewish Population Survey (NJPS 2000–01)[10] sponsored by The Jewish Federations of North America (JFNA), and (3) local Jewish community studies sponsored by local Jewish federations.[11] All these studies have utilized the most advanced, and most expensive, methodology—state-of-the-art random digit dialing telephone surveys.

The Pew Research Center 2013 survey[12] completed 2,786 surveys with "Jews by Religion" and 689 surveys with "Jews of No Religion" for a total sample size of 3,475.

The sample size of NJPS 2000–01 is also larger than that for most other studies. For the more Jewishly connected" sample in NJPS 2000–01, the sample size is 3,927; for persons who did not answer that their religion was Jewish, but were connected culturally or ethnically to the Jewish people (secular Jews), the sample is 359, for a total sample size of 4,286. NJPS 2000–01 and the local Jewish community studies contain a much richer set of variables measuring religiosity than do other studies. A drawback to the NJPS 2000–01 data set is that these data are now 15 years old.

Many previous descriptions of American Jews' political behavior have relied upon the American Jewish Committee's (AJC) annual survey of American Jewish Public Opinion. While these surveys are a valuable source of information, particularly because of their time-series nature (that is, as data collected annually over decades), the AJC sample is not nearly as representative of American Jewry as the surveys employed in this chapter.[13] One of the principal problems one encounters is that the AJC surveys generally include only interviews with Jews who state that their religion is

Jewish, omitting many Jews (22% according to Pew 2013) who identify as being ethnically Jewish, but who would respond in a survey of religious identification that they are atheists, agnostics, of no religion, and so on.[14] The Workmen's Circle Survey and Jewish Values Survey referenced in the following are based upon Internet surveys of randomly selected panels, but like the AJC surveys, cannot claim the randomness and sample size of Pew 2013 or NJPS 2000–01.

The problem with much of the data from such national polls as Gallup, Roper, and Quinnipiac is that, even when 1,000 interviews with Americans are completed nationwide, given that Jews are only about 2 percent of the population, no more than about 30 Jews are usually interviewed.

While measuring the votes and opinions of persons who are known to have actually voted, exit polls often suffer from a small Jewish sample. Moreover, to obtain a satisfactory size for the Jewish sample, pollsters may oversample regions with heavy Jewish concentrations. For example, in Florida, pollsters often sample the largely Jewish Aventura area of north Miami-Dade County that is comprised mostly of retirees and immigrants from Israel, Russia, and Latin America. Jews living in such areas are often different demographically, religiously, and politically from Jews living in areas of lower Jewish density.[15]

PART I. THE REASONS JEWS PLAY A SIGNIFICANT ROLE IN AMERICAN POLITICS: GEOGRAPHY AND DEMOGRAPHY

Two major reasons may be posited for the significant role Jews play in American politics. First, Jews are a much higher percentage of voters than they are of the American population. Second, the geographic concentration of Jews in a small number of states and the Electoral College system magnify the impact of the Jewish community at the national level, and the concentration of Jews in a few major cities and in a relatively small number of congressional districts is instrumental in providing the Jewish community with local impact.

While only about 2 percent of the American population, Jews form a higher percentage of the actual electorate for three reasons: First, about 81 percent of the members of Jewish households are of voting age, compared to 76 percent of all Americans. Second, Jews register to vote at a much higher percentage than do all Americans. About 90 percent of adults in Jewish households claim to be registered to vote[16] compared to about 64–74 percent of all Americans. Third, registered Jews actually vote in a much higher percentage than do all Americans. According to the American National Election Study of 2008,[17] 96 percent of Jews who were registered to vote actually did so, compared to 79 percent of Blacks and 76 percent of non-Jewish whites.

An analysis from *The New York Times* illustrates the impact. While Jews are only 2 percent of all Americans compared to 16 percent for Hispanics (in 2008), of about 20 million Hispanics who were eligible to vote in 2008, only about 12 million were registered to vote and only about 9 million actually voted. Given the higher registration rate and voter turnout rate for Jews, the comparable figure for Jews may be about 4.5 million. Thus, although there are eight times as many Hispanics as Jews, there are likely only twice as many actual Hispanic voters, as compared to Jewish voters (Figure 4.1).

Jewish political influence in Presidential elections, however, derives not from being perhaps 3.5–4.0 percent of the national voting electorate, but rather from the Electoral College, which effectively makes one's vote "worth more" in more populous states with more electoral votes. In 2014, 70 percent of Jews lived in just five states: New York, California, Florida, New Jersey, and Pennsylvania. Of the 270 electoral votes needed to be elected president, 147 are in these five states: New York with 8.9 percent Jewish, California with 3.2 percent, Florida with 3.3 percent, New Jersey with 5.8 percent, and Pennsylvania with 2.3 percent (Table 4.1). The top 10 states for Jewish population have a total of 244 electoral votes. Thus, it is not the percentage of Jews nationwide, but their geographic concentration

Figure 4.1
Hispanic Voting over Time

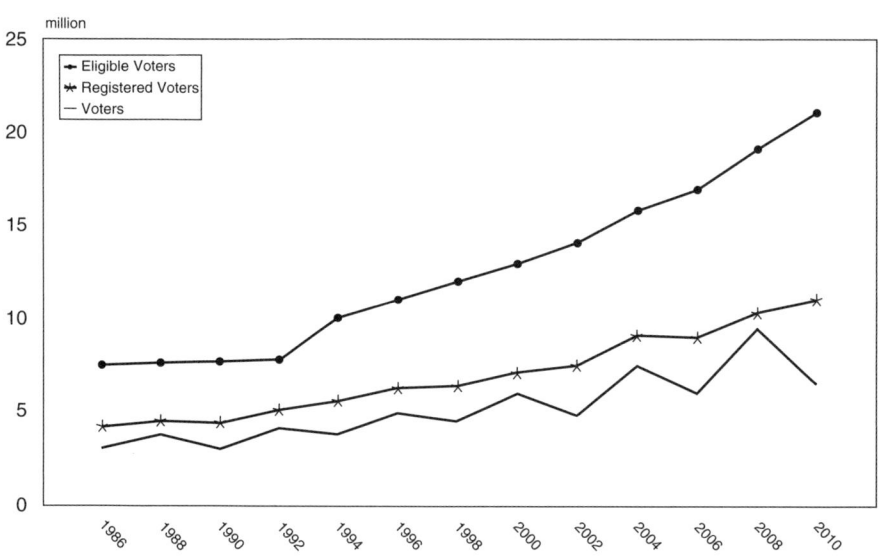

Source: *New York Times*, June 9, 2012.

Table 4.1
Jewish Population in the United States by State, 2014

State	Number of Jews	Total Population[a]	Percentage Jewish	% of Total U.S. Jewish Population	Number of Electoral Votes
Alabama	8,800	4,833,722	0.2	0.1	9
Alaska	6,175	735,132	0.8	0.1	3
Arizona	106,300	6,626,624	1.6	1.6	10
Arkansas	1,725	2,959,373	0.1	0.0	6
California	1,232,190	38,332,521	3.2	18.2	55
Colorado	103,020	5,268,367	2.0	1.5	9
Connecticut	117,850	3,596,080	3.3	1.7	7
Delaware	15,100	925,749	1.6	0.2	3
D.C.	28,000	646,449	4.3	0.4	3
Florida	638,985[b]	19,552,860	3.3	9.4	27
Georgia	127,470	9,992,167	1.3	1.9	15
Hawaii	7,280	1,404,054	0.5	0.1	4
Idaho	1,525	1,612,136	0.1	0.0	4
Illinois	297,885	12,882,135	2.3	4.4	21
Indiana	17,220	6,570,902	0.3	0.3	11
Iowa	6,170	3,090,416	0.2	0.1	7
Kansas	17,425	2,893,957	0.6	0.3	6
Kentucky	11,300	4,395,295	0.3	0.2	8
Louisiana	10,675	4,625,470	0.2	0.2	9
Maine	13,890	1,328,302	1.0	0.2	4
Maryland	238,200	5,928,814	4.0	3.5	10
Massachusetts	274,680	6,692,824	4.1	4.1	12
Michigan	83,255	9,895,622	0.8	1.2	17
Minnesota	45,635	5,420,380	0.8	0.7	10
Mississippi	1,575	2,991,207	0.1	0.0	6
Missouri	59,175	6,044,171	1.0	0.9	11
Montana	1,350	1,015,165	0.1	0.0	3
Nebraska	6,150	1,868,516	0.3	0.1	5
Nevada	76,300	2,790,136	2.7	1.1	5
New Hampshire	10,120	1,323,459	0.8	0.2	4
New Jersey	516,450	8,899,339	5.8	7.6	15
New Mexico	12,725	2,085,287	0.6	0.2	5
New York	1,757,270	19,651,127	8.9	26.0	31
North Carolina	32,075	9,848,060	0.3	0.5	15
North Dakota	400	723,393	0.1	0.0	3

(continued)

Table 4.1 (continued)

State	Number of Jews	Total Population[a]	Percentage Jewish	% of Total U.S. Jewish Population	Number of Electoral Votes
Ohio	150,615	11,570,808	1.3	2.2	20
Oklahoma	4,625	3,850,568	0.1	0.1	7
Oregon	40,650	3,930,065	1.0	0.6	7
Pennsylvania	293,240	12,773,801	2.3	4.3	21
Rhode Island	18,750	1,051,511	1.8	0.3	4
South Carolina	13,570	4,774,839	0.3	0.2	8
South Dakota	250	844,877	0.0	0.0	3
Tennessee	19,600	6,495,978	0.3	0.3	11
Texas	158,505	26,448,193	0.6	2.3	34
Utah	5,650	2,900,872	0.2	0.1	5
Vermont	5,985	626,630	1.0	0.1	3
Virginia	95,595	8,260,405	1.2	1.4	13
Washington	45,885	6,971,406	0.7	0.7	11
West Virginia	2,310	1,854,304	0.1	0.0	5
Wisconsin	28,255	5,742,713	0.5	0.4	10
Wyoming	1,150	582,658	0.2	0.0	3
Total	6,768,980	316,128,839	2.1	100.0	538

Source: Sheskin and Dashefsky (2014).

[a] Source: www.census.gov (July 1, 2013 estimates).

[b] Excludes 74,875 Jews who live in Florida for three to seven months of the year and are counted in their primary state of residence.

in several states that is important. For example, in the much disputed 2000 election between George W. Bush and Al Gore, had Florida not had a large Jewish population who voted overwhelmingly for Al Gore, the election would not have been in dispute.

The concentration of Jews in states with many electoral votes has increased over the past four decades, despite a small reduction in their overall geographic concentration. Table 4.2 shows the changes in the geographic distribution of Jews, by Census Region and Census Division, from 1971 to 2013, which, to some extent, reflects the changing geographic distribution of Americans in general. The percentage of Jews who live in the Northeast decreased from 63 percent in 1971 to 44 percent in 2014. The 12 percent who live in the Midwest remained virtually unchanged during this period, while the percentage living in the South increased from 12 percent to 21 percent and the percentage residing in the West increased from 13 percent to 24 percent. In sum, the Jewish population has shifted from the Northeast to the West and the South, with little change in the Midwest.

Table 4.2
Changes in Jewish Population in the United States by Census Region and Census Division, 1971–2014

Census Region/ Division	1971 Number of Jews	1971 Percentage Distribution	2014 Number of Jews	2014 Percentage Distribution	Percentage Change
Northeast	3,828,135	63.2	3,008,235	44.4	(21.4)
Middle Atlantic	3,420,265	56.4	2,566,960	37.9	(24.9)
New England	407,870	6.7	441,275	6.5	8.2
Midwest	732,610	12.1	712,435	10.5	(2.8)
East North Central	592,800	9.8	577,230	8.5	(2.6)
West North Central	139,810	2.3	135,205	2.0	(3.3)
South	694,850	11.5	1,408,110	20.8	102.6
East South Central	41,425	0.7	41,275	0.6	(0.4)
South Atlantic	560,835	9.3	1,191,305	17.6	112.4
West South Central	92,590	1.5	175,530	2.6	89.6
West	804,135	13.3	1,640,200	24.2	104.0
Mountain	57,275	0.9	308,020	4.6	437.8
Pacific	746,860	12.3	1,332,180	19.7	78.4

Source: Sheskin and Dashefsky (2014).

The final column of Table 4.2 shows that the number of Jews living in the Northeast decreased by 22 percent (822,000) from 1971 to 2013, the number in the Midwest decreased by 3 percent (22,000), but the number living in the South and the West each doubled from 1971 to 2013. The number of Jews residing in the South increased by 693,000 from 1971 to 2013 as the number in the West increased by 814,000.

From 1971 to 2014, significant increases were seen in the number of Jews in California (511,000), Florida (379,000), Georgia (102,000), Arizona (85,000), Nevada (73,000), Texas (91,000), Colorado (77,000), and Virginia (54,000). From 1972 to 2012, these eight states were allocated an additional 50 electoral votes, because of general population growth. The only significant decreases in Jewish population from 1971 to 2013 are seen in New York (minus 779,000) and Pennsylvania (minus 179,000). Their electoral votes were reduced by 19 between 1972 and 2012, but both retain large Jewish populations. A statistically significant relationship is seen between the number of Jews and the number of electoral votes in a state ($R = 0.711$, $\alpha = 0.000$).[18]

Examined in another way, of the five swing states in the 2012 presidential election with 10 or more electoral votes, only Wisconsin (10 electoral votes, 28,000 Jews) does not have a significant Jewish population (Table 4.1).

For the 1972 presidential election, 73 percent of Jews lived in just five states: New York (13.8%), California (3.6%), Pennsylvania (4.0%), New Jersey (5.7%), and Illinois (2.5%). In 1972, these five states cast only 119 electoral votes, compared to the 147 votes that are cast by the top five states for Jewish population in 2013. Thus, the significant geographic shift of American Jews over the past four decades has actually concentrated Jews even more in states with many electoral votes.

Jewish political influence in Congressional elections is affected by geographic concentration within states. Examining the Jewish population in the top 20 Metropolitan Statistical Areas (MSAs) (Table 4.3), we see that 79 percent of Jews are concentrated in these 20 MSAs, compared to only 38 percent of the general population. Note as well that almost 65 percent of American Jews live in just seven MSAs (New York, Los Angeles, Miami, San Francisco, Chicago, Boston, and Washington, D.C.). Thus, Jews are concentrated within certain congressional districts.[19] With many elections decided by less than 5 percentage points, Jews do have the ability to significantly affect election outcomes in these areas.

Jewish geographic concentration at the MSA level helps to explain the 9 Jewish Senators and the 26 Jewish representatives from 21 different states elected to the 114th Congress. Importantly, however, some Jewish Senators and Representatives were elected from states, such as Minnesota (0.8% Jewish), Oregon (1.0% Jewish), and Tennessee (0.3% Jewish), which actually have tiny Jewish populations. This is probably an indicator of a lessening of anti-Semitism in the United States, as large numbers of non-Jews are clearly voting for Jewish candidates. Jewish politicians are not being elected "because they are Jewish" but for other reasons important to voters.

Thus, the significant migration of American Jews over the past few decades has *not* dissipated American Jews' political influence, because as American Jews migrated, they mostly relocated to states with large numbers of electoral votes.

Changes in the Size of the American Jewish Population

The 1990 National Jewish Population Survey (NJPS 1990)[20] and NJPS 2000–01 suggest that the Jewish population *decreased* by about 5 percent, from 5.5 million in 1990 to 5.2 million in 2000, although a subsequent correction to the 2000–01 estimate by DellaPergola[21] suggests that the number did not decrease from 1990 to 2000. The estimates provided in the 1990 and 2000 *American Jewish Year Book* available at www.jewishdatabank.org suggest that the Jewish population *increased* by about 3 percent, from

Table 4.3
Jewish Population in Top 20 Metropolitan Statistical Areas (MSAs) in the United States, 2014

MSA Rank	MSA Name	Population Total[a]	Jewish	Percentage Jewish
1	New York-Northern New Jersey-Long Island, NY-NJ-PA	19,949,502	2,067,500	10.4
2	Los Angeles-Long Beach-Anaheim, CA	13,131,431	617,480	4.7
3	Chicago-Naperville-Elgin, IL-IN-WI	9,537,289	294,280	3.1
4	Dallas-Fort Worth-Arlington, TX	6,810,913	75,005	1.1
5	Houston-The Woodlands-Sugar Land, TX	6,313,158	45,640	0.7
6	Philadelphia-Camden-Wilmington, PA-NJ-DE-MD	6,034,678	283,350	4.7
7	Washington-Arlington-Alexandria, DC-VA-MD-WV	5,949,859	217,390	3.7
8	Miami-Fort Lauderdale-West Palm Beach, FL	5,828,191	555,125	9.5
9	Atlanta-Sandy Springs-Roswell, GA	5,552,942	119,800	2.2
10	Boston-Cambridge-Quincy, MA-NH	4,684,299	249,060	5.3
11	San Francisco-Oakland-Hayward, CA	4,516,276	295,850	6.6
12	Riverside-San Bernardino-Ontario, CA	4,380,878	22,625	0.5
13	Phoenix-Mesa-Scottsdale, AZ	4,398,762	82,900	1.9
14	Detroit-Warren-Dearborn, MI	4,294,983	67,000	1.6
15	Seattle-Tacoma-Bellevue, WA	3,610,105	39,700	1.1
16	Minneapolis-St. Paul-Bloomington, MN-WI	3,459,146	44,500	1.3
17	San Diego-Carlsbad, CA	3,211,252	100,000	3.1
18	Tampa-St. Petersburg-Clearwater, FL	2,870,569	58,350	2.0
19	St. Louis, MO-IL	2,801,056	54,200	1.9
20	Baltimore-Columbia-Towson, MD	2,770,738	115,400	4.2
	Total Population in Top 20 MSAs	120,106,027	5,329,280	4.4
	Total U.S. Population	316,128,839	6,768,980	2.1
	Percentage of Population in Top 20 MSAs	38.0%	78.7%	

Source: Sheskin and Dashefsky (2014).

Note:

1) See www.census.gov/population/metro/files/lists/2009/List1.txt for a list of the counties included in each MSA.

2) The total Jewish population of 5,293,080 excludes 75,875 part-year residents who are included in MSAs 8, 12, and 18.

[a] Source: www.census.gov.

5.9 million in 1990 to 6.1 million in 2000. From 2000 to 2014, Sheskin and Dashefsky[22] show a 10 percent increase in the Jewish population, but attribute this not to an actual increase but to methodological improvements used to measure the U.S. Jewish population. Using a meta-analysis of many U.S. surveys, Tighe et al.[23] found the same 10 percent increase as Sheskin and Dashefsky, but posited that the increase reflected a real change. This seems highly implausible, as the U.S. white, non-Hispanic population increased by only 1.2 percent during the decade.[24]

In fact, if the U.S. Jewish population has remained about the same in recent years, or even if it has shown a small increase (as DellaPergola and Sheskin and Dashefsky posit), it is clear that the U.S. Jewish population is likely to decrease in the future. First, in 2000, 16 percent of American Jews were elderly, compared to 12 percent for all Americans. Second, for a population to replace itself naturally, women need to average 2.15 children. According to NJPS 2000–01, Jewish women age 40–44, that is, women at the end of their child-bearing years, average 1.86 children each, not all of whom are raised as Jews. According to Pew 2013, Jewish adults age 40–59 report an average of 1.9 children each (4.1 for Orthodox Jews, 1.8 for Conservative Jews, 1.7 for Reform Jews, and 1.4 for other Jews).[25] Thus, it is likely that the number of deaths in the Jewish community will continue to be higher than the number of Jewish births.

It is also likely that the number of Jews migrating into the United States[26] will continue to surpass the number leaving the country. To some extent, the large Jewish immigration from the former Soviet Union (FSU) has counteracted, until recently, the loss due to Jews "opting out" of being Jewish by simply rejecting their Jewish identity. In sum, while the Jewish population may have been relatively stable over the past decade, mostly due to the large number of FSU migrants, most observers believe that the Jewish population will decrease in the coming years, as it is unlikely that any significant immigration will occur to offset the losses resulting from more deaths than births and the number of persons who opt out in the future.

The likelihood of a future decrease in the U.S. Jewish population certainly has political implications, although at least in the short run, the impact will probably not be significant. Given the Population Reference Bureau's estimate of 423 million Americans by 2050,[27] it is likely that only about 1.5 percent of Americans will be Jewish. On its face, such a decrease would imply a decrease in political influence, but for the same reasons that it currently may not matter whether Jews constitute 1.7 or 2.2 percent of the American population; so likewise, it may not matter if the percentage of Jews in the American population decreases to 1.5 percent.

Other Reasons for Significant Jewish Political Influence

Two additional reasons may be posited for the significant influence of the Jewish community on the American political process: (1) the political activism and significant financial contributions of the Jewish community and (2) the inflated perception of the American public concerning the percentage of Americans who are Jewish.

The first reason for Jewish political influence is that Jews "are extremely active in American political life."[28] NJPS 2000–01 asked their Jewish respondents if they attended any political meetings or rallies, contributed money to a political party or candidate, or contacted or wrote a government official in the past year. About one-third of Jewish adults responded in the affirmative. In Washington, D.C., for the same question, 45 percent responded affirmatively[29] and in Bergen County, New Jersey, 34 percent did so.[30] This political activism springs out of one of the guiding principles of Judaism—that humankind is God's partner in healing, repairing, improving, and transforming the world; thus, by implication, Jews feel it is necessary to be involved in activities that do so. Helping Jews meet this obligation through political activism are numerous Jewish organizations, which operate in the public square,[31] such as the American Jewish Committee, the Anti-Defamation League, the Jewish Council for Public Affairs, the American-Israel Public Affairs Committee, the National Jewish Democratic Council, the Republican Jewish Coalition, and the World Jewish Congress.[32]

While reliable data are hard to find, it is significant that estimates of the percentage of total donations to the Democratic Party that were derived from Jews range from "as much or more than about one-third"[33] to "as much as 60%."[34] Jewish money donated to the Republican Party is also significant, even without counting the millions donated by Sheldon Adelson, the Jewish Las Vegas casino mogul who was the largest single donor during the 2012 election cycle.[35]

Second, non-Jews seem to have an inflated impression of the percentage of the U.S. population who are Jewish. Nadeau, Niemi, and Levine[36] show that almost 40 percent of Americans think that 20 percent of the U.S. population is Jewish and about 60 percent think that 10 percent or more is Jewish. Only 18 percent think that less than 5 percent of Americans are Jewish. More recent evidence[37] using the 2000 General Social Survey shows that non-Hispanic whites estimate that 17 percent of Americans are Jewish; Blacks, 22 percent; and Hispanics, 20 percent.

PART II. POLITICAL PARTIES AND POLITICAL IDEOLOGY OF AMERICAN JEWS

We will now examine the political parties and political views of American Jews. Three important findings should be emphasized in Part II. First, in 2013, the percentage of Jews who are Democrats (55%) or lean Democrats (15%) is 70 percent. The 55 percent Democratic in 2013 compares to 56 percent in 2000–2001. The 13 percent Republican in 2013 compares to 15 percent in 2000–2001. Thus, the recent claim of the Republican Jewish

Coalition of an increase in Jewish Republicans is not borne out by the facts. It is also not true that younger Jews are more likely to be Republicans than older Jews, although the Orthodox are increasingly Republican, particularly during the Obama years. Also, 70 percent of Jews are Democratic/lean Democratic compared to 49 percent of all Americans.

Second, from 2000–2001 to 2013, the percentage liberal has decreased from 56 to 51 percent and the percentage conservative has decreased from 23 to 19 percent. The percentage moderate has increased from 21 to 30 percent. Thus, there is also no evidence to support the concept that Jews are becoming more conservative. Also, in 2013, 51 percent of Jews are liberal compared to 22 percent of all Americans; 19 percent of Jews are Conservative compared to 40 percent of all Americans.

Third, the demographics of Democrats and Republicans and liberals and conservatives suggest that the current pattern, which indicates that the majority of Jews are Democrats and liberals, will not change in the foreseeable future.

Political Party

The generally held perception that American Jews are Democrats is shown to be mostly true (Table 4.4). Pew 2013 shows that 70 percent of Jews are either Democratic (or lean Democratic) while only 22 percent are Republican (or lean Republican) with 8 percent being independents or something else. The low percentage independent in the Pew survey may be due to the fact that the Pew data combine "Democrat" and "lean Democrat" and "Republican" and "lean Republican." In a first question, Pew respondents were asked: "In politics *today*, do you consider yourself a Republican, Democrat, or independent?" In a second question, respondents selecting independent or volunteering no preference, other party, or don't know in the first question were asked: "As of today do you lean more to the Republican Party or more to the Democratic Party?" As measured by Pew, Jews are significantly less likely to be Republicans/lean Republicans by 22 to 39 percent and much more likely to be Democrats/lean Democrats by 70 to 49 percent, than all Americans.

In Pew 2013, 78 percent of Jews of No Religion are Democrats or lean Democratic compared to 68 percent of Jews by Religion. About 24 percent of Jews by Religion are Republicans, compared to 12 percent of Jews of No Religion.

NJPS 2000–01 asked, "Generally speaking, do you think of yourself as Republican, Democrat, independent, or something else?" Without the "encouragement" that Pew used to move respondents out of the independent category, NJPS 2000–01 found that 56 percent of Jews are Democrats, 15 percent are Republicans, 22 percent are independents, and 7 percent are *something else* (Table 4.4). Jews are significantly less likely

Table 4.4
Political Party Community Comparisons

		Base: Jewish Respondents			
Community	Year	Republican (%)	Democrat (%)	Independent (%)	Something Else (%)
Washington	2003	11	69	17	4
Los Angeles	1997	11	69	9	11
Minneapolis	2004	9	66	19	6
St. Paul	2004	13	63	18	6
Bergen	2001	11	63	19	6
Seattle	2000	8	63	25	4
San Francisco	2004	9	61	12	18
Columbus	2001	15	58	22	5
NJPS (More Jewishly-Connected)	2000–2001	14	61	20	6
NJPS (Secular Jews)	2000–2001	16	34	35	15
NJPS (Total Sample)	2000–2001	15	56	22	7
Pew (Jews by Religion)	2013	24	68	8	
Pew (Jews of No Religion)	2013	12	78	12	
Pew (Total Sample)	2013	22	70	8	
United States	2012	27	31	40	2
United States (Pew)	2013	39	49	12	

Source: Sheskin 2013, Section 35 at www.jewishdatabank.org; United States 2012 data from Jones 2012; Pew data from Pew Research Center 2013.

Note:
1) The Pew data combine "Democrat" and "Lean Democrat" and "Republican" and "Lean Republican." In a first question, respondents were asked: "In politics *today*, do you consider yourself a Republican, Democrat, or independent?" In a second question, respondents selecting independent or volunteering no preference, other party, or don't know in the first question were asked: "As of today do you lean more to the Republican Party or more to the Democratic Party?" This may be the reason fewer independents appear in the Pew survey.
2) The Pew survey "Jews by Religion" can be equivalenced to the NJPS 2000–01 "More Jewishly-Connected" sample and the Pew survey "Jews of No Religion" can be equivalenced to the NJPS 2000–01 "Secular Jews."
3) The United States 2012 data reflect the question asked in NJPS 2000–01 and the local Jewish community studies, while the United States 2013 data reflect the question asked by Pew.

to be Republicans by 15 to 27 percent, much more likely to be Democrats by 56 percent to 31%, and much less likely to be independents by 22 to 40 percent than all Americans.[38] These results are consistent with those of Mellman, Strauss, and Wald,[39] who found that, for the 2000–2008 Congressional elections, Jews were 28 percentage points more likely to vote for the

Democratic candidate than were Americans in general. In addition, from 2004 to 2008, a noticeable increase was seen in Jewish support for Democratic Congressional candidates. Greenberg and Wald[40] discovered that between 1990 and 2000, only 39 percent of "white, college-educated, urban middle-class non-Jews" identified as Democrats, compared to 60 percent of Jews with the same profile.

Note that the Republican percentage for the "Secular Jewish" sample in NJPS 2000–01 is not significantly different from the "More Jewishly-Connected" sample, unlike in Pew 2013 where Jews by Religion were twice as likely to be Republican or lean Republican. The real difference is that the "Secular Jewish" group, reluctant to categorize their religion as Jewish, may also be reluctant to categorize their political preference, with 35 percent indicating they are independent and 15 percent providing a response categorized as "something else."

Table 4.4 presents these results as well as those of eight local Jewish community studies, which demonstrate that the Democratic percentage varies in the eight communities from 58 to 69 percent and the Republican percentage, from 8 to 15 percent. Thus, while it is true that a majority of Jews identify as Democrats, and only a small minority identify as Republicans, certainly not all Jews are Democrats. Moreover, significant numbers classify themselves as independents. Note that while differences do exist by community, Mellman, Strauss, and Wald[41] found that, at least since 1988, very little difference has existed in the percentage of Democratic voters across the four major geographic areas (Northeast, South, Midwest, and West).

In recent years, some Jewish Republicans have forwarded claims of significant increases among their number, particularly among younger Jews and Orthodox Jews. The Republican Jewish Coalition website,[42] states that "the last decade has seen tremendous growth in the number of Jews identifying with Republican ideas and the GOP"; however, no statistical evidence is offered to support this statement. In fact, the evidence is quite to the contrary. First, the 56 percent Democratic in NJPS 2000–01 compares to 55 percent Democratic in Pew 2013 (not including the "lean" percentages). The 15 percent Republican in NJPS 2000–01 compares to 13 percent Republican in Pew 2013 (not including the "lean' percentages). Second, Mellman, Strauss, and Wald[43] show that, based on exit polls, the percentage of Jews who self-identify as Republicans has been relatively stable. Figure 4.2 shows the self-identification of Jewish voters from 1972 to 2008. At least since 1980, with the exception of two years, self-identification as Republican has remained at 15 percent or lower. Thus, Windmueller's projection[44] of an increase in Republican Jews is not borne out by these results, as Windmueller[45] himself realizes in his analysis of the 2008 election.

Likewise, the hypothesis that younger Jews are more likely to be Republicans than are older Jews is not supported by either Pew 2013 or

Figure 4.2
Self-Identified Partisanship among Jewish Voters, 1972–2008

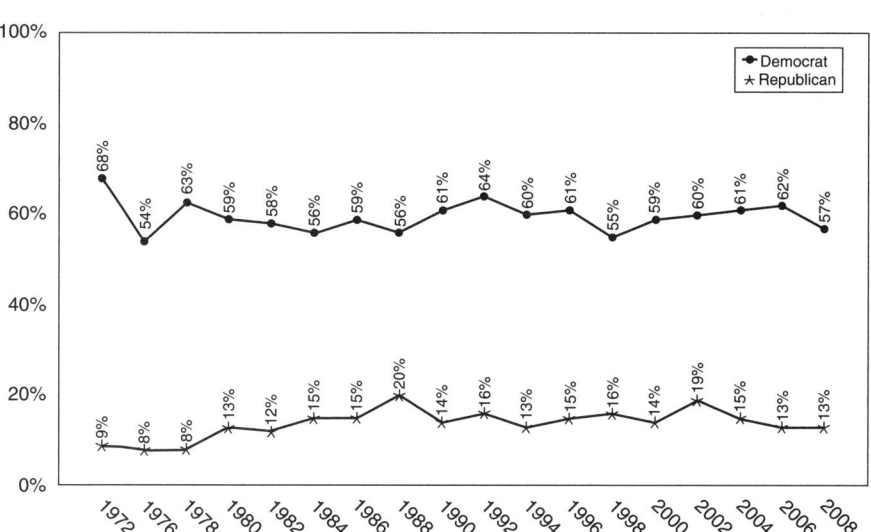

Source: Mellman, Strauss, and Wald (2012, 17).

the NJPS 2000–01findings, which suggest that nationally the percentage of Jews who are Republican is no different for younger Jews than for older Jews (Table 4.5). In fact, for Pew 2013, the lowest percentage Republican (17%) is for respondents age 18–29. Among the eight local Jewish community studies, only those in Los Angeles (32%), Minneapolis (17%), and Bergen (22%) support the contention that younger Jews, those under age 35, are more likely to be Republican and the Los Angeles data are quite dated (1997). In Bergen, this is because a large percentage of younger Jews are Orthodox. Hence, while younger Jews in some areas may be more likely to be Republican, such is not the case nationwide, either in 2000 or in 2013. Mellman, Strauss, and Wald[46] found that while for the period 2000–2008, Jewish voters under 30 were less likely to vote Democratic than older Jews—75 percent for Jews under 30, 77 percent for Jews 30–60, and 84 percent for Jews 60 and over—Jewish voters under 30 have become *more* Democratic over time.

The claim of a greater percentage of Republicans among Orthodox Jews (Table 4.5) is verified by both Pew 2013 data (57%) and the NJPS 2000–01 data (25%) and is true as well in Washington (28%), Los Angeles (26%), the Twin Cities (Minneapolis/St. Paul) (45%), and San Francisco (19%). However, Orthodox Jews constitute only about 10 percent of all American Jews (Pew Research Center 2013) nationally, and while participation in Orthodox institutions appears to have increased in the past

Table 4.5
Percentage Republican for American Jews

		Base: Jewish Respondents					
Community	Year	Under 35 (%)	35–49 (%)	50–64 (%)	65–74 (%)	75+ (%)	Orthodox (%)
Washington	2003	9	13	10	13	6	28
Los Angeles	1997	32	8	19	5	5	26
Minneapolis	2004	17	13	6	5	3	45
St. Paul	2004	8	19	7	16	10	
Bergen	2001	22	14	10	6	4	12
San Francisco	2004	12	8	8	7	13	19
Columbus	2001	18	13	19	12	5	17
Seattle	2000	0	13	28	2	2	9
NJPS (Total Sample)	2000–2001	15	16	15	13	11	25
Pew (Total Sample)	2013	18–29 17	30–49 24	50–64 24	65+ 20		57

Source: Sheskin 2013, Section 35 at www.jewishdatabank.org; Pew data from Pew Research Center 2013.

decade, the percentage of American Jews identifying as Orthodox has not changed significantly since 1971.[47] Thus, even if Orthodox Jews were to become increasingly Republican, they are only a small minority of American Jews. The fact that more traditionally religious Jews, the Orthodox, are more likely to be Republican is consistent with the findings of Putnam and Campbell[48] that religious voters tend to support the Republican Party. These results are also consistent with the findings of much earlier studies.[49] Interestingly, the Pew 2013 data show no statistically significant difference between percentage Republican for ultra-Orthodox (58%) and modern Orthodox (56%).

Why are Orthodox Jews identifying as Republican much more frequently than non-Orthodox Jews? First, Orthodox Jews are generally closer to the views of the Republican Party on the social issues. For example, while 82 percent of all Jews indicate in Pew 2013 that homosexuality should be accepted by society (as do 57% of all Americans), such is the case for only 32 percent of the Orthodox (20% of the ultra-Orthodox and 30% of the modern Orthodox). Second, Orthodox Jews are generally closer to the views of the Republican Party on economic matters. Pew 2013 shows that while 54 percent of all Jews indicate that they prefer a bigger government (as do 40% of all Americans), such is the case for only 34 percent of the Orthodox. Third, Orthodox Jews seem to be distrustful of Barack Obama, particularly with regard to his stance on Israel and Iran. While 60 percent of all Jews in Pew 2013 indicate approval of the way Obama is handling the nation's policy on Israel (as do 41% of all

Americans), such is the case for only 36 percent of Orthodox Jews. While 52 percent of all Jews in Pew 2013 indicate approval of the way Obama is dealing with Iran (as do 45% of all Americans), such is the case for only 27 percent of Orthodox Jews.

NJPS 2000–01 results showed that 25 percent of Orthodox Jews identified as Republican compared to the 57 percent in Pew 2013. One possible explanation for this increase is that the distrust of Obama has caused the defection of Orthodox Jews from the Democratic Party. This suggests that when the Democratic Party is under different leadership, support by the Orthodox for the Republicans may wane.

The 2011 Jewish Community Study of New York[50] shows that the percentage of Jews who are Orthodox in the eight-county New York area (New York City, Long Island, and Westchester) increased significantly from 27 percent in 2002 to 32 percent in 2011. Because Orthodox fertility, and particularly ultra-Orthodox fertility, in New York is very high, 64 percent of Jewish children in New York are being raised in Orthodox households, many of them in ultra-Orthodox households. Since Orthodox Jews are more likely to be Conservative and Republican than are other Jews, this suggests that, at least in New York, one might expect to see an increase in Jews voting for Republicans in the future. This phenomenon will probably not be seen nationwide since, as noted, only about 10 percent of persons nationwide are Orthodox and the percentage of ultra-Orthodox outside New York is very low.

Figure 4.3 provides an alternative method for examining claims of a recent upsurge in Jewish Republicans. While it is true that the percentage of Jews voting for the Republican candidate in presidential elections has increased recently from 16 percent for Bush in 1992 to 30 percent for Romney in 2012, the percentage of Jews voting for the Republican candidate from 1972 to 1988 was, on average, 32 percent. So, one could argue that the recent increase from 16 to 30 percent merely returns that percentage to just below the average level from 1972 to 1988. Moreover, voting for a Republican candidate does not necessarily mean that a particular voter identifies as a Republican.

Percentage of Democrats by Demography and Religiosity

NJPS 2000–01 data allow further examination of the relationship between demographics and political party.[51] Overall, in 2000–2001, 56 percent of Jews were Democrats. The Democratic percentage increased from 49 percent of persons under age 35 to 56 percent of persons aged 35–64, 60 percent of persons aged 65–74, and 68 percent of persons aged 75 and over. The decrease for the younger age cohorts does not, as shown here, imply an increase in younger Republicans. Rather, younger persons were more likely to indicate that they are "independent" or "something else."

Figure 4.3
Percentage of Jews Voting for the Republican Candidate for President

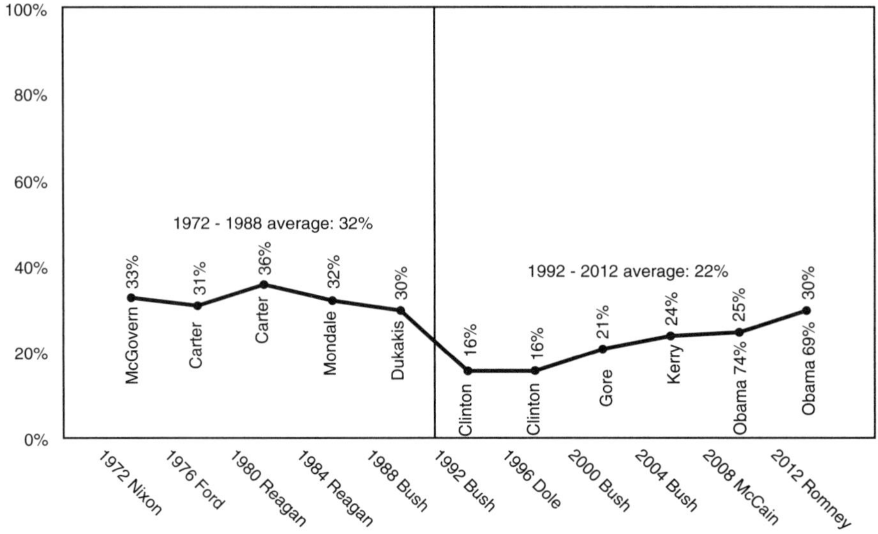

Year/Candidate	%
1972 Nixon (McGovern)	33%
1976 Ford (Carter)	31%
1980 Reagan (Carter)	36%
1984 Reagan (Mondale)	32%
1988 Bush (Dukakis)	30%
1992 Bush (Clinton)	16%
1996 Dole (Clinton)	16%
2000 Bush (Gore)	21%
2004 Bush (Kerry)	24%
2008 McCain (Obama 74%)	25%
2012 Romney (Obama 69%)	30%

1972 - 1988 average: 32%
1992 - 2012 average: 22%

Source: Weisberg (2012) for data through 2008. Due to methodological issues, two alternative histories are available: Maisel and Forman (2001) and Mellman, Strauss, and Wald (2012). While each presents slightly different results, the general pattern shown in the figure prevails in both analyses.

Note: In 1980, 19 percent of Jews voted for John Anderson; in 1992, 10 percent voted for Ross Perot.

This percentage was much higher for females (65%) than for males (46%). This result is consistent with Mellman, Strauss, and Wald,[52] who discovered that in 2008, Jewish females were 18 percentage points more likely to self-identify as Democrats than were Jewish males. This gender gap is consistent with the gender gap for all Americans.

Fifty-one percent of respondents in Jewish households with children were Democrats, a percentage not much different from the overall percentage of Americans. To the extent that children follow their parents politically, this suggests that the Democratic percentage will be maintained in the future. Podhoretz[53] posits that all the evidence supports that political attitudes and affiliations have a strong correlation from parent to child.

The percentage of Jews identifying as Democrats increased from 46 percent of persons with no high school degree to about 53 percent of persons with a high school through a college degree and 63 percent of persons with a graduate degree. Mellman, Strauss, and Wald[54] also showed that in 2008, Jews with a college degree were 14 percentage points more likely to vote for Obama than Jews without a college degree.

No variation was seen in the Democratic percentage by Jewish household income. This is consistent with the findings of Mellman, Strauss, and

Wald,[55] who found that no significant differences exist among income groups in the percentage of Jews who self-identify as Democratic between 1976 and 2008.

Orthodox Jews identified as Democrats (49%) at a much lower rate than Conservative (65%), Reconstructionist (66%), and Reform (62%) Jews. Respondents from in-married households, that is, households where both partners are Jewish (64%) were more likely to be Democrats than respondents in intermarried households (45%). Since it is Jews in intermarried households who are least likely to be involved in Jewish causes and most likely not to raise their children as Jewish, this finding also suggests that the Democratic percentages of Jews will not change significantly in the foreseeable future.

Synagogue members (60%) and Jewish Community Center (JCC) members (61%) were no more likely to be Democratic than nonmembers (61% and 60%, respectively). Jewish organization members (66%), belonging, for example, to B'nai B'rith and Hadassah, were more likely to be Democratic than were nonmembers (58%). Donors to the local Jewish Federation in the past year (66%) were also more likely to be Democrats than were nondonors (57%).

The findings concerning Jewish organization member households and Jewish Federation donors are, at first glance, not consistent with the findings by Mellman, Strauss, and Ward,[56] which revealed that, in 2000, Jews who never attended synagogue services were 15 percentage points more likely to vote Democratic than Jews who attended services once per week or more.[57] This is no doubt because the vast majority of Jews, who attend services weekly, are Orthodox. Since, as noted earlier, the Orthodox are only about 10 percent of American Jews, when we examine the non-Orthodox, some evidence is seen that involved Jews[58] were more likely to be Democrats than were less involved Jews.

Percentage of Republicans *by Demography and Religiosity*

Overall, in 2000–2001, 15 percent of Jews nationally were Republican. The percentage of Jewish Republican did not vary significantly by age, although the percentage was higher for males (18%) than for females (11%). In households with children, 18 percent of respondents were Republicans, a percentage not significantly different from the overall percentage. Again, to the extent that children adopt their parents' partisan identification, this suggests that the percentage Republican will maintain itself in the future. As noted before, this is likely to be different for the New York metropolitan area, where an increase in Orthodox Jews may well lead to an increase in Jews voting Republican, against the broader, national trend.

The percentage of Jews identifying as Republican was much higher for persons with no high school degree (27%) than for persons with a high school education or higher (14%).

The Republican percentage was much higher for households earning $200,000 and over (25%) than for households earning under $200,000 (14%).

While 25 percent of Orthodox households were Republican, the 13 percent for Conservative households did not differ significantly from the 15 percent for Reform households. Only 5 percent of Reconstructionist households were Republican. Respondents in intermarried households (18%) were slightly more likely to be Republican than were respondents from in-married households (15%).

No significant differences were seen in the percentages identifying as Republican between synagogue, JCC, and Jewish organization members, and nonmembers. The 12 percent of local Jewish Federation donors in the past year who identify as Republican was slightly less than the overall percentage (15%).

Political Ideology

Pew 2013 shows that 51 percent of Jews identify as liberal, 30 percent as moderate and 19 percent as conservative. Jews by Religion (45%) are much less likely to be liberal than Jews of No Religion (68%) and are much more likely to be conservative (23%) than Jews of No Religion (11%).

The NJPS 2000–01 data in Table 4.6 show that nationally 56 percent of Jews identified themselves as liberal, 21 percent as moderate, and 23 percent as conservative. Unlike the case for political party and unlike the Pew 2013 data, the responses of "Secular Jews" differ little from the "More Jewishly-Connected" sample.

The percentage identifying as liberal increased from 47 percent in 1990 to 56 percent in 2000–2001, but then decreased to 51 percent in 2013. The percentage identifying as conservative remained constant at about 22–23 percent from 1990 to 2000, but decreased to 19 percent by 2013. The percentage identifying as moderate decreased, from 32 percent in 1990 to 21 percent in 2000–2001, but then increased again to 30 percent in 2013.

For the six local communities shown in Table 4.6, the percentage self-identified as liberal varies from 47 to 63 percent, the percentage for conservative from 8 to 20 percent, and the percentage for moderate from 18 to 42 percent.

Mellman, Strauss, and Wald (2012, 19) found that, since 1976, at most 21 percent of Jews self-identified as conservative and that since 1996, with the exception of 2002, no more than 13 percent of American Jews identified themselves as conservative.

As of Pew 2013, Jews are significantly more likely than are all Americans to be liberal by 51 to 22 percent, much less likely to be moderate by 30 to 38 percent, and much less likely to be conservative by 19 to 40 percent.

Table 4.6
Political Ideology of American Jews

		Base: Jewish Respondents		
Community	Year	Liberal (%)	Moderate (%)	Conservative (%)
Seattle	2000	63	29	8
Columbus	2000	63	18	20
San Francisco	2004	59	28	12
Washington	2003	52	37	11
Los Angeles	1997	50	33	17
Bergen	2001	47	42	11
NJPS	1990	47	32	22
NJPS (More Jewishly-Connected)	2000–2001	56	21	22
NJPS (Secular Jews)	2000–2001	54	23	23
NJPS (Total Sample)	2000–2001	56	21	23
Pew (Jews by Religion)	2013	45	32	23
Pew (Jews of No Religion)	2013	68	21	11
Pew (Total Sample)	2013	51	30	19
United States	2011	21	35	40
United States (Pew)	2013	22	38	40

Source: Sheskin 2013a, Section 35 at www.jewishdatabank.org; United States 2011 data from Saad 2012; Pew data from Pew Research Center 2013.

Note:

1) NJPS 2000–01 respondents were asked: "Do you consider yourself extremely liberal, liberal, slightly liberal, moderate, slightly conservative, conservative, or extremely conservative. Pew respondents were asked: "In general, would you describe your political views as very conservative, conservative, moderate, liberal, or very liberal?"

2) The Pew survey "Jews by Religion" can be equivalenced to the NJPS 2000–01 "More Jewishly-Connected" sample and the Pew "Jews of No Religion" can be equivalenced to the NJPS 2000–01 "Secular Jews."

Using NJPS 2000–01 allows further examination of the relationship between demographics and political ideology. Overall, in 2000–2001, 56 percent of Jews were liberal. This percentage did not vary significantly by age but was much higher for females (61%) than for males (51%).

Fifty-two percent of respondents in households with children were liberal, a percentage not much different from the overall percentage. To the extent that children follow their parents politically, this suggests that the percentage of liberals will be maintained in the future.

Percentage of liberals increased from 47 percent of persons with no high school degree and 43 percent with only a high school degree to 54 percent with some college or a two-year college degree, 58 percent with a four-year college degree, and 65 percent with a graduate degree.

The percentage of liberals was higher for households earning $25,000 and over (58%) than for households earning under $25,000 (50%).

Only 23 percent of Orthodox Jews identified themselves as liberal, compared to 64 percent of Reform, 50 percent of Conservative, and 83 percent of Reconstructionist Jews. Respondents in in-married household did not differ in percentage liberal from respondents in intermarried households.

Synagogue members (51%), JCC members (48%), and Jewish organization members (52%) were less likely to be liberal than were nonmembers (61%, 59%, and 58%, respectively). Local Jewish Federation donors in the past year were about as likely as nondonors to be liberal.

Overall, in NJPS 2000–01, 23 percent of Jews self-identified as politically conservative. The percentage increased from 19 percent of persons under age 35 to 26 percent aged 35–64, but then decreased to 21 percent of persons age 65–74 and 17 percent age 75 and over. The percentage is higher for males (26%) than for females (19%).

Twenty-five percent of respondents in households with children were conservative, a percentage not significantly different from the overall percentage. Again, to the extent that children follow their parents politically, this suggests that the percentage of Jewish conservatives will continue to be constant into the future.

The percentage of conservatives decreased from 30 percent of persons with no high school degree and 34 percent with only a high school or technical school degree to 24 percent with some college or a two-year degree, 20 percent with a four-year college degree, and 16 percent with a graduate degree.

The percentage of Jewish conservatives showed no correlation with household income.

Orthodox Jews (50%) were more likely to be politically conservative than were Conservative Jews (Conservative denomination) (26%), Reform Jews (17%), and Reconstructionist Jews (8%). Respondents from in-married households did not differ from respondents in intermarried households.

Synagogue members (26%) and JCC members (27%) were more likely to be conservative than were nonmembers (20% and 21%, respectively). Jewish organization members did not differ from nonmembers. The percentage of conservatives among local Jewish Federation donors in the past year was somewhat lower (20%) than among nondonors (24%).

Thus, none of the relationships between demographics and political party and political ideology suggest that any significant change in the political orientation of American Jews may be expected in the future. The data also suggest that most American Jews are as wedded to the Democratic Party and to liberalism, in general, as has been the case since.[59] Perhaps as important for American Jews as a whole is a recognition that,

Table 4.7
Political Party and Political Ideology of American Jews

Base: Jewish Respondents	
Category	Percentage (%)
Liberal Republican	2
Moderate Republican	3
Conservative Republican	9
Liberal Democrat	41
Moderate Democrat	9
Conservative Democrat	7
Liberal Independent	10
Moderate Independent	7
Conservative Independent	5
Other	7
Total	100

Source: Calculated by author from NJPS 2000–01.

as of 2000–2001, only 41 percent of Jews identified as liberal and Democratic, 10 percent as liberal and independent, and 9 percent as moderate and Democrat (Table 4.7). When representing their community, many Jewish leaders generally speak from a liberal Democratic viewpoint, which is the modal preference at 41 percent, but not the preference of a majority of American Jews.[60]

PART III. THE REASONS MOST JEWS CONTINUE TO VOTE DEMOCRATIC

In the run-up to the 2012 election, the Republican Party and supporters such as the Republican Jewish Coalition expended an enormous amount of money and effort, attempting to overcome Jewish resistance to voting for conservatives and Republicans. This unprecedented targeted effort, partly funded by tens of millions of dollars donated by Las Vegas casino magnate Sheldon Adelson, led many to question whether Obama would lose a significant percentage of the Jewish voters who had supported him in 2008.[61] In fact, the Jewish vote for Obama decreased from 74 percent in 2008 to 69 percent in 2012. Given the small sample size for the 2012 data, the 69 percent in 2012 is within the statistical margin of error of the 2008 result of 74 percent.

To some extent, Jews defy the "natural progression" from the Democratic to Republican Party that at least some observers note for immigrant groups. The sociographer Milton Himmelfarb's aphorism that "Jews earn like Episcopalians, but vote like Puerto Ricans"[62] clearly applies. That is, one might expect that, as Jews have "made it" in American society, with a 2012 median income of $87,500 compared to $54,000 for all Americans, they would have become more conservative and vote for Republicans. Such has not happened. Wald and Calhoun-Brown[63] state that "Collectively an affluent religious group, Jews nonetheless hold liberal political views that seem contrary to their economic self-interest."

At least five reasons may be posited for the persistent Democratic Jewish vote: (1) the concepts of *tikkun olam* and *tzedaka*; (2) the tendency of Jews to maintain their ideology over the ages; (3) the Democratic/liberal urban environment in which most Jews reside; (4) the movement of the Republican Party toward the religious right; and (5) the ability of the Democratic Party to "control" its left wing, some of whom tend to be anti-Israel.

First, two concepts from Jewish *culture* contribute to the Jewish population's continuing Democratic and liberal viewpoints. The first concept, alluded to previously, is *tikkun olam*, a Hebrew phrase from the Talmud that means "repairing the world" and implies that it is humanity's shared responsibility with God to repair, heal, transform, and perfect the world. The second concept is *tzedakah*, sometimes translated as "charity," but really meaning "justice." Jews are commanded to "uphold the rights of the orphan; defend the cause of the widow" (Isaiah 1:17) and in general to do justice by taking care of those less fortunate. The 2012 Jewish Values Survey suggests that 72 percent of American Jews see *tikkun olam* as a somewhat or very important value and more than 80 percent see *tzedakah* as a somewhat or very important value that informs their political beliefs and activities.[64] Podhoretz,[65] however, takes issue with the contention that Jewish liberalism springs from these concepts, noting that those who are most observant, the Orthodox, are also the most conservative.[66] Jews have always felt that the ideals and positions of the Democratic Party better represent *tikkun olam* and *tzedakah* than those of the Republican Party.

Second, by virtue of the fact that they have clung to their identity for thousands of years, Jews have shown that they are a "stiff-necked" people (Exodus 32:9), that is, a stubborn people who, once committed to a particular path, will continue down that path. Perhaps "once a Jew, always a Jew" easily segues into "once a Democrat, always a Democrat." Jews were historically on the left of the political spectrum because more anti-Semitism sprang from the right than the left.[67] Podhoretz[68] goes on to posit that for many Jews, liberalism has replaced Judaism as their religion.[69]

Third, as shown in Table 4.3, Jews overwhelmingly live in the nation's largest cities, areas that tend to be both Democratic and liberal. Living and working in an environment, in which Jews associate with others who share their Democratic and liberal standards, reinforce these values.

Fourth, changes in the Democratic and Republican parties themselves have provided an incentive for some Jews to remain within or even return to the former and turn away from the latter. As shown by Putnam and Campbell,[70] decades ago one could find the highly "religious" in both political parties. More recently, Christian fundamentalists and evangelists have become the base of the Republican Party. While the organized Jewish community appreciates Republican support on issues related to Israel, the Democratic Party's core beliefs are much closer to those of the vast majority of American Jews on issues such as evolution, abortion, gay marriage, immigration, Medicare, the Affordable Care Act ("Obamacare"), Social Security, the government's role in the economy, and the use of diplomacy in international relations. Republicans of more recent vintage increasingly support matters like prayer in the public schools and, in a debate most thought was over, 2012 Republican presidential candidate Rick Santorum even spoke out against birth control. Missouri Republican Senate candidate Todd Akin discussed "legitimate rape" and Richard Murdock indicated that pregnancies resulting from rape were events that God intended. Even though both comments were disavowed by Republican presidential nominee Mitt Romney, many Jews had difficulty finding a "home" in a party that (1) includes spokespersons espousing such points of view;[71] (2) includes those with Tea Party views; and (3) nominates someone like Sarah Palin, whom many considered anti-intellectual (Rubin 2010). Jews are also concerned by evangelical denominations' efforts to convert Jews to Christianity.[72]

While Windmueller[73] points to some Jewish support for Tea Party *ideas* based on a 2010 Pew Research Center study, he relates a statement by Fred Zeidman, a Jewish Republican leader in Texas: "The idea of the Tea Parties scares the hell out of the Jewish community, and I can't tell you it's unjustified in some cases. There are some candidates out there that are clearly unqualified." In addition, Windmueller points to the neo-isolationism of some in the Tea Party as running counter to the pro-Israel agenda of the American Jewish community. Furthermore, Berkowitz (2010) points to the use of Holocaust imagery in an insensitive way by the Tea Party and the fact that some Tea Partiers have blamed Jews for the country's economic problems.

Differences between Jews and the base of the Republican Party are illustrated by the following examples. While 48 percent of Americans believe that evolution is the best explanation for the origin of life on earth, 77 percent of American Jews believe so.[74] While 52 percent of Americans favor allowing gay and lesbian couples to marry legally, 81 percent of American Jews support this. While 54 percent of all Americans think abortion should be legal in all or most cases,[75] 90 percent of Jews support this.

A fifth reason Jews remain Democrats is that, even as some Democrats have moved further left, espousing support for racial and ethnic immigration quotas and harboring anti-Israel attitudes, the Democratic Party's leadership continues to reject these more extreme forms of radical-left ideology.[76] Thus, for example, Jewish liberalism and Democratic Party membership have both pushed back against the rise of anti-Semitism's that has occurred in some radical black circles.[77]

Two counter trends to Democratic voting by the Jewish community may be noted. First, as mentioned earlier, the percentage of Jews who are Orthodox is liable to increase in the future and Orthodox Jews tend to vote Republican.

Second, Jewish immigrants from the FSU, who together with their children now number about 500,000–700,000 and may be as much as 10 percent of American Jews[78] have tended to vote Republican as their FSU background has tended to set them against big government. They hold conservative views on taxes and Israel (to which many of them have very strong emotional attachments), which outweigh their more liberal views on the social issues.[79] But, ameliorating this source of Republican votes is that the children of these Russian-speaking immigrants are tending to vote Democratic.[80]

Voting Democratic in 2012

Most arguments made by Republicans during the 2012 presidential election to sway Jews to vote for their ticket revolved around Obama's actions and views on Israel and, in particular, that he had not, as president, visited Israel during his first term. While one could certainly attribute some of the failure of the peace process during Obama's first term to the White House, other charges are more questionable. Though Obama visited Israel before becoming president, it is true that he did not travel there during his first term. But this was also the case for Republican presidents Nixon, Ford, Reagan, and George H. W. Bush. Moreover, George W. Bush failed to visit the Holy Land until his eighth year in office. Also in play was the "cold" relationship between Obama and Israeli prime minister Netanyahu; yet, Obama's policies benefitted Israel sufficiently to lead Israeli defense minister, and former prime minister, Ehud Barak to state, "I can hardly remember a better period of American support and backing."[81]

But these arguments are, in fact, not all that relevant to American Jews' ultimate voting decision, as they do not vote solely, or even mainly, on the issue of Israel. In an American Jewish Committee survey of 15 issues before the 2008 presidential election, Jews ranked Israel as the eighth most important issue behind, among others, health care, gas prices, energy, taxes, and education. When asked to name their top three issues, only 15 percent, mostly Orthodox Jews, chose Israel as one of the three. This does not mean that American Jews do not care about Israel or a candidate's Israel policy. They do. Pew 2013 shows that 69 percent of American Jews are very or somewhat attached to Israel (the same percentage as in NJPS 2000–01) and only 9 percent are not at all attached. According to Pew 2013, about 43 percent of American Jews have visited Israel. Thus, while American Jews are attached to Israel, they have not yet perceived enough of a difference in the candidates' positions on Israel so that the issue would surface and play a significant role in their choice.

In the Workmen's Circle/Arbeter Ring 2012 American Jews' Political Values Survey, three main groups of factors were found that influence Jewish voting:

1. a social justice commitment, including abortion, environment, same-sex marriage, and health insurance;
2. an economic justice commitment, including tax fairness, raising taxes on the affluent, the threat of banks, support for labor unions, and the need for government assistance to the poor;
3. economic conservatism, including concern for high taxes, the business climate, and jobs.

A multiple regression analysis showed the following factors impacting the Jewish vote: party identification (0.38), social issues (0.27), economic justice (0.21), economic conservatism (0.12), and attachment to Israel (0.07). The numbers in parentheses are standardized regression coefficients, and their relative values reflect the relative importance of each factor. Party identification is thus more than five times more important in determining votes than is the issue of Israel.[82]

Note that almost all polls show that significant U.S. support for Israel derives, in part, from the backing of all Americans, not just American Jews. A poll released in March 2013 revealed that American public support for Israel matched its all-time high.[83] In this poll, 64 percent of Americans sympathized more with the Israelis, while only 12 percent indicated support for the Palestinians, with the remainder (23%) indicating both, neither, or no opinion. Thus, of the 76 percent who have an opinion, 84 percent are pro-Israel. American support of Israel, then, is clearly not only dependent on the approximately 2 percent of the population that is Jewish but also upon Americans in general. Support for Israel tends, thus, to be bi-partisan.

Summary and Conclusions

While there is no agreement on the number of Jews in the United States, nor whether that number is increasing or decreasing, it probably matters little in the ability of American Jews to influence the American political system, given their changed geographic distribution over the past four decades that has served to further enhance Jewish influence in the electoral process. Also contributing to their influence is the tendency for Jews to participate, both with time and money, in the democratic process.

The plurality of Jews is both liberal and Democratic, but Jews of all political stripes are evident. This finding is unlikely to change over the next generation. Nationwide, younger Jews are *not* more likely to be Republican, although such is the case in some local Jewish communities.

Nationally and in some Jewish communities, Orthodox Jews are more likely to be Republican. Jews as a whole have not become more Republican.

For a variety of reasons related to history, Jewish cultural values, the differences between most Jews' positions on social issues and numerous core beliefs held by the contemporary base of the Republican Party, it is most probable that their overwhelming support for the Democratic Party will continue. Even after the unprecedented spending of the Republican Party in 2012 to convince Jews to vote for Mitt Romney, the Jewish vote for Obama did not decrease appreciably. And perhaps most importantly, for the vast majority of the Jewish population, a candidate's stand on Israel is not the determining factor in their voting decision.

NOTES

1. See Berman Jewish Databank, www.jewishdatabank.org.
2. Dashefsky and Sheskin, *American Jewish Year Book*; DellaPergola, "Was it Demography"; DellaPergola, "World Jewish Population, 2014"; Kotler-Berkowitz et al., *Strength, Challenge and Diversity in the America Jewish Population*; Tighe et al., *Estimating the Jewish Population of the United States: 2000–2010*; Pew Research Center, "Portrait of Jewish Americans"; Sheskin, "Four Questions about American Jewish Demography."
3. Sheskin and Dashefsky, "Jewish Population in the United States, 2006."
4. DellaPergola, "How many Jews in the United States."
5. See, for example, Zeveloff, "U.S. Jewish Population Pegged at 6 Million" and Sheskin, "Will U.S. Jews Vote for Barack Obama in 2012?"
6. United States Census Bureau, www.census.gov.
7. Pew Forum on Religion and Public Life, *U.S. Religious Landscape Survey*.
8. Sheskin, "Why All the Emphasis on the Jewish Vote?"
9. Pew Research Center, "Portrait of Jewish Americans."
10. Kotler-Berkowitz, et al., *Strength, Challenge and Diversity in the American Jewish Population*.
11. Berman Jewish Databank, www.jewishdatabank.org.
12. Pew 2013.
13. Perlman, *American Jewish Committee's Annual Opinion Surveys*.
14. Kosmin and Keysar, "American Jewish Secularism."
15. Weisberg, "Reconsidering Jewish Presidential Voting Statistics."
16. Sheskin, *Comparisons of Jewish Communities*; Pew Research Center, "Portrait of Jewish Americans."
17. American National Election Studies, www.electionstudies.org.
18. The Pearson correlation coefficient (R) varies from -1 to $+1$. A value of $R = 0$ indicates that no relationship exists between two variables. A value of $R = +1$ indicates that a perfect positive relationship exists between two variables. A value of $R = -1$ indicates that a perfect negative relationship exists between two variables. In a positive relationship, as the values of one variable increase, the values of the other variable also increase. In a negative relationship, as the values of one variable increase, the values of the other variable decrease. The α value tests whether a particular value of R is statistically significantly different from 0, in which case we can conclude that a relationship exists between two variables. Alpha gives the

exact probability of being wrong in concluding that a relationship exists. In this case, we conclude that a positive relationship exists between the number of Jews and the number of electoral votes in a state ($R = 0.711$). That is, states with larger Jewish populations also have more electoral votes. In reaching this conclusion, we are 95 percent certain that we are taking less than 1 chance in 1,000 of erring in our conclusion ($\alpha = 0.000$).

19. Comenetz, *Jewish Maps of the United States by Congressional District—revised January 2014.*
20. Kosmin, et al., *Highlights of the CJF 1990 National Jewish Population Survey.*
21. DellaPergola, "World Jewish Population, 2013."
22. Sheskin and Dashefsky, *American Jewish Year Book, 2014.*
23. Tighe, et al., *Estimating the Jewish Population of the United States: 2000–2010.*
24. Calculated by author from data available at www.census.gov.
25. Note that Orthodox Jews are only 10 percent of the Jewish population. Thus, their high level of fertility has a relatively small impact on the total fertility rate for all Jews.
26. Gold, "Patterns of Adaptation."
27. www.prb.org.
28. Wald and Calhoun-Brown, *Religion and Politics in the United States*, 266.
29. Sheskin, *Jewish Community Study of Greater Washington.*
30. Sheskin, The UJA Federation of Bergen County and North Hudson Community Study.
31. Mittleman, Sarna, and Licht, *Jewish Polity and American Civil Society.*
32. For a relatively complete listing of Jewish advocacy organizations, which advocate both for Jewish and general causes, see Sheskin and Dashefsky (2014, Chapter 20). Jewish political activism is further documented in Goldberg, *Jewish Power*; Maisel and Forman, *Jews in American Politics*; Medoff, *Jewish Americans and Political Participation*; and Feingold, *Jewish Power in America.*
33. Tobin, "Jews, Money, and 2012."
34. Edsall and Cooperman, "GOP Uses Remarks to Court Jews."
35. Cline, "Sheldon Adelson Willing to Spend $100 Million to Beat Obama."
36. Nadeau, Niemi, and Levine, "Innumeracy about Minority Populations," 335.
37. Herda, "Innocuous Ignorance?."
38. Gallup, www.gallup.com; Jones, "Record-High 40% of Americans Identify as independents in '11."
39. Mellman, Strauss, and Wald, *Jewish American Voting Behavior 1972–2008*, 15.
40. Greenberg and Wald, "Still Liberal after All These Years?" 174.
41. Mellman, Strauss, and Wald, *Jewish American Voting Behavior 1972–2008*, 14.
42. www.rjchq.org.
43. Ibid., 17.
44. Windmueller, *Are American Jews becoming Republican.*
45. Windmueller, *Revisiting the 2008 American Presidential Election.*
46. Mellman, Strauss, and Wald, *Jewish American Voting Behavior 1972–2008*, 9.
47. Massarik and Chenkin, "United States National Jewish Population Study."
48. Putnam and Campbell, *American Grace.*
49. Cohen, *American Modernity and Jewish Identity*; Cohen and Liebman, "American Jewish Liberalism."
50. Cohen et al., *Jewish Community Study of New York*, 123.

51. While the Pew 2013 *report* is available as of this writing, the *data set* has not yet been made available to researchers, so the Pew data cannot be used for this analysis.
52. Mellman, Strauss, and Wald, *Jewish American Voting Behavior 1972–2008*, 21.
53. Podhoretz, *Why Are Jews Liberals?*, 272.
54. Mellman, Strauss, and Wald, *Jewish American Voting Behavior 1972–2008*, 11.
55. Ibid., 24.
56. Ibid., 12.
57. Note that service attendance was the only religiosity variable available to Mellman, Strauss, and Ward.) While the level of involvement in one's faith for Christian groups can be measured satisfactorily by church attendance, many Jews, while not synagogue members and while not attending synagogue services regularly, are involved in home religious practices (lighting candles on Friday night, attending a Passover Seder, etc.), that have no equivalent in the Christian world. In addition, other Jews, while not at all religious, are involved Jewishly in an ethnic sense in their participation in Jewish cultural activities and in support of Israel.
58. Calculated by author from data available at www.census.gov.
59. Podhoretz, *Why Are Jews Liberals?*, 258.
60. For further analysis of the relationship between various aspects of Jewish ethnicity and political party and political ideology, see Kotler-Berkowitz, "Ethnicity and Political Behavior among American Jews."
61. Sheskin, 2012.
62. Berger, "Milton Himmelfarb."
63. Wald and Calhoun-Brown, *Religion and Politics in the United States*, 266.
64. Jones and Cox, *Chosen for What*.
65. Podhoretz, *Why Are Jews Liberals?*, 277.
66. Lazerwitz, Winter, and Dashefsky, "Localism, Religiosity, Orthodoxy, and Liberalism."
67. Podhoretz, *Why Are Jews Liberals?*, 269.
68. Ibid., 282.
69. Wald and Calhoun-Brown, *Religion and Politics in the United States*, 266.
70. Putnam and Campbell, *American Grace*.
71. Schrag, "American Jews and Evangelical Christians."
72. Wald and Calhoun-Brown, *Religion and Politics in the United States*, 273.
73. Windmueller, "Jews and the Tea Party Movement."
74. Pew Forum on Religion and Public Life, *U.S. Religious Landscape Survey*.
75. Pew Forum Survey of 2013.
76. Kotler-Berkowitz, "Ethnicity and Political Behavior among American Jews," 135.
77. Wald and Calhoun-Brown, *Religion and Politics in the United States*, 271.
78. Berger, "How Many Russian Jews Are in the U.S.?"
79. Berger, "Among New York's Soviet Immigrants, Affinity for G.O.P."
80. Simpson, "Poll Finds Generation Gap Emerging in Russian Vote."
81. http://www.njdc.org/blog/post/BarakCorrectsGreta080411.
82. Workmen's Circle, *Workmen's Circle/Arbiter Ring, 2012 American Jews' Political Values Survey.*
83. Saad, "Americans' Sympathies for Israel Match All-Time High."

REFERENCES

Berger, Joseph. "Among New York's Soviet Immigrants, Affinity for G.O.P." *New York Times* 8 May 2012.

Berger, Joseph. "Milton Himmelfarb, Wry Essayist, 87, dies." *New York Times* 15 January 2006.

Berger, Paul. "How Many Russian Jews Are in the U.S.?" *Forward* 25 November 2011.

Berkowitz, Bill. "The Tea Party Movement's Jewish Problem." 13 January 2010. http://www.truth-out.org/buzzflash/commentary/the-tea-party-movements-jewish-problem/8640-the-tea-party-movements-jewish-problem.

Cline, Seth. "Sheldon Adelson Willing to Spend $100 Million to Beat Obama." *US News and World Report*. 14 June 2012. http://www.usnews.com/news/articles/2012/06/14/sheldon-adelson-willing-to-spend-100-million-to-beat-obama

Cohen, Steven M. *American Modernity and Jewish Identity*. Vol. 140. New York: Tavistock, 1983.

Cohen, Steven M., and Charles S. Liebman, "American Jewish Liberalism: Unraveling the Strands." *Public Opinion Quarterly* 61 (1997): 405–430.

Cohen, Steven M., et al. *Jewish Community Study of New York*. New York: UJA-Federation of New York, 2012.

Comenetz, Joshua. "Jewish Maps of the United States by Congressional District—Revised January 2014." http://www.jewishdatabank.org/Studies/details.cfm?StudyID=719.

DellaPergola, Sergio. "How Many Jews in the United States: The Demographic Perspective." *Contemporary Jewry* 33.1–2 (2013): 15–42.

DellaPergola, Sergio. "Was It the Demography: A Reassessment of U.S. Jewish Population Estimates, 1945–2001." *Contemporary Jewry* 25.1 (2005): 85–131.

DellaPergola, Sergio. "World Jewish Population, 2014." *American Jewish Year Book, 2014*. Ed. Arnold Dashefsky and Ira M. Sheskin. Dordrecht: Springer, 2014. 301–393.

Edsall, Thomas B., and Alan Cooperman. "GOP Uses Remarks to Court Jews." *Washington Post* 13 March 2013: A01. http://www.stat.unc.edu/visitors/temp/NYT/Jcontrib.html.

Feingold, Henry L. *Jewish Power in America: Myth and Reality*. Piscataway, NJ: Transaction, 2011.

Gold, Steven J. "Patterns of Adaptation among Contemporary Jewish Immigrants to the US." *American Jewish Year Book*, forthcoming 2015. Ed. Arnold Dashefsky and Ira Sheskin. American Jewish Year Book, 2015, Vol. 115. Dordrecht: Springer, 2015.

Goldberg, Jonathan J. *Jewish Power: Inside the American Jewish Establishment*. Reading, MA: Perseus, 1997.

Greenberg, Anna, and Kenneth D. Wald. "Still Liberal after All These Years?" *Jews in American Politics*. Ed. L. Sandy Maisel and Ira Forman. Lanham: Rowman & Littlefield, 2001.

Herda, Daniel. "Innocuous Ignorance? Perceptions of the American Jewish Population Size." *Contemporary Jewry* 33 (2013): 1–15.

Jones, Jeffrey M. "Record-High 40% of Americans Identify as Independents in '11." 9 January 2012. http://www.gallup.com/poll/151943/record-high-americans-identify-independents.aspx

Jones, Robert P., and Daniel Cox. *Chosen for What? Jewish Values in 2012, Findings from the 2012 Jewish Values Survey.* Washington, D.C.: Public Religion Research Institute, Inc., 2012.

Kosmin, Barry, and Ariella Keysar. "American Jewish Secularism: Jewish Life beyond the Synagogue." *American Jewish Year Book, 2012.* Ed. Arnold Dashefsky and Ira M. Sheskin. : Dordrecht: Springer, 2013. 3–54.

Kosmin, Barry A., et al. *Highlights of the CJF 1990 National Jewish Population Survey.* New York: Council of Jewish Federations, 1991.

Kotler-Berkowitz, Laurence. "Ethnicity and Political Behavior among American Jews: Findings from the National Jewish Population Survey 2000–01." *Contemporary Jewry* 25 (2005): 132–157.

Kotler-Berkowitz, Laurence, et al. *Strength, Challenge and Diversity in the American Jewish Population.* New York: United Jewish Communities, 2003. http://www.jewishdatabank.org/studies/downloadFile.cfm?FileID=1490

Lazerwitz, Bernard, J. Alan Winter, and Arnold Dashefsky. "Localism, Religiosity, Orthodoxy, and Liberalism: The Case of Jews in the United States." *Social Forces* 67 (1988): 229–242.

Maisel, L. Sandy, and Ira Forman, eds. *Jews in American Politics.* Lanham: Rowman & Littlefield, 2001.

Massarik, Fred, and Alvin Chenkin. "United States National Jewish Population Study: A First Report." *American Jewish Year Book 1972.* New York: American Jewish Committee and the Jewish Publication Society, 1973. 264–306.

Mellman, Mark S., Aaron Strauss, and Kenneth D. Wald. *Jewish American Voting Behavior 1972–2008: Just the Facts.* The Solomon Project, 2012. http://images.politico.com/global/2012/07/solomonsurvey072012op.pdf.

Mittleman, Alan, Jonathan D. Sarna, and Robert Licht. *Jewish Polity and American Civil Society.* Lanham, MA: Rowman & Littlefield, 2002.

Nadeau, Richard, Richard G. Niemi, and Jeffrey Levine. "Innumeracy about Minority Populations." *Public Opinion Quarterly* 57.3 (1993): 332–347.

Perlman, Joel. *The American Jewish Committee's Annual Opinion Surveys: An Assessment of Sample Quality.* Annandale-on-Hudson, NY: The Levy Economics Institute of Bard College, 2007.

Pew Forum on Religion and Public Life. . *Religious Landscape Study.* 2008. http://www.pewforum.org/religious-landscape-study/.

Pew Research Center. "A Portrait of Jewish Americans." Washington, DC: Pew Research Center, 2013.

Podhoretz, Norman. *Why Are Jews Liberals?* New York: Doubleday, 2009.

Putnam, Robert D., and David E. Campbell. *American Grace: How Religion Divides and Unites Us.* New York: Simon & Schuster, 2012.

Saad, Lydia. "Americans' Sympathies for Israel Match All-Time High." 15 March 2013. http://www.gallup.com/poll/161387/americans-sympathies-israel-match-time-high.aspx.

Schrag, Carl. "American Jews and Evangelical Christians: Anatomy of a Changing Relationship." *Jewish Political Studies Review* 17.1–2 (2005): 171–181.

Sheskin, Ira M. *Comparisons of Jewish Communities: A Compendium of Tables and Bar Charts*. Storrs, CT: Mandell Berman Institute, Berman Jewish Data Bank and The Jewish Federations of North America, 2015. http://www.jewishdatabank.org/Studies/details.cfm?StudyID=777

Sheskin, Ira and Arnold Dashefsky. "Jewish Institutions." *The American Jewish Year Book*, 2014. Ed. Arnold Dashefsky and Ira M. Sheskin. Dordrecht: Springer, 2014. 397–740.

Sheskin, Ira M. "Four Questions about American Jewish Demography." *Jewish Political Studies Review* 20.1–2 (2008): 23–42. http://jcpa.org/article/four-questions-about-american-jewish-demography/.

Sheskin, Ira M. *The Jewish Community Study of Greater Washington*. Rockville, MD: The Kaplan Foundation, 2004.

Sheskin, Ira M. *The UJA Federation of Bergen County and North Hudson Community Study*. River Edge, NJ: The UJA Federation of Bergen County and North Hudson, 2001.

Sheskin, Ira M. "Why All the Emphasis on the Jewish Vote?" *St. Louis Jewish Light* 24 October 2012. http://www.stljewishlight.com/opinion/commentaries/article_3bf32bbc-1e00-11e2-a404-001a4bcf887a.html.

Sheskin, Ira M. "Will U.S. Jews Vote for Barack Obama in 2012?" *The Jerusalem Post* 21 March 2012. http://www.jpost.com/Opinion/Op-Ed-Contributors/Will-US-Jews-vote-for-Barack-Obama-in-2012.

Sheskin, Ira M., and Arnold Dashefsky. "Jewish Population in the United States, 2006." *American Jewish Year Book, 2006*. Ed. David Singer and Lawrence Grossman. Vol. 106. New York: American Jewish Committee, 2006. 133–193. http://www.jewishdatabank.org/Studies/downloadFile.cfm?FileID=3018

Sheskin, Ira M., and Arnold Dashefsky. "Jewish Population in the United States, 2014." *The American Jewish Year Book*, 2014. Ed. Arnold Dashefsky and Ira M. Sheskin.: Dordrecht: Springer, 2014. 215–283.

Simpson, Willie. "Poll Finds Generation Gap Emerging in Russian Vote." *Sheepshead Bites*. 18 October 2012. http://www.sheepsheadbites.com/2012/10/poll-finds-generation-gap-emerging-in-russian-vote/.

Tighe, Elizabeth, et al. *American Jewish Population Estimates: 2012*. Waltham, MA: Brandeis University, Steinhardt Social Research Institute, 2011. http://www.brandeis.edu/ssri/noteworthy/amjewishpop.html.

Tobin, Jonathan. "Jews, Money, and 2012." *Commentary* March 2012. https://www.commentarymagazine.com/article/jews-money-and-2012/.

Wald, Kenneth D., and Allison Calhoun-Brown. *Religion and Politics in the United States*. 6th ed. Lanham, MA: Roman & Littlefield, 2011.

Weisberg, Herbert F. "Reconsidering Jewish Presidential Voting Statistics." *Contemporary Jewry* 32.3 (2012): 215–236.

Windmueller, Steven. *Are American Jews Becoming Republican? Insights into Jewish Political Behavior*. Jerusalem Viewpoints No. 509. Jerusalem: Jerusalem Center for Public Affairs, 2003. http://jcpa.org/article/are-american-jews-becoming-republican-insights-into-jewish-political-behavior/.

Windmueller, Steven. "Jews and the Tea Party Movement." *Sh'ma*. 1 December 2012. http://shma.com/2012/12/jews-and-the-tea-party-movement/.

Windmueller, Steven. *Revisiting the 2008 American Presidential Election: Reflections on the Jewish Vote*. Changing Jewish Communities No. 44. Jerusalem: Jerusalem Center for Public Affairs, 2009.

Workmen's Circle. *Workmen's Circle/Arbiter Ring, 2012. American Jews' Political Values Survey*, 2012. http://www.bjpa.org/Publications/details.cfm?PublicationID=14166.

Zeveloff, Naomi. "U.S. Jewish Population Pegged at 6 million." *Jewish Daily Forward* Accessed 9 July 2013. http://forward.com/articles/149492.

Chapter 5

The Persisting Liberalism of (Most) American Jews: The Pew Survey of 2013 in Historical Context

Samuel J. Abrams and Steven M. Cohen

The mystery of American Jewish liberalism and its durability have intrigued observers for decades. As early as 1928, American Jews turned out in massive numbers for a Democratic presidential candidate, Al Smith, the first Roman Catholic candidate from a major party. Ultimately, Jews were on the losing side, as Smith lost to Herbert Hoover.

By the 1930s, Jewish support for Democrats was so pronounced that a Republican Jewish judge complained that his fellow Jews lived in three worlds (or *velten* in Yiddish): *di velt* (this world), *yene velt* (the next world), and Roosevelt. In the 1930s and 1940s, it was not at all surprising heavily working-class, urban-dwelling, and recently arrived Jews and their children to support Democratic candidates. But then in the 1950s, 1960s and 1970s, their suburban and more affluent children kept the Jewish liberal proclivity alive, as they sponsored open housing laws and agitated for civil liberties, civil rights, nuclear test bans, ending the Viet Nam war, and feminism. In more recent times, with the possible exception of the 1980 presidential election in which John Anderson siphoned a good number of Jewish votes from Jimmy Carter, Jews remained firmly in the Democratic voting column in Presidential and Congressional elections and even at the local level. The Gallup Poll[1] regularly reported that Jews supported Democrat Barak Obama over Republican Mitt Romney by a margin of 2–1 in the 2012 presidential election, and numerous media reports touted the close relationships between President Obama and the American Jewish population.[2]

Clearly, and somewhat paradoxically, Jewish liberalism persisted beyond the working-class period and the immigrant or second-generation status. Its endurance into the late-20th century prompted Milton Himmelfarb,[3] the distinguished conservative essayist, to quip that Jews "earn like Episcopalians and vote like Puerto Ricans." In saying so, he expressed the apparent anomaly between Jews' high social standing and their continuing identification with liberalism—the political camp most inclined to champion the interests of the poor and most prone to call for raising, or at least maintaining, the level of taxation on the most affluent.

Rising affluence is only one reason why some have predicted the demise of Jewish liberalism, or wondered about its persistence. Another factor is their decades-long mobilization on behalf of Israel. In the larger population, Israel's hard-line policies find more favor among American conservatives than they do among liberals, and among Evangelical Christians more than among mainstream Protestants and their typically more liberal church leaders. Indeed, in recent years Evangelicals have raised charitable funds for Israel while several mainstream Protestant church leaders have seemed more sympathetic to Palestinian claims and to calls for boycotting Israel. If American Jews care about Israel, as most still do, and they support its government's policies, as many still do, then how do they manage to lend their votes, activism, and financial contributions to the political party and the ideological camp that seem less aligned with Israel's policies, if not with its interests? In short, if American Jews are pro-Israel, how can they remain so staunchly pro-liberal?

The mystery of American Jews' enduring liberalism continues when considering the role of their waning sense of societal marginality. Through much of the 20th century, Jews were treated as outsiders. They were excluded from certain neighborhoods, universities, big businesses, country clubs, philanthropic boards, and prestigious social circles. Their outsider status, or societal marginality, had political consequences. Jews aligned with other marginalized groups in society to challenge the cultural and political hegemony of Northern white Protestant men as expressed in the Republican Party and the conservative camp. The famed Democratic coalition of mid-century brought together an incongruous array of the socially marginalized.

Yet this prop to American Jews' liberalism also faded as, in more recent decades, the growing acceptance of Jews has proceeded apace. In one study in the early 1960s, Jews were among the lowest ranking white ethnic groups, in terms of social prestige. But as Robert Putnam reported in *American Grace*,[4] by 2009 their social standing had advanced to where they now ranked as the most admired religious group in America. At the same time, Jews have been intermarrying at extraordinary rates: since 2000, 58 percent of all Jews who married did so with non-Jews; for the non-Orthodox, the number climbed to 72 percent; and for those raised Reform, the recent intermarriage rate reached 82 percent. With so many non-Jews willing to marry Jews, and even more involved in nonmarried romantic relationships with them, Jews must have some inkling that they are increasingly accepted in America. The high rate at which Jews say they are proud to be Jewish—94 percent—itself is testimony to the greater comfort Jews feel in the larger society. Shouldn't these signs and components of increased acceptance and diminished marginality have nudged Jews toward the center, or even toward conservative precincts that look to maintain the prevailing social order and patterns of privilege rather than try to disrupt them?

Still other processes should also have eroded Jews' liberal commitment. First is the matter of "assimilation," loosely defined. Insofar as liberalism is associated with Jewish group identity, and insofar as Jews assimilate, that is, lose their attachment to Jewish social identity, shouldn't a decline in Jews' liberalism be observed, especially among those who intermarry and particularly among the children of the intermarried? In short, if being distinctively Jewish means being disproportionately liberal, what happens when Jews are less distinctively Jewish? Why don't they become less liberal and move toward the American political center?

In point of fact, earlier and largely unnoticed research has noted the very selective nature of Jews' liberalism, once their sociodemographic characteristics are considered. They remain liberals with respect to their partisan and ideological identities; social and sexual norms; church state and spending. But at the same time, Jewish liberalism is far from comprehensive and universal. Cohen and Liebman (1997) found almost two decades ago that "on issues of poverty, race, capital punishment, and civil liberties, American Jews, in the past twenty years [now almost forty years], are not liberal. . . . Jews may earn like Episcopalians and vote like Hispanics; they think like Episcopalians. In this respect, contrary to what others have argued, there is no anomaly of excessive Jewish liberalism (p. 6).[5]

This chapter presents the historical and contemporary data on the state of Jews' political ideology, showing where historical Jewish liberalism persists and where it recedes or even does not exist. We will show that the Jewish population is not entirely homogenous; moreover, much of the extant work on the Jewish population uses tools such as exit polls which overstate the strength of Jewish political ideology and make it appear far more uniform than it truly is.[6] With original data and data from the Pew survey on Jewish Americans,[7] we present a balanced portrait of the state of

Jewish political opinion and behavior in the United States, which is strong, but not absolute.

PARTISANSHIP AND BEHAVIOR

Due to modern advances in polling and big data, the academic and policy communities can paint an empirical picture of the Jewish population's attachment to liberalism and the Democratic Party since the 1950s, as large-scale public opinion surveys began in earnest. Figure 5.1 presents pooled decadal data from the American National Election studies to generate sample sizes of Jewish Americans that range from a high of 256 in the 1970s to a low of 139 in the 2000s. These raw numbers are not huge and do not permit much examination of internal differences within the Jewish population, however, the data do enable a general examination of the population's opinions and behaviors.

Stated partisanship and ideology are two measures that are regularly queried historically and, while incomplete and subject to bias, these can paint a comparative picture of Jewish positions relative to the average American. Figure 5.1 plots a collapsed version of stated partisanship along a seven-point scale, where respondents indicated if they were independents, leaning toward a party, strong partisans, or weak partisans. The top half of Figure 5.1 presents the often reported and widely examined (Fiorina and Abrams 2009) national trend where strong and weak Republican identifiers have not moved much in almost 70 years and hovered in the mid to high 20 percent range. Meanwhile, those who identified as strong and weak Democrats have declined from a high of 46 percent in the 1960s to a low of 36 percent in the 2000s while there has been a concurrent rise of independents and leaners from the high 20s in the 1950s and 1960s to a high of almost 40 percent in the 2000s. While these trends have been unpacked elsewhere, it is worth noting them here for they provide context for studying the Jewish population's positions along the same dimensions.

The Jewish population's responses are plotted in the bottom half of the figure and reveal a drastically different set of trends compared to the national data in the top half of the figure. The first clear finding is that the trend lines are fairly flat over time, and while there are some shifts over the decades, all three categories are at approximately the same values in the 2000s as they were in the 1950s. Therefore, Jewish opinion seemingly appears fairly stable compared to the national trend, which has shifted notably away from Democrats over time. The second notable finding is that where Jews place themselves on the seven-point scale is appreciably different with a small number of Jews identifying as Republican, hovering around 10 percent with a recent uptick, and the lion's share going to Democratic identifiers with 60 percent. The remaining 30 percent are for independents and leaners, and this group has declined slightly in recent

Figure 5.1
Partisanship: Jewish Identifiers and the General Population

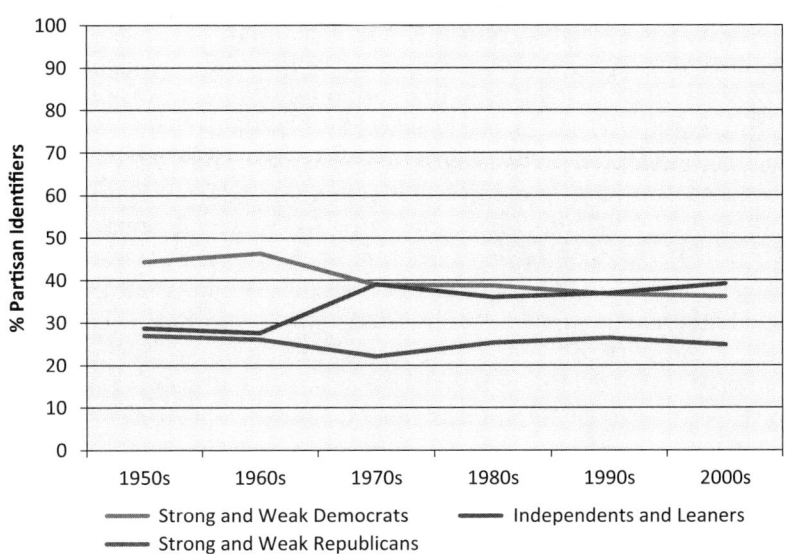

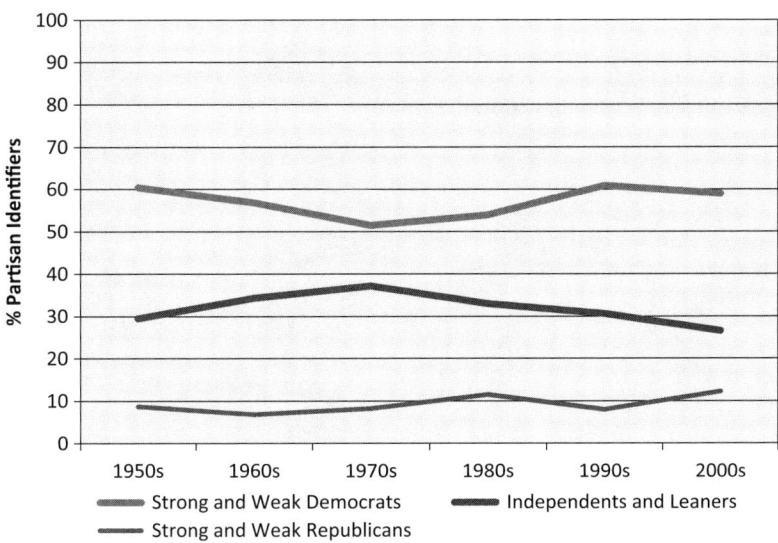

Source: ANES.

decades while Democratic identifiers have grown steadily since a low point in the 1970s. Given the data presented here, it is hardly surprising why so many academics, pundits, and politicos continue to assert that there is a persistent Democratic and left lean among American Jews.

In addition to self-reported data on partisan choice, which is an imperfect measure, exit polling data with moderately large samples of American Jews (from roughly 400 to over 3,000) have regularly been collected that enable us to evaluate Jewish voting and partisan preferences. These data (see Figures 5.2 and 5.3), reveal, like Figure 5.1, a stable and enduring trend of support toward Democratic candidates. In Figure 5.2, we compared the Democratic percentage of the two- party vote for Democratic candidates for members of the House of Representatives. The national trend hovers between 50 and 60 percent. The Jewish trend, in contrast, is considerably greater in support of Democratic House candidates with the trend line being fairly stable and 20 points higher, at almost 80 percent with a spike at 90 percent in 2006. Again, this Jewish tendency is markedly different from the national picture and in line with the partisan data.

Figure 5.3 presents exit poll data on presidential vote choice and these data show not only a strong Jewish preference over time for Democratic presidential candidates but also an increasingly stronger level of support over time from the 1970s through the 2000s. The national sample of the two-party presidential vote fluctuated regularly, the range of Democratic

Figure 5.2
The Jewish Vote in Congressional Elections, 1972–2008

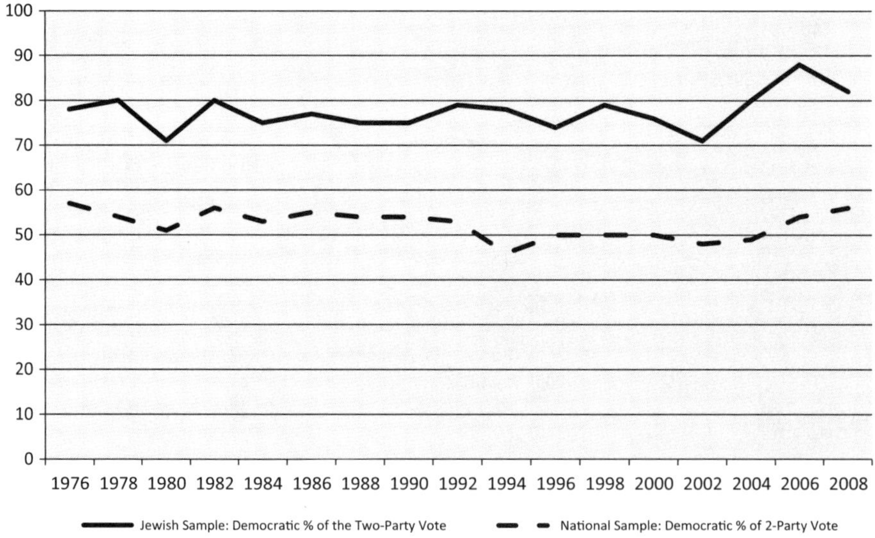

Source: NAEP.

Figure 5.3
The Jewish Vote in Presidential Elections, 1972–2008

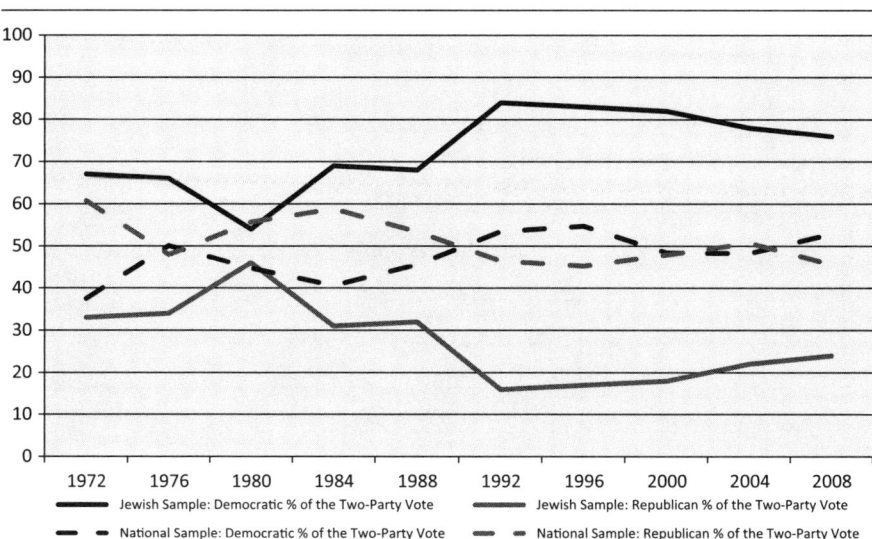

Source: NAEP.

presidential support moved from a low of the high 30s in 1972 during the Nixon-McGovern race to highs in the mid-50s during the Clinton era. Moreover, the majority supporting one candidate over another candidate fluctuated over time. The Jewish trend line, on the other hand, revealed a strong majority of Jews voting for Democratic presidential candidates since 1972, and at no point did support a dip below 55 percent. In fact, the average percentage of support over the 36-year period was 72 percent in favor of the Democratic presidential candidate, with the number generally climbing from a low of 55 percent in 1980. The overall level of support declined from a high of 94 to 76 percent from 1992 to 2008, but the cumulative effect remains that Jews are far more supportive of Democratic presidential candidates compared to Republicans.

Finally, some additional context about these voting and partisan trends is warranted, as it accentuates the unique nature of the American Jewish population. The first appears in Figure 5.4, which compares self-reported turnout data from the American National Election Studies over time. While self-reported data overstate the realities of turnout,[8] the ANES data represent a fairly useful measure to examine how American Jews compare with the national behavior of Americans over time. The data in Figure 5.4 show a nontrivial difference between Jews and Americans as a whole. On average, Jews vote at a rate of 85 percent compared to 68 percent for the average American. The two trend lines track ebbs and flows over time, but

Figure 5.4
Jewish and National Self-Reported Turnout

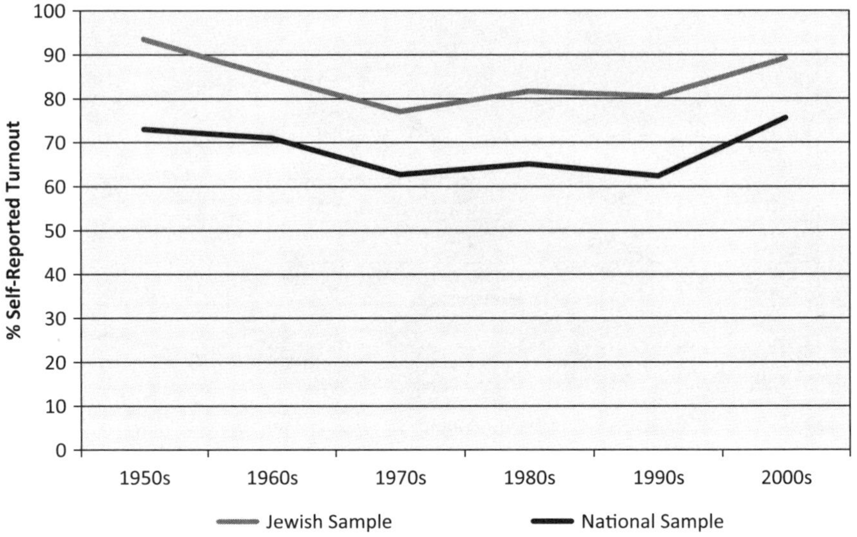

[Line graph showing % Self-Reported Turnout from 1950s to 2000s. Jewish Sample line starts around 93% in 1950s, declines to ~77% in 1970s, rises slightly through 1980s-1990s (~80-82%), and climbs to ~90% in 2000s. National Sample line starts around 73% in 1950s, declines to ~63% by 1970s, stays around 63-65% through 1990s, rising to ~75% in 2000s.]

Source: ANES.

Jews participate at a rate almost 20 percent higher than the general population. This turnout reality, coupled with the fact that, as Figure 5.5 shows, the Jewish population has a greater than average and growing number of individuals who identify as partisans (defined as strong and weak partisan identifiers on the seven-point scale) contributes to the sense that there is an enduring and strong left-lean to the American Jewish population. Figure 5.5 also plots the Jewish partisan trend line next to the national partisan trend, the differences are striking. More specifically, the national trend has been a secular decline in partisanship that is captured with partisans decreasing from levels in the 70th percentile range in the 1950s to the 60th percentile range today. Jews have declined a bit from the 1950s to the 1970s with a low of the 60th percentile. However, from the 1970s through the present, partisanship increased notably among the Jews, climbing to the 85th percentile range by the 2000s. Jews today are almost 25 points higher than the American population at large in terms of being partisan identifiers and that fact, coupled with higher rates of turnout, certainly contributes to the widespread knowledge of American Jewish liberalism and influence.

Viewing Figures 5.1–5.5 comprehensively, it certainly appears that Jewish left-leaning behavior is not only persistent but also has been increasing over time; however, these figures can be misleading. Not only are the sample sizes small, but the variables of interest are crude. Measures of partisanship and voting preferences often conflate choices with true preferences. Jews, like all Americans, live in a world of ever-increasing

Figure 5.7
Ideological Positions Compared

Issue: Government should provide many fewer services; Reduce spending a lot vs. Government should provide many more services; increase spending a lot

%	1 Fewer Services	2	3	4 Neutral	5	6	7 More Services
Jewish Sample	15.5	8.8	11.5	21.4	20.0	15.5	7.4
	24.3			52.9			22.9
National Sample	7.1	9.4	11.7	23.5	22.3	12.0	13.9
	16.5			57.5			25.8

Source: ANES

Issue: Greatly decrease defence spending vs. Greatly increase defense spending

%	1 Less Spending	2	3	4 Neutral	5	6	7 More Spending
Jewish Sample	15.5	18.6	18.5	21.7	12.7	6.1	7.0
	34.1			52.9			13.1
National Sample	8.1	8.1	11	24	18	11	8
	16.2			53.0			19.0

Source: ANES

Issue: The government should do more to help needy Americans, even if it means going deeper into debt. vs. The government today can't afford to do much more to help the needy.

%	1 Help	2	3 Neutral	4	5 can't Afford
Jewish Sample	13.3	26.2	28.2	15.9	16.4
	39.5		28.2		32.3
National Sample	33	8	8	13	37
	41		8		5.1

Source: Pew

Issue: Poor people today have it easy because they can get government benefits without doing anything in return vs. Poor people have hard lives because government benefits don't go far enough to help them live decently.

%	1 Have It Easy	2	3 Neutral	4	5 Not Enough Support
Jewish Sample	14.8	16.5	25.3	23.6	19.6
	31.3		25.3		43.4
National Sample	29	12	12	12	35
	51		12		47.0

Source: Pew

Issue: Women and Men should have equal roles vs. A woman's place in the home

%	1 Equal Roles	2	3	4 Neutral	5	6	7 In the Home
Jewish Sample	72.0	10.1	5.7	7.1	2.2	1.4	1.5
	82.1						
National Sample	64	15	5	10	3	2	2
	79.1						

Source: ANES

Issue: Government regulation of business is necessart to portect the public interest. vs. Government regulation of business usually does more harm than good.

%	1 Necessary	2	3 Neutral	4	5 Does Harm
Jewish Sample	32.1	25.2	14.6	15.3	12.8
	57.3		14.6		28.1
National Sample	33	14	8	10	35
	47.0		8		45.0

Source: ANES

Issue: Too much power is concentrated in the hands of a few large companies. vs. The largest companies do NOT have too much power.

%	1 Too Much	2	3 Neutral	4	5 Nor Too Much
Jewish Sample	44.8	22.3	18.5	8.5	5.9
	67.1		18.5		14.4
National Sample	66	12	6	7	9
	78		6		16

Source: Pew

Issue: Business corporation make too much profit. vs. Most corporations make a fair and reasonable amount of profit

%	1 Too Much	2	3 Neutral	4	5 Reasonable
Jewish Sample	28.2	24.0	20.4	14.5	12.8
	52.2				27.3
National Sample	47	7	7	13	26
	54				39

Issue: Immigrants today strenthen our country because of their hard work and talents. vs. Immigrants today are a burden on our country because they take our jobs, housing and health care.

%	1 Strengthen	2	3 Neutral	4	5 A Burden
Jewish Sample	28.1	32.3	22.5	9.6	7.4
	60.4		22.5		17
National Sample	33	12	12	9	35
	45.0		12		44

Source: The Pew Foundation and the ANES.

Figure 5.8
Ideological Positions Compared

Issue: Gay Marriage

%	Favor	Oppose
Jewish Sample	78.0	22.0
National Sample	47	43

Pew Research Center. April 4-15, 2012. N = 1,514 adults nationwide. Margin of error±2.9.

"Do you strongly favor, favor, oppose, or strongly oppose allowing gay and lesbian couples to marry legally?"
EXCEPT for 5/08, 6/08, 8/09, 4/12: "Do you strongly favor, favor, oppose, or strongly oppose allowing gays and lesbians to marry legally?"

Issue: Abortion

	Jewish Sample	National Sample
By law, abortion should never be permitted	1.3	15
The law should permit abortion only in the case of rape, incest, or when the woman's life is in danger	11.4	27
The law should permit abortion for reasons other than rape, incest, or danger to the woman's life, but only after the ne.	12.5	18
By law, a woman should always be able to obtain an abotyion as a matter of personal choice	74.8	40

Source: ANES

Issue: Climate Change

	Jewish Sample	National Sample
Climate Change–Occurring	71.9	54
Global climate change has been established as a serious problem, and immediate action is necessary.	45.8	23
There is enough evidence that climate change is taking place and some action should be taken.	26.1	31
Climate Change–Not Occurring	28.0	46
We don't know enough about global climate change, and more research is necessary before we take any actions.	13.3	29
Concern about global climate change is exaggerated. No action is necessary.	8.7	12
Global climate change is not occurring; this is not a real issue.	6.0	5

NBC News/Wall Street Journal Poll conducted by the polling organizations of Peter Hart (D) and Bill McInturff (R.) Dec. 11-14, 2009. N = 1,008 adults nationwide.

Issue: Medicare Changes

	Jewish Sample	National Sample
Complete Overhaul	11.3	15
Major Changes	26.1	27
Unsure	9.1	4
Minor Modifications	44.1	39
OK the way it is	9.3	15

NBC News/Wall Street Journal Poll conducted by the polling organizations of Peter Hart (D) and Bill McInturff (R.) Aug. 16-20, 2012. N = 1,000 registered voters nationwide. Margin of error ± 3.1.

population as each issue has been measured linearly in either the General Social Survey or the American National Election Studies over time and therefore provide a strong national baseline for comparison against the Jewish population as a whole.

Services/Spending: Both the national sample and our Jewish sample overwhelmingly placed themselves in the central, neutral category on the debate between fewer services and reducing spending compared to increasing spending and services with each group in the mid-50 percentile range. With the remaining percentages, the general population leaned right of center on this metric with almost 10 more points in favor of more spending and services, the Jewish population was essentially evenly split in the mid-20s.

Defense Spending: This item closely resembles an item in Figure 5.6 and the results here are cognate for the Jewish population. Here the Jewish population again placed itself with its majority in the neutral category, but the remaining Jews were three times more likely to be in favor of reducing defense spending, which differed significantly from the national sample whose nonneutral votes leaned to spending more on defense.

Helping the Needy: This question asked respondents to balance helping the poor with concerns about the national debt, and the responses between Jews and the national sample differed sharply here. Americans were not neutral here at all, but split their positions between the two choices with a slight, 10-point preference for not helping the needy. Jews, on the other hand, were far more divided, with a plurality (40%) supporting the idea that helping the needy was more important than taking on more debt. Roughly 30 percent of the population each supported either not going into more debt or was neutral.

Poor/Mobility: Similar the notion of debt and the poor, this item queried the salience of government benefits in helping the poor move forward and the general attitude of respondents toward the poor. Here, the national sample was split, with only a small number of respondents placing themselves in the neutral center and the remainder dividing themselves between believing that the poor were either lazy or lacked enough support to get ahead. The Jewish population was split, in contrast, with the plurality believing that the poor did not have enough support and about a third believing that the poor had it easy. About a quarter of Jews were neutral here and this again shows that the Jewish population was not as ideologically dogmatic but uncertain for many salient and challenging policy issues.

Gender Roles: There is little to say here and little variance for large majorities in the same proportions for Jews, and Americans in general support the idea that men and women have equal roles in society.

Government/Business: On the question of the relationship between the public good and government regulation of business, there is a clear difference between Jews and the national sample. While the national sample was not neutral (8%), the population splits evenly (47%–45%) between regulation and free markets. The Jewish population clearly leaned toward the position that government regulation of business was necessary to protect the public interest, with almost 60 percent of the respondents supporting that view compared to almost 30 percent in the other direction. In this case, there seems to be a stronger liberal position with the Jewish population on the whole.

Corporate Power: In contrast to the issue of regulation and public interest item, the question of large companies having too much power produced responses among Jews and Americans that were fairly similar. Large majorities in both groups supported the notion that there was too much power in companies, with roughly 15 percent in each group believing that there was not too much power—we have relative parity here.

Corporate Profit: With respect to profit, Jews and Americans in general were on the same page in the mid-50 percentile range in thinking that business corporations earned too much profit. Jews were slightly more liberal, as 39 percent of Americans are satisfied with the rates of corporate profit, compared to only 27 percent of Jews approving the amount of corporate profit and 20 percent in an undecided neutral position.

Immigration: Liberalism on the part of the Jewish population came through in terms of beliefs about the value of immigrants in the United States compared to the population as a while. About 60 percent of Jews believed that immigrants strengthen the United States with ~20 percent or so unclear and 17 percent seeing immigrants as a burden. The national picture, in contrast, was split with almost 45 percent in each direction, suggesting a divided sense of the role of newcomers to the United States compared to the strong support that such individuals had within the Jewish population.

In addition to these nine linear scales, we queried Jews on four additional items and compared those responses with national samples responding to the same issue items. These data are presented in Figure 5.8 and the subfigure on gay marriage demonstrates another stark difference between Jews and typical Americans quite clear. Gay marriage has been a polarizing issue for decades and the national sample showed a clear split with 47 percent in support and 43 percent in opposition. The Jewish division was different with a ratio of 3:1 in support of gay marriage—a nontrivial difference on the liberal side for Jews.

With respect to the abortion Jews were also more liberal when compared to the national average. The abortion table in the upper right quadrant plots the response percentage to the question ""Which one of the opinions on this page best agrees with your view?"[11] The national sample revealed that 40 percent believed that a woman has the right to an abortion under any circumstance and divided the balance in various cases with 15 percent believing that it should never be permitted. The Jewish population in this case was again fairly liberal compared to the nation as a whole.

The final two tables, in the bottom half of Figure 5.8, show mixed positions for the Jewish population in relation to the average American. On the left, we plotted data related to issues of climate change and Jews were 20 points higher than the national sample in stating that climate change is occurring and this position tended to resonate on the liberal side of the ideological spectrum. With respect to changes in Medicare, there was relative parity here among Jews and those in the national sample. Equal numbers wanted to see a complete overhaul (15%) and major changes (27%) and similar amounts wanted to see minor modifications (~40%). Of course, all of the items in Figure 5.8 are imperfect measures of ideological leanings, but they offered a sense of where people stood on these issues and allowed us to gain a better sense of where the Jewish population stood with respect to the rest of the nation.

Taking all of these 13 items into consideration, the portrait of the Jewish population in America as a stalwart liberal group is called into question. While it is the case that long-term trends with respect to partisanship and voting again show an affinity for the left and for the Democrats, political choices made in a polarized world do not necessarily equate with true ideological positions and preferences. Our survey items, asked in isolation, also seemingly revealed a deep and committed left-bent to most policy issues. However, the data in Figures 5.7 and 5.8, revealed a liberalism for certain issues—abortion, gay rights, and immigration—but marked centrism in and parity with Americans on others. Moreover, those issues on which Jews are often very liberal are rarely salient in "most important issue" lists. More specifically, these social issues—issues that dominate the so called culture wars and the news—are simply not significant in the political calculus of most Americans. The Gallup Poll for decades has asked the question of "What is the most important problem facing the country?" and 66 percent of the responses to that question in May 2012 were economic in nature, from the economy in general to jobs, and the federal deficit. Noneconomic problems are simply not particularly important to most of the American public at the present time and social issues are rarely mentioned in response to survey questions on the most important problem facing the county.

ORTHODOX EXCEPTIONALISM

The foregoing discussion applies to the 90 percent of American Jewish adults who defined themselves as other than Orthodox. As a group, however, the Orthodox are exceptional. Both Modern Orthodox and Haredi Orthodox often align with other fervently religious groups in America, particularly around cultural issues pertaining to abortion, gay rights, and related matters. Moreover, the profound attachments of Orthodox Jews to Israel and their relative hawkishness on Israeli policies also tend to propel them toward conservative Republicans.

Figure 5.9 makes the Orthodox/non-Orthodox distinction quite clear by plotting vote choice in the past two presidential elections. In both elections, non-Orthodox readily supported Obama but the Orthodox community

Figure 5.9
Orthodox and Non-Orthodox Presidential Voting

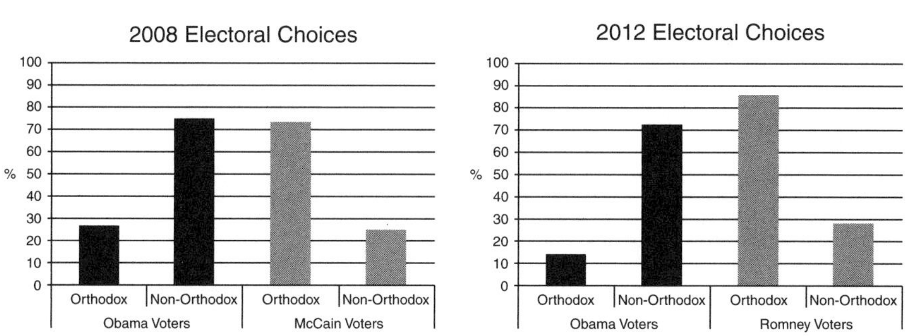

Source: 2012 WC/AR Social Activist Survey.

Figure 5.10
Jewish Ideology from the Pew Religious Landscape Survey

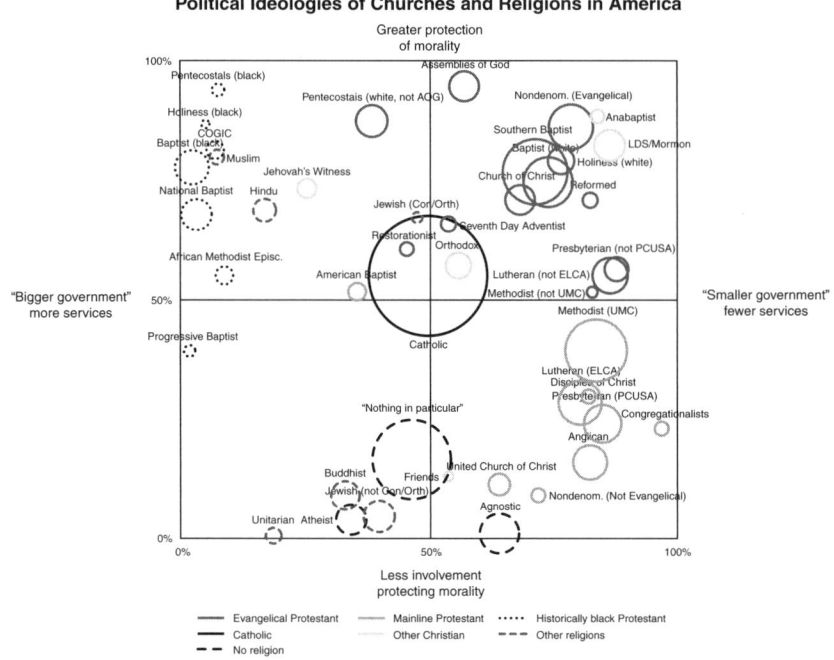

Source: http://tobingrant.religionnews.com/2014/08/27/politics-american-churches-religions-one-graph/.

voted strongly in favor of the Republican candidates. Figure 5.9 presents a notably different portrait than Figure 5.3, supporting our argument that just examining the traditional measures is flawed and incomplete and that change may be on the horizon. Moreover, a similar picture of a cleavage within the Jewish population emerges in Figure 5.10, which plots data from the Pew Religious Landscape Survey with a sample size that enabled scholars to break down Jewish religiosity. What emerged from this analysis (Figure 5.10) is that all Jews were fairly moderate and centrist on the economy. But there was a morality divide and that affected the issues mentioned earlier, such as gay rights, homosexuality, and abortion. While Figure 5.10 is not the complete story, it does again demonstrate that demographic change, coupled with this internal heterogeneity, should give pause to those who state that the Jewish population is a singular liberal entity.

THE PEW SURVEY OF 2013

Given all the changes in the American Jewish population and its relationships with the larger society, one may question whether American Jewish liberalism indeed persists, and, if it does, whether newly emerging trends are beginning to erode their historic commitment to the Democratic Party and more broadly to the liberal camp.

To examine the current state of American Jewish liberalism, we turn to a social scientific study of American Jewry: the Pew survey of American Jews, conducted in 2013. In the course of locating its massive national sample, Pew interviewed 3,475 respondents who qualified as Jewish [either "Jewish by Religion" (N = 2,786, representing 4.0 million people), or "Jewish with No Religion" (N = 689, representing 1.2 million people)]. In addition, Pew interviewed 1,190 respondents of "Jewish Background," as they identified them, or 2.6 million such people. These Jewish Background respondents did not identify as Jewish or identified with a non-Jewish religion, but had a Jewish parent or were raised as Jews.

FIVE MEASURES OF POLITICAL IDENTITY AND ATTITUDES

For purposes of this analysis, we focused on five particularly relevant and instructive questions contained in the Pew survey:

1. *Ideological Identity:* Respondents were asked to describe their political views on a five-point scale ranging from very conservative to very liberal. In Tables 5.1–5.4 in the following, these answers are translated into scores ranging from 0 to 100, from political right to left.
2. *Approval of Obama:* "Do you approve or disapprove of the way Barack Obama is handling his job as president?" We report the percentage that approved.
3. *Big government:* "If you had to choose, would you rather have a smaller government providing fewer services, or a bigger government providing more services?" We report the percentage favoring bigger government.
4. *Acceptance of homosexuality:* Preferring "Homosexuality should be accepted by society" versus "Homosexuality should be discouraged by society." We report the percentage that thought homosexuality was acceptable.
5. *Party identification:* Republican (scored as 0), Independent (50) or Democrat (100).

In all instances, higher scores reflected greater liberalism: more identification as a liberal, higher approval of Obama, support for bigger government, favoring acceptance of gay people and greater identification with the Democratic Party.

LIBERAL LEANINGS ACROSS THE BOARD

Where do American Jews overall stand on the political spectrum? Are they still situated left of the American center? Table 5.1 presents answers.

On all five political attitude measures, the Jewish population leaned to the left, and sometimes decidedly so. On the matter of their ideological identity on the political spectrum, Jewish liberals vastly outnumbered Jewish conservatives, 50 to 20 percent. In fact, looking at the "extreme" answers alone, those who said they were "very liberal" outnumbered those who were "very conservative" by almost 5–1 (19% vs. 4%). In contrast, most surveys of American society find the general public favoring conservatives over liberals.

Among the Jews surveyed, President Obama's approval ratings at the time (the first half of 2013) stood at 69 percent, far higher than in the American public where slim majorities—at best—expressed approval of his job performance.

The evidence for Jewish liberalism extended to other measures as well. We found that those favoring big government outnumbered those favoring smaller government or who were "not sure" by 56 percent to 44 percent. Those favoring acceptance of homosexuality reached as high as 84 percent. Finally, Democrats outnumbered Republicans by 4–1 (56% vs. 14%). These lopsided margins also underscored the contrasts between Jews and other Americans, as national polls in this period regularly showed the two parties virtually tied among the American public.

In short, on any of these questions (and surely others as well), if we can speak of a statistical center to the American public, Jewish citizens stood well to the left of that center. This is not to say that all Jews are liberals. But it is to say that the middle of the Jewish political spectrum is to the left of its counterpart in American society and that Jews abide far more liberalism, and especially "extreme" liberalism, than is found in the American population. At the same time, Jews include a relatively small number of conservatives, especially of the more "extreme" variety.

Is it possible to anticipate the perpetuation of Jewish liberalism? Do the internal differences within the Jewish population predict an ongoing commitment to the liberal camp, or do they suggest a turn toward the center or even the right?

MODERN ORTHODOX ON THE RIGHT, HAREDIM EVEN MORE SO

One critical issue, mentioned earlier, entails the variations between Orthodox and non-Orthodox Jews in America. How deep is this division, and how wide is the gap in political terms?

Table 5.1 suggests that the (currently) small numbers of Orthodox Jews sharply break from the overall liberal tendencies of the rest of American Jewry. All five indices show fairly similar interdenominational differences. The differences are present, but muted, for self-described political

Table 5.1
Political Variables by Denomination

Denomination Now	Very Liberal (100) to Very Conservative (0): Mean Score on 0–100 Scale	% Approving of Obama	% Favoring Bigger Government with More Services (vs. Opposed & Not Sure)	% Who Agree Homosexuality Should Be Accepted by Society	Democrat (100), Independent (50), or Republican (0): Mean Score
Haredi	31	34	37	21	38
Modern Orthodox	42	43	33	53	42
Conservative	53	65	50	81	69
Reform	65	73	58	93	79
No Denomination, Other	68	75	62	89	78
Total	61	69	56	84	73

Source: National data collected by the authors.

ideology. However, rather large gaps differentiate the Orthodox from other Jews in terms of support for Obama, preferring bigger government, accepting homosexuality, and party identification.

With respect to party identification, both Orthodox groups score about 40 (the Republican side of Independent), while the Conservative Jews average 69 (Democratic side of Independent) and Reform Jews display a mean of 79, putting them squarely in the Democratic camp. In other words, most Orthodox Jews are Republicans or Independents. Most Reform Jews are "soft" Democrats or strong Democrats.

As noted, these variations are highly consistent with previous research. Given the sharp differences between the Orthodox and the others, as well as our interest in learning how the various expectations associated with several major axes of social differentiation play out, Tables 5.1–5.3 focus entirely on the 90 percent of the adult Jewish population that defines itself as other than Orthodox. It is among the non-Orthodox, largely liberal Jews that we search for signs of persisting or eroding liberal identity.

SLIGHTLY MOUNTING LIBERALISM AMONG THE YOUTH

In the absence of measuring political attitudes at different points in time, the age variations in political attitudes at any one point offer a useful indicator of impending changes in political direction. Age-related differences are no certain sign of population-wide changes. Younger people may differ from their elders simply because they are young, single, without children, in early career stages, residentially unsettled, and economically vulnerable. Yet, younger people may also differ because they exhibit birth cohort or more enduring generational effects. Indeed, musical tastes, reading habits, technological capacity, and political attitudes all exhibit the effects of birth cohort, that is, the period in which one is born exerts significant impact upon a range of social characteristics.

Hence, with a degree of caution, we must ask: How do younger people differ from their elders? In which directions are political attitudes and identities headed? In short, are younger Jews (non-Orthodox) more liberal, more conservative, or about the same as their parents' and grandparents' generations? And what might that mean for the future of American Jewish liberalism?

In Table 5.2 on all five measures, those 18–29 were clearly more liberal than their elders; they were more liberal than the averages for the population as a whole, and they were more liberal than those 30–49. With respect to political identity (identifying as liberal, moderate, or conservative), each decline in age brought with it a very modest increase in liberal identity (or decline in conservative identity).

Table 5.2
Political Variables by Age, Four Groups, Non-Orthodox Only

Age	Very Liberal (100) to Very Conservative (0): Mean Score on 0–100 Scale	% Approving of Obama	% Favoring Bigger Government with More Services vs. Opposed & Not Sure	% Who Agree Homosexuality Should be Accepted by Society	Democrat (100), Independent (50), or Republican (0): Mean Score
18–29	68	78	67	97	81
30–49	64	71	55	89	75
50–64	63	69	55	87	76
65+	60	71	58	84	76
Total	64	72	58	89	77

Source: National data collected by the authors.

Table 5.3

Political Variables by Income, Four Groups, Non-Orthodox Only

	Very Liberal (100) to Very Conservative (0): Mean Score on 0–100 Scale	% Approving of Obama	% Favoring Bigger Government with More Services vs. Opposed & Not Sure	% Who Agree Homosexuality Should Be Accepted by Society	Democrat (100), Independent (50), or Republican (0): Mean Score
$150,000+	66	74	52	95	78
$100–$150,000	67	77	55	95	79
$50–$100,000	65	67	60	93	78
Less than $50,000	63	73	65	80	76
Total	65	73	59	90	78

Source: National data collected by the authors.

In short, at least the age results point to continued persistence of Jewish liberalism. But what about affluence? For Jews, do high incomes erode support for Democrats and for the liberal camp overall?

EARNING LIKE EPISCOPALIANS: THE LIMITED IMPACT OF INCOME

To address this other major question in the discourse on Jewish liberalism, we examine variations in political attitudes and identities tabulated by income. If affluence curtails Jewish liberalism, then we should see lower scores among those earning the most money.

But contrary to expectations, as a general rule, Jewish incomes appeared to have very little relationship with the political measures. We found few differences by income for three of the five measures: political ideology, Obama approval, and party identity.

However, we do see noticeably less approval of homosexuality among the least affluent, reflecting, in part older age and lower levels of educational attainment. In other words, a modicum of financial security is associated with greater acceptance of homosexuality, in large part because of the other social factors associated with low income.

But in one area we observed the corrosive impact of affluence on staunch liberalism, that is, we saw a slight softening of support for big government as the income ladder rose. This one item may indicate a more conservative posture among wealthier Jews with respect to related issues such as taxation and social welfare spending. To be sure, the turn is very modest at best. Jews earning like Episcopalians (actually, earning more than this most prestigious religious group) may come into play in views on economic justice, taxation, and other economic matters. However, such dynamics do not seem to have affected (yet?) their attachment to liberalism and the Democratic Party.

The survey did not contain information on wealth or on super-incomes. The views of the top 1 percent, who may comprise 3 percent or more of American Jews, may well be more conservative on economic matters than those of less affluent Jews.

INTERMARRIAGE: LITTLE EFFECT IN THIS GENERATION

The consequences of intermarriage may be revealed in two ways. The intermarried derive from and situate themselves in less religiously active parts of the Jewish population. As such, they might be expected to exhibit even greater liberalism than their in-married counterparts. At the same time, intermarriage is associated with more frequent relationships with non-Jewish family members and friends. Insofar as Jews are distinctively liberal, more Jewish relationships should reinforce liberalism, while more non-Jewish relationships, in theory, should diminish liberalism.

In Table 5.4, those married to a non-Jewish spouse exhibited views that were slightly to the left (generally, 5 points on a 100-point scale) than those who married other Jews. The nonmarried were aligned with or ever so slightly with the left of the intermarried, suggesting only a small effect, at most.

We cannot credit (or blame) in-marriage for these political gaps. First, they were very small. Second, the in-married were generally older and more denominationally Conservative. With controls for these and other correlative factors, in-marriage bore little causal relationship with political identities or attitudes.

INTERMARRIAGE: MOVING RIGHT IN THE NEXT GENERATION

While intermarriage may exert little impact on the political views of those marrying, it may well influence the next generation's move somewhat to the right. Owing to the high rates of intermarriage in recent years, the Pew data set contains large numbers of people who identify as Jewish and have one Jewish parent, the children of the intermarried. In fact, among the non-Orthodox, who are Jewish or no longer Jewish but had a Jewish parent, the number of such people with one Jewish parent only slightly trailed the number with two Jewish parents (almost 3 million vs. about 3.7 million adults).

The political effects of intermarriage on the next generation of people with Jewish parents may be counterintuitive. Among those with two Jewish parents, almost all (88%) continue to identify as Jews today. Among those with one Jewish parent, just 43 percent identify as Jews. Among those with Jewish parentage, then, we have four types of individuals: those with one Jewish parent, or two; those who identify as Jews and those who do not.

The extent to which these four groups identify with liberalism is very instructive. Fifty-five percent of those who identify as Jews also identify as liberals, regardless of parentage, and just a third (34%) of those who do not see themselves as Jews, or identify as liberal. The differences in political ideology between those with one or two Jewish parents are miniscule, while the differences in political ideology between Jews and non-Jews with Jewish parents are large. However, this is *not* to say that in-marriage and intermarriage are irrelevant. Rather, intermarriage leads to erosion of liberal commitment by way of eroding Jewish identity. Those who leave the Jewish community also leave its distinctively liberal political ethos and environs.

Table 5.4
The Non-Orthodox In-married, Intermarried, and Nonmarried

	Very Liberal (100) to Very Conservative (0): Mean Score on 0–100 Scale	% Approving of Obama	% Favoring Bigger Government with More Services vs. Opposed & Not Sure	% Who Agree Homosexuality Should Be Accepted by Society	Democrat (100), Independent (50), or Republican (0): Mean Score
Married to a Jewish Spouse	60	68	51	91	72
Married to a Non-Jewish Spouse	65	72	56	88	78
Not Married	65	74	63	89	78
Total	64	72	58	89	77

Source: National data collected by the authors.

CONCLUSION

Periodically, an article based on recent data that reaffirms the durability and persistence of Jewish liberalism is needed that draws upon data from one of the most authoritative sources of information on American Jews. In this chapter, the Pew data revealed in five diverse ways that Jews exhibit political views and identities that place them, as a group, well to the left of the American center. Of course, as we have seen numerous times before, the Orthodox—both Modern and Haredi—constitute an exception to this generalization.

Jews' liberal tilt does not extend to all issue areas. They identify as Democrats more than would be expected on the basis of their political views. In this research, relatively strong liberal leanings appeared with respect to gay marriage and other social justice issues, immigration, and defense spending. At the same time, Jews' liberalism was not so pronounced in regulation of business and their profit, Medicare and health care regulation, and the role of government benefits in supporting the needy. We have every reason to believe that Jews' liberalism is also restrained, if at all present, in other areas examined in prior research, such as economic regulation, issues of diplomacy and international relations, and issues of fairness and socioeconomic mobility.

Moreover, old-young comparisons among the non-Orthodox reaffirm the likely persistence of Jews' liberal tendencies as they mature. Higher income does not seem to blunt Jewish political liberalism, with the possible exception of matters relating to economic justice. Intermarriage does not bring about much change in Jewish political attitudes. However, insofar as intermarriage produces children who choose not to identify as Jews, these children also tend not to identify as liberals to the extent that typifies their counterparts who identify as Jewish.

While the proportion of non-Orthodox Jews who hold liberal views, albeit selectively, seems rather durable, the number of such Jews may well be in decline. While Orthodox numbers are increasing, below-replacement fertility levels and high rates of intermarriage among the non-Orthodox (reaching 72% overall and 82% among those raised Reform) may well be setting the stage not only for the numerical decline of engaged Jews outside of Orthodoxy but also as a corollary for the number of Jews with decidedly liberal inclinations. Raising Jewish fertility rates and their rates of in-marriage are essential to preserving the liberal character of American Jewry in the mid-21st century.

NOTES

1. http://www.gallup.com/poll/155111/mormons-widely-favor-romney-jewish-voters-back-obama.aspx.

2. http://www.jewishworldreview.com/1010/obama_remorse.php3#.VAZayvldWSo; Boyer, "Obama Aims to Shore Up Jewish Support"; Rosner, "So,

Arab immigration and an interest in Arab culture, Syrian-Americans might have Americanized themselves out of existence."[6]

There is no such concern today. A community with deep ethnic pride and shared heritage, culture, language, and concerns undoubtedly exists as a key constituency. Further, that established community of descendants of Arab immigrants continues to welcome new immigrants into its fold. The dynamic nature of the Arab American community has long been maintained by the constant turmoil in the Middle East. With each major conflict or war, additional immigrants arrived prepared to resume their new life in America. We see that today with increased arrivals from Egypt, Syria, and Iraq. But unlike earlier generations, these immigrants arrive to find well-established communities dispersed across the country. With their ethnic identify firmly established, Arab Americans sought to gain their rightful place in American politics. Like previous constituencies, they organized around common concerns; they established organizations to represent their interests; and they supported policy-makers who supported them. Further, they have established plans to help elect representatives from their own communities and leadership programs training the next generation of Arab Americans for public service. While profound challenges abound—particularly in a post-9/11 America—Arab Americans are poised to confront them as an organized constituency representing a fourth-generation attorney from Massachusetts and a recent arrival that may have just settled in Michigan. And central to that empowerment effort, as it has always been, is breaking down barriers through voting and political engagement.[7]

AN EMPOWERED COMMUNITY: BECOMING ARAB AMERICAN VOTERS

In 2014, 3.7 million Arab Americans lived in all 50 states, with two-thirds concentrated in just 10 states—California, Michigan, New York, Florida, Texas, New Jersey, Illinois, Ohio, Pennsylvania and Virginia- most of which are hotly contested during presidential elections (see Figure 6.1).

Arab American voters are generally well educated and upwardly mobile. Compared to 28 percent of Americans at large, 43 percent of Americans of Arab descent have a bachelor's degree or higher.[8] The Arab American voting bloc is known to vote for issues and candidates rather than political parties and have a high rate of political participation. And contrary to prevailing perceptions, they are not a single-issue constituency. Jobs and the economy regularly rank as their top issue.[9] Arab American voters also carry a strong sense of pride in their ethnic identity, which can determine the issues that matter the most to the bloc. For instance, U.S. policy in the Middle East is consistently one of the top three issues that matter most to Arab American voters.

Figure 6.1
States with the Largest Populations of Arab Americans.[10]

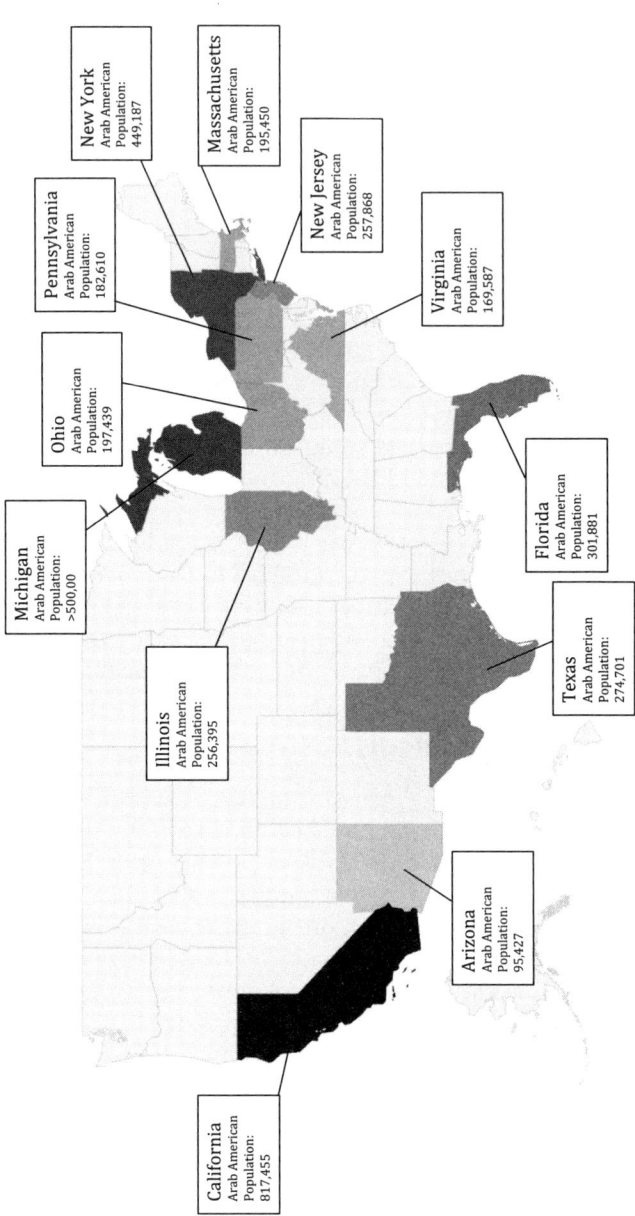

States with the Largest Populations of Arab Americans

*Note: These numbers have been adjusted for undercounting. Research by AAI and Zogby International suggest that the numbers provided by the Census are significantly lower than the actual number of Arab Americans in each state. The Census Bureau identifies only a portion of the Arab American population through a question on "ancestry" on the American Community Survey. Reasons for the undercount include the placement of and limit of the ancestry question (as distinct from race and ethnicity); the effect of the sample methodology on small, unevenly distributed ethnic groups; high levels of out-marriage among the third and fourth generations; and distrust/misunderstanding of government surveys among recent immigrants.

Source: http://www.aaiusa.org/demographics.

Political Participation

While Arab Americans have historically faced some unique challenges to their participation in electoral politics, including the most egregious examples of the rejection of campaign contributions, they successfully organized in spite of the obstacles. Indeed, one can make the case that the organized political response of the community was because of such tactics that came to be known as the "politics of exclusion," referring to the phenomena of Arab-baiting and the desire to "exclude Arab American constituencies from politics."[11] For example, the campaign of George McGovern rejected the endorsement of Arab Americans in 1972. President Jimmy Carter allowed a committee in 1976, but it had to be called "Lebanese Americans for Carter." The first presidential campaign cycle with established Arab American support committees came in 1984 with committees formed in support of both President Ronald Reagan and Reverend Jesse Jackson. That historic effort to court Arab Americans, with its debates and platform battles, led to the first organized effort of the community to impact electoral politics on a national scale during the 1988 election. Coming on the heels of the founding of the Arab American Institute in 1985, the 1988 presidential cycle marked a great success for Arab Americans, as a critical political point was first noted: "Even 5 to 10 percent of highly motivated Arab American voters, when placed in situations of low-turnout caucuses, reaped a higher level of accomplishment than in larger, highly contested elections or primaries."[12] Leveraging the power of the proportionately well-placed Arab American vote began.

Despite some setbacks along the way, success eventually defined the 1990s for Arab American political power. The Clinton administration brought the first Arab American cabinet appointment: Secretary of Health and Human Services Donna Shalala.

By 2014, Arab Americans had one of the highest voter participation rates among ethnic minorities. Over 88 percent of the community is registered to vote and of those registered, around 90 percent say they are likely to vote in upcoming national elections.[13] Arab Americans are very likely to visit a presidential candidate's website, donate to a presidential candidate, and watch a presidential debate.[14] With high concentrations of Arab Americans living in some of the most politically contested states, such as California, Florida, Illinois, Michigan, Ohio, Texas, and Virginia, the high rate of political participation in the community makes Arab Americans a key demographic. In Michigan, Arab American voters represent about 5 percent of the electorate.[15] Those seeking office learned that they cannot ignore such an active community in these states, and candidates from Bill Clinton to George Bush courted the bloc during their campaigns.

Ethnic Pride and Issues

The top three issues that matter to Arab American voters have consistently been jobs and the economy, foreign policy in the Middle East, and health care. Civil rights and civil liberties, immigration, and the budget have also occasionally been cited as top concerns for the bloc. Although in considering the issues that most concern them, Arab Americans cite many of the same issues as the general American public cites. Emotional and familial ties to their countries of origin continue to put foreign policy issues—from the Iraq war, to Palestine, to U.S.-Arab relations—at the forefront of their political concerns.

Despite diversity in their country of origin, religion, and generation, Arab Americans generally have a consensus on their views of the Middle East and U.S. policy in the region, meaning that on these issues especially, the community votes as a bloc.[16] The community's particular concern with foreign policy can significantly impact their support for public officials. In the 2008 election, polls indicated that one-third of the supporters of each candidate would change their vote if they disagreed with their candidate's Middle East positions.[17] In advance of the 2012 presidential election, when asked which candidate would do a better job with the Israeli-Palestinian conflict, 50 percent of Arab American voters chose Barak Obama while only 28 percent selected Romney. When asked about U.S. outreach to the Arab world or Muslim-majority countries, 59 percent chose Obama and 21 percent picked Romney. These preferences were reflected in the overall candidate choices made by the community, which favored Obama to Romney 52 to 28 percent.[18]

Party Identification

While Arab American voters have traditionally been split fairly evenly along party lines, with 40 percent identifying as Democrats and 38 percent as Republicans in 2000, support for the Republican Party has significantly diminished since the 2000 election, with more and more Arab Americans choosing to identify as Independent.[19] In 2012, only 22 percent of Arab Americans identified as Republican, while 46 percent identified as Democrats and 24 percent as Independents (see Figure 6.2).[20]

Despite remaining party affiliations, Arab American voters tend to vote by candidate or issue and less based on party loyalty. Recent immigrants and Arab American Muslims are the two groups most likely to switch parties. This base of independent voters and the tendency of Arab Americans to eschew party loyalty mean that the community has supported candidates of both parties, making it an important swing voting bloc. In 1996, 51.5 percent of Arab Americans voted for the Democratic candidate, Bill Clinton, and four years later in 2000, 45.5 percent supported the Republican candidate, George W. Bush.[21] The shift was caused by multiple factors, including

Figure 6.2

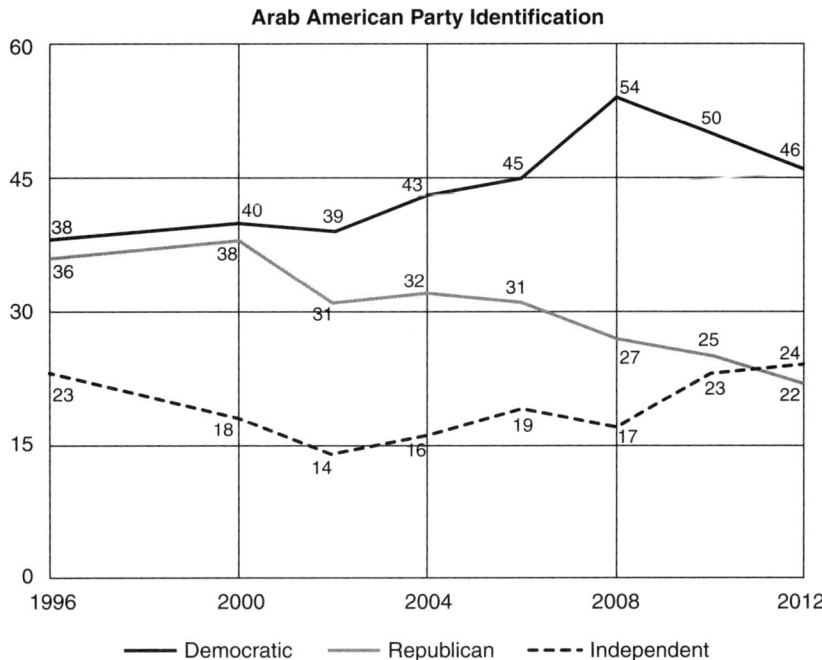

the Clinton administration's handling of the Arab-Israeli conflict and the Bush campaign's successful outreach to the Arab American community.

COURTING THE ARAB AMERICAN VOTE: THE 2000 PRESIDENTIAL ELECTION

The 2000 presidential election was a turning point for Arab Americans. For the first time in history, both candidates courted the Arab American vote. The presence of concentrated Arab American communities in several battleground states drew the notice of both campaigns. Arab American voters comprised 2 percent of the vote in Ohio, Pennsylvania, and Florida, and 5 percent in Michigan, which was particularly close for the two candidates that year.[22] Eighty-eight percent of Michigan's Arab American community was registered to vote, and 90 percent of those registered were expected to vote. Realizing Arab American voters could sway the outcome of the Michigan's electoral votes and impact the national election, both the Gore and Bush campaigns addressed the community, meeting with Arab American leaders to hear the community's concerns. Both campaigns formed support committees, placed ads in ethnic press outlets, and sent targeted mail pieces highlighting their support for community priorities.

Michigan voters were keenly aware of the attention and significance placed on their vote that year. That awareness made national news when for the first time, Arab Americans were mentioned in a national presidential debate on October 11, 2000. While answering a question about support for a federal law that banned racial profiling by government authorities, Bush specifically mentioned the Arab American community, noting, "Arab-Americans are racially profiled in what is called secret evidence. People are stopped, and we have to do something about that. My friend, Senator Spencer Abraham of Michigan, is pushing a law to make sure that Arab-Americans are treated with respect."[23] Although political expediency was the motive and candidate Bush had incorrectly conflated the use of secret evidence and the profiling of passengers, the fact that Bush addressed real policy concerns of Arab Americans on a national platform won the approval of the Arab American community. In the weeks following the debate, a number of Arab American and American Muslim organizations endorsed Governor Bush's candidacy.

Despite that fact that 51.5 percent of the community voted for Clinton in the previous presidential election, Bush received 45.5 percent of the Arab American vote in the 2000 election.[24] Overall, Bush received 7.5 percent more of the Arab American vote than Gore. Though Arab Americans only make up a small percentage of the electorate, their presence and engagement can make a difference. In Ohio that year, where the community comprised 2 percent of the vote—Bush won by only 165,000 votes.[25]

BLOCK THE VOTE: THE UNIQUE BARRIERS TO ARAB AMERICAN EMPOWERMENT

Barriers to voting can take different forms from literacy tests to voter identification laws. Arab American voters have encountered obstacles affecting their ability and decision to cast their ballots on Election Day.

LANGUAGE

The history of disenfranchisement of African American voters is well known and well documented. Indeed, equal access to the ballot was a major factor in the civil rights movement of the 1960s and several activists tragically lost their lives fighting for that basic right.[26] But it was not until the infamous attack that came to be known as "Bloody Sunday" when hundreds of peaceful marchers were met with violence from police after crossing the Edmund Pettus Bridge in Selma, Alabama, on March 7, 1965, that policy makers understood federal action was necessary. Just five months later, President Lyndon Johnson signed into law the landmark Voting Rights Act on August 6, 1965, bringing an end to overt racial discrimination in voting.

Understanding that limited English proficiency can also be a barrier, Congress acted again to protect voters' rights with the enactment of Section 203 of the Voting Rights Act in 1975. Section 203 requires jurisdictions to provide election material and assistance to four prescribed language minority groups: Asian Americans, Hispanics, American Indians, and Alaska Natives.

VOTER INTIMIDATION

Facing Political Realities: Arab American Voters Post-9/11

The Bush administration's handling of both domestic and foreign policy in the years after 9/11 had a drastic effect on support for his administration. President Bush's approval rating among Arab Americans dropped 40 percent between 2001 and 2004.[27] It also impacted how Arab Americans were identifying with political parties. Change in party support from the 2000 election evolved over the next four years. Despite a majority of the community supporting Bush in 2000, Arab American voters backed Kerry in the 2004 election.[28]

In fact, since 2002, the Republican Party gradually lost the community's support. Disappointment with the Bush administration's handling of national security measures after 9/11, the war in Iraq, and the administration's neglect of the peace process turned Arab Americans away from the Republican Party. Initially, both Arab Americans and American Muslims were reassured by President Bush's support for their community. Only six days after the tragic attacks of 9/11, President Bush gave a short speech at the Islamic Center of Washington, D.C. His remarks emphasized the importance of distinguishing between those who planned the terrorist attacks and those who follow the Islamic faith. Further, and perhaps most significantly, President Bush explicitly condemned acts of hate against American Muslims and Arab Americans.[29]

A poll conducted in October 2001 found that 90 percent of Arab Americans were reassured by President Bush's conduct and comments.[30] However, by October 2002, the number dropped to 46 percent, with 38 percent saying they did not feel reassured.[31] When looking at the issues that determined the community vote, the declining support for President Bush from the Arab American community can be attributed to the administration's Middle East policy and encroachments on civil liberties in the aftermath of 9/11.

Heading into the 2004 presidential election, 68.5 percent of Arab Americans indicated that Middle East policy would be important in determining their vote, while another 53 percent specified civil liberties and the treatment of immigrants as important issues.[32] Discrimination and profiling were of great concern to the community, with nearly 60 percent of respondents indicating that they were concerned about long-term discrimination against Arab Americans and more than one-third saying that they were worried about being profiled at airports—direct consequences of programs put in place by the Bush administration following 9/11.

Approval of the administration's Middle East policy was low as well. In July 2004, President Bush received a 56 percent unfavorable rating for his policy in the region, and the low rating indicated a lack of trust in the president by the Arab American community. At the time, only 12 percent of Arab Americans believed the administration remained committed to supporting a two-state solution to the Palestinian Israeli conflict. The war in Iraq was another divisive subject with 55 percent of the community opposed to the war.

These policy concerns, both domestic and foreign, led to a decisive drop in support for the president. As previously noted, President Bush's approval rating fell from 83 percent in 2001 to 43 percent in 2004, and in the 2004 election, Arab Americans supported Kerry. However, approximately half of Arab American voters who supported Kerry were motivated by "anti-Bush sentiments and not necessarily by strong support for the Massachusetts senator."[33]

2008 Presidential Election

Through President Bush's second term, Arab American support continued to erode. At the time of the 2000 election, 40 percent of Arab Americans identified as Democrats and 38 percent identified as Republicans. By the 2008 election, 54 percent identified as Democrats and only 27 percent identified as Republicans. The Bush administration's foreign policy and increased implementation of policies that infringed on the civil liberties of the community, continued to turn away Arab American voters. At the same time, the Obama campaign's promise of change gave hope that the policies of the Bush administration that had worried and excluded Arab Americans could be improved.

Polls in the lead up to the general election placed Senators McCain and Obama neck and neck in Michigan.[34] Once again, the Arab American community's concentration in key states meant they would play an important role. Two months before the 2008 Presidential Election, Arab American voters overwhelmingly favored Obama to McCain 54 to 33 percent in a two-way matchup.[35]

But the energy of the 2008 election season was marred by the presence of anti-Muslim and anti-Arab bigotry on the campaign trail. With the candidacy of an African American named Barack Hussein Obama, elements of the far right in America saw an opportunity to paint Obama as "not like us." Regrettably, casting Obama as the other meant suggesting he was foreign-born or even worse, Muslim. Negative stereotypes of

Arabs and Muslims played a large role in the 2008 election, where fear of the two communities was exacerbated and leveraged for political gain. On the Republican side, an independent group that strongly supported the McCain campaign delivered copies of the Islamophobic film "Obsession: Radical Islam's War Against the West" to 28 million households in the United States.[36] The distribution of the anti-Muslim "documentary" across the United States is indicative of the use of fear in the election. With demands for a birth certificate and the highlighting of his African Muslim father, the campaign rhetoric would turn ugly. Events and rallies held for McCain and Alaska Governor Sara Palin were characterized by the bigotry and divisiveness of some in the crowds.

Rally attendees for the GOP candidates often used hateful, violent rhetoric when speaking about Obama. Calling the candidate a terrorist and communist and questioning his patriotism were common as was implying that he was Arab or Muslim—as if either identity was derogatory. Eventually, McCain did address the discriminatory rhetoric of his supporters, but in doing so made the disparaging way in which the American public had come to think about Arabs and Muslims excruciatingly clear. During a campaign town hall when a woman began to tell Senator McCain that she could not trust Senator Obama because he was an Arab, McCain took the microphone from her and said, "No, ma'am. No, ma'am. He is a decent family man, citizen that I just happen to have disagreements with on fundamental issues. And that's what this campaign is all about. He's not."[37] McCain was praised for "defending" his opponent and rectifying misconceptions sparked by the campaign. But in forcefully assuring the crowd that Obama was, in fact, not an Arab, McCain bolstered the implication that an Arab couldn't be a "decent family man." The idea that being Arab made a person untrustworthy and unfit for the position of president generally went unchallenged on the national campaign conversation.

The Obama campaign was not free from the pervasiveness of anti-Muslim and anti-Arab bigotry either. At Obama's rally in Detroit, Michigan, in July 2008, two Arab American campaign supporters were prevented from sitting behind the podium where then Senator Obama would be speaking. The two young women were Muslim and both were wearing headscarves. At the rally with other friends, both women noticed that their friends were pulled aside by volunteers and asked to sit behind the podium, where they would appear in photos of Obama at the rally. Both times, the volunteers told the women that they were not allowed in the seating area while wearing hijabs, the traditional headscarf worn by some Muslim women. In the case of Heba Aref, a 25-year-old lawyer and Detroit native, the volunteer was specific in telling her it was because she was an American Muslim. A friend that was with her at the time told the media that the volunteer had explained to him "that because of the political climate and what's going on in the world and what's going on with Muslim Americans, it's not good for [Aref] to be seen on TV or associated with Obama."[38] Although apologies were given to both women, the Obama campaign had played directly into the anti-Arab and Islamophobic rhetoric that had been driving the opposition that season. By excluding the women from the stands solely based on their headscarves suggested that the campaign was actively trying not to associate itself with Arabs and Muslims, and in doing so, regrettably perpetuating the negative stereotypes of the two groups.

2012 Presidential Election

The 2012 presidential election found Arab American voters once again favoring Barack Obama. However, failures to deliver on promises of change on some foreign and domestic policies had dropped support from the community. Whereas Obama had led McCain in the community 67 to 28 percent, polls leading up to the election put Obama ahead of Romney 52 to 28 percent, with 16 percent of Arab American voters undecided.[39] Arab Americans continued to see the economy and foreign policy as the issues that mattered most in determining their vote, and many were still deeply concerned about profiling and discrimination.

The real story of the 2012 election season for Arab Americans, however, was on a much more local scale. A 2011 redrawing of New Jersey's districts resulted in a primary between two incumbent Democratic Congressmen, Steve Rothman and Bill Pascrell. The new Ninth district encompassed the city of Paterson, home to one of the largest concentrations of Arab Americans in the country. The race, already controversial because of Rothman's decision to challenge his long-time friend Pascrell, grew ugly when opponents of Pascrell and several pro-Israel and right-wing bloggers decided to characterize the race in terms of a strange, false dichotomy: Arabs versus Jews on the Palestinian-Israeli conflict.

Both Rothman and Pascrell shared very similar voting records, and both supported Israel, including voting for aid to Israel and U.S.-Israeli military cooperation. Pascrell, however, was singled out as being a "harsh critic of Israel" and even of practicing "Islamic anti-Semitism."[40] The rhetoric was based on only a few of Pascrell's actions, the Congressman had spoken out against Israel's blockade of Gaza, and on multiple occasions, spoke out against bias and discrimination toward the Arab American and American Muslim communities.

Pascrell had been engaged with the local Arab American community for much of his political career and often defended his constituents against discriminatory policies. As a congressman he had denounced New York Representative Peter King's anti-Muslim hearings, opposed discriminatory practices stemming from the PATRIOT Act, and spoke out against the New York Police Department (NYPD) profiling of Arab and Muslim communities.[41] As one supporter would explain with complete clarity, "He comes to our events, he attends our church and mosque services and some on his staff are Arab American. It only makes sense that the community would rally behind a candidate who has reached out time and time again. This race is not about Israel."[42] The Arab American community in the district had rallied to support the Congressman that had invested so much in their community over his 16-year career.

Local groups raised money for the campaign, held voter registration drives, and participated in phone banking and door-to-door outreach. Their efforts paid off, with well over 1,000 new registered voters. Pascrell won the district with 61 percent of the vote, despite polling that put the race as too close to call. Precincts with large Arab American populations had "such lopsided totals as 134 for Pascrell to 3 for Rothman, and 222 to 6 and 195 to 6 and 290 to 20."[43] The victory showed that the political participation of Arab Americans could have a direct influence on key races. Further in refusing to accept the false narrative of a local election being about support for Israel, the community did not allow itself to be vilified in the public sphere. The takeaway for Arab Americans and election observers alike was that an organized constituency could successfully define itself, tell its own story, and help determine the outcome of an election. Indeed, it also showed that though the community had not picked that fight, it could defend itself and soundly reject divisive politics by simple political organizing and GOTV efforts.

Regrettably, some had a different takeaway. In a 1 minute and 20 second ad produced by a group identified as iVoteIsrael, the Rothman-Pascrell race was characterized as an ominous sign of an "Arab" victory and closed with the alarmist "don't let them win."[44] The ad did not refer to the community as Arab American but rather only as Arab and stated, "On June 5, radical anti-Israel elements of the New Jersey Arab community flexed their political muscle. . . . Arabic campaign posters rallied the Arab New Jersey community. They mobilized their base." With images of the Yalla Vote logo, the highly successful nonpartisan GOTV campaign created by Arab Americans, appearing on screen, the message was clear: Arab Americans remained a foreign, single-issue constituency whose presence in American electoral politics was insidious. A president of a pro-Israel political action committee was even more direct when he was quoted as saying, "It's a little bit scary" in reference to voter registration drives that added 6,000 new Arab American voters.[45] While the attempt to cast community organizing as sinister was ultimately rejected, it is important for those examining Arab American voter engagement efforts to note that such politicizing of an ethnic constituency are not rare when it comes to Arab Americans. The zero-sum approach to the politics of the Arab-Israeli conflict has had a harmful impact on the political empowerment of Arab Americans, including their desire to cast their vote as a bloc in support of the many issues they care deeply about.

CONCLUSION

The Issues That Matter: Profiling of Arab Americans

Unfairness and discrimination are generally frowned upon as un-American. The practice of profiling and selective treatment of some is when an individual's race, ethnicity, religion, or national origin is used by law enforcement as a proxy for criminal behavior. Under federal law, profiling violates the Fourth Amendment, which guarantees an individual the right to be safe from unreasonable search and seizure without probable cause, and the Fourteenth Amendment's "equal protection" clause, which requires all citizens to be treated equally under the law. Profiling should offend our most basic sensibilities regarding justice. However, profiling has been used as a security technique by the U.S. government for decades, alienating many minority groups and stripping away the civil liberties granted by the constitution in the process. For many Arab Americans, being profiled in airports or by their local police in the name of national security is a common occurrence. The incorporation of this practice into the methods used by government authorities strips away the civil rights and civil liberties guaranteed to each citizen by the constitution.

Following the tragic attacks of September 11, 2001, the profiling of Arab Americans emerged in public discourse as a security measure against terrorism. Profiling as a method of maintaining national security has been legitimated with the passage of the PATRIOT Act, ironically through guidance issued in 2003 to ostensibly ban profiling and, most recently, with the surveillance of Arab Americans and American Muslims by the NYPD. However, profiling had been around far longer than the renewed security efforts following 9/11 would suggest. In the 1970s, OPERATION BOULDER, a program under the Nixon administration, put many Arab Americans and organizations under surveillance. During the Gulf War, the Federal Bureau of Investigation began conducting interviews with Arab Americans, looking for connections to terrorism in Iraq.[46] In fact, some new methods, including increased profiling in airports by the Transportation Security Administration, were built on existing systems of profiling formed prior to 9/11.[47] In the aftermath of the 1996 explosion of the TWA Flight 800, a new computerized profiling system was introduced into American airports. Despite assurance from officials that the system did not screen based on criteria such as ethnicity or religion, it was largely recognized that the system, called the Computer-Assisted Passenger Screening system (CAPS), singled out Arabs and Arab Americans.

In 1998, the House Committee on Transportation and Infrastructure held a hearing on the newly implemented aviation security techniques, with a focus on the criteria used for passenger profiling. At the hearing, then Congressman Ray LaHood made a statement addressing the concerns of Arab Americans noting that they "are often the target of such profiling attempts," and expressing his opinion that "If passenger profiling must take place . . . it should be based on behavior instead of indicators, such as race, religion, and national origin, that are subject to generalizations and stereotypes."[48] Despite the statement of Representative LaHood and the testimony of prominent organizations such as the Arab American Institute, the American-Arab Anti-Discrimination Committee, and the American Civil Liberties Union, the practice of profiling at airports, and the bias toward a selection of Arab Americans and American Muslims for further screening, continued.[49] The issue would again be brought into the spotlight by the presidential election of 2000, when discrimination against Arab Americans was thrust into the national spotlight during a presidential debate.

The 2000 presidential election was a turning point in Arab American voter influence. Empowered by expanded inclusion in the previous administration and positioned in several key states in the election—including Florida, Michigan, New York, New Jersey, Pennsylvania, Ohio, and Illinois—Arab Americans emerged as a key bloc of voters. It was the first election in U.S. history in which both major party nominees were inclusive of Arab Americans; both parties were courting their votes.[50] The desire to gain votes by the campaign of Governor Bush gave legitimacy to the concerns of Arab American voters, specifically profiling, and that manifested itself in an influx of support for the Republican candidate despite the voting bloc having supported the Clinton campaign in the previous election.

Working with Arab American Republican Party organizers, Governor Bush had successfully met with bipartisan leaders of Michigan's Arab American community and had been briefed on the issues that concerned the community by the time of the second presidential debate on October 11, 2000. When the moderator asked the candidates whether they would support or sign a federal law that banned racial profiling by government authorities, both responded that they would. But while Vice President Gore focused on the profiling of African Americans, a group that already strongly supported the Democratic Party, Bush drew attention to another group that experienced profiling at the hands of the government—Arab Americans. "Secondly, there is other forms of racial profiling that goes on in America. Arab-Americans are racially profiled in what is called secret evidence. People are stopped, and we have to do something about that. My friend, Senator Spencer Abraham of Michigan, is pushing a law to make sure that Arab-Americans are treated with respect."[51]

It didn't matter that the governor had conflated the issues of secret evidence and profiling, as it was the first time that a presidential candidate had addressed the concerns of Arab Americans on a national platform. Two days later, Bush received an endorsement from the Michigan-based Arab American Political Action Committee (AAPAC), a group of Arab American Professionals that had organized in metropolitan Detroit. Shortly after the endorsement, *The Arab American News*, a bilingual newspaper based in Dearborn, published a portion of the letter Bush had sent to AAPAC asking for their endorsement:

> I am a uniter, not a divider. I will work every day to unite all Americans around common goals—regardless of background, religion, or place of origin. I will fight discrimination wherever it happened and on this subject I know that Arab Americans have special concerns. The present administration has pursued policies that, in practice, have adversely affected your community. My administration will act with more fairness. . . . Under the Clinton-Gore administration, Arab-American air travelers have experienced harassment and delay simply because of their ethnic heritage. Such uses of passenger profiling are a violation of Constitutional rights and must be stopped.[52]

The letter's reference to Vice President's Gore's involvement in the implementation of profiling as a security measure at airports was a political point at best but it was used effectively by the Bush campaign as a liability against Gore with Arab American voters. Following the 1996 TWA Flight 800 explosion, Vice President Gore served as chair of the White House Commission on Aviation and Security. It was this commission that, despite there being no evidence of terrorism in the TWA 800 disaster, recommended the use of more intensive security efforts at airports, including the CAPS.[53] The Commission would issue a report whose appendix included nine guidelines from a Civil Liberties Advisory Panel that dealt with concerns regarding profiling. Despite assurance from officials that the system did not screen based on criteria such as ethnicity or religion, Arab Americans were consistently singled out in the process. The Bush campaign had successfully highlighted that fact and made Vice President Gore's chairmanship of the commission as an issue for Arab American voters in Michigan. This, combined with Gore cancelling and having to reschedule a meeting with Arab American leaders in Michigan, helped the Bush campaign's overtures create stronger connections to the community, and ultimately to effectively sway Arab American voters. Further, this effort to court the Arab American voting bloc in Michigan had broader national implications.

A Zogby poll taken in 2000 indicated that 40 percent of Arab Americans identified as Democrats, 38 percent as Republican, and 22 percent as Independent. In the presidential election, 38 percent of Arab Americans voted for Gore, while 45.5 percent voted for Bush.[54] In the 1996 presidential election, 51.5 percent of Arab Americans had voted for Clinton, and 31.5 percent voted for Dole. The shift in support from a Democratic to Republican ticket demonstrates that the Arab American voting bloc, with its positioning in key election states, can serve as a key demographic in elections.[55] The response of Arab American community groups to Bush's discourse on profiling during the election suggest that Arab Americans will swing their vote based on issues, like profiling, that deeply affect the community.

The Issues That Matter: Foreign Policy Concerns of Arab Americans

When asked to identify, in their own words, the top two issues facing the country, Arab Americans consistently include foreign policy. Over the years, their concerns have centered on U.S. policy toward the Middle East, beginning with Palestine and including issues such as the Lebanese Civil War, the wars in Iraq, the current crisis in Syria, and the more contemporary Israeli-Palestinian Peace Process.[56] The issues continually factor in to the electoral choices made by the Arab American community (see Figure 6.3).

Arab Americans have a strong sense of cultural heritage with 82 percent of the community taking pride in their ethnic identity.[57] Emotional attachment to their country of origin has remained fairly constant in the

Figure 6.3

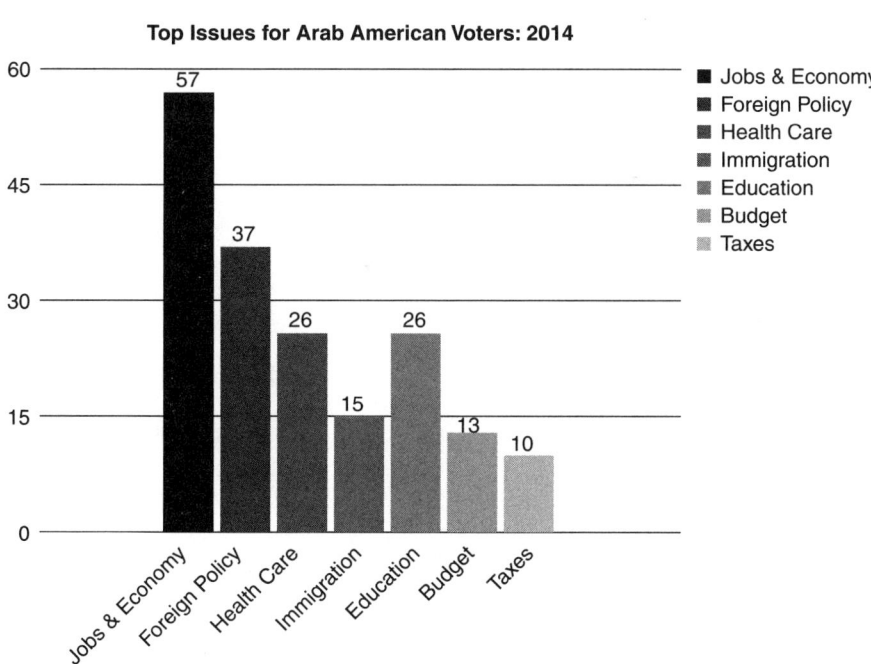

144   Minority Voting in the United States

Arab American community. In 2001, 64.8 percent of Arab Americans said that they had somewhat strong or very strong emotional ties to their country of origin (see Figure 6.4).[58] By 2004, the number had grown slightly to 77.1 percent (see Figure 6.5).[59] Recent immigrants were more likely than those born in the United States to indicate that they had a "very strong" emotional attachment to their country. It's not hard to see the connection between the strength of emotional ties of Arab Americans

Figure 6.4

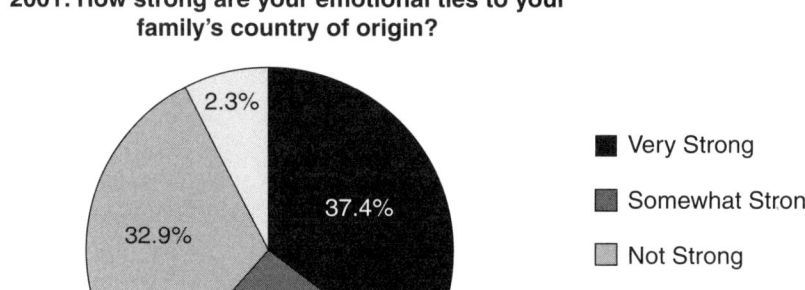

Figure 6.5

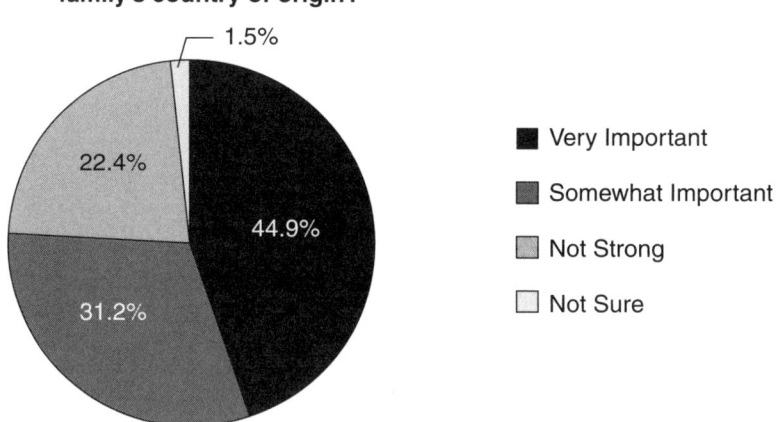

New Jersey

In New Jersey, Congressman Bill Pascrell recently penned an Op-Ed piece calling for a better U.S. policy on Syrian refugees.[69] In the piece, he noted that Paterson, New Jersey—located in Passaic County and part of his district—is "home to one of the largest Syrian American communities in the United States." He has sponsored legislation to prevent the further use of chemical weapons in Syria.[70] New Jersey is home to close to 240,000 Arab Americans, the largest concentration of which can be found in Passaic County.

Virginia

Congressman Jim Moran, of the eighth district of Virginia, was an outspoken opponent of the Iraq war. He coauthored the Democratic alternative resolution that required President Bush to exhaust all forms of diplomatic action before taking military action.[71] The eighth district is home to 39 percent of the 135,000 Arab Americans that currently reside in Virginia.[72]

Michigan

In Michigan, Detroit is represented by Rep. John Conyers and Dearborn was represented by Rep. John Dingell for nearly six decades before his retirement in January 2015. Detroit and Dearborn are located in Wayne County, which houses 46 percent of the nearly 490,000 Arab Americans that reside in Michigan. Around one-third of the city of Dearborn claims Arab heritage.[73] Congressman Dingell supported President Obama's pursuit of a diplomatic resolution to the Israeli-Palestinian conflict, repeatedly called for increased aid to ease the suffering in Gaza, and advocated for freer movement for Palestinians. An opponent of the Iraq war, Rep. Dingell approved the gradual withdrawal of troops from both Iraq and Afghanistan.[74] Rep. Conyers has supported continued aid to Palestinians[75] and urged National Security Advisor Susan Rice to establish partnerships between United States Agency for International Development and Syrian refugee and relief organizations.[76]

NOTES

1. Hitti, *Syrians in America*, 25.
2. Immigration Act of 1924, also known as the Johnson-Reed Act or the National Origins Act.
3. Naff, "Arabs in America," 22.
4. Israel's overwhelming victory and the hostility in the American press toward the Arab side would serve to unify the Arab American community and

prompt it to establish organizations in support of Arab American empowerment. These included the Association of Arab-American University Graduates in 1968, the National Association of Arab Americans in 1972, the American-Arab Anti-Discrimination Committee in 1980, and the Arab American Institute (AAI) in 1985. Of these, AAI is the only one that adopted political engagement and electoral politics as its core mission, which continues to today.

 5. Naff, "Arabs in America," 23.
 6. Ibid.
 7. Zogby, James, *Arab Voices*, 181.
 8. "Demographics." Arab American Institute.
 9. Ibid.
 10. Arab American Institute. *Map of States with the Largest Population of Arab Americans.* Numbers in Figure 6.1 have been adjusted for undercounting. Research by AAI and Zogby International suggest that the numbers provided by the Census are significantly lower than the actual number of Arab Americans in each state. The Census Bureau identifies only a portion of the Arab American population through a question on "ancestry" on the American Community Survey. Reasons for the undercount include the placement of and limit of the ancestry question (as distinct from race and ethnicity); the effect of the sample methodology on small, unevenly distributed ethnic groups; high levels of out-marriage among the third and fourth generations; and distrust/misunderstanding of government surveys among recent immigrants.
 11. Arab American Institute. *Arab American Voters 2014.*
 12. James Zogby and Helen Samhan coined the phrase in their seminal document, *The Politics of Exclusion: A Report on Arab-Baiting in the 1986 Elections*, published by the Arab American Institute in 1987.
 13. Samhan, "Arab Americans and the Elections of 1988."
 14. Arab American Institute. *What Ethnic Americans Really Think.*
 15. Ibid.
 16. Arab American Institute. *2008 Election: The Arab American Vote.*
 17. The 15-year Lebanese Civil War challenged community unity on foreign policy issues during the 1970s and 1980s, just as the Syrian armed conflict is now doing since protests began in March 2011.
 18. Ibid.
 19. Arab American Institute. *Arab American Vote 2012.*
 20. Ibid.
 21. Ibid.
 22. Arab American Institute. *Arab American Vote 1996, 2000, 2002.*
 23. Cole, "John McCain's Arab-American Problem."
 24. "October 11, 2000 Debate Transcript." Commission on Presidential Debates.
 25. Arab American Institute. *Arab American Vote 1996, 2000, 2002.*
 26. Cole, "John McCain's Arab-American Problem."
 27. Most notably the national attention given to the brutal murder of civil rights activists James Earl Chaney, Andrew Goodman, and Michael Schwerner on June 21, 1964 in Philadelphia, Mississippi. The three were part of the "Freedom Summer" campaign to register African American voters in Mississippi.
 28. Zogby, James. "An Early Look at Arab Americans and the 2004 Elections."

29. Cole, "John McCain's Arab-American Problem."
30. "Remarks by the President at Islamic Center of Washington, D.C." The White House Archives.
31. Arab American Institute. "Poll of Arab Americans since the Terrorist Attack on the United States."
32. Zogby, "Early Look at Arab Americans and the 2004 Elections."
33. Arab American Institute. "The Arab American Vote in 2004."
34. Zughbi, "Arab-Americans Turning Away From Bush."
35. Martelle, "Polls Look Ahead to Fall Showdown between Barack Obama and John McCain."
36. Arab American Institute. *2008 Election: How Arab Americans Will Vote and Why*.
37. Zogby, "Exploiting Fear."
38. "McCain Counters Obama 'Arab' Question (Video)." Associated Press.
39. Smith, Ben. "Muslims Barred from Picture at Obama Event."
40. Zogby, "Arab American Vote: 2012."
41. Zogby, "Big Election for Arab Americans."
42. Ibid.
43. Tewfik, Omar. "Arab American Support for Pascrell."
44. Zogby, "Big Election for Arab Americans."
45. Tewfik, "Arab American Political Participation under Attack."
46. Tewfik, "Arab American Support for Pascrell."
47. Hanna, J. "FBI Questioning Irks Some Arabs in U.S."
48. National Commission on Terrorist Attacks upon the United States. *Aviation Security System and the 9/11 Attacks*.
49. U.S. House. Subcommittee on Aviation of the Committee on Transportation and Infrastructure. *Status of Aviation Security Efforts*.
50. Michigan Advisory Committee to the U.S. Commission on Civil Rights. "Civil Rights Issues Facing Arab Americans in Michigan."
51. Isikoff, "New Fight for Arab Votes."
52. October 11, 2000 Debate Transcript. Commission on Presidential Debates.
53. Malek, *A Country Called Amreeka*.
54. White House Commission on Aviation Safety and Security. *Final Report to President Clinton*.
55. Arab American Institute. *Arab American Vote 1996, 2000, 2002*.
56. Zogby, *How Arab Americans Voted and Why*.
57. Arab American Institute. *Arab American Opinion Polls*.
58. Arab American Institute. *The Arab American Vote 2012*.
59. Arab American Institute. *Poll (2001)*.
60. Arab American Institute. *Poll (2004)*.
61. Arab American Institute. *Poll (2000)*.
62. Arab American Institute. *Poll (2004)*.
63. Arab American Institute. *Poll (2002)*.
64. Arab American Institute. *Detailed State Profiles*.
65. Arab American Institute. *How Arab Americans Will Vote and Why*. http://www.aaiusa.org/the-2008-election-how-arab-americans-will-vote-and-why.
66. "McDermott Statement on End of U.S. Military Operations in Iraq."

67. Arab American Institute. *Washington Demographics.*
68. Congressman Keith Ellison.
69. Arab American Institute. *Minnesota Demographics.*
70. Pascrell, "Pascrell: Of Marathon Champs and War Refugees."
71. Pascrell, *Congressional Record Online.*
72. Congressman Jim Moran.
73. Arab American Institute. *Detailed State Profiles.*
74. Ibid.
75. Congressman John Dingell.
76. Congressman John Conyers Jr.
77. Arab American Institute. *Congressional Scorecard: 113th Congress.*

REFERENCES

Arab American Institute. *Arab American Opinion Polls.* Accessed 25 May 2014, from http://www.aaiusa.org/opinion-polls.

Arab American Institute. *The Arab American Vote 1996, 2000, 2002.* Zogby International. 2002. Accessed 26 September 2014, from http://b.3cdn.net/aai/260a504a326ad34a52_05m6b8xft.pdf.

Arab American Institute. "The Arab American Vote in 2004." Zogby International. 2004. Accessed from http://b.3cdn.net/aai/74bc457b1c7340217d_qtm6br2y9.pdf.

Arab American Institute. *The Arab American Vote 2012.* JZ Analytics. 2012. Accessed 26 September 2014, from http://b.3cdn.net/aai/f3ae1a15536d25538b_yym-6bcp79.pdf.

Arab American Institute. *Arab American Voters 2014: Their Identity and Political Concerns.* Zogby Analytics. 24 November 2014. Accessed from http://b.3cdn.net/aai/701da5a04425f92a58_1qm6btv55.pdf.

Arab American Institute. *Congressional Scorecard: 113th Congress.* 2013. Available at http://b.3cdn.net/aai/ed944398d4919141db_sfm6v3uzp.pdf.

Arab American Institute. "Demographics." Accessed 26 September 2014. http://www.aaiusa.org/demographics.

Arab American Institute. *Detailed State Profiles.* Accessed 29 May 2014, from http://www.aaiusa.org/state-profiles-detailed.

Arab American Institute. *Minnesota Demographics.* Accessed 25 May 2014, from http://b.3cdn.net/aai/35108f356238080fef_8om6i6sw4.pdf.

Arab American Institute. "A Poll of Arab Americans since the Terrorist Attacks on the United States." Zogby International. 10 October 2001. Accessed from http://b.3cdn.net/aai/56ee89620552ada2d6_06m6yviv3.pdf.

Arab American Institute. Poll. Zogby International. 2000. https://d3n8a8pro7vhmx.cloudfront.net/aai/pages/9748/attachments/original/1438880696/AA_2001.pdf?1438880696

Arab American Institute. Poll. Zogby International. 2001. https://d3n8a8pro7vhmx.cloudfront.net/aai/pages/9747/attachments/original/1431961550/WhatEthnicAmericansReallyThink_2001.pdf?1431961550

Arab American Institute. Poll. Zogby International. 2002. https://d3n8a8pro7vhmx.cloudfront.net/aai/pages/9749/attachments/original/1438880781/AA_Vote_1996-2002.pdf?1438880781

Arab American Institute. Poll. Zogby International. 2004. https://d3n8a8pro7vhmx.cloudfront.net/aai/pages/9745/attachments/original/1438880470/AA_Vote_2004.pdf?1438880470

Arab American Institute. *The 2008 Election: How Arab Americans Will Vote and Why*. Zogby International. 2008. Accessed from http://www.aaiusa.org/page/-/Polls/ArabAmericanOpinion/HowArabAmericansWillVote_2008.pdf.

Arab American Institute. *The 2008 Election: The Arab American Vote*. Zogby International. 2008. Accessed 26 September 2014, from http://b.3cdn.net/aai/95fef06f09792bccf1_fbfm60kgc.pdf.

Arab American Institute. *Washington Demographics*. Accessed 25 May 2014, from http://b.3cdn.net/aai/f4ae62df45b0b5e01d_17m6iib1w.pdf.

Arab American Institute. *What Ethnic Americans Really Think*. Zogby International. 2001. Accessed 26 September 2014, from http://www.aaiusa.org/what-ethnic-americans-really-think-2001.

Cole, Juan. "John McCain's Arab-American Problem." *Salon*. 28 May 2008. Accessed 23 September 2014. http://www.salon.com/2008/05/28/mccain_69/.

Congressman Jim Moran. Accessed 2 June 2014, from http://moran.house.gov/.

Congressman Keith Ellison. Accessed 2 June 2014, from http://ellison.house.gov/.

Hanna, J. "FBI Questioning Irks Some Arabs in U.S." *Chicago Tribune*. 10 January 1991. Accessed 19 May 2014, from http://articles.chicagotribune.com/1991-01-10/news/9101030477_1_arab-americans-fbi-agents-interviews.

Hitti, Philip K. *The Syrians in America*. New York: George Doran, 1924. 25.

Isikoff, M. "A New Fight for Arab Votes." *Newsweek*. 22 October 2000.

Malek, Alia. *Courted. A Country Called Amreeka: U.S. History Retold through Arab-American Lives*. New York: Free Press, 2009.

Martelle, Scott. "Polls Look Ahead to Fall Showdown between Barack Obama and John McCain." *Los Angeles Times*. 21 May 2008. Accessed 21 October 2014. http://latimesblogs.latimes.com/washington/2008/05/barack-obama--4.html.

"McCain Counters Obama 'Arab' Question (Video)." *Associated Press*. 11 October 2008. Accessed 22 October 2014. https://www.youtube.com/watch?v=jrnRU3ocIH4.

McDermott Statement on End of U.S. Military Operations in Iraq. 16 December 2011. Accessed 19 May 2014, from http://mcdermott.house.gov/index.php?option=com_content&view=article&id=555:mcdermott-statement-on-end-of-us-military-operations-in-iraq&catid=25:press-releases&Itemid=20.

Michigan Advisory Committee to the U.S. Commission on Civil Rights. Civil Rights Issues Facing Arab Americans in Michigan. *Statements of Elected Officials*. May 2001.

Naff, Alixa. "Arabs in America: A Historical Overview." *Arabs in the New World: Studies on Arab-American Communities*. Ed. Sameer Y. Abraham and Nabeel Abraham. Detroit: Wayne State University Press, 1983. 22–23.

National Commission on Terrorist Attacks upon the United States. *The Aviation Security System and the 9/11 Attacks: Staff Statement No. 3*. Accessed 19 May 2014, from http://www.9-11commission.gov/staff_statements/staff_statement_3.pdf.

"October 11, 2000 Debate Transcript." Commission on Presidential Debates. 11 October 2000. Accessed 19 October 2014. Accessed 15 May 2014, from http://www.debates.org/index.php?page=october-11-2000-debate-transcript.

Pascrell, B. "Pascrell: Of Marathon Champs and War Refugees." *Special to the Herald News*. 5 May 2014.

Pascrell, Rep. [NJ]. *Congressional Record Online*. THOMAS. Available at http://thomas.loc.gov/cgi-bin/bdquery/R?d113:FLD003:@1%28Rep.+Pascrell+Bill%29.

"Remarks by the President at Islamic Center of Washington, D.C." *The White House Archives*. 17 September 2001. Accessed 21 October 2014. http://georgewbush-whitehouse.archives.gov/news/releases/2001/09/20010917-11.html.

Representative John Dingell. Accessed 2 June 2014, from http://dingell.house.gov/.

Samhan, Helen Hatab, *Arab Americans and the Elections of 1988: A Constituency Come of Age*. Arab Studies Quarterly 11.2&3 (Sprint/Summer 1989): 248.

Smith, Ben. "Muslims Barred from Picture at Obama Event." POLITICO. 18 June 2008. Accessed 22 October 2014. http://www.politico.com/news/stories/0608/11168_Page2.html.

Tewfik, Omar. "Arab American Political Participation under Attack." Arab American Institute. 24 June 2012. Accessed 22 October 2014. http://www.aaiusa.org/arab-american-political-participation-under-attack.

Tewfik, Omar. "Arab American Support for Pascrell: It's about Engagement, Not Israel." Arab American Institute. 5 June 2012. Accessed 22 October 2014. http://www.aaiusa.org/arab-american-support-for-pascrell-its-about-engagement-not-israel.

U.S. Congressman John Conyers, Jr. Accessed 2 June 2014, from https://conyers.house.gov/index.cfm/home.

U.S. House. Subcommittee on Aviation of the Committee on Transportation and Infrastructure. *Status of Aviation Security Efforts with a Focus on the National Safe Skies Alliance and Passenger Profiling Criteria*. 14 May 1998.

White House Commission on Aviation Safety and Security. *Final Report to President Clinton*. 12 February 1997.

Zogby, James. "The Arab American Vote: 2012." Arab American Institute. 1 October 2008. Accessed 22 October 2014. http://www.aaiusa.org/the-arab-american-vote-2012.

Zogby, James. *Arab Voices: What They Are Saying to Us, and Why It Matters*. New York: Palgrave Macmillan, 2010: 181.

Zogby, James. "A Big Election for Arab Americans." Arab American Institute. 11 June 2012. Accessed 22 October 2014. http://www.aaiusa.org/a-big-election-for-arab-americans.

Zogby, James. "An Early Look at Arab Americans and the 2004 Elections." Arab American Institute. 14 July 2003. Accessed 21 October 2014. http://www.aaiusa.org/w071403.

Zogby, James. "Exploiting Fear." Arab American Institute. 26 September 2008. Accessed 22 October 2014. http://www.aaiusa.org/exploiting-fear.

Zogby, James. *How Arab Americans Voted and Why*. 18 December 2000. Accessed 19 May 2014, from http://www.aaiusa.org/w121800/.

Zughbi, Mona. "Arab-Americans Turning Away From Bush." *NBC News*. 22 September 2004. Accessed 21 October 2014. http://www.nbcnews.com/id/6056602/ns/politics/t/arab-americans-turning-away-bush/#.VEkgV_nF98F.

Chapter 7

The Political Incorporation and Mobilization of American Muslims

Farid Senzai

The political behavior of minority groups in the United States has interested social scientists for several decades. Much of the research has focused on the political incorporation and mobilization of African Americans, Asian Americans, and Latinos through such political activities as elections and voting behavior, political representation, and the influence of grassroots movements on national debates.[1] More recently, research has generated new insight into such aspects of minority political behavior as the growth, development, and mobilization of ethnic and racial minority groups; the conditions that facilitate or impede political coalitions; the relative impact of religion, gender, social capital, transnational ties, class, national origin, immigrant status, and other social identities on civic engagement; and other forms of ethnic/racial political participation at the local, state, and national levels.[2]

The leading scholars of Latino politics pioneered a landmark study of Latino political behavior in 1992.[3] DeSipio's work on Latino ethnicity and voting laid much of the groundwork for how we think about how racial identification affects political action, and F.C. Garcia's *Pursuing Power: Latinos and the Political System* resulted in a whole new field: Latino politics in America.[4] There is also increasing scholarship on the political participation of Asian Americans, most notably the work of Pei-te Lien and colleagues analyzing the Pilot National Asian American Political Study and the work of Lai.[5]

There remains, however, a dearth of data and analysis on the political participation of American Muslims. Until recently, political scientists paid little attention to, and had little interest in, understanding and analyzing this minority's political incorporation and mobilization. With the exception of a few academic journal articles, very little data on this emerging minority group exist within the literature.[6] This leads one to ask: Are American Muslims politically incorporated? What political activities are American Muslims involved in, and are these similar to or different from other minority groups? What are their major political behaviors, and how active are they in the political process? These and other questions are posed to outline and analyze the landscape for American Muslim political incorporation, while examining the "identity to politics" link by drawing on national survey data from Zogby International and the Pew Research Center.

Given that politics and identity seem inextricably intertwined, American Muslims are drawing circles of identity and producing meaning. Michael Dawson's concept of a "linked fate," created to explain the African American experience, has relevance here, even if not to the same extent. In his *Behind the Mule: Race and Class in African American Politics*, Dawson argued that blacks tend to elevate race above class interests and will support policies that they perceive as in the interests of blacks as a group, even if such programs appear to violate their class interests.[7] This same tendency seems to apply to American Muslims as a racial and ethnic minority group. As such, across the country they have been unifying, especially since 9/11, which has generated claims of a politicized and "racialized" group identity that has politically mobilized this particular community.

American Muslims are increasingly engaging in politics and asserting their voice in the political process.[8] While naysayers within the community believe that political participation will lead to assimilation and the loss of a distinct "Islamic identity," others within the community believe that political participation is the best way to ensure their rights. These conflicting views are mirrored in the different views Muslims have of their place in America.

This chapter draws on several different surveys on the political activity of American Muslims including the 2001 and 2004 Zogby International's Muslim Americans in the Public Square (MAPS) project, as well as the 2007 and 2011 Pew Research Center surveys, which investigated how group identity affects political participation, as measured by electoral and nonelectoral activities.[9] I served on the research team and conducted the focus groups for the Pew surveys. It should be noted, however, that most surveys of American Muslim public opinion have several limitations. First, the lack of data on the community's subgroups prevents any analysis of differences in a diverse Muslim population. Second, most surveys examine a specific aspect of American Muslim opinion rather than painting a comprehensive picture. Finally, the lack of continuity between follow-up questionnaires creates a problem for those attempting to assess trends. American Muslims have never been surveyed via probability methods on the national level.[10]

THE HISTORICAL INTEGRATION OF AMERICAN MUSLIMS

Based on the Muslim world's ethnic and racial diversity, one should expect the Muslim population in America to be equally diverse.[11] This has been corroborated by MAPS and the Pew survey, both of which found that its members are predominantly of South and Southeast Asian, Arab, African American, Iranian, Latino, and African descent. The majority of them have come to this country from nearly 70 countries, beginning in the 1980s, to live, work, or study.[12] Others, including a large number of African Americans who converted or chose to reconnect with their ancestors' Islam, have been here for more than a century.[13] These different historical and social experiences have also shaped each group's pattern of political incorporation.

The earliest known Muslims arrived on American shores as slaves during the first half of the 16th century.[14] They combined their African roots with their Islamic identity and established the first Muslim presence on what would become American soil. It became the foundation upon which future generations of immigrant Muslims expanded.[15] Over time, however, links to Islam were weakened and even lost in many African American communities, only to be rediscovered during the 20th century. At that time, "black movements and black Muslim movements ran parallel, often overlapping and invariably drawing from each other . . . and gave African Americans a sense of common aspirations and dreams."

Middle Eastern Arabs and South Asians migrated to the United States in waves beginning in the late 19th century.[16] While some of the early Muslims, including blacks and Arabs arriving at the turn of the 20th century sought opportunities to engage politically and became active in the public sphere, the majority of those who arrived after 1980 were unfamiliar and less comfortable with such practices. For many of them, such activities seemed both alien and theologically problematic (discussed in more detail in the following). Furthermore, their small numbers, ethnic diversity, and lack of experience in playing the democratic game impeded their political integration.[17]

Differences between the experiences of African American and immigrant American Muslims are reflected in their respective levels of social, economic, and political integration. Demographic patterns reveal that, regardless of their largely immigrant status, South Asian and Arab Muslim immigrants are similar to Asian American immigrants and more likely than their African American counterparts to be economically integrated into broader suburban American society. In particular, higher levels of formal education among immigrant Muslims led to white-collar occupations and higher income levels.[18] Taken together, these resources produced an immigrant population that was less likely to reside in ethnic enclaves and more likely than other minority groups to live in racially integrated suburban neighborhoods and attend racially diverse schools.[19] Earlier studies of minority politics focused on socioeconomic status as a determinant of political engagement. Political scientists have often viewed this particular status as the most critical variable in explaining variations in political participation rates across racial and ethnic groups.[20] Other groundbreaking studies include theories on blacks' "overparticipation," that is, higher participation than whites when controlling for socioeconomic status.[21] To the extent that classic assimilation models are correct, this level of economic and residential integration suggests that immigrant Muslims will more quickly become incorporated into American society.[22] These assimilation models also suggest that along with structural incorporation, individuals begin to lose their former ethnic attachments, and while ethnic identities may not be completely lost, they instead become symbolic, perceived as optional identities.

When discussing immigrant Muslims, however, one must note that they, like Asian, Latino, and many other minority groups, have other cultural allegiances that exert a pull beyond their religious identity. As Nagel noted, ethnicity has multiple layers and American Muslims often choose between national origin and ethnic attachments versus religious attachments.[23] By attaching one all-encompassing religious identity to American Muslims, a very diverse set of people are homogenized. This may be problematic for American Muslims themselves, who perceive clear distinctions by national origin. Multiple identities have also been noted among Asian Americans.[24] Some American Muslims continue to place their national origin and ethnicity above their religious identity. Just as many Asian Americans understand, a link created through a shared race that requires an additional set of loyalties may not always be so easy to forge.[25] Cultural connections as Afghans, Pakistanis, Turks, and Syrians occasionally engender feelings of closeness with one's national origin and eclipse a sense of religious identification. One must underscore that racial formation and definitions applied to racial categories in the United States are uniquely American constructs, and thus are new categories to immigrant American Muslims.

As we have seen, immigrant and African American Muslim experiences have generally not coincided, the American Muslim community's integration has developed through a sophisticated disaggregation of country-specific cultural norms from Islamic orthodoxy, and a subsequent integration of American norms that fit with this new Islamic orthodoxy.[26] For many Muslims this resulted in the evolution of a unique American Muslim identity.[27]

AMERICAN MUSLIM POLITICAL INCORPORATION

The community's political incorporation has been a gradual process not unlike that of other minority communities. Immigrant American Muslims, like Asian Americans, are a maturing community, and along with numerical growth and age comes political sophistication. National surveys have validated this view. For instance, the 2007 Pew survey found that most American Muslims were politically engaged and had integrated fairly well with nearly two out of three (66%) registered to vote.[28] Equal percentages of Muslim men and women are registered to vote, with more women registering as Democrats and more men registering independent. Furthermore, the majority of American Muslims (38%) hold moderate political views, while 25 percent are conservative, and 27 percent are liberal.[29] Muslims between the ages of 18 and 44 are most likely to describe themselves as political moderates, with less than 30 percent identifying with either end of the political spectrum. Among Muslims aged 45 to 64, political views are evenly split among liberal, conservative, and moderate.[30] Seven out of ten American Muslims identify themselves as Democrats or as leaning toward the Democratic Party and favor a bigger government that provides more social services. Only 11 percent say they are Republicans or lean toward that party, and 10 percent are independent and unaffiliated with either party.[31] American Muslims are a generally well-informed group, since 64 percent claim to follow government and public affairs most of the time. This varies a little along geographic or partisan lines, although those who self-identify as "progressive" were more likely to say that they follow government affairs most of the time (81% of "progressives"). The 2007 Pew study found similar results: nearly 70 percent claimed to be paying attention to politics either "most" or "some" of the time.

Yet the degree of political incorporation clearly depends upon the segment of the community one examines. The incorporation of African American Muslims is consistent with the pattern found generally among blacks. The same can be said about Arab Muslims who have lived in the United States since the early 1920s. Their incorporation followed the pattern found among other Arab Christians arriving at the turn of the 20th century. The largest of these communities are Detroit's Muslim and Christian Arabs, who began significant involvement in the country's labor movement rather than political engagement in the early 1900s.[32] Many began to think of themselves as Americans during the 1910s, particularly after the outbreak of World War I. The political incorporation of those South Asian and Arab immigrants who mostly arrived from the 1980s onward and now constitute nearly 66 percent of the community has been more gradual, for many of them initially viewed politics with disenchantment and, at times, even disdain. But over the years many of them have become more receptive toward political engagement. Similar to other religious minorities who arrived earlier, many of them wondered whether they should maintain a distinctive culture or enter the mainstream?[33] Furthermore, are "these Muslims—immigrants and their descendants—any different from other large waves of immigrants to Western countries, who went through a similar process of acculturation, dropping ethnic characteristics and gathering themselves into religious categories?" How can one understand the level of this very diverse group's political engagement with the American social fabric?

One way is to locate the community's level of acculturation along a political spectrum. Levels of engagement can be viewed along a spectrum featuring isolation at one end and complete assimilation at the other end. Integration would thus fall somewhere between the two poles (Figure 7.1).

The isolationists choose to segregate themselves from the broader society by establishing enclaves or ghettos and have little interest in engaging with the public sphere whether by voting or other types of external social networking, for example, civic engagement and community activism. Religiously, they are represented by ultra-conservative Salafi Muslims or other groups, for example, the Tablighi Jamaat, who choose to physically distance themselves from the broader American society. For many Salafi Muslims, maintaining a pure Islamic identity is paramount, with any political engagement seen as a threat, something religiously forbidden and to be shunned. Some isolationists adopt this approach to maintain cultural purity. Holding onto both cultural and Islamic norms, they insist that any mixing with the West is likely to dilute one's culture and faith. Other

Figure 7.1
Level of Engagement

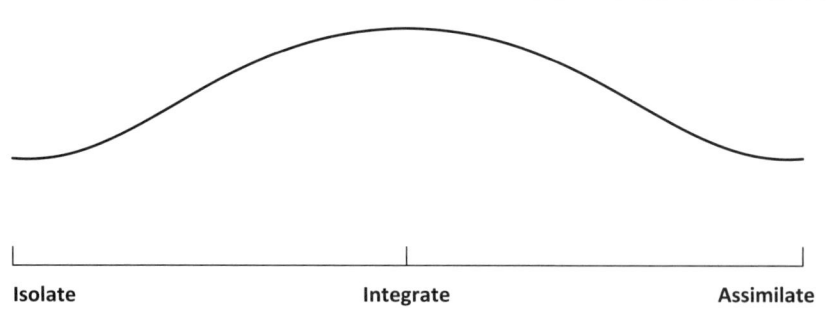

For American Muslims, the 9/11 tragedy and its aftermath heightened their sense of a "linked fate" cutting across cultural and racial lines. Certainly religion plays a role in developing group consciousness, especially for religious minorities. The role of religion, and not just of minority religions, in this case as well as in increased political participation has been noted by scholars, including in the Muslim American Public Opinion Survey (MAPOS).[62] Matt Barreto, Masuoka, and Sanchez found that discrimination, religiosity, and diversity are the major predictors of the formation of Muslim commonality. The authors concluded that religion is a major foundation of a shared group identity, with language and religious practice being the largest factors of that identity. They found that 44 percent of the Muslims surveyed had much in common with other Muslims, that 67 percent said they shared a similar fate, and that there were no differences in these results among Arabs, African Americans, and South Asians.[63]

In light of post-9/11 stereotypes and Islamophobia, American Muslims are often perceived as "foreigners" or "the other" and viewed through a "security lens" with the implication that they are a "threat" to America. This narrative has the effect of a glass ceiling, despite the group's economic success, and thus prevents them from full social integration. The same experience has been shared by Asian Americans. Tuan contends that the "forever foreigner" stereotype serves as a common racialized connection shared by both communities, regardless of national origin or how long they have lived in the country. Studies have documented a shared racial identity among Asian Americans.[64] In addition, evidence of a distinctively Asian American racial experience can be found in public opinion data, where Asian American respondents are more likely to feel that they have been discriminated against when compared to whites and, in some cases, Latinos.[65]

In this post-9/11 environment, American Muslim identity has become increasingly prevalent in self-identification and voting decisions.[66] According to the 2004 MAPS study, nearly 70 percent of American Muslim voters stated that being a Muslim is important when deciding how they should vote. African Americans were more likely than all Muslims to assert that their Muslim identity was *very* important in this regard (67% compared to 51%, respectively). The overwhelming majority of American Muslims (86%) said that it is important for Muslims to participate in politics, seven times those who said it is not important. This held across all geographic regions. Yet despite this, Muslims were not yet fully engaged politically in 2004. By a 3–1 margin (73% vs. 24%), they did not consider themselves active members of their political party. This was less pronounced among Democrats, where the margin drops to 2–1 (65% vs. 33%). Republicans mirrored the overall trend, while among self-described independents the margin was 80 percent to 17 percent. Democrats, Africans, and African Americans were the most likely to be active party members; South Asians were the least likely. Muslims were more likely to have volunteered time for a political candidate (33%) than to be active party members. About 40 percent had visited a political website, with younger Muslims the most likely to have done so, and 50 percent had written a letter to a political figure or the media. African American Muslims were more likely than immigrant Muslims to have written a letter on an issue that concerned them, as well as contacted a politician or the media, had attended a rally, boycotted, or contributed financially to a candidate.[67]

Muslims have also expressed a strong desire for political unity within their religion. Approximately 80 percent of American Muslims agreed with following the agenda of the American Muslim Taskforce on Civil Rights and Elections (AMT), a coalition of the 10 largest national Muslim organizations. A majority of American Muslims said that American Muslims should vote as a bloc for president in 2004. Around 70 percent of American Muslims said the AMT's endorsement of a presidential candidate would be important. Voting patterns shifted dramatically in 2004: 82 percent of all registered American Muslims voted for Kerry, whereas only 7 percent voted for Bush.[68] American Muslims tested their commitment to bloc voting again in the 2008 presidential elections. Most observers predicted that they would vote strongly in favor of Barack Obama. Yet Muslims did not merely support Obama because his father was Muslim and his middle name is Hussein; they voted for him largely because they felt that Republicans, especially under the Bush administration, had promoted a climate of fear and distrust of Muslims. AMT chairman Agha Saeed pointed out that the 2008 presidential election was a national (irrespective of religious affiliation) referendum on the Bush administration. Muslims watched a president who had promised to protect them and then, after 9/11, chip away at their civil liberties with legislation like the PATRIOT Act.[69]

Throughout the 2008 election year, Imam Mahdi Bray, executive director of the MAS Freedom Foundation, said repeatedly that it "is time for Muslims to step up to the plate in 2008 and take their souls to the polls."[70] Hoping to build upon the 2004 Muslim vote, the "MAS Voting is Power" program launched Muslim voter registration drives nationwide and added thousands of new Muslims to the rolls in such swing states as Pennsylvania, Virginia, North Carolina, Florida, and Michigan. An assortment of Muslim organizations, all of which pledged to generate a record Muslim voter turnout in 2008, joined this effort. During the 2008 presidential election, an ATF survey as well as the survey results from Gallup polls suggested that nearly 90 percent of registered American Muslims voted for Obama, while only 2 percent chose John McCain. The 2011 Pew study puts the number at 92 percent. Yet despite their overwhelming support for Obama, fewer American Muslims (64%) reported voting in the 2008 election, compared to the general public (76%). According to the 2012 Pew study, American Muslims "continue to be somewhat less engaged in several key elements of the political process than the public as a whole."[71] The study asked Muslim citizens if they were registered to vote: 66 percent said that they were, compared to 79 percent of the general public (numbers that had not changed since 2007).[72] On the other hand, younger Muslim citizens and those with higher levels of education were more likely to be registered and to vote.

At the local level, American Muslims have made some political inroads: a Muslim was elected mayor of San Carlos, CA, and others were elected to city council positions in Oakland, Detroit, and Chattanooga. Similarly, there are now several American Muslims in prominent federal government positions: Rashad Hussain as President Obama's special envoy to the Organization of Islamic Conference, Representative Keith Ellison (DFL-MN) elected in 2007, and Representative André Carson (D-IN) elected in 2008. Tate's work on black electoral behavior is illustrative here. Her study emphasized the importance of Jackson's presidential candidacy in explaining higher levels of voter turnout, while Bobo and Gilliam stressed the importance of political empowerment, that is, black office holding, in local politics.[73] My findings supported this idea with Muslims mobilizing and leading the charge to reelect both Ellison and Carson. The prominence of elected Muslim officials further reinforced the Muslims' desire to become politically active. It is surely evident in the number of local fund-raising events hosted by Muslims across the country to reelect Ellison and Carson.

In 2011, 75 percent of American Muslims expressed satisfaction with Obama's presidency, citing approval of his job performance, compared to only 14 percent who disapproved.[74] This level of satisfaction is significantly higher than that of the general public, which was split more evenly: 46 percent approving and a similar percentage disapproving. American Muslims "clearly see a friend in Obama, who came into office in 2009 pledging to improve relations with the Muslim world," with 64 percent saying he is "generally friendly" toward American Muslims, 4 percent considering him as unfriendly, and 27 percent perceiving him as neutral.[75] Along similar lines, American Muslims considered the Democratic Party friendlier than the Republican Party. Despite their high levels of support, the community was less likely than the general public to view Obama as a Muslim.

Several studies conducted by CAIR, including those completed in 2008 and 2012 supported many of the political trends revealed by MAPS between 2001 and 2004. The CAIR Poll showed that American Muslims continue to move away from the Republican Party; by 2008, only 8 percent identified as Republicans. This shift, however, increased the numbers of Independents rather than Democrats. The percentage of American Muslims identifying as independents rose to 36 percent from the 2004 figure of 31 percent. The survey shows that American Muslims, as a group, are gaining political self-identity and flexing their political muscle, both of which stand in stark contrast with some of the results in the 2001 survey.[76]

THE MOSQUE AS A CATALYST FOR POLITICAL MOBILIZATION

Researchers have found that religious institutions will often increase political participation. For instance, the 1990 Citizen Participation Study discovered that those attending/active in church-related matters had access to resources that increased their likelihood of participation. Paul Djupe and J. Grant showed that 75 percent of active church members were politically active in some way, compared to only 53 percent of those who were not active.[77]

A 2012 CAIR survey suggested that mosque leaders overwhelmingly endorsed involvement in American society that over 98 percent of mosque leaders agreed that Muslims should be involved in American institutions, and that 91 percent agreed that Muslims should be politically active. A similar number said it was important to them that their children be active as well. Similarly, researchers identified a link between mosque attendance and political participation among American Muslims: those who regularly attended the Friday prayer services were twice as likely to be highly politically involved compared to those who seldom attended such services. Amaney Jamal examined different ethnic groups and demonstrated that mosque involvement increased political participation for Arab Americans, but not for South Asians and African Americans.[78] For South Asians, mosque involvement led to higher levels of civic engagement and involvement with civic groups. "This raises the possibility of community leaders using mosques as a mobilizing platform to push Muslim Americans toward greater civic engagement."[79] Also, the more involved Arabs and African Americans were in their mosques, the more aware they were of discrimination against Muslims in America. This was not the case for South Asians.

This link has been confirmed by studying other religious communities, including the large-scale comparative study of political activity among African Americans, Latinos, and Whites.[80] Their project revealed that religious affiliation as a resource for political activity was associated with race and ethnicity. Church membership among African Americans was higher than that of any other ethnic/racial group. Thus they were more likely to be exposed to political messages and given greater opportunity to develop civic skills through their church. Exposure to political messages, through church meetings on political issues and political discussions by clergy from the pulpit, were reported more often by African Americans than Whites or Latinos. Similarly, African Americans were more likely to engage in civic activities for example, writing letters, planning meetings, or giving a speech in a church setting, than Whites or Latinos. Comparably,

African American Muslims are more likely to participate in such activities than immigrant Muslims.

Berman and Witting noted that African Americans have historically looked to the church for political mobilization, for it has traditionally provided the resources needed for action. Further, they confirmed that group consciousness defines African Americans as a disadvantaged group and that the church both facilitates and serves as a receptacle for this consciousness and provides the resources needed for mobilizing the community for political action.[81] Similarly, M. Calhoun found that the church continues to play its role, albeit a smaller one than before, for African Americans. She found that church attendance and political church membership were associated with group identification that politicizing that identity led to a group consciousness, that some churches were more political than others, and that members of more political churches had a stronger, positive relation to the development of a group consciousness.[82]

Religion and religious institutions may play a similar role for Muslims of all ethnicities. Kenneth Wald adds the role of religion, particularly for Arabs, when he concludes that "many Muslims clung to Islam as the primary means of expressing Arab identity and maintaining contact with the larger Arab world."[83] Jen'nan Read expanded on this phenomenon by identifying three components of a religious identity: a political religious identity, namely, attitudes toward Muslims and their participation in the political system; an organizational religious identity, that is, one based on mosque attendance/involvement; and a subjective religious identity, that is, the frequency of prayer and the general importance of religion in one's daily life.[84] Beyond the Arab American racial group, the title "American Muslim" encompasses multiple racial groups. Much like pan-ethnic identities, this title includes multiple races having a group consciousness related to religious identification. Read found that subjective religious identity had no influence on their degree of political involvement; rather, their organizational and political religious identity encouraged political consciousness and activity. In particular, she noted that mosque attendance increased the Arabs' group consciousness.[85]

In 2010, Representative Peter King (R-NY) held congressional hearings and expressed concern that mosques have a radicalizing and alienating effect on the country's Muslims. The 2007–2008 MAPOS study delved deeper into this issue and showed empirically that the opposite was true: that an association exists between higher levels of involvement in mosque-related activities and political participation.[86] Thus mosques, like churches and synagogues, were shown to be associated with a higher level of civic engagement and to contribute significantly to the creation of a more informed and engaged electorate. These findings also revealed that those American Muslims who are more actively engaged with their mosque tend to believe that Islam is compatible with the American political system. Those with no connection or involvement to a mosque reported an average of 1.7 acts of political participation per year (out of a scale of 0–4 acts). In contrast, those who said they were very involved with the mosque reported an average of 2.6 political acts per year, a 53 percent increase in civic engagement. Thus, rather than having a radicalizing or alienating effect, as some have suggested, American mosques have shown empirically to help Muslims integrate into American political life.

CONCLUSION

This broad overview of the American Muslim community suggests that the community has slowly become more comfortable with political engagement and entering into the political system. While African American Muslims have been politically active since the civil rights movement of the 1960s, immigrant South Asian and Arab Muslims have gradually increased their level of participation since the 1980s. Those who had historically considered American politics as a *kufr* (unbelieving) system are now organizing political campaigns, initiating voter registration drives, and building political institutions nationwide. Many of them are recognizing that flexing their political muscle is a necessity.

Since 9/11, American Muslims have further mobilized following a more hostile political environment, increased government scrutiny, and higher levels of discrimination. The post-9/11 environment has accelerated group identity and group consciousness. Given the community's diversity in terms of national origin and immigration, some note it is difficult to attribute American Muslim participation and attitudes to a distinctive racial group identity. Some have interpreted this reality as evidence that American Muslims' racial identity is irrelevant to their political affiliation and attitudes. At the same time, however, as we have seen, there has been a unifying of American Muslims across the country, especially since 9/11, which generated claims of a politicized and "racialized" group identity that mobilized the American Muslim community. Park 51 often referred to as the *Ground Zero* Mosque, was one such example. The incident unified the community across all racial and ethnic lines. Similarity exists with other minority groups, including Latino efforts to galvanize the community behind a particular cause. For instance, Hardy-Fanta argued that "group activities socialize individuals, establishing [thereby] social ties and developing interpersonal connections. When these social ties are developed, individuals are more likely to participate, particularly when the issues are important to the Latino community, for example, government housing or social welfare programs, when political leaders encourage such involvement."[87] During these periods, the community mobilized itself by engaging in more protests, civic engagement, and political activism nationwide. The common bond between the community and many of its leaders was their shared religious experience as American Muslims.

Soon after the Park 51 controversy erupted onto the national stage, American Muslims formed national leadership groups in order to respond to the anger leveled at the mosque's developers. The national attention that it garnered galvanized American Muslims across the nation, serving as a catalyst for the development of organizations devoted to protecting the community's right to freely build places of worship.

Muna Ali suggests that although American Muslims feel that their faith is under attack, they have not yet crystallized the meaning of "American Muslim." She notes that "American Muslim group consciousness, as a distinct group of Muslims in the *ummah* (global Muslim community), and Muslim American group consciousness, as a distinct group of Americans, are quite fluid."[88] While the relationship between identity and politics is not fixed, we have, at times, seen signs of convergence. If nothing more, the identity to politics dynamic continues to evolve as the community matures. Moving forward, the challenge for the community is how they might crystallize their religious identity as American Muslims and channel it into political influence.

NOTES

1. Navarro and Mejia, *Latino Americans and Political Participation*; Tate, *From Protest to Politics*; Garcia, *Latino Politics in America*; Alvarez and Bedolla, "Foundations of Latino Voter Partisanship," 31–49; Leal, "Political Participation by Latino Non-Citizens in the U.S.," 353–370; Leighley, *Strength in Numbers?*; Lien, *Making of Asian America*; Pantoja, Ramirez, and Segura, "Citizens by Choice, Voters by Necessity," 729–750; Canon, *Race, Redistricting, Representation*; Garcia, "Hispanic Political Participation and Demographic Correlates," 44–71; Arvizu and Garcia, "Latino Voting Participation," 104–128; DeSipio, *Counting on the Latino Vote*; Hero and Campbell, "Understanding Latino Political Participation," 129–141.

2. Saito, *Race and Politics*; Nagel, *American Indian Ethnic Renewal*; Jennings, *Blacks, Asians, and Latinos in Urban America*; Hardy-Fanta, *Latina Politics, Latino Politics*; Espiritu, *Asian American Panethnicity*; Padilla, *Latino Ethnic Consciousness*.

3. De la Garza, et al., *Latino Voices*; DeSipio, "Making Citizens or Good Citizens?" 194–213; F. C. Garcia, *Latinos and the Political System*; J. A. Garcia, *Latino Politics in America*.

4. DeSipio, "Making Citizens or Good Citizens?"; F. C. Garcia, *Latinos and the Political System*; J. A. Garcia, *Latino Politics in America*.

5. Lien, *Making of Asian America*; Lien, Conway, and Wong, *Politics of Asian Americans*; Lai, *Asian American Political Action*.

6. Jamal, "Political Participation and Engagement of Muslim Americans," 521–544; Djupe and Green, "Politics of American Muslims."

7. Dawson, *Behind the Mule*.

8. Senzai, *Engaging American Muslims*.

9. Pew Research Center, *Muslim Americans: Middle Class and Mostly Mainstream*.

10. Sandoval and Jendrysik, "Convergence and Divergence in Arab-American Public Opinion," 303–314.

11. Abedin and Abedin, "Muslim Minorities in Non-Muslim Societies," 112.

12. By some accounts, Islam is now the fastest growing religion in the United States. It is probably not an exaggeration to say that this community is the most diverse one in the Muslim world (Pew Research Center, *Muslim Americans: Middle Class and Mostly Mainstream*; Read, "Muslims in America.")

13. Smith, *Islam in America*; Yvonne Haddad, "Muslims in United States Politics."

14. Blassingame, *Slave Community*; Gomez, "Muslims in Early America," 671; Diouf, *Servants of Allah*.

15. Turner, *Islam in the African-American Experience*, 11–46; McCloud, *African American Islam*.

16. Mehdi, *Arabs in America, 1492–1977*; Coleman, "Individualizing Justice through Multiculturalism," 1093.

17. Haddad, "Muslims in United States Politics."

18. While high socioeconomic standing is an average across all people classified as Asian American, it is important to note that the distribution of educational and income resources within the Asian American community is bimodal. Southeast Asian and many new Chinese immigrant Asian Americans occupy the lower end of the economic spectrum.

19. Lai and Arguelles, *New Face of Asian Pacific America*.

20. Verba, Schlozman, and Brady, "Race, Ethnicity, and Political Resources."

21. Guterbock and London, "Race, Political Orientation, and Participation," 439–453; Olsen, "Social and Political Participation of Blacks," 682–697; Verba and Nie, *Participation in America*; Williams, Babchuk, and Johnson, "Voluntary Associations and Minority Status."

22. Dahl, *Who Governs?*

23. Nagel, *American Indian Ethnic Renewal*.

24. Espiritu, *Asian American Panethnicity*; Lien, *Making of Asian America through Political Participation*; Lien, Conway, and Wong, *Politics of Asian America*.

25. Espiritu, *Asian American Panethnicity*; Nagel, *American Indian Ethnic Renewal*.

26. McCloud, *African American Islam*.

27. Haddad, "Muslims in United States Politics"; Metcalf, *Making Muslim Space in North America and Europe*; Nyang, *Islam in the United States of America*.

28. Pew Research Center, *Muslim Americans: Middle Class and Mostly Mainstream*.

29. Ibid.

30. Gallup, 2009.

31. Pew Research Center, *Muslim Americans: Middle Class and Mostly Mainstream*.

32. For further discussion of the "Political Participation of American Muslims in Detroit," see Chapter 8 in this volume.

33. Haddad and Esposito, *Muslims and the Americanization Path?*; Haque, *Muslims and Islamization in North America*; Abraham, "Arab-American Marginality," 17–45; Muhammad, "Some Factors Which Promote and Restrict Islamization in America," 1.

34. Khalidi, "Living as a Muslim in a Pluralistic Society and State."

35. Johnson, "Political Activity of Muslims in America," 113.

36. Nyang, "Convergence and Divergence in an Emergent Community," 238–239.
37. Hashem, "Assimilation in the American Life: An Islamic Perspective," 83–97.
38. Abd-Allah, "Islam and the Cultural Imperative."
39. Haddad and Smith, *Muslim Communities in North America*; Haddad, *Becoming American?*; Khan, *American Muslims: Bridging Faith and Freedom*.
40. Zogby International, *Muslims in the American Public Square*; Pew Research Center, *Muslim Americans: Middle Class and Mostly Mainstream*; Pew Research Center, *Muslim Americans: No Signs of Growth in Alienation or Support for Extremism*.
41. Pew Research Center, *Muslim Americans: No Signs of Growth in Alienation or Support for Extremism*.
42. Ibid.
43. Muhammad, "Some Factors Which Promote and Restrict Islamization in America"; Haddad and Esposito, *Muslims and the Americanization Path?*; Haque, *Muslims and Islamization in North America*.
44. Freeland, "Treatment of Muslims."
45. Haddad, *Muslims of America*.
46. Pew Research Center, *Muslim Americans: Middle Class and Mostly Mainstream*.
47. Haddad, "Muslims in United States Politics."
48. Ibid.
49. Zogby International, *Muslims in the American Public Square*.
50. Ibid.
51. Dawson, *Behind the Mule*.
52. Leighley, *Strength in Numbers?*
53. Hardy-Fanta, *Latina Politics, Latino Politics*.
54. Leighley, *Strength in Numbers?*
55. Bakalian and Bozorgmehr, *Backlash 9/11*.
56. Howell and Jamal, "Detroit Exceptionalism and the Limits of Political Incorporation."
57. Verba and Nie, *Participation in America*.
58. Jamal and Naber, "Mainstream America's Silence."
59. Dawson, *Behind the Mule*.
60. Verba and Nie, *Participation in America*.
61. Dawson, *Behind the Mule*.
62. Dana, Barreto, and Oskooii, "Mosques as American Institutions."
63. Barreto, Masuoka, and Sanchez, "Discrimination and Group Consciousness among Muslim Americans," 1.
64. Lien, Conway, and Wong, *Politics of Asian Americans*.
65. DeSipio, *Counting on the Latino Vote*; Lien, Conway, and Wong, *Politics of Asian Americans*.
66. Ba-Yunus and Kone, *Muslims' Place in the American Public Square*.
67. Zogby International, *Muslims in the American Public Square*.
68. Ibid.
69. Brachear, "Why Did Muslims Vote for Obama?"
70. Lee, "Muslim Vote in the United States Presidential Race."

71. Pew Research Center, 2011.
72. Pew Research Center, *Muslim Americans: No Signs of Growth in Alienation or Support for Extremism*.
73. Bobo and Gilliam, "Race, Sociopolitical Participation, and Black Empowerment," 377–393.
74. Pew Research Center, *Muslim Americans: No Signs of Growth in Alienation or Support for Extremism*.
75. Ibid.
76. Bagby, Perl, and Froehle, "The Mosque in America: A National Portrait."
77. Djupe and Grant, "Religious Institutions and Political Participation in America."
78. Jamal, "Political Participation and Engagement of Muslim Americans," 521–544.
79. Gallup, 2009.
80. Verba, Schlozman, and Brady, "Race, Ethnicity, and Political Resources," 453–497.
81. Berman and Michele, "Intergroup Theories Approach."
82. Calhoun, "Political Behavior, Group Consciousness and African American Churches."
83. Wald, "Homeland Interests, Hostland Politics," 282.
84. Read, "More of a Bridge than a Gap," 1072–1091.
85. Ibid.
86. Dana, Barreto, and Oskooii, "Mosques as American Institutions."
87. Leighley, *Strength in Numbers?*
88. Ali, "Muslim American/American Muslim Identity," 356.

REFERENCES

Abd-Allah, Umar Faruq. "Islam and Cultural Imperative." *Nawawi Foundation Paper*. 2004. http://www.nawawi.org/wp-content/uploads/2013/01/Article3.pdf

Abedin, Syed Z., and Saleha M. Abedin. "Muslim Minorities in Non-Muslim Societies." *Oxford Encyclopedia of the Modern Muslim World*. Vol. III. Oxford: Oxford University Press, 1994. 112.

Abraham, Nabeel. "Arab-American Marginality: Mythos and Praxis." *Arab Americans: Continuity and Change*. Ed. Baha Abu-Laban and Michael W. Suleiman. Belmont, MA: Association of Arab-American University Graduates, Inc., 1989. 17–45.

Akhtar, Muhammad Salim. "95% Muslim Voter Turnout, 89% for Obama." 7 November 2008. www.americanmuslimvoter.net.

Ali, Muna. "Muslim American/American Muslim Identity: Authoring Self in Post-9/11 America." *Journal of Muslim Minority Affairs* 31.3 (2011): 356.

Alverez, R. Michael, and Lisa Garcia Bedolla. "The Foundations of Latino Voter Partisanship: Evidence from the 2000 Elections." *Journal of Politics* 65.1 (2003): 31–49.

Bagby, Ihsan, Paul M. Perl, and Bryan T. Froehle. "The Mosque in America: A National Portrait." Washington, D.C.: Council on American Islamic Relations, 2001.

Bakalian, Anny, and Mehdi Bozorgmehr. *Backlash 9/11: Middle Eastern and Muslim Americans Respond.* Berkeley: University of California Press, 2009.

Barbara Daly, Metcalf, ed. *Making Muslim Space in North America and Europe.* Berkeley: University of California Press, 1996.

Barreto, Matt, Natalie Masuoka, and Garbriel Sanchez. "Discrimination and Group Consciousness among Muslim Americans." *Conference Papers—Western Political Science Association* 1 (2008).

Ba-Yunus, Ilyas, and Kassim Kone. *Muslims' Place in the American Public Square: Hope Fears and Aspirations.* Ed. Zahid H. Bukhari, et al. Walnut Creek: Alta Mira Press, 2004.

Berman, Schuyler L., and Michele A. Witting. "An Intergroup Theories Approach to Direct Political Action among African Americans." *Group Processes & Intergroup Relations* 7.1 (2004): 19–34.

Blassingame, John. *The Slave Community: Plantation Life in the Antebellum South.* Oxford: Oxford University Press, 1979.

Bobo, Lawrence, and Franklin D. Gilliam Jr. "Race, Sociopolitical Participation, and Black Empowerment." *The American Political Science Review* 84. 2 (June 1990): 377–393.

Brachear, Manya A. "Why Did Muslims Vote for Obama?" *Chicago Tribune* 8 November 2008. http://www.islamicity.org/3391/why-did-muslims-vote-for-obama/.

Calhoun, M. A. *Political Behavior, Group Consciousness and African American Churches: Motivating Voters in the Black Community.* Atlanta, GA: Emory University Press, 1995.

Coleman, Doriane Lambelet. "Individualizing Justice through Multiculturalism: The Liberals' Dilemma." *Columbia Law Review* 96 (1996): 1093.

Dahl, Robert. *Who Governs?: Democracy and Power in an American City.* New Haven, CT: Yale University Press, 1961.

Dana, Karam, Matt Barreto, and Kassra Oskooii. "Mosques as American Institutions: Mosque Attendance, Religiosity and Integration into the American Political System." *Religions* 2.2 (September 2011).

David, Canon T. *Race, Redistricting, and Representation.* Chicago: University of Chicago Press, 1999.

Dawson, Michael. *Behind the Mule: Race and Class in African American Politics.* Princeton, NJ: Princeton University Press, 1994.

De la Garza, Rodolfo, et al. *Latino Voices: Mexican, Puerto Rican, and Cuban Perspectives on American Politics.* Boulder, CO: Westview Press, 1992.

DeSipio, Louise. *Counting on the Latino Vote: Latinos as a New Electorate.* Richmond: University of Virginia Press, 1996.

DeSipio, Louis. "Making Citizens or Good Citizens? Naturalization as Predictor of Organizational and Political Behavior among Latino Immigrants." *Hispanic Journal of Behavior Sciences* 18 (1996): 195–213.

Diouf, Sylviane. *Servants of Allah: African Muslims Enslaved in the Americas.* New York: New York University Press, 1998.

Djupe, Paul A., and J. T. Grant. "Religious Institutions and Political Participation in America." *Journal for the Scientific Study of Religion* 40.2 (2001): 303–314.

Djupe, Paul A., and John C. Green. "The Politics of American Muslims." *From Pews to Polling Places: Faith and Politics in the American Religious Mosaic.* Ed. J. Matthew Wilson. Washington, DC: Georgetown University Press, 2007.

Espiritu, Yen Le. *Asian American Panethnicity: Bridging Institutions and Identities.* Philadelphia: Temple University Press, 1992.
Freeland, Richard. "The Treatment of Muslims in American Courts." *Islam and Christian Muslim Relations* 12.4 (2001): 449–463.
Garcia, John A. "Hispanic Political Participation and Demographic Correlates." *Pursuing Power.* Ed. F. Chris Garcia. Notre Dame, IN: University of Notre Dame Press, 1997. 44–71.
Garcia, John A. *Latino Politics in America: Community, Culture, and Interests.* Lanham: Rowman & Littlefield Publishers, 2011.
Garcia, F. Chris. *Latinos and the Political System.* Notre Dame, IN: University of Notre Dame Press, 1988.
Gomez, Michael. "Muslims in Early America." *The Journal of Southern History* 60 (November 1994): 671.
Guterbock, T. M., and B. London. "Race, Political Orientations, and Participation: An Empirical Test of Four Competing Theories." *American Sociological Review* 43 (1983): 439–453.
Haddad, Yvonne. *Becoming American? The Forging of Arab and Muslim Identity in Pluralist America.* Waco, TX: Baylor University Press, 2011.
Haddad, Yvonne. *The Muslims of America.* New York: Oxford University Press, 1993.
Haddad, Yvonne. "Muslims in United States Politics: Recognized and Integrated, or Seduced and Abandoned." *SAIS Review* 21.2 (Summer–Fall 2001).
Haddad, Yvonne, and John Esposito. *Muslims and the Americanization Path?* Atlanta, GA: Scholar's Press, 1998.
Haddad, Yvonne, and Jane I. Smith, eds. *Muslim Communities in North America.* Albany: State University of New York Press, 1994.
Haque, Amber, ed. *Muslims and Islamization in North America: Problems and Perspectives.* Beltville, MD: Amana, 1999.
Hardy-Fanta, Carol. *Latina Politics, Latino Politics: Gender, Culture, and Political Participation in Boston.* Philadelphia: Temple University Press, 1993.
Hashem, Mazen. "Assimilation in the American Life: An Islamic Perspective." *American Journal of Islamic Social Sciences* 18 (Spring 1991): 83–97.
Howell, Sally, and Amaney Jamal. "Detroit Exceptionalism and the Limits of Political Incorporation." *Being and Belonging: Muslims in the United States since 9/11.* Ed. Katherine Pratt Ewing. New York: Russell Sage Foundation, 2008.
Jamal, Amaney. "The Political Participation and Engagement of Muslim Americans: Mosque Involvement and Group Consciousness." *American Politics Research* 33.4 (July 2005): 521–544.
Jamal, Amaney, and Nadine Naber. "Mainstream America's Silence: The Racialization of Arab Americans." *Race and Arab Americans after 9-11: From Invisible Citizens to Visible Subjects.* Syracuse University Press, February 2008.
Jennings, James, ed. *Blacks, Latinos, and Asians in Urban America.* Westport, CT: Praeger, 1994.
Johnson, Steve A. "Political Activity of Muslims in America." *The Muslims of America.* Ed. Yvonne Y. Haddad. New York: Oxford University Press, 1991. 113.
Khalidi, Omar. "Living as a Muslim in a Pluralistic Society and State: Theory and Experience." *Muslims' Place in the American Public Square: Hope, Fears, and Aspirations.* Ed. Zahid Bukhari, et al. Walnut Creek: Alta Mira Press, 2004.
Khan, M. A. Muqtedar. *American Muslims: Bridging Faith and Freedom.* Beltsville, MD: Amana Publications, 2002.

Lai, Eric, and Dennis Arguelles, eds. *The New Face of Asian Pacific America: Numbers, Diversity and Changes in the 21st Century.* San Francisco: AsianWeek, 2003.

Lai, James S. *Asian American Political Action: Suburban Transformations.* Boulder, CO: Lynne Rienner Publishers, 2011.

Leal, David. "Political Participation by Latino Non-Citizens in the U.S." *British Journal of Political Science* 32 (2002): 353–370.

Lee, Umar. "The Muslim Vote in the United States Presidential Race." *IslamOnline.* Accessed 21 October 2008. http://www.onislam.net/english/politics/americas/431212.html.

Leighley, Janet E. *Strength in Numbers? The Political Mobilization of Racial and Ethnic Minorities.* Princeton, NJ: Princeton University Press, 2001.

Lien, Pei-Te. *The Making of Asian America through Political Participation.* Philadelphia: Temple University Press, 2001.

Lien, Pei-Te, M. Margaret Conway, and Janelle Wong. *The Politics of Asian Americans.* New York: Routledge Press, 2004.

McCloud, Aminah Beverly. *African American Islam.* New York: Routledge, 1995.

Mehdi, Beverlee T. *The Arabs in America, 1492–1977.* New York: Oceana, 1978.

Muhammad, Akbar. "Some Factors Which Promote and Restrict Islamization in America." *American Journal of Islamic Social Sciences* 1 (1984).

Nagel, Joane. *American Indian Ethnic Renewal.* New York: Oxford University Press, 1997.

Navarro, Sharon A., and Armando Xavier Mejia. eds. *Latino Americans and Political Participation.* Santa Barbara: ABC-CLIO Press, 2004.

Nyang, Suleyman S. "Convergence and Divergence in an Emergent Community: A Study of Challenges Facing United States Muslims." *The Muslims of America.* Ed. Yvonne Haddad. New York: Oxford University Press, 1991. 238–239.

Nyang, Suleyman S. *Islam in the United States of America.* Chicago: ABC International Group, 1999.

Olsen, Marvin. "Social and Political Participation of Blacks." *American Sociological Review* 35 (1970): 682–697.

Padilla, Felix M. *Latino Ethnic Consciousness.* Notre Dame, IN: University of Notre Dame Press, 1985.

Pantoja, Adrian D., Ricardo Ramirez, and Gary M. Segura, "Citizens by Choice, Voters by Necessity: Patterns in Political Mobilization by Naturalized Latinos." *Political Research Quarterly* 54.4 (December 2001): 729–750.

Pew Research Center. *Muslim Americans: Middle Class and Mostly Mainstream.* Washington, D.C.: Pew Research Center, 2007.

Pew Research Center. *Muslim Americans: No Signs of Growth in Alienation or Support for Extremism.* Washington, DC: Pew Research Center, 2011.

Read, Jen'nan Ghazal. "More of a Bridge than a Gap: Gender Differences in Arab-American Political Engagement." *Social Science Quarterly (Blackwell Publishing Limited)* 88.5 (2007): 1072–1091.

Read, Jen'nan Ghazal. "Muslims in America." *Contexts* 7.4 (2008).

Saito, Leland. *Race and Politics: Asian Americans, Latinos and Whites in a Los Angeles Suburb.* Urbana: University of Illinois Press, 1998.

Sandoval, Jose Miguel, and Mark Stephen Jendrysik. "Convergence and Divergence in the Arab-American Public Opinion." *International Journal of Public Opinion Research* 5.4 (Winter 1993): 310–311.

Senzai, Farid. *Engaging American Muslims: Political Trends and Attitudes*. Detroit, MI: Institute for Social Policy and Understanding, April 2012.

Smith, Jane. *Islam in America*. New York: Columbia University Press, 1999.

Tate, Katherine. *From Protest to Politics: The New Black Voters in American Elections*. Boston: Harvard University Press, 1998.

Tuan, Mia. *Forever Foreigner or Honorary White: The Asian Ethnic Experience Today*. New Brunswick, NJ: Rutgers University Press, 1999.

Turner, Richard Brent. *Islam in the African-American Experience*. Bloomington: Indiana University Press, 1997. 11–46.

Verba, Sidney, and Norman H. Nie. *Participation in America*. Chicago: University of Chicago Press, 1987.

Verba, Sidney, Kay Lehman Schlozman, and Henry E. Brady. *Voice and Equality: Civic Voluntarism in American Politics*. Boston: Harvard University Press, 1995.

Wald, Kenneth D. "Homeland Interests, Hostland Politics: Politicized Ethnic Identity among Middle Eastern Heritage Groups in the United States." *International Migration Review* 42.2 (2008): 282.

Williams, J. Allen, Jr., Nicholas Babchuk, and David R. Johnson. "Voluntary Associations and Minority Status: A Comparative Analysis of Anglo, Black, and Mexican Americans." *American Sociological Review* 38 (1973): 637–646.

Younis, Mohamed. *Muslim Americans Exemplify Diversity, Potential*. Gallup Poll, Report, Gallup Center for Muslim Studies, 2009. http://www.gallup.com/poll/116260/muslim-americans-exemplify-diversity-potential.aspx.

Zogby International. *Muslims in the American Public Square*. Georgetown University's Muslims in the American Public Square (Project MAPS). Washington, DC: Zogby International, 2004.

Chapter 8

Political Participation of American Muslims in Detroit

Juris Pupcenoks and Farid Senzai

Individual political participation among American Muslims with an immigrant background remains an understudied topic, although several projects have been conducted in the post-9/11 era.[1] These studies generally conclude that these citizens are politically active and that their political activism is peaceful,[2] and mostly suggest that while their level of political involvement may be increasing, the group's impact remains limited. With the exception of voting patterns, political participation among Muslims living in the Greater Detroit area largely resembles patterns of other minority and immigrant-background communities in the West. In general, minority communities tend to choose one of two broad avenues: voting (citizens) and nonelectoral political engagement. Minority voters tend to turn out at the polls in lower numbers and vote mainly for parties on the left of the political spectrum than is the case with nonminority voters.[3] American Muslim nonelectoral political participation largely resembles those activities engaged in by other minority communities. Among the issues of great concern are "issues of material justice,"[4] and thus immigrant mobilization efforts largely focus on them. Other issues among the better-established individuals in Britain and elsewhere in Europe include mobilizing against perceived societal ills, for example, racism, discrimination, lack of representation, and the lack of various rights.[5] Additionally, conditions of vulnerability and the lack of rights among undocumented immigrants have spurred many of them to work with advocacy organizations to establish popular movements calling for their documentation, such as the San-Papiers movement in France, the Sin-Papeles in Spain, or the Strangers into Citizens in the United States.[6]

With regard to the evolution of and challenges to participation, Mark J. Miller's classic study of immigrant-background community's political participation identified five key channels for immigrant and minority political participation: the extra-parliamentary avenue, for example, street protests and hunger strikes; consultative institutions, that is, forming organizations that represent minority group interests when interacting with governmental representatives; participation in unions and factory councils; participation through political, religious, and civic organizations; and these communities' ability to impact homeland politics through diplomatic channels.[7] Since at least the 1980s, immigrants and minorities in the West have been politically active in many ways, even though, until recently, social science research has largely overlooked such activism.[8] Furthermore, more recent studies suggest that immigrants mobilize cross-ethnically and along class lines.[9] A similar pattern is evident in Detroit. In some instances, politically mobilized minority and migrant voting blocs acquired major political roles. For example, Jews who migrated from the former Soviet Union have significantly affected the results of Israel's elections from 1992 onward. By the late 2000s, such "Russian" Jews constituted 15 percent of the electorate.[10] Quebec's immigrants voted overwhelmingly against the province's secession from Canada in the 1996 referendum and decisively influenced the slim margin by which its sovereignty was rejected. Naturalized Eastern European citizens acted as an important voting bloc that enabled Angela Merkel to win the German chancellorship.[11]

A significant portion of American Islam is indigenous, for African Americans have been part of American history for centuries. Nationally, immigrant Muslims have become a more politically active segment of the American Muslim population. As Ali Mazrui notes, "the groups that have been most politically active for the cause of Islam in the United States may well be immigrant Muslims, many of whom came to the United States in the postwar era and, more especially, in the past three decades."[12]

This chapter assesses the political participation of Detroit's American Muslim community, for its members constitute a sizeable percentage of the population, especially in such suburbs as Dearborn. Over time, this community has become increasingly active, as can be seen in its higher levels of political mobilization and incorporation.[13] Much has been written about the development of increasingly influential Detroit Arab institutions and their participation in both local politics and the affairs of their former homelands.[14] This discussion shows that political participation among Detroit's Muslim minority community increasingly resembles that of other Muslim communities nationwide. As it has matured, its members have become more active and politically engaged. Their preferred form of political participation, organized locally, has evolved from protest politics and other kinds of nonelectoral participation to voting, lobbying, and running for office. Furthermore, although Detroit's Muslims remain committed to foreign policy issues and conflicts in the Middle East, their interests have gradually shifted toward domestic issues. This trend is similar to what Farid Senzai's chapter (Chapter 7) in this volume highlights: a Muslim shift toward domestic issues at the national level. But internal community divisions still stifle effective political participation, for although Detroit's Muslims have gained a notable influence on local politics, their impact on national politics and foreign policy remains negligible. Sources of information for this case study come from field research, the Muslim American Public Opinion Survey (MAPOS) study, and available quantitative data on the community. Lessons from Detroit's Muslims may predict the key types of political participation, issues of concern, the challenges of political mobilization, and the impact of political participation for other American Muslim communities in future years.[15] The chapter begins with an overview of Muslims in the greater Detroit area, including basic demographic information, and then examines each of these topics in turn.

AMERICAN MUSLIMS IN THE GREATER DETROIT AREA

The Greater Detroit area hosts one of the largest populations of Arab and Muslim Americans in the country. Many Muslim immigrants from what was known as Greater Syria (including Syria, Lebanon, Jordan, and Palestine) began arriving in the early years of the 20th century for economic reasons, mainly to work in the automobile industry.[16] Muslim population estimates vary widely. The University of Michigan's exhibit, "Building Islam in Detroit," estimates that there are 150,000 Muslims;[17] a 2004 Institute of Social Policy and Understanding (ISPU) study estimates the number as being somewhere between 125,000 and 200,000 and roughly equally divided among Arabs, South Asians, and African Americans.[18] Despite the variation, it is reasonable to estimate that by 2010 this community had over 200,000 members,[19] including religious Arab, South Asian, and indigenous Muslims, as well as those less-observant and secular Muslims for whom Islam remains a basis for identity. The largest Muslim concentration is in Dearborn, where the predominant Muslim Arab group constitutes 30 percent of its total population.

Many of Greater Detroit's Muslims share an Arab heritage. Given that ethnicity serves as one of the community's most important mobilizing factors, Arab-background Muslims have the most influence. Community advocates often argue that the 2000 U.S. Census greatly underestimated the Arab American population "due to the fact that Arab Americans are not an official minority."[20] The 2005 U.S. Census' American Community Survey estimates suggested that Michigan's Arab population rose from 116,331 in 2000 to 153,843 in 2005, a 32 percent increase.[21] The Arab American Institute and Zogby International estimate that the state's Arab-American population stood at 490,000. The community is almost equally comprised of Muslims and Christians. The Detroit Arab-Muslim community differs from American Muslims elsewhere in two important ways: (1) it contains a very significant number of Shi'as and (2) while most Muslims nationwide are generally highly educated and working professionals, a larger segment of Detroit's Muslims are akin to European Muslims, for example, they tend to come from poor, working-class families and often distrust the government's policies.[22] Additional information about the community's composition can be obtained from survey data.

The MAPOS survey conducted by Karam Dana and Matt Barreto is one of the major studies of Muslims in the United States.[23] Michigan was one of the 22 sites surveyed between December 2006 and December 2008, with the bulk of the survey conducted in the Detroit metro area. The 96 respondents answered questions related to demographics, level of religiosity, and civic and political engagement. Figure 8.1 shows the community's racial composition. This information was collected in Detroit, and therefore Arabs were naturally the highest percentage of respondents, followed by South Asians. The general American Muslim population is more diverse than the data suggest, as Arab Americans are overrepresented.[24]

Figure 8.1
Racial Composition of Muslims in Michigan

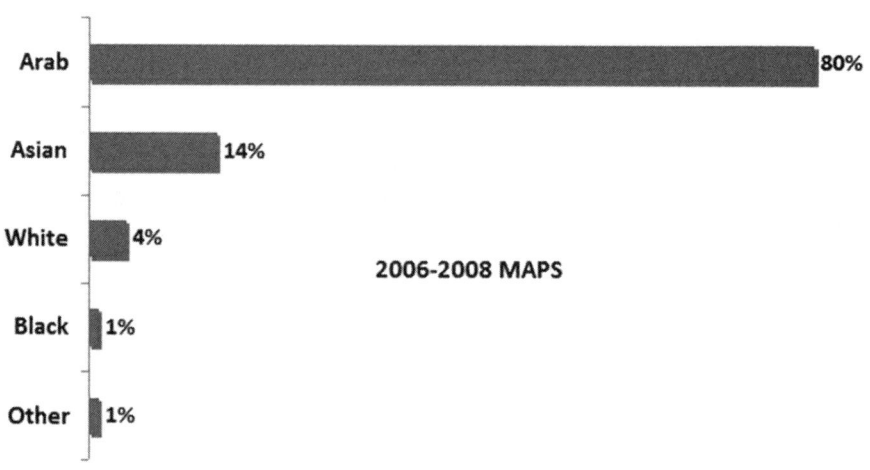

Figure 8.6
Acts of Political Participation by Generation

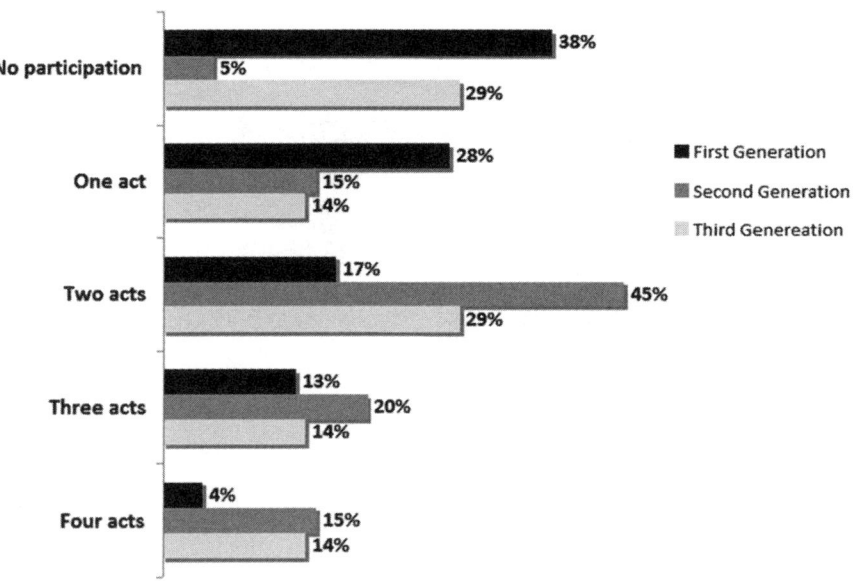

Muslims were the most politically active (Figure 8.6). This is consistent with similar studies. The longer that individuals live in the United States, the more they participate in its politics, which is unsurprising considering such factors as decreasing linguistic and cultural barriers and acquiring citizenship.

EVOLUTION OF TYPES OF PARTICIPATION

During the 1960s and 1970s, many foreign-born university students established Muslim Student Associations (MSAs) and eventually the Islamic Society of North America. But today, native-born American Muslims dominate the MSAs. The national MSA leaders address political issues more aggressively than their elders ever did. Especially since 9/11, many MSA members continue to insist on their right to protest American foreign policy and to take advantage of the national focus on Islam to expand educational outreach activities.[28] They have made new political coalitions with Japanese Americans and Latino Americans, and, at times, have gained unexpected allies, namely, Just Act, the gay-rights organization that was among the first to publically support Muslims after the

Figure 8.4
Acts of Political Participation by Gender

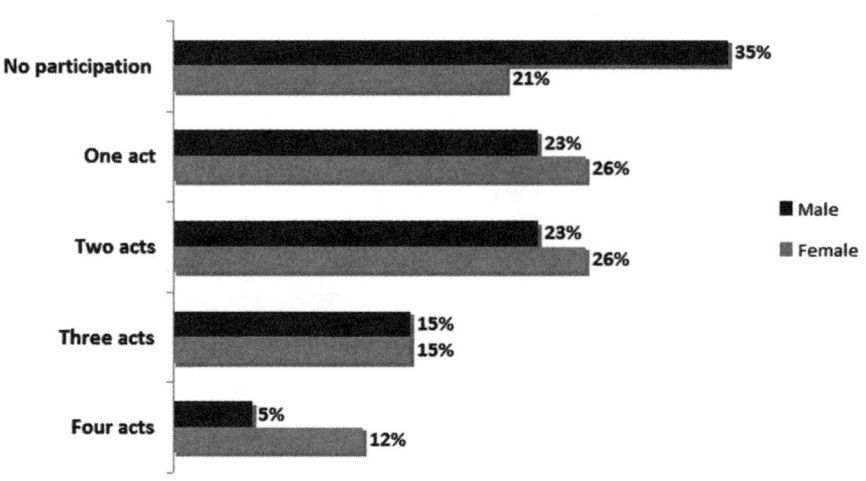

Figure 8.5
Acts of Political Participation by Educational Attainment

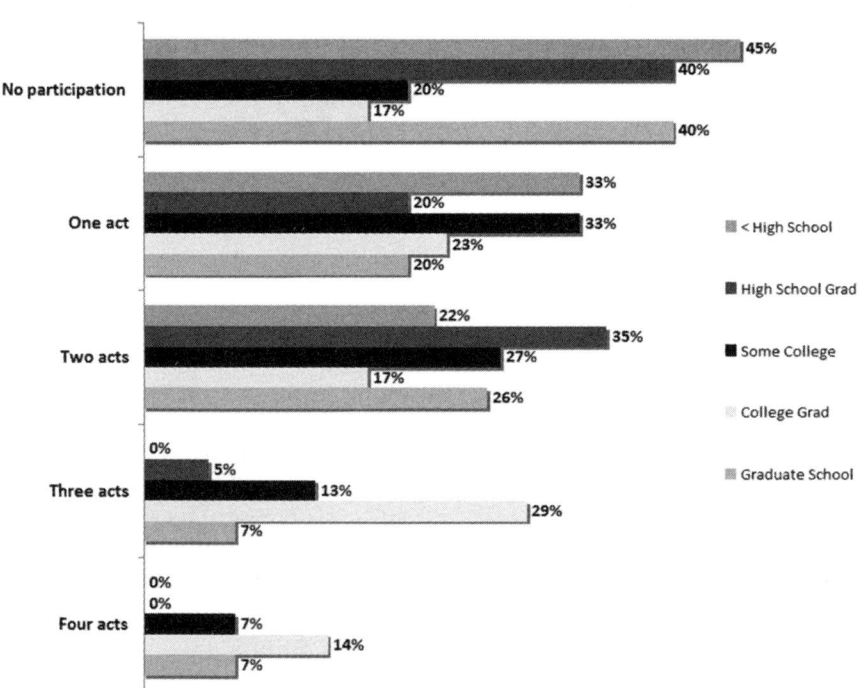

0 to 4. Because relatively older people tend to participate more, Figure 8.3 presents the extent of political participation. When compared with other minority groups, particularly Latino Americans, the American Muslim community is relatively more active.

Data from the MAPOS study suggest similar patterns to those found among the larger American population; for example, as people age they tend to become more politically involved.[26] Among younger American Muslims, political participation is relatively high when compared to their peers in other minority groups. This suggests that they are encouraged by the benefits of participation and therefore are more likely to be involved and to understand the overall significance of politics.

Exploring this further, we found that American Muslim women in Michigan were more politically active than their male counterparts (Figure 8.4). This contradicts the stereotype that Muslim women are disengaged from or uninterested in political activity. In fact, many of our interviewees suggested that women have often been a driving force in their communities, an assertion that these data fully support.

Education is often positively associated with an individual's level of political participation. Detroit's Muslim community is no exception (Figure 8.5). American Muslims generally tend to be highly educated.[27]

Analyzing the level of political participation according to one's immigrant status, we found that second- and third-generation American

Figure 8.3
Acts of Political Participation by Age

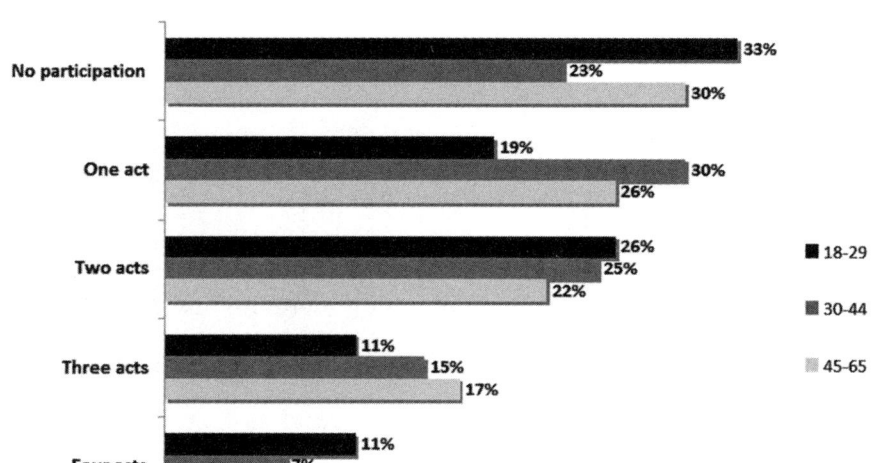

Arab Muslims in Detroit often lead the Muslim community in level of political engagement. Detroit is also among the first places the American media descends upon when conflict in the Middle East or the Muslim world at large generates headlines. The city often finds itself in the spotlight as journalists survey the views of Arab and Muslim Americans about the latest eruption in the Middle East. Although the city has witnessed street protests, lobbying, and other kinds of political protest as tensions rise in Lebanon, Iraq, or Palestine, the community has generally shunned violence and demonstrated peacefully.[25] Given the current political environment, the community follows events from Iraq, Afghanistan, and Palestine, and the Arab Spring to American policies in the Middle East.

An oft-debated question within the community is whether Islam and participation in Western-style democracy are compatible, a question previously explored by scholars and academics. The MAPOS survey asked respondents what they thought about this. Thirty percent replied that they were "very much" compatible, and 28 percent said they were "somewhat" compatible. Thus a total of 58 percent saw a certain degree of compatibility, whereas 14 percent saw none at all (Figure 8.2).

The MAPOS study inquired about the respondents' level of political participation, for example, writing to a public official, participating in a protest or rally, attending a community meeting, and donating to a public candidate/campaign, and rated their responses on a scale ranging from

Figure 8.2
Are Islamic Teachings Compatible with Participation in the American Political System?

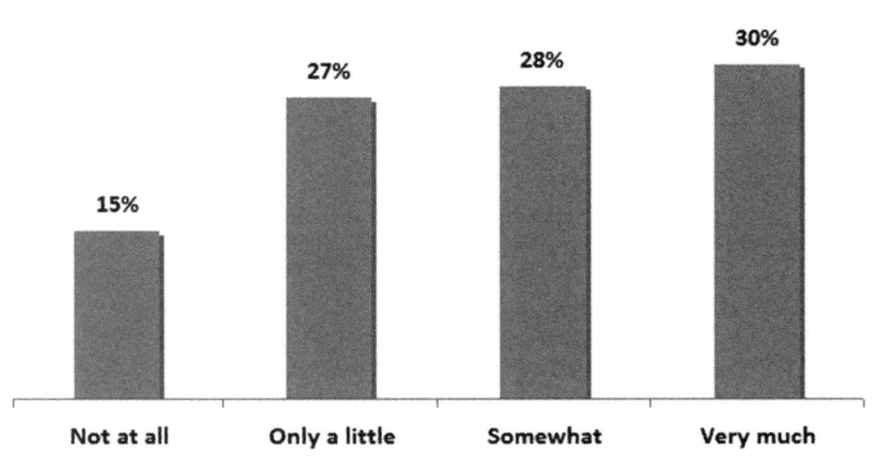

9/11 tragedy. MSA leaders also used the Internet very aggressively to rally support and strengthen their Muslim identity.[29] Work by younger Muslim academics reflects this self-confidence and claiming of political rights.[30]

Muslim political activism has been on the rise nationwide for the last two decades. Growing numbers of American Muslims are registering to vote and seeking to influence candidates during elections. For example, "in the 1994 elections, Muslim groups backed 77 congressional and gubernatorial candidates. This year, for the first time, a coalition of Muslim groups will back a presidential candidate."[31] Some limited success has been achieved in electing Muslims to local positions.

The 2001 MAPS project, conducted by Georgetown University and Zogby International, was helpful because it asked several questions about political views and voting behavior. A major finding was that 79 percent of Muslims were registered to vote; African Americans and women comprised the highest groups. Among those registered participants who answered the questions, 40 percent were Democrats, 23 percent Republicans, and 28 percent Independents or small-party members. African Americans were the most likely to be Democrats and Pakistanis were the most likely to be Republicans; Arabs were almost evenly divided among the three categories.[32] Although over 905 of the respondents favored big government solutions to issues like health care and poverty, respondents were very conservative on social issues.[33] American foreign policy concerns were clear: 84 percent wanted Washington to support a Palestinian state, 70 percent wanted it to reduce financial aid to Israel, and 61 percent wanted it to reduce its support of undemocratic regimes in the Muslim world. Fifty-seven percent thought mosques should express views on questions of the day: 37 percent disagreed. Again, African Americans and women had the highest percentage rates.[34] Finally, a healthy percentage of African Americans (39%) were raised as Muslims ("born Muslims" as opposed to "new Muslims"), while 98 percent of Arabs and 95 percent South Asians were raised Muslim.[35]

A similar evolution in political participation methods is occurring in Detroit. Street protests, a popular traditional response to calamities in the Middle East, are still common reactions to foreign policy events. The Congress of Arab American Organizations (CAAO) often organizes major demonstrations in Dearborn under its umbrella. Escalating tensions in the greater Middle East are very likely to trigger demonstrations. In the planning stages, leaders of various organizations come together, issue press releases, and schedule demonstrations. Vast text messaging and e-mailing campaigns frequently accompany these efforts. In Dearborn, demonstrations often start on Warren Avenue and end at Dearborn City Hall, which is located on Michigan Avenue. More recently, however, political participation has transcended protests and now largely focuses on voting and running for office, charitable giving, organization building and lobbying, and outreach.

Voting and Running for Office

In national terms, Muslims are considered an "unreliable" constituency because although they tend to vote for Democrats, they are also inclined to support Republican positions on social and foreign policies. In 1996, according to Mazrui, "[i]n Middle Eastern politics, American Muslims have noted that Republican administrations have sometimes shown greater ability to stand up to Israel than Democratic administrations."[36] It is, however, beneficial to examine studies addressing Arab American political participation in Detroit first, as many of them are Muslim.

Two main political parties' increasingly favorable treatment of Arab Americans suggests that their political significance has increased over time. During the 1980s, Senator Walter F. Mondale (D-MN) returned Arab American donations to his 1984 presidential campaign, and Governor Michael S. Dukakis (D-MA) told a group of Arab Americans during his 1988 presidential campaign that he was not interested in their vote.[37] In 1996, Bill Clinton's reelection organization tried to woo new ethnic voters, and Arab Americans were seen as key voters in the 2004 and 2008 presidential elections. But in 1988, the "unreliable" Arab Americans in Michigan strongly supported liberal Democrat's Jesse Jackson presidential bid, while two years later they endorsed John Engler, a conservative Republican, in the state's gubernatorial race.[38]

An ever-growing number of Detroit's Arab Americans are registering to vote and stand for election. In Dearborn, this figure has grown steadily from 1,200 (1990), to 9,800 (the 2000 election), and 12,000 (the 2004 national election).[39] Arab Americans constituted 5 percent of all Michigan voters in the closely contested 2004 election.[40] In 2008, voter turnover among Dearborn's Arabs was high. In a record turnout, almost 70 percent of registered voters in Dearborn, among whom Arabs featured prominently, voted; however, their turnout in the 2012 election was lower (65%). Furthermore, studies and reports on exclusively Detroit Muslim voters suggest that their political influence is increasing as well.

Recent presidential elections offer a window into the significance of the Muslim vote. In 2000, the Republican leadership had closed-door meetings with imams in Michigan to enact a Muslim bloc vote for Governor George W. Bush (R-TX). In 2008, Senator Barack Obama's (D-IL) campaign had no such meetings; rather, its members relied on the senator's family background and policy pronouncements to mobilize Muslims as part of the broader campaign. This turned out to be an effective strategy. To some Muslims, even though Obama was Christian, having a Muslim father and Muslim family members implied that he would be more sensitive and understanding toward them. To other Muslim voters, his declarations to shut down Guantanamo and end the war in Iraq were even more of a catalyst for acquiring their bloc vote. The 2012 elections did contain several important policy-related hurdles for Obama: discriminatory counterterrorism laws at home, continued drone strikes in Muslim countries with civilian casualties abroad, and the slow recovery following the 2008–2009 economic crisis, among others. These made many Michigan Muslims wary about voting for him again. Nevertheless, the majority of American Muslims, including those in Michigan, voted for Obama in the 2012 election.[41]

According to Michigan Democratic Party records, there are a total of 82,117 registered Muslim voters. But this is surely an underestimation, for Muslim voter projections utilize name recognition software. Out of this total, 48,562 registered Muslim voters voted at least once or twice in the last three even-year election cycles: 2006, 2008, and 2010. The remaining either did not vote at all or probably—but not definitively—voted in any of the last three even-year election cycles.

The potential Muslim voting bloc is greatest in Michigan's congressional districts (CDs) 9, 14, 12, and 11. Although absolute voter numbers underestimate the true number of voters across all ethnicities and religions, the comparisons among ethnic groups and religions are noteworthy.[42] For example, the DNC categorized Muslims as the Middle Eastern voting bloc, which is much larger than the Latino, Jewish, and Hindu voting blocs. In the case of some CDs, for example CD 14 (includes the large Muslim enclave of Hamtramck) and CD 12 (includes Dearborn), the Muslim voting bloc is much greater than the Asian voting bloc. In other CDs, like CD 9 (includes the Muslim enclave of Warren) and CD 11 (includes Muslim enclaves of Canton, Bloomfield Hills, Troy, and others), the two voting blocs are approximately the same size.

Most registered Muslim voters participate, or sometimes participate, in local elections in addition to national elections. This is understandable due to the great increase in Muslim candidates running for elected office in recent years who reach out to voters through mosques as well as partisan, bipartisan, and nonprofit organizations. In November 2010, four Bangladeshi Muslims and one Yemeni Muslim ran for the House from fifth district; this split the Muslim vote in five ways and allowed a non-Muslim candidate, John Olumba, to win by slightly less than 2,000 votes. In the 2012 election, a Muslim candidate, Syed Taj, was the Democratic candidate for Congress from Michigan's 11th district; he lost in the general election to his Republican opponent, Kerry Bentivolio, by 6 percentage points.[43]

Overall, three of Dearborn's current seven counselors, and nine of all of its elected officials, are Arab Americans. In the 2009 primaries, 8 of the 25 initial candidates were Arab American: five ran for the 2009 City of Dearborn Council (seven seats) and three were reelected. There are currently no Arabs or Muslims serving in the Detroit City Council proper;

two Arab Americans, one Muslim and one Christian, serve in Michigan's House of Representatives. In addition, the Detroit metropolitan area has several elected and appointed Arab and Muslim judges.[44] Furthermore Detroit-born-and-raised Representative Keith Ellison (DFL-MN), an African American Muslim, was the first Muslim elected to the U.S. Congress. He represents Minnesota's fifth CD. However, no Muslim American represents Michigan in the U.S. Congress.

Building Arab and Muslim Political Organizations

Local partisan and bipartisan Arab and Muslim organizations have played important roles in encouraging Michigan's and Detroit's Muslim to participate in the political arena. Some of the main organizations include the Muslim Political Action Committee (MPAC), the Arab American Political Action Committee (AAPAC), the Yemeni American Political Action Committee (YAPAC), the Pakistani American Public Affairs Committee (PAKPAC), the Bangladesh Political Action Committee (BAPAC), and the Michigan Muslim Democratic Caucus (MMDC).

MPAC was formed in 1996 and has the honor of being Michigan's oldest Muslim political organization. As part of its effort to create access to government for Muslims and to establish an Islamic presence within government, it endorses a slate of candidates during every presidential and gubernatorial race. The endorsement or selection process involves reviewing the candidates' issues and voting records, followed by printing and distributing its endorsements at the polls on Election Day. The AAPAC, the oldest Arab political organization, was founded in January 1998 by a group of Arab American professionals (initially Osama Siblani and Abed Hammoud) to organize and encourage Arab American political activities. It is nonpartisan and independent of any other existing organization or interest group. AAPAC's membership base comprises 100 active members: approximately 20 voting members attend its annual endorsement meeting, and approximately 80 members annually volunteer on Election Day. The Yemeni American Public Affairs Council was established in 2005 with two key missions for the Yemeni American community and society at large: public affairs and political involvement. As such, its political action committee (YAPAC) is strictly involved in politics, whereas its parent organization (Yemeni American Public Affairs Council) limits its activities to nonprofit educational public engagements and services. Since 1989, PAKPAC has actively encouraged Pakistani Americans to participate in the political process by supporting candidates of their choice or by running for office themselves. Formed in 2004, BAPAC encourages Bangladeshi Americans to promote awareness of their rights and responsibilities as American citizens and their political rights as a group. Finally, MMDC was founded in 2010 to strengthen the voice of Michigan Muslims in local and national politics.

Building Community, Advocacy, and Research Organizations

A recent study found that 39 percent of all Detroit metro area Arabs were involved with an ethnic Arab organization and that a majority of those surveyed found them effective.[45] These well-established institutions assist the Arab and Muslim communities integrate and voice their grievances. Among the key organizations are the Arab Community Center for Economic and Social Services (ACCESS), the Council for American Islamic Relations-Michigan (CAIR-MI), the American-Arab Anti-Discrimination Committee-Michigan (ADC-MI), and the Institute for Social Policy and Understanding (ISPU). Additionally, major local Muslim leaders have worked tirelessly to influence public opinion.

Since its inception in 1971 in Dearborn, ACCESS has committed itself to supporting the Arab American community's economic and cultural growth. As of 2014, it has five locations in Dearborn and Hamtramck to help with community members with their job searches, immigration issues, and health services. CAIR seeks to promote understanding of Islam, protect civil liberties, empower American Muslims, and to build coalitions to promote justice and mutual understanding. Led by Imam Dawud Walid, the powerful CAIR-MI chapter has served the entire state since 2000. Founded in 1980, ADC is the largest Arab American grassroots civil rights organization in the country. Its Michigan chapter is led by Imad Hamad. ISPU, an independent nonprofit research organization dedicated to studying the issues impacting Muslims both here and abroad, was established in Detroit in 2002. A decade later, ISPU expanded its effort in the policy arena and subsequently opened an office in Washington, DC. Media outlets, including Arab American News (http://www.arabamericannews.com/news/) and portal www.arabdetroit.com, cater to the community's interests. In addition, the ever-increasing volume of local Muslim novels and other literary works offers outsiders insights into the daily lives of Detroit Muslims.

Finally, local religious leaders are engaged in shaping public opinion. Detroit religious leaders led street demonstrations both for and against the 2003 American invasion of Iraq. Imam Mohammad Ali Elahi writes op-eds in *The Detroit News*, while Imam Husham Al-Husainy regularly contributes commentaries on various issues to media outlets. Imam Steve Alturk of Warren, a Detroit suburb, offers podcasts of his *khutba*s, some of which focus on political issues, for example, the situation in Palestine, on his organization's website: the Islamic Organization of North America (http://www.ionamasjid.org/).

Community Outreach and Interfaith Efforts

Since 9/11, Muslims in Detroit and nationwide have worked closely with government and law enforcement officials to address sectarian tensions, and have engaged in extensive interfaith work. Federal Bureau of Investigation (FBI) officials enjoy a close working relationship with the community, and the Central Investigation Agency (CIA) is actively engaged in trying to recruit Detroit's Arab and Muslims.[46] Following 9/11, more than 4,000 Detroit Arabs called to volunteer for the FBI and CIA.[47] Anecdotal stories suggest that a number of them work for the agency; for obvious reasons, however, there is little evidence for this claim.

Detroit Muslims lead American Muslims in a number of innovations and promote mutually beneficial cooperation with the government. Following the 2003 invasion of Iraq, ADC initiated the BRIDGES program to enable local Muslims and government leaders to hold regular meetings to reflect on issues that the community considers important. This project became a national model for community–law enforcement relations,[48] and ADC's Imad Hamad traveled to the United Kingdom to share this success story. Together with local government officials, ADC also hosts an annual U.S. Citizenship Ceremony to swear in new citizens; 200 new citizens were naturalized during the 2010 ceremony.

Community leaders have also worked to address intracommunity sectarian tensions. The state's Sunni and Shi'a leaders began to meet regularly to promote cooperation following the February 22, 2006, bombing of the Golden Mosque of Samarra (Iraq), one of the Shi'a's most holy shrines.[49] On May 10, 2007, a few months after Saddam Hussein's execution, many local religious leaders signed a "Muslim Code of Honor" that condemned sectarian violence and hate speech. The agreement has been on display at prominent locations in local mosques ever since. The accord was initiated by the Council of Islamic Organizations of Michigan, and similar measures were replicated in Muslim communities in California and New York.

Since the 1990s, Detroit's Arabs and Muslim communities have created a "guest room" for outsiders seeking to visit, learn more about, or to engage with the community. This guest room consists of local institutions that outsiders can contact or visit, mainly such organizations as ACCESS, Warren Avenue's famous New Yasmeen Bakery (Dearborn), the Arab American National Museum, the Islamic Center of America (ICA), and other larger mosques.[50] ACCESS has particularly benefited from federal grants and its close interaction with local governments.

Another important institution, Dearborn's Islamic Center of America, formerly the largest mosque in the country, is one of the Detroit Muslim community's most visible components. The mosque, which offers tours, is frequently visited by members of the media and government and operates an Office of Interfaith Outreach directed by Eide Alawan. Other larger area mosques also employ designated individuals to engage with the broader community. Another key individual in interfaith efforts is Imam Hisham Al-Huseiny, a Shi'a who holds regular interfaith gatherings in his Karbalaa Islamic Education Center in Dearborn. Through the work of these organizations, as well as extensive interfaith efforts by others, the community projects a positive image to outsiders and informs insiders, including new immigrant Muslims, that integration is the way to success.

ISSUES OF CONCERN

Foreign policy issues surrounding Israel have been of particular interest to Arab and Muslim Americans. The Arab American community in particular has been politically active since the 1930s. In their attempt to prevent the partition of Palestine (1947–1948), both Christian and Muslim Arabs lobbied fervently for an "undivided Palestine." Even today, the Arab American population in the United States remains more Christian than Muslim. But after the establishment of Israel, the "Palestinian cause" in this country became increasingly identified with Muslims alone.

During the decade following 9/11, the key foreign issues for Detroit's Muslim community centered on events taking place in Palestine, Lebanon, and Iraq.[51] More recently, the Arab Spring and its subsequent transformative changes have been of special concern. The community has a long history of political activism in support of various Palestinian and Lebanese causes, despite the disagreements over endorsing the American-led invasion and subsequent war in Iraq.[52] The majority of Shi'as supported the war, whereas the Sunnis opposed it. The resulting impasse rendered the community incapable of taking a strong position; some lobbying and street protests on both sides took place during the lead-up period to the 2003 invasion. Dearborn's Sunni leaders organized one of the more visible antiwar protests on the eve of the war. This event was accompanied by an anti-Saddam Hussein counterprotest led by local Shi'a Imams Hisham al-Huseiny and Sayid Hassan Al-Qazwini.

Detroit's Muslim student groups tend to be particularly outspoken when it comes to foreign policy.[53] Henry Ford Community College and the University of Michigan, both of which are located in Dearborn, host a number of active Muslim and Arab student groups. Besides organizing awareness-raising events on issues involving Lebanon and Palestine, student groups also embraced the opposition to the Iraqi invasion and subsequent war of 2003 to a greater extent than the broader local Muslim community did. A University of Michigan-Dearborn male Lebanese student group leader explained how, on the fifth anniversary of the United States' involvement in Iraq, the local Arab Student Union organized an Iraq Awareness Week that featured a series of seminars and a rally that exhibited 167 crosses, each one representing a fallen Michigan soldier.

Meanwhile, Abed Hammoud (former chairman of the influential CAAO), Imad Hamad (director of a local ADC office), and several other senior community leaders have acknowledged a relative decline in the community's support for the Palestinian cause.[54] They report that pro-Palestinian events are no longer as well attended, a trend attributed to growing disillusionment with the situation in Palestine after decades of largely futile activism. Furthermore, the post-9/11 environment has made many Muslims reluctant to express their support out of fear of being labeled "sympathetic to terrorism." Yet, as seen during pro-Palestinian demonstrations in Dearborn following Israel's 2009 incursion into Gaza, community members are still quick to pour into the streets to protest any dramatic deterioration in Palestine.

Additionally, Detroit is home to a sizeable and financially secure Lebanese community that actively reacts to troubles in that particular country. The community witnessed a great deal of activism during Israel's 2006 bombardment of Hezbollah positions in southern Lebanon. Among the largest rallies in the Detroit Metropolitan area was a 10,000-person march in Dearborn to oppose Israel's actions. While some celebrate such community activism, others fear being labeled "terrorist sympathizers." Although Washington has designated Hezbollah as "sympathetic to terrorism," during Israel's 2006 bombardment of Lebanon many Muslims in Detroit and particularly the Lebanese Shi'a continued to defend it, viewing it as a resistance group protecting Lebanon against Israeli aggression.

While foreign policy issues are important to Detroit's Muslims, their main focus is local. An overwhelming majority of interviewees noted the importance of domestic issues over foreign ones. For example, for many of Detroit's African American Muslims, crime in the inner city is a significantly more pressing issue than injustice in Palestine.[55] CAIR-MI director Walid sees the community's Muslims as united by having shared local issues, including discrimination in schools and universities, the 2001 PATRIOT Act, profiling in airports, and the targeting of Muslim charities.[56]

When interviewed about reactions to foreign policy events, most community leaders emphasized that bread-and-butter and domestic issues are more important and spoke of the need to improve the weak economic situation, create jobs, focus on education, engage in interfaith work, counter prejudices, and repeal discriminatory post-9/11 domestic antiterrorism laws.

CHALLENGES TO PARTICIPATION

While Detroit's Muslims are united on some issues, several internal divisions hinder their political activism. Several sociologists have noted that Detroit is among one of the country's most segregated areas. This is also true about the Muslim community, which is divided along racial, ethnic, socioeconomic, and sectarian lines.[57] The resulting divisions create challenges when sections of the local community remain segregated or even mutually antagonistic, instead of moving toward broader political mobilization as Muslims.

Internal fragmentation, for example, poor English proficiency, and a nonunderstanding of the American political process, present various challenges to Detroit Muslims' political participation. Republican Susan Sareini, a Muslim elected official who serves on the Dearborn City Council, noted that even after being in office for 20 years she still hears the same lack of understanding about the role of local officials, for example, the mayor or a city council member, among Arab American Muslim voters.[58] An estimated two-thirds of Detroit's Arab Americans speak fluent English,[59] whereas many of the more recent immigrants speak little English. Furthermore, because many of them come from such authoritarian states as Saddam Hussein's Iraq, adjusting to the American democratic processes can take years. In recent decades, the strength of ACCESS and other Detroit institutions have facilitated their adjustment.

Muqtedar Khan (2002), a political scientist who taught at Adrian College outside Detroit, is concerned about the polarization between what he calls "Muslim Democrats," who focus on American democracy, and "Muslim Isolationists," who focus on American foreign policy. These groups have very different views of the country's role in the world, American social issues, and issues of freedom and pluralism or multiculturalism. Khan believes that the destiny of American Muslims is to play the role of *mujaddid*, a reviver and reformer of Islam. He discusses the transformative power of what Muslims themselves are now calling an "American Muslim perspective." Arguably, this and other expressions of the community's aspiration to lead the *umma*, the global Muslim community, are partially based upon the freedoms and strengths present in the United States and upon the country's vision of itself as leader of the world.[60]

IMPACT OF PARTICIPATION

Muslims made some domestic gains during the Clinton administration. While it continues to be viewed as more pro-Israeli than any other since the time of Lyndon Johnson, in domestic terms, the Clinton administration made friendly gestures toward American Muslims. The president sent greetings to Muslims during the Ramadan fast in 1996, and the First Lady hosted an Id al-Fitr celebration in the White House in April 1996 to mark its end.[61] At the time President Bill Clinton also received an Arab American delegation in the White House to discuss a wide range of domestic and international issues, and National Security Adviser Anthony Lake met with a Muslim delegation to discuss the ramifications of the Bosnian crisis. Moreover, American Muslim Council representatives met with State

Department and Department of Justice officials to voice their concerns about the antiterrorism bill and to lobby against provisions that were felt unfair to Muslims.[62]

These meetings have continued, but they have been few and far between. Nationally, American Muslims still have no influence on domestic or foreign policy issues. In Detroit, largely due to the emergence of effective organizations and the increasing level of electoral participation, the community has gained a certain visibility and influence on the local level. As previously discussed, more of Detroit's Muslims are voting and running for elected offices in Dearborn and the surrounding towns. Muslim candidates have experienced little success at the state and the national levels, but Muslims in general have been particularly successful in building institutions.

Effective Arab and Muslim organizations, for example, ACCESS, ADC, CAIR, and AAPAC, exert much influence and have grassroots support in Detroit. Muslim cultural and religious institutions are flourishing. In certain instances, contrary to national debates over whether Muslims should be able to build community centers in New York City (Park 51) and elsewhere, Detroit Muslims have occasionally received support to create new places of worship. In 2007, Imam Alturk had a hard time obtaining a city permit to operate a mosque in a commercial building that IONA had purchased, despite being strongly supported by interfaith group (mainly Christian) partners. However, the greatest help came from the U.S. Department of Justice, which intervened on IONA's behalf to ensure that the permit was granted. Additionally, on the local level, Dearborn schools offer the option of *halal* lunches.[63]

Detroit's Muslims have taken stances on certain foreign policy issues, but their activism has, at best, brought them only symbolic policy gains. In a largely symbolic move, local municipalities held hearings on some of the foreign policy issues that were important to the community. Dearborn's City Council went a step further in 2009 by passing a resolution condemning Israeli attacks on civilians during its 2009 assault on Gaza. Representative John Dingell (D-MI) occasionally refused to denounce Hezbollah, which some of his Muslim constituents do not perceive as a terrorist group.

CONCLUSION

Despite its relative sophistication when compared to other domestic Muslim communities, the Detroit community's internal divisions prove to be a major obstacle to its effective political participation on the local level. Its members' political advancement is partially hindered by their internal racial, ethnic, socioeconomic, sectarian, and generational differences. Yet the city's Muslims are relatively more successful than most other American

Muslim communities, for they have been able to create effective political institutions and make some local inroads. Community members have been politically active for decades; however, since 2000 they have found more direct means to engage with the political process. Since the 1980s, Detroit's Muslims have become more concerned with domestic politics, especially those on the local level, while continuing to voice strong opinions on American foreign policy and the politics of their home countries.

The Muslims of Detroit continue to have only a limited impact at the national level. It is clear that the community is becoming more politically active, but the sophistication needed to reach the upper tiers of the political echelon is lacking, due in part to the fact that the majority are immigrants and continue to play catch-up with other voting blocs.

NOTES

1. Jamal, "Political Participation and Engagement of Muslim Americans," 521–544.
2. Strum, *American Arabs and Political Participation*; Bagby, "American Mosque in Transition," 120–137.
3. Castles and Miller, *Age of Migration*, 277–298; Messina, *Logics and Politics of Post-World War II Migration to Western Europe*.
4. Pero and Solomos, "Migrant Politics," 1–18.
5. Ibid., 4; Solomos, *Race and Racism in Britain*.
6. Pero and Solomos, "Migrant Politics," 5.
7. Miller, *Foreign Workers in Western Europe*.
8. Pero, and Solomos, "Migrant Politics."
9. Hamlin, "Immigrants at Work," 300–322; Hearn, *Learning from the Cleaners*.
10. Castles and Miller, *Age of Migration*, 288.
11. Ibid.; Wust, "New Citizens—New Voters?" 560–567.
12. Mazrui, "Between the Crescent," 500.
13. Senzai, *Engaging American Muslims*.
14. Abraham and Shryock, *Arab Detroit*; Howell and Amaney, "Detroit Exceptionalism."
15. Similar trends were found in the recent study of American Muslims in the San Francisco Bay Area. See Senzai and Bazian, *Bay Area Muslim Study*.
16. Bagby, *Portrait of Detroit Mosques*.
17. "The 'Building Islam in Detroit' Exhibit," University of Michigan-Dearborn, Bertkowitz Library.
18. Bagby, "Portrait."
19. Pupcenoks, "Religion or Ethnicity," 174.
20. Hassoun, *Arab Americans in Michigan*, 80; Bakalian and Bozorgmehr, *Backlash 9/11*, 68.
21. Shryock and Lin, "Limits," 282.
22. Ibid., 278.
23. Karam, Barreto, and Oskooii. "Mosques as American Institutions," 504–524.
24. For further details on the diversity of Muslims in America, see the 2004

Muslims in American Public Square Study; 2007 Pew Study, "Muslim Americans: Middle Class and Mostly Mainstream"; 2009 Gallup Study, "Muslim Americans Exemplify Diversity, Potential"; and 2011 Gallup Study, "Muslim Americans."

25. Abraham and Schryock, *Arab Detroit*; Detroit Arab American Study Team.
26. Karam, et al., "Mosques."
27. 2009 Gallup Poll.
28. Leonard, *Muslims in the United States*, 121.
29. Ibid.
30. Khan, *American Muslims*; Leonard, *Muslims*, 121.
31. Mazrui, "Between the Crescent," 501.
32. Leonard, *Muslims*, 102.
33. Ibid.
34. Ibid.
35. Ibid.
36. Mazrui, "Between the Crescent," 503.
37. Holmes, "Influx of Immigrants in Changing Electorate."
38. Ibid.
39. Curiel, "Arab Americans Could Help Sway Crucial States"; Alexander, "How Did Muslims Vote in 2000?" 13–27.
40. Ibid.; Rose, "How Did Muslims Vote?"
41. For example, see Delinda Hanley, "How Muslim and Arab Americans 'Rocked the Vote' in 2012," 30–31.
42. Michigan Democratic Party data as generated by the Democratic National Committee.
43. Rushin, "Islam, Muslims, and the 2012 Election," 21–35.
44. Sinno and Tatari, "Towards Electability," 315–346.
45. Howell and Jamal, "Detroit Exceptionalism."
46. Stanek, "CIA in Recruitment Pitch to Arab-Americans."
47. Howell and Jamal, "Backlash, Part 2," 94.
48. Bakalian and Bozormergh, *Backlash*, 154.
49. Voice of America, "Iraq Sectarian Violence Affects American Muslims."
50. Shryock, personal communication with Juris Pupcenoks, November 23, 2009.
51. Other specific events that generated political activism included Qur'an flushing in Guantanamo (2005), the Prophet Muhammad cartoon controversy (2006), and the November 19, 2008, Israeli siege of Gaza (Walid, Interview with Juris Pupcenoks).
52. Pupcenoks, "Religion or Ethnicity?"
53. Nevertheless, a number of youth leaders interviewed in 2009 insisted that even while in college, their primary focus was on domestic issues and interfaith work.
54. Hamad, Interview with Juris Pupcenoks.
55. Walid, "5 Years with CAIR in Michigan."
56. Walid, Interview with Juris Pupcenoks.
57. Walid, "5 Years with CAIR in Michigan."
58. Senzai and Ahmad, "Galvanizing the Muslim Vote in Michigan."
59. *Psychiatric News*, "Mich. Has Largest U.S. Muslim Population," 13.

60. Leonard, *Muslims*, 106.
61. Mazrui, "Between the Crescent," 498–499.
62. Ibid.
63. Dotinga, "Public Schools Grapple with Muslim Prayer," 1.

REFERENCES

Abraham, Nabeel, and Andrew Shryock, eds. *Arab Detroit: From Margin to Mainstream*. Detroit: Wayne State University Press, 2000.
Alexander, Rose. "How Did Muslims Vote in 2000?" *Middle East Quarterly* 8.3 (2001): 13–27.
Bagby, Ihsan. "The American Mosque in Transition: Assimilation, Acculturation, and Isolation." *Muslims and the State in the Post-9/11 West*. Ed. Erik Bleich. London and New York: Routledge, 2006. 120–137.
Bagby, Ishan. *A Portrait of Detroit Mosques: Muslim Views on Policy, Politics, and Religion*. Canton, MI: Institute for Social Policy and Understanding, 2004.
Bakalian, Anny, and Mehdi Bozorgmehr. *Backlash 9/11: Middle Eastern and Muslim Americans Respond*. Berkeley: University of California Press, 2009.
"The 'Building Islam in Detroit' Exhibit." University of Michigan-Dearborn, Bertkowitz Library, 2009.
Castles, Steven, and Mark J. Miller. *The Age of Migration*. 4th ed. New York and London: The Guilford Press, 2009.
Curiel, Jonathan. "Arab Americans Could Help Sway Crucial States." *SF Gate*. 28 October 2004. http://articles.sfgate.com/2004-10-28/news/17448462_1_arab-american-institute-muslim-voters-muslim-americans.
Dana, Karam, Matt Barreto, and Kassra Oskooii. "Mosques as American Institutions: Mosque Attendance, Religiosity, and Integration into American Society." *Journal of Religions* 2.4 (2011): 504–524.
Detroit Arab American Study Team, eds. *Citizenship and Crisis: Arab Detroit after 9/11*. New York: Russell Sage, 2009.
Dotinga, Randy. "Public Schools Grapple with Muslim Prayer." *The Christian Science Monitor*. 12 July 2007. http://www.csmonitor.com/2007/0712/p01s03-ussc.html.
Gallup. "Muslim Americans Exemplify Diversity, Potential." 2 March 2009. http://www.gallup.com/poll/116260/muslim-americans-exemplify-diversity-potential.aspx.
Gallup. "Muslim Americans: Faith Freedom, and the Future." 2 August 2011. http://www.gallup.com/poll/148931/presentation-muslim-americans-faith-freedom-future.aspx.
Hamad, Imad. Interview with Juris Pupcenoks. Detroit.11 November 2009.
Hamlin, Rebecca. "Immigrants at Work: Labor Unions and Noncitizen Members." *Civic Hopes and Political Engagement*. Ed. S. K. Ramakrishnan and I. Bloemraad. New York: Russell Sage Foundation, 2008. 300–322.
Hanley, Delinda. "How Muslim and Arab Americans 'Rocked the Vote' in 2012." *The Washington Report on Middle East Affairs* 32.1 (2013): 30–31.
Hassoun, Rosina J. *Arab Americans in Michigan*. East Lansing: Michigan State University Press, 2005.

Hearn, Julie. *Learning from the Cleaners: Migrant Workers and Trade Union Mobilization at the University of London*. UK: Identity, Citizenship and Migration Centre, University of Nottingham, 2009.
Holmes, Steven A. "Influx of Immigrants in Changing Electorate." The New York Times. 30 October 1996. http://www.nytimes.com/1996/10/30/us/influx-of-immigrants-is-changing-electorate.html.
Howell, Sally, and Amaney Jamal. "Backlash, Part 2: The Federal Law Enforcement Agenda." *Arab Detroit 9/11: Life in the Terror Decade*. Ed. Detroit Arab American Study Team. New York: Russell Sage, 2011. 87–104.
Howell, Sally, and Amaney Jamal. "Detroit Exceptionalism and the Limits of Political Incorporation." *Being and Belonging: Muslims in the United States since 9/11*. Ed. Katherine Pratt Ewing. New York: Russell Sage, 2008. 47–79.
Jamal, Amaney. "The Political Participation and Engagement of Muslim Americans: Mosque Involvement and Group Consciousness." *American Politics Research* 33.4 (2005): 521–544.
Khan, Muqtedar M. A. *American Muslims: Bridging Faith and Freedom*. Beltsville, MD: Amana Publications, 2002.
Leonard, Karen I. *Muslims in the United States: The State of Research*. New York: Russell Sage, 2003.
Mazrui, Ali. "Between the Crescent and the Star-Spangled Banner: American Muslims and US Foreign Policy." *International Affairs* 72.3 (2006): 493–506.
Messina, Anthony M. *The Logics and Politics of Post-World War II Migration to Western Europe*. New York: Cambridge University Press, 2007.
Miller, Mark J. *Foreign Workers in Western Europe: An Emerging Political Force*. New York: Praeger, 1981.
Muslims in American Public Square (MAPS) Study.19 October 2004. http://explore.georgetown.edu/news/?ID=1310.
Pero, Davide, and John Solomos, eds. "Migrant Politics and Mobilization: Exclusion, Engagement, Incorporation." *Special Issue of Ethnic and Racial Studies* 33(1) (2010): 1–156.
Pero, Davide, and John Solomos. "Migrant Politics and Mobilization: Exclusion, Engagements, Incorporation." *Ethnic and Racial Studies* 33.1 (2010): 1–18.
Psychiatric News. "Mich. Has Largest U.S. Muslim Population." 40.2 (2005). http://psychnews.psychiatryonline.org/doi/full/10.1176/pn.40.2.00400013b.
Pupcenoks, Juris. "Religion or Ethnicity?: Middle Eastern Conflicts and American Arab-Muslim Protest Politics." *Nationalism and Ethnic Politics* 18.2 (2012): 170–192.
Rushin, David. "Islam, Muslims, and the 2012 Election." *Middle East Quarterly* 20(3) (2013): 21–35.
Senzai, Farid. *Engaging American Muslims: Political Trends and Attitudes*. Washington, DC: Institute for Social Policy and Understanding, 2012.
Senzai, Farid, and Sema Ahmad. "Galvanizing the Muslim Vote in Michigan for the 2012 Elections: Why and How?" Unpublished Report. 2011.
Senzai, Farid, and Hatem Bazian. *The Bay Area Muslim Study: Establishing Identity and Community*. Washington, DC: Institute for Social Policy and Understanding, 2013.
Shryock, Andrew. Personal Communication with Juris Pupcenoks. 23 November 2009.

Shryock, Andrew, and Ann Chih Lin. "The Limits of Citizenship." *Citizenship and Crisis: Arab Detroit after 9/11*. Ed. The Detroit Arab American Study Team. New York: Russell Sage, 2009: 265–286.

Sinno, Abdulkader H., and Eren Tatari. "Towards Electability: Public Office and the Arab Vote." *Arab Detroit 9/11: Life in the Terror Decade*. Ed. Detroit Arab American Study Team. New York: Russell Sage, 2011: 315–346.

Solomos, John. *Race and Racism in Britain*. 3rd ed. Basingstoke, UK: Palgrave Macmillan, 2003.

Stanek, Steven. "CIA in Recruitment Pitch to Arab-Americans." *The National*. 20 November 2009.

Strum, Philippa.. *American Arabs and Political Participation*. Washington, DC: Woodrow Wilson International Center for Scholars, 2006.

Voice of America. "Iraq Sectarian Violence Affects American Muslims." 10 May 2007.

Walid, Dawud. Interview with Juris Pupcenoks. Detroit. 19 November 2009.

Walid, Dawud. "5 Years with CAIR in Michigan." Speech. The Building Islam in Detroit symposium, Mardigan Library, University of Michigan-Dearborn. 14 November 2009.

Wust, Andreas. "New Citizens—New Voters? Political Preferences and Voting Intentions of Naturalized Germans: A Case Study in Progress." *International Migration Review* 34.2 (2000): 560–567.

Part VII

Asian American Voters

Chapter 9

Asian American Voting Rights

Glenn D. Magpantay

ASIAN AMERICAN ACCESS TO THE VOTE

History of Exclusion

Like African Americans, Asian Americans have also been denied access to the electoral franchise. Beginning with the Chinese Exclusion Act, Asians were denied the ability to naturalize and become citizens of the United States until 1943.[1] The Supreme Court upheld this bar in the infamous *Chae Chan Ping v. United States*, 130 U.S. 581 (1889). Only whites and former slaves were eligible to become citizens through naturalization. When Asian foreign nationals sought to become citizens of the United States, the Supreme Court held that they were not white and therefore ineligible to naturalize.

In *Ozawa v. United States*, 260 U.S. 178 (1922), the Court ruled that Asians, specifically Japanese, who spoke English, were educated in U.S. schools and understood American civics, resided in the United States for two decades, and often had light skin tone were not sufficiently "Caucasian" and therefore ineligible to naturalize. The Court went further in *United States v. Thind*, 261 U.S. 204 (1923) and rejected the application for citizenship by a high caste Asian Indian, with Arian lineage. They too were not considered Caucasian or white for the purpose of naturalization. The Court ruled that Europeans, namely people of English, French, German, Italian, and

Scandinavian ancestry "blended well" with the American population, and therefore were eligible to naturalize. Incidentally, people of Mediterranean heritage, as well as Arabs and Middle Easterners were ruled to be Caucasian or white as the Court held in *Dow v. United States*, 226 F. 145 (1915). It was not until 1943 that Congress lifted restrictions from immigration law to allow people from Asian nations to become U.S. citizens.

Of course, under the Fourteenth Amendment, any person born in the territory of the United States could become a citizen by virtue of the location of one's birth, as the Court held in *United States v. Wong Kim Ark*, 169 U.S. 649 (1898).

Discrimination on Election Day

Today, Asian Americans can become U.S. citizens through naturalization, and once naturalized, can register to vote. Yet, when they tried to vote, they faced a series of barriers on Election Day. Several incidents were reported to the U.S. Department of Justice or the Asian American Legal Defense and Education Fund (AALDEF), and a representative sample follows.

Poll Sites on Election Day

To this day, Asian Americans have been segregated into separate voting lines. Though the incidents are admittedly few, they are unconscionable. In Annandale, Virginia, during the 2012 election, an election officer stated, "All Koreans stand in this line." Poll workers separated all Korean American voters into the second line because "there were so many" and that line was a language assistance line, but the Electoral Board provided no Korean interpreters to assist Korean-speaking voters.[2] In Boston during the 2004 election, poll workers in Mission Hill also segregated voters by race, and made Chinese voters form one line and white voters form another. They claimed that the separate lines for limited English proficient voters would speed the process, but in the end, whites voted first while Asian voters waited.[3]

Poll workers were also found to be unnecessarily rude and selectively hostile toward Asian American voters. During the 2010 elections in Boston's South End, a South Asian voter felt that she was improperly racially profiled and temporarily detained at her poll site by a police officer. In Philadelphia, a poll worker mocked a Korean American voter, publically embarrassing her.[4]

Some poll workers made disparaging remarks about Asian Americans. Poll workers said the following during specific elections:

- "There are just too many Asians here" and "They [Asians] should have to learn English" in Flushing, New York, in 2008[5]

- When a Gujarati- or Hindi-speaking voter appeared, she would "send them to the nearest gas station" in Edison, New Jersey, in 2005[6]
- All Middle Eastern voters "looked like terrorists to [him]" in Brooklyn, New York, in 2008[7]
- "I'll talk to [Asian voters] the way they talk to me when I call to order Chinese food," which was then followed with random English phrases with a mock Chinese accent in Queens, New York, in 2004[8]

Sometimes Asian American voters were simply treated with less courtesy than white voters, or they were simply ignored.

These incidents create an unwelcoming, if not hostile, environment at poll sites for Asian American voters, which discourage Asian Americans from voting.

Political Campaigns

Increasingly Asian Americans are running for political office. Though they have enjoyed some success, their campaigns have occasionally been marred by racial appeals and hostility.

In the 2009 race for New York City Council, District 19, Kevin Kim, a Korean American, won the Democratic nomination in the mostly Democratic district. One resident of District 19 found that her Kim campaign lawn sign was set on fire. A group of white male teenagers targeted campaign volunteers for Kim. They used racial slurs and made disparaging racial comments, chanting "White Power!" and "White Supremacy!" One of the white males assaulted one of the Korean volunteers. Police investigated the incident as a hate crime. Campaigners for the white Republican candidate also made racial appeals. They told voters that "Halloran's opponent is some Chinese guy" and complained that the "neighborhood is getting really Asian. Chinese people are taking over."[9]

In the 2004 race for mayor of Edison, New Jersey, on April 25 commentators Craig Carton and Ray Rossi on the "Jersey Guys" radio show on NJ 101.5 FM delivered a tirade of anti-Asian remarks and disparaged Jun Choi, a Korean American candidate for mayor. On the air, Mr. Carton said, "Chinese should never dictate the outcome of an election, Americans should. . . . Damn Orientals and Indians." Advocates were concerned about this broadcast's effect on voters and those administering the elections. The Department of Justice dispatched federal monitors to observe the election.[10]

During the 1999 election in Hamtramck, Michigan, a traditionally Polish city, when an Arab American ran for City Council, Bangladeshi, Arab, and Muslim voters encountered racial profiling and intimidation. City officials dispatched police officers to poll sites to confirm the citizenship of voters and interrogate them about their vote. The following year, the U.S.

Department of Justice brought suit against the city for violations of the Voting Rights Act and the U.S. Constitution.[11]

After the 2007 School Board race in Fort Lee, New Jersey, a losing candidate charged that Korean American voters illegally voted because they did not live in Fort Lee or were not U.S. citizens. He persuaded the local sheriff to issue subpoenas to the voters at their Fort Lee addresses in the early morning hours, and forced them to present passports and naturalization certificates. Voters complained that they felt punished for voting.[12]

In Annandale, Virginia, in 2004, elderly Asian American voters were tricked due to their limited English proficiency. A bilingual partisan campaign worker assisted Korean Americans as the ballots were only in English. The campaigner not only showed voters how to vote but also who to vote for. Two years prior, this same person encouraged Korean American voters to apply for absentee ballots, promising to translate them. The voters did not hear from her again and on Election Day they returned to vote at their polling place, but were told that their ballots were already cast for them.[13]

The history of anti-Asian voter discrimination continues to this day with racial appeals and expressions of anti-Asian animus at poll sites. Because Asian Americans continue to encounter a range of barriers in exercising their right to vote, Congress enacted the Language Assistance Provisions, codified at Section 203, of the federal Voting Rights Act to remediate past discrimination and expand access to the fundamental right to vote.

Language Assistance—VRA Section 203

In the early 1970s, Congress found that limited English proficiency was a serious barrier to political participation of Asian Americans, Latinos, and Native Americans.[14] Asian Americans and Latino citizens were registered to vote at much lower rates than non-Hispanic whites.[15] As a result, Congress enacted the Language Assistance Provisions of the Voting Rights Act, codified at Section 203.[16] Section 203 mandates bilingual ballots, translated voting materials, and oral language assistance at voting booths and polling sites. The law has helped ensure that countless more Asian Americans, Latinos, and Native Americans will have equal access to the ballot.

Need for Language Assistance

Today, Asian Americans are one of the fastest-growing minority groups in the nation, estimated to number almost 15.5 million.[17] More are becoming U.S. citizens through naturalization and are registering to vote. Asian citizens of voting age numbered 3.9 million in 1996, rose from 4.7 million in 2000, and to 6.7 million in 2004. Asian American voter turnout is also steadily increasing, from 1.7 million in 1996, to nearly 3 million in 2004,[18] and 3.4 million in 2008.[19]

Asian Americans expect to vote when eligible, but they are often unfamiliar with American electoral processes.[20] Many come from Asian countries with very different political systems or which lack a tradition of voting. Seventy percent of Asian Americans are citizens, almost half (47%) acquired citizenship through naturalization.[21] Many do not understand the basic political procedures, such as operating voting machines, the need to register to vote by a certain date, or to register to vote under a party label to vote in primary elections, where required.

Nationally, more than half (52%) of Asian Americans over 18 are limited English proficient. Eighty-one percent speak a language other than English in their homes.[22]

In 2012, nonpartisan, multilingual exit polls revealed that 37 percent of Asian American voters were limited English proficient, 79 percent were foreign born, naturalized citizens.[23] Twenty-one percent had no formal education in the United States, which is notable because U.S. schools teach American civics. Only 18 percent identified English as their native language.[24] Moreover, 27 percent of all respondents stated that the November 2012 elections were the first U.S. elections in which they had voted. See Table 9.1.

Beyond a doubt, language assistance is needed to preserve access to the vote for Asian Americans. In the 2012 elections, 22 percent responded that they preferred some form of language assistance to vote. Korean

Table 9.1
AALDEF's Multilingual Exit Poll, November 2012: Respondents

All	First-Time Voter	Foreign-Born	No Formal U.S. Education	English as Native Language	Limited English Proficient	Largest Ethnic Groups
Total: 9,096	27%	79%	24%	18%	37%	31% Chinese 30% South Asian 12% Vietnamese 11% Korean 9% Filipino
By Ethnic Group						
Chinese	23%	75%	26%	16%	55%	NA
Korean	20%	84%	37%	18%	67%	NA
Filipino	23%	74%	12%	26%	7%	NA
South Asian	34%	88%	26%	*	25%	45% Indian 40% Bangladeshi 10% Pakistani
Vietnamese	26%	83%	20%	9%	59%	NA

Source: AALDEF's Multilingual Exit Poll, November 2012: Respondents.

Table 9.2
AALDEF Exit Poll Results, November 6, 2012

All Voters Surveyed	First-Time Voter (%)	Foreign-Born (%)	No Formal U.S. Education (%)	English as Native Language (%)	Limited English Proficient (%)	Largest Asian Groups Surveyed
Total: 9,096	27	79	24	18	37	31% Chinese 30% South Asian 12% Vietnamese 11% Korean 9% Filipino
By State						
New York	29	82	32	17	45	Chinese 43% Bangladeshi 20% Korean 12% Asian Indian 11%
New Jersey	23	87	51	11	49	Korean 57% Asian Indian 15% Filipino 8%
Massachusetts	25	74	23	21	47	Chinese 52% Vietnamese 32%
Pennsylvania	28	79	31	10	53	Chinese 35% Vietnamese 24% Cambodian 12% Asian Indian 6%
Michigan	29	77	17	17	23	Bangladeshi 34% Asian Indian 20% Arab 15%
California	16%	57	6	40	9	Filipino 62% Vietnamese 16% Chinese 9%

(*continued*)

Table 9.2 (continued)

All Voters Surveyed	First-Time Voter (%)	Foreign-Born (%)	No Formal U.S. Education (%)	English as Native Language (%)	Limited English Proficient (%)	Largest Asian Groups Surveyed
Illinois	18	83	46	17	27	Korean 67% Asian Indian 17%
Virginia	24	74	14	24	20	Chinese 21% Asian Indian 20% Korean 20% Vietnamese 10%
Georgia	31	85	16	14	28	Asian Indian 33% Korean 24% Chinese 14%
Maryland	26	75	12	22	24	Chinese 26% Asian Indian 20% Korean 17% Vietnamese 11%
Texas	28	86	12	11	32	Vietnamese 31% Asian Indian 25% Chinese 18% Pakistani 11%
Louisiana	29	84	21	8	67	Vietnamese 98%
Nevada	26	71	7	35	5	Filipino 67% Other 18% Chinese 6%
Florida	0	100	27	27	55	Chinese 100%
District of Columbia	18	47	14	40	22	Chinese 49% Korean 19% Asian Indian 12%

Source: AALDEF Exit Poll Results, November 6, 2012.

Table 9.3
Asian Language Coverage under VRA Section 203 after Census 2010

Alaska		
	Aleutians East Borough	**Filipino**
	Aleutians West Census Area	**Filipino**
California		
	Alameda	Chinese, **Filipino, Vietnamese**
	Los Angeles	Chinese, Japanese, Korean, Filipino, Vietnamese, **Indian, Other (not specified)**
	Orange	Chinese, Korean, Vietnamese
	Sacramento	**Chinese**
	San Diego	Filipino, **Chinese, Vietnamese**
	San Francisco	Chinese
	San Mateo	Chinese
	Santa Clara	Chinese, Filipino, Vietnamese
Hawaii		
	Honolulu	Chinese, Filipino, Japanese
	Maui	Filipino
Illinois		
	Cook	Chinese, **Indian**
Massachusetts		
	Quincy city	**Chinese**
Michigan		
	Hamtramck city	**Bangladeshi**
Nevada		
	Clark	Filipino
New Jersey		
	Bergen	Korean
New York		
	Kings (Brooklyn)	Chinese
	New York (Manhattan)	Chinese
	Queens	Chinese, Korean, **Indian**
Texas		
	Harris	Vietnamese, **Chinese**
Washington		
	King	Chinese, **Vietnamese**

Source: Asian Language Coverage under VRA Section 203 after Census 2010.
Note: New languages since the 2010 Census are identified in the table in bold.

Americans exhibited the greatest rates of limited English proficiency at 67 percent, followed by Vietnamese Americans at 59 percent, Chinese at 55 percent, and Bangladeshis at 45 percent. See Tables 9.2, 9.3, and 9.4 for detailed findings.

Even though Asian Americans may be citizens, their right to vote is futile when ballots and voting instructions cannot be understood.

Table 9.4
AALDEF Multilingual Exit Poll, November 2012: Language Minority Groups

State-Locality	Language Minority Group	Limited English Proficient (%)	Prefers Voting with Assistance of Interpreter or Translated Materials (%)
California			
- San Diego	Vietnamese	28	17
District of Columbia			
- District of Columbia	Chinese	36	27
Georgia			
- Dekalb Co.	Vietnamese	18	9
- Gwinnett Co.	Korean	61	22
	Vietnamese	48	12
	Chinese	21	3
Louisiana			
- New Orleans	Vietnamese	67	41
Maryland			
- Montgomery Co.	Chinese	23	16
	Korean	41	19
	Vietnamese	42	17
Massachusetts			
- Boston	Chinese	53%	44
	Vietnamese	68	37
- Malden	Chinese	51	42
- Quincy	Chinese	26	17%
Michigan			
- Wayne Co.	Bangladeshi	44	36
New Jersey			
- Bergen Co.	Korean	72	28
- Hudson Co.	Asian Indian	26	11
New York			
- Brooklyn	Chinese	56	42
	Bengali	48	17
- Manhattan	Chinese	56	45
- Queens	Chinese	45	27
	Korean	71	38
	Bengali	48	28
Pennsylvania			
- Philadelphia	Chinese	74	52
	Vietnamese	68	33
Texas			
- Houston	Vietnamese	62	32
	Chinese	62	27

(continued)

Table 9.4 (continued)

State-Locality	Language Minority Group	Limited English Proficient (%)	Prefers Voting with Assistance of Interpreter or Translated Materials (%)
Virginia			
- Arlington Co.	Chinese	35	22
- Fairfax Co.	Korean	39	14
	Vietnamese	49	14

Source: AALDEF Multilingual Exit Poll, November 2012: Language Minority Groups.

Bilingual ballots help Asian American voters to fully participate in elections.

Statutory Scheme and Legal Requirements

Congress adopted the language assistance provisions of the Voting Rights Act in 1975, and reauthorized them in 1982, 1992, and 2006. In 2006, after extensive hearings and additional findings of continued discrimination and noncompliance, Congress extended the provisions for another 25 years.[25] In enacting these provisions, Congress found that:

> [T]hrough the use of various practices and procedures, citizens of language minorities have been effectively excluded from participation in the electoral process. Among other factors, the denial of the right to vote of such minority group citizens is ordinarily directly related to the unequal educational opportunities afforded them resulting in high illiteracy and low voting participation. The Congress declares that, in order to enforce the guarantees of the fourteenth and fifteenth amendments to the United States Constitution, it is necessary to eliminate such discrimination by prohibiting these practices, and by prescribing other remedial devices.[26]

A trigger formula determines if a jurisdiction will be covered under Section 203, and for what language.[27] The statute requires that "no covered State or political subdivision shall provide voting materials only in the English language."

The Voting Rights Act mandates language assistance when the census reports that a jurisdiction has 5 percent or more than 10,000 voting-age (over 18 years old) citizens who speak the same Asian, Hispanic, or Native American language, have limited English proficiency, and, as a group, have a higher illiteracy rate than the national illiteracy rate.[28]

Section 203 was amended in 1992 to include the numeric approach. Before 1992, under the 5 percent approach, no political subdivision, except for San Francisco and some counties in Hawai'i, provided materials in any Asian language.[29] This spurred a grassroots movement to change the coverage formula. After the 1992 amendment, under the numeric approach, 10 counties in New York, California, and Hawai'i were mandated to provide translated ballots and voting materials in four Asian languages: Chinese, Japanese, Filipino, and Vietnamese.[30]

After the 2000 census, 16 counties in 7 states were required to provide assistance in one or more Asian languages. Korean was covered for the first time. New York remained as the only state on the East Coast to require language assistance in any Asian language.

After the 2010 census, commensurate with the growth of the Asian American population, 22 counties in 11 states were required to provide assistance in one or more Asian languages. Four new states were included. South Asian languages were covered for the first time in three jurisdictions: Chinese, Korean, Filipino, Vietnamese, Japanese, Asian Indian, Bangladeshi, and "Asian Other." The languages of Asian Indians were locally determined to be Hindi in Los Angeles and Chicago, whereas it was Bengali in New York. "Asian Other" in Los Angeles was determined to be Khmer for Cambodian American and Thai for Thai Americans.[31] The following counties and languages were covered under Section 203:[32]

Once covered, the jurisdictions must provide bilingual assistance to voters. The types of assistance include:

(1) translated written materials, including ballots,[33] voter registration forms,[34] voting instructions, notifications, and announcements;
(2) oral assistance such as interpreters, bilingual poll workers, and bilingual/multilingual voter hotlines;[35] and
(3) publicity regarding the elections and availability of bilingual assistance,[36] such as signs at polling sites, announcements in language minority radio, television, and newspapers, and direct contact with language minority community organizations.

The covered jurisdiction can devise a system to "target" certain areas to receive translated materials or language assistance.[37]

The goal is to ensure that covered language minority groups can effectively vote in elections.[38] In determining whether a jurisdiction's language assistance is sufficiently effective to comply with Section 203, the Attorney General considers (1) whether the materials and assistance are provided in a way designed to allow members of the applicable language minority group to be effectively informed of and participate effectively in voting connected activities; and (2) whether the affected jurisdiction has taken all reasonable steps to achieve that goal.[39]

In addition, the Voting Rights Act's bilingual requirements also include Section 208, which gives voters who are unable to read English the right to be assisted by persons of their choice.[40] These individuals can be anyone, including the voters' relatives or friends, but not their employers or union representatives, and the assistors may accompany the voters inside the voting booth to translate the ballots for the voters.

Implementation and Effectiveness

The language assistance provisions promote integration by encouraging limited English proficient citizens to participate in the American political process.[41] In 2005, testimony to Congress showed that bilingual assistance had helped 672,750 Asian Americans fully participate in the political process.[42] Certainly the numbers have increased since then. Translated ballots have enabled Asian American voters to exercise their right to vote independently and privately inside the voting booth. In jurisdictions covered for bilingual ballots, exit polls consistently found high rates of limited English proficiency among covered language minority groups.

Section 203 has also aided grassroots efforts to increase Asian American voter registration. In California, from 1998 to 2004, Asian American voter registration increased 61 percent.[43] In New York, from 2001 to 2004, multilingual voter registration forms required under Section 203 have helped increase Asian American voter registration by 40 percent.[44] In both states, the increase greatly outpaced the overall growth of the Asian American population.

Most importantly, Section 203 has contributed to Asian American electoral success. In 2001, the first Asian American was elected to the New York City Council. In 2004, the first Asian American was elected to the New York State Assembly. In the same year, the first ever Vietnamese American was elected to the state legislature from Harris County, Texas, after the county became covered for Vietnamese under Section 203.[45]

Although Section 203 has made voting more accessible, covered jurisdictions have had several problems in initial implementation.[46] Ever since strengthening Section 203 in 1992, Asian American civil rights groups have monitored its local compliance.[47] Poll monitoring uncovered numerous violations.[48]

The Department of Justice has dispatched federal attorneys to monitor for Section 203 compliance.[49] Before 2000, the Department filed only a few lawsuits to remedy these deficiencies, all of which concerned Spanish speakers.[50] From 2000 to 2008, the Department filed several lawsuits to remedy deficiencies.[51] Civil rights groups have also filed their own cases on behalf of Asian American community voters.[52] All have more forcefully ensured that jurisdictions fully comply with Section 203.

Poll monitoring for compliance with Section 203 uncovered numerous violations. Ballots have not always been fully and accurately translated. In New York City, during the 2000 presidential election, ballots flipped the Chinese translated party headings, with Republican candidates listed as

Democrats and Democrats as Republicans.[53] For four elections since 2010, the Board of Elections refused to provide ballots translated into Bengali.[54]

Observers found that poll workers have kept translated materials hidden and unavailable to voters. This repeatedly occurred in New York City[55] and Los Angeles,[56] Orange, San Francisco,[57] and San Jose, in California.[58] On a number of occasions, poll workers never opened the supply kit containing translated materials. Translated signs were posted in obscure locations or not posted at all. During the 2012 election, in Hamtramck, Michigan, translated Bengali precinct signs were printed in very small font and placed in locations hidden from view, such as behind voters when they entered the building and around corners but not in the main hallways of poll sites.[59] Likewise in Bergen County, New Jersey, there were few signs in Korean directing voters to the polling place.[60]

Voters have also complained about too few interpreters or interpreters who spoke the wrong language or dialect, for example, in Hamtramck, Bergen County, and Harris County, Texas. In New York, Chinese American voters have been directed to Korean interpreters.[61]

Notwithstanding federal mandates, poll workers were ignorant of or hostile to providing language assistance to voters. In one election when was asked about translated materials, a poll worker sarcastically replied, "What, are we in China? It's ridiculous."[62]

Fully translated and navigable election websites pose another dilemma. Much more information from election agencies is conveyed through the Internet and websites. Yet technological obstacles make compliance with Section 203 challenging.

Translated materials were often posted online as PDF documents to download.[63] Users had to navigate an English page to find the specific resources, and then point and click to a file that contained the translated version.[64] Some jurisdictions provided no access to translated voting information or had elections websites that were difficult, if not impossible, to navigate. The Bergen County, New Jersey's Superintendent of Elections' website[65] has links in English to translated Korean information. Clicking on the "Instructions for Voting (Korean video)" brings the viewer to a video that is entirely in English. The elections website of Cook County, Illinois,[66] had a hyperlink to a translated webpage that was named "Language" written in English. The City of Hamtramck, Michigan's elections website does not have any voting materials that are available in Bengali.[67] The City of Quincy, Massachusetts's elections website[68] contains links that list Chinese and Vietnamese as the options for language assistance, however, they link to the City of Quincy's home page, which is in English.

Election websites have also contained poor, inaccurate translations. Cook County's elections website[69] uses Google Translate, which left several errors throughout the website. For example, if the viewer searches for voter information to confirm a registration or find an assigned poll site by using the Chinese translation function, the voter is instructed to input the "last 4 nuclear submarines," instead of the last four digits of the social security number.

When voters searched for a translated listing of candidates and their party affiliations on the "Candidate Filing" page, they found comical errors. The abbreviation "DEM" was not translated into Chinese as "Democratic Party" but rather as "*Digital Elevation Model.*" The Cook County Board of Elections website was replete with translation errors.

In addition to mistranslating terms, Google Translate also directly translates any errors in the original, English version. Though errors, such as extra spaces in words, are not problematic in the English version, they cause nonsensical results when translated into another language using Google Translate.

Jurisdictions have failed to review the translated webpages of their elections websites. Simple translation errors can be easily corrected. Elections officials have not taken the same care in ensuring that limited English proficient voters can read and navigate websites as easily as fully English proficient voters.

Compliance with Section 208 (Assistance by Persons of Choice)

In companion to Section 203, voters have the right to be assisted by persons of their choice under Section 208 of the Voting Rights Act.[70] Unlike Section 203, this provision applies across the nation. These assistors may accompany voters inside the voting booth to translate the ballot. The only exception under this federal law is that they may not be the voters' union representatives or employers. Poll workers, however, have obstructed this right.

In New Orleans, Louisiana, poll workers did not allow limited English proficient voters to bring interpreters with them into the voting booth for the entire day. Poll workers stated that anyone who wanted to be accompanied by an interpreter because of illiteracy in English needed to have preclearance. When voters chose someone to render assistance, poll workers objected. Many voters complained about the lack of interpreters.[71]

At poll sites in Fort Bend and Harris Counties, Texas, poll workers did not allow limited English proficient voters to bring interpreters with them into the voting booth. One elderly voter with limited English proficiency was denied her granddaughter's assistance inside the voting booth and was forced to cast her vote without the language assistance to which she was entitled.[72]

The Voting Rights Act's language assistance provisions have been exceedingly helpful in expanding access to the vote for Asian Americans. However, access is only the first step toward meaningful political empowerment.

ASIAN AMERICAN POLITICAL BEHAVIOR AND PARTICIPATION

Asian Americans are one of the fastest-growing minority groups in the nation, estimated to number almost 12 million, with many becoming U.S. citizens and increasingly registering to vote. Sixty-six percent of Asian Americans are citizens, yet most (53%) acquired citizenship through naturalization.[73] Asian American citizens of voting age numbered 3.9 million in 1996, and rose from 4.7 million in 2000 to 6.7 million in 2004. Asian American voter turnout also steadily increased, from 1.7 million in 1996, to nearly 3 million in 2004.[74]

Notwithstanding this growth, Asian American voters are overlooked by the mainstream media and by candidates for political office. Exit polls typically break down election returns along racial lines using whites, African Americans, Latinos, and "other" as categories. When Asian American votes were reported, the data were skewed. In the 1996 presidential election, for example, Voter News Service (VNS) surveyed only 170 Asian Americans nationwide, out of 16,000 voters polled, and conducted their poll only in English. It reported that Asian Americans favored Republican presidential candidate Bob Dole over Bill Clinton by 48 percent to 43 percent. But multilingual community exit polls in New York and California found that Asian American voters supported Clinton by wide margins, up to 75 percent in immigrant neighborhoods.[75] When the media neglects the Asian American vote, candidates usually follow suit.

Since 1988, the AALDEF has conducted nonpartisan, multilingual exit polls of Asian American voters and monitored elections to document instances of anti-Asian voter disenfranchisement.[76] AALDEF's multilingual exit polls reveal vital information about Asian American voting patterns that are regularly overlooked in mainstream voter surveys. They also provide a snapshot of Asian American voter preferences on candidates, political parties, language needs, and other issues of vital importance to their communities.

On November 6, 2012, AALDEF conducted a nonpartisan, multilingual exit poll of 9,096 Asian American voters in 14 states: California, Florida, Georgia, Illinois, Louisiana, Maryland, Massachusetts, Michigan, Nevada, New Jersey, New York, Pennsylvania, Texas, Virginia, and Washington, D.C.[77] AALDEF's exit poll, the largest survey of its kind in the nation, surveyed 9,096 Asian American voters at 81 poll sites in 38 cities. The exit poll was conducted in English and 11 Asian languages: Arabic, Bengali, Chinese, Gujarati, Hindi, Khmer, Korean, Punjabi, Tagalog, Urdu, and Vietnamese. Survey takers were also conversant in 32 Asian languages and dialects (see Figure 9.1).

The largest Asian ethnic groups polled were Chinese (31%), Asian Indian (13%), Bangladeshi (12%), Vietnamese (12%), Korean (11%), Filipino (9%), Pakistani (3%), Indo-Caribbean (1%), and Cambodian (1%). The

Figure 9.1
Limited English Proficiency by Language Group

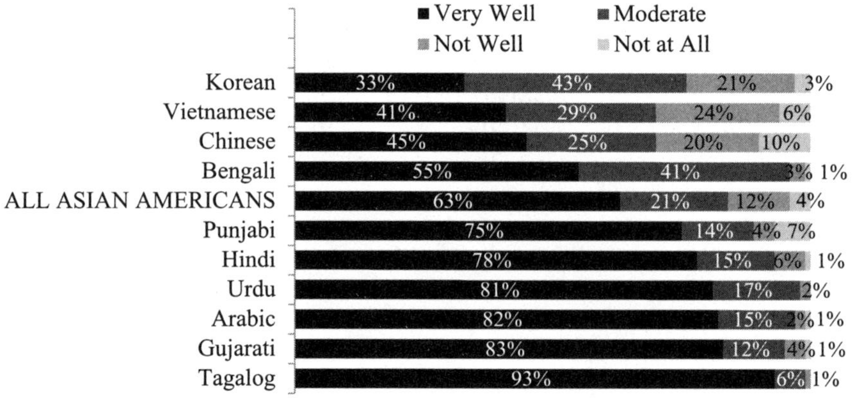

Language	Very Well	Moderate	Not Well	Not at All
Korean	33%	43%	21%	3%
Vietnamese	41%	29%	24%	6%
Chinese	45%	25%	20%	10%
Bengali	55%	41%	3%	1%
ALL ASIAN AMERICANS	63%	21%	12%	4%
Punjabi	75%	14%	4%	7%
Hindi	78%	15%	6%	1%
Urdu	81%	17%	2%	
Arabic	82%	15%	2%	1%
Gujarati	83%	12%	4%	1%
Tagalog	93%		6%	1%

Source: AALDEF Multilingual Exit Poll, November, 2012: Language Minority Groups.

remaining respondents were of other Asian ethnicities, such as Japanese, Thai, Nepalese, and multiracial Asians.

Multilingual exit polls provided a more comprehensive portrait of Asian American voters than surveys done only in English. Twenty-nine percent of respondents completed Asian language questionnaires, while 71 percent completed the English version. Some voters required assistance and had the questions read aloud to them. AALDEF's exit poll revealed details about the Asian American community, including voter preferences on candidates, political parties, issues, and language needs.

A Growing Segment of the Electorate

Asian Americans are a growing segment of the electorate. Twenty-seven percent of Asian Americans said that they voted for the first time in the November 2012 presidential election. The highest rates of first-time voters were among South Asians, with 45 percent of Bangladeshi, 35 percent of Pakistani, 29 percent of Asian Indian, and 28 percent of Indo-Caribbean Americans voting for the first time.

Asian Americans are gravitating more toward the Democratic Party. The majority (57%) of Asian American respondents were registered in the Democratic Party, 14 percent in the Republican Party, while 27 percent of all Asian American respondents were not registered at all (see Figure 9.2).

There was some variation among ethnicities. Democratic Party registration was highest among South Asian ethnicities. Eighty-four percent of Indo-Caribbean, 79 percent of Bangladeshi, 73 percent of Pakistani, and

Figure 9.2
Asian American Party Enrollment by Ethnicity

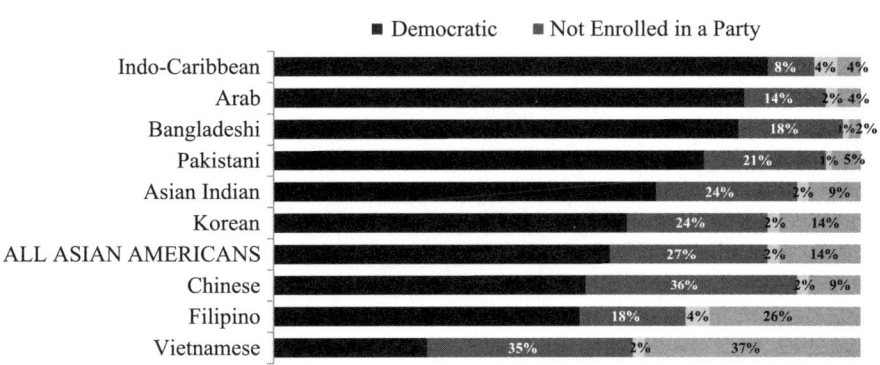

Source: AALDEF Multilingual Exit Poll, November 2012: Language Minority Groups.

65 percent of Asian Indian American voters were enrolled as Democrats, compared to 57 percent of all Asian Americans surveyed nationally. Vietnamese American respondents exhibited higher rates of enrollment in the Republican Party at 37 percent. Thirty-six percent of Chinese Americans and 35 percent of Vietnamese Americans were not enrolled in any political party, the highest rates of all the groups surveyed.

The Asian American Vote for President

Over the past 15 years, Asian Americans have increasingly voted more Democratic in presidential races. This has been especially true in swing states, such as Nevada, Virginia, Pennsylvania, and Michigan, where Asian Americans are relatively large segments of the electorate. Moreover, Asian Americans demonstrated political unity, even across ethnic lines (see Figure 9.3).

In 2012, the majority of Asian Americans (77%) favored Barack Obama over Mitt Romney for president; 21 percent favored Mitt Romney. The most important factors influencing the vote for president were the economy/jobs (53%), health care (35%), education (27%), and civil rights/immigrant rights (26%). Other important factors included women's issues (14%) and terrorism/security (11%).

With the exception of Vietnamese American voters, every Asian ethnic group voted as a bloc for Obama. Support for Obama was particularly strong among first-time voters and South Asian voters. South Asian voters demonstrated the strongest support for Obama, a trend that was consistent over the past several presidential elections. In the 2012 presidential election, 90 percent of South Asian voters voted for

Figure 9.3
Vote for President by Ethnicity

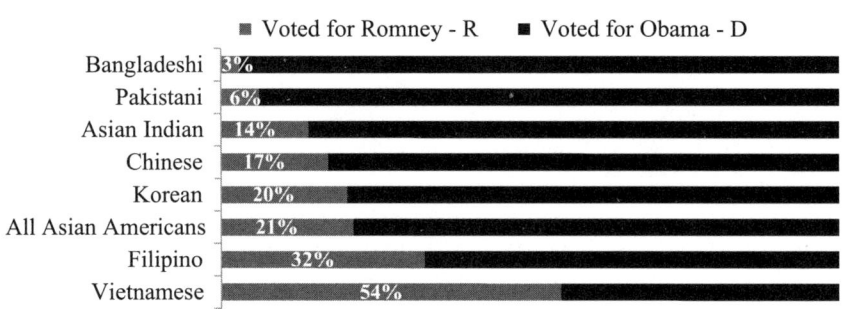

Source: AALDEF Multilingual Exit Poll, November 2012: Language Minority Groups.

Obama, 93 percent for Obama in 2008, and 90 percent for John Kerry in 2004. In November 2012, 96 percent of Bangladeshi, 91 percent of Pakistani, and 84 percent of Asian Indian Americans voted for Obama at a higher rate than Asian Americans nationally. Among Vietnamese American voters, on the other hand, 54 percent voted for Romney and 44 percent voted for Obama. But this was a decrease from the 67 percent support that John McCain received from Vietnamese voters in the 2008 presidential election (see Figures 9.4 and 9.5).

South Asian, Chinese, and Korean Americans have consistently shown strong support for Democratic presidential candidates. In the 2012 presidential election, 81 percent of Chinese Americans and 78 percent of Korean Americans voted for Obama. In the 2008 election, 73 percent of Chinese Americans and 64 percent of Korean Americans backed Obama. In the 2004 presidential election, 72 percent of Chinese Americans and 66 percent of Korean Americans gave their votes to Senator Kerry.

First-time voters favored Barack Obama by a wide margin, a trend consistent over the past presidential election that AALDEF surveyed. Eighty-two percent of Asian American first-time voters went for Obama, compared to the 16 percent who voted for Romney. Similarly, in the 2008 presidential election, 81 percent of Asian American first-time voters voted for Obama and 18 percent for McCain. In the 2004 presidential election, 78 percent of Asian American first-time voters voted for Senator Kerry.

Crossover voting favored Obama over Romney. A larger percentage of Asian Americans enrolled in the Republican Party (13%) crossed party lines to vote for Obama for president, in comparison to registered Democrats (3%) who crossed party lines to vote for Romney. Of those not enrolled in a political party, the majority favored Obama over Romney by a 3–1 margin (73 to 24%).

Figure 9.4
Vote for President by Election Year

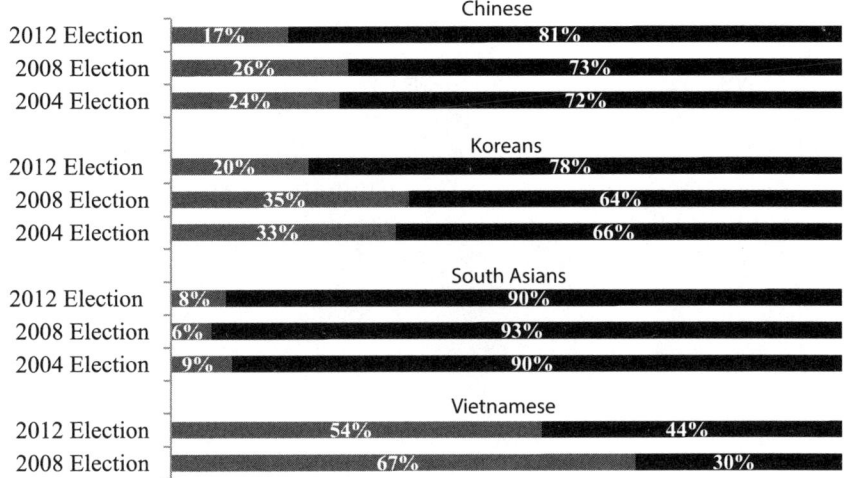

Source: AALDEF Multilingual Exit Poll, November 2012.

Figure 9.5
Vote for President by Party Affiliation

Voted for ...	Asian American Democrats	Asian American Republicans	Not Enrolled in Any Party
Barack Obama—D	96%	13%	73%
Mitt Romney—R	3%	85%	24%

Source: AALDEF Multilingual Exit Poll, November 2012: Language Minority Groups.

There was overwhelming support for Obama across all age levels, especially voters under age 40. The strongest support for Obama came from voters between the ages of 18 to 29, in which 86 percent voted for Obama. In that age category, only 10 percent of respondents voted for Romney, compared to 16 percent of those between 30 and 39, 26 percent of those between 40 and 49, 26 percent of those between 50 and 59, and 27 percent between 60 and 69. Although 23 percent of voters over 70 voted for Romney, 76 percent voted for Obama.

This was different from 2008, where support for Obama had steadily declined as age increased. For example, in 2008, 88 percent of voters between the ages of 18 to 29 voted for Obama, but 59 percent of those over the age of 70 voted for Obama. The gap was not as large in the 2012 presidential election.

In prior presidential elections, voter support for Democratic presidential candidates over Republican candidates was consistent.

- In 2008, Asian Americans favored Barack Obama over Republican John McCain, 76 percent to 22 percent, with 2 percent voting for other candidates.
- In 2004, Asian Americans favored Democratic Senator John Kerry over Republican President George W. Bush, 74 percent to 24 percent, with 2 percent voting for other candidates.
- In 2000, Asian Americans favored Democrat Al Gore over Republican George W. Bush. Only 1 percent voted for Independent Ralph Nader.

The Asian American Vote for Congress

In most of the congressional races surveyed, the majority of Asian Americans also supported Democratic candidates. This has been significant in certain key races.

U.S. Senate Races

Asian Americans were important constituencies in certain U.S. Senate races. During the November 2006 midterm elections, Democrats seized control of both houses of Congress for the first time in 12 years. They won a majority in the Senate with 51 of 100 seats, and a majority in the House of Representatives with 233 of 435 seats.[78]

In the midst of this historical shift in power, Asian American voters heavily favored Democratic candidates in particular states. Four out of every five (80%) Asian Americans voted for the Democratic candidates in the top-ballot races, and 17 percent voted for the Republican candidates. Two races were key. In the Virginia Senate race, 76 percent of Asian Americans voted for Democratic challenger Jim Webb, while 22 percent voted for Republican incumbent George Allen. Among all Virginia voters, Webb defeated Allen by less than 8,000 votes, a 0.3 percent margin of victory. In the Pennsylvania Senate race, 70 percent of Asian Americans supported Democratic candidate Bob Casey Jr., while 28 percent voted for incumbent Republican Rick Santorum. Among the general electorate, Casey carried 59 percent of the total vote and Santorum held 41 percent. Asian Americans were credited with helping deliver the U.S. Senate to the Democrats in 2006.

Table 9.5
Asian American Vote for Congress (Selected Districts)

State	Congressional District	Democratic Candidate	Asian American Vote (%)	Republican Candidate	Asian American Vote
CA	52	Scott Peters*	55	Brian Bilbray	41
GA	4	Hank Johnson*	58	J. Chris Vaughn	38
	6	Jeff Kazanow	73	Tom Price*	27
	7	Steve Reilly	49	Robert Woodall*	50
LA	2	Cedric Richmond*	25	Dwayne Bailey	71
MA	5	Edward Markey*	89	Tom Tierney	11
	7	Michael Capuano*	88	N/A	N/A
	8	Stephen Lynch*	75	Joe Selvaggi	24
MD	3	John Sarbanes*	78	Eric Knowles	20
	8	Chris Van Hollen*	74	Ken Timmerman	24
MI	3	Steve Pestka	92	Justin Amash*	0
	11	Syed Taj	68	Kerry Bentivolio*	29
	12	John Dingell*	90	Cynthia Kallgren	8
	14	Gary Peters*	97	John Hauler	2
NJ	9	Bill Pascrell*	81	Shmuley Boteach	18
	10	Donald Payne Jr.*	85	Brian Kelemen	15
NV	1	Dina Titus*	81	Chris Edwards	17
NY	3	Steve Israel*	91	Steven Labate	7
	5	Gregory Meeks*	89	Allan W. Jennings Jr.	10
	6	Grace Meng*	88	Daniel Halloran	11
	7	Nydia Velázquez*	76	N/A	N/A
	9	Yvette Clark*	89	Daniel J. Cavanagh	8

(continued)

Table 9.5 (continued)

State	Congressional District	Democratic Candidate	Asian American Vote (%)	Republican Candidate	Asian American Vote
	10	Jerrold Nadler*	98	Michael Chan	1
	12	Carolyn Maloney*	87	Christopher R. Wight	7
	14	Joseph Crowley*	91	William F. Gibbons Jr.	8
PA	1	Robert Brady*	92	John Featherman	8
	2	Chaka Fattah*	80	Robert Mansfield	17
	13	Allyson Schwartz*	90	Joseph J. Rooney	10
TX	9	Al Green*	49	Steve Mueller	44
	22	Kesha Rogers	62	Pete Olson*	34
VA	2	Paul O. Hirschbiel Jr.	44	Scott Rigell*	53
	7	Wayne Powell	56	Eric Cantor*	31
	8	Jim Moran*	77	J. Patrick Murray	20
	11	Gerry Connolly*	77	Chris S. Perkins	22

*Winning candidate.

Source: AALDEF Multilingual Exit Poll, November 2012: Language Minority Groups.
Note: Larger cells indicate a larger number of poll sites surveyed.

Asian Americans continued to vote for Democratic candidates in the 2012 Senate elections. Massachusetts has been a solidly Democratic state but in an enormous surprise, Republican Scott Brown was elected to finish the remaining term for Ted Kennedy after his death. In the 2012 election, 79 percent of Asian Americans voted for Democratic U.S. Senator Elizabeth Warren, while only 17 percent voted for Republican candidate Scott Brown. In comparison, 53 percent of the Massachusetts electorate voted for Warren.

Asian Americans also voted for Democratic candidates in certain swing states, stronger than the overall electorate in 2012:

- In Michigan, 81 percent of Asian Americans voted for Democratic U.S. Senator Debbie Ann Stabenow, while only 12 percent voted for Republican candidate Pete Hoekstra. In comparison, 59 percent of the Michigan electorate voted for Stabenow.

- In Nevada, 79 percent of Asian Americans voted for Democratic candidate Shelley Berkley, and 17 percent voted for Republican U.S. Senator Dean Heller. The Nevada electorate was split in this race, with 45 percent voting for Berkley and 46 percent voting for Heller.
- In Pennsylvania, 76 percent of Asian Americans voted for Democratic U.S. Senator Bob Casey, while only 10 percent voted for Republican candidate Tom Smith. In comparison, 54 percent of the Pennsylvania electorate voted for Casey and 45 percent for Smith.
- In Virginia, 70 percent of Asian Americans voted for Democratic U.S. Senator Timothy Kaine, while 26 percent voted for Republican candidate and former Senator George Allen. In comparison, 53 percent of Virginians voted for Kaine and 47 percent for Allen.

U.S. House of Representative Races

Likewise, most Asian Americans polled voted for the Democratic House candidates (74%) than for the Republican candidates (17%) in 2012. Results sometimes varied by congressional district (see Table 9.5).

Asian American Solidarity with Black and Latinos

Asian Americans often exhibited political support for minority office holders. Obviously, most Asian Americans supported Asian American candidates for office, even across ethnic lines. For example, in Edison, a Korean American candidate was elected to mayor in 2005 with the near total (97%) support of mostly South Asian and Chinese voters. The race was decided by only 273 votes. Asian Americans have also consistently supported African American and Latino candidates for office.

Asian Americans have consistently supported Latino candidates. Latinos office holders typically intimately understand the immigrant experience and need for language services. During the 2012 election, 76 percent of Asian Americans in New York voted for Nydia Velázquez, the first Puerto Rican-born Member of Congress. During the 2006 U.S. Senate race, 77 percent of Asian Americans in New Jersey voted for Democratic incumbent Senator Bob Menendez, while 20 percent voted for Republican challenger Thomas Kean Jr.

Asian Americans have also supported African American candidates for office. Some examples of U.S. House of Representatives races include Pennsylvania representative Chaka Fattah at 80 percent Asian American support; New Jersey representative Donald Payne Jr. at 81 percent support; and New York representatives Gregory Meeks at 89 percent; and Yvette Clark at 89 percent. It is important to note that Yvette Clark is a Caribbean American whose mother is a foreign-born naturalized citizen from Jamaica. She represents a large Asian immigrant community in Brooklyn.

Similarly Gregory Meeks represents a large South Asian population in Queens and once served as chair of the Subcommittee on India and South Asia of the House Foreign Affairs Committee.

In the 2006 Massachusetts gubernatorial race, 75 percent of Asian Americans voted for Democratic candidate Deval Patrick, while 21 percent voted for Republican candidate Kerry Healey. Additionally, although most Vietnamese American respondents were not registered Democrats, a majority (53%) of Vietnamese Americans voted for Patrick. Among all voters, Patrick defeated Healey 56 to 35 percent and became the first African American governor of Massachusetts and the second elected in U.S. history.

Likewise, Asian American candidates for office have often received support from African American and Latino voters. This includes Los Angeles Congresswoman Judy Chu and New York City comptroller John Liu who credit their victories with support for Latino and African voters, respectively.

Though the news media sometimes illustrates divisions between Asian and Black and Latinos in the political process, communities of color are united.

Summary of the Asian American Vote

Asian Americans are a growing segment of the electorate and are sizable in numbers in certain swing states. Over the past 15 years, Asian Americans have become a more reliable and consistent Democratic voting constituency.

Compared to other racial and ethnic groups, Asians Americans voted in higher percentages for Democrats than white voters, but in lower percentages than African Americans. In 2000 and 2008, Asians Americans more closely resembled the voting patterns of Latinos statewide. But then in 2012, Asian Americans were the second strongest Democratic voting group for Obama, again just after African Americans.

Asian Americans are diverse, coming from different countries and speaking different languages. In the political arena, however, they share common political interests even across ethnic lines. During major national and state elections, Asian American voters cast their ballots as a bloc for the same candidates and identified common reasons for their votes.

CONCLUSION

Like other minority groups, Asian Americans have suffered from a history of political exclusion. While they are increasingly naturalizing and registering to vote, they have often encountered discriminatory barriers at the polls. They have been racially profiled, segregated into separate voting lines, and political campaigns have used racial appeals and intimidation. Congress enacted the Language Assistance Provisions (Section 203) of the federal Voting Rights Act expand access to the right to vote for language minorities.

Under the Act, many jurisdictions must provide bilingual ballots and interpreters. However, there have also been several deficiencies in implementation, such as a lack of interpreters, mistranslations, a disregard for translated voting materials, and some materials not being translated at all. More work is needed to ensure full compliance.

Once assistance is sufficiently provided, Asian Americans will be able to fully exercise their right to vote and can secure greater electoral success. The growing Asian Americans electorate is more cohesive and more aligned with other communities of color in supporting Democratic candidates. But mainstream news media and politicians have, at times, overlooked the Asian American vote. With the tremendous Asian population expansion in the United States, their political power can no longer be ignored.

NOTES

1. *Chinese Exclusion Laws: Background*, National Archives.
2. Asian American Legal Defense and Education Fund, *Asian American Access to Democracy in the 2012 Election*, 14.
3. Ibid., 16.
4. Asian American Legal Defense and Education Fund Complaint Letter to Voting Section, Civil Rights Division, U.S. Department of Justice, "Violations of the Voting Rights," 3–4.
5. Asian American Legal Defense and Education Fund, *Asian American Access to Democracy in the 2008 Election*, 22.
6. Asian American Legal Defense and Education Fund, *Asian American Access to Democracy in the 2004 Election*, 16.
7. Asian American Legal Defense and Education Fund, *Asian American Access to Democracy in the 2008 Election*, 21.
8. Asian American Legal Defense and Education Fund, *Asian American Access to Democracy in the 2004 Election*, 16.
9. Asian American Legal Defense and Education Fund, Complaint Letter to Voting Section, Civil Rights Division, U.S. Department of Justice, "Racial Discrimination against Asian Americans."
10. Barca, *Feds to Watch Edison Vote*, Home News Trib.
11. *United States v. Hamtramck* (E.D. Mich. 2000).
12. Asian American Legal Defense and Education Fund, Complaint Letter to Voting Section, Civil Rights Division, U.S. Department of Justice, "Voter Intimidation in Fort Lee School Board Election."
13. Asian American Legal Defense and Education Fund, *Asian American Access to Democracy in the 2004 Election*, 16.
14. Voting Rights Act, Section 203, 42 U.S.C. Sec. 1973aa-1a (2004).
15. See Senate Commission on the Judiciary Report, July 2, 1992, Voting Rights Act Language Assistance Amendments of 1992, Report 102–315, Calendar No. 537, 102 Cong., 2d Session, at 4.
16. Voting Rights Act, Section 203, 42 U.S.C. Sec. 1973aa-1a (2010).
17. U.S. Census Bureau, "Asian/Pacific American Heritage Month: May 2010." For a fuller discussion on the need for language assistance for Latino and Native

American voters, in addition to Asian American voters, see Tucker, *Enfranchising Language Minority Citizens*.

18. Oversight Hearing on the Voting Rights Act: Section 203-Bilingual Election Requirements, Part I Before the House Subcomm. on the Constit., Comm. on the Judiciary (Nov. 8, 2005) (statement of Margaret Fung, Exec. Dir., AALDEF) [hereinafter AALDEF VRA Testimony before Congress, 2005].

19. U.S. Census Bureau, Current Population Survey.

20. Language Assistance Provisions of the Voting Rights Act, Hearing on S. 2236 Before the House Subcomm. on Civil and Constitutional Rights, House Judiciary Committee, 102 Cong. at 1 (April 1, 1992) (statement of Margaret Fung, Executive Director, Asian American Legal Defense and Education Fund); Senate Report 102–315, Calendar No. 537 July 2, 1992, at 12 (on file with author) [hereinafter Fung, Testimony on Language Assistance Provisions].

21. U.S. Census Bureau, Current Population Survey, Annual Social and Economic Supplement, 2009, http://www.census.gov/population/www/socdemo/race/ppl-aa09.html.

22. U.S. Census Bureau, 2005–2009 American Community Survey, "Age by Language Spoken at Home."

23. Asian American Legal Defense and Education Fund, *The Asian American Vote in the 2012 Presidential Election*, 2.

24. Limited English proficiency is determined by one's ability to read English less than "very well." Letter from Robert Kominski, U.S. Census Bureau, Population Division, to Paul Siegel, Chief of Education & Social Stratification Branch, U.S. Census Bureau, Population Division (February 4, 1985) (on file with author).

25. The Fannie Lou Hamer, Rosa Parks, and Coretta Scott King Voting Rights Act Reauthorization and Amendments Act of 2006, S. 2703, 109 Cong. §2 (2006). Reauthorization did not come about easily. Many members of Congresses opposed bilingual ballots with nativists and anti-immigrant arguments. See generally Ao, *When the Voting Rights Act Became Un-American*.

26. Voting Rights Act, Section 203, 42 U.S.C. Sec. 1973aa-1a.

27. 42 U.S.C. Sec. 1973aa-1a (b) (1).

28. 42 U.S.C. Sec. 1973aa-1a (b) (2) (A).

29. Language Assistance Provisions of the Voting Rights Act, Hearing on S. 2236 Before the House Subcomm. on Civil and Constitutional Rights, House Judiciary Committee, 102 Cong. at 12 (April 1, 1992) (statement of Margaret Fung, Executive Director, Asian American Legal Defense and Education Fund); Senate Report 102–315, Calendar No. 537 July 2, 1992, at 12.

30. Implementation of the Voting Rights Act Regarding Language Minority Groups, 28 C.F.R. Part 55 (Appendix, 105–107). The counties and languages include Alameda County, CA (Chinese), Los Angeles County, CA (Chinese, Filipino, Japanese, Vietnamese), Orange County, CA (Vietnamese), San Francisco County, CA (Chinese); Honolulu County, HI (Filipino, Japanese), Kauai County, HI (Filipino), Maui County, HI (Filipino); Kings County, NY (Chinese), New York County, NY (Chinese), Queens County, NY (Chinese).

31. See City of Los Angeles Office of the City Clerk Election Division, Multilingual Service Program, 76 Fed. Reg. 63602, 63603 (October 13, 2011) (to be codified at 28 C.F.R. pt. 55).

32. 67 Fed. Reg. No. 144, 48871–77 (July 26, 2002) (Notices).

33. 28 C.F.R. §§ 55.15, 55.19.
34. 28 C.F.R. § 55.18 (c).
35. 28 C.F.R. §§ 55.18, 55.20. Sometimes assistance must be provided in more than one dialect of the language. For instance, although there is one written form of Chinese, there are several spoken dialects, like Cantonese, Mandarin, Toisan, and others. 28 C.F.R. § 55.20.
36. See 28 C.F.R. § 55.20.
37. See 28 C.F.R. § 55.17.
38. 28 C.F.R. §§ 55.2, 55.15, 55.19, 55.20.
39. 28 C.F.R. § 55.2 (b) (1), (2).
40. 42 U.S.C. § 1973aa-6 (2001).
41. Tucker, *Enfranchising Language Minority Citizens*.
42. Asian American Legal Defense and Education Fund, *Lowering the Numerical Trigger to Improve the Effectiveness of Section 203* (Fact Sheet).
43. Avila, Lee, and Ao, *Voting Rights in California: 1982–2006*.
44. Endo, *Asian-American Voters Could Swing Mayoral Election*.
45. Tucker, *Enfranchising Language Minority Citizens* [citing Voting Rights Act: Section 203—Bilingual Election Requirements (Part I): Hearing Before the Subcomm. on the Constitution of the H. Comm. on the Judiciary, 109th Cong. 12 (2005) (statement of Bradley J. Schlozman, Acting Assistant Attorney General, Civil Rights Division, Department of Justice)].
46. See generally, U.S. Government Accountability Office, Bilingual Voting Assistance: Selected Jurisdictions' Strategies for Identifying Needs and Providing Assistance, GAO-08–182 (January 2008), available at http://www.gao.gov/new.items/d08182.pdf.
47. See, for example, National Asian Pacific American Legal Consortium, *Access to Democracy* (July 2000); Asian American Legal Defense and Education Fund, Asian American Access to Democracy in the 2008 Election (2009); Asian Pacific American Legal Center and Chinese for Affirmative Action, Language Barriers to Voting: Findings from APALC and CAA's November 2006 Poll Monitoring in Los Angeles, Orange and San Francisco Counties (2006); Chinese for Affirmative Action, 2006 Poll Monitoing in San Francisco County 1 (2006); Asian Law Alliance and Asian Law Caucus, Obstacles to Full and Equal Access to the Ballot for Limited English Proficient Voters, November 9, 2010; Law Foundation of Silicon Valley, A Report on the Law Foundation of Silicon Valley Poll Monitoring Project for the November 4, 2008, Presidential General Election, July 2009 (San Jose, 2008).
48. Magpantay, *Asian American Access to the Vote*, 11 ASIAN L.J. 31, 40–42 (2004).
49. Voting Rights Act § 5, 42 U.S.C. § 1973c (2004); Juan Cartagena, *Voting Rights in New York City: 1982–2006*, 17 S. CAL. REV. L. & SOC. JUST. 501, 516–517 (2008) (describing federal observers in New York).
50. The Department of Justice is responsible for enforcement of Section 203 of the Voting Rights Act. 28 C.F.R. § 55.2 (b) (1), (2). The Department has already used three jurisdictions for Section 203 compliance for Spanish language assistance. *See United States of America v. Passaic County* (D.N.J.) (Consent Decree) June 1999; *United States of America v. City of Lawrence*, Civ. 98 CV 12256 (WGY) (D. Mass.) 1999 (Settlement Agreement and Order); and *United States of America v. Bernalillo County*, Civ. CV-98-156 (BB, LCS) (D.N.M.) April 22, 1998 (Consent Decree).

51. See, for example, *United States v. City of Rosemead* (C.D. Cal. 2005) (for Chinese and Vietnamese voters); *United States v. San Diego County* (S.D. Cal 2004) (for Filipino and Vietnamese voters); *United States v. City of Boston* (D. Mass. 2005) (for Chinese and Vietnamese voters); *United States v. City of Walnut, CA* (C.D. Cal. 2007) (for Chinese and Korean voters). For a full listing of cases filed by the U.S. Department of Justice, Voting Section, go to http://www.usdoj.gov/crt/voting/litigation/caselist.htm.

52. *Chinatown Voter Education Alliance v. Ravitz*, 06 CV 913 (NRB) (S.D.N.Y. May 23, 2008).

53. Murphy, Cheng, Lowe, *Spirit Willing, System Weak; Bungled Ballots in Chinatown*.

54. *Alliance of South Asian American Labor v. NYC Board of Elections*, 13 CV 3732 (RJD) (MDG) (E.D.N.Y. July 2, 2013).

55. *Complaint, Chinatown Voter Education Alliance, et al. v. Ravitz, et al.* (S.D.N.Y. 2006) (No. 06. Civ. 913) at 9; AALDEF, *Asian American Access to Democracy in the 2008 Election* 13 (2009).

56. Asian Pacific American Legal Center and Chinese for Affirmative Action, Language Barriers to Voting Findings from APALC and CAA's November 2006 Poll Monitoring in Los Angeles, Orange and San Francisco Counties (2006).

57. Asian Law Alliance and Asian Law Caucus, Obstacles to Full and Equal Access to the Ballot for Limited English Proficiency Voters, November 9, 2010; Chinese for Affirmative Action, 2006 Poll Monitoring in San Francisco County 1 (2006).

58. Law Foundation of Silicon Valley, A Report on the Law Foundation of Silicon Valley Poll Monitoring Project for the November 4, 2008, Presidential General Election, July 2009.

59. Asian American Legal Defense and Education Fund, Asian American Access to Democracy in the 2012 Election, 14.

60. Ibid.

61. Asian American Legal Defense and Education Fund, Asian American Access to Democracy in the 2004 Election, 10.

62. Asian American Legal Defense and Education Fund, Complaint Letter to New York City Board of Elections, November 2, 2003, at 6.

63. Sometimes, voter information on website was not even fully translated. *First Amended Complaint, Chen et al. v. State of Hawaii, et al.*, Civ. No. 10–00245 SOM-BMK (D. Haw. July 28, 2010) at 9–10.

64. Board of Elections in the City of New York, Chinese-Korean Language Assistance Plan (April 5, 2007) *Settlement, Chinatown Voter Education Alliance, et al. v. Ravitz, et al.* (S.D.N.Y. 2006) (No. 06. Civ. 913) at 3.

65. *Bergen County Superintendent of Elections*, http://www.co.bergen.nj.us/elections/default.html (last visited October 2, 2012).

66. *Elections—Suburban Cook County*.

67. *Elections*, City of Hamtrack, MI.

68. *Elections*, City of Quincy.

69. *Elections—Suburban Cook County*. http://www.cookcountyclerk.com/elections/pages/default.aspx (last visited October 2, 2012).

70. 42 U.S.C. § 1973aa-6 (2001).

71. Asian American Legal Defense and Education Fund, *Asian American Access to Democracy in the 2012 Election*.

72. Ibid.

73. Census 2000 identified 11,898,828 individuals who are of Asian heritage. Asian American growth since 1990 was 72.2 percent. U.S. Census Bureau, Census 2000 PHC-T-1 (Tables 3, 4) and Summary File 3 "PCT63D."

74. Oversight Hearing on the Voting Rights Act: Section 203-Bilingual Election Requirements, Part I before the House Subcomm. on the Constit., Comm. on the Judiciary (November 8, 2005) (statement of Margaret Fung, AALDEF).

75. VNS later supplemented its national poll with state polling data and found that 53 percent of Asian Americans supported Clinton, with 40 percent voting for Dole. VNS was disbanded after the 2000 election debacle.

76. For a full review of AALDEF's exit poll and election monitoring activities, see Magpantay, *Ensuring Asian American Access to Democracy in New York City*, 2 *AAPI Nexus Journal: Policy, Practice, and Community* 87 (2004). In 2006, AALDEF surveyed 4,726 Asian American voters in nine states; in 2004, 10,789 voters in eight states; and in 2002, over 3,000 voters in four states.

77. The cities and states selected for the exit poll were among those with the largest or fastest-growing Asian American populations according to the 2010 U.S. Census. Poll sites with large concentrations of Asian American voters were selected based on voter registration files, census data, interviews with local elections officials and community leaders, and a history of voting problems.

78. Oversight Hearing on the Voting Rights Act: Section 203-Bilingual Election Requirements, Part I before the House Subcomm. on the Constit., Comm. on the Judiciary (November 8, 2005).

REFERENCES

Alliance of South Asian American Labor v. NYC Board of Elections. 13 CV 3732. RJD. MDG. E.D.N.Y. 2 July 2013.

Asian American Legal Defense and Education Fund. *Asian American Access to Democracy in the 2004 Election*. 2005.

Asian American Legal Defense and Education Fund. *Asian American Access to Democracy in the 2008 Election*. 2009.

Asian American Legal Defense and Education Fund. *Asian American Access to Democracy in the 2012 Election*. 2013.

Asian American Legal Defense and Education Fund. Complaint Letter to New York City Board of Elections. 2 November 2003.

Asian American Legal Defense and Education Fund. Complaint Letter to Voting Section. Civil Rights Division. U.S. Department of Justice. "Racial Discrimination against Asian Americans in New York City Council Race for 19th District." Fall 2009. 15 June 2010.

Asian American Legal Defense and Education Fund. Complaint Letter to Voting Section. Civil Rights Division. U.S. Department of Justice. "Violations of the Voting Rights Act and Help America Vote Act during the General Elections on November 2, 2010." 2011.

Asian American Legal Defense and Education Fund. Complaint Letter to Voting Section. Civil Rights Division. U.S. Department of Justice. "Voter Intimidation in Fort Lee School Board Election, Bergen County, NJ, on April 17, 2007." 8 April 2008.

Asian American Legal Defense and Education Fund. *Lowering the Numerical Trigger to Improve the Effectiveness of Section 203*. Fact Sheet submitted to House Subcommittee on the Constitution. Committee on the Judiciary. 14 November 2005.

Asian Law Alliance and Asian Law Caucus. *Obstacles to Full and Equal Access to the Ballot for Limited English Proficient Voters*. 9 November, 2010.

Asian Pacific American Legal Center and Chinese for Affirmative Action. *Language Barriers to Voting Findings from APALC and CAA's November 2006 Poll Monitoring in Los Angeles, Orange and San Francisco Counties*. 2006.

Avila, Joaquin G., Eugene Lee, and Terry M. Ao, "Voting Rights in California: 1982–2006." *Southern California Review of Law & Social Justice* 17 (2007): 131–181.

Barca, Jerry. "Feds to Watch Edison Vote." *New Brunswick Home News Tribune*. 2 November 2005. http://www.thnt.com/apps/pbcs.dll/article?AID=/20051102/NEWS/511020421/1001.

Board of Elections in the City of New York. Chinese-Korean Language Assistance Plan. 5 April 2007.

Cartagena, Juan. "Voting Rights in New York City: 1982–2006." *Southern California Review of Law & Social Justice* 17 (2008): 501, 516–517.

Chen, et al. v. State of Hawaii, et al., First Amended Complaint. Civ. No. 10-00245 SOM-BMK. D. Haw. 28 July 2010.

Chinatown Voter Education Alliance, et al. v. Ravitz, et al., Complaint, 06 CV. 913 NRB. S.D.N.Y. 23 May 2008.

Chinatown Voter Education Alliance, et al. v. Ravitz, et al., Settlement. S.D.N.Y. 2006. No 06. Civ 913.

Chinese for Affirmative Action. *Poll Monitoring in San Francisco County*. 2006.

City of Los Angeles Office of the City Clerk Election Division. Multilingual Service Program. 76 Fed. Reg. 63602, 63603. 13 October 2011.

Editors. "Bungled Ballots in Chinatown." *New York Times*. 1 January 2001. (Editorial).

Endo, Sandy. "Asian-American Voters Could Swing Mayoral Election." *New York 1 News*. 9 February 2005.

The Fannie Lou Hamer, Rosa Parks, And Coretta Scott King Voting Rights Act Reauthorization And Amendments Act Of 2006. S. 2703. 109 Cong. §2. 2006.

Kominski, Robert. Letter. U.S. Census Bureau, Population Division, to Paul Siegel, Chief of Education & Social Stratification Branch, U.S. Census Bureau, Population Division. 4 February 1985. (On file with author).

Language Assistance Provisions of the Voting Rights Act. Hearing on S. 2236 before the House Subcomm. on Civil and Constitutional Rights. House Judiciary Committee. 102 Cong. at 1. 1 April 1992. Statement of Margaret Fung, Executive Director, Asian American Legal Defense and Education Fund.

Law Foundation of Silicon Valley. *A Report on the Law Foundation of Silicon Valley Poll Monitoring Project for the November 4, 2008, Presidential General Election, July 2009*. San Jose, 2008.

Magpantay, Glenn D. "Asian American Access to the Vote: The Language Assistance Provisions (Section 203) of the Voting Rights Act and Beyond." *Asian Law Journal* 11 (2004): 31, 40–42.

Murphy, William, Mae Cheng, and Herbert Lowe. "Spirit Willing, System Weak: Bungled Ballots in Chinatown." *Newsday*. 8 November 2000. A10.

National Archives. *Chinese Exclusion Laws: Background*. http://www.archives.gov/pacific/education/curriculum/4th-grade/chinese-exclusion.html.

National Asian Pacific American Legal Consortium. *Access to Democracy: Language Assistance and Section 203 of the Voting Rights Act*. July 2000.

Oversight Hearing on the Voting Rights Act: Section 203-Bilingual Election Requirements. Part I Before the House Subcomm. On the Constit., Comm. on the Judiciary. 8 November 2005. Statement of Margaret Fung, Exec. Dir., AALDEF.

Senate Comm. on the Judiciary Report. 2 July 1992. Voting Rights Act Language Assistance Amendments of 1992. Report 102-315. Calendar No. 537. 102 Cong., 2nd Session, at 4.

Senate Report 102-315, Calendar No. 537. 2 July 1992, at 12.

67 Fed. Reg. No. 144, 48871-77. 26 July 2002. Notices.

Tucker, James Thomas. *Enfranchising Language Minority Citizens: The Bilingual Election Provisions of the Voting Rights Act*. 10 N.Y.U. J. Legislation and Public Policy. 195 (2006–2007).

28 C.F.R. Part 55. Appendix, 105-107.

United States of America v. Bernalillo County. Civ. CV-98-156. BB, LCS. D.N.M. 22 April 1998. Consent Decree.

United States of America v. City of Lawrence. Civ. 98 CV 12256. WGY. D. Mass. 1999. Settlement Agreement and Order.

United States of America v. Passaic County. D.N.J. Consent Decree. June 1999.

United States v. City of Boston. D. Mass. 2005.

United States v. City of Rosemead. C.D. Cal. 2005. For Chinese and Vietnamese Voters.

United States v. City of Walnut, CA C.D. Cal. 2007.

United States v. Hamtramck (E.D. Mich. 2000).

United States v. San Diego County (S.D. Cal 2004) (for Filipino and Vietnamese voters).

U.S. Census Bureau, 2005–2009 American Community Survey. "Age by Language Spoken at Home by Ability to Speak English for the Population 5 Years and Over."

U.S. Census Bureau, Asian/Pacific American Heritage Month: May 2010. http://www.census.gov/newsroom/releases/pdf/cb10-ff07.pdf.

U.S. Census Bureau, Census 2000 PHC-T-1 (Tables 3, 4) and Summary File 3. "PCT63D."

U.S. Census Bureau, Current Population Survey. Annual Social and Economic Supplement, 2009. http://www.census.gov/population/www/socdemo/race/ppl-aa09.html.

U.S. Census Bureau, Current Population Survey. "Table 2. Reported Voting and Registration, by Race, Hispanic Origin, Sex, and Age, for the United States." November 2008.

U.S. Government Accountability Office. Bilingual Voting Assistance: Selected Jurisdictions.' Strategies for Identifying Needs and Providing Assistance. GAO-08-182. January 2008, at http://www.gao.gov/new.items/d08182.pdf.

Voting Rights Act. Section 5. 42 U.S.C. § 1973c. 2004.

Voting Rights Act. Section 203. 42 U.S.C. Sec. 1973aa-1a. 2010.

Chapter 10

South Asian Americans: New American Voters in a Changing Nation

Deepa Iyer[1]

The ability to fully engage in the civic and political process is an important milestone that immigrant communities in the United States strive to reach in their lives. It represents a coming of age in terms of political consciousness, of feeling "American," and of being part of the decision-making process in one's city, state and nation. For immigrants who often feel disconnected and disengaged from their adopted nation, the ability to vote can be particularly meaningful. This is the case for many recent immigrants in America, who are making their way toward naturalization and subsequently, the polling booths in greater numbers. South Asian Americans comprise a growing segment of this electorate of new minority voters.

For over a century, South Asian Americans have traveled a winding path to accessing their fundamental right to vote. South Asian immigrants who settled in the United States at the turn of the 20th century faced considerable barriers that restricted them from the naturalization process, and thereby, the polling booth. Today, South Asians are a sought-after voting bloc due to the large numbers of individuals applying for naturalization, the potential for political leadership from within the community, and the community's growing influence in various sectors. Demographic changes in the South Asian population, coupled with a more politically savvy South Asian electorate, could magnify the community's influence on U.S. elections in future decades. Moreover, South Asian voters could help amplify the opinions of minority voters as a whole if they vote in tandem with them in elections. At the same time, South Asian American voters continue to face challenges and barriers to the right to vote.

WHO ARE SOUTH ASIAN AMERICAN VOTERS?

South Asians are the fastest-growing ethnic population in the country. Over 3.5 million South Asians live in the United States, tracing their ancestry to Bangladesh, Bhutan, India, the Maldives, Nepal, Pakistan, Sri Lanka,[2] and to the South Asian diaspora.[3] Between 2000 and 2010, census data reveal that the South Asian community grew by 78 percent. As Table 10.1 demonstrates, certain segments of South Asians, especially Bangladeshis and Pakistanis, experienced significant population growth since 2000.

Not surprisingly, the South Asian community's population expansion has also generated many more potential voters. Indeed, between 2000 and 2010, the number of U.S. citizens of voting age in the South Asian community swelled by 99 percent for Indian Americans and 471 percent for Bangladeshi Americans. Table 10.2 shows the population changes for South Asian voters between 2000 and 2010.

It is likely that the numbers of potential South Asian voters will increase in the future as more individuals become eligible for naturalization, and

Table 10.1
Changes in South Asian American Population, 2000–2010[4]

	Single Ethnicity Reported			Single and Multiple Ethnicities Reported		
	2000	2010	% Change	2000	2010	% Change
Bangladeshi	41,280	128,792	212	57,412	147,300	157
Bhutanese	n/a	15,290	n/a	n/a	19,439	n/a
Indian	1,678,765	2,843,391	69	1,899,599	3,183,063	68
Nepali	n/a	51,907	n/a	n/a	59,490	n/a
Pakistani	153,533	363,699	137	204,309	409,163	100
Sri Lankan	20,145	38,596	92	24,587	45,381	85
Total South Asians	n/a	3,441,675	n/a			
Total for Four Census 2000 Groups	1,893,723	3,374,478	78			

Table 10.2
Changes in Population of South Asian Americans of Voting Age, 2000–2010[5]

	U.S. Citizens			Non-U.S. Citizens		
	2000	2010	% Change	2000	2010	% Change
Bangladeshi	8,527	43,829	414	19,249	37,323	94
Indian	576,784	1,154,308	100	660,714	932,851	41
Pakistani	52,755	161,036	205	58,356	85,726	47
Sri Lankan	5,944	14,464	143	8,468	17,642	108

as more U.S.-born South Asians turn 18. Indeed, in 42 states, South Asians rank among the top 10 countries of birth for immigrants who naturalized in the 2000s, with Indians leading the people naturalizing in New Jersey, Virginia, and West Virginia. States where Pakistanis were among the top 10 groups of voting-age citizens who naturalized between 2000 and 2009 include Alaska, Arkansas, Connecticut, Illinois, Indiana, Louisiana, Texas, Virginia, and West Virginia.[6]

TRENDS AND PATTERNS IN SOUTH ASIAN AMERICAN VOTING

Exit polls and surveys of South Asian American voters[7] during elections in the 2000s have revealed three clear trends or patterns: (1) South Asians increasingly compose a large segment of the Asian American electorate, especially first-time voters; (2) South Asians increasingly lean toward candidates affiliated with the Democratic Party; and (3) South Asians are motivated by issues such as health care, economy, and immigration when selecting their candidates of choice.

First-Time Voters on the Rise

The Asian American Legal Defense and Education Fund (AALDEF)'s exit polls conducted in 2006,[8] 2008,[9] and 2012[10] reveal that South Asians comprised the largest segment of first-time voters of all Asian American surveyed voters. In the 2012 election, for example, South Asians comprised the highest rates of first-time voters who were surveyed, with 45 percent of Bangladeshis, 35 percent of Pakistanis, 29 percent of Indians, and 28 percent of Indo-Caribbeans indicating that they were voting for the first time. Similarly, in the 2008 elections, South Asian voters comprised the top four ethnic groups of first-time voters, with 40 percent of Bangladeshis, 36 percent of Indo-Caribbeans, 34 percent of Indians, and 34 percent of Pakistanis indicating that they were casting a ballot for the first time. In the 2006 mid-term elections, the groups with the highest rates of first-time voters included Pakistanis (24%) and Bangladeshis (18%).

The consistently high rates of first-time South Asian voters strongly suggests that South Asians are utilizing the naturalization process and eagerly exercising their right to vote as U.S. citizens quickly. Political parties have taken note of the growing South Asian electorate and are engaging in various forms of outreach to attract South Asian voters.

Democrat Leaning

According to the 2012 National Asian American Survey,[11] among the surveyed Asian Americans who identified with a political party, more were affiliated with the Democratic Party (33%) than the Republican Party (14%). In fact, AALDEF's exit polls consistently show that South Asian voters affiliated with the Democratic Party in greater numbers than all other Asian ethnic groups. The 2012 exit poll found that 84 percent of Indo-Caribbeans, 79 percent of Bangladeshis, 73 percent of Pakistanis, and 65 percent of Indian voters were registered as Democrats.

Registration patterns translated to voter choice on Election Day as well. In 2012, the National Asian American Survey (NAAS) postelection survey found that two-thirds of Asian Americans and Pacific Islanders voted for President Obama. In fact, 84 percent of Indian Americans voted for President Obama and only 16 percent voted for Mitt Romney, the Republican challenger.

South Asians are likely to vote for Democratic candidates based on the issues that are most important to them. These issues may explain why South Asians have historically been aligned with the Democratic Party.

Voter Choice

Results from AALDEF's exit polls and the NAAS show that Asian American voters generally identify particular issues as significant factors in deciding which candidates to support. These issues tend to cluster around the economy, health care, education, and immigration. This is also the case with South Asian voters. For example, the NAAS revealed that 52 percent of Indian Americans surveyed had a favorable opinion on the importance of health care reform, and that 72 percent of Indians (larger than any other Asian ethnic group surveyed) believed that environmental protection should be prioritized over economic growth.[12]

In addition, the post-September 11 environment has also affected the political orientation of many South Asians. Since September 11, South Asians, Arab Americans, Muslims, and Sikhs have endured higher levels of discrimination, as well as the brunt of policy initiatives ranging from the USA PATRIOT Act to the National Security Entry/Exit Registration

System (NSEERS). In addition, many community members oppose the use of surveillance tools by law enforcement to spy on mosques and Muslim student associations, as well as the anti-immigrant and Islamaphobic rhetoric espoused by some elected leaders. South Asian voters may believe that conservative candidates do not take strong civil rights or pro-immigrant positions to ameliorate conditions in the post-9/11 environment. As a result, South Asian voters may lean toward Democratic or independent candidates who might more accurately reflect their values and policy goals.

BARRIERS TO VOTING

Despite their growing influence on the minority electorate, South Asians continue to experience a variety of barriers and obstacles to becoming completely engaged civically and politically in the United States. South Asians have historically faced attempts to prevent their civic and political participation. In fact, at the turn of the 20th century, South Asians who were not born in the United States could not be naturalized. This changed with *In re Mozumdar* (1913) in which a federal court in Washington State granted citizenship to an Indian-born individual based upon the argument that Indians were "Caucasians" who could be considered "white" and therefore eligible for naturalization under existing laws. Yet, this ruling was quickly reversed in *U.S. v Bhagat Singh Thind* (1923) in which the U.S. Supreme Court held that people from the Indian subcontinent were ineligible for naturalization because they were not "white," as this term was interpreted "in accordance with the understanding of the common man." In its decision, the U.S. Supreme Court validated perceptions of South Asians and other Asian immigrants as being foreign and incapable of and undesirable for integration within U.S. society. It was not until Congress enacted the Luce-Celler Act of 1946, which allowed Indians to naturalize, that the *Thind* decision was overturned. But it would not be until 1965—with the passage of the Immigration and Naturalization Act—when all race-based restrictions on citizenship were eliminated.

Over the past two decades, South Asians have faced different types of voting barriers including (1) voting discrimination; (2) lack of language access to the polls; and (3) xenophobic political discourse referencing "others," namely South Asians, in the post-9/11 environment.

Voting Problems

One of the significant cases that demonstrates the extent of voting discrimination in the United States since 1999 is related to South Asian and Arab American voters in Hamtramck, Michigan. Hamtramck is home to a vibrant community of Arab Americans and Bangladeshi Americans. In the

November 1999 elections there, Arab Americans and Bangladeshi Americans were required by poll workers to take an oath of citizenship before they could vote. This requirement was not imposed upon white voters. As a result, the U.S. Department of Justice investigated the City of Hamtramck's election procedures. The city and the federal government entered into an agreement to establish a training program for election officials; provide notices in English, Arabic, and Bengali to inform voters of new election practices; and hire bilingual poll workers on Election Day.[13]

While the Hamtramck incident may have been particularly egregious, there are examples of voting rights violations which often fall under the radar of media attention but are just as significant. Asian American voters, including South Asians, identified voting problems ranging from improper requests for identification, missing or misspelled names in voter rolls, and hostile poll workers.[14]

Language Access

Under Section 203 of the Voting Rights Act, certain jurisdictions with more than 10,000, or 5 percent of all voting-age citizens, being part of the same language minority group and are limited English proficient (LEP), are required to provide linguistic assistance, including translated ballots or interpreters, to those voters. For the first time in 2012, Section 203 required Asian language assistance in several jurisdictions. For example, in New York City, Chinese language assistance is required in Brooklyn and Manhattan. In Queens, Chinese, Korean, and Bengali, assistance is required. In Cook County, Chicago, Indian language assistance is required, which is designated as Hindi.

With growing numbers of LEP individuals of South Asian descent, community members benefit from increased assistance in certain South Asian languages, specifically Bengali and Hindi, in particular parts of the country that fall under Section 203 coverage.

Xenophobic Political Rhetoric

Even as South Asians emerge as a visible and effective political force and broadly engage in civic life, the community faces a growing trend of xenophobic and racist rhetoric that limits the exercise of its full potential. Like other immigrant communities and people of color, the South Asian community has shouldered the burden of having to prove its loyalty and "American-ness." In the wake of September 11, 2001, South Asians have witnessed a spike in rhetoric in the political sphere that promotes stereotypes of South Asians as criminals and terrorists, thereby contributing to the ill will and misconceptions held by the general public and the media. This dynamic, coupled with policies and initiatives that target particular communities—such as NSEERS, surveillance, and racial and religious profiling—has led to a climate of intolerance and bigotry targeting many South Asian communities.

With this context in mind, xenophobic comments made by elected and public officials that reinforce terrorism-related stereotypes contribute to an environment condoning retaliation against South Asians and validate policies and public actions that discriminate against the community. An example of this occurred shortly after September 11 when former representative John Cooksey (R-LA) stated that if "someone who comes in that's got a diaper on his head and a fan belt wrapped around the diaper on his head, that guy needs to be pulled over." Cooksey's comments were harmful because they degraded religious symbols worn by Sikhs or Muslims and provided a clear image to the general public of whom he believed could or could not be trusted in America based upon their appearance or religion. His comments also signaled an approval of religious and racial profiling, a tactic that links suspicious behavior to individuals on the basis of religious or racial appearance unrelated to criminal conduct. Representative Cooksey's comments were met with criticism from groups around the country, but he did not apologize for them.

While incidents of intolerant rhetoric that labeled South Asians as *terrorists* escalated following September 11, xenophobic comments that played upon broader anti-immigrant sentiment and "fear of the foreigner" continued. In August 2006, former Virginia Senator George Allen's comment aimed at a 20-year-old South Asian staffer working for his opponent led to immediate criticism and national media attention. Senator Allen's comments, made on the campaign trail before a predominantly Caucasian audience, were as follows: "Let's give a warm welcome to Macaca here. Welcome to America and the real world of Virginia." Senator Allen was roundly criticized for his remarks, which implied that the South Asian staffer, despite the fact that he was born and raised in Virginia, did not belong in America because of his appearance and ethnic background. The use of the word "macaca"—a racial slur in some parts of the world—only intensified the impact of Senator Allen's remarks.

Almost a year later, former representative Bill Sali (R-ID) attacked efforts to recognize pluralism in American society through his rhetoric. His remarks followed the momentous occasion of a prayer offered by a Hindu priest in July 2007 at the beginning of Senate proceedings. Sali stated, "We not only have a Hindu prayer being offered in the Senate, we have a Muslim member of the House of Representatives now, Keith Ellison from Minnesota." Sali continued, "Those are changes—and they are not what was [sic] envisioned by the Founding Fathers." He went on to state that the United States was built on Christian principles and that when a Hindu prayer is offered to "a different god" it "creates problems for the longevity of this country." One of America's cornerstones is the freedom to practice religion without interference. The statements of former representative Sali promote the notion that diverse religions are not welcome in the United States, and could potentially foster bias incidents and discriminatory policies against religious and ethnic minorities.

In the 2008 election, the South Asian community participated at unprecedented levels in terms of turnout, voter mobilization, and campaign contributions. While the Democratic and Republican parties recognized the significant influence that South Asians had in the elections and embraced the support that the community provided, the presidential candidates of both parties also made remarks that perpetuated the foreignness of South Asians living in the United States. For example, a memorandum released by Obama's presidential campaign included references to former presidential candidate Senator Hillary Clinton and the Indian American community's financial influence in her campaign. The document labeled Senator Clinton as "Hillary Clinton (D-Punjab)" and discussed her "[p]ersonal, [f]inancial, and [p]olitical [t]ies [w]ith India." It also implied that Senator Clinton's financial support from the Indian American community was of concern, and could lead to lost jobs or a weaker economy due to outsourcing.

The memorandum from Obama's campaign troubled leaders in the community because it blamed Indian Americans for the outsourcing of jobs abroad. In addition, labeling Senator Clinton as a representative of Punjab implied that she was being influenced by foreign entities, and that South Asians in the United States prioritized interests of their home countries over those of the United States. Obama's campaign later apologized for the memo, stating that it "was not a memo that reflected [his] views or [his] attitudes, and didn't reflect [his] long-standing friendship with the Indian-American community."

On the Republican side, in September 2007, former presidential candidate Senator John McCain remarked in an interview that the prospect of a Muslim candidate for President made him uncomfortable. When asked whether a Muslim candidate would be able to lead the country, Senator McCain stated: "[S]ince this nation was founded primarily on Christian principles . . . personally, I prefer someone who I know who has a solid grounding in my faith. But that doesn't mean that I'm sure that someone who is Muslim would not make a good president. I don't say that we would rule out under any circumstances someone of a different faith. I just would—I just feel that that's an important part of our qualifications to lead." Senator McCain later attempted to clarify, stating, "I would vote for a Muslim if he or she was the candidate best able to lead the country and defend our political values."

Xenophobic rhetoric made by elected officials and public figures at the local, state, or national levels can produce several consequences: it can chill civic and political participation by minority communities and new

American voters, put community members in the position of proving their loyalty and "American-ness," and send conflicting messages to the growing pool of new voters in today's diverse electorate.

COURTING THE NEW ELECTORATE

In recent years, political parties have observed that South Asians are a potential source of new, influential voters, as well as gatekeepers to financial resources and campaign support. A new model of South Asian-centered political participation emerged in 2004, and matured with the 2008 and 2012 elections. In the 2004 elections, South Asians for Kerry organized political fund-raisers, including the first South Asian fund-raiser to net $1 million for a presidential candidate, phone banking, and canvassing activities targeting South Asians around the country. In the 2008 and 2012 presidential elections, groups such as South Asians for Obama and to a lesser extent, South Asians for McCain and South Asians for Romney, were active in fund-raising and registering South Asian voters, as well as providing input into policy priorities. In 2014, the Republican Party began an outreach effort tailored to Asian Americans in order to shore up the demographic of minority voters that seem disenchanted with its priorities.

Simultaneously, nonpartisan and community-based initiatives reached South Asian voters through larger-scale voter outreach, registration, and mobilization efforts. Groups such as South Asian Americans Leading Together (SAALT), a national nonprofit organization that addresses issues affecting South Asians through a social change framework, developed a range of voter education materials for dissemination around the country. At the local level, Chhaya CDC in New York City worked with a coalition of Asian and South Asian groups in Queens to increase voter registration and mobilization, and the South Asian Network in Southern California launched an outreach effort called *DesiVote* to raise awareness about the provision of Hindi ballots as well as encourage voters to make it to the polls on Election Day.

What's Ahead for South Asian Communities?

South Asians' voting behavior should be examined in light of broader civic actions, especially given that there are still large segments of South Asians who are unable to vote. A broader context reveals how South Asian voters are influenced in terms of the political parties with which they affiliate and for whom they ultimately vote.

For example, South Asians have become involved in the civic and political process in many ways. Civic participation by South Asians has taken many forms, including naturalization and voting, running for elected office, serving on local governmental and educational commissions and committees, and becoming involved with the infrastructure of political campaigns. Moreover, many South Asians have become more attuned to political issues, especially in the post-9/11 environment. South Asians have developed views and opinions on issues such as civil rights, immigration, and national security.

In the years ahead, it is likely that South Asians will comprise a larger part of the Asian American electorate. South Asian voters might even become important swing voters in certain parts of the country such as Queens County, New York, where they comprise a large segment of the population or vote similarly as other Asian or immigrant voters. Political parties that seek to court South Asian voters can be successful only if they also demonstrate their genuine interest in and support of issues that matter to this community. Anti-immigrant rhetoric and policies are likely going to move South Asian voters away from a particular candidate or party.

South Asian voters, donors, and political candidates will continue influence the state of the American electorate, domestic and international policies, and U.S. values. Programs to strengthen voter engagement and mobilization will buttress this new electorate to become a powerful force in the American political landscape.

NOTES

1. Deepa Iyer is senior fellow at the Center of Social Inclusion. A lawyer, writer, and activist, she served as the executive director of South Asian Americans Leading Together (SAALT) for nearly 10 years. In this article, I draw upon previous writing with Priya Murthy found at Iyer, Deepa and Murthy, Priya (2009), "Courting the South Asian Vote: One Step Forward, Two Steps Back," *Journal of Civil Rights and Economic Development*: Vol. 24: Iss. 2, Article 2. Available at: http://scholarship.law.stjohns.edu/jcred/vol24/iss2/2.

2. A Demographic Snapshot of South Asians in the United States, compiled by SAALT (July 2012), U.S. Census Bureau. Last accessed at www.saalt.org.

3. Members of the South Asian diaspora include individuals who trace their ancestry to Bangladesh, Bhutan, India, the Maldives, Nepal, Pakistan, and Sri Lanka. The community also includes members of the South Asian diaspora—past generations of South Asians who originally settled in other parts of the world, including Africa, Canada, the Caribbean, Europe, the Middle East, and other parts of Asia and the Pacific Islands.

4. U.S. Census Bureau; Demographic Factsheet produced by SAALT and the Asian American Federation (July 2012).

5. Ibid., ii.

6. http://csii.usc.edu/RockTheNaturalizedVote_maps.html; http://csii.usc.edu/documents/Naturalization_and_Voting_Age_Population_web.pdf

7. This chapter focuses on exit polls conducted by the Asian American Legal Defense and Education Fund (AALDEF) in 2006, 2008, 2010, and 2012, and the National Asian American Survey (NAAS).

8. On November 7, 2006, AALDEF and its partners conducted a nonpartisan, multilingual exit poll of over 4,700 Asian American voters in 23 cities across nine states (New York, New Jersey, Massachusetts, Michigan, Pennsylvania, Maryland, Virginia, Illinois, and Washington) and the District of Columbia. The poll questionnaire was available in English and nine Asian languages. In 2006, 27 percent of the surveyed voters were of South Asian descent.

9. AALDEF and its partners conducted a nonpartisan, multilingual exit poll of 16,665 Asian American voters who voted in the presidential election in 2008. The survey took place in 11 states (New York, New Jersey, Massachusetts, Pennsylvania, Michigan, Illinois, Virginia, Maryland, Texas, Nevada, and Louisiana), and the District of Columbia. 5,204 South Asians completed the AALDEF survey.

10. On November 6, 2012, AALDEF and its partners conducted a nonpartisan, multilingual exit poll of 9,096 Asian American voters at 81 poll sites in 38 cities across 14 states (California, Florida, Georgia, Illinois, Louisiana, Maryland, Massachusetts, Michigan, Nevada, New Jersey, New York, Pennsylvania, Texas, and Virginia) and the District of Columbia. The poll was conducted in English and 11 Asian languages. Thirty percent of the respondents were of South Asian descent.

11. The National Asian American Survey is a scientific, independent and nonpartisan effort to understand the political opinions of Asian Americans and Pacific Islanders in the United States. In 2012, the NAAS conducted 3,376 interviews.

12. Ramakrishnan and Lee, *Policy Priorities and Issue Preferences of Asian Americans and Pacific Islanders*, National Asian American Survey, 2012.

13. *Consent Decree in U.S. v. City of Hamtramck, MI (2000)*, accessible at http://www.justice.gov/crt/about/vot/sec_2/hamtramck_cd.pdfw

14. 2012 Asian American Vote (AALDEF).

Chapter 11

Voting Patterns among Pacific Islanders

Peggy Spitzer Christoff

This chapter describes the constitutional and legal rules throughout American history that have, at times, restricted, and at other times, allowed Pacific Islanders access to the polls, and it charts the shifting social and political values of Pacific Islanders in the United States and its territories.

There are at least seven ways Pacific Islanders have been identified and categorized in the United States: by ethnicity, demographics (in terms of languages spoken), geography (rural/urban/suburban, military bases, and neighborhoods), family history, social status, political history (relating to colonialism), and cultural practices. Because group identities overlap somewhat, the classification system for Pacific Islanders in the United States and its territories is fluid. In 2010, the United States Census Bureau recognized 16 primary Pacific Island ethnic groups: Carolinian, Chamorro, Chuukese, Fijian, Guamanian, Hawaiian, Kosraean, Marshallese, Native Hawaiian, Niuean, Palauan, Pohneian, Samoan, Takelauan, Tongan, and Yapese. Before 2000, the Bureau classified all of these as "Asian." Since 2000, in order to incorporate both race and ethnicity, the Bureau configured a Native Hawaiian and Pacific Islander (NHPI) classification scheme.[1]

The 2011 U.S. Census estimated that 1.2 million NHPIs resided within the United States, representing 0.4 percent of the U.S. population. Roughly half lived in Hawaii and California, 355,816 and 286,145, respectively. As Table 11.1 shows, other states have experienced NHPI population growth,

Table 11.1
U.S. Census Bureau Data on Populations, 2010 and 2012

State	2010	2012	% Change
Alabama	3,169	5,914	86.6
Alaska	5,515	11,154	102.2
Arizona	13,415	25,106	87.1
Arkansas	3,129	7,849	150.8
California	221,458	286,145	29.2
Colorado	10,153	15,200	49.7
Connecticut	4,076	5,397	32.4
Delaware	671	1,216	81.2
District of Columbia	785	1,320	68.2
Florida	23,998	39,914	66.3
Georgia	9,689	15,577	60.8
Hawaii	282,667	355,816	25.9
Idaho	2,847	5,094	78.9
Illinois	11,848	13,546	14.3
Indiana	4,367	6,385	46.2
Iowa	2,196	3,847	75.2
Kansas	3,117	4,938	58.4
Kentucky	3,162	5,111	61.6
Louisiana	3,237	4,879	50.7
Maine	792	988	24.7
Maryland	6,179	9,826	59
Massachusetts	8,704	10,257	17.8
Michigan	7,276	9,348	28.5
Minnesota	5,867	6,206	5.8
Mississippi	1,901	2,776	46
Missouri	6,635	11,296	70.2
Montana	1,077	1,732	60.8
Nebraska	1,733	2,823	62.9
Nevada	16,234	32,848	102.3
New Hampshire.	777	1,160	49.3
New Jersey	10,065	12,999	29.2
New Mexico	3,069	4,698	53.1
New York	28,612	36,423	27.3
North Carolina	8,574	14,774	72.3
North Dakota	475	782	64.6
Ohio	6,984	10,525	50.7
Oklahoma	5,123	8,206	60.2
Oregon	16,019	25,785	61
Pennsylvania	8,790	12,424	41.3
Rhode Island	1,783	2,260	26.8
South Carolina	3,778	5,880	55.6
South Dakota	556	920	65.5
Tennessee	4,587	7,785	69.7

(continued)

Table 11.1 (continued)

State	2010	2012	% Change
Texas	29,094	47,646	63.8
Utah	21,367	36,777	72.1
Vermont	308	465	51
Virginia	9,984	15,422	54.5
Washington	42,761	70,322	64.5
West Virginia	887	1,254	41.4
Wisconsin	4,310	5,117	18.7
Wyoming	614	1,063	73.1
Puerto Rico	2,894	2,628	−9.2

Source: The % change was calculated from figures provided in the 2010 and 2012 U.S. Census Bureau reports.

including Washington, Texas, Florida, New York, Utah, Nevada, Oregon, Alaska, and Arkansas.

In 2010, approximately 35 percent of NHPIs were under the age of 18. Since then, those who have become eligible to vote have increased and it is sure to be the case that population trends will continue in an upward direction. In fact, population data reveal a 40 percent growth rate among the NHPI population between 2000 and 2010, compared to an overall 10 percent growth rate of the total population in the United States. Much of this increase is due to migration from the Pacific Islands, in particular, American Samoa and Tonga.

Historically, the U.S. government has refused to recognize the sovereignty of Pacific Islanders. America's interest in controlling the region began at the end of the 19th century and took the form of denying sovereignty to the U.S. territories of American Samoa, Guam, Hawaii, and the Northern Mariana Islands. Once NHPIs began to migrate to the United States in large numbers at the turn of the 21st century, community leaders began to identify communities in the United States mainland and involve NHPIs in the political process. Key factors that affect the level of political participation are education, income, health care, and English language fluency. The Office of Minority Health reported the following:[2]

Educational Attainment: In 2010, 88.5 percent of Native Hawaiians/Pacific Islanders, alone or in combination, have at least a high school diploma, as compared to 91 percent for whites; 20.1 percent of Native Hawaiians/Pacific Islanders have a bachelor's degree or higher compared to 31 percent of whites; 5.3 percent of Native Hawaiians/Pacific Islanders have graduate degrees while the white percentage is 11.7 percent; and 30 percent of Native Hawaiians/Pacific Islanders speak a language other than English at home.

Economics: According to the 2010 Census, the average Native Hawaiian/Pacific Islander family median income was $59,521 compared to $67,892 for non-Hispanic White families. In 2010, the U.S. Census Bureau reported that 17 percent of Native Hawaiian/Pacific Islander families were living at the poverty level, while 10.6 percent of non-Hispanic Whites experienced the same condition.

Insurance Coverage: In 2010, 60.9 percent of Native Hawaiians/Pacific Islanders used private health insurance as compared to 75.1 percent of non-Hispanic whites. Also in 2010, 28.1 percent of Native Hawaiians/Pacific Islanders relied on public health insurance compared to 28.0 percent of non-Hispanic whites. Finally, 17.4 percent of Native Hawaiians/Pacific Islanders, in comparison to 10.9 percent of non-Hispanic whites, were uninsured.

English Language Fluency: As of 2010, among the entire population of Pacific Islanders, 71 percent speak English; 29 percent speak English as well as their native language; and only 8 percent have limited English proficiency. Thus, as represented in Figure 11.1, through

Figure 11.1
Percentage of Pacific Islander Population with English-Language Proficiency (2010)

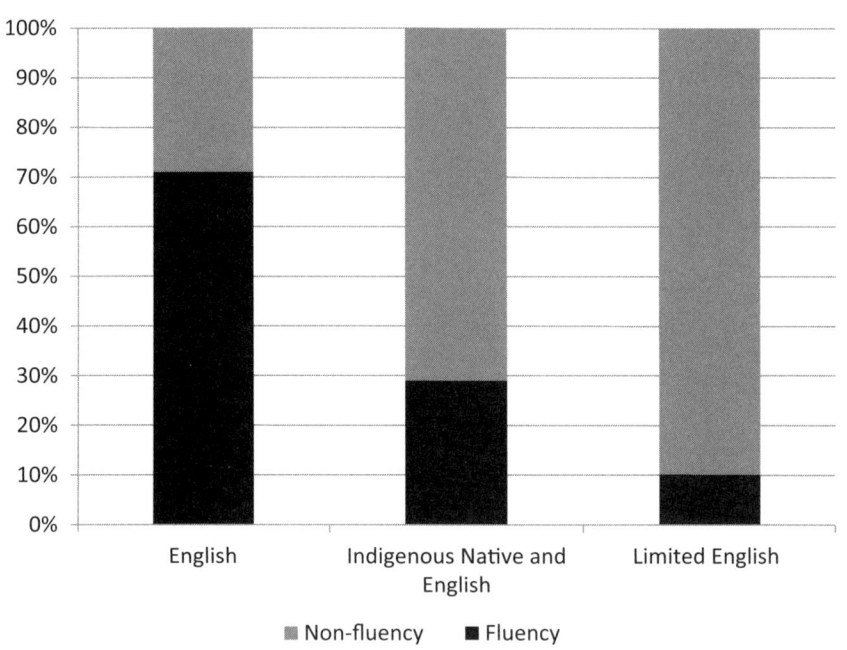

the lens of voter education, NHPIs are in the process of acquiring the language tools necessary to become involved in local, state, and national politics.

A report issued by a coalition of the Asian American Justice Center, Asian and Pacific Islander American Vote, and National Asian American Survey (NAAS), noted that NHPI voter turnout in 2012 for the presidential election was relatively high, close to 80 percent; and that there was an increase in political participation among NHPI communities in the United States. Still, the report noted that NHPI communities are suspicious of the American government's intentions vis-à-vis sovereignty for the Pacific Islands.

A brief history of American involvement in Hawaii, American Samoa, Guam, and the Northern Marianas reveals the specific ways that the U.S. government has marginalized NHPIs both in the United States and in the territories. I will also discuss the extent to which elected officials in Hawaii and the Pacific territories represent the interests of NHPIs in the U.S. Congress.

HISTORICAL CONTEXT

Hawaii

Hawaii has been of interest to Europeans since the late 1700s when Captain James Cook inadvertently discovered the "the Sandwich Islands," which he named after the British 4th Lord of Sandwich. The discovery led to increased European travel to and explorations of the islands.[3] By 1810, with the help of European advisors, King Kamehameha unified the eight major islands, and nearly a decade later, on the advice of his stepmother, Ka'ahumanu, Kamehameha II abolished *kapu*, the ancient system of Polynesian rule. Europeans accelerated their efforts to govern, however, by the mid-1800s, King Kamehameha III challenged the European initiatives, especially those represented by Catholic missionaries who sought to affiliate with the wealthy Polynesian monarchy. The British navy also attempted to claim the Hawaiian Islands but its mission failed, and King Kamehameha III exerted Hawaii's sovereignty, which is represented today in Hawaii's state motto: "The life of the land is perpetuated in righteousness."

The Reciprocity Treaty of 1875 allowed the United States to obtain sugar, duty free, in exchange for developing and dividing Hawaii's agricultural base into sugarcane plantations. Under the treaty, Pearl Harbor and Ford Island were ceded to the United States, and Hawaii was defined "on paper" as an independent and sovereign nation. Twelve years later, the Bayonet Constitution stripped King Kalakaua of his imperial authority and imposed strict regulations on voting rights, allowing only those who owned property and had a substantial income to vote. According to Kioni and Keoloha, new voting rights were so stringent—and so carefully constructed—that elections were effectively controlled by the white community, referred to as the *haole*. In ranking order, the House of Nobles controlled the cabinet, and because the cabinet controlled the king, Kalakaua was forced to sign the reciprocity treaty and give the United States government full rights to Pearl Harbor.[4]

By 1893, a European and American "Committee of Safety" was formed to annex Hawaii. It was not until 1921 that the " Hawaiian Homes Commission Act" (HHCA), passed by Congress and signed into law by President Warren Harding (chapter 42, 42 Stat. 108), allowed native Hawaiians, that is, those who had a blood quantum level of 50 percent, to lease land through a government-sponsored homesteading program.[5]

When Japan attacked Pearl Harbor in 1941, the United States imposed martial law on Hawaii, which lasted until the end of World War II. Less than a decade later, the Democratic Revolution in Hawaii lobbied for statehood and, on March 18, 1959, President Eisenhower signed the "Hawaii Admissions Act." Ninety-three percent of the total population on Hawaii (mostly white Americans and other foreigners) favored statehood status.[6] Only 15 percent of the population (76,620) was Native Hawaiian.

Until the 1960s, the U.S. President appointed all governors and judges on Hawaii. A movement to honor and promote Native Hawaiian cultural identity began with a heightened awareness of racism in the United States. In 1993, Senators Daniel Akaka and Daniel Inouye spearheaded legislation and encouraged Congress to pass an "Apology Resolution" in which the U.S. government expressed regret to Native Hawaiians for the deprivation of their rights to self-determination. Subsequently, the "Native Hawaiian Government Reorganization Act of 2009" (S1011/HR2314) recognized Native Hawaiians as first settlers, in a way that was similar to the recognition of Native American Indian tribes in the American West. Currently, the Office of Hawaiian Affairs (OHA) supports cultural and Hawaiian language immersion programs and organizes the community to preserve and protect the rights of Native Hawaiians.[7]

American Samoa

In the present day, more American Samoans live overseas than live on the islands.[8] Those who returned to American Samoa did so to rejoin family members and because they could not find jobs on the U.S. mainland.[9] Traditionally, the chiefly *Fa'amatai* system held society together in which family connections and kinship formed the basis of governance. Similar to Hawaii's ancient *kapu* ruling system, the *Fa'amatai* system was radically altered by European colonialism, beginning with French explorers in the 1700s and continuing after the Congregationalist London Missionary

Society exerted its influence in the 1800s. In 1879, the United States took possession of the eastern half of Samoa where it established a naval coaling station in Pago Pago Bay. Twenty years later, in a three-party agreement among Germany, the United States, and the United Kingdom, American Samoa was officially established.

While the Samoan Congregational Church became an *indigenous* religious institution in the South Pacific, *institutional* claims to territory were established with the 1929 Ratification Act. This act was the basic constitutional document that provided all islands of American Samoa, including Tutuila and Manu'a, with a government of civil judicial and military powers *as directed by the U.S. president*. As a territory under U.S. law in 1951, Executive Order 10264 delegated responsibility to governing the territory to the U.S. secretary of the interior. After World War II, many American Samoans began migrating to Hawaii and California, became even more interested in pursuing career paths in the military, and enlisted in the U.S. military as a way of developing closer ties to the United States.[10] The migrations were based on family connections. Once a community was established, often near military bases or factories, other family and church members followed. One negative result was that subsistence agriculture, which was a primary source of income in American Samoa, disappeared.[11]

In 1966, the secretary of the interior issued The Constitution of American Samoa, which was approved in general elections by the majority of Samoan voters. By 1983, the spirit of the Samoan constitution was diluted with the passage of a law by the U.S. Congress that stipulated that *only* the United States Congress could amend the constitution. Since 1983, the secretary of the interior holds all power as, in the eyes of many Samoan residents, "a benevolent dictator." Correspondingly, the constitution is recognized as "a giant deceit." One result is a dramatic increase in migration to the United States. American Samoans have developed a direct migration line from Pago Pago to Los Angeles, San Diego, and Salt Lake City.[12]

Guam and the Northern Marianas

The culmination of ethnic identity, economic interests, and to a lesser extent religious zeal, has influenced voting patterns in Guam as well as in the unincorporated dependent territory of the Northern Marianas. The Chamorros people are considered the indigenous population.[13] According to Spickard, Guam became an American colonial project in 1898 when the U.S. Navy sought to Americanize Chamorros men by introducing organized sports. The Navy characterized Chamorros as "degenerate and potentially troublesome."[14] Eventually the region was divided politically into the U.S. territory of Guam and the U.S. Commonwealth of the Northern Mariana Islands.

In what is now acknowledged as an extension of Manifest Destiny, the U.S. Navy captured Guam in 1898 to use it as a way station in the Pacific.

Because U.S. naval history fundamentally is tied to claims to the Philippines, Guam became an island naval station or jumping-off point. Between 1941 and 1944, Guam's occupation by the Japanese led the Chamorros people to regard the American military favorably because they drove out the Japanese. One particular point is that the Japanese military had forced Chamorros women to serve as "comfort women" or sex slaves.

As Guam later became a forward operation base for the U.S. Navy and Air Force, island residents became resentful of the U.S. military's attempts to dominate and control Guam. Until 1950, the U.S. military opposed any type of civilian government in Guam. By 1952, the Immigration and Nationality Act (Section 307) granted U.S. citizenship "to all persons born on the island after April 11, 1899." However, Camacho notes, colonial and wartime experiences fueled long-standing tensions among the Chamorros population. Furthermore, commemorations honoring American involvement in Guam have masked differences within the community and have made it difficult to address the needs of those who are marginalized.[15]

Guam developed a limited, sovereign identity. In 1968, the Elective Governor Act (Public Law 90–497) specified that Guamanian residents could elect their own governor and lieutenant governor. In 1972, the Guam Virgin Islands Delegate Act allowed one delegate each in the U.S. Congress's House of Representatives to have a voice in debates and vote in committees but not to vote on the floor of the House. Several attempts to draft a constitution led to the passage of the Guam Delegate Act and the creation of a status commission. This resulted in the formation of the Second Political Status Commission in 1975, the Commission on Self-Determination in 1980, and the Commission on Decolonization in 1996. The latter investigated various options for Guam's political status and provided for the establishment of a public education system. Trask states: "Sovereignty, for us, promises the institutional and psychological opposite of racism. . . . Sovereignty is the assertion that what we are—culturally, emotionally, and physically—is what we prefer to be."[16]

The Asian economic crisis of the late 1990s had grave consequences for Guam's tourism industry. Guam was important to the United States primarily as a military installation in the Pacific Ocean, especially after the United States moved its military operations to Guam from the Philippines. In 2014, a U.S. objective is to relocate military forces from Okinawa to Guam, but the local Guamanian population has resisted this plan. On the other hand, a new generation of the Chamorro population is less interested than previous generations in preserving traditional culture and more interested in assimilating to American culture, resulting in increased migration to the United States.

Rondilla noted that a pan-ethnic Pacific Islander group identity, separate from an Asian identity, is likely to endure. Unlike Filipinos, Pacific Islanders have no cultural ties or common ancestry with Asia. Linkages do exist, however, because of a related history of American colonizing projects, first in the Philippines and then throughout the Pacific region.[17] Rondilla cited the views of political activist, Lemuel F. Ignacio, noting that NHPIs formed a bloc with Asian Americans in order to confront power structures in the United States.[18] Rondilla wrote, "Almost all prominent leaders and scholars of so-called Asian and Pacific Islander America are descendants from mainland East Asia. Filipino and Pacific Islander voices go almost unheard."[19]

In a study published by the NAAS titled "Public Opinion of a Growing Electorate: Asian Americans and Pacific Islanders in 2012," 62 percent of Native Hawaiians and 54 percent of Samoans are "likely voters."[20] A growing number of NHPIs live in the battleground state of Nevada. One particular question to be addressed is whether congressional delegates or elected officials in the U.S. House of Representatives and the U.S. Senate represent the interests of NHPIs.

ISSUES, DELEGATES, AND ELECTED OFFICIALS

As noted earlier, U.S. government policies historically have not acknowledged the equal status of native Hawaiians. Residents in the U.S.-controlled territories of Guam, American Samoa, and the Northern Marianas Islands do not vote in U.S. elections though they do elect nonvoting delegates to the U.S. House of Representatives. In order to identify shifting social and political values of Pacific Islanders in the United States and its territories, this section examines the platform issues of the total, that is, the 34 U.S. congressional delegates and representatives between 1900 and 2013.[21]

Twenty-six of these officials represented Hawaii, three represented American Samoa, four represented Guam, and one represented the Northern Marianas. Eleven of the 34 delegates self-identified as Native Hawaiian and/or Pacific Islander. Seven representatives were women: five were Democrats and two were Republicans. The only female delegate outside of Hawaii was from Guam.

As of 2014, three American Samoan delegates represented American Samoa and one American Samoan represented Hawaii; three Chamorros delegates were from Guam and one was from the Northern Marianas Islands; and three Native Hawaiians served constituencies in Hawaii, two prior to statehood and one after statehood, both beginning in the House of Representatives and then moving to the Senate.

One particularly difficult question is how to identify platform positions that address the concerns or priorities of NHPIs. It is not clear whether independence for American Samoa, Guam, the Northern Marianas, and Hawaii would serve to preserve or isolate so-called indigenous cultures. It is possible that programs that attempt to celebrate ethnic traditions are interpreted in ways that exoticize or infantilize and further marginalize

NHPI communities. On a broader scale, programs that reform educational systems throughout the state or territories may increase the number of skilled jobs and have a positive impact on the NHPI population.

There does appear to be one natural break, or shift, in social and political trends. At one end are the 16 politicians in Hawaii who began their public careers between 1900 and 1965. At the other end are the 18 who were in Congress between 1970 and 2013—four delegates from American Samoa, four delegates from Guam, nine congressional representatives (including both houses) from Hawaii and one delegate from the Northern Marianas.

VOTERS AND ISSUES

Prior to 1970, Native Hawaiians were the only indigenous people of the Pacific region who were defined as part of the American electorate. The U.S. Congress did not grant Guam and American Samoa delegate status until 1970 and 1973, respectively. The remaining U.S. territory, the Northern Marianas, did not have a congressional delegate until 2008.

Between 1970 and 2013, U.S. congressional delegates from the Pacific region were ethnically diverse, with five Caucasians, four Asians, and nine NHPIs (including American Samoans, Native Hawaiians, and Chamorros). This is in stark contrast to the earlier period between 1900 and 1969 when, in representing Hawaii, Caucasians held 10 congressional seats, Asian Americans 4 seats, and Native Hawaiians 2 seats.

Another shift in NHPI representation occurred on the U.S. mainland in the late 1970s, when American Samoans began to migrate to the United States. This migration started with the relocation of individuals who worked on U.S. military bases; and was followed by a surge of extended family members. In fact in 2014, more American Samoans lived and voted in the state of Utah than in American Samoa.

Using the 34 congressional delegates who served the Pacific region in the U.S. Congress between 1900 and up to the present day as a baseline, it is possible to identify the types of issues and programs that were most likely of interest to NHPIs. While longitudinal data on NHPI voting patterns are not available, it is possible to examine the types of programs promoted by congressional delegates representing the Pacific region from 1900 to the present day and draw some conclusions about specific issues of concern to NHPI communities. In some cases, the "issues" reflect specific historic changes, such as the establishment of Hawaiian statehood in 1959; in other cases, the issues reveal gradual shifts in interests and priorities, such as championing voting rights among indigenous people.

In the early period prior to Hawaiian statehood, the Republican (and the Home Rule) Party dominated, thereafter and in line with the 1960s civil rights movement on the U.S. mainland, congressional delegates represented the Democratic Party. Democrats eventually outnumbered Republicans as congressional delegates by a margin of approximately 2–1 (22 Democrats to 10 Republicans, and one from the Home Rule Party).

In chronological order, from 1900 to the present day, seven issue areas appeared to generate the greatest interest: (1) maintaining territorial sovereignty/integrity in the Pacific region; (2) protection of the region vis-à-vis U.S. military presence and national security; (3) replacing Christian-based institutions with secular social welfare programs; (4) influencing the establishment of local political institutions; (5) drafting business and economic development plans for the Asia-Pacific region; (6) passing government programs addressing the quality of life (e.g., from education to health care) throughout NHPI communities and, combined with this, (7) attempting to reach out to underrepresented ethnic and indigenous groups. A more detailed explanation of these issues follows, along with a graphic representation in Figure 11.2, of changes in priorities and interests.

Maintaining territorial sovereignty/integrity was the first "issue" to emerge in the early 1900s. Initially, the public debate focused on whether Hawaii should become a U.S. state, and how to classify indigenous people on the islands who could lease or own land and consequently vote in

Figure 11.2
Issues and Programs by Congressional Delegates Representing NHPI Constituencies between 1900 and 2013

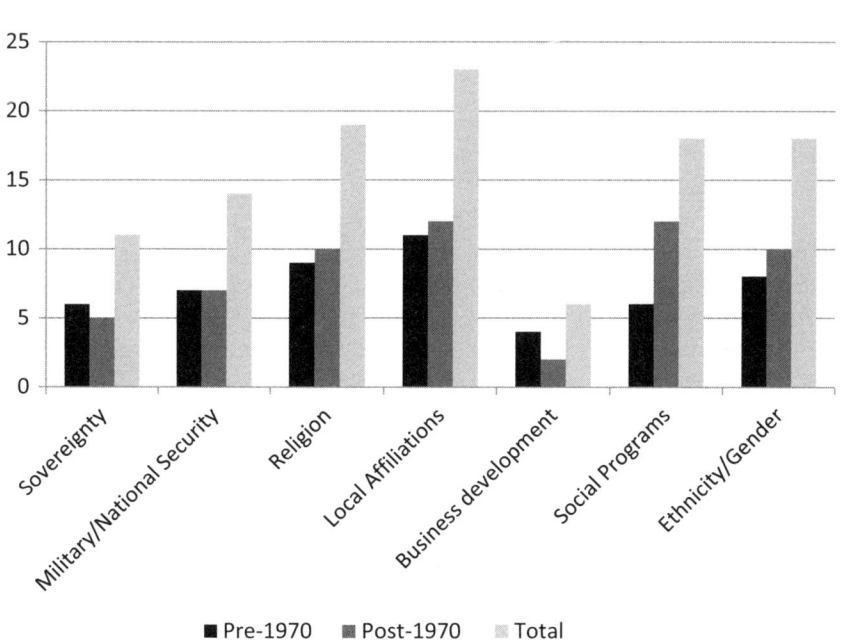

elections. By the 1980s, the issue of sovereignty had a different meaning. The central debate became how to acknowledge and maintain indigenous cultural traditions and incorporate diverse groups into the political landscape. Within this, the notion of inclusion was intended to ensure greater transparency in the election process.

Beginning at the turn of the 20th century and into the present day, protection of the Asia Pacific region vis-à-vis U.S. military presence on the islands was a major concern. In fact, 42 percent of the congressional delegates representing the Pacific region served in the military, including the U.S. Navy and Army and the all-Nisei 442nd Regimental Combat Team, during World War II. There is a continued commitment through government programs to grant educational and other benefits to active-duty military.

Since the turn of the 20th century, NHPI communities have been influenced by Christian missions. In the early period, Christian missions were the only "institutions" that addressed the native population's needs, particularly Roman Catholic, United Methodist, and Disciples of Christ missionaries, who established schools. After 1970, identification with religious values and institutions on the islands continued to enhance the credentials of congressional delegates. However, since 1990, religiously conservative Christian groups that support the Defense of Marriage Act and banning gay marriage have migrated to the United States, for example, from American Samoa to Mormon communities in Utah. In the Pacific islands, there appears to be a relaxed acknowledgment of the diverse religious backgrounds among congressional delegates, who were Congregationalists, Mormons, nondenominational Christians, Buddhists, Jews, and Hindus, perhaps reflecting a partial understanding of the importance of secular democratic societies in establishing public and governmental institutions. Although they still provide many important services, especially in private education, Catholic and Protestant institutions are considered by some as vestiges of early 20th century colonization efforts.

Over time, the issue that has been consistently important to the electorate is ensuring that congressional representatives have a track record supporting and developing state and local governments. This means that, in order to be considered credible to local residents, congressional representatives must have a degree of fluency in native languages and dialects; have experience holding a public office such as in the State House or Senate, as attorney general, or in law enforcement; actively promote tourism that is a fundamental source of revenue, which also acknowledges the importance of the local culture and customs; and have experience with local radio and print media to build constituencies throughout the islands.

Drafting business and economic development plans for the Asia-Pacific region initially was an important issue because it demonstrated to the U.S. mainland that Hawaii, Guam, American Samoa, and the Northern Marianas could be viable economies without depending upon massive infusions of U.S. aid. Resulting programs addressed the economic climate and encouraged the success of minority-owned businesses and other small business ventures. An additional component of the local economy remains supporting the mainland's initiatives vis-à-vis free trade in Asia, which is a double-edged sword. On the one hand, the Pacific region's traditional economy depended on long-term trading relations with individual Asian countries, but on the other hand, NHPI populations suffered economically from fluctuations that naturally occurred as a result of "free trade" policies.

By far, the most significant issue over time for NHPI populations is ensuring that social programs increase the quality of life for all sectors of society. Prior to U.S. civil rights legislation, social programs in the Pacific region focused primarily on developing schools and civil service institutions, including health care facilities, early childhood education, and women's education equality. But by the 1970s, the number of "quality of life" programs burgeoned to address the environment, including submerged land legislation, consumer protection, the aging population, veterans' education through the G.I. bill, food stamps and in-state college tuition on par with the U.S. mainland, Job Corps and other labor rights concerns, immigration, and marriage rights.

Finally and most important for extending voting rights to minority populations in the Pacific region, there has been an increase among congressional representatives that brought more NHPIs into the political process. In the early 1900s, it took the form of ensuring that a percentage of ethnic Hawaiians occupied positions in local government and distinguishing U.S. presence as different from the "civilizing" colonial initiatives that unfortunately characterized America's relations in the Philippines. In the early 1900s in Hawaii, there was controversy around whether blood quantum levels could be used to classify an individual as "native Hawaiian," and whether the levels should determine who could lease land and vote in elections. By the 1970s, as the number of Asian-Pacific congressional delegates from different ethnic backgrounds, including Chinese American, Japanese American, Samoan, and Chamorran increased, the earlier issue became irrelevant vis-à-vis voting rights. Furthermore, NHPIs have become *somewhat* more involved in the political process. Problems remain, however, with developing and implementing voter education programs among populations that were historically disenfranchised and did not have access to basic education and economic advancement opportunities.

CONCLUSIONS ABOUT VOTER ENGAGEMENT

A 2002 report, "Asian American Electoral Participation," highlighted the discrepancies in gathering data on voting patterns. An election analyst for the Congressional Research Service at the Library of Congress, Kevin J. Coleman, noted that, in 1990, the Census Bureau used a broad designation,

Asian and Pacific Islander, to include many different ethnic and national identities—Chinese, Filipino, Japanese, Asian Indian, Korean, Vietnamese, Cambodian, Hmong, Laotian, Thai, Other Asian, Hawaiian, Samoan, Guamanian, and Other Pacific Islander.[22] This group was negligible, however, in terms of affecting electoral outcomes. By 1998, the Asian Pacific American (APA) population was engaged in the American political process;[23] however, data indicate that voter turnout rates were comparatively low for four reasons. First, 70 percent of APAs were born outside of the United States and were not yet U.S. citizens; second, immigrants generally did not trust political involvement, perhaps as a carryover from inhibitions in their home countries; third, there was a low level of English language fluency; and fourth, as a relatively young population (the median age was around 30 years old), APAs were among those who traditionally did not vote.[24]

A more recent publication, *Behind the Numbers: Post-Election Survey of Asian American and Pacific Islander Voters in 2012*, a collaborative effort of the Asian American Justice Center, Asian and Pacific Islander American Vote, and NAAS, noted that community organizations significantly increased mobilization efforts for the 2012 election and that the communities' population growth led them to become more politically active.[25]

An interview with Alisi Tulua, of Empowering Pacific Islander Communities, revealed that a great deal of work was done to reach eligible voters.[26] In addition to encouraging people to vote, community organizations focused on improving knowledge of the voting process, especially targeting the new immigrant community.

In response to the question of how community organizations knew where APAs had settled in the United States, Ms. Tulua responded that cross-country connections began during World War II when significant numbers of Pacific Islanders first migrated from Guam and American Samoa. The "community" expanded in the early 1960s with a second wave of migrants from Fiji and Tonga. Migrants often settled around U.S. military bases, and because the numbers were rather small, she noted that it was relatively easy to locate and contact Pacific Islanders. Migrants from Micronesia settled in Arkansas, for example, to work at the Tyson Food's chicken processing plant. Many first families settled in Nevada, commonly known as the Ninth Pacific Island because of the diaspora, Utah, including Mormons from American Samoa, Texas, Washington, Oregon, and California.

Both the authors of *Behind the Numbers* and community organizer Tulua note that Pacific Islanders did not affiliate with one particular political party, though in the 2012 election, most supported President Obama. In grassroots organizing to "get out the vote," Tulua noticed that many of the younger and well-educated Pacific Islanders are attracted to Christian agendas and generally favor issues promoted by the Republican Party. For example, many supported Proposition 8's ban on same-sex marriage in California. Other issues that seemed to draw attention were affirmative action proposals, relating to financial aid for college students, and immigration reforms. In contrast to *Behind the Numbers*, which concluded that "the economy" and "jobs" were high-priority issues, Tulua stated, "Most Pacific Islanders either are independent contractors or labourers and, frankly, don't see jobs and economic security as connected. They are more likely to be interested in voting on highly publicized and controversial issues. There are a few elected officials and community leaders, as well as athletes, who influence public opinion among PIs. Presently, the most visible is Congresswoman Tulsi Gabbard. While PIs never have considered themselves 'Asian,' we are fortunate that many Asian and Asian American organizations, in particular the Asian American Justice Center, reach out to us."

In terms of reaching potential voters in the Pacific Islander community across the United States, Ms. Tulua noted that, in 2012, social media was the best method, particularly Facebook, Instagram, and Twitter. Using social media, Tulua developed an outreach strategy that was replicated by other community organizations to increase Pacific Islander voter turnout. A second highly effective method was contacting church pastors to help register and educate voters, and promote community gatherings. Methods that proved unsuccessful were phone banking and community forums. The Pacific Islander community is spread out across the United States—even to Alaska—and Tulua was surprised to find that the younger generation, primary users of social media, were very active in motivating the older generation to vote.

An interview with Krystal Ka'ai, executive director of the Congressional Asian Pacific American Congress also shed light on key issues in NHPI representation.[27] She noted that NHPIs are overrepresented in the military and in athletics, and that those who migrate to the mainland do so to join family members or to attend college. NHPI populations tend not to be as engaged in the political process; however, issues around sovereignty are vital. In Hawaii, because the monarchy historically supported the voting rights only of landowners, most Native Hawaiians were excluded from the political process. Presently, ballots are in the Hawaiian language in Hawaii, in Chamorro in Guam, and Gagana Samoa in American Samoa. Because migration patterns traditionally have not included an interest in voting, a key link to political participation is through popular figures, including famous athletes and actors/entertainers. In addition, the OHA overturned discriminatory practices, including the use of blood quantum levels to decide who is native Hawaiian, first used in the 1920s and abandoned in the 1970s.

In order to assign appropriate meaning and significance to the constitutional and legal rules and sociopolitical values that influence the voting behavior of NHPIs, this study utilized multiple methods. It was important especially to understand the way in which NHPIs defined "sovereignty" vis-à-vis the U.S. mainland's interests in the Pacific region. Certainly, the indigenous systems of rule and consensus building became less important over time as did NHPI loyalty to colonial-based Christian values and institutions. While NHPIs have been subsumed under the APA voting bloc, deriving resources and influence from the larger organization, those who have not migrated to the mainland still are uniquely psychologically overshadowed by the U.S. government's foreign policy toward Asia. In voting behavior, the consistent affiliation has been with U.S. military objectives and, since the 1970s, recognition of the need for proactive social programs that engage in the political process diverse ethnic groups living in Hawaii and the greater Pacific region. The major issue that retards the process for Guam, American Samoa, and the Northern Marianas, "the elephant in the room," is the nonvoting status of congressional delegates in the U.S. House of Representatives.

NOTES

1. According to Rondilla, unlike Filipinos, Pacific Islanders have no cultural ties and no common ancestry with Asians. However, there is some linkage between Filipinos and other Pacific Islanders: In 1972, a "brown" Asian Caucus was established to represent Filipinos, Guamanians, Hawaiians, and Samoans; Spickard, Rondilla, and Wright, "Pacific Diaspora," 60–61.
2. Information gathered from the Office of Minority Health website (http://minorityhealth.hhs.gov/templates/browse.aspx?lvl=2&lvlID=71).
3. It is believed—though there is no precise documentation—that Polynesians migrated to Hawaii during the Neolithic period. The earliest written records of "Native Hawaiians" are from the late 1700s.
4. Dudley and Agard, "History of Dispossession," in Spickard et al., 309–321.
5. Between 1921 and 1960, a federal agency, the Hawaiian Homes Commission was responsible for administering the HHCA. In 1960, a state agency, the Department of Hawaiian Home Lands, took over these responsibilities and continues to do so.
6. Historians often consider the treatment of Native Hawaiians as similar to that of Native American Indians in the United States.
7. See Office of Hawaiian Affairs, Review of website. http://www.oha.org/. Accessed 15 September 2013.
8. Connell, "Paradise Left?" in Spickard et al., 85.
9. Ibid., 80.
10. Janes, "From Village to City," in Spickard et al., 130.
11. Connell, "Paradise Left?" 78; Janes, "From Village to City," 130.
12. Cowling, "Motivations for Contemporary Tongan Migration," in Spickard et al., 109.
13. In 2000 BC, people moved from Malaysia, Indonesia, and the Philippines migrated to the region. In 1521, Magellan provided the first written documentation of the existence of Pacific Islanders, though not in a positive light: He described them as "thieves." Claimed by Spain in 1565, Jesuit missionaries and traders travelled to Guam and wrote about their encounters with the Chamorro people. It was not until the Mexican Revolution concluded in 1815 that a number of scientists, whalers, and travelers from Russia, France, and England wrote detailed accounts of their encounters.

14. Diaz, "Fight Boys," in Spickard et al., 180–181.
15. See Camacho, "Cultures of Commemoration."
16. Trask, "Pacific Island Women and White Feminism," in Spickard et al., 253.
17. Hunt and Levine, "The Philippines, 1899–1902," in *Arc of Empire*, 10–63.
18. Spickard et al., 60.
19. Ibid., 61.
20. Asian American Justice Center, "Behind the Numbers," 3.
21. Special thanks to Camille Salas, formerly at the Library of Congress, Office of Strategic Initiatives and my research assistant, Luo Luo Fang at Stony Brook University, Department of Asian and Asian American Studies, for their help in developing the following view: http://viewshare.org/share/9bc242d8-1bea-11e3-9ee9-4040e007d488/.
22. Coleman, "Introduction," in Lee, 6.
23. Coleman, "Asian Pacific American Political Participation and Representation in Elective Office," in Lee, 43.
24. One caveat is that the 2000 Census changed the classification system to include both nationality and ethnicity; and respondents were able to self-identify as one or more races. Thus, the data collected from the 1990 census or earlier censuses is not directly comparable to the Census 2000 data.
25. Asian American Justice Center, "Behind the Numbers," 1.
26. Tulua, Program Manager for Empowering Pacific Islander Communities. Interview.
27. Ka'ai, Executive Director of the Congressional Asian Pacific American Congress (CAPAC). Interview.

REFERENCES

Asian American Justice Center. "Behind the Numbers: Post-Election Survey of Asian American and Pacific Islanders Voters in 2012." *Asian Pacific Islander American Vote, and National Asian American Survey*. Arlington, VA: APIAVote, April 2013.

Camacho, Keith L. *Cultures of Commemoration: The Politics of War, Memory and History in the Mariana Islands*. Honolulu: Center for Pacific Islands Studies, School of Pacific and Asian Studies. University of Hawai'i, Maānoa: University of Hawai'i Press, 2011.

Christoff, Peg. "Key Statistics on Voting Behavior among Asian Americans." Last Accessed 15 September 2013. http://www.asiamattersforamerica.org/node/626.

Hunt, Michael H., and Steven I. Levine. *Arc of Empire: America's Wars in Asia from the Philippines to Vietnam*. Chapel Hill: University of North Carolina Press, 2012.

Ka'ai, Krystal. Executive Director of the Congressional Asian Pacific American Caucus. Interview on 13 June 2013.

Lee, John W., ed. *Asian-American Electoral Participation*. New York: Novinka Books, 2002.

Office of Hawaiian Affairs. Late Accessed 15 September 2013. http://www.oha.org/.

Spickard, Paul, Joanne L. Rondilla, and Debbie Hippolite Wright, eds. *Pacific Diaspora: Island Peoples in the United States and Across the Pacific*. Honolulu: University of Hawaii Press, 2002.

Chapter 12

Filipino American Voting

Joaquin Jay Gonzalez III

IS THERE SUCH A THING AS A FILIPINO AMERICAN VOTING BLOC?

Official demographic data point to a "Filipino American voting bloc" that has solidified incrementally during the past century from hundreds to present-day millions. The bloc's existence in the U.S. Census Bureau's statistics began with a mere 160 respondents in 1910, while the 2010 Census revealed that Filipinos numbered 3,416,840, a million more Filipino residents than in the 2000 Census, which is a 44.5 percent jump in a decade. Except for the 1930s, when their population rose by 0.8 percent, the decade-by-decade increases have been notable as seen in Table 12.1.

Because of their increasing numbers, Filipino American (aka FilAm) influence on the ballot box has gained considerable attention from political parties and individual candidates. Political parties are aware that FilAms have the third highest naturalization rate behind Mexico and India—as reported in the U.S. Department of Homeland Security's Yearbook of Immigration Statistics.[1] Filipinos have led all immigrants from Asia in citizenship rates since the 1990s.[2] This is notable considering there are 52 possible U.S. immigrant-originating countries in Asia.

Thus, at naturalization ceremonies in major U.S. cities, many political parties jockey to attract new Filipino voters. They know that the Filipino

Table 12.1
Filipino American Population Rise

Year	Population	Percentage of Change
1910	160	—
1920	5,603	+3,401.9
1930	45,208	+706.9
1940	45,563	+0.8
1950	61,636	+35.3
1960	176,310	+186.1
1970	343,060	+94.6
1980	774,652	+125.8
1990	1,406,770	+81.6
2000	2,364,815	+68.1
2010	3,416,840	+44.5

Source: U.S. Census Bureau.

voter registration rate is higher than the national average and they parallel the U.S. average in going to the polls. Their registration and voting rates are second to the Japanese and the highest among Asian Americans.[3] As new U.S. citizens, Filipinos are also easier to "inform and register" because of their relatively higher English proficiency, political awareness, and educational attainment.

The Filipino Americans' primary source of political information and outreach derives from a mix of mainstream and ethnic FilAm media. Besides their local news channels, many also view FOX News and CNN, while some also watch MSNBC, Al Jazeera, or the BBC. However, a large segment also supplements its cable TV subscriptions with The Filipino Channel (TFC) and wouldn't want to miss the popular "Balitang America" show. The more tech-savvy 1.5th generation[4] and second-generation FilAms gravitate to their Internet and social media sources, including www.inquirer.net and www.gmanetwork.com/news/. At Manilatowns or Asiatowns, FilAm newspapers are readily available at Asian or Filipino restaurants and food outlets, convenience stores and supermarkets, and other commercial places in the community where people gather. The languages are English, Filipino (Tagalog), and Taglish (mix of Tagalog and English).

The stock of eligible FilAm voters is only expected to increase given that they are currently the fourth largest, legal, permanent residence-receiving ("green card") group. Adding to this stock annually are immigrant visa recipients from the 10–15 year backlog waiting in the Philippines. They are lined up to join their American families who have petitioned for them under the "family reunification" provisions of the U.S. Immigration and

Nationality Act of 1965. Hence, the Filipino bloc will continue to surge into the future at a rate of 100,000 annually or one million new Filipino Americans every 10 years.

Given these demographic shifts, Filipinos have established themselves as the second ranked Asian American political bloc after the Chinese. The Filipino population is followed closely by Asian Indians, Vietnamese, Koreans, and Japanese with each group also numbering more than one million. As Asian American numbers grow, so too will their political, economic, and social influences.

From a regional perspective, Filipino Americans are the largest group of Asian Americans in 10 of the 13 Western states: Alaska, Arizona, California, Hawaii, Idaho, Montana, Nevada, New Mexico, Washington, Wyoming, as well as the territory of Guam. FilAms are also the largest group of Asian Americans in South Dakota.[5] Table 12.2 illustrates the percentage distribution of Filipinos vis-à-vis the total population in the top 10 states with large Filipino populations.

Examining the Census data, it appears that Filipino Americans will have their largest impact in California because the state has 1.5 million FilAms, the most among the 50 states. Following California, the battle to sway FilAm voters is in Hawaii, with more than 300,000, followed by Illinois, Texas, Washington, New Jersey, New York, Nevada, and Florida with more than 100,000 FilAms each. The 10th state is Virginia with close to 100,000 FilAms.

In terms of proportion, however, the greatest political influence of FilAms at the municipal and state level will be in Hawaii, which reported that more than one-quarter of its population is ethnically Filipino. In the

Table 12.2
Top 10 U.S. States with Filipino Populations

State	State Population	Filipino Population	Percentage of Filipinos
California	37,253,956	1,474,707	3.95
Hawaii	1,360,301	342,095	25.15
Illinois	12,830,632	139,090	1.08
Texas	25,145,561	137,713	0.55
Washington	6,724,540	137,083	2.03
New Jersey	8,791,894	126,793	1.44
New York	19,378,102	126,793	0.65
Nevada	2,700,551	123,891	4.59
Florida	18,801,310	122,691	0.65
Virginia	8,001,024	90,493	1.13
50 states + D.C.	308,745,538	3,416,840	1.11

Source: U.S. Census Bureau.

last decade, FilAms have overtaken Japanese Americans as the largest Asian American group in the state.

The effects have already been felt with Filipinos and Filipinas in Hawaii achieving political firsts. In 1994, Benjamin Cayetano was elected Hawaii's fifth Governor and the first Filipino American Governor in the United States. Previously, he was elected the first Filipino American Lieutenant Governor in the United States. Most recently, in January 2013, long-time State House representative and State Senator Donna Mercado Kim made history as the first Filipina American State Senate president.

Thus, it has become common to see Hawaiians of Filipino descent elected to state and municipal positions. For instance, in the 2012 state-wide contests, a record 11 first- and second-generation FilAms easily won seats in the State's House of Representatives. Many ran unopposed. For some districts it was a choice between two FilAms. As a side note, the high FilAm population proportion in Hawaii is equaled by the U.S. territory of Guam. Hence, as in Hawaii, Guam FilAms are becoming more visible in both elected and appointed public offices.

Nevada, a crucial swing state, is an interesting case for the FilAm bloc. From 2000 to 2010, the state's Filipino population soared 142 percent. Like Hawaiians, Filipinos have become the largest Asian American group in the state, comprising 4.59 percent of the total population. Close to 124,000 reside in metropolitan Las Vegas, Clark County, where their votes were critical in tightly contested statewide and local elections. In 2010, when Senate Majority Leader Harry Reid was seriously challenged by Republican Sharron Angle, he turned to the popularity of Philippine Congressman Manny Pacquiao to assure him the Filipino vote, particularly in Clark County. Pacquiao not only helped solidify his Democratic FilAm vote, while also charming undecideds, Independents, and even FilAm Republicans.

Nevertheless, the idea of FilAms running for Nevada public office remains novel. There are no elected FilAms in municipal and state positions. Very few second-generation FilAms are interested in working for Nevada politicians. New FilAm organizations, including the recently established nonpartisan Filipino-American Political Organization With Equal Representation, intend to change things. They already have a FilAm milestone: in the November 2012 elections, Clark County issued ballots and election materials in Filipino (Tagalog) language.

California is where the Filipino voting bloc has the greatest potential to influence electoral contests at the national level, especially during presidential elections, while its influence at the state and municipal levels is strongest in Hawaii. Forty-three percent of FilAms live in California. All of the state's 58 counties experienced an increase in the number of Filipino residents since the 1960s. Interestingly, the only exemption to the trend is

San Francisco County, whose Asian population has increased significantly but the number of Filipinos has declined from a peak of 42,652 in 1990 to 36,347 in 2010.

Table 12.3 demonstrates that in Northern California, FilAm constituents have increased significantly, specifically in Santa Clara, Alameda, San Mateo, Contra Costa, and Solano counties. Daly City in San Mateo County has the highest concentration of FilAms in any municipal jurisdiction in the United States, more than 30 percent of 101,123 residents.

Southern California contains the highest density, nationally, of FilAms. Approximately 10 percent of Filipinos in the United States and more than 20 percent of Filipinos in California live in Los Angeles County. The Westlake section of the Los Angeles City hosts one of the country's oldest Filipinotowns. The largest jumps are in the vote-rich counties of Los Angeles, San Diego, Orange, Riverside, and San Bernardino. Ranked second, after Los Angeles County in FilAms, is San Diego County, which has also seen a marked increase in its FilAm population from 121,147 to 146,618 between 2000 and 2010. But the most notable increase during this 10-year period is in Riverside County, which saw more than 30,000 additional FilAm residents in a traditionally Republican jurisdiction.

Table 12.3
Filipinos in the United States and Major California Counties

	1910	1990	2000	2010
United States	160	1,406,770	2,364,815	3,416,840
California	5	731,648	918,678	1,474,707
Northern				
Santa Clara	0	61,518	76,060	87,412
Alameda	0	53,760	69,127	82,406
San Mateo	0	44,732	59,047	70,191
Contra Costa	0	24,663	34,595	48,418
Solano	0	28,390	36,576	43,366
Southern				
Los Angeles	2	219,653	260,158	322,110
San Diego	0	95,945	121,147	146,618
Orange	0	30,356	48,946	71,060
Riverside	0	12,748	20,850	51,003
San Bernardino	0	16,171	25,919	41,702

Source: U.S. Census Bureau.

Thus, FilAm voting blocs are slowly electing FilAm mayors, vice-mayors, council members, school board members, and college board members in the San Francisco, Los Angeles, and San Diego regions. But FilAm voters in California have not had similar results as FilAms in Hawaii in electing one of their own to the state legislature. The first major breakthrough occurred recently when Alameda vice-mayor Rob Bonta won a seat in the State Assembly during the 2012 elections. Two other Northern California FilAm candidates lost.

In Southern California, no FilAm ran for any elective position from community college board to city council member that was open in 2012. Nonetheless, despite not having sufficient ethnic elected and appointed representation in state and local executive and legislative offices, FilAm community leaders and organizations have successfully influenced policies and pressured politicos through aggressive advocacy, lobbying, and activism.

The Filipino American voting bloc is not all about numbers. Wealth is power. According to the 2010 American Community Survey (ACS), Filipinos possess the capacity to transform their reported economic strength to political muscle, because the median annual individual earnings for FilAm full-time, year-round workers are $43,000, higher than for all U.S. adults overall ($40,000) but lower than for all Asian Americans in general ($48,000). But among U.S. households, the median annual income for Filipinos is $75,000, higher than for all Asians ($66,000) and significantly higher than all U.S. households ($49,800). FilAms are far less likely to live in poverty than other immigrant groups. Although it is important to add that FilAms reported larger households of 3.4 persons compared to the average American household, which is at 2.6 persons. Larger households also mean more potential voters.[6]

Based on ACS data, more than 6 in 10 Filipino Americans (62%) own a home, compared with 58 percent of all Asian Americans and 65 percent of the U.S. population overall. Their very low poverty rate, at 6.2 percent, is remarkable, since this is only half of both the United States (12.8%) and Asian (11.9%) averages. In the eyes of politicians and parties, they are more than just voters and constituents but important taxpayers and campaign contributors as well.

HISTORY OF FILAM IMMIGRATION AND INCORPORATION

For more than three centuries, the Philippines was a valued Spanish colony and integral part of global commerce. On October 18, 1587, the Spanish galleon Nuestra Señora de Esperanza laden with products from "the East," mainly China, landed in Morro Bay, California. Part of the crew sent ashore to search for food and supplies were the first Filipinos to land in North America. Many other recorded and unrecorded landings of Filipino sailors and navigators probably occurred during the 250 years (1565–1815) of the lucrative Manila-Acapulco galleon trade.

The first recorded Filipinos permanent settlement was in 1763 in Saint Malo, Saint Bernard Parish fronting the bayous and marshes of Louisiana. Former Spanish-speaking Filipino sailors and navigators, nicknamed "Manilamen," abandoned ship to escape the brutality of their Spanish masters. They built houses on stilts, caught fish and shrimp, and thus were the first Filipino constituents of a future U.S. territory. To demonstrate patriotism to their new homeland, many of them fought against the British in the Battle of New Orleans.

In California, on August 10, 1779, Spanish priest Junipero Serra administered the rite of confirmation to Vicente Tallado, "indio de la Panpangua en Philipinas, marinero" [native of Pampanga, Philippines, seaman]. This event was recorded in the Confirmation Records of California's Monterey mission, which was less than 100 miles from San Francisco. Two years later, Filipino Antonio Miranda Rodriguez Poblador, along with 44 other individuals, was sent by the Spanish government from Mexico to establish a settlement, which eventually became the city of Los Angeles.

Filipino disdain for America's discriminatory immigration policies was palpable. On April 29, 1888, while Philippine national hero, Jose P. Rizal was on board the *SS Belgic* attempting to enter San Francisco, his U.S. port of entry, he was held up by immigration officials. To keep himself busy during the long, bureaucratic delay, Rizal penned a letter to his parents:

> Here we are in sight of America since yesterday without being able to disembark, placed in quarantine on account of the 642 Chinese that we have on board coming from Hong Kong where they say smallpox prevails. But the true reason is that, as America is against Chinese immigration and now they are campaigning for the elections, the government, in order to get the vote of the people, must appear to be strict with the Chinese, and we suffer. On board there is not one sick person.[7]

The Spanish-American War erupted on April 25, 1898. With serious defeats in Cuba and the Philippines, the Spanish government had no choice but to seek peace. Therefore, in December 10, 1898, the Treaty of Paris was signed ending the war. Under the agreement, Spain surrendered Cuba, Puerto Rico, Guam, and the Philippines to the United States. Eleven days after the treaty was signed, U.S. president William McKinley announced a policy of "benevolent assimilation" of the Philippines. Many Filipino revolutionaries denounced and resisted the U.S. arbitrary takeover, and the Philippine-American War ensued.

Nevertheless, annexation brought rights as U.S. nationals to Filipinos on April 11, 1899, when the Treaty of Paris went into effect. But as U.S. nationals, and not U.S. citizens, they were granted limited political, social, and economic rights. Filipinos in the Philippines did not have U.S. voting rights and were not eligible for U.S. passports. However, unlike Japanese and Chinese workers, they had visa-free entry and the ability to work and reside anywhere in the United States. Like many Asian workers though, they were restricted from owning property and businesses. As U.S. nationals, they were not affected by the Asian exclusion provisions of the Immigration Act of 1917 and National Origins Act of 1924.

Filipinos born in the United States and of U.S. parentage gained automatic U.S. citizenship. Filipinos from the Philippines as U.S. nationals were eligible to gain U.S. citizenship and the voting rights that came with it through the naturalization process. In many states, Filipino Americans, like other racial minorities, were only able to exercise this political right fully after the passage of civil rights legislation in the 1950s and 1960s, especially the Voting Rights Act.

Citizen or not, socially, Filipinos in America experienced discrimination through antimiscegenation laws, which prohibited them from marrying, cohabiting, or having sex with whites or blacks. Because of the increasing number of Filipino residents in their jurisdictions, the California, Arizona, Maryland, Nevada, South Dakota, Utah, and Wyoming amended their antimiscegenation laws to specifically include "Filipinos" in their prohibitions.

Starting in 1901, the U.S. Navy began recruiting Filipinos. Between 1903 and 1934, many came on all-expenses paid U.S. government scholarships to study at American universities under the Pensionado Act passed by the Philippine Commission. Between 1906 and 1910, Hawaiian plantations systematically recruited them for the island's booming agricultural industry. Hiring expanded to the West Coast in subsequent years, but many who worked in the fields of Hawaii, California, Oregon, and Washington were paid low wages and had to live and work in poor conditions. Not having political influence through the ballot box, many eventually joined forces with Mexican American farm workers to form labor rights organizations. Pinoys[8] Philip Vera Cruz and Larry Itliong, along with Chicano Cesar Chavez, were among the fathers of California's militant labor movement.

Unrestricted entry ended in 1934 with the passage of the Philippine Independence Act (or Tydings-McDuffie Act). It also reclassified Filipinos in the United States from "nationals" to "aliens" and restricted immigration to 50 per year. Based on U.S. Census data, the law had a significant effect on the number of Filipinos between 1930 and 1940 during which only 355 people entered. This number is staggeringly low when compared to the previous decade, when the number of Filipinos grew eight-fold from just 5,603 to 45,208. Even with the introduction of the Filipino Repatriation Act of 1935, only around 1,900 of the more than 45,000 chose to leave the United States.

World War II ushered in a new wave of Filipinos to the United States as "stewardsmen" for the U.S. Navy. They cooked as well as cleaned, washed, scrubbed, and shined the decks of navy ships, equipment, weapons, and infrastructures on bases around the world. During that time, many Filipinos who were from the United States and who were U.S. citizens fought gallantly alongside these nonnationals. Later, they created another wave of Filipino (actually Filipina!) migration when they returned home to the United States with "war brides" from the Philippines.

The end of World War II, the passage of the 1965 U.S. Immigration Act, and the 1972 declaration of Martial Law in the Philippines intensified the conditions that drew Filipinos to the United States. Many Filipinos who served in the military during World War II as soldiers and civilians decided to follow the promises of a productive postmilitary life in America.

Joining these soldiers were beneficiaries of the Immigration Act of 1965, which encouraged highly skilled professionals such as doctors, nurses, engineers, and accountants to immigrate to the United States. Many brought their immediate families—spouses and children—and upon gaining permanent residency status or U.S. citizenship, petitioned to bring others, mainly their parents, siblings, and other relatives.

The deplorable state of the Philippine economy in the 1970s and 1980s also forced a mass exodus of migrants to San Francisco. Some came to the United States on nonimmigrants visas (B-1/B-2 Tourist visa, F-1 Student, J-1 Exchange Visitor, etc.) and later overstayed their short-term visitor visas. Some of them married American citizens to legalize their stay, while others paid for "green card" marriages. Later, the 1986 general illegal immigration amnesty enabled many to legalize. Filipino migrants who became illegal or undocumented after the 1986 amnesty have been insulated from federal scrutiny by San Francisco's "INS Raid-free Zone" and "City of Refuge" resolutions, and most recently by a Sanctuary City Ordinance. For current unauthorized FilAms, both their churches and their city are their safe havens.

The dot-com boom in the Silicon Valley in the late 1980s also increased the numbers of highly skilled Filipino migrants to the San Francisco Bay region with an expanded working visa (H-1) category. Interestingly, the dot-com bust did not decrease immigration, but instead brought a new population of Filipino migrants, since the health care industry successfully lobbied Congress to allow more health care professionals, particularly nurses, to migrate with their families directly as legal permanent residents. Filipino nurses and caregivers were needed to alleviate an acute health care shortage that has been exacerbated by an ever-growing number of aging baby boomers who require care and medical attention. Thus, America's hospitals, assisted living centers, hospices, and clinics experienced a boom in highly trained and caring FilAm nurses and caregivers.

A DISCUSSION AND ANALYSIS OF THE FILIPINO BLOC'S AFFILIATION WITH ONE OR MORE PARTIES OVER TIME

Answering the question of whether Filipino Americans lean Democrat or Republican is difficult. Because while past anecdotal evidence and media reports seem to indicate that they support Democrats, recent independent surveys indicate mixed results.

If we rely on the question "If you had to choose, would you rather have a smaller government providing fewer services or a bigger government providing more services?" from the PEW Research Center 2012 survey,[9] then the answer is Filipinos lean Democrat. This is because 58 percent of the Filipinos surveyed responded, "bigger government, more services." Their response aligns with most Asian Americans, particularly the Chinese (50%), Korean (68%), and Vietnamese communities (69%). Not surprisingly, this trend runs counter to the U.S. national average of 39 percent supporting this statement.

Moreover, if we examine the record of past and present elected officials of Filipino descent an overwhelming majority ran as Democrats. For instance, Table 12.4 shows that 19 out of 20 FilAm winners in the 2012 were Democrats.

But how does one explain the findings of both the PEW Survey and a 2012 National Asian American Survey[10] that among Asian Americans only 50 percent of Filipinos voted for candidate Barack Obama in 2008, the lowest among major Asian American groups? Comparatively, both the PEW and NAAS polls indicated that Indian, Chinese, Japanese, and Korean American voters enthusiastically supported Obama. In addition, the NAAS study reported that only 45 percent of Filipino respondents perceived President Obama doing a good job, again, the lowest among Asian American respondents. While in the PEW research, 61 percent expressed "dissatisfaction with the way the United States is run."

Do these results suggest that Filipino Americans are Republicans? There seems to be some empirical evidence in support of an affirmative answer. It is accurate to infer from the two current and several past studies that Filipinos are one of the largest source of Asian American Republican Party votes. There is a segment of the Filipino voting bloc that sympathizes with the views of conservative Filipina blogger Michelle Malkin and relies on Fox News for information. In predominantly Democratic San Francisco, successful business owner, Juanita Nimfa Yamsuan Gamez, and community activist, Rudy Asercion, go against the

Table 12.4
2012 Filipino American Election Winners

Candidate	Position	Party
Robert C. Scott	U.S. Representative, Virginia, 3rd district	Democratic
Rob Bonta	California State Assembly, 18th district	Democratic
Dennis Rodriguez Jr.	Guam Senate	Democratic
Donna Mercado Kim	Hawaii Senate, 14th district	Democratic
Will Espero	Hawaii Senate, 19th district	Democratic
Donovan Dela Cruz	Hawaii Senate, 22nd district	Democratic
Gilbert S. Keith-Agaran	Hawaii House of Representatives, 9th district	Democratic
Della Au Belatti	Hawaii House of Representatives, 24th district	Democratic
Romy Cachola	Hawaii House of Representatives, 30th district	Democratic
Henry Aquino	Hawaii House of Representatives, 38th district	Democratic
Ty Cullen	Hawaii House of Representatives, 39th district	Democratic
Rida Cabanilla-Arakawa	Hawaii House of Representatives, 41st district	Democratic
Jose Esteves	Mayor, City of Milpitas	Republican
Tony Daysog	Alameda City Council	Democratic
Stewart Chen	Alameda City Council	Democratic
Jim Navarro	Union City Council	Democratic
Wendy Ho	Trustee, San Jose Evergreen Valley Community College Board	Democratic
Rudy Nasol	Trustee, San Jose Evergreen Community College District	Democratic
Jonas Dino	Trustee, New Haven Unified School District, Union City	Democratic
Vince Songcayawon	Trustee, Evergreen School District Board	Democratic

Source: Various election results.

grain by touting GOP views and interests. This conservative cluster probably explains why many Filipino Democratic political candidates lose during elections, especially if they rely primarily on the Filipino voting bloc to support them.

The major influence on Filipino views and ballot decisions may not be a political party and its platform but an entrenched social institution that upholds conservative teachings: the Church. The role of religion and faith are quite strong among Filipino Americans, particularly Christianity. This is documented in many studies including some written by the authors.[11]

The largest beneficiary of the Filipino bloc's church-based conservatism is the Republican Party.[12] Filipino Americans who grew up in the Philippines are swayed by the power of the pulpit, pastoral letters, and the religious views that were passed down to them in their other homeland. A majority of FilAms are Catholics. They are influenced politically by the pronouncements of the Vatican and the conservative interpretations of their pastors. Some Filipino Americans are followers of homegrown independent Philippine churches like the Iglesia ni Christo (Church of Christ) and charismatic preachers like Brother Mike Velarde of El Shaddai. Still others are affiliated with the multitude of American evangelical churches. There are also networks of nationwide church-related organizations, which may sway their ballot decisions like the Couples for Christ (including Youth for Christ) and Bukas Loob sa Diyos.

In the Philippines, Catholic and Christian Churches' influence is codified through specific provisions in the fundamental laws of the land. For instance, Article XV, Section 2 of the Philippine Constitution provides, "Marriage, as an inviolable social institution, is the foundation of the family and shall be protected by the State." Hence, divorce is not a comfortable topic to many churchgoers. Neither is abortion as proclaimed in Article II, Section 12, "The State shall equally protect the life of the mother and the life of the unborn from conception."

Perhaps an even more important political affiliation question is: Are Filipino Americans "independents?" This is an important question since, nationally, there is a trend toward registering independent among mainstream and minority voters.[13] As reported by the National Asian American Surveys in Table 12.5, Filipino Americans seem to be following the trend. There is a growing segment of Filipinos who are unhappy with the party choices and so opt to be "independent minded," "have no party," or "be aligned with other parties," like the Libertarian or Green. Many state that they would like to place the candidate's stand on issues above party loyalty. This is not surprising to those who study politics in the Philippines, where there are multiple parties to choose from, and personal connection with a candidate, or patronage, transcends party loyalty.

FilAm Democratic and Republican Clubs exist throughout the United States. The most active ones are in California, New York, and Hawaii. They are seen organizing strategic activities year-round, not just Get Out the Vote campaigns, canvassing, and membership drives. These groups also sponsor FilAm social, cultural, and economic events to project visibility. Members also appear on The Filipino Channel and write opinion

Table 12.5
Filipino American Party Identification

	Respondents	Democrat (%)	Republican (%)	Independent/ Other Party/ No Party (%)
2008 Survey	603	34	16	50
2012 Survey	396	24	27	49

Source: NAAS Surveys, 2008 and 2012.

pieces and blogs in the many FilAm newspapers and blog sites. Leaders and representatives of the parties are regular commentators after State of the Nation addresses and November elections. They participate in community and city hall town hall meetings. Most FilAm Democrats and Republicans are more active in the Asian and Pacific Islander Clubs, as opposed to the FilAm Club.

In California, the most active political clubs are in the San Francisco Bay Area. There are numerous chartered FilAm Democratic clubs representing the various cities and towns in the area. For instance, the Filipino American Democratic Club is one of 26 chartered clubs in the City of San Francisco. The various FilAm Democratic clubs from around the state are networked together under the banner of the Filipino American Democratic Caucus of California or FADC. The FADC affiliates directly with California and County Democratic Central Committees. The FilAm Democratic clubs endorse candidates and ballot initiatives during elections. Filipino American Republicans are represented nationally by National Organization of Filipino American Republicans. Only a handful of FilAm Democrats and FilAm Republicans are members of their respective Central Committees. An even smaller number have made it to their party's national convention.

In San Francisco, as Table 12.6 illustrates, the most effective venue to reach out, build networks, and disseminate information to FilAms is through their hometown associations. This may be true in the cities and counties where there are large concentrations of Filipinos, like Los Angeles, San Diego, Honolulu, or Guam.

As of 2008, there are more than 400 Philippine hometown associations in the San Francisco Bay Area. These hometown associations represent the regions, provinces, cities or towns, or linguistic group where the FilAm came from. They mainly organize dances, language classes, beauty pageants, or neighborhood cleanups. But they also organize fund-raisers for local and international causes. They are at the core of annual citywide FilAm events. Every June, it's the Philippine Independence Day celebration and parade on downtown Market Street. Every October, it's Filipino

Table 12.6
Types of FilAm Organizations in the San Francisco Bay Area

Type	Number	Percentage
Hometown/Regional	170	41
Spiritual/Religious	37	9
Professional	36	9
Cultural and Recreational	34	8
Filipino American Social Clubs	31	8
Political and Civic	26	6
Senior's and Elderly	22	5
Veterans	19	5
Educational/Alumni	16	4
Philippine Development	13	3
Lions Clubs	7	2
Total	411	100

Source: Gonzalez, 2012.

American History Month or Filipino American Heritage throughout the United States. Every December, there is a Parol (Christmas lantern) stroll and contest on Mission Street. FilAm Quezonians, that is, from the Quezon Province, make time for a Pahiyas harvest festival every May. FilAm Cebuanos, that is, from Cebu City and Province, look forward to the feast of the Sinulog religious festival praising the Santo Niño de Cebu every January, the most popular Philippine icon. FilAm Bicolanos, from the Bicol region, create an American version of the Peñafrancia thanksgiving festival every September.

In the aftermath of the super typhoon Haiyan, Filipino American hometown associations, particularly from provinces directly affected, raised millions of dollars and sent thousands of care boxes for the relief and rehabilitation efforts. Recognition and support of these hometown association activities are keys to getting the political sympathy and respect of the FilAm voting bloc.

WHAT ARE THE MOST IMPORTANT ISSUES THAT INFLUENCE THE FILIPINO VOTING BLOC'S BALLOT DECISION?

The single most important political issue for the Filipino American voting bloc is immigration. As mentioned in the previous section and illustrated in Table 12.7, the waiting period for a family member from the Philippines to come to the United States is too long. For instance, the U.S. Embassy in Manila is currently processing the immigrant visas of petitions filed on August 8, 1990, for F4 category, Brothers and Sisters of Adult U.S. Citizens, a 24-year wait!

Hence, the Washington politician, Democratic or Republican, who is able to pass legislation addressing this backlog will certainly gain the FilAm voting bloc's debt and gratitude for many elections to come.

Most in the FilAm bloc are concerned about the lawful and legal immigration of their relations. They believe that comprehensive immigration reform should prioritize this issue over amnesty to unauthorized immigrants.

The Office of Immigration Statistics has estimated that 270,000, or 2 percent, of the approximately 10.8 million unauthorized immigrants in 2009 are Philippine-born. This is a 33 percent increase from the 200,000 estimate in 2000. Comparatively, this figure is still much smaller than the estimated seven million unauthorized immigrations from Mexico. *TNT*, for Tago Nang Tago, is the Filipino slang term for the unauthorized, which literally means "in perpetual hiding." A majority of TNTs came to the United States on nonimmigrant visas, for example, tourist, student, and working, and decided to stay after their visa expired. Some were brought to the United States before adolescence and hence have no connection to the Philippines.

The FilAm voting bloc was divided on whether to support their TNT brothers and sisters until unauthorized immigrant and Pulitzer prize-winning FilAm author Jose Antonio Vargas made the cover story of *Time* magazine and CNN. He was one of those brought to the United States by a relation as a child. When Vargas's revelation that he was unauthorized went viral in the mainstream and social media, the FilAm bloc's sympathy for a path to legalization for the unauthorized,

Table 12.7
U.S. State Department Visa Bulletin for February 2014

Category	China	India	Mexico	Philippines
F1	01JAN07	01JAN07	01OCT93	15AUG01
F2A	08SEP13	08SEP13	01SEP13	08SEP13
F2B	08JUL06	08JUL06	01MAY93	22MAY03
F3	15MAY03	15MAY03	01JUN93	08FEB93
F4	22OCT01	22OCT01	08NOV96	08AUG90

Source: travel.state.gov.

Note: (F1) Unmarried Sons and Daughters of U.S. Citizens, (F2A) Spouses and Children of Permanent Residents, (F2B) Unmarried Sons and Daughters, (F3) Married Sons and Daughters of U.S. Citizens, and (F4) Brothers and Sisters of Adult U.S. Citizens.

especially those who were brought to the country at a young age, somewhat shifted.

The second issue lingering within the FilAm voting bloc is the veteran's benefits equalization issue for the aging and dwindling Filipino World War II veterans and their families. During the height of war preparations, General Douglas MacArthur and President Franklin D. Roosevelt issued a call for volunteers in the Philippines to enlarge the United States Armed Forces of the Far East (USAFFE). 22,532 young Filipino men heeded the call that included a promise of U.S. citizenship and veteran benefits.

But their expectations were dashed when Congress passed two Rescission Acts after the conflict essentially invalidating MacArthur and Roosevelt's promises. It partially corrected in 1990 when U.S. president George H. Bush signed the Immigration and Naturalization Act granting Filipino World War II veterans U.S. citizenship. Many finally arrived in the country for which they fought and risked their lives. However, most were elderly and suffering from physical and mental wounds. Although these gallant warriors were given citizenship, they were not granted much deserved veteran's benefits. In effect, they languished in their new homeland, relying on welfare and social security benefits. For many, being a citizen welfare recipient was tough to swallow.

On January 17, 2009, 60 years after the 1946 Rescission Acts, President Barack Obama signed the American Recovery and Reinvestment, also known as the "Stimulus Package," which included a $198 million earmark for the remaining FilAm World War II veterans and their families. Under the law, each veteran was entitled to receive $15,000. However, they still were not provided full G.I. bill benefits, meaning the battle continues for many.

The economy, jobs, and health care are political issues that align Filipino Americans with mainstream American society. Many FilAms were affected by the economic downturn that began in 2008 when their mortgage investments suffered, because like many Asian Americans, a large segment of the FilAm population invested in real estate and fell victim to easy-to-secure loans, which they were unable to afford long term. Some lost their jobs. Some FilAm engineers and medical professionals, who thought themselves in safe occupations, received pink slips.

The implementation of the Affordable Care Act was watched closely by FilAm Democrats and Republicans. Despite the fact that Filipinos have one of the lowest rates of noninsurance among minorities (around 2%–3%), there are still at-risk subgroups in the population who needed to be reached and enrolled, especially in states like California and New York. The at-risk population includes the elderly, adult Pinays, who are susceptible to breast cancer and heart disease, adult Pinoys, who are prone to lung and prostate cancer, as well as children, who are prone to obesity.

CONCLUSION

This chapter sketched in broad strokes the relative size, magnitude, history, and key issues associated with Filipino American voting. The demographic and historical trend is clear: there is a FilAm bloc and it will continue to grow for the decades to come. The bloc is comprised of FilAms who report themselves as Republican, Democratic, or Independent, but who may vote outside of party affiliation depending on the issue and their various community and socialization influences. In Hawaii, the large FilAm voter population has allowed them to gain many elective posts in municipal and state elections. In California, they are an important swing vote. Immigration policy and politics is of utmost importance to this FilAm bloc.

Three points stand out when examining the events that have the potential of shaping and reshaping future Filipino American voting trends.

First, the passage of a comprehensive immigration reform law that legalizes those who are currently unauthorized as well as addresses the backlog of legal family petitions. Both will definitely spike their voting numbers even further.

Second, for first-generation FilAms, who comprise the majority, the passage of the Philippine dual citizenship law, or The Philippine Citizenship Retention and Re-acquisition Act of 2003 allowed them to own property, vote, and exercise the rights and privileges of citizens of both countries. Will FilAms then experience voter burnout having to participate in too many electoral contests?

Third, as the Filipino diaspora increases in scale and complexity, U.S. politicians and parties should give serious consideration to balancing their message because of the FilAms contradictory psyche: "Republican in the U.S., but Democratic in the Philippines." In other words, FilAms are conservative in their views but quite liberal in their welfare support of families and hometowns. FilAm constituents sent their Philippine kin more than $10 billion in remittances (*padala*) on top of over a million care boxes (*balikbayan boxes*). How these factors will affect future Filipino American voting behavior could be the subject of further research.

NOTES

1. U.S. Department of Homeland Security, *Yearbook of Immigration Statistics*.
2. Lien, "Asian Americans and Voting Participation," 493–517; See also Magpantay, "Asian American Political Participation," 11–24; Oh, "Group Membership," 137–160.

3. Taylor, *Rise of Asian Americans*, 163.
4. FilAm immigrants who arrived in the United States before adolescence.
5. Lott, *Common Destiny*.
6. Takei and Kim, "Socioeconomic Attainments," 198–212.
7. Gonzalez, *Filipino American Faith*, 21.
8. Nickname for Filipinos while Filipinas are Pinays.
9. PEW sample size: 504 Filipino American respondents.

10. NAAS 2012 sample size: 396 Filipino American respondents. Both landline and cell phone calls. In the NAAS 2008 Survey, a slightly higher percentage (58%) of the 603 Filipino respondents said that they voted for Obama.

11. Gonzalez, *Filipino American Faith*; Lorentzen, et al., *Religion at the Corner of Bliss*.

12. Ramakrishnan, et al., *National Asian American Survey*; Ramakrishnan and Lee, *Public Opinion of a Growing Electorate*.

13. Hajnal and Lee, *Why Americans Don't Join the Party*.

REFERENCES

Gonzalez, Joaquin Jay. *Diaspora Diplomacy: Philippine Migration and its Soft Power Influences*. Minneapolis, MN and Manila, Philippines: Mill City Press and De La Salle University Publishing-Anvil Press, 2012.

Gonzalez, Joaquin Jay. *Filipino American Faith in Action: Immigration, Religion, and Civic Engagement*. New York: New York University Press, 2009.

Hajnal, Z. L., and Taeku Lee. *Why Americans Don't Join The Party: Race, Immigration, And The Failure (Of Political Parties) To Engage The Electorate*. Princeton, NJ: Princeton University Press, 2011.

Lien, P. "Asian Americans and Voting Participation: Comparing Racial and Ethnic Differences in Recent U.S. Elections." *International Migration Review* 38.2 (2004): 493–517.

Lorentzen, L., et al. *Religion at the Corner of Bliss and Nirvana: Politics, Identity, and Faith in New Migrant Communities*. Durham and London: Duke University Press, 2012.

Lott, Juanita Tamayo. *Common Destiny: Filipino American Generations*. New York: Rowman and Littlefield, 2006.

Magpantay, G. D. "Asian American Political Participation in the 2008 Presidential Election." *Asian American Policy Review* 18 (2009):11–24.

Oh, S. "Group Membership and Context of Participation in Electoral Politics among Korean, Chinese, and Filipino Americans." *Development and Society* 42.1 (June 2013): 137–160.

Ramakrishnan, Karthick, and Taeku Lee. *Public Opinion of a Growing Electorate: Asian Americans and Pacific Islanders in 2012*. Los Angeles, California: National Asian American Survey, 2012.

Ramakrishnan, Karthick, et al. *National Asian American Survey, 2008*. Ann Arbor, MI: Inter-university Consortium for Political and Social Research, 2008.

Takei, I., A. Sakamoto, and C. Kim. "The Socioeconomic Attainments of Non-immigrant Cambodian, Filipino, Hmong, Laotian, Thai, and Vietnamese Americans." *Race and Social Problems* 5 (2013): 198–212.

Taylor, P., ed. *The Rise of Asian Americans*. Washington, D.C.: Pew Research Center, 2013.

U.S. Census. Various Years.

U.S. Department of Homeland Security. *Yearbook of Immigration Statistics*. Washington, D.C.: Department of Homeland Security, 2012.

Chapter 13

Minority Voting in the United States: East Asian Americans

Jeanette Yih Harvie and Pei-te Lien

INTRODUCTION

East Asian Americans constitute two-fifths of the present-day Asian American population and are characterized by rapid population growth, a high foreign-born rate, and relative socioeconomic affluence, even if there are significant inter- and intraethnic differences within the community. In the 2012 general elections, more than two-thirds of East Asian Americans voted for President Barack Obama.[1] This result might not be surprising to scholars, given that the Democrat vote share among Asian Americans has steadily grown since the early 1990s when such data became available.[2] Nonetheless, the long-term sustainability of a Democratic voting bloc among East Asian Americans and the larger Asian American community remains an open question, in part because of the continuous expansion and diversification of the minority population in the post-1965 era. This chapter focuses on East Asian Americans and starts by asking: who are the East Asian Americans? What have been the historical barriers to their voting? What are the historical and contemporary voting trends that exist within the voting bloc? What are the issues that influence the voting decisions of those within the East Asian American community? Also, what has been their relationship with the two major parties in the United States? Finally, we speculate on the likely voting behavior and prospective electoral influence of East Asian Americans as a voting bloc in the near future.

WHO ARE EAST ASIAN AMERICANS?

"Asian Americans" are generally defined as individuals who reside in the United States on a long-term basis and with ancestral roots in Asia.[3] East Asian Americans can trace their ancestral origins to countries or places in East Asia, such as mainland China, Japan, and the Korean Peninsula. For a long time, people of Chinese descent, who migrated from mainland China, Hong Kong, or Taiwan, were all called Chinese Americans by the U.S. government and society. However since 2000, ethnic Chinese, who migrated from Taiwan and entered their ethnic identity as "Taiwanese" in response to the race questions in the U.S. Census, are listed separately as Taiwanese Americans.[4]

Table 13.1 shows that there were 3.8 million Chinese Americans and over 230 thousand Taiwanese Americans in 2010. Together, they constituted nearly a quarter of the Asian American population. There were over 1.7 million Korean Americans, almost all originating from South Korea, who constituted roughly 10 percent of the Asian American population in 2010. In addition, there were over 1.3 million Japanese Americans, who made up less than 8 percent of the Asian American population. Between 2000 and 2010, the population growth rate of these communities are all higher than the U.S. average, but only one group, Taiwanese, has a growth rate that is higher than the Asian American average, while another group, Japanese, has the lowest growth rate of all Asian groups. Differences in population growth rates reflect the immigration history of these ethnic communities, but other factors, such as U.S. domestic and international relations as well as conditions in the homelands in Asia, also play a decisive role.

The Chinese were the first East Asian group to enter the United States in large and persistent numbers. They started arriving in 1848, lured by the prospects of finding gold in the western United States and a reprieve from overcrowding, drought, warfare, and other problems they experienced in their homeland of southern China. However, anti-Chinese sentiment rose soon after their arrival. The large and sudden influx of the "heathen Chinese," coupled with language barriers, economic depression, and tight political party competition, resulted in the passage of the Chinese Exclusion Act in 1882. This barricade to Chinese immigration was not lifted until World War II, and it was not until the mid-1960s that racist quotas against all Asian nationalities were lifted. The slow loosening of

Table 13.1
Key Demographic Indicators of East Asian Americans, 2010

	Chinese Americans	Korean Americans	Japanese Americans	Taiwanese Americans	Asian Americans	U.S. Total
Population (×1000, 2010)	3,795	1,707	1,304	230	17,321	308,746
% Among Asians	22	10	8	1	100	n/a
% Growth from 2000 to 2010	39	39	14	59	46	10
% Foreign-Born	61	65	28	68	60	13
% Naturalized	60	54	33	67	57	43
% Limited English Proficiency	42	41	18	43	32	9
% in Poverty	12	13	8	12	11	14
Per Capita Income	$30,061	$26,118	$31,831	$38,312	$28,342	$27,100

Source: Asian American Center for Advancing Justice, A Community of Contrasts: Asian Americans in the United States, 2011. 2012. Table compiled by authors from the report.

restrictions on Chinese immigration and the final opening of Asian immigration almost two decades later brought about a new and ongoing wave of ethnic Chinese immigration, first from Hong Kong and Taiwan, then directly from mainland China after the Communist regime liberalized its closed-door policy in the late 1970s.

Major labor immigration from Japan did not occur until after Chinese migration stopped in 1882. Japanese laborers were recruited to work on sugarcane and pineapple plantations in Hawaii, but a significant number relocated to the West Coast at the turn of the 20th century to seek better economic opportunities and to fill the labor market need created by the Chinese exclusion. Anti-Asian sentiment forced the Japanese government to agree to halt its labor migration in 1907, even if migration of wives and children of the laborers was permitted by the U.S. government until the passage of the de facto Asian exclusion legislation in 1924. Although Japanese immigration restriction was lifted in 1952, relatively few Japanese were able to take advantage of the opportunity due to the minuscule national origin quota. The internment of Japanese Americans during World War II and the relative affluence of Japan in the postwar era have mostly accounted for fewer new migrants from Japan in the post-1965 era.

The first major wave of Korean immigration to the United States occurred between 1903 and 1905, when about 7,200 predominantly male Koreans were recruited for plantation labor in Hawaii. The entry of Korean immigrants was subject to the same restrictions placed on the Japanese after the occupation and annexation of the Korean Peninsula by the Japanese Empire between 1910 and 1945. A small and steady flow of Korean women entered as war brides in the 1950s. Major immigration from Korea did not occur until after the mid-1960s, and these immigrants tended to settle in the Los Angeles area.

Like most other Asian American groups, immigration from Taiwan is predominantly a post-1965 phenomenon, motivated by the fear of political instability, aspirations for economic and education opportunities, and a search for better quality of life. Democratic political change in the homeland did not stem the tide of emigration from the overcrowded, relatively affluent, but resource-limited island that is literally under the shadow of mainland China.[5] A gradual shift in ethnic identity from being Chinese to Taiwanese in the past three decades has resulted in an increased enumeration of Taiwanese Americans in the U.S. Census.[6]

Today because of this immigration history, the majority of the Chinese, Korean, and Taiwanese American populations are foreign-born, whereas the reverse is true among Japanese Americans. Table 13.1 also shows that, except for the Japan-born, a majority of those born in other places in East Asia have become naturalized citizens, with the highest percentage recorded by those born in Taiwan and identified as Taiwanese. Again, with the exception of Japanese Americans, more than two in five Chinese,

Koreans, and Taiwanese Americans were identified as limited in English proficiency; they also reported higher levels of people living in poverty than Japanese Americans. Taiwanese Americans, however, reported the highest per capita income among East Asian Americans, while Korean Americans reported the lowest.

Immigration history and contemporary demographic characteristics among East Asian Americans reveal both commonalities and differences in their experiences and group resources for political participation. How will they affect the formation of a voting bloc in present-day politics? Before we examine the empirical evidence from recent election studies, we will discuss the barriers to their voting rights throughout history.

HISTORICAL BARRIERS TO VOTING

Like other racial minorities, East Asian Americans have overcome obstacles to vote. However, unlike native-born minorities such as African Americans, most of the limitations the East Asian community confronted were at a more fundamental level: not the barrier to voting per se, but rather roadblocks erected by the U.S. government in terms of discriminatory immigration and naturalization policies. Together, they significantly impeded the ability of East Asian Americans to participate in mainstream electoral politics in the past and impaired the pace of their social and political incorporation.

Historically, the U.S. government's position on immigration oscillated between periods of relative openness and claims of nativism. A large part of the anti-immigration policies were especially directed at nonwhite newcomers.[7] The Chinese Exclusion Act of 1882 marked the first time in U.S. history when a people was singled out and banned from entering the United States as immigrants.[8] The Gentlemen's Agreement made between the Japanese and the U.S. governments in 1907 blocked labor migration of Japanese (and Korean) males but permitted the entry of "picture brides" and allowed the formation of families in America. This opportunity was erased by the passage of the National Origins Act of 1924, which effectively halted all immigration from East and South Asia.[9] Comparatively during the same time period, the U.S. government allowed "the annual entry of 17,853 [immigrants] from Ireland, 5,802 from Italy, and 6,524 from Poland."[10] Because the overall flow of Asian immigration to the United States was effectively stifled, the 1924 Act prevented the Asian American community from keeping the same pace and capacity for natural growth experienced by other European immigrants in the same period.

Before 1952, Asian nationals, who were able to enter the United States, were explicitly banned from naturalization. According to the 1790 Nationality Act, eligibility for naturalization was limited to "free white persons."[11] In *Ozawa v. United States* (1922), the decision to deny U.S. citizenship to

Takao Ozawa, a Japanese national who lived and was educated in the United States, was based solely on the premise that Ozawa was not and cannot racially be classified as "white."[12] Essentially, the Court ruled against Ozawa's request to naturalize based on his racial ineligibility. This decision had a deleterious effect on East Asian Americans as a class, and created institutional barriers for all Japanese Americans, citizen or not, to petition for equal protection during World War II, when over 110,000 of them, two-thirds of whom were American-born, were ordered to evacuate from their homes along the Pacific Coast and interned in inland areas because of their ancestry. Ultimately, the lack of citizenship status not only "impeded [Asian Americans'] assimilation and social mobility" but also "denied them a device for political adaptation, for achieving personal legal security, and for a useful symbolic declaration of Americanism."[13] This was the political and social reality of East Asian immigrants who came to the United States prior to World War II.

Several changes and iterations to immigration and naturalization legislation in the mid- to late 20th century slowly allowed East Asian Americans to naturalize and fulfill the basic requirement to participate in U.S. electoral politics. The Chinese Exclusion Repeal Act of 1943, also known as the Magnuson Act, passed in Congress as a friendly gesture to a wartime ally in East Asia, not only repealed the 1882 Chinese Exclusion and subsequent acts and opened a symbolic quota of 105 per year for China but it also permitted the naturalization of Chinese immigrants from that point on. The Immigration Act of 1952, heavily lobbied by the postinternment Japanese Americans, cracked open the door of naturalization for Japanese and Korean immigrants. Finally, the 1965 Immigration Act was landmark in that it lifted racist national origin quotas for all Asian Americans.

U.S.-born Asian Americans were also subject to discriminatory and restrictive policies that hindered their ability to preserve and exercise their citizenship rights. In the case of *United States v. Wong Kim Ark* (1898), an American-born Chinese man was prohibited from reentering the United States after a visit to his grandparents in China. In an unusual victory for its time, the U.S. Supreme Court ruled that U.S.-born children of aliens ineligible for citizenship could make claims to their birthright citizenship. Still, their voting rights were infringed by the suppression of the Fifteenth Amendment in many Western states.[14] Ratified after the Civil War, the Fifteenth Amendment prohibited a state from denying a citizen's right to vote regardless of race, color, and previous servitude.[15] However in reality, many states, especially in the South and West, subjected their citizens to a variety of electoral qualifiers, such as poll-taxes or literacy tests, as prerequisites to exercising their voting rights. This unfairly discriminated against many minorities at the time, including East Asian Americans, because of their concentration in the Western states.

With the passage of the Voting Rights Act in 1965 and subsequent amendments that broadened the protection to language minorities, Asian Americans were not only ensured equal access to the ballots, but also among them those with difficulties reading voting materials written in English were provided with language assistance according to Section 203, if they resided in jurisdictions where more than 5 percent of the voting-age population, or more than 10,000 residents in a particular language group, are limited in English proficiency. Research has shown that language assistance on electoral ballots has significant impact on the access to political knowledge for many Asian Americans.[16] And 8 in 10 among those who showed or described themselves as demonstrating low-levels of English proficiency in the 2008 National Asian American Survey (NAAS) indicated that they would use language assistance at the voting sites. However, observations made on Election Day 2012 showed varying degrees of compliance by jurisdictions and common problems dealing with translated materials, lack of adequate notices of availability of assistance, lack of bilingual poll workers or lack of their identification, and failure of poll workers to have adequate knowledge or to proactively approach voters needing language assistance.

PATTERNS OF HISTORICAL VOTING BEHAVIOR

The narrative of voting and political participation barriers for East Asian Americans is a manifestation and reflection of their history of discrimination by the U.S. government and society, their status as immigrants to the United States, and their settlement patterns in the United States. Prior to the 1970s, it was uncommon for East Asian Americans to run for public office with any success, except in Hawaii and among Japanese and Chinese Americans.[17]

Japanese American, particularly Nisei (second-generation Japanese American), involvement in electoral politics can be traced to Hawaii with the Republican Party recruitment of Japanese membership in 1917.[18] By 1922, Japanese voters were 3.5 percent of the electorate.[19] Noboru Miyake was the first Japanese American to be elected in 1930 as county supervisor. By 1940, Japanese Americans in the Hawaiian electorate had risen to 31 percent; 15.6 percent of the legislators elected were also Nisei. Nonetheless during World War II, no Japanese Americans served in Hawaii's territorial legislature.[20] Because Japan was an enemy of the United States, many prospective Japanese American voters at the time "found that they had to go [to] greater lengths to prove their citizenship and eligibility to register [to vote]."[21] Ironically, during Japanese American internment, the Wartime Relocation Authority allowed Issei (first-generation) Japanese Americans to vote for the first time in an attempt to "socialize Japanese immigrants to . . . American democratic politics."[22]

Heroic efforts by Japanese Americans in World War II successfully propelled many Nisei veterans into the political arena after the war, first at the local level and later to highly visible, national-level electoral offices. One of the most prominent figures was Daniel Inouye, who was elected to the U.S. House of Representatives in 1959 and then to the U.S. Senate in 1963, becoming President pro tempore of the U.S. Senate before dying in December 2012. Between the mid-1950s and mid-1980s, Japanese and Chinese Americans occupied more than half of the leadership positions in the Hawaiian state legislature as president of the Senate, Speaker of the House, and chairs of key committees.[23] By 1990, Japanese Americans made up "22 percent of [Hawaii's] population, 35 percent of the registered voters, 37 percent of legislators, and 55 percent of the civil service administrators."[24]

Because of their earlier arrival on the island, the Chinese in Hawaii had a relatively larger U.S.-born generation and voting numbers than the Japanese in 1919, when Chinese voters constituted 4.3 percent of registered voters, and William Heen was elected as the city and county attorney in Honolulu. Chinese Americans were elected to a number of territorial and county positions before 1930.[25] One of the most prominent Hawaiian Chinese Americans, Hiram Fong, became the first U.S. Senator elected from Hawaii and served continuously from 1959 to 1977. By 1990, Hawaiian Chinese Americans were one-tenth of the state's population and made up 8 percent of registered voters, 9 percent of legislators, and 9 percent of civil service administrators.[26]

On the U.S. mainland, Chinese and Japanese Americans were also slowly incorporated into American electoral politics. Although there was no systematic documentation of Asian American voting on the mainland, "American-born Chinese [were] increasingly aware that their vote was their primary protection against discrimination."[27] Before 1950, the only recorded history of electoral success on the mainland was Wing F. Ong of Phoenix, Arizona. In 1946, he became the first Asian elected to a state house, becoming an example for winning high electoral offices with an immigrant background and without a large number of ethnic votes.[28]

In the next few decades, East Asian Americans slowly found success in the political arena, mainly in California and other Western states. Some examples include March Fong Eu, a third-generation Chinese American from California, who was elected to various offices in California and whose political career spanned from 1956 to 1994. She was also the first Asian woman from the U.S. mainland to win an elective office. Seiji Horiuchi of Brighton, Colorado, was the first Nisei elected to a state legislature on the mainland in 1961. Alfred Song, a third-generation Korean American (Hawaiian-born), became the first Asian elected to the California General Assembly in 1962. Paul Shing, another Korean American, was elected to the Washington State Legislature in 1992.[29] By the late 1970s, Asian

Americans' electoral success had expanded widely into state assemblies, city governments, and school boards from the Pacific Northwest, California, and the Mountain West, to the South and East.[30]

PATTERNS OF CONTEMPORARY VOTING PARTICIPATION

Studying (East) Asian American voting behavior is challenging in that generally accepted theories about American electoral behavior often do not apply. Whereas conventional scholarship in American politics examines the roles of socioeconomic status, demographic background, social network, and political context, some of these factors are less useful than others in explaining Asian American voting.[31] For example, socioeconomic status is not as significant as length of stay in the United States, English language proficiency, immigration generation, and citizenship in explaining Asian American political participation.[32] Acquisition of citizenship is influenced, in turn, by the length of stay in the United States: those who are younger, with higher English proficiency, and with more U.S. education are also more likely to naturalize and acquire citizenship.[33] Additionally, the presence of an "intraethnic" gap in participation rates among Asian Americans could be the result of "widespread differences in the length, condition, and demographic makeup of ethnic immigration and settlement."[34] Fundamentally different from predominantly native-born groups, voting participation for Asian Americans is best viewed as a "three-step process" that involves becoming naturalized and registered to vote before foreign-born adults can be eligible to vote in U.S. elections.[35]

Today, mostly because of the large presence of the foreign-born in the East Asian community, their voting turnout and voter registration rates at first glance appear rather low. Nonetheless, their average naturalization rate is not lower than that of non-Hispanic whites. An examination of the 2004 Current Population Survey (CPS) shows the Taiwanese American community to have a significantly higher naturalization rate (74%) than the other East Asian communities. Table 13.2 also shows that among East American ethnicities, only about one-third of voting-age Chinese and Korean Americans are registered voters, which is comparable to the rate among all Asians. Japanese Americans have a higher level of voter registration at 39 percent and Taiwanese Americans have the highest level at 48 percent.

When citizenship is taken into consideration, Table 13.2 demonstrates that over half of Chinese, Japanese, and Korean American citizens are registered to vote and their registration rates are not that different from each other or from the Asian average (51%). However, Taiwanese Americans again have the highest rate of voting registration at 62 percent. Nonetheless, this figure remains significantly lower than the 75 percent of voting registration among non-Hispanic white citizens.

Table 13.2
Voting and Registration in November 2004 Elections among East Asian Americans

Place of Birth/Race	China (%)	Korea (%)	Japan (%)	Taiwan (%)	Asian Total (%)	Non-Hispanic White (%)
Foreign-Born	88	93	54	87	86	5
Citizenship	64	64	70	78	65	98
Among the Foreign-Born	59	61	44	74	59	60
Registration Among the Voting-Age	32	34	39	48	33	74
Among Citizens	51	53	55	62	51	75
Foreign-Born	47	54	46	60	53	70
U.S.-Born	66	41	61	74	46	75
Voting Among the Voting-Age	29	29	35	30	28	66
Among the Registered	89	87	91	80	85	89
Foreign-Born	90	87	95	80	85	91
U.S. Born	87	83	89	84	85	89
Weighted N (×1000)	1,731	886	412	432	8,523	151,410

Source: U.S. Dept. of Commerce, Bureau of the Census. Current Population Survey: Voter Supplement File, November 2004 [Computer file]. ICPSR04272-v1. Washington, DC: U.S. Dept. of Commerce, Bureau of the Census [producer], 2005. Ann Arbor, MI: Inter-university Consortium for Political and Social Research [distributor], 2006.

Note: Except for the "Non-Hispanic White" column, figures reported are among voting-age persons who themselves or at least one of the parents were born in Taiwan, China, Japan, Korea, or anywhere in Asia.

When nativity, or place of birth, is considered, China-born citizens are registered at a significantly lower rate, 47 percent, than their U.S.-born counterparts, who are at 66 percent. Similarly, Japan-born citizens are registered at a lower rate, 46 percent, than their U.S.-born counterparts, who are at 61 percent. Also among Taiwanese Americans, 74 percent of the U.S.-born are registered to vote compared to the 60 percent among naturalized citizens born in Taiwan. Conversely among Korean Americans, the voting registration rate among foreign-born citizens, 54 percent, is higher than the 41 percent among the U.S.-born.

Turning to voting rates, though the overall rate among the voting-age population is rather low because noncitizens and new immigrants in the community are rather large, turnout rates among East Asian American registered voters are indeed quite impressive. Examining Table 13.2, among registered voters, 89 percent are Chinese Americans, 87 percent are Korean Americans, 91 percent are Japanese Americans, and 80 percent are Taiwanese Americans. When analyzed by nativity status, foreign-born Chinese, Korean, and Japanese American citizens all report voting at a higher rate than their native-born counterparts. Taiwanese Americans are the exceptions, as native-born citizens voted at a slightly higher rate than foreign-born citizens. Importantly, except for the Taiwanese, East Asian Americans, who are registered to vote, have turnout rates that are higher than the Asian average and comparable to the voting rate among non-Hispanic whites.

ASIAN AMERICAN POLITICAL PARTY AFFILIATION

Historically, Asian Americans were not heavily targeted and recruited by either Republicans or Democrats when compared to Irish Americans or Italian Americans. Some early instances of partisan recruitment include the Republican Party's enlistment of second-generation Japanese in Hawaii for membership in 1917.[36] Before 1940, second-generation Japanese and other Asian workers on the plantations were introduced only to Republican candidates and instructed to vote only for the approved GOP slate.[37] And in New York, the Democratic Party organized the Chinese American Voting league as part of a coalition to stimulate minorities, labor interests, and support for Franklin D. Roosevelt's presidential campaign in 1932 and 1936.[38]

While recent surveys targeting Asian Americans have generally shown that Asian Americans tend to favor the Democratic Party over the Republican Party, an accurate understanding of partisanship within the Asian American community must consider factors of ethnic diversity and the large proportion of the foreign-born.[39] East Asian Americans of Chinese, Japanese, Korean, and Taiwanese origin are found to be more Democratic or Democratic-leaning as recently as the 2000–2001 Pilot National Asian American Political Survey (PNAAPS) and the 2008 National Asian American Survey (NAAS), even if this is not the case for all Asian American ethnic groups.[40] And despite the inclination for East Asian American adults to identify themselves as Democrats, data in both Tables 13.3 and 13.4 show that their degrees of identification with the Democratic Party are weaker in 2008 than in 2000. Moreover, there are substantial proportions of the "nonidentifiers" within the community.[41] This means that a large segment of East Asian Americans do not think in traditional partisan terms and that Democratic and Republican labels do not hold the same political implications, such as what each of the major parties stands for, possible or assumed, policy positions of those political parties, and the overall partisan image as generally understood in the U.S. society.

It is often assumed in party identification theory that survey respondents have the ability to accurately place themselves on the American party identification continuum. But scholars who study the partisanship of predominately immigrant communities, such as Asian Americans and Latinos, understand that in order for partisanship to have meanings, respondents in these minority groups need to be able to "grapple with what it means to be a partisan" before they can give a genuine and satisfactory answer about where they accurately stand along the party continuum.[42] This may be more difficult for many Asian Americans because a majority of them are foreign-born.

Table 13.3 shows that among those who responded about partisanship, as high as 55 percent of Chinese Americans and 51 percent of Taiwanese Americans are simply ambivalent or do not identify with either of the two major American political parties. Similarly, Table 13.4 indicates that 39 percent of Chinese Americans and 36 percent of Taiwanese Americans are nonidentifiers. The proportions of adults in these two East Asian groups who identify themselves as partisan Independents are also significantly higher than those found in the other two East Asian groups and the Asian American community as a whole. In both surveys, relatively more Korean and Japanese Americans identify with either the Democratic or the Republican Party than Chinese or Taiwanese Americans. A comparison of results in both surveys also shows a significant decrease in the percentage

Table 13.3
Political Partisanship and Presidential Vote Choice among East Asian Americans

Place of Origin	China (%)	Korea (%)	Japan (%)	Taiwan (%)	Asian Total (%)
Partisanship					
Democrat	32	43	40	27	36
Independent	4	12	20	3	13
Republican	9	22	12	19	16
No/Not Sure	55	23	28	51	35
Presidential Vote Choice in 2000					
For Gore	66	44	56	46	55
For Bush	18	32	18	37	26

Source: Lien, Pei-te. The Pilot National Asian American Political Survey (PNAAPS), 2000–2001. ICPSR 3832. Van Nuys, CA: Interviewing Service of America, Inc. [producer], 2001. Ann Arbor, MI: Inter-university Consortium for Political and Social Research [distributor], 2004.

Table 13.4
Political Partisanship among East Asian Americans in 2008

Place of Origin	China (%)	Korea (%)	Japan (%)	Taiwan (%)	Asian Total (%)
Partisanship					
Democrat	26	34	39	20	31
Independent	30	8	17	33	21
Republican	7	21	15	9	15
No/Not Sure	39	34	26	36	30

Source: Ramakrishnan, et al. National Asian American Survey, 2008. ICPSR31481-v2. Ann Arbor, MI: Inter-university Consortium for Political and Social Research [distributor], 19 July 2012.

of Chinese and Taiwanese Americans who do not identify as Democrats or Republicans from 2001 to 2008. Importantly, we note a corresponding rise in the proportion of Independents in these two communities during the same timeframe. Movements in the partisanship of Korean and Japanese American communities are less stark and in the opposite direction. Namely, there is significant growth in the proportion of the nonidentifiers among Korean Americans and of Republican identifiers among Japanese Americans.

Despite doubts about the solidarity level of East Asian American adults' identification with the Democratic Party in the 2008 survey, East Asian American voters' presidential choices during recent elections are most certainly with the Democratic Party. In the highly contested 2000 presidential election between Al Gore and George W. Bush, two-thirds of Chinese Americans and the majority of Japanese Americans as well as close to half of Korean Americans and Taiwanese Americans opted for Gore (Table 13.3). Meanwhile, fewer than 2 in 10 Chinese Americans and Japanese Americans, but about 1 in 3 Korean Americans and Taiwanese Americans, voted for Bush. Compared to Asian American voters as a whole, Chinese and Japanese American voters gave more support to the Democratic candidate, while Taiwanese and Korean American voters gave more support to the Republican candidate in 2000. In the 2012 contest between President Barack Obama and Governor Mitt Romney, 69 percent of Chinese, 70 percent of Japanese, and 66 percent of Korean American voters, as compared to 68 percent of all Asian American voters, voted for the Democrat Obama.[43] A multistate post-2008 election survey also found 73 percent of Chinese and 64 percent of Korean Americans voted for Obama, as compared to the 76 percent among all Asian American voters in that exit poll.[44] These findings suggest the solidification of the Democratic bloc vote among East Asian American voters.

ASIAN AMERICAN POLICY ISSUES AND BALLOT PREFERENCES

Surveys that include East Asian Americans have focused on several "hot button" issues, particularly abortion, immigration policy, and universal health care. In the 2008 NAAS survey, Asian Americans, in general, were found to strongly favor universal health care at 81 percent. This is much higher than the support at the national level, 60 to 54 percent.[45] Within East Asian groups, Taiwanese Americans are the most supportive of the federal government offering universal health care at 86 percent (Table 13.5). More than 8 in 10 Chinese Americans and Korean Americans are also in support of this policy. Japanese Americans' level of support is relatively lower at 70 percent. Additionally, this survey also shows that noncitizens are slightly more supportive of universal health care than citizens and voters on this issue.[46]

As to whether abortion should be legal in all cases, the 2008 NAAS shows that on the whole, Asian Americans display a relatively more liberal view than the American public, with 35 percent indicating support for this policy position, compared to an average of 17 percent among Americans in general.[47] Within East Asian Americans (Table 13.6), over two in five of Chinese and Taiwanese Americans are supportive of this policy position, while less than two in five of Korean Americans also share this view. And Japanese Americans are the most supportive of this policy position with close to half of the population in agreement that abortion should be legalized in all cases.[48] These numbers show that East Asian Americans are even more liberal on the issue of abortion compared to most Asian Americans, who are already much more liberal than the U.S. average.

The 2008 NAAS findings also provide insights on Asian American attitudes on immigration. In recent years, the U.S. government has proposed different aspects of reform on immigration policies and one of those is that the government would "favor people with professional qualifications over those who already have family in the U.S."[49] Although the Asian American

Table 13.5
Support for Universal Health Care

	Chinese Americans (n = 1,248)	Japanese Americans (n = 540)	Korean Americans (n = 614)	Taiwanese Americans (n = 101)
Somewhat Agree	22	30	18	26
Strongly Agree	61	40	64	60
All Agree	83	70	82	86

Source: Ramakrishnan, et al. National Asian American Survey, 2008. ICPSR31481-v2. Ann Arbor, MI: Inter-university Consortium for Political and Social Research [distributor], 19 July 2012.

Note: Question wording—*The federal government should guarantee health care for everyone.*

Table 13.6
Support for Legalizing Abortion

	Chinese Americans (n = 1248)	Japanese Americans (n = 540)	Korean Americans (n = 614)	Taiwanese Americans (n = 101)
Somewhat Agree	20	25	16	20
Strongly Agree	22	24	20	22
All Agree	42	49	36	42

Source: Ramakrishnan, et al. National Asian American Survey, 2008. ICPSR31481-v2. Ann Arbor, MI: Inter-university Consortium for Political and Social Research [distributor], 19 July 2012.

Note: Question wording—Abortions should be legal in all cases.

Table 13.7
Support for Favoring Admitting Professional Immigrants

	Chinese Americans (n = 1,248)	Japanese Americans (n = 540)	Korean Americans (n = 614)	Taiwanese Americans (n = 101)
Somewhat Agree	27	25	20	28
Strongly Agree	31	9	23	34
All Agree	58	34	43	62

Source: Ramakrishnan, et al. National Asian American Survey, 2008. ICPSR31481-v2. Ann Arbor, MI: Inter-university Consortium for Political and Social Research [distributor], 19 July 2012.

Note: Question wording—U.S immigration policy should favor people with professional qualifications over those who already have family in the United States.

population appears to be split on this issue, about two-thirds of Taiwanese Americans, but also 58 percent of Chinese Americans and 43 percent of Korean Americans are strongly supportive of an immigration policy that favors H1B over family reunification applications (Table 13.7). Only Japanese Americans appear to be lower than the Asian American average (49%) with about one-third in agreement with this aspect of reform in immigration policy.[50]

On the issue of permitting a path to citizenship for unauthorized immigrants, there appears to be a general reservation or lack of support for such within the overall Asian American community with 32 percent supporting and 46 percent opposing the idea.[51] Table 13.8 shows that among East Asian Americans, the Chinese, Taiwanese, and Japanese respondents are even less enthusiastic about this issue. However, over two in five Korean Americans favored the U.S. government providing a path to citizenship for unauthorized immigrants.

Table 13.8
Support for Providing a Path to Citizenship

	Chinese Americans (n = 1,248)	Japanese Americans (n = 540)	Korean Americans (n = 614)	Taiwanese Americans (n = 101)
Somewhat Agree	17	21	26	19
Strongly Agree	11	10	21	9
All Agree	28	31	47	28

Source: Ramakrishnan, et al. National Asian American Survey, 2008. ICPSR31481-v2. Ann Arbor, MI: Inter-university Consortium for Political and Social Research [distributor], 19 July 2012.

Note: Question wording—*The United States should provide a path to citizenship for people in this country illegally.*

Whereas political partisanship is typically a good explanatory factor for white voters on issue opinions and candidate preferences, it needs to be reconsidered when explaining Asian American policy stands and candidate choices due to the large numbers in the community who could not identify with either of the major political parties.[52] As scholars analyzed the votes in the 1990s for and against California's Proposition 187, which prohibited noncitizens and unauthorized immigrants from using health care, public education, and other social services, and Proposition 209, which prohibited state government and institutions from considering race, sex, or ethnicity in the areas of public employment, public contracting or public education, Asian Americans who identified with the Republican Party are not any more likely to support the two propositions compared to those who identified with the Democratic Party.[53] In fact, Cain and Tam concluded that Asian Americans are unique in their policy preferences because their interests are shaped by "other" factors, such as their status as foreign-born but legal immigrants.[54] A similar finding was echoed by Lien and her associates, who discovered that, in general, neither political partisanship nor political ideology is a significant predictor of the Asian American attitudes towards affirmative action as a principle and the provision of language assistance for immigrant communities.[55] Regardless, the preceding discussion also suggests that Asian Americans have become more Democratic-leaning and liberal on several contentious policy areas in recent years. And East Asian Americans appear to be even more liberal on issues of abortion, universal health care, and immigration than the average Asian Americans.

CONCLUSION AND OUTLOOK FOR EAST ASIAN AMERICAN INFLUENCE ON ELECTIONS

Our research on the four East Asian groups of Chinese, Japanese, Korean, and Taiwanese Americans indicates that they neither share the same history of immigration nor current demographic outlook, even if they were subject to the same race-based discrimination in accessing the franchise in both historical and contemporary contexts. Because of the distinct group history and demography, scholars of Asian American politics have cautioned against the assumption of a monolithic political identity for Asian Americans. For example, in the election of California's March Fong Eu in the early 1990s, Wendy Tam discovered that while a large proportion of support for Eu came from Asian American Democrats, there were electoral variations within the community based on other demographic characteristics such as age and generational status.[56] Furthermore, Pei-te Lien and her associates found that, when disaggregated, Asian American political identity and voting behavior vary considerably by ethnic national origins.[57] Our research established that there are not only interethnic differences among East Asian Americans but also intraethnic differences between Chinese Americans and Taiwanese Americans. Still, we observed an overall movement toward the Democratic Party among voters and a largely progressive voting bloc in 2012.

Under what conditions can East Asian Americans think and act together and be conceived as an influential voting bloc? According to James Lai, there is qualitative evidence that when the Asian American population is concentrated in several metropolitan communities and vote in sufficiently large numbers, they can potentially affect electoral outcomes in state and local races.[58] He argues that because of the suburbanization of Asian American politics, small- to medium-sized suburbs are increasingly the primary sites for community mobilization and electoral gains and that this is not just a California phenomenon.[59] In their study of the 2000 elections, Pei-te Lien and her associates found that having a sense of linked fate with fellow Asian Americans helped predict greater identification with the Democratic Party and support for Asian American candidates, other conditions being equal.[60] Thus despite the internal diversity in their political experiences, perspectives, and orientations, East Asian American respondents in recent surveys are able to coalesce around shared political interests and are increasingly rallying behind Democratic Party candidates. Past research suggested that the formation of a Democratic bloc vote was driven in part by the shared political ideology, interest, and knowledge of Asian American issues, but it was also influenced by ethnic group-based activism and experience of ethnic discrimination.[61]

Looking forward, as long as there is no drastic change in issue positions or platforms taken by the major parties and their attitudes toward racial and ethnic minorities, including Chinese and other Asian Americans and the respective homeland governments in East Asia, the Democratic-leaning voting bloc among East Asian Americans will likely be sustained. Their bloc vote could be decisive in tight races, especially in state and local elections. On the other hand, failure to deliver campaign promises such as friendly immigration reforms and universal health care as well as protection of voting and other minority rights may turn them away from supporting Democrats. More importantly, a significant segment of the prospective voters in each East Asian American community has yet to be aligned with either of the major parties. Their mobilization as a bloc vote may fortify or fracture the extant partisan and issue alignments, and should be a force to be reckoned with by any serious political organization and contender for high offices. In a nutshell, East Asian Americans are waiting for the parties to reach out and mobilize their identification and participation. Their growing presence in U.S. society and the electorate and their swing vote potential warrants serious contention by the major parties and candidates for their votes in future elections.

NOTES

1. "President Exit Polls," *New York Times*; AALDEF, "New Findings."
2. Wong, et al., *Asian American Political Participation* (New York: Russell Sage Foundation, 2011), 127.
3. Lien, Conway, and Wong, *Politics of Asian Americans*, 2–4; Aoki and Takeda, *Asian American Politics*.
4. For more information on the U.S. Census enumeration of the Taiwanese American population, see Lien and Harvie, "Political Incorporation of Taiwanese Americans in Comparative Perspective," 128–153.
5. Ibid.
6. Yu and Chiang, "Assimilation and Rising Taiwanese Identity," 115–160.
7. Tichnor, *Dividing Lines*.
8. Takaki, *Strangers from a Different Shore*.
9. Ibid., Okihiro, *Margins and Mainstreams*.
10. Takaki, *Strangers from a Different Shore*, 14.
11. Ibid., Okihiro, *Margins and Mainstreams*.
12. *Takao Ozawa v. United States*, 260 U.S. 178 (1922).
13. Ueda, "Changing Path to Citizenship," 202–216.
14. Stanley, "Frank Pixley and the Heathen Chinese," 224–228.
15. Ibid.
16. Wong et al., *Asian American Political Participation*.
17. Lien, *Making of Asian American through Political Participation*.
18. Ibid., 86; Hosakawa, *Nisei: The Quiet Americans*.
19. Lien, *Making of Asian American through Political Participation*, 86.
20. Haas, *Institutional Racism*.
21. Lien, *Making of Asian American through Political Participation*.
22. Ibid., 109.
23. Cooper and Daws, *Land and Power in Hawaii*.
24. Haas, *Institutional Racism*.
25. Lien, *Making of Asian American through Political Participation*.
26. Ibid., 88.
27. Ibid., 109; Tsai, *Chinese Experience in America*.
28. Nagasawa, *Summer Wind*.
29. Lien, *Making of Asian American through Political Participation*, 87.
30. Ibid., 99.
31. Verba and Nie, *Participation in America*; Brady, Verba, and Schlozman, "Beyond SES," 271–294; Verba, Schlozman, and Brady, *Voice and Equality*; Rosenstone

and Hansen, *Mobilization, Participation, and Democracy in America*; Abramson, Aldrich, and Rohde, *Change and Continuity in the 2004 and 2006 Elections*.

32. Lien, et al., "Asian Pacific-American Public Opinion and Political Participation," 625–630.

33. Ibid., 628; Nakanishi, "Beyond Redress."

34. Lien, et al., "Asian Pacific-American Public Opinion and Political Participation," 626.

35. Ibid.

36. Hosakawa, *Nisei: The Quiet Americans*.

37. Lien, *Making of Asian American through Political Participation*, 87.

38. Chen, "Chinese Community in New York, 1920–1940."

39. Lien, et al., "Asian Pacific-American Public Opinion and Political Participation"; Wong, et al., *Asian American Political Participation*.

40. Proportionally, more than half of the partisan identifiers within the Vietnamese American community are Republican. S. Karthick Ramakrishnan and Taeku Lee, "Public Opinion of a Growing Electorate"; NAAS, "Different or Similar?"; Lien, Margaret Conway, and Janelle Wong, *Politics of Asian Americans*.

41. Wong, et al., *Asian American Political Participation*.

42. Hajnal and Lee, *Why Americans Don't Join the Party*.

43. AAJC, "Strength in Numbers."

44. Lee, "Asian American Vote in the 2008 Presidential Election."

45. Wong, et al., *Asian American Political Participation*.

46. NAAS, "Different or Similar?."

47. Ibid.; Smith and Pond, "Slight But Steady Majority Favors Keeping Abortion Legal"; Wong, et al., *Asian American Political Participation*, 234.

48. NAAS, "Different or Similar?."

49. Ibid.

50. Ibid.

51. Ibid.

52. Cain and Cho, "Asian Americans as the Median Voters."

53. Ibid., 149.

54. Cain and Cho, "Asian Americans as the Median Voters."

55. Lien, Conway, and Wong, *Politics of Asian Americans*

56. Eu is a popular secretary of state who served in California. Tam, "Asians—a Monolithic Voting Bloc?" 223–249.

57. Lien, *Making of Asian American through Political Participation*; Lien, Conway, and Wong, *Politics of Asian Americans*.

58. Lai, "Asian Pacific Americans and the Pan-Ethnic Question."

59. Lai, *Asian American Political Action*.

60. Lien, Conway, and Wong, *Politics of Asian Americans*.

61. Ibid.

REFERENCES

AALDEF. "New Findings: Asian American Vote in 2012 Varied by Ethnic Group and Geographic Location." 17 January 2013. http://aaldef.org/press-releases/press-release/new-findings-asian-american-vote-in-2012-varied-widely-by-ethnic-group-and-geographic-location.html.

Abramson, Paul, John H. Aldrich, and David W. Rohde. *Change and Continuity in the 2004 and 2006 Elections*. Washington, D.C.: Congressional Quarterly Press, 2007.

Aoki, Andrew L., and Okiyoshi Takeda. *Asian American Politics*. Malden: Polity Press, 2008.

Asian American Center for Advancing Justice (AACAJ). "A Community of Contrasts: Asian Americans in the United States, 2011." http://napca.org/wp-content/uploads/2012/11/AAJC-Community-of-Contrast.pdf.

Asian Americans Advancing Justice (AAJC). "Strength in Numbers: Infographics from the 2012 AAPI Post-Election Survey." http://www.advancingjustice-aajc.org/sites/aajc/files/sin_final.pdf.

Brady, Henry, Sidney Verba, and Kay Lehman Schlozman. "Beyond Ses: A Resource Model of Political Participation." *American Political Science Review* 89.2 (1995): 271–294.

Cain, Bruce, and Wendy K. Tam Cho. "Asian Americans as the Median Voters: An Exploration of Attitudes and Voting Patterns on Ballot Initiatives." *Asian Americans and Politics: Perspectives, Experiences, Prospects*. Ed. Gordon H. Chang. Stanford: Stanford University Press, 2001. 133–152.

Chen, Hsuan Julia. "The Chinese Community in New York, 1920–1940." PhD Dissertation, American University, 1941.

Cooper, George, and Gavan Daws. *Land and Power in Hawaii*. Honolulu: Benchmark Books, 1985.

Haas, Michael. *Institutional Racism: The Case of Hawaii*. Westport: Praeger, 1992.

Hajnal, Zoltan, and Taeku Lee. *Why Americans Don't Join the Party: Race, Immigration, and the Failure (of Political Parties) to Engage the Electorate*. Princeton: Princeton University Press, 2011.

Hosakawa, Bill. *Nisei: The Quiet Americans, the Story of a People*. New York: Morrow, 1969.

Lai, James S. *Asian American Political Action: Suburban Transformations*. Boulder, CO: Lynne Rienner Publishers, 2011.

Lai, James S. "Asian Pacific Americans and the Pan-Ethnic Question." *Minority Politics at the Millennium*. Ed. Richard A. Keiser and Katherine Underwood. New York: Garland Publishing, 2000. 203–226.

Lien, Pei-te. *The Making of Asian American through Political Participation*. Philadelphia: Temple University Press, 2001.

Lien, Pei-te, Margaret Conway, and Janelle Wong. *The Politics of Asian Americans*. New York: Routledge, 2004.

Lien, Pei-te, and Jeanette Yih Harvie. "The Political Incorporation of Taiwanese Americans in Comparative Perspective." *Taiwan in Comparative Perspectives* 4 (2012): 128–153.

Lien, Pei-te, et al. "Asian Pacific-American Public Opinion and Political Participation." *PS: Political Science and Politics* 3 (2001): 625–630.

Nagasawa, Richard. *Summer Wind: The Story of an Immigrant Chinese Politicians*. Tuscson: Westernlore Press, 1986.

Nakanishi, Don Toshiaki. "Beyond Redress: The Future of Japanese American Politics on the Mainland." *The Politics of Minority Coalitions*. Ed. Wilbur C. Rich. Westport: Praeger Publishers, 1996.

National Asian American Survey (NAAS). "Different or Similar? Asian American Public Opinion and Intergroup Relations." http://www.naasurvey.com/resources/Publications/naas-ajconf-2009-final.pdf.

Okihiro, Gary Y. *Margins and Mainstreams*. Seattle: University of Washington Press, 1994.

"President Exit Polls." *New York Times*. http://elections.nytimes.com/2012/results/president/exit-polls.

Ramakrishnan, S. Karthick, and Taeku Lee. "Public Opinion of a Growing Electorate: Asian Americans and Pacific Islanders in 2012." NAAS, 2012.

Rosenstone, Steven J., and John Mark Hansen. *Mobilization, Participation, and Democracy in America*. New York: Pearson Education, Inc., 2003.

Smith, Gregory, and Allison Pond. "Slight But Steady Majority Favors Keeping Abortion Legal; Most Also Favor Restrictions." 2008.

Stanley, Gerald. "Frank Pixley and the Heathen Chinese (a Phylon Document)." *Phylon (1960–)* 40.3 (1979): 224–228.

Takaki, Ronald. *Strangers from a Different Shore*. Boston: Little, Brown and Company, 1989.

Tam, Wendy. "Asians—A Monolithic Voting Bloc?" *Political Behavior* 17 (1995): 223–249.

Tichnor, Daniel J. *Dividing Lines*. Princeton: Princeton University Press, 2002.

Tsai, Shih-Shan Henry. *The Chinese Experience in America*. Bloomington: Indiana University Press, 1986.

Ueda, Reed. "The Changing Path to Citizenship: Ethnicity and Naturalization During World War Two." *The War in American Culture*. Ed. Lewis A. Erenberg and Susan E. Hirsch. Chicago: University of Chicago Press, 1996. 202–216.

Verba, Sidney, and Norman Nie. *Participation in America: Political Democracy and Social Equality*. New York: Harper and Row, 1972.

Verba, Sidney, Kay Lehman Schlozman, and Henry Brady. *Voice and Equality: Civic Voluntarism in American Politics*. Cambridge, MA: Harvard University Press, 1995.

Wong, Janelle, et al. *Asian American Political Participation*. New York: Russell Sage Foundation, 2011.

Yu, Zhou, and Lan-hung Nora Chiang. "Assimilation and Rising Taiwanese Identity: Taiwan-born Immigrants in the United States, 1990–2000." *Journal of Population Studies* 38 (2009): 115–160.

Chapter 14

From Central Cities to Ethnoburbs: Asian American Political Incorporation in the San Francisco Bay Area

James S. Lai

INTRODUCTION: POLITICAL INCORPORATION BEYOND CENTRAL CITY LIMITS

Asian Americans are increasingly more active and visible in local politics, extending beyond central city limits. While central cities such as San Francisco, Los Angeles, Seattle, Houston, and New York City remain vibrant 21st-century gateways for contemporary Asian immigrants and community formation, a majority of the U.S. Asian American population currently resides in suburban cities. Between 2000 and 2010, Asian American population growth in the suburbs reached 1.7 million, which was nearly four times the growth during the same period for those Asian Americans living in central cities.[1] Approximately 62 percent of the U.S. Asian American population is situated in the suburbs compared to 59 percent for Latinas/os, 51 percent for African Americans, and 78 percent for whites.[2] Variations of suburban settlement exist among Asian ethnic groups with Asian Indians being the most likely to live in the suburbs at 56 percent followed by Filipinos (54%), Koreans (54%), Japanese (52%), Vietnamese (50%), and Chinese (45%).[3]

In 2010, the national Asian American population reached 17.9 million in 2010, an increase of 250 percent from 1990.[4] California and New York remain the two most prominent states with Asian American populations at 32 percent and 9 percent of the national Asian American population, respectively. Each of these states contains different variations of Asian ethnic populations. In California, the San Francisco Bay Area and Los Angeles metro area contain the most diverse Asian ethnic groups among central cities in the state with significantly large numbers of Filipinos (27%), Chinese (26%), Asian Indians (11%), Japanese (9%), and Koreans (8%).[5] In New York, New York City's Asian American population is tilted toward Chinese (39%) and Asian Indians (23%).[6] While California and New York are major destination states, they are by no means alone. Nevada, Arizona, North Carolina, North Dakota, and Georgia each witnessed their respective Asian American populations' growth between 80 and 116 percent from 2000 to 2010.

Nearly 3.9 million Asian Americans, or 3 percent of the electorate, voted in the 2012 elections. This represented an increase of 547,000 voters from 2008.[7] The impact of the growing Asian American voter base in the suburbs of battleground states was witnessed during the 2012 U.S. presidential election. For example, in the suburbs of Northern Virginia, outside of Richmond, the Asian American population has doubled during the past decade, according to the 2010 U.S. census. These Asian-influenced suburbs were the focus of both President Obama and Republican challenger Mitt Romney in their efforts to sway potential Asian American swing voters. According to Shawn Steel, a Republican National Committee member and an outspoken evangelist about the importance of the Asian American vote for his party: "We've got to get communicating (with Asian American voters). We've got to get on it, and we're running out of time."[8] Both political parties are likely to contend for Asian American voters in key battleground states such as Nevada, Virginia, Texas, Ohio, and Florida.

The Asian American Voter: Trending toward the Democratic Party

According to the 2012 National Election Pool (NEP) exit polls, 73 percent of Asian American voters supported President Obama. This percentage was comparable to the 71 percent support among Latinas/os and 76 percent among lesbian, gay, and bisexual voters. Indeed, according to the NEP, Asian Americans were the only demographic group that Obama was able to build upon from 62 percent in 2008 to 73 percent in 2012. National political commentators such as the *New York Times* columnist David Brooks and *Bloomberg News* editor Albert Hunt began to postulate about the GOP's inability to capture a majority of the Asian American electorate, which shared many of the party's core values—family, faith, education, and business. Given these traits, why did Asian Americans overwhelmingly vote Democratic in the 2012 presidential election?

Before addressing this question, it is important to note that the 2012 Democratic turn of Asian American voters did not happen overnight but was the result of a steady progression since 1992. In the presidential election, Bill Clinton received only 31 percent of the Asian American vote. Since then, every election year has witnessed an increase in Asian American support: 43 percent in 1996, 54 percent in 2000, 58 percent in 2004, 62 percent in 2008, and the most recent 73 percent in 2012. Even with this upward trend, the Asian American vote has not yet crystallized for the Democratic Party. According to a 2012 National Asian American Survey (NAAS) finding, the month prior to the November 2012 election, 30 percent of Asian American voters were undecided. A different set of opportunities and challenges exist for both Democrats and Republicans when it comes to recruiting and incorporating this emerging electorate.

The voting trend toward the Democratic Party is due to a multitude of policy issues that influence Asian American voters such immigration, higher education, fair pay, and health care reform. A 2012 NAAS study found that a majority of Asian Americans supported Obama's Affordable Care Act, a pathway to legal status for undocumented immigrants, higher taxes for the wealthy, and even affirmative action policies in education and employment.[9] While socioeconomic traits help predict how a racial minority group will vote, perceptions of the two parties around the future direction of this group on these critical policies can also shape voter attitudes that transcend socioeconomic status. Whether fair or not, the Republican Party has been perceived by Asian Americans and other racial minorities as a party for only wealthy white males and social conservatives whose interests are counter to those of racial minority groups, regardless of median family income and educational attainment levels. Conversely, the Democratic Party has been perceived as more inclusive of racial and ethnic group interests. For example, a 2013 NAAS postelection survey found that among the 43 percent of Asian American voters who identified "immigration reform" as a very important issue, 70 percent supported Obama compared to 30 percent for Romney. For the 54 percent of Asian American voters who identified "racial discrimination" as a very important issue, 74 percent favored Obama compared to 26 percent for Romney.[10]

Another influential factor on Asian American voters is the nebulous issue of racial and ethnic identity. For example, in a 2008 NAAS finding on racial and ethnic self-identification,[11] 52 percent of Asian American respondents in the San Francisco Bay Area identified with the "Ethnic American" category followed by 35 percent for "Ethnic Group," 23 percent for "Asian American," 19 percent for "Asian," 4 percent for "American," and 3 percent for "Other."[12] These percentages varied by Asian ethnic group with Korean American respondents having the highest percentages across all identification categories. Another key finding was 57 percent of the Asian American respondents in the San Francisco Bay Area stated they would vote for a coethnic candidate.[13] Similar to racial and ethnic self-identification, these percentages varied by Asian ethnic group with 53 percent of Chinese, 63 percent of Filipinos, 60 percent of Japanese, 88 percent of Koreans, and 63 percent of Vietnamese answering "Yes" to whether they would vote for a co-ethnic candidate. Such findings support previous findings on coethnic candidate support such as the 2000–2001 Pilot Study of the National Asian American Political Survey.[14]

These NAAS findings suggest that racial and ethnic identity has yet to crystalize as a key mobilizing factor among Asian American voters. However, the findings suggest that Asian Americans are gradually developing a pan-ethnic or an Asian American identity as illustrated by the percentage of respondents identifying with the "Ethnic American" and "Asian American" categories among the various ethnic groups. While the percentages vary by Asian ethnic group, factors such as acculturation, geographic location, and racial discrimination (real or perceived) are likely facilitating the gradual formation of a racial group identity. The importance of Asian American elected leadership and community-based organizations at the local and state level that can articulate and foster pan-ethnic coalition-building among the ethnically diverse Asian American population will be central to future group political action in central cities and suburbs.[15]

A key question for the political future of Asian Americans is whether they can continue political incorporation efforts that extend beyond voting in cities and counties with significant Asian American populations. The concept of political incorporation is defined as "the extent to which group interests are effectively represented in policy making."[16] This broad definition includes political behaviors such as voting, donating to campaigns, participating in political coalitions, and running for elected office. For Asian Americans, contemporary political incorporation efforts begin at the local level in the context of central cities and suburbs. Perhaps nowhere on the continental United States is this more evident than the San Francisco Bay Area.

THE SAN FRANCISCO BAY AREA AS THE EPICENTER OF ASIAN AMERICAN POLITICAL INCORPORATION

The San Francisco Bay Area, which includes the counties of San Francisco, Alameda (East Bay), San Mateo (West Bay), Santa Clara (South Bay), is a prime example of the dramatic Asian American demographic shifts occurring in both central city and suburban contexts and how this has positively impacted their local political incorporation. Since the Immigration Act of 1965, a monumental congressional act that allowed mass Asian emigration to the United States for the first time in U.S. history, Asian American community formation patterns have taken dramatic shape in all major regions throughout the continental United States.[17] These population shifts have simultaneously redefined the political identities of neighborhoods and districts in the cities within this region.[18] For example, in San Francisco, Asian Americans currently account for 33 percent of the entire citywide population, the second largest population behind whites.

The San Francisco Bay Area's rapid Asian American population growth has been followed by gradual local political incorporation as evidenced by the increasing numbers of Asian Americans elected to represent local political districts. Among San Francisco's 11 Board of Supervisors (BOS) districts, five are currently represented by Asian Americans. Two districts contain Asian American majority populations. District Four has elected five successive Asian American supervisors dating back to the 1990s. This level of political incorporation in San Francisco is both unprecedented and a fairly recent phenomenon, as BOS supervisors Mar and Chiu were elected in 2008, supervisor Kim in 2010, and supervisor Yee in 2012.

San Francisco's central city is not alone in experiencing seismic demographic and political shifts. In the South Bay, several suburbs have undergone similar demographic transformations in their respective Asian American populations that rival or even surpass San Francisco. During the 1980s, the Los Angeles County suburb of Monterey Park, known as the "first suburban Chinatown," was the sole Asian American majority city on the continental United States.[19] Thirty years later, according to the 2010 U.S. Census, 15 California cities contained Asian American majority populations.[20] One-third of these Asian American majority cities were in the South Bay: Daly City, Fremont, Cupertino, Milpitas, and Union City. Scholars have termed these Asian-influenced suburban cities as "ethnoburbs"—cities transformed by transpacific capital and immigration and whose economies are interconnected by these linkages.[21] These majority Asian American suburbs are characterized as small- to medium-size cities with total populations ranging from 35,000 to 110,000.

Asian American candidates in small- to medium-size suburbs have demonstrated a critical marker for political power, namely, the ability to elect and replace outgoing ethnic city council members.[22] The reasons for Asian American candidates' success in the suburban context are factors such as the presence of a majority or significant population base, issue saliency around public education, and electoral procedures, such as citywide elections as opposed to district, which allow ethnic candidates to parlay citywide Asian American voters.[23] A large population base is the first but not sole step necessary for successful group mobilization as seen with African American and

Latina/o districts in large urban cities.[24] Even within the context of majority Asian American suburbs, successful Asian American candidates must foster multiracial political coalitions in diverse cities regardless of the Asian American population size due to this group's low voter turnout.[25]

No other region on the continental United States, with the exception of the ethnoburbs in San Gabriel Valley in the eastern part of Los Angeles County, has achieved a level of local political incorporation as measured by the number of Asian American elected officials than the San Francisco Bay Area. Its long and rich history dates to the Chinese contract laborers, who arrived in San Francisco during the California Gold Rush in the mid-1800s, formed communities and settlement patterns, and helped to establish North America's oldest Chinatown. Since the Immigration Act of 1965, this region has served as a major gateway for Asian immigrants from a variety of socioeconomic classes. The Bay Area's Asian American population grew from 1.4 million in 2000 to 1.9 million in 2010, becoming the second largest racial group behind whites. While the Bay Area's total population increased 5 percent from 2000 to 2010, the Asian American population increased 31 percent.[26] San Francisco County witnessed a 14 percent growth in the Asian American population during this period compared to 4 percent for the general population. Other counties, particularly in the South Bay and East Bay, have witnessed more rapid growth. Approximately one-third of the entire Asian American Bay Area population currently resides in the South Bay region of Santa Clara County with Asian American majority suburbs like Cupertino, Sunnyvale, Milpitas, and Fremont leading the way. In the East Bay's Alameda County, the Asian American population grew from 20 percent in 2000 to 26 percent in 2010 with Asian Indians representing the largest population growth, at 74 percent increase, for any ethnic group.

Asian American immigrants are making the San Francisco Bay Area suburbs in the South and East Bay regions key destinations with the exception of Daly City, which is the nation's largest Asian American majority city located south of San Francisco. Asian American majority cities in the East Bay, for example, Union City, and South Bay, for example, Cupertino and Milpitas, are taking shape as a result. Approximately one-third of the entire Asian American Bay Area population currently resides in the South Bay region of Santa Clara County that has facilitated the rise of Asian American majority suburbs like Cupertino, Sunnyvale, Milpitas, and Fremont.

With the invention of the microprocessor in 1971, Santa Clara County, also known internationally as Silicon Valley, emerged as home to highly educated Asians recruited and trained in the United States and abroad, immigrant entrepreneurs, and blue-collar workers.[27] In 1990, nearly 9,000 Asian Americans accounted for 47 percent of the total 19,000 blue-collar workers in Silicon Valley. In 2013, Asian Americans surpassed whites, for the first time, to become the majority of Silicon Valley's high-tech workers. High-tech companies such as Google, Intel, and Apple have contributed to this diversity with their recruitment of HI-B visa workers, an overwhelming majority of whom are from India and China. In 2010, the Asian American population in Santa Clara County was 32.9 percent compared to 58.4 and 27.2 percent for whites and Latinas/os, respectively.[28] These shifts have made Santa Clara County an important region for understanding the recent evolution of Asian American politics in California, where over 40 percent of the entire Asian American population resides and but also for speculating what the future portends for the political incorporation of this group in these regions and localities.

Table 14.1 captures the Bay Area's ethnically diverse population of Asians and Pacific Islanders. Asian American population growth presents

Table 14.1
Ethnic Diversity of the Bay Area Asian and Pacific Islander Population, 2010

Ethnic Group	Number
Chinese (except Taiwanese)	630,467
Filipino	457,857
Indian	264,533
Vietnamese	205,766
Japanese	109,879
Korean	86,497
Taiwanese	34,095
Native Hawaiian	19,385
Cambodian	16,024
Pakistani	15,368
Samoan	14,770
Laotian	14,288
Thai	12,388
Tongan	12,083
Guamanian or Chamorro	11,249
Fijian	10,153
Burmese	8,778
Indonesian	8,119
Nepalese	3,277
Sri Lankan	2,280
Malaysian	2,095
Bangladeshi	1,980
Hmong	1,523
Bhutanese	410
Marshallese	99

Source: U.S. Census Bureau, 2010 Census SF1 Tables QT-P8 and QT-P9.

both political promise and challenges for this community with regard to issues related to pan-ethnic identity construction and political action.[29] Yet despite such challenges, one fact is certain, successful Asian American candidates today, whether in a central city or ethnoburb, must build multiracial coalitions that articulate common interests and ideologies through strong leadership, regardless of the size of the Asian American population, due to low U.S. naturalization rates for a majority immigrant community that may result in low voter turnout. For example, Ed Lee was elected in 2011 as San Francisco's first Asian American mayor, despite the 150-year history of Asian Americans in the "City by the Bay."

ED LEE, THE MODERATE GOVERNING COALITION, AND THE 2011 SAN FRANCISCO MAYORAL ELECTION

Ed Lee's historic election as San Francisco's first Asian American mayor in 2011 represents an analogy for the larger shifts taking place in one of the most famous cities of the Pacific Rim. Like much of the San Francisco Bay Area, San Francisco's demographics are rapidly changing. In 2010, Asians and Pacific Islanders accounted for 33 percent of the entire citywide population. In various neighborhoods such as Sunset and Excelsior, Asian Americans account for the majority populations. In the Tenderloin, a blighted and historically African American neighborhood, Asians and Pacific Islanders are now the plurality population. These demographic shifts would fuel future political shifts at the BOS level and the mayor's office along with competing progressive and moderate coalitions within the city.

While the 1995 San Francisco mayoral election was described as the "perfect storm" that unseated two-time political veteran Willie Brown from office, the 2011 mayoral election was described as the "perfect confluence of intersections" that brought Ed Lee to the city's most powerful position with the electoral backing of the city's moderate governing coalition in the form of votes, political endorsements, and campaign contributions.[30] One critical juncture of Asian American political incorporation in San Francisco history took place during the 2000 BOS elections in which the city's governing moderate coalition supervisors decreased from three to two during an anti-Mayor Willie Brown movement.[31] The 2000 election further exacerbated the political disconnect between the growing liberal coalition led by former Supervisor Bevan Dufty, BOS District 8, the liberal Democratic County Central Committee (DCCC), and the emerging Asian American electorate. The city's liberal coalition had historically relegated Asian Americans to peripheral status, but it was the moderate coalition that began to see political opportunity with the emerging Asian American electorate and worked to incorporate them. Such a strategy that marginalized Asian American voters pursued by the liberal coalition will likely prove to be political suicide as politicians in San Francisco must give attention to the emerging Asian American electorate.

Since the watershed 2000 election that empowered the liberal coalition, the DCCC has missed important opportunities to reach out to the city's growing Asian American population. One recent example was in 2011 when it failed to endorse any of the four Asian American mayoral candidates, including Ed Lee, among its top three endorsed candidates for San Francisco mayor. Instead, the DCCC endorsed two Latinos, Supervisor John Avalos and City Attorney Dennis Herrera, as its first and second choice, respectively, with no third choice identified. The result was public anger among Asian American political activists and leaders. Attorney Doug Chan's public statement captured this feeling:

> In San Francisco, four Chinese American officeholders—the Mayor, President of the Board of Supervisors, A State Senator, and the Assessor—are running, and the Democratic County Central Committee could not find a way to endorse any of them for even a third choice? This is either a tribute to the political pluralism in my community, or the DCCC is a seriously disturbed institution in a hypocritical manner? The DCCC fumbled its history-making moment badly. Here we are in San Francisco, the Capital City of Chinese America, where eight generations of Chinese Americans have done their part to contribute not only to the building of a great metropolitan area and the American West for more than 160 years. The DCCC had three chances to endorse for election to the highest city office a qualified Chinese American, and it went small.[32]

The DCCC may have chosen to court the emerging Latino vote in San Francisco by endorsing the two most visible Latino candidates in Avalos and Herrera, a progressive and moderate. However, DCCC's reluctance to endorse any of the four Chinese American candidates with the third choice in some ways represents how the liberal coalition failed to understand the intersections of identity and ideology for Asian Americans, even as Asian Americans increased their number on the BOS to five. Concomitantly, the progressive coalition's reluctance to endorse an Asian American candidate led to a political opportunity for the ruling moderate coalition given the common interests and ideology with the city's expanding Asian American electorate. All that was needed to complete the coalition was a strong, symbolic leader such as Ed Lee, a long-time, San Francisco political insider with a strong reputation for building grassroots alliances. Indeed, Lee's emergence as the city's governing moderate coalition figurehead was by no means an accident, rather largely attributable to two intersections in development since the 1970s that facilitated the moderate governing coalition's willingness to include Asian Americans: (1) race and geopolitical space and (2) identity and ideology.

Intersection One: Race and Geopolitical Space

In San Francisco, the intersection of race and geopolitical space has extended well beyond the pre-1965 urban core of Old Chinatown, BOS District 3. In the post-1965 immigrant-influenced communities, new Asian American majority and plurality districts have added the following BOS Districts: District 1 (Richmond), District 4 (Sunset), District 6 (South of Market/Tenderloin), and District 10 (South San Francisco). In 1960, non-whites accounted for only 18 percent of San Francisco's population. By 1990, the figure increased to 53 percent making it a "minority majority city."[33] Asian Americans represented the city's largest minority racial group at 33 percent, followed by Latinos at 14 percent, and African Americans at 11 percent. As mentioned, a primary factor facilitating this demographic shift in the 1960s was the Immigration Act of 1965, which allowed Asians to immigrate en masse as a racial group. Previously, the 1924 National Origins Act excluded all Asians on the basis of their race. The counterbalancing factors that drew Asian immigration to and resettlement in San Francisco during this period included established ethnic communities, such as Old Chinatown, that provided security and social services to recent immigrants, San Francisco's prime location as a U.S. gateway for the Pacific Rim, and the subsequent globalization that created the need for both cheap and professional labor that complemented the skill sets of the post-1965 Asian immigration.

Population growth presents unique challenges for local Asian American candidates. Since 1965, the large foreign-born population influx along with the early-20th-century Asian pioneer immigrants and their descendants of Old Chinatown created two cleavages: pre- and post-1965 immigrants, and Chinese and "Other" Asians. The latter cleavage is important to consider given that the Immigration Act greatly diversified the Asian American community beyond the large, historic Chinese and Japanese American communities to include other Asian ethnicities, such as Taiwanese, Filipinos, Vietnamese, Laotian, Cambodian, and Korean as well as Pacific Islanders, namely Hawaiian and Samoan. Whether these recent Asian ethnic groups can identify with and participate in local politics as Asian Americans with other single- and mixed-race Asians has been a great challenge at the local and state levels.[34]

In 2004, San Fransisco's Districts 1 (Richmond), 3 (Chinatown/North Beach), 4 (Sunset), 6 (South of Market/Tenderloin), and 7 (W. Twin Peaks) contained Asian American populations between 32 and 92 percent. Since then, the 2010 census findings confirmed that Asian Americans are the city's fastest-growing racial group. The Asian American population grew 31.5 percent from 2000 to 2010. With the city's Asian American population now at 33 percent—265,700, it is likely to surpass the white population, which currently stands at 42 percent—337,451—by 2020. The Latino population grew the second fastest with a 27.8 percent increase.[35] In comparison, the white and African American populations grew by 6.4 percent and 1.6 percent, respectively, from the 2000 census.

What is significant about the Asian American population growth is not only the magnitude but also the community settlement patterns throughout San Francisco's neighborhoods. Prior to 1970, the largest Asian American population base was located in Old Chinatown, BOS District 3. However, from 1980 to 2000, the Asian American population extended into the new immigrant communities of Richmond, BOS District 1, and Sunset, BOS District 4, which are known as the New Chinatowns. For example, the 2010 census revealed that Old Chinatown's Asian population decreased to 86.2 percent from 92 percent in 1990, making Old Chinatown less Asian.[36] At the same time, the white population in Old Chinatown rose from 6.7 percent (1990) to 10 percent (2010). In adjacent Nob Hill and Russian Hill, which contain parts of Old Chinatown, the Asian American population also declined. In Nob Hill, the Asian American population declined from 47.8 percent in 1990 to 36.5 percent in 2010. Similarly in Russian Hill, the Asian American population declined from 48.9 percent in 1990 to 40.6 percent in 2010.

While the Asian American population stagnated and declined in the District 3 neighborhoods of Chinatown, Russian Hill and Nob Hill, the opposite was occurring in other areas located in the city's western, eastern, and southern regions. These areas include significant Asian American and Latino population growth in the Outer Mission, Excelsior, Sunset, and Parkside. In contrast, the white population decreased, but more affluent neighborhoods, such as the Marina district, Pacific Heights, the Presidio, the Castro, and Glen Park, remain the whitest neighborhoods. The impact of these community formation patterns extended well beyond mere population and into the political realm. Given the increasingly diverse, multiracial and ethnic characteristics, the importance of multiracial coalition building becomes more salient, and it provides political opportunity for a candidate who can construct and maintain such coalitions.

Intersection Two: Identity and Ideology

Identity and ideology matter in the context of contemporary racial politics in America's cities for African Americans and Latinos.[37] A 2008 national, multilingual survey of 5,000 Asian American voters found a similar trend emerging.[38] As the Asian American community continues to grow in San Francisco, the interplay between identity by which they see themselves through the lenses of race or ethnicity, and ideology, defined as a set of beliefs that deeply affects political opinions, will become increasingly salient factors in determining the city's future political coalitions.

The emergence of a vibrant Chinese American community, specifically, and the Asian American community, generally, illuminates the intersection of racial ideology and identity during the 2011 mayoral election. According to a recent national survey of Asian Americans, residential location was not a strong predictor of Asian American voter support for Asian American candidates in gateway cities.[39] However, this was not the case in San Francisco during the 2011 mayoral election, as a majority of Asian Americans in election precincts located in highly populated Asian American BOS districts ranked-ordered Ed Lee as their first choice. The strong support that Lee received from Asian American voters over other Asian American candidates may likely be the influence of Lee's racial identity on Asian American voters' candidate preferences. Other contributing factors include Lee's front-runner status and the historical significance of this mayoral election that galvanized many Asian Americans to Lee's support despite the presence of four other Asian American candidates.

According to the San Francisco Progressive Voter Index (PVI), in 2004, the top four BOS districts containing the largest Asian American populations in relation to their ideological identification were District 4 (57.8%)/Mostly Conservative; District 11 (51.4%)/Moderate-Conservative; District 3 (45.7%)/Moderate-Conservative, and District 1 (44%)/Moderate-Conservative. The identity/ideology overlap occurring at the BOS district level throughout San Francisco appears to align Asian American voter interests with the moderate governing coalition's interests.

The intersection of racial ideology and identity combined with the intersection of race and geopolitical space made Ed Lee an attractive figurehead for the moderate governing coalition. With no strong, white moderate candidate emerging among the 2011 mayoral candidates, Lee became the symbolic leader to represent the new face of San Francisco's changing demographics and the moderate coalition's newest partner. With the progressive coalition's backing of Avalos in 2011, it will be interesting to see how future Latina/o and Asian American candidates and voters are courted by the rival coalitions.

2011 San Francisco Mayoral Election Results

In the 2001 citywide, mayoral election that featured ranked choice voting, Ed Lee won after the 12th round of vote redistribution with 84,457 votes for 59.6 percent. Although Lee received a majority after the first round, he was the top vote getter with 59,775 votes for 30.8 percent followed by John Avalos (37,445 votes for 19.3%), Dennis Herrera (21,914 votes for 11.3%), David Chiu (17,921 votes for 9.2%), and Leland Yee (14,609 for 7.5%). Among the field of 16 candidates who officially entered the mayoral election, 5 of them were Asian American, which could have potentially divided the large, diverse Asian American electorate. Moreover, there were three high-profile candidates: David Chiu, then BOS president and supervisor of District 3: California Senator Leland Yee, who began his political career as supervisor of District 4; and then Interim Mayor Ed Lee. With the support of various San Francisco city elites, Lee withstood the ethnic competition, and defeated other Asian American mayoral candidates in their former or current supervisor districts. In District 4, Lee received 44 percent, the highest of all candidates, in the first round of votes compared to Yee's 11 percent, and in District 3, Lee received 37 percent, again the largest total and more than double that of Chiu's 15 percent.

Lee's victory was due, in part, to the strategy of reaching out to the city's Asian American voters through the absentee vote process. The nonpartisan Chinese American Voter Education Committee (CAVEC) executive director David Lee estimated that the grassroots voter outreach and bilingual education media campaign resulted in the targeting of 78,000 Asian American voters to vote by absentee ballot.[40] The result of this strategy likely benefitted Lee's campaign the most, as 63.4 percent of his votes came from absentee ballots compared to second place finisher Avalos with 46.1 percent.[41]

Asian American leadership's gradual incorporation into the city's moderate coalition has continued to facilitate further political shifts since the 2011 mayoral election. In the 2012 BOS District 1 election, where Asian Americans comprised nearly 44 percent of the population, the moderate coalition led an unprecedented effort in support of David Lee, the executive director of CAVEC, to unseat Eric Mar, the incumbent, with liberal coalition backing. Lee's supporters spent a record-setting sum nearing $1 million, or an expenditure of $94 per vote cast in this election. Of this amount, nearly $700,000 was soft money spent by independent expenditure committees against Mar, the largest amount for any San Francisco BOS election.[42] Despite this unprecedented amount, Mar was successful in winning nearly 54 percent compared to Lee's 38 percent. Mar later declared his victory over Lee the result of people power over financial power.[43]

THE ETHNOBURBS OF SILICON VALLEY: POLITICAL INCORPORATION IN CUPERTINO

Approximately 45 miles south of San Francisco County is Santa Clara County, which comprises of 15 incorporated cities and towns. Among these municipalities is the region's central city of San Jose, the nation's

10th largest city in 2010. Beyond the city limits, the region contains multiple 21st-century ethnoburbs with significant and majority Asian American populations. For example, the small suburb of Cupertino, corporate headquarters of Apple Computers, has become the archetype California Asian-influenced suburb, with the Asian American population increasing from less than 10 percent in 1980 to 63 percent in 2010.

Cupertino may be the archetype Asian-influenced ethnoburb but it is certainly not alone in Santa Clara County. Table 14.2 illustrates that Cupertino is among six other emerging ethnoburbs, such as Milpitas with 62 percent, Sunnyvale with 41 percent, and Santa Clara with 32 percent Asian American populations. Over the past decade, each ethnoburb underwent varied stages of political incorporation for local elected positions. Cupertino led the way, electing five Asian Americans to the five-person city council since 1995. In 2007, Cupertino became the first Asian American majority city council in Santa Clara County with three Asian American members. In contrast, Santa Clara city has never elected an Asian American to its city council while the cities of Mountain View and Sunnyvale have elected one and two Asian Americans, respectively.

Unlike many central cities, such as Los Angeles, where the Asian American community's interests and ideologies are often splintered around ethnic factions, small ethnoburbs like Cupertino are better able to circumvent such divisions if two important components are present: first, strong, community-based organizations and leadership; and second, a guiding political ideology that unifies the community. Strong leadership and vision are necessary to guide and establish the latter, a strong ideology. Ideology represents a key reason why Asian Americans in Cupertino have been able to mobilize their large population base and successfully

Table 14.2
Santa Clara County Cities by Race, 2010

Santa Clara County City	% Asian American	% Latina/o	% African American	% White
Majority-Minority Cities				
Cupertino	63	4	4	29
Gilroy	7	58	4	31
Milpitas	62	17	7	15
Mountain View	26	22	7	46
San Jose	32	33	6	29
Santa Clara	37	19	7	36
Sunnyvale	41	19	6	35
Subtotal	35	29	6	30

elect Asian Americans to the city council. The presence of a strong political ideology and strategy in the Asian American community has guided its leadership's quest around a common goal: descriptive representation. Its ideology and strategy are modeled after the Asian American Movement of the 1960s, which advocated self-determination and group empowerment for Asian Americans in civil rights and access to higher education in public universities.[44] In many ways, Cupertino politics today represents a continuation of this movement into the field of electoral politics, focusing on Asian American political incorporation and self-determination to achieve descriptive representation in city government.

One of the most influential Asian Americans who helped to establish the foundation for Asian American politics in Cupertino during the mid-1990s is Dr. Michael Chang, the first Asian American elected to the Cupertino city council in 1995 and who also directs the Asian Pacific American Leadership Institute at De Anza College in Cupertino. The vision that guided Chang to run for city council was based on the need for increased Asian American elected representation in city government. Underlying this need for greater elected representation were the principles of the Asian American Movement of the 1960s. Chang, who earned a doctorate from Stanford University and teaches Asian American Studies at De Anza Community College, was a participant in the student movements of the sixties that defined the Asian American Movement's origins. He applied these principles to the electoral arena. After his election, Chang began appointing Asian Americans to key citywide commissions and recruiting future Asian American council members, with the goal of creating a future candidate pool for local elected offices so that political power could be sustained over time.

Another Asian American who was instrumental in establishing the Asian American Movement as the primary ideology guiding Asian American politics in Cupertino is Paul Fong, a former professor of political science and Asian American studies at Evergreen Community College in San Jose. He was elected to the California State Assembly from District 28, which contains Santa Clara County cities and communities of Burbank, Cambrian Park, Campbell, Cupertino, Fruitdale, Lexington Hills, Los Gatos, Monte Sereno, San Jose, Santa Clara, and Saratoga. Fong, like Michael Chang, also participated in the Asian American Movement in the Bay Area. During the late 1960s, he was concerned with minority students' access to public, higher education institutions like San Francisco State, UC Berkeley, and CSU San Jose State. Fong realized the necessity of extending the Asian American Movement beyond higher education to other public sectors, such as city government, through Asian American political action by creating local political institutions that reflected their group's interests and concerns.

Cupertino's suburban dynamics not only fostered the development of an Asian American ideology that focused on pan-ethnic or shared identities rather than the typical ethnocentric interests that have limited Asian American political representation in larger cities but it also helped to establish active and vital community-based institutions that reflect and practice these ideological interests. In Cupertino, not only do Asian Pacific American community-based organizations exist, but many of them work together for a common purpose—the local political incorporation of Asian Americans. An example can be seen with Chang's Asian Pacific American Leadership Institute (APALI), which trains future generations of high school students for civic participation and education. A Senior Fellow program, headed by both Chang and Ruben Abrica, the first elected Latino city councilmember of East Palo Alto, was established to train both Latina/o and Asian American professionals for civic engagement and to understand the common historical and contemporary issues within both communities as they become more politically engaged in racially commingled communities throughout Santa Clara County/Silicon Valley. Asian Americans and Latinas/os together represent over 65 percent of Santa Clara County's 2010 total population with additional increases likely in the future. Consequently, Chang and Abrica foresee the need to establish common ground among the region's future Asian American and Latina/o candidates. APALI is arguably the first local, nonpartisan institute of its kind in the nation with this particular focus and mission.

The sponsorship for many of APALI's events, including the summer institute aimed at college students and recent graduates, comes from many local nonprofit Asian American community organizations such as the Robert Chang Foundation, Asian Americans for Community Involvement, the Asian Pacific Bar Association of Silicon Valley, Chinese Historical & Cultural Project, and Vision New America, a local, nonpartisan organization that seeks to improve Asian American awareness through civic education and participation. Unlike many urban cities, where similar organizations exist but are hampered by competing interests, these organizations pull their resources together to support important institutions like APALI and Asian American candidates, due to the establishment of a pan-ethnic model based on the Asian American Movement ideology.

As seen in mature, Asian American suburbs like Cupertino, the pathway to political incorporation that begins with elected representation is arguably moving faster in the suburbs than in central cities.[45] As political pipelines are established, suburbs with large Asian American populations serve as a foundation for future Asian American candidates at the local, state, and federal levels. One vivid example is current U.S. Congressional Representative Judy Chu, who began her political career on the school board and city council of Monterey Park before her election to the State Assembly and later to Congress.

New Challenges to the South Bay Asian American Coalition

Despite positive trends of political incorporation in local cities, Asian Americans still face challenges creating and maintaining pan-ethnic coalitions, whose leadership is often dominated by Japanese and Chinese Americans among Santa Clara County's ethnically diverse Asian American population. In particular, emerging Asian ethnic groups, such as Vietnamese and Asian Indians, are seeking political representation in Santa Clara, which raises the question of whether these groups should align themselves with the established Asian American Democratic coalition or challenge it. This question was at the heart of the high-profile 2014 California Congressional District 17 election, which pitted two Asian American Democrats against each other in the nation's first majority Asian American congressional district on the continental United States.

Michael Honda, the symbolic leader of the region's Asian American-led Democratic coalition defeated fellow Democrat Ro Khanna, a 36-year-old Indian American attorney, in the 2014 general election with 51.8 percent (69,561 votes) compared to Khanna's 48.2 percent (64,847 votes). In 2016, Honda will again square off with Khanna, who has already announced that he will run again.

In 2012, Khanna raised nearly $1.2 million for a Congressional run against Democrat incumbent Congressman Fortney "Pete" Stark in District 13.[46] Instead, Khanna decided to run in the 2014 Congressional District 17 election against Congressman Honda. The reaction by Honda's supporters and the Democratic coalition's members was that Khanna should have run against Democrat Stark in 2012 when he had a chance to win, and most importantly, would have received the support from the Asian American Democratic coalition. According to Paul Fong, California State Assemblyman, District 28, "We could have gotten behind Ro if he ran against Stark, but he's going against our leader. Mike is the leader of the Asian Pacific Islander Movement."[47]

Other Asian American elected officials and community leaders feel this is necessary, however. Milpitas's former mayor, Jose Estevez, who rallied Filipino Americans in support of Khanna's 2014 campaign, said: "Ro is more focused on Silicon Valley."[48] Despite Khanna's support from local leaders, Honda received major political endorsements from Democratic Party leaders such as President Obama and Representative Nancy Pelosi. Given Khanna's ethnic background, another significant challenge to the South Bay Asian American coalition is whether it can maintain its pan-ethnic nature as emerging Asian American groups, such as Asian Indians, flex their political muscle and challenge the status quo. The political emergence of rising Asian ethnic groups such as Asian Indians and Filipino Americans, who are challenging the established Asian American coalition led by Chinese Americans and Japanese Americans such as Congressman

Honda in the South Bay, should not be viewed as surprising with the Bay Area's increased Asian American immigration and ethnic diversity. Time will tell whether Asian Indians and Filipino Americans will align with the established Asian American coalition or with another coalition that will determine the future impact of Asian American voters in local and state elections in the region. This represents a unique situation for Asian Americans, and it speaks to why the South Bay region is vital to understand the challenges facing contemporary Asian American political incorporation.

CONCLUSION

With its rich and long Asian American history, the San Francisco Bay Area is undergoing new political shifts that are redefining the demographic and political identities in its various cities as illustrated by San Francisco and its South Bay suburbs. Since 1965, San Francisco and its suburbs have been shaped by a stable influx of Asian immigration. As these Asian American communities within the metropolitan region mature, so to have their levels of political incorporation. Asian Americans are key partners in central city governing coalitions that allow for Asian American elected representation to not only continue but also flourish. In San Francisco, Asian American elected officials now represent 5 of the city's 11 BOS districts and the mayor's office. Meanwhile, South Bay ethnoburbs, such as Cupertino, serve as political incubators for horizontal, or citywide, and vertical, or county and state levels, political incorporation bolstered by an extensive network of Asian American community-based organizations that cultivate and support Asian American candidates through political action at the local and state levels. As California and the San Francisco Bay Area transform into majority minority populations containing large, ethnically diverse Asian American populations, the ability to build multiracial and pan-ethnic coalitions will become even more critical to the future success of Asian American and non-Asian candidates. Asian Americans now find themselves as a central component of a multiracial political equation in the San Francisco Bay Area that is unrivaled and will serve as a blueprint for future Asian American political engagement in other regions throughout the United States.

NOTES

1. Frey, *Melting Pot Cities and Suburbs.*
2. Ibid.
3. Logan and Zhang, "Separate but Equal."
4. Hoeffel, et al., *Asian Population.*
5. Logan and Zhang, "Separate but Equal."
6. Ibid.

7. Asian and Pacific Islander American Vote, "Behind the Numbers."
8. Goldmacher, "Undecided Asian Americans Prove to be a Powerful Voting Bloc."
9. Lee and Ramakrishnan, "The 2012 Asian American Vote?"
10. Ibid.
11. For this finding, the 2008 National Asian American Survey asked the following: "People of Asian descent in the United States use different terms to describe themselves. In general, do you think of yourself as . . . ?" The respondent was then read the following categories: Ethnic American, Ethnic Group, Asian American, Asian, American, and Other.
12. Wong, et al., *Asian American Political Participation*.
13. Wong, et al., *Asian American Political Participation*; this question asked: "Suppose you have an opportunity to decide on two candidates for political office, one of whom is (respondent ethnic group)-American. Would you be more likely to vote for the (respondent ethnic group)-American candidate, if the two candidates are equally experienced and qualified?"
14. Lien, et al., "Summer Report of the Pilot Study," 80–95.
15. Lai, *Asian American Political Action*.
16. Browning, Marshall, and Tabb, *Racial Politics in American Cities*.
17. Lai, *Asian American Political Action*.
18. Worth, "San Francisco Neighborhoods Have Changed Faces"; Singer, Hardwick, and Brettell, *Twenty-First Century Gateways*.
19. Fong, *First Suburban Chinatown*.
20. These majority Asian American suburbs in 2010 were the following California cities: Daly City, Fremont, Monterey Park, Walnut, Cupertino, Milpitas, Cerritos, San Gabriel, Rosemead, Rowland Heights, Arcadia, Temple City, Alhambra, Diamond Bar, and Union City. All of these cities are from 25,000 to 110,000 in total population.
21. Lai, *Asian American Political Action*; Li, *Ethnoburb*.
22. Lai, *Asian American Political Action*; Lai and Geron, "When Asian Americans Run," 62–88.
23. Lai and Geron, "When Asian Americans Run," 62–88.
24. Browning, Marshall, and Tabb, *Racial Politics in American Cities*.
25. Lai, *Asian American Political Action*.
26. Asian American Center for Advancing Justice 2013, *Community of Contrasts*.
27. Park, "Asians Matters," 155–168.
28. Nakaso, "Asian Workers Now Dominate Silicon Valley Tech Jobs."
29. Lai, *Asian American Political Action*.
30. DeLeon, *Left Coast City*.
31. Ibid.
32. SFNewsfeed.us, "San Francisco Democratic Party Locks Out Asian Candidates."
33. DeLeon, *Left Coast City*, 14.
34. Junn and Masouka, "Asian American Identity," 729–740; Masouka, "Political Attitudes and Ideologies of Multiracial Americans," 253–267.
35. Fagan, "Census Shows Big Gains by Asian Americans, Latinos."
36. Worth, "San Francisco Neighborhoods Have Changed Faces over Two Decades."

37. Sonenshein, "Do Asian Americans Count in L.A.?"; Browning, Marshall, and Tabb, *Racial Politics in American Cities*; Bowler and Segura, *The Future Is Ours*.
38. Wong, et al., *Asian American Political Participation*.
39. Ibid.
40. Lee, "Presentation Slides."
41. Ibid.
42. Sabatini, "Record-Setting Spending by Challenger in District 1 Didn't Out Mar."
43. Ibid.
44. Omatsu, "Four Prisons and the Movements of Liberation," 135–162.
45. Lai, *Asian American Political Action*; Lai and Geron, "When Asian Americans Run," 62–88.
46. Pulcrano, "Is Rho Khanna the Valley's Next Big Thing?"
47. Onishi, "Rivalries Begin to Emerge in a New Seat of Power."
48. Ibid.

REFERENCES

Asian American Center for Advancing Justice. *A Community of Contrasts: Asian Americans, Native Hawaiians, and Pacific Islanders in California*. 2013. http://www.calstate.edu/externalrelations/partnerships/documents/Communities_of_Contrast_California_2013.pdfAsian and Pacific Islander American Vote. "Behind the Numbers." 2013. http://www.naasurvey.com/resources/Presentations/2012-aapipes-national.pdfBowler, Shaun, and Gary Segura. *The Future Is Ours: Minority Politics, Political Behavior, and the Multiracial Era of American Politics*. Los Angeles, CA: Sage Press, 2012.

Browning, Rufus, Dale Rogers Marshall, and David H. Tabb. *Racial Politics in American Cities*. 3rd ed. New York: Pearson Press, 2003.

DeLeon, Richard. *Left Coast City: Progressive Politics in SF, 1975–1991*. Lawrence: University of Kansas Press, 1992.

Fagan, Kevin. "Census Shows Big Gains by Asian Americans, Latinos." *SF Gate* 9 March 2011. http://www.sfgate.com/bayarea/article/Census-shows-big-gains-by-Asian-Americans-Latinos-2472173.php.

Fong, Timothy. *The First Suburban Chinatown*. Philadelphia, PA: Temple University Press, 1994.

Frey, William H. *Melting Pot Cities and Suburbs: Racial and Ethnic Change in Metro America in the 2000s*. Washington, D.C.: Brookings Institution, 2011. http://www.brookings.edu/~/media/research/files/papers/2011/5/04 census ethnicity frey/0504_census_ethnicity_frey.

Goldmacher, Shane. "Undecided Asian Americans Prove to be a Powerful Voting Bloc." *National Journal* 29 October 2012. http://www.nationaljournal.com/thenextamerica/politics/undecided-asian-americans-prove-to-be-powerful-voting-bloc-20121029.

Hoeffel, Elizabeth, et al. "The Asian Population: 2010." 2010 *Census Briefs C2010BR-11*. Washington, D.C.: U.S. Census Bureau, 2012.http://www.census.gov/prod/cen2010/briefs/c2010br-11.pdf.

Junn, Jane, and Natalie Masuoka. "Asian American Identity: Shared Racial Status and Political Context." *Perspectives on Politics* 6.4 (2008): 729–740.

Lai, James S. *Asian American Political Action: Suburban Transformations.* Boulder, CO: Lynne Rienner Publishers, 2011.
Lai, James S., and Kim Geron. "When Asian Americans Run: The Suburban and Urban Dimensions of Asian American Candidates in California Local Politics." *California Politics & Policy* 10.1 (2006): 62–88.
Lee, David. "Presentation Slides." 15 November 2011. https://docs.google.com/file/d/0B-EK0tbETbAiMTRiMjUyNzUtNjg4OC00MDU1LWE2YjctYTIzYzE3YTYwZjJk/edit?pli=1.
Lee, Taeku, and Karthick Ramakrishnan. "The 2012 Asian American Vote: A Pivot to Blue?" *2013 National Asian American Political Almanac.* 15th ed. Ed. Don T. Nakanishi and James S. Lai. Los Angeles, CA: UCLA Asian American Studies Center Press, 2013.
Li, Wei. *Ethnoburb: The New Ethnic Community in Urban America.* Honolulu: University of Hawaii Press, 2011.
Lien, Pei-te, et al. "A Summer Report of the Pilot Study of the National Asian American Political Survey." *2001–02 National Asian American Political Almanac.* 10th ed. Ed. Don T. Nakanishi and James S. Lai. Los Angeles, CA: UCLA Asian American Studies Center Press, 2001. 80–95.
Logan, John R., and Weiwei Zhang. "Separate But Equal: Asian Nationalities in the U.S." New York: Russell Sage Foundation, 2013. http://www.s4.brown.edu/us2010/Data/Report/report06112013.pdf.
Masuoka, Natalie. "Political Attitudes and Ideologies of Multiracial Americans: The Implications of Mixed Race in the U.S." *Political Research Quarterly.* 61.2 (2008): 253–267.
Nakaso, Dan. "Asian Workers Now Dominate Silicon Valley Tech Jobs." *San Jose Mercury News* 30 November 2012. http://www.mercurynews.com/business/ci_22094415/asian-workers-now-dominate-silicon-valley-tech-jobs.
Omatsu, Glenn. "The Four Prisons and the Movements of Liberation: Asian American Activism from the 1960s to the 1990s." *Asian American Politics: Law, Participation, and Policy.* Ed. Don T. Nakanishi and James S. Lai. Lanham, MD: Rowman & Littlefield Publishers, 2003. 135–162.
Onishi, Normitsu. "Rivalries Begin to Emerge in a New Seat of Power." *New York Times* 26 February 2013. http://www.nytimes.com/2013/02/27/us/asian-american-diversity-in-potential-california-race.html?pagewanted=all&_r=0.
Park, Edward. "Asians Matters: Asian American Entrepreneurs in the High Technology Industry in Silicon Valley." *Reframing the Immigration Debate.* Ed. Bill Ong Hing and Ronald Lee. Los Angeles, CA: LEAP and UCLA Asian American Studies Center Press, 1996. 155–168.
Pulcrano, Dan. "Is Rho Khanna the Valley's Next Big Thing?" *San Jose Inside* 13 March 2013. http://www.sanjoseinside.com/news/entries/ro_khanna_silicon_valley/.
Sabatini, Joshua. "Record-Setting Spending by Challenger in District 1 Didn't Out Mar." *San Francisco Examiner* 13 November 2012. http://archives.sfexaminer.com/sanfrancisco/record-setting-spending-by-challenger-in-district-1-didnt-out-mar/Content?oid=2318406S-FNewsfeed.us. "San Francisco Democratic Party Locks Out Asian Candidates." 19 August 2011. https://www.facebook.com/media/set/?set=a.10150280150320817.330797.171020735816&type=3.

"San Francisco Democratic Party Locks Out Asian Candidates." 19 August 2011. https://www.facebook.com/media/set/?set=a.10150280150320817.330797.171020735816&type=3.

Singer, Audrey, Susan W. Hardwick, and Caroline B. Brettell, eds. *Twenty-First Century Gateways: Immigrant Incorporation in Suburban America*. Washington, D.C.: Brookings Institution Press, 2008.

Sonenshein, Raphael. "Do Asian Americans Count in L.A.?" *Los Angeles Times* 28 February 2005. http://articles.latimes.com/2005/feb/28/opinion/oe-sonenshein28.

Wong, Janelle, et al. *Asian American Political Participation*.

Worth, Katie. "San Francisco Neighborhoods Have Changed Faces Over Two Decades." *San Francisco Examiner* 20 March 2011. http://archives.sfexaminer.com/sanfrancisco/san-francisco-neighborhoods-have-changed-faces-over-two-decades/Content?oid=2171602.

Chapter 15

Korean American Voting Behavior

Yoon M. Lee

INTRODUCTION

In studying immigrant groups' electoral behavior, two theoretical approaches are available. First, traditional assimilation theory[1] posits that the length of time immigrants spend in the U.S. significantly predicts to successful assimilation. The theory assumes that the longer immigrants remain in the United States, the more likely they are to become naturalized citizens, which often improves their socioeconomic condition. As immigrants become more integrated into their communities and more accepting of U.S. institutions and social customs, they are more likely to register and vote.[2] Electoral participation is an indicator of the loss of immigrant identity and incorporation into the majority society. Most studies that employ the linear assimilation hypothesis to explain immigrants' electoral participation assume that socioeconomic resources, such as education and income, increase over time in the United States; yet, researchers discovered that foreign-born persons, regardless of the duration of their U.S. residence, consistently voted at lower rates than the second generation.[3] The effects of education and income on registration and voting are more evident with naturalized Asian and Latino American citizens the longer these citizens lived in the United States.[4]

The second theory posits that political mobilization predicts increased voter turnout. This approach emphasizes the importance of external forces shaping voters' extrinsic motivation to participate than by voluntary decision-making. Therefore, mobilization theory does not consider socioeconomic status and resources as critical factors.[5] Most research on voter mobilization relies heavily on survey data, on self-reporting by respondents about whether they have been contacted and encouraged to vote by a party or other organization, and whether they have voted. Yet, there are limitations to studying mobilization using survey data, especially exit poll data, because researchers do not have control over the type or quality of contact and cannot be certain whether a contact actually occurred, resulting in uncertainty whether higher turnout rates among those who indicated that they had been mobilized are really attributable to contact or to other factors.[6] Moreover, organizations like political parties are most likely to target high propensity voters; therefore, higher turnout may be biased toward the contact organizations.[7]

Studies of Korean American Electoral Behavior

Almost no academic research has targeted Korean Americans alone as a voting group using either theoretical model. Election studies cited in this chapter mostly employ exit polls, and Koreans exhibit their unique cultural behavior, as do all other Asian groups. Despite the limitations of inferring Korean Americans' electoral behavior from a handful of comparative studies of Asian American electorates, researchers must rely on them because of the paucity of information on Korean Americans.

In this chapter, I reexamined data on Korean Americans' electoral behavior using the U.S. Census[8] and the Pew Research 2012 Asian American Survey.[9] I focused on electoral behavior as a dependent variable at key stages under Gordon's seven stages of assimilation model.[10]

Description of the Korean American Voting Bloc

Asian Americans are one of the fastest-growing racial groups in the United States. The modern Asian immigration wave is nearly a half-century old, and it pushed the total Asian American population to a record 18.2 million in 2011, or 5.8 percent of the total U.S. population, up from less than 1 percent in 1965.[11]

Korean Americans have been in the United States over 110 years, and are included among the six largest Asian American ethnic groups. The first wave of Korean immigrants to the United States started in January 1903 and ended in July 1905, when Japan colonized Korea. By then about 7,200 Koreans arrived in Hawaii to work on sugar plantations. The Immigration Act of 1924 completely barred Asian immigration, and nearly ended

Table 15.1
Number of Korean Immigration and Population

Decades	Immigrants in Decade	Decennial Census	N in Decennial Census
1965–1970	27,283	Year 1970	69,130
1971–1980	265,069	Year 1980	354,593
1981–1990	338,872	Year 1990	798,849
1991–2000	171,323	Year 2000	1,228,427
2001–2010	222,146	Year 2010	1,706,822

Source: U.S. Census; Immigration and Naturalization Service, The 1965–1978 Annual Reports and the 1979–2001 Statistical Yearbooks; Office of Immigration Statistics, The 2002–2012 Yearbooks of Immigration Statistics. (Compiled by Pyong Gap Min)

Korean immigration. Following the implementation of the Immigration and Nationality Act of 1965, the influx of Korean Americans soared by more than 30,000 a year in the 1980's, reaching a high of 35,849 in 1987. But the 1988 Seoul Olympics triggered the downturn of Koreans immigration to the U.S. In 2011, the annual number of Korean immigrants was reported at 22,824, but only 5,243 were new arrivals, while the remaining 77 percent were status adjusters who came to the United States earlier on nonimmigrant visas or without visas.[12] In the 2010 census, Korean Americans were estimated at 1.7 million, including mixed-race Koreans (see Tables 15.1 and 15.3). Because a quarter million mixed-race Koreans may exhibit behavior as other than Korean, they were excluded from the studies of Korean Americans, and only those identifying as Korean, estimated at 1,418,962, were included.

Growth of Korean American Voters

According to the Census Bureau's Current Population Survey (CPS), the Asian American electorate grew by 76 percent from 4.7 million in 2000 to approximately 8.3 million in 2012 (see Table 15.2). Applying the Koreans' proportion (8.8%) among Asian Americans in the 2010 Census to the 2012 CPS electorate, approximately 730,400 Korean Americans were voters in 2012. Using the numbers and rates in Table 15.2 with the same logic, 411,215 Korean Americans registered to vote while 345,479 Korean Americans voted in the 2012 November election.

Of the 1,418,962 identifying as purely Korean, Korean Americans of voting age, 18 years and older, are estimated at 1,105,157. Among them, 702,847 (63.6%) are estimated as eligible American voters. Of those voters, 534,112 (48.3%) are first-generation, naturalized voters, and 168,735 (16.2%) are second-generation voters born in the United States. Meanwhile, 410,020

Table 15.2
Growth of Asian American Voting Power

Year	Number (millions)	% Registered	% Voted
2000	4.7	52.4	43.3
2002	6	49.2	31.2
2004	6.3	51.8	85.2
2006	6.6	49.1	32.4
2008	7.1	55.3	47.6
2010	7.6	49.3	30.8
2012	8.3	56.3	47.3

Source: U.S. Census Bureau, Current Population Reports. Voting and Registration in the election of multi years combined by Y. Lee.

(36.4%) of the voting-age group are noncitizens, who could be targeted by the Korean political parties as potential voters in Korean elections.

Problem of Delayed Naturalization

Immigrants may view citizenship as a resource for self-protection in a hostile environment of the host society and rush to acquire citizenship as soon as they qualify. But only 54.7 percent of adult Korean immigrants are naturalized citizens. This analysis of U.S. Census and Pew 2012 data reveals that time of entry into the United States is the most important factor related to naturalization. Evidently, those arriving in the United States since 2000 might not have had enough time to opt for naturalization. Additionally, the ability to speak English had a moderate but significant positive relationship with naturalization (see Table 15.4). Because educational attainment, occupation, and income had no significant effect on naturalization, shortcomings in the social resource model's ability to explain immigrant Korean Americans' electoral behavior were revealed.

Acquiring citizenship is not simply a matter of individual choice. Naturalization is a collective behavior associated with minority status, systematically and differentially affected within the political context.[13] For example, restrictive measures taken in the late 1990s regarding access to welfare and other services, for example, the 1996 Welfare Reform Act, greatly influenced senior Korean American's naturalization decisions at that time. The character of the culture-personality of the group and the socioeconomic-political environment in the country of origin may also have a consistent effect on opting to naturalization in the new country. The "homeland pull" effect[14] on delaying naturalization is explored further in Section 6.

Table 15.3
Korean American Eligible Voters (Age 18 or Older) by State

State	U.S.-born	Naturalized	Non-citizen	Total	State	U.S.-born	Naturalized	Non-citizen	Total
Alabama	430	2,249	2,319	4,998	Montana	12	685	181	878
Alaska	308	1,773	545	2,626	Nebraska	182	1,337	689	2,208
Arizona	2,432	5,140	4,354	11,926	Nevada	1,471	5,188	3,164	9,823
Arkansas	116	1,153	559	1,828	New Hampshire	265	643	249	1,157
California	54,438	171,824	132,009	358,271	New Jersey	6,600	31,212	27,700	65,512
Colorado	3,396	8,722	5,296	17,414	New Mexico	414	1,189	505	2,108
Connecticut	820	3,270	2,293	6,383	New York	17,363	51,744	44,041	113,148
Delaware	219	707	446	1,372	North Carolina	1,972	6,209	5,035	13,216
District of Columbia	760	783	404	1,947	North Dakota	32	224	107	363
Florida	3,619	10,467	6,788	20,874	Ohio	2,185	4,969	3,759	10,913
Georgia	5,390	16,922	18,065	40,377	Oklahoma	505	2,580	1,272	4,357
Hawaii	8,513	10,138	5,724	24,375	Oregon	2,257	6,774	4,063	13,094
Idaho	199	530	607	1,336	Pennsylvania	4,551	14,651	11,200	30,402
Illinois	9,357	25,626	14,672	49,655	Rhode Island	463	347	734	1,544
Indiana	1,086	2,742	3,133	6,961	South Carolina	437	2,256	899	3,592
Iowa	415	2,618	1,715	4,748	South Dakota	19	632	161	812
Kansas	900	2,082	1,538	4,520	Tennessee	1,142	3,435	3,091	7,668
Kentucky	633	1,794	1,055	3,482	Texas	6,398	22,894	21,651	50,943
Louisiana	451	1,251	1,113	2,815	Utah	1,079	2,392	1,924	5,395
Maine	243	376	142	761	Vermont	74	446	111	631
Maryland	4,880	19,452	11,331	35,663	Virginia	5,840	26,788	18,956	51,584
Massachusetts	3,641	6,725	8,398	18,764	Washington	6,692	26,648	14,407	47,747
Michigan	2,530	7,855	6,778	17,163	West Virginia	97	429	193	719
Minnesota	1,016	8,168	2,754	11,938	Wisconsin	1,196	3,167	2,302	6,665
Mississippi	303	689	824	1,816	Wyoming	136	140	168	444
Missouri	1,258	4,077	2,886	8,221	Total	168,735	534,112	402,310	1,105,157

Source: 2010 ACS, tabulated by Y. Lee.

Table 15.4
English Proficiency of Foreign-Born Koreans

Ability to speak English	Naturalized citizen	Non-citizen	Total
Veiy well	56.4%	43.6%	100.0%
Well	49.8%	50.2%	100 0%
Not well	43 2%	56.8%	100.0%
Not at all	35.6%	64.4%	100.0%
Total	54.3%	45.7%	100.0%

Source: 2010 ACS, tabulated by Y. Lee.

Korean American's Struggle for Voting Rights

The majority of Korean Americans arrived at the end of the 1960s during the Civil Rights Movement, and never experienced a struggle to achieve their voting rights as African Americans had. Ironically, Korean Americans showed more interest in sharing in the battle for national security and democracy against dictators in their homeland from the 1970s through the 1980s. Indeed, they continue to demonstrate interest in their homeland's politics as well as the security issues that divide the Korean peninsula. Nonetheless, Korean Americans are encouraged to participate in American politics by Korean language media in major metropolitan areas as well as by the Korean government, suggesting that they model Jewish Americans. In addition, their unique "middleman minority" experiences[15] as victims of boycotts and riots in inner city neighborhoods strengthened ethnic solidarity and increased interest in political outcomes. Meanwhile, Korean Americans gained prominence through political representation, as 31 Korean Americans were elected as city councilmen and mayor at the state and municipal levels.[16]

Problems Encountered by Korean American Voters

There is no systematic documentation of Korean Americans encountering problems with political participation; however, the AALDEF study dramatically identified challenges encountered by Korean Americans while voting.[17] For example, of the 998 Korean American respondents in the AALDEF's 2012 November Election Survey, 337 were required to show identification, though 272 of them were not first-time voters, 22 were required to prove their U.S. citizenship, 23 were informed that their names were missing or experienced errors with the list of voters at poll sites. Furthermore, 13 had to vote by provisional ballot, 30 voters indicated that poll workers did not know the rules, 22 voters indicated that poll workers were rude or hostile, 43 voters complained that no interpreters or translations were available when needed, and 8 voters were directed to the wrong polling site or voting machine or table within a site.

Removing Obstacles: Language Barriers

Lack of English proficiency has frequently been blamed by various immigrant groups as a barrier to naturalization, voter registration, and voting at polling places. To alleviate this problem, language assistance provisions were added under the Voting Rights Act. Section 203 mandated bilingual ballots, translated voting materials, and interpreters in counties where immigrants are concentrated. But results are varied among Asian groups, and bilingual ballot provision had no effect on Koreans' voting based on the state-level data (Logan, Oh, and Darrah 2012). As Korean American voter numbers are relatively small, few counties meet the bilingual ballot requirement.[18]

Mobilization for Voting by Korean American Organizations

Although Korean Americans, like other Asian Americans, lack civil rights organizations with longevity and intensity, efforts to advance voting rights and mobilize political participation are growing. A number of pan-Asian American organizations have embraced constituents, including Korean Americans, on an individual basis, and collaborated with Korean American organizations. Among the organizations that actively conduct nationwide campaign are Asian and Pacific Islander American Vote (APIAVote), Asian American Justice Center (AAJC), and the Asian American Legal Defense Education Fund (AALDEF). In 2012, about 6 Korean American organizations partnered with over 75 Asian American organizations in 15 states to enhance civic participation within the Asian American community. On Election Day 2012, APIAVote and AAJC hosted an "election protection" hotline with operators conversant in Chinese, Korean, Vietnamese, and Thai, an unprecedented and extensive outreach by grassroots organizations.

Since the 2008 election, Korean American organizations devoted to promoting registration and voting became more active at the local level. As many Korean American organizations compete nationwide or locally, a few exemplary cases are introduced. In the East, the Korean American Civic Empowerment (KACE) was established in 1996 in Flushing, New York, and then expanded into New Jersey. KACE is one of the most active, grassroots organizations mobilizing Korean-Americans community by promoting voting rights and educating Korean American citizens. KACE registered over 25,000 Korean Americans to vote in New York and New Jersey, and raised the Korean American turnout from 5 percent in 1996 to over 68 percent in 2008. In advance of the 2012 presidential election, KACE accessed the voter registration records from 62 New York counties, establishing a foundation for future elections.[19]

In Los Angeles following the civil unrest of the early 1990s, the anti-immigrant, sociopolitical backlash that followed caused Korean community-based organizations to form the National Association of Korean American Educational Centers (NAKASEC). NAKASEC's purpose is to project a national, progressive voice on major civil rights and immigrant issues and to promote the full participation of Korean Americans for social change. It has affiliates in Annandale, Virginia, and Chicago, where the organizations assists Korean American voters with voter registration, voter education, voter mobilization, voter assistance, voter research, and voting rights advocacy. The Korean Resource Center (KRC), a NAKASEC affiliate in Los Angeles, has coordinated a multifaceted civic participation campaign since the 1996 presidential elections.[20]

In the Midwest, the Korean American Resource and Cultural Center in Chicago, a member of NAKASEC, and the Korean American Voter Organizing Initiative & Community Empowerment have been active in voter registration and mobilization. Two groups organized the Korean American Early Voting Day event before the November 2012 election with the cooperation of the Cook County Election Commission, and reprised it in the March 2014 primary election.

Mobilizing Likely Voters by Political Parties

A key factor in voter turnout is mobilization, that is, recruiting people registered to vote to actually do so on Election Day. Neither the major parties nor their candidates actively or sufficiently engage Korean Americans or other Asian American groups. According to the 2012 National Asian American Survey (NAAS), voter mobilization rates targeting Asian Americans (31%) fall noticeably short of those targeting whites (43%) or African Americans (39%). Moreover, Korean Americans in the NAAS 2012 Survey were more likely to be contacted about the election than all other Asian Americans, 42 to 35 percent, respectively. However, the survey found that outreach efforts by political parties, candidates, and community advocacy organizations were not effective in influencing Korean Americans' votes.[21]

Patterns of Korean Americans' Voting Behavior

The majority of Korean immigrants have lived in the United States only about five decades, and their absolute numbers are very small, therefore, it is premature to develop a theoretical model to explain Korean American voting behavior that employs either the linear assimilation or social mobilization model. It is possible to speculate about the level of Korean American participation in the electoral process.

Voter Registration

In the CPS data, 4.7 million Asian American citizens reportedly registered to vote, or 56.3 percent of the 8.3 million eligible Asian Americans (see Table 15.2). Applying this voter registration rate (56.3%) to the 702,847 Korean Americans eligible to vote estimated by the 2010 census, there are an estimated 404,949 Korean American registered voters. In the Pew 2012 Survey, 74.4 percent of the 316 Korean American respondents were registered to vote,[22] and extrapolating from this rate (74.4%), there appears to be approximately 522,918 registered Korean American voters.

Voting at Polling Places

According to the CPS data presented in Table 15.2, approximately 3.9 million, or 47.3 percent of the 8.3 million Asian American eligible voters, reportedly voted in the 2012 presidential election, which is approximately the same figure offered by the National Asian American Survey (NAAS)—3.85 million: a record number of Asian Americans and Pacific Islanders turned out in 2012 election. When the 2012 Asian American voting rate in the CPS data (47.3%) is applied to Korean American eligible voters (702,847), approximately 332,446 Korean Americans voted in the 2012 election. In the Pew 2012 Survey sample, 60.2 percent of the 316 Korean American respondents voted in the 2008 election.[23]

Applying this 60.2 percent to 702,847 Korean American eligible voters, it is likely that 423,113 Korean Americans could have voted in the 2012 November election. Based on the few available voting rates for registered voters, approximately 316,281 to 423,113 Korean Americans could have voted in November 2012 election as shown in Table 15.5.

Table 15.5
Estimates of Korean Americans Who Voted in November 2012 Election

	Voter Base Number in 2010 ACS	Rate Voted	Estimates of Voted
CPS, Asian American Registered Voters in 2012	702,847	47.3%	332,446
Pew 2012 Survey, Korean Voters Voted in 2008	702,847	60.2%	423,113
NAAS, Korean Registered Voters in 2012 Election	702,847	79.0%	555,249

Socioeconomic Resources

There are several significant factors affecting Korean Americans' voter registration and turn out. First, socioeconomic factors do not appear to influence Korean Americans' electoral behaviors. Oh found[24] that higher levels of educational attainment, a simplified measure of socioeconomic resources, did not necessarily correlate with higher levels of registration and voting for all Asian groups compared to non-Hispanic whites. It appears that longevity has a stronger effect than socioeconomic factors. My analyses of the 2012 Pew data do not support the socioeconomic resources model as sufficient to explain Korean American citizens' electoral behavior. Korean Americans with higher education levels voted less in the 2008 presidential election, while occupation and income had no apparent impact on their votes as well. Alternatively, the immigration period had a significant positive effect on voting in 2008. Citizens arriving between 2000 and 2010 were less likely to have voted in the 2008 presidential election. Clearly, a better understanding of the negative relationship between levels of education and levels of political participation is needed.

Limited English Proficiency and Voting

With Asian and Latino immigrants in particular, English proficiency is an important resource. Language barriers seem to work significantly against foreign-born Korean Americans' electoral participation. Cho posited[25] that the observed racial and ethnic group differences in voting and registration among racial minorities can be explained primarily by the interaction between English-speaking ability and foreign-born status. She argued that language barriers can significantly diminish or eliminate the effects of socioeconomic and demographic factors on electoral activities. Oddly enough, foreign-born Korean Americans have the lowest rate of English proficiency among six major Asian groups.[26] Analyses of the 2012 Pew Survey data partially support such assertions, showing English proficiency is not related to registration, but it is related to having voted in 2008 election. The turnout rate is 71.3 percent for those who speak English "very well," compared to 45 percent for those who speak English "not at all" (see Figure 15.1).

Approximately half of Korean American voters (56%) reported "Limited English Proficiency" as problem in the AALDF's 2012 exit poll. In addition, 26 percent preferred voting with assistance, 22 percent used an interpreter, and 23 percent used translated written materials. Only 5 percent needed no interpreter and 8 percent required no translated written materials. However, the hypothesis that limited English proficiency causes low electoral participation is not supported by most research.

Figure 15.1
English Proficiency and Voting Behavior (Korean Americans)

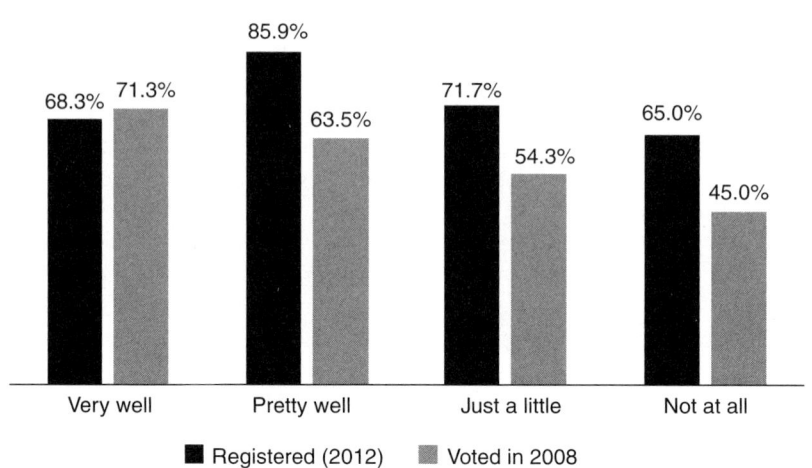

Korean Americans' Influence to the Election Outcome

There is a general perception that the impact of Asian Americans, particularly that of Korean Americans, on the national level election is insignificant. The major reasons for such a perception are their relatively small numbers coupled with their low turnout rate. However, according to T. Lee's account,[27] Korean Americans' lopsided preference for Democratic candidates has been obvious since the 2004 election, when 65 percent of Korean Americans voted for John Kerry. Also, the Korean American's vote for Obama increased from 64 percent in 2008 to 78 percent in 2012. Their support for President Obama was consistent across voters of all age groups and all categories including first-time voters (80%), foreign-born voters (77%) and native-born voters (87%), and limited English proficiency voters (78%).

Another reason for the poor perception of Asian American voters' influence impact could be that Asian Americans are less likely to reside in presidential battleground states than whites or blacks.[28] Moreover, reports of mobilization among Asian Americans living in presidential battleground states are not higher than those living in non-competitive states. Yet, Asian Americans and Pacific Islanders are nationally the fastest-growing groups, and are rapidly expanding in battleground states. One in six Asian Americans (17%) lived in a battleground state during the 2012 presidential election, and Korean Americans in the battleground states are increasing (see Table 15.2).[29] Although no significant differences were found between battleground and non-battleground states in their support of candidates, Asian American voters contributed decisively to Obama's victories in 2008 and 2012. Korean American voters, as a part of the Asian American community, could have contributed in two elections to Democratic victories as Ramakrishnan asserted.[30]

Important Issues That Influence Korean American Voters

Liberal Issues and Democratic Party Preference

Among 316 Korean American citizens in the 2012 Pew Survey, evidence supports increasing liberalism within the Korean American electorate. Extreme political views seem to be related to more active political participation, that is, those holding extreme political opinions were more likely to register and vote compared to those with moderate opinions (see Figure 15.2).

The most important policy issues influencing Korean American voters in the 2012 presidential election were the economy and jobs (48%) according to the NAAS study. Civil rights was the second most important issue (36%) when immigrant's rights were included, followed by education (18%), women's issues (18%), health care (17%), and terrorism/security (8%). Among Korean Americans who voted, their issue preferences were not much different than typical American voters.[31] On the other hand, the important issues among the general public, such as women's rights, abortion, and homosexuality were not as critical to Korean Americans. Korean Americans, more than other Asians and the general public, were more likely to prefer liberal issues, according to the 2012 Pew Survey (see Table 15.6).

Figure 15.2
Political Ideology and Voting Behavior

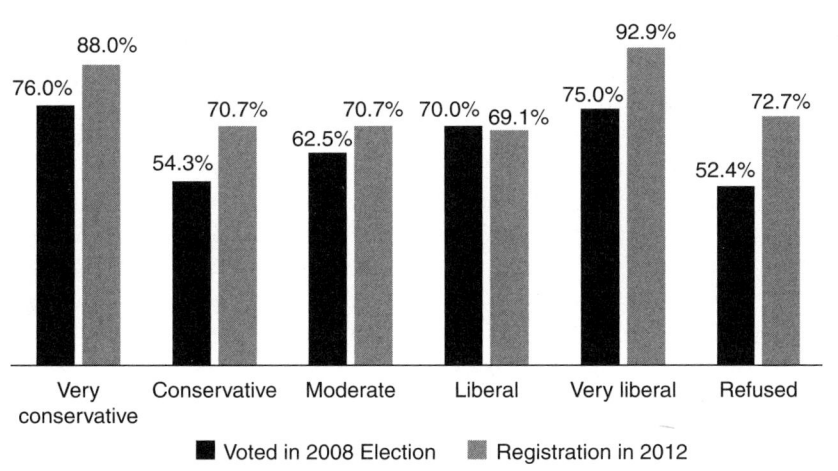

Table 15.6
Preference of Liberal Issue among Korean Americans

	Korean	All Asian	General Public
Discrimination a major problem	24%	13%	N/A
Against homosexuality	56%	40%	32%
Prefer a big government	68%	55%	52%
Prefer a smaller government	26%	36%	39%

Table format: Y. Lee from Pew 2012 Asian American Survey Report.

Specifically, Korean Americans' support for comprehensive immigration reform was consistent in 2012 election among all age groups, according to the AALDEF survey. With immigration policy, the effects of Korean Americans' support for Obama were statistically significant, even after considering key demographic factors and partisanship. Korean Americans also supported Obama's other policies, such as taxing the rich by 79 percent, citizenship for undocumented aliens by 74 percent, and the recent Korea-U.S. Free Trade Agreement (KORUS-FTA) by 75 percent. T. Lee asserted that the high level of support for liberal issues and for the KORUS-FTA were strong factors for Korean Americans, controlling for other variables, contributing to their votes for President Obama in 2012.[32]

Korean Homeland Issues

Conservative Korean American groups, found mostly in large cities, are dedicated to homeland issues rather than American political issues, such as Koran Associations in large cities, Pyung-Tong (Korea Peaceful Unification Advisory Council), Korean culture project groups, and Korean military veterans groups. For many years, they advocated against North Korea's policies on unification of the homeland. In the 2010s, conservative Korean Americans became seriously engaged in "Comfort Women" issues[33] and so-called Dong Hae Byungi campaign to add the name of the East Sea to the map of the Sea of Japan. These are extensions of the homeland's anti-Japan affective movement and policy. They have been partially successful in passing Congressional resolutions and legislation at state level. Additionally, the anti-North Korean campaign repeatedly emerges as an ideological dispute or organized confrontation among Korean groups in major U.S. metropolitan areas. It appears that conservative Korean Americans than liberal Korean Americans are more likely to focus on homeland issues while delaying naturalization and electoral participation in the United States.

Discussion and Analysis of Korean Americans' Party Affiliation

Theoretically, party identification may be coupled with ideological interests. Early studies of Latinos and Asian Americans political behavior hypothesized that large, immigrant-based groups might ally with the Republican Party because of foreign policy interests.[34]

Asian Americans more than any other voting blocs have shifted dramatically from the Republican Party over the since the 1990s. The shift in Asian American political sentiments started during the Clinton years in response to the appeal of the Democratic Party that was seemingly more welcoming of minorities. Comparative studies of recent elections involving Korean Americans concur that although Korean Americans were twice as likely to identify as Democratic than Republican, more than one-third to one-half preferred to identify as independent.

Korean Americans' heavy preference for Democrats appears less obvious in the 2012 Pew Survey than in other political surveys. It is noteworthy that party identification is not static but fluctuates depending on how questions are worded. According to the Pew data, Korean Americans leaned more Democratic (32% leaning toward Republican, 48% leaning toward Democrat) than their party identification indicated (23% as Republican vs. 36% as Democrat). A summary of Korean Americans' party preferences from available sources is presented in Table 15.7.

Table 15.7
Korean American Party Preferences

	Democrat	Republican	Independent	Not Enrolled	Others or N/A	Total
2006 Midterm Elections Asian American survey	56%	12%		34%		102%
AALDEF Asian American Survey, 2012 November Elections	60%	14%		24%	2%	100%
NAAS Exit Poll for 2012 November Elections	41%	18%	32%	9%		100%
Pew 2012 Asian American Survey	36%	23%	28%	5%	8%	100%

Table format: by Y. Lee; Source: Glenn. D. Magpantay, 2006.

Issues and Party Preference and Voting

Before President Clinton, many Korean Americans, who had political interests, were concerned with their homeland's security vis-à-vis communist North Korean, and so identified with the Republican Party, because of its strong anticommunist platform. That preference remains among conservative, aged Korean Americans. Interestingly, my analysis of Pew data revealed that longevity in the United States significantly differentiated Korean Americans along party identification and party preference. Republican identification was prevalent among those who came to the United States before 1979, but the tendency reversed to favor Democrats among those who arrived between 1980 and 2010.

A second hypothesis is that immigrant groups that experienced improvements material well-being are more likely to support the Republican Party and its candidates,[35] but there was little evidence from the 2012 NAAS data to support it. To the contrary, Korean Americans on average were quite liberal across a wide range of policies and their liberal views correlated to their voting behavior in 2012. Korean Americans' party identifications do not vary significantly as a function of educational attainment, occupation, income, or English proficiency based on my analyses of the 2012 Pew data; however, those with higher education and with higher English proficiency leaned Republican.

Taeku Lee (2012) found that although issues correlated to party identification rather than demographic factors, candidate favorability had stronger effect on Korean American's support of Democrats. President Obama's popularity with Asian Americans, in general, and with Korean Americans specifically, turned them to the Democratic Party. My analysis of the 2012 Pew 2012 data also supported T. Lee's findings. Although party identification had no significant effect on voter registration, it had a weak, yet significant, relationship with casting a vote in the 2008 election. The 2008 voting rate was slightly higher among those who identified as Democratic (67.2%) than among those who identified as Republican (65.1%) and among Independents (60.8%). Favoring a party had no significant effect on voter registration. There was no gap in the registration rate between Republican sympathizers (65.4%) and Independents (65.1%), while the Democratic sympathizers' registration rate increased to (81.1%). Korean Americans shift toward the Democratic Party had a significant impact on voting in the 2008 election. The 2008 voting rate was slightly higher among Democratic sympathizers (72.2%) than among Republican sympathizers (56.0%) and those who had no preference for party (40.3%).

Speculation on Future Korean Americans' Voting Behavior

Those holding optimistic views on the growth of Korean Americans' voting power may want to focus only on their rapid, expanding influence, but the reality is much more sobering because Korean Americans make up only a small percentage of the total U.S. electorate and because of their general attitude toward their adopted country.

Intra-Networks and Delay of Civic Identity

Earlier in this chapter, a lapse in naturalization by foreign born adult Korean Americans was noted. There could be many reasons why immigrants delayed becoming U.S. citizens. Korean Americans voluntarily dispersed across America and the majority live in suburban residential areas, but they are highly concentrated in terms of community networks, primarily by Korean language media and community organizations, particularly by churches and homeland-related organizations. Korean Americans are a unique Asian group who favor ethnic language daily papers and full-time broadcasting outlets franchised in the homeland. These networking entities may complicate assimilation and adversely affect the development of American civic identity.

As a measure of social networking, primary group ties may be examined. In the 2012 Pew Survey, more Korean Americans (58%) than all Asian Americans (41%) were likely to say that all or most of their friends shared their ethnic heritage.[36] Although the number of close Korean friends in the United States had no significant relationship with voter registration, the primary group tie had a weak yet significant inverse relationship with voting in 2008, according to my analyses of the 2012 Pew data. Voter turnout was 52.5 percent among those whose friends were all Korean compared to 64.9 percent among those who had "hardly any" Korean friends. Additionally, Korean Americans were most likely to respond that it was very important to them that future generations of Koreans living in the United States speak their ancestral language (62%), but the number of cases were too small to establish any significant relationship with the ability to use Korean language on naturalization, voter registration, and having voted in the 2008 election.

Homeland Sentiments and Civic Identity

Emotional attachment to the homeland and a rational calculation of the costs and benefits may explain Korean American reluctance to cut their homeland ties, even more so when the homeland offers greater incentives such as an economically thriving Korea. Koreans who registered with the Korean government to immigrate to the United States in 2013 declined to 3,185, a drop of 70 percent from 2012.[37] Meanwhile, Korean Americans who sought return to their homeland and registered for a permanent address in Korea rose to 40,421 in 2013 from 31,734 in 2009.[38]

Some media accounts and scholarly articles suggest that Asian Americans participate less in American politics because they focus on their home countries' politics. However, the 2012 NAAS data did not support the "homeland pull" hypothesis.[39] Contrary to common misconceptions about a trade-off between political engagement in one's homeland and engagement in U.S. politics, transnational political activity appeared to boost participation in activity. In the 2012 Pew Survey, the majority of Korean Americans acknowledged the rapid economic growth in Korea, and that 63 percent of Korean Americans still had close family living in the homeland. However, they rated the current conditions in the United States better (68%) and the "opportunity to get ahead is better in the United States (69%) than in Korea. And if they had to make a choice again, a majority (68%) would still immigrate to the United States than remain in Korea (23%). Analyzing the Pew data, most of the homeland push-pull items were not significantly related to voter registration or voting in the 2008 election, partially supporting the 2012 NASA findings. For example, having immediate family members such as a spouse, parents, siblings, or children, in the homeland did not have any relationship with registration or voting in the 2008 election, but did have a significant relationship with naturalization. Choosing "come to the U.S. if they had to do it over again" is not significantly related to registration or having voted in 2008 election. As stated before, the homeland pull factors affect decisions on naturalization, not electoral behavior.

Conflicts, Group Consciousness, and Voting

The "ethnic community hypothesis" posits that minority groups generate a sense of solidarity in reaction to discrimination, which then motivates group efforts to overcome disadvantages through political engagement.[40] African Americans' high voting rates, despite deficits in socioeconomic and other resources, have been attributed to group consciousness, mobilizing institutions, and other features specific to their race. This approach suggests that the political potency of group membership is linked to racial identification, and argues that a sense of "linked fate" stimulates participation or group solidarity.[41] However, there are studies[42] that find no positive relationship between group consciousness and voting. But did experiences with discrimination influence Korean American group consciousness and affect their political behavior? Only one-fifth of the Koreans in the 2012 Pew sample (95 out of 504) personally experienced discrimination and 12 percent had been called offensive names within the last year. Among those who reported personally experiencing discrimination or unfair treatment during the past 12 months, 67.2 percent registered to vote, while 75.8 percent of those had not experienced discrimination. Yet, the discrimination hypothesis was not supported because only one-fifth of Koreans in the 2012 Pew sample

Table 15.8
Perceived Discrimination as Problem and Voting

	Registered for Voting	Voted in 2008 Election
Major problem	83.3%	81.7%
Minor problem	68.8%	67.3%
Not a problem	71.8%	72.9%
Refused to answer	60.0%	75.0%

Tabulated by Y. Lee from 2012 Pew Survey Data.

experienced discrimination, and those who did not have English proficiency were significantly less likely to report personally experiencing discrimination.

On the other hand, in the 2012 Pew sample, 33.9 percent of Korean Americans' perceived discrimination as a "Major problem," the highest among all Asian groups and more than twice as high as all Asians (14.9%). In my analysis of the 2012 Pew sample, the perception of discrimination was significantly associated with 316 Korean Americans' voter registration. The highest voter registration rate (83.3%) and voting rate (63.0%) were seen among those who perceived discrimination as a "Major problem," declining among those who perceived discrimination as "Not a problem." Yet, these two discrimination items did not have a significant relationship with having voted in the 2008 election (see Table 15.8).

Future of Korean American Voting Power

Korean Americans' small population, coupled with its low naturalization rate and poor English proficiency, puts them at a political disadvantage. In addition, insufficient voter education and nonintensive outreach and mobilization by the major parties are also problems. Therefore, a large portion of Korean American eligible voters are marginalized during campaigns and remain without political party identification, and stay aloof on polling days. Moreover, pull factors from the homeland are increasing in quantitative measures and in intensity, although their effect on civic assimilation has not been conclusively demonstrated. Such incentives are available even to the U.S.-born Korean descendants. Without greater effort to internal and external mobilization, Korean American political participation dominated by the first generation immigrants may be unlikely to increase dramatically in the near future.

It is, however, possible that U.S.-born Korean American citizens may not follow in the political footsteps of their father's generation.

Oh suggested[43] that there is consistent generational progress that second-generation Asian Americans are more likely to participate in American politics than their first-generation counterparts, and that Asian ethic groups differences in both voter registration and voting rates seem to fade away for second generation and later generations. This finding suggests that a significant Asian American identity convergence across the nationality groups is forthcoming in political participation as generational progress. Thus, greater convergence across Asian ethnic groups may be expected in terms of political participation, despite cultural differences and somewhat divergent socioeconomic attainments. This implies a potential increase in validity for the pan-Asian American category, blurring the Korean American identity.

Future Korean identity will blur further with the drastic increase in mixed marriage. U.S.-born Koreans who married a U.S.-born Korean declined to 44.8 percent for males and 24.1 percent for females. The Korean Americans' in-marriage rate declined most rapidly among all races with progression of generations.[44]

Optimists' views about Korean Americans' voting strength may persist until other scenarios emerge and demonstrate plausibility. For instance, T. Lee's considered the future of Korean Americans in electoral politics. Specifically, he argued that the size of the Korean American population will continue to grow; that Korean Americans' party preference is not stable, even as a solid majority decide not to identify with either party; that Korean American voters preferred candidates based on their positions on issues relevant to Korean American voters, and that neither party should view Korean Americans as a one-party voting bloc.

But it is unwarranted to expect steady growth in Korean Americans' voting strength. To have the number of Korean Americans become comparable with other Asian groups' growth, there needs to be a sudden surge of Koreans willing to migrate to the United States. Such a scenario may only be triggered if a sociopolitical upheaval, such as unification of the Korean peninsula or the collapse of the North Korean regime occurred. It remains to be seen whether the number of Korean Americans will rebound or follow the pattern of Japanese Americans, who no longer immigrate in large numbers from Japan.

NOTES

1. Gordon, *Assimilation in American Life*, 70–71.
2. Alba and Nee, *Remaking the American Mainstream*.
3. DeSipio, "Making Citizens," 194–213.
4. Bass and Casper, "Differences in Registering and Voting," 483–511.
5. Lijphart, "Unequal Participation," 1–14.
6. Green and Gerber, "Reclaiming the Experimental Tradition," 805–832.

7. Leighley, *Strength in Numbers?*
8. I use the Census Bureau's 2010 American Community Survey (ACS) 5 percent data compiled in three years.
9. Pew Research Center, *The Rise of Asian Americans*, 2013.
10. I frequently refer to Stage 1 Cultural assimilation (measured with English proficiency and socioeconomic status); Stage 2 Structural assimilation (measured with primary group relations); Stage 4 Identification assimilation (sense of people hood of the United States); Stage 6 Behavioral receptional assimilation (absence of discrimination).
11. This is an official estimate of the size of the Asian American population was released in May 2012 by the Census Bureau based on the 2010 Census, which included mixed-race Asians. As I use the 2010 ACS data, the total base number of Asian Alone is 16,213,197.
12. *Source:* U.S. Department of Homeland Security.
13. Logan, Oh, and Darrah, "Political and Community Context," 535–544.
14. This refers to the psychological-economic incentives by "pulling forces" from ones' country of origin. See note 38.
15. The term *middleman minorities*, coined by Hubert Blalock (1967), refers to minority entrepreneurs who mediate between the dominant and subordinate groups. Their customers are typically members of marginalized racial or ethnic groups that are segregated from the majority group.
16. Yun and Chung, *Korean American Elected Politicians.*
17. AALDEF, New Findings, Press Release, March 27, 2013.
18. For example, in the City of Chicago, only Chinese language voting assistance is available because Koreans and other Asian groups are not geographically concentrated as in Chinatown.
19. KACE calculated that 53.5 percent of the estimated 72,517 Korean American citizens age over 18 in the state of New York are eligible voters and that 3,103(8%) could not be contacted by the Election Commission. KACE estimated there would be 38,818 Korean American registered to vote among the 11,866,845 registered voters in the state of New York. KACE even projected Korean Americans' voting rate at 40 percent (which represents 21.5% of the Korean American eligible voters in the state of New York) in the 2012 November election.
20. KRC set a goal is in the 2013 city elections to increase Korean American turnout and vote share by encouraging voter registration, educating about vote by mail, providing voter guides to households, phone banking and knocking on doors, providing hotlines and daily assistance workshops, getting voters pledge cards, and direct one-on-one voter outreach.
21. NAAS, AAPI Post-Election Survey.
22. According to 2012 Pew Survey, Korean American adults' voter registration rate is slightly lower than that of the average Asian Americans (72%) or the General public (75%).
23. Ibid.
24. Oh, "Immigrant Assimilation," 137–160.
25. Cho, "Naturalization, Socialization," 1140–1155.
26. The proportion of those who speak English "very well" among 1,048,099 foreign-born Korean Americans is only 28.2 percent compared to 41.7 percent of all foreign-born Asian Americans according to the 2010 Census. Even the majority

(68.1%) of the naturalized Korean American citizens spoke English less than "very well." Also in the 2012 Pew Survey, 30 percent of foreign-born Korean adults could carry on a conversation in English "very well" compared to 49 percent of all Asian American counterparts.

27. Lee, "Korean American Vote."

28. Wong, et al., *Asian American Political Participation*.

29. The following are considered battleground states: Ohio, Virginia, Florida, New Hampshire, Iowa, Colorado, Wisconsin, Michigan, Pennsylvania, Missouri, Nevada, and North Carolina.

30. Ramakrishnan, *Findings from the 2012 NAAS*.

31. Lee, "Korean American Vote."

32. Lee, "Korean Americans and the U.S. Presidential Elections"; in the 2012 NAAS data, 64 percent of Korean American voters either "strongly favor" or "somewhat favor" the 2010 Affordable Care Act (ACA), which the Republican candidate opposed. This support for the 2010 health care reform legislation is a significant predictor of Korean Americans' likelihood of voting for Obama in 2012.

33. A Korean nationalist movement demanding Japan's apology for forcing Korean women into prostitution camps during the World War II.

34. Uhlaner, Cain, and Kiewiet, "Political Participation," 195–231; Cain, "Acquisition of Partisanship," 390–422.

35. Ibid.

36. Those with better English skills have a more mixed social circle. Among the foreign-born Koreans who speak English "Very well," 36.1 percent say that all or most of their friends are Korean; this compares with 83.7 percent "Just a little" and 82.4 percent of those who speak English "Not at all" saying that all or most of their friends are Korean.

37. *The Korea Times-Chicago*, 17 February 2014.

38. Ibid.

39. 2012 NAAS study found that citizens in the sample who followed U.S. foreign policy in their countries of origin were 4 percent more likely to be registered to vote and 8 percent more likely to have reported voting in the 2008 elections. Also, it found that contact with family and friends and sending money to one's home country have nearly no effect on either one's likelihood of voter registration or having voted in the 2008 presidential elections.

40. Harris, "Something within Religion," 42–68.

41. Dawson, *Black Visions*; Chong and Rogers, "Racial Solidarity," 347–374.

42. Uhlaner, Cain, and Kiewiet, "Political Participation," 195–231; Lien, "Ethnicity and Political Participation," 237–264.

43. Oh, "Immigrant Assimilation," 137–160.

44. By tabulating the 2010 Census data, C. N. Le, also Y. Lee separately, found the following trend of decreasing internal marriage of Koreans: 61.1 percent of 1.5 generation Korean males married either Korea-born female or U.S-born Korean female, and 44.8 percent of U.S-born Korean males married U.S-born Korean female. In the case of females, 35.4 percent of 1.5 generation married either Korea-born male or U.S-born Korean male, and 24.1 percent of second-generation U.S-born Korean females -married U.S-born Korean males. Available on http://www.asian-nation.org/index.shtml; and http://www.hansainstitute.org.

REFERENCES

Alba, Richard, and Victor Nee. *Remaking the American Mainstream: Assimilation and Contemporary Immigration.* Cambridge, MA: Harvard, 2003.
Asian American Justice Center. "Behind the Numbers: Post-Election Survey of Asian American Voters in 2012." *Preliminary Report, 2012.* http://www.naasurvey.com/resources/Presentations/2012-aapipes-national.pdf
Bass, L.E., and L.M. Casper. "Differences in Registering and Voting between Native Born and Naturalized Americans." *Population Research and Policy Review* 20.6 (2001): 483–511.
Blalock, Hubert M. *Toward a Theory of Minority-Group Relations.* New York: Wiley, 1967.
Cain, Bruce E., D. Roderick Kiewiet, and Carole J. Uhlaner. "The Acquisition of Partisanship by Latinos and Asian Americans." *American Journal of Political Science* 35 (1991): 390–422.
Cho, W.K.T. "Naturalization, Socialization, Participation: Immigrants and (Non-) Voting." *Journal of Politics* 61.4 (1999): 1140–1155.
Chong, D., and R. Rogers. "Racial Solidarity and Political Participation." *Political Behavior* 27.4 (2005): 347–374.
Dawson, Michael. *Black Visions: The Roots of Contemporary African-American Ideologies.* Chicago: University of Chicago Press, 2001.
DeSipio, L. "Making Citizens or Good Citizens? Naturalization as a Predictor of Organizational and Electoral Behavior among Latino Immigrants." *Hispanic Journal of Behavioral Sciences* 18.2 (1996): 194–213.
Gordon, Milton M. *Assimilation in American Life: The Role of Race, Religion, and National Origin.* New York: Oxford Press, 1964.
Green, Donald P., and Alan Gerber. "Reclaiming the Experimental Tradition in Political Science." *State of the Discipline.* Vol. III. Ed. Helen Milner and Ira Katznelson. New York: W.W. Norton & Company, Inc., 2002. 805–832.
Harris, F.C. "Something Within-Religion as a Mobilizer of African-American Political Activism." *Journal of Politics* 56.1 (1994): 42–68.
Lee, Taeku. "The Korean American Vote: A Report on the Multilingual Exit Poll from the 2012 Presidential Election." A Special Presentation of *The Asian American Legal Defense and Education Fund.* 2012.
Lee, Taeku. "Korean Americans and the U.S. Presidential Elections." Korea Economic Institute, Academic Paper Series. 24 January 2013. His Presentation on YouTube. http://www.youtube.com/watch?v=JV0DndDAEH8.
Leighley, Jan E. *Strength in Numbers? The Political Mobilization of Racial and Ethnic Minorities.* Princeton, NJ: Princeton University Press, 2001.
Lien, P.T. "Ethnicity and Political Participation: A Comparison between Asian and Mexican Americans." *Political Behavior* 16.2 (1994): 237–264.
Lijphart, Arend. "Unequal Participation: Democracy's Unresolved Dilemma." *The American Political Science Review* 91.1 (March 1997): 1–14.
Logan, John R., Sookhee Oh, and Jennifer Darrah. "The Political and Community Context of Immigrant Naturalization." *Journal of Ethnic Migration Studies* 38.4 (2012): 535–554.
National Asian American Survey (NAAS). *Behind the Numbers: Post-Election Survey of Asian American and Pacific Islander Voters in 2012.* http://www.naasurvey.com/resources/Presentations/2012-aapipes-national.pdf.

Oh, Sookhee. "Immigrant Assimilation and Political Participation: Group Membership and Context of Participation in Electoral Politics among Korean, Chinese, and Filipino Americans." *Development and Society* 42.1 (June 2013): 137–160.

Pew Research Center. *The Rise of Asian Americans*. 2013. http://www.pewsocialtrends.org/files/2013/04/Asian-Americans-new-full-report-04-2013.pdf.

Ramakrishnan, Karthick. *Findings from the 2012 NAAS and the 2012 AAPI Post-Election Survey.* AAPI PES. April 2013.

Uhlaner, Carole J., Bruce Cain, and D. Roderick Kiewiet. "Political Participation of Ethnic Minorities in the 1980s." *Political Behavior* 17 (1989): 195–231.

Wong, Janelle, et al. *Asian American Political Participation: Emerging Constituents and Their Political Identities*. New York: Russell Sage Foundation, 2011.

Yun, Claire, and Thomas Chung. *Korean American Elected Politicians, Influential Administrative Officials, and Judicial Appointees.* The Research Center for Korean Community, Queens College of CUNY. Community Research Report No. 2. November 2013.

Chapter 16

Electoral Turnout among Vietnamese Americans

Loan K. Le and Phi Hong Su

INTRODUCTION

From the first reports of refugees arriving in the United States in the aftermath of the Vietnam War, public officials struggled with how best to integrate into American life Vietnamese immigrant families. They were depicted in the mainstream media as desperate, poor, lacking proficiency with the English language, and foreign to Western culture. And yet during the last decade, Vietnamese Americans have made considerable strides in politics, with the election of Van Tran and Hubert Vo to the California and Texas state legislatures, respectively, in 2004, and the election of Anh "Joseph" Cao (R-LA) to the U.S. Congress in 2008. Given several decades of Vietnamese American integration and substantial heterogeneity in the group's population, we ask: do patterns in electoral participation differ across waves of Vietnamese immigrants? We complement an analysis of voter turnout with an examination of citizenship and voter registration because voting requires successfully meeting a number of formal requirements. One hypothesis is that regardless of their immigration wave, Vietnamese American subgroups will exhibit no differences in their citizenship, registration, and voting patterns. Another, consistent with the classical assimilation school,[1] is that previous immigrant groups will be more assimilated than later groups, with steady increases over time along each of the political dimensions under study. A third hypothesis, consistent with what we call the "immigrant cohort" hypothesis, is that the distinct socialization of immigrant waves will shape their eventual political incorporation.

Among social scientists, the political incorporation of recent immigrant groups is a young but flourishing research field. Yet, research on immigrant integration into politics is complicated by competing explanatory factors, including individual-level socioeconomic resources, contexts of exit (pre-migration experiences within the country of origin) and contexts of reception (post-migration experiences within the country of destination).[2] Due to data limitations, analyses are often conducted at the level of pan-ethnic groups (Asian, Latino, etc.) and for particular regions rather than with a nationally representative sample. Using national surveys in this study with large subgroup sample sizes, we argue that even within a given immigrant group with similar exit characteristics, substantial diversity in immigrant socialization during the initial contact and resettlement period apropos the destination country is a key imprinting moment. Unpacking how membership in a "wave" of immigration to a new destination country—a question that has been understudied to date—predicts patterns in immigrant political integration is this chapter's contribution to developing scholarship in political science and sociology.

In this study, we analyze the most recent survey data available for two nationally representative data sets: November 2012 Voting and Registration Supplement to the Current Population Survey (CPS) and 2008[3] National Asian American Survey (NAAS). We consider whether membership in a given immigrant wave predicts patterns of naturalization, voter registration, and turnout, while controlling for individual-level social and demographic characteristics in a series of logistic regression models. We also provide a descriptive analysis of reports for the "most important problem" and partisan attachments among respondents, concluding with recommendations for future research.

POLITICAL INCORPORATION

The political incorporation of immigrant groups in the electoral arena de facto occurs in stages. Unlike their native-born counterparts, immigrants must become citizens before they can register to vote or cast a ballot. Many studies examine early stages of political incorporation processes, but immigration scholars "have paid considerably less attention to voting and other forms of political participation"[4] that occur after naturalization. This chapter examines each of the three pivotal stages requisite to participation at the ballot box among immigrants: (1) acquisition of citizenship, (2) voter registration, and (3) voter turnout.

Among the characteristics that matter in the electoral arena, political scientists have long concluded that educational attainment is one of the most powerful for predicting the likelihood of voting, as more education implies that individuals have more politically relevant skills.[5] Income additionally functions as a good predictor of participatory behaviors, although its effects diminish once other social and demographic characteristics such as education and race are accounted for.[6] Ethnicity and gender are also important factors influencing political behavior.[7]

To complement an analysis of social and demographic characteristics, we specifically investigate the socialization processes that occur among members of one immigrant group. We first consider our study in the context of competing schools of thought on political socialization based on the persistence of preadult attitudes versus lifelong learning. The persistence hypothesis argues that attitudes formed during one's impressionable years of adolescence are largely stable throughout the life course; in contrast, the lifelong learning hypothesis advances that individuals are open to learning and malleable throughout adulthood.[8] Using the case of Vietnamese Americans, we advance the immigrant cohort hypothesis, which considers the particular combination of exit and reception as a political imprinting experience.

CONTEXTS OF EXIT AND RECEPTION

A pre- versus post-migration political learning perspective is reflective of the dichotomous way that migration has traditionally been perceived, with a sharp division between old and new country. The central puzzle regarding contexts of exit is embodied by the consideration: Do origins shape destinies?[9] Min Zhou and Carl L. Bankston,[10] among others, have noted the turbulent exit for Vietnamese immigrants and refugees to the United States in the years following 1975. In truth, contexts of exit for first-wave Vietnamese were not as jarring as for those in subsequent waves because many first-wave elites spoke English and had years of exposure to French and American influences. Moreover, later waves of refugees were distinct from the first, with lower levels of education and less proficiency in English language skills, and so on. This heterogeneity in individual-level resources amongst immigrants in the same ethnic group, ceteris paribus, likely impacts trajectories of immigrant incorporation. However, recognition of within-group complexity for conditions of exit has seldom been centered in social scientific analysis.

Across refugee groups, hypotheses based on pre-migration human capital would suggest the successful integration of largely educated, early elite Cuban refugees, and falsely predict the failure of Vietnamese refugees who have lower overall levels of human capital. The recent political successes among both Cuban and Vietnamese refugee groups suggest that pre-migration characteristics are not deterministic of long-term successful incorporation. Moreover, using solely an exit perspective, one cannot explain why Cubans and Vietnamese experienced such disparate outcomes compared with Salvadorans and Guatemalans, who similarly fled political violence. While the former have naturalized[11] in large numbers and (by socioeconomic measures) are generally doing well, the uncertain legal status of many Guatemalans and Salvadorans limits not only citizenship acquisition but also educational attainment and socioeconomic advancement."[12]

For the contexts-of-exit and reception frameworks, the idea that "the context that receives immigrants plays a decisive role in their process of adaptation, regardless of the human capital the immigrants may possess" is highly salient.[13] Vietnamese refugees arriving in the United States encountered a complex environment laden with ambivalence about the Vietnamese. By 1972, less than 30 percent of Americans agreed with the Vietnam War and marked protests against the draft, which affected over 1.7 million males between the ages of 20 to 26, were regular occurrences.[14] Harris and Gallup polls throughout the 1970s to 1990s showed that although the government responded favorably to the plight of many refugee families fleeing war's aftermath, the American public's acceptance of large waves of incoming refugees reflected substantial reservations, particularly during a period when the United States was struggling with difficult economic times. Rubén Rumbaut[15] noted that in the recession years of the 1990s, American nativism spiked, particularly in California. The economic recession also constrained employment opportunities[16] so that many Vietnamese immigrants were either unemployed or underemployed.

Furthermore, the receiving ethnic community in the destination country is also significant for contexts of reception. In addition to Portes and Böröcz,[17] other scholars have also noted the significance of a preexisting coethnic community.[18] Later arrivals were met with more established immigrant enclaves, ethnic media, and ethnic markets than were earlier immigrants.[19] Given such conflicting and changing dimensions of reception, we consider each wave as having encountered a distinctive public, economic, and coethnic reception.

To this exit/reception dichotomy, we contribute an emphasis on differences in immigration experiences for ethnic subgroups. Some combination of exit, reception, and the space between is necessary to construct a portrait of the web of interrelated forces and conditions that shape immigrant incorporation in varying ways. Our findings highlight that although third-wave Vietnamese Americans immigrated with lower levels of human capital than those in the first wave, they are more likely to be politically active as members of the American electorate.

WAVES OF VIETNAMESE MIGRATION

To preview our analysis, we first outline and categorize Vietnamese migration experiences according to period ("waves of immigration"). We summarize developing government policy and public responses, two key dimensions shaping the contexts of exit and contexts of reception for each immigrant group. Next, we examine the human capital characteristics of each immigrant wave in order to account for individual-level characteristics that might confound an understanding of factors shaping immigrant experiences. Refugees are characteristically those who flee a country for fear of violence or political persecution, though, of course, flight is a necessary but insufficient condition for receiving asylum. Potentially, circumstances of exit really do imprint themselves on immigrants arriving in a country of destination. Unfortunately, any investigation of this is complicated by simultaneity; analyses of contexts of exit and reception should include individual characteristics. Though the studies cited here have discussed the different compositions of waves of Vietnamese and Cuban refugees coming to the United States and their average levels of human capital, they did not have not have the advantage of contemporary data with sufficient samples for different waves and multiple measures of long-term political incorporation in their empirical analysis. We attempt to remedy this by situating waves of immigration, above and beyond human capital and other factors, as our primary predictor variable in studying party and voter registration among Vietnamese Americans, all other factors being equal.

Defining a Wave

While it is generally accepted that extended migration streams tend to take on "waves," characterized by differences in mode of exit, motives, human capital, and reception, defining a wave for a particular national origin group becomes quite messy, and scholars vary in their classification of the waves.[20] For the purposes of this analysis, we focus on three primary streams of immigration that define U.S. policy toward those who would become Vietnamese Americans. We include some mention of pre-1975 immigrants as a comparison group, but our "first wave" (1975–1979) includes South Vietnamese immigrants with high educational attainment and those who worked with Americans in the South Vietnamese government or military. The "second wave" (1980–1994) includes those who fled by boat or over land following the collapse of the Vietnamese economy in the late 1970s and early 1980s. This "second wave" also includes beneficiaries of the Orderly Departure Program (ODP) such as mixed-race Amerasians and former political prisoners.[21] Our "third wave" (1995–2012) includes many immigrants who were able to join their families through the family reunification policies available to them under the Immigration and Nationality Act of 1965. Although we are unable to trace from the available data exactly how immigrants left Vietnam, these categories approximate divisions in each group's immigration experiences.[22]

Wave I: Asylum and Post Hoc Legislation, 1975–1979

The United States' decision to accept refugees is a direct result of American involvement in the Vietnam War and a sense of responsibility for the conflict that created the Southeast Asian refugee crisis. On May 23, 1975, the 94th Congress approved the Indochina Migration and Refugee Assistance Act (H.R. 6755), which provided for refugee relocation and resettlement. Drawing from the Migration and Refugee Assistance Act of 1962, this legislation applied to "aliens who (A) because of persecution or fear of persecution on account of race, religion, or political opinion, fled from Cambodia or Vietnam; (B) cannot return there because of fear of persecution on account of race, religion, or political opinion; and (C) are in urgent need of assistance for the essentials of life." Additionally, the legislation called for a committee to describe plans for the resettlement of refugees in processing centers, and for keeping records of those who indicated interest in returning. Alongside H.R. 6755, Congress passed Appropriations for Vietnamese and Cambodian Refugees (H.R. 6894), providing $305,000,000 for the relocation and resettlement of refugees from Vietnam and Cambodia.[23]

A 1977 Amendment to the Indochina Migration and Refugee Assistance Act (H.R. 7769) extended assistance to refugees through September 30, 1981.[24] This legislation created a record of admission for permanent residence. These benefits applied "to any alien ... [who] was paroled into the United States as a refugee from those countries under section 212 (d) (5) of the Immigration and Nationality Act subsequent to March 31, 1975, but prior to January 1, 1979." Once immigrants were granted permanent residency, they became eligible to sponsor spouses and children.

In reality, large numbers of Vietnamese refugees arrived in the United States from the 1970s onward. Early immigrant settlement was characterized by dispersion. There was no preexisting coethnic community with which to greet the first wave of Vietnamese refugees, and officials directed the settlement of new arrivals so that they were dispersed across different regions of the country, thereby minimizing the likelihood of excessive strain on any one local economy. However, Vietnamese-origin immigrants en masse soon engaged in secondary migration, gravitating toward California, Texas, and places with warmer weather.

Wave II: Standardization and Orderly Departure, 1980–1994

1980 marked a series of watershed legislative moments for Vietnamese migration to the United States. On the American side, Congress passed the Refugee Act of 1980, institutionalizing protocols for refugee admission. Previously, immigration legislation regarding economic or political refugees had been in response to refugee inflows, without explicit procedures for defining or dealing with resettlement.[25] In the same year, the government of Vietnam, along with the United Nations High Commissioner for Refugees, established the ODP to allow those in Vietnam to migrate for purposes of family reunification. While ODP was criticized as being "far from orderly; instead, it was a bureaucratic nightmare,"[26] the years following 1980 were marked by efforts to standardize resettlement procedures. Another example in this vein is the 1982 Amerasian Immigration Act, which amended the Immigration and Nationality Act to provide preferential access to mixed children of United States citizens. Registries for the purposes of family reunification cropped up during this time, including Amerasian Registry and Amerasian Child Find.

When the second Vietnamese wave arrived in the 1980s, some ethnic communities were forming into Vietnamese ethnic enclaves. The most prominent overseas Vietnamese community in Orange County, California, was formally designated "Little Saigon" by a sign alongside a freeway ramp in 1988. Because of the nature of family reunification, second-wave Vietnamese immigrants did not experience the same large-scale dispersion across the United States as did their first-wave counterparts.

Despite having a preexisting ethnic community and legal provisions for resettlement and integration, Vietnamese refugees were nevertheless embedded in broader struggles over the nation's immigration policy on legal and unauthorized immigration from other countries. While there was hesitancy over refugee admissions immediately following Saigon's fall, news reports indicated that substantial segments of the public blamed Vietnamese refugees for crime and economic ills. Although many Americans sympathized with those fleeing war-torn countries, compassion fatigue had set in by 1980, according to Senator Alan K. Simpson, who was working with the administration on refugee policy. In the early 1990s, former South Vietnamese soldiers recently released from "re-education" camps arrived in the United States with their families en masse. Before ODP ended on September 30, 1994, it is estimated that the program provided for the resettlement of 167,000 former detainees and their family members, 89,700 Amerasian children and accompanying family, and 523,000 other refugees, immigrants, and parolees to resettle in the United States.[27]

Wave III: After ODP, 1995 to the Present

While the admission and resettlement of refugees from Southeast Asia, as well as the former Soviet Union and Cuba, figured heavily into U.S. immigration policy and geopolitics throughout the years of the Cold War, the face of immigration in the late 1990s and the first decade of the 21st century transitioned to that of skilled labor and, later, undocumented immigration. Though family reunification provisions remained, President George H.W. Bush's signing of the Immigration Act of 1990 specified an increase in visa allowances for high-skilled immigrants.[28]

By 1994, President Bill Clinton's OPERATION GATEKEEPER reflected the shifting discourse toward the illegality of immigration from the south. Much legislation at state and national levels has been aimed at comprehensive immigration reform or, conversely, increasing efforts to police the United States' southern border. Vietnamese continue to immigrate to the United States, even after the perceived refugee crisis has long fallen out of public discourse.[29] While the proportion of those arriving under provisions for family reunification have increased over the years, some admits are still refugees.

After ODP, Vietnamese immigration continued to contribute to the growth of ethnic communities, which also served as primary destinations for immigrants arriving under family reunification, student visas and other policies. Today, Little Saigon in Orange County is a thriving Vietnamese American hub with numerous businesses, ethnic media, and concentration of cultural and financial capital among the overseas Vietnamese. Other areas of concentration in the United States include Houston and San Jose. Because of the formation of ethnic communities, many Vietnamese shop, eat, and navigate social life in their native language.

HYPOTHESIS

Given the varying conditions confronting and confronted by Vietnamese Americans during their various waves of arrival, how might we expect these very different socialization processes to impact long-term political engagement across immigrant waves? Patterns of association between wave of immigration and political integration should vary according to the dimension under study, as the pathways to naturalization and electoral participation are different. The acquisition of citizenship in the United States is best predicted by duration of time in the destination country, and this relationship should hold for our analysis, as earlier waves are more likely to have gained citizenship than later waves. Obviously, they are advantaged over the more recent immigrants from later waves, who may have an interest in naturalization but lack knowledge, eligibility or access to other resources. Overall, refugees have no real options to return to their country of origin, and even if that were not the case, Vietnam is a distant land.

In the realm of voter participation, however, later waves may be advantaged. Due to the circumstances of their exit and reception in which many early refugees suffered the greatest status loss, we might expect that refugees from the "first wave" will exhibit behaviors that are more directed toward the homeland than subsequent waves, as reflected in greater participation in protest politics than in electoral politics. For the "first-wave" cohort, voters do not have much opportunity to influence how the Vietnamese government is run from the U.S. ballot box.[30]

Those in the second wave of immigration may be split between participating in protests and electoral politics. Like the first-wave cohort, they also survived difficult journeys to the destination country and bear recent memories of the war; nevertheless, they had access to a growing coethnic community that facilitated information sharing about domestic issues that mattered to group members. These immigrants also received substantial resettlement assistance from the government. Members of the second-wave cohort might, therefore, split their attention between the politics in Vietnam and the United States. Those in the third wave, many of whom arrived in the United States under family reunification policies, faced a different incentive structure. These individuals were not escaping a repressive regime under dire circumstances, and they were not the recipients of the same resettlement benefits from the United States government. Hence, they may be more focused on and willing to influence domestic politics by casting their ballots for advantageous candidates or policies. We consider these hypotheses and their implications below, and conclude with a discussion of the study's limitations for future important trends among Vietnamese Americans.

RESULTS

We first discuss the profiles for each immigrant wave using bivariate statistics to show that immigrant groups have shifted in composition over time. Next, we review our multivariate logistic regression models for citizenship, naturalization and voting, holding constant social and demographic characteristics of respondents.

Bivariate Statistics: Demographic Characteristics by Nativity and Waves of Immigration

Increasingly, recent Vietnamese migration streams are composed of younger adults than earlier stages of migration. Across the first, second, and third waves, the proportion of respondents between the ages of 25 and 44 increased from 21 to 44 percent, while the number of middle-aged adults (45 to 64) decreased from 60 to 36 percent (see Table 16.1). The proportion of older adults (aged 64 to 74) similarly declined from 11 percent in the first wave to 7 percent after 1994. Migration has either been disproportionately female (as in the years before 1975 and after 1994) or split equally between males and females (as in the years 1975 to 1994).

Bivariate Statistics: Political Incorporation Outcomes by Waves and Generation

Reported Citizen. Previous scholarship noted the high rates of naturalization among Vietnamese Americans. The CPS (2012) sample in our survey corroborates these claims, with 97 percent of first-wave immigrants reporting holding citizenship (see Table 16.2). The proportion of those who have naturalized fell to 87 percent by the second wave and 69 percent by

Table 16.1
Social and Demographic Characteristics by Nativity and Waves of Immigration

	Pre-1975	%	Wave 1 (1975–1979)	%	Wave 2 (1980–1994)	%	Wave 3 (1995–2012)	%	Native-Born	%
Age										
18–24 yrs	0	0	0	0	19,994	4	28,240	8	122,579	43
25–44 yrs	3,599	12	30,334	21	180,205	33	153,511	44	120,017	42
45–64 yrs	19,464	63	87,840	60	269,147	49	125,486	36	25,249	9
65–74 yrs	7,902	26	16,261	11	49,193	9	25,722	7	6,036	2
75–90 yrs	0	0	12,340	8	25,881	5	13,104	4	9,935	4
Female	21,061	68	73,474	50	268,892	49	225,485	61	335,029	50
Male	9,904	32	73,301	50	275,530	51	143,659	39	329,820	50
Education										
Less HS degree	3,487	11	17,943	12	81,522	15	77,351	22	83,575	24
HS degree	10,696	35	36,186	25	186,739	34	129,133	36	71,371	21
Some college	7,106	23	40,003	27	115,884	21	77,168	22	117,421	34
College degree	2,786	9	34,036	23	123,916	23	45,351	13	42,679	12
Grad school	6,889	22	18,605	12	36,359	7	24,989	7	27,031	8
Income										
Up to 25k	11,271	36	27,462	19	63,753	12	87,093	24	114,731	1
25k to 50k	7,359	24	37,028	25	106,931	20	72,499	20	127,274	19
50k to 100k	3,015	10	59,242	40	211,728	39	149,102	40	231,751	35
More than 100k	9,320	30	23,043	16	164,010	30	60,449	16	191,092	29

Source: November 2012 Voter Supplement to the U.S. Current Population Survey, U.S. Census Bureau.

Table 16.2
Citizenship, Voter Registration, and Voter Turnout among Vietnamese Americans, by Nativity and Immigrant Wave

	Reported Citizen		Reported Registered		Reported Voted	
	Number	% of Group	Number	% of Group	Number	% of Group
Immigrants						
Pre-1975	30,965	100	8,905	41	8,321	33
Wave 1 (1975–1979)	142,249	97	70,428	74	52,096	53
Wave 2 (1980–1994)	474,936	87	238,720	62	203,899	50
Wave 3 (1995–2012)	254,642	69	135,851	69%	122,594	61
Native-Born	664,849	100	118,823	62	93,923	49

Source: November 2012 Voter Supplement to the U.S. Current Population Survey, U.S. Census Bureau.

Notes:
(1) Data are weighted. Missing data are excluded from the analysis.
(2) Citizenship totals are limited to the foreign-born. Registration and Voting totals are limited to the citizen population.
(3) All specifications are limited to the sample population who are 18 years and older.

the third. All respondents who immigrated prior to 1975 reported attaining citizenship. Lastly, native-born children of Vietnamese immigrants are, by definition, citizens.

Reported Registered. While 100 percent of pre-1975 immigrants have citizenship, less than half (41%) reported having registered to vote in the 2012 presidential election. In contrast, 74 percent of first-wave immigrants and 69 percent of third-wave immigrants reported having registered. Registration rates for second-wave and native-born respondents were 62 percent. Rates of voter registration, like citizenship, declined from Wave 1 to Wave 2 but resurged again for Wave 3.

Reported Voted. While first-wave respondents were more likely than all other waves to have naturalized, they were not the group most likely to have voted in the 2012 election. While 61 percent of third-wave citizen respondents reported having voted, only half of each of the first-wave (53%), second-wave (50%) and native-born citizen respondent groups (49%) reported having voted. Pre-1975 immigrants were the least likely to have reported voting (33%). We next tested the relationship between waves of migration and electoral outcomes, controlling for social and demographic factors.

Multivariate Statistics: Predictors of Political Incorporation Outcomes

Model 1: Citizenship. Findings for our citizenship model supported the linear, upward trajectory of success predicted by the classical assimilation model. Holding age, gender, educational attainment, and family income constant, wave of immigration was negatively correlated with the acquisition of citizenship. Membership in the second wave (versus first wave) was associated with a 24 percent decline in the likelihood of obtaining citizenship among the Vietnamese foreign-born, net of other variables (see Table 16.3). Similarly, membership in the third wave (versus first wave) was associated with a 53 percent decline in the chance of becoming naturalized. This is consistent with the bivariate data on decreasing levels of naturalization across waves.

Age, education, and family income have positive effects on the likelihood of obtaining citizenship (OR 3.83, 8.87, and 2.72, respectively, $p < 0.001$), if all else remains equal. Moving from the minimum to maximum values for each independent variable, the coefficients correspond with a 21, 32, and 17 percent increase in the predicted probabilities of reporting citizenship. Finally, being female (vs. being male) was associated with a 0.24 ($p < 0.001$) increase in the log-odds of naturalizing, holding all else constant.

Model 2: Registration. Findings for our registration model highlight group differences that are consistent with our immigrant cohort hypothesis. Holding all else constant, membership in the second wave (versus first wave) is associated with a 0.32 ($p < 0.001$) decrease in the log-odds of registration. However, the pattern starts to reverse with the next wave of immigration. Membership in the third wave (versus first wave) is associated with a 0.17 ($p < 0.001$) decrease in registration, all else constant. These data are consistent with the bivariate findings of first- and third-wave immigrants as more likely to have registered to vote than members of the second wave. The native-born are also less likely to be registered to vote than the first-wave group (5% decline in the likelihood).

Age of respondents and educational attainment are the two most powerful explanatory variables in our voter registration model. A discrete change in the age of respondents, moving from the minimum age category of 18 to the maximum age category of over 85 years, corresponded to a 33 percent increase in the predicted probability of having reported registration. For education, those with some graduate school experience (vs. those with some high school education or less) benefited from a 37 percent increase in the predicted probability of having reported successful voter registration. Being female (vs. being male) increased the log odds of registration by .18 ($p < 0.001$), controlling for other variables. Notably, there was

Table 16.3
Political Incorporation of Vietnamese Americans

	Model 1: Citizenship		Model 2: Registration		Model 3: Voting	
	Odds Ratios	Pr(Change) min-> max	Odds Ratios	Pr(Change) min-> max	Odds Ratios	Pr(Change) min-> max
Wave 2	0.24	−24%	0.68	−9%	1.09	2%
Wave 3	0.04	−53%	0.83	−4%	1.56	11%
Native-Born	n/a	n/a	0.80	−5%	1.23	5%
Age (18+)	3.83	21%	4.83	33%	5.01	38%
Female	1.24	4%	1.18	4%	1.16	4%
Educ. Attain	8.87	32%	5.46	37%	4.43	35%
Family Income	2.72	17%	0.98	0%	1.30	7%
Number of obs		418		320		329
Log Likelihood		−539484.47		−583229.20		−632006.36
M1: LR chi^2(6) M2&3: LR chi^2(7)		342038.45		59100.76		57473.97
Prob. > chi^2		0.00		0.00		0.00
Pseudo R^2		0.24		0.05		0.04

Source: November 2012 Voter Supplement to the U.S. Current Population Survey, U.S. Census Bureau.

Notes:

(1) Base category is Wave 1 Vietnamese Refugees.

(2) All coefficients are significant at $p < 0.001$.

(3) "Pr(Change) min->max" denotes the difference in the predicted value as one independent variable changes values from its minimum to its maximum while all others are held constant at the mean. "Number of obs" denotes the number of observations.

(4) All variables are coed from 0 to 1.

(5) Data are weighted. Missing data are excluded from the analysis.

(6) Citizenship model is limited to the foreign-born. Registration and Voting models are limited to the citizen population. All models are limited to the sample population who are 18 years and older.

almost no difference in the likelihood of voter registration between those in the highest versus lowest family income categories.

Model 3: Voting. Results from our voter registration model directly contradicted the classical assimilation model and instead supported the immigrant cohort hypothesis. Model findings consistent with classical assimilation theory would have illustrated a positive association between length of stay in the United States and voter turnout. We found instead that members of the immigrant third wave were most likely to have cast their ballots in the November 2012 election, with an 11 percent advantage over the first wave in the likelihood of having reported voting. Albeit modestly, members of the second wave and the native-born were also more likely to vote than first-wave immigrants (2% and 5% gains in predicted probability). Affiliation with the third wave (versus first wave) was associated with an 11 percent increase in the predicted probability of having voted in the November 2012 election.

Once again, age and education are the most powerful explanatory variables in our model, with increases of 38 and 35 percent, respectively, in the chances of having reported voting for a discrete change in each independent variable. Controlling for other variables, being female was associated with a 0.16 ($p < 0.001$) increase in the log-odds of voting in the November 2012 election, which corresponds with a modest 4 percent increase in the predicted probability of having reported voting. Given a discrete change in family income from the minimum to maximum value, the increase in the likelihood of voting is 7 percent.

DISCUSSION

These findings support the idea that there are substantive within-group differences among Vietnamese Americans and that the classical linear assimilation hypothesis does not adequately explain political incorporation. Although naturalization does appear to increase steadily over time, with earlier waves more likely to have acquired citizenship, the same pattern of associations does not appear for our analyses of registration and voting. Notably, it was the third wave of Vietnamese immigrants who were most likely to cast ballots in the last presidential election.

Issue Trends: Limitations and Directions for Future Research

Thus far, we have provided a discussion of the behavioral incorporation of Vietnamese Americans, such as their likelihoods of acquiring citizenship, registering, and voting. What of the issue preferences that shape the Vietnamese American electorate? Since applicable NAAS 2008 measures for Vietnamese Americans, such as report of actual ballot cast, are absent or have substantial missing data, we will not formulate predictive models of factors that shaped vote choice. We can, however, delineate the contours of issues that are important to this group of voters. The survey queried, "What do you think is the most important problem facing the United States today?" Sixty-two percent of Vietnamese Americans chose the "economy in general" as the most important problem, and this priority was consistent across all waves of immigrants and for the native-born as well. However, only 24 percent of the pre-1975 immigrant group chose this category in contrast to at least 61 percent of all other Vietnamese American groups (see Table 16.4). The pre-1975 group was also concerned about "fuel/oil/gas prices" (20%), "terrorism" (29%), and "education" (13%). Among the remaining problems, the Iraq War was ranked as the most important problem for between 6 and 13 percent across waves of Vietnamese American immigrants and the native-born. Nevertheless, a "Don't Know" response was relatively common (8% to 12%) among almost all groups except for the opinionated pre-1975 immigrants.

Overall, during the 2008 presidential election seasons, Vietnamese Americans favored Republicans over Democrats, but many were not incorporated into the two-party system. According to the same weighted sample of Vietnamese Americans in the National Asian American Survey of 2008, more Vietnamese American registered voters were Republicans (46%) than Democrats (22%), but much of the group is not formally affiliated with either of the major two parties. The third most popular category among registered voters was "Don't know" (18%), followed by Independent/declined to state (9%), "Other" party (4%), and Refused (1%). The NAAS survey was fielded before the 2008 presidential election occurred, but registered voters were asked about their preferences or intentions. The question wording was: "Do you plan to vote for John McCain the Republican, or Barack Obama the Democrat, or another candidate for president

Table 16.4
Most Important Problem among Vietnamese Americans, by Wave of Immigration and Nativity

Most Important Problem	Pre-1975 Migrant	First Wave	Second Wave	Third Wave	Native-Born	Overall
Iraq War	13	9	9	6	8	8
Economy in General	24	65	64	61	63	62
Unemployment/Jobs	0	5	4	7	5	5
Terrorism	29	5	4	4	5	5
Ethics/Morality/Family	0	0	0	0	0	0
Education/Educational	13	0	2	1	2	1
Poverty/Homelessness/	0	0	0	0	0	0
Lack of/Cost of Health Care	0	0	1	0	1	1
Fuel/Gas/Oil Prices	20	3	5	8	5	6
Race/Ethnic Relations	0	0	0	0	0	0
Other	0	4	2	2	2	2
Don't Know	0	9	8	12	9	8
Refused	0	0	0	0	0	0
Weighted N	6,368	114,201	506,201	218,102	98,134	949,027

Source: 2008 National Asian American Survey.

Notes:

(1) Estimates shown are percentages who noted "the most important problem," using sample weights.

(2) *Question wording:* What do you think is the most important problem facing the United States today?

of the United States, or are you unsure at this point in time?" Leading up to the November elections, Vietnamese Americans who were registered or who intended to register to vote *and* who expressed a preference for either one of the two major parties heavily favored John McCain (75%), Republican candidate for president in 2008, over Barack Obama (25%), Democratic candidate for president. Nevertheless, many survey respondents indicated that they were still unsure (21%).

Lastly, we draw on some points of interest from past surveys and reports to provide some suggestions for what the electorate future of Vietnamese Americans may look like. The NAAS "Behind the Numbers: Post-Election Survey of Asian American and Pacific Islander Voters in 2012"[31] report noted a historic shift in the partisanship of Vietnamese Americans from Republican to Democratic with a striking ratio of 39:61. This shift begs the question of whether the trend will hold in future elections, as the NAAS "Public Opinion of a Growing Electorate: Asian Americans and Pacific Islanders in 2012"[32] reported that Vietnamese (and Filipinos) still lean toward Republicans more than other Asian American groups, despite the former's comparatively high number of Independents. In future analyses, we will assess the hypothesis that this shift is driven not in major part by the changing partisanship of the existing Vietnamese electorate, but rather by the coming-of-age and voter registration of young Vietnamese Americans whose actions are changing historic partisanship trends. We believe that lower levels of Republican support will continue in the near future.

Other points of interest concern particular policies relevant to Vietnamese Americans. As noted by an Asian American Legal Defense and Education Fund (AALDEF) study, "Asian American Vote in 2012,"[33] 59 percent of Vietnamese American respondents identified as English-deficient—a relatively high proportion when compared to other Asian immigrant groups. This suggests the importance of initiatives for in-language voter outreach and education as means by which to bolster participation among Vietnamese American voters. Lastly, the AALDEF reports that, compared with numbers from the overall Asian American population, Vietnamese Americans support comprehensive immigration reform at lower rates (49%). Only with future developments will we be able to assess whether this trend, as with partisanship, will start to approximate that of the overall Asian American population and result in higher support for comprehensive immigration reform.

A final thematic point of interest for the future of the electorate concerns comprehensive health care. In comparison to other Asian ethnic groups, Vietnamese and Koreans were least likely to report their health as excellent, very good, or good. A NAAS study, "Opinions of Asian Americans and Pacific Islanders: Affordable Care Act"[34] found that merely 61 percent of Vietnamese Americans, compared to 88 percent of Indian Americans, rated their health positively. A potential issue that could underscore group differences among Asian Americans for future elections, then, may be in the realm of heath disparities, health care coverage and general approaches to individual and community well-being for future elections, then, may be in the realm of health care coverage.

CONCLUSION

In this chapter, we described three primary waves of Vietnamese migration to the United States and examined their associations with patterns of citizenship, naturalization and voting, all else equal. We believe that these findings provide some support for our "immigrant cohort" hypothesis, but more investigation in this promising domain is merited.

We distinguished socialization processes due to unique experiences during a critical imprinting experience among Vietnamese immigrants from an explanation that relies on duration of time spent in the United States. Immigrant cohorts, as instantiated in waves of immigration, are of course related to years spent in the destination country, but we argue for in-depth analysis of immigrant cohorts above and beyond duration of time in the United States. If there is support for our argument that socialization during the immigration experience matters, all else equal, then the relationships described above will vary across waves and across dimensions of political participation. If duration in the United States explains political incorporation, then the data should illustrate a steady, linear and increasing pattern of association, with more years in the destination country tied to increases in naturalization, registration and voter participation. Where patterns of political incorporation across waves are nonlinear, accounting for other variables, we argue that more investigations should be directed to intraethnic group differences, to complement extant analyses of inter-group differences. Immigrant experiences vary even within the growing Vietnamese American community. Though we cannot say for certain which issues will drive Vietnamese American voting patterns in the future, we suggest some potentially fruitful directions for future research, including attitudes toward government, health care, the environment, gender differences in politics, racialization and socioeconomic advancement across Asian American ethnicities and in relation to other groups more broadly.

NOTES

1. Gordon, *Assimilation in Everyday Life*.
2. See also Portes and Rumbaut, *Immigrant America*, a foundational work on contexts of exit and reception.
3. Though the 2012 NAAS has been conducted, data were not yet available to researchers at the time of this study.
4. Ramakrishnan and Espenshade, "Immigrant Incorporation and Political Participation in the United States," 871.

5. Wolfinger and Rosenstone, *Who Votes?*
6. Wolfinger and Hoffman, "Registering and Voting with Motor Voter," 85–92.
7. Leighley and Nagler, "Individual and Systemic Influences on Turnout," 718–740.
8. Alwin, *Political Attitudes over the Life Span*; Merelman, "Adolescence of Political Socialization," 134–166; Valentino and Sears, "Event-Driven Communication and the Preadult Socialization of Partisanship," 127–154.
9. Rumbaut, "Origins and Destinies," 583–621.
10. Zhou and Bankston, *Growing Up American*.
11. Portes and Mozo, "Cubans and Other Ethnic Minorities"; Võ, "Constructing a Vietnamese American Community," 84–109; Bloemraad, *Becoming a Citizen*.
12. Hagan, Jacqueline Maria. *Deciding to Be Legal: A Maya Community in Houston*. Philadelphia: Temple University Press, 1994.
13. Portes and MacLeod, "Educational Progress of Children of Immigrants," 257.
14. Ip, "Looking Back: The End of the Vietnam War."
15. Rumbaut, "Origins and Destinies."
16. Menjívar, "Immigrant Kinship Networks and the Impact of the Receiving Context," 104–123.
17. Portes and Böröcz, "Contemporary Immigration."
18. Landolt and Da, "Spatially Ruptured Practices of Migrant Families," 625–653; Menjívar, "Liminal Legality," 999–1037; Reitz, "Host Societies and the Reception of Immigrants," 1005–1019; Zhou and Bankston, *Growing Up American*.
19. However, some have questioned the utility of an existing ethnic community for immigrants, for example, Borjas, "Ethnic Enclaves and Assimilation," 89–122. He reported a negative association between residing in an ethnic enclave and wage growth.
20. Kelly, "Coping with America," 138–149; Gordon, "Southeast Asian Refugee Migration to the United States," 153–173.
21. Collet, "The Significance of Madison Nguyen," 131–150.
22. Due to limitations of CPS multiyear groupings of year of arrival in the United States, we approximate our waves: wave 1 encompasses respondents who arrived in the United States between 1975 and 1979. In our data, the coding for wave 2 includes those arriving between 1980 and 1993, though ideally it should correspond to those arriving between 1980 and 1994. Wave 3 of the CPS corresponds to those arriving between 1994 and 2012, though ideally it would encompass only those arriving between 1995 and 2012.
23. Through a 1976 Amendment to the Indochina Migration and Refugee Assistance Act (S. 2760), provisions were made eligible to refugees from Laos as well.
24. Because our second wave encompasses 1980–1994, we recognize that some of the earliest arrivals under family reunification overlap with the extension of funds. Because Orderly Departure was not enacted until 1980, however, and funds for the fiscal year ending September 30, 1981, were nearly depleted, we maintain that 1980–1994 constitutes a more cohesive time frame to capture contexts of reception under family reunification.
25. Moore, "Developments: The Refugee Act of 1980," 155–159.
26. Robear, "The Dust of Life," 128.
27. Campi, "From Refugees to Americans."
28. Council on Foreign Relations, "Timeline: U.S. Postwar Immigration Policy."
29. Between 2000 and 2008, for example, 149,865 persons born in Vietnam immi-

grated to the United States (see Moore, "Developments: The Refugee Act of 1980").

30. Although we do not examine protest politics in this chapter, first-wave immigrants may be more likely to participate in protests against the communist regime in Vietnam and in support of the advancement of human rights developments than those who arrived later. Differences across waves in participation vis-à-vis protest versus electoral politics merit examination in future research.

31. Asian American Justice Center, Asian and Pacific Islander American Vote, and National Asian American Survey. "Behind the Numbers: Post-Election Survey of Asian American and Pacific Islander Voters in 2012." Accessed 21 July 2015. http://www.naasurvey.com/resources/Presentations/2012-aapipes-national.pdf.

32. Ramakrishnan, Karthick, and Taeku Lee. "Public Opinion of a Growing Electorate: Asian Americans and Pacific Islanders in 2012." 25 September 2012. http://www.naasurvey.com/resources/Home/NAAS12-sep25-election.pdf.

33. Asian American Legal Defense and Education Fund. "New Findings: Asian American Vote in 2012 Varied by Ethnic Group and Geographic Location." 17 January 2012. http://aaldef.org/press-releases/press-release/new-findings-asian-american-vote-in-2012-varied-widely-by-ethnic-group-and-geographic-location.html.

34. Ramakrishnan, Karthick. "Opinions of Asian Americans and Pacific Islanders: The Affordable Care Act." 1 October 2013. http://www.naasurvey.com/resources/Home/NAAS12-ACA-report-oct2013.pdf.

REFERENCES

Alwin, Duane. *Political Attitudes over the Life Span: The Bennington Women after Fifty Years.* Madison: University of Wisconsin Press, 1991.

Bloemraad, Irene. *Becoming a Citizen: Incorporating Immigrants and Refugees in the United States and Canada.* Berkeley: University of California Press, 2006.

Borjas, George. "Ethnic Enclaves and Assimilation." *Swedish Economic Policy Review* 7 (2000): 89–122.

Campi, Alicia. "From Refugees to Americans: Thirty Years of Vietnamese Immigration to the United States." Policy brief for the American Immigration Law Foundation, 2005.

Collet, Christian. "The Significance of Madison Nguyen and the Rise of the Vietnamese American Voter in San Jose, California: Analysis and Commentary." *Doshisha American Studies* 43 (2007): 131–150.

Council on Foreign Relations. "Timeline: U.S. Postwar Immigration Policy." Accessed 20 August 2013. http://www.cfr.org/immigration/timeline-us-postwar-immigration-policy/p30191.

Gordon, Linda. "Southeast Asian Refugee Migration to the United States." *Center for Migration Studies Special Issue: Pacific Bridges* 5 (1987): 153–173.

Gordon, Milton. *Assimilation in Everyday Life: The Role of Race, Religion, and National Origins.* New York: Oxford University Press, 1964.

Ip, Michael. "Looking Back: The End of the Vietnam War." *ABC News.* 29 March 2013. http://abcnews.go.com/blogs/headlines/2013/03/looking-back-the-end-of-the-vietnam-war/.

Kelly, Gail. "Coping with America: Refugees from Vietnam, Cambodia, and Laos in the 1970s and 1980s." *Annals of the American Academy of Political and Social Science* 487 (1986): 138–149.

Landolt, Patricia, and Wei Da. "The Spatially Ruptured Practices of Migrant Families: A Comparison of Immigrants from El Salvador and the People's Republic of China." *Current Sociology* 53 (2005): 625–653.
Leighley, Jan, and Jonathan Nagler. "Individual and Systemic Influences on Turnout: Who Votes? 1984." *Journal of Politics* 54 (1992): 718–740.
Menjívar, Cecilia. "Immigrant Kinship Networks and the Impact of the Receiving Context: Salvadorans in San Francisco in the Early 1990s." *Social Problems* 44 (1997): 104–123.
Menjívar, Cecilia. "Liminal Legality: Salvadoran and Guatemalan Immigrants' Lives in the United States." *American Journal of Sociology* 111 (2006): 999–1037.
Merelman, Richard. "The Adolescence of Political Socialization." *Sociology of Education* 45 (1972): 134–166.
Moore, Peter. "Developments: The Refugee Act of 1980." *Journal of International Law and Policy* 10 (1980): 155–159.
Portes, Alejandro, and József Böröcz. "Contemporary Immigration: Theoretical Perspectives on Its Determinants and Modes of Incorporation." *International Migration Review* 233 (1989): 606–630.
Portes, Alejandro, and Dag MacLeod. "Educational Progress of Children of Immigrants: The Roles of Class, Ethnicity, and School Context." *Sociology of Education* 69 (1996): 257.
Portes, Alejandro, and Rafael Mozo. "Cubans and Other Ethnic Minorities in the United States." *International Migration Review* 19 (1985): 35–63.
Portes, Alejandro, and Rubén Rumbaut. *Immigrant America: A Portrait*. Oakland: University of California Press, 1990.
Ramakrishnan, S. Karthick, and Thomas J. Espenshade. "Immigrant Incorporation and Political Participation in the United States." *International Migration Review* 35 (2001): 871.
Reitz, Jeffrey. "Host Societies and the Reception of Immigrants: Research Themes, Emerging Theories and Methodological Issues." *International Migration Review* 36 (2002): 1005–1019.
Robear, Earnest. "The Dust of Life: The Legal and Political Ramifications of the Continuing Vietnamese Amerasian Program." *Dickinson Journal of International Law* 8 (1989): 128.
Rumbaut, Rubén. "Origins and Destinies: Immigration to the United States since World War II." *Sociological Forum* 9 (1994): 583–621.
Valentino, Nicholas, and David Sears, "Event-Driven Communication and the Preadult Socialization of Partisanship." *Political Behavior* 20 (1998): 127–154.
Võ, Linda Trinh. "Constructing a Vietnamese American Community: Economic and Political Transformation in Little Saigon, Orange County." *Amerasia* 34 (2008): 84–109.
Wolfinger, Raymond, and Jonathan Hoffman. "Registering and Voting with Motor Voter." *Political Science and Politics* 34 (2001): 85–92.
Wolfinger, Raymond, and Steven Rosenstone. *Who Votes?* New Haven, CT: Yale University Press, 1980.
Zhou, Min, and Carl L. Bankston. *Growing Up American: How Vietnamese Children Adapt to Life in the United States*. New York: Russell Sage Foundation, 1998.

Part VIII

Lesbian, Gay, Bisexual, and Transgender American Voters

Chapter 17

The Voting Behavior of Lesbian, Gay, Bisexual, and Transgender People in the United States

Barry L. Tadlock

The chapter's title suggests an introduction to the voting behavior of a unified group of people that includes lesbian, gay, bisexual, and transgender (LGBT) individuals. To a degree, it does precisely that; however, it must be emphasized that the LGBT community is, in many ways, an assemblage of several smaller groups, two of which contain even smaller subdivisions within them. For example, the terms "bisexual" and "transgender" are essentially overarching terms for somewhat disparate groups that may or may not have unified electoral and political goals. Furthermore, for those who fall within either the bisexual or transgender umbrella, many have expressed feelings of marginalization with respect to the larger LGBT community. Another division exists between lesbian, gay, and bisexual (LGB) people in contrast to transgender people, partially resulting from a perception that LGB people are focused on issues relating to sexual orientation, while transgender people are focused on issues related to gender identity. Even among lesbians and gay men, differences exist. One difference is a consequence of what some lesbians perceive as sexism among many gay men. Finally, across the entire LGBT community, there are historical differences between those who have pursued an assimilationist political strategy and those who have pursued a liberationist political strategy. To the extent possible, this chapter documents the LGBT community as a single minority group, but when necessary, attention is given to issues that divide the larger community.

DEFINITIONS AND DESCRIPTIONS

To generalize, the LGBT community consists of those whose sexual orientation and/or gender identity challenge notions of what is considered by many to be mainstream or normal. More specifically, lesbians and gay men are united in their sexual attraction to members of the same sex. *Bisexual* is an umbrella term for people who have emotional, romantic, or sexual feelings about more than one sex, which may include pansexual, fluid, omnisexual, and other people.[1] In terms of the relative size of the LGB subdivisions within the larger LGBT community, a recent national-level survey of 1,197 LGBT individuals reported that 40 percent identified as bisexual, 36 percent as gay, and 19 percent as lesbian.[2]

Transgender is an umbrella term used to refer to *transsexuals* (those whose gender identity is different from their assigned sex at birth), *genderqueer* (used by some individuals who identify as neither entirely male nor entirely female), *two-spirit* (a term that references multiple-generation traditions in many First Nations cultures), *cross-dressers*, and others.[3]

It is extraordinarily hard to obtain systematic information about transgender individuals. This is an issue that is discussed more thoroughly in this volume's chapter by Paschall. One reason is that some transgender people do not self-identify. Other reasons result from difficulties related to polling instruments, including the difficulty in writing intelligible questions, that is, questions that do not confuse non-transgender people, and also the fact that many surveys fail to make a distinction between LGB and transgender people. Furthermore, within a traditional sample of 1,100–1,200 individuals, the sample size of transgender people is likely to be miniscule. As was the case in the aforementioned LGBT survey, the percentage of transgender people was 5 percent of the sample. Such a small percentage makes it impossible to identify any statistically significant findings.[4]

How large is the overall LGBT community? National-level surveys and exit polls typically reveal that between 1 percent and 4 percent of the overall sample are LGBT-identified individuals.[5] In terms of raw numbers of voters, a recent estimate derived from an extensive gay-supported voter registration drive suggests that there are nine million gay and lesbian voters. If true, that number exceeds the number of Jewish American voters.[6]

While the LGBT acronym is now common in its usage among citizens, politicians, and the media, its wide utilization dates only from the latter third of the 20th century, which accompanied the rise of the modern gay and lesbian movement that many view as developing less than 50 years ago.

FORMING A SOCIAL MOVEMENT AND GAINING ACCESS INTO THE ELECTORAL ARENA

In order to understand the voting behavior of LGBT people, it is first necessary to understand how those who identify as LGBT coalesced into a movement and gained entry into the U.S. political system. The earliest instance of lesbian and gay activism is most often connected to several so-called homophile groups. Ronald Hunt described the Mattachine Society (for gay men) and the Daughters of Bilitis (for lesbians) as having "paved the way for the more ambitious agenda of future gay and lesbian activists."[7] It is worth noting that these groups tended towards an assimilationist stance, trying to fit into mainstream American politics. Also, they tended not to enter into coalitions with other movements, such as the women's or civil rights movements. These groups' assimilationist orientation was not embraced by all lesbians and gay men. For example, the Mattachine of Washington, D.C. (MOW) chapter, headed by Frank Kameny, assumed a liberationist stance. MOW's focus on the uniqueness and apartness of gay men was at odds with other Mattachine chapters. Despite the presence of groups with differing political strategies, it took a catalytic event—the Stonewall raid—to foster an LGBT social movement.

Haider-Markel dates 1969 as the "birth year of the modern gay and lesbian social movement."[8] Why 1969? On June 27 of that year, police in New York City conducted a raid at the Stonewall Inn, a Greenwich Village gay bar. Raids on bars frequented by lesbians and gay men were nothing new. However, at this particular point in time the formation of a viable gay and lesbian liberation movement was due "in large part because of the radical movements that had so inflamed much of American youth during the 1960s."[9] Activists, "with the model of the civil rights movement in front of them, . . . argued that political action, rather than self-help or education, was the path to equality."[10] In a mere four years their work bore fruit, as evidenced by the fact that the number of LGBT groups grew from 50 in 1969 to 800 in 1973, which was the same year that the American Psychological Association removed homosexuality from its list of mental disorders.[11]

LGBT political and cultural movements proceeded on parallel tracks during the 1970s. The former focused on, among other things, beginning electoral work and also "laid the foundation for gay and lesbian political stature."[12] The cultural reformers, however, mostly eschewed politics.[13] Another key distinction existed within the broader LGBT movement. D'Emilio noted that there were parallel movements for gay men and lesbians, in part because lesbians believed gay men to be sexist and women to be hostile, which explained why lesbians did not seek to achieve their goals within the women's movement.[14]

Note the preceding discussion centered on gay men and lesbians, but not bisexual or transgender people. The reason is captured within the concept of secondary marginalization. Phelan argued that lesbians and gay men define their identity by sexual object choice, and such a definition is problematic for bisexual individuals: "In communities defined by object choice, a desire that fluctuates must necessarily be problematic."[15] Inclusion of transgender people is also subject to secondary marginalization, because "they are vilified as embarrassments to the 'normal' homosexuals."[16] A tendency toward secondary marginalization is exacerbated by tactics used by LGBT movement leaders. This has occurred when the messaging used in electoral campaigns makes transgender people invisible. For example, legislation related to public bathroom access is an issue of great importance to many transgender individuals. However, such issues are sometimes swept under the carpet rather than cause the primary electoral communications in a political campaign to move off-message.[17] Hunt drew attention to another aspect of secondary marginalization within the LGBT movement when he discussed racism "within the gay and lesbian community" in bars and by groups and "apathy . . . toward the movement for social justice."[18] As with any minority group, LGBT people inevitably depend upon allies, whether they be racial minorities or others, when they enter into the field of electoral politics. Therefore, issues related to secondary marginalization are highly problematic.

VOTING BEHAVIOR AT THE LOCAL, STATE, AND NATIONAL LEVELS

Having established that the LGBT social movement is largely a modern phenomenon, it stands to reason that its voting history is short when compared with other minority groups. LGBT voters and activists often are first exposed to the electoral arena at the local level, which is where anti-LGBT legislation is sometimes introduced. Perhaps the single most famous instance occurred in south Florida in 1977, when both pro-LGBT and anti-LGBT forces mobilized in response to "the Dade County, Florida antigay referenda spearheaded by Anita Bryant and her organization, the Save Our Children Network."[19] Bryant's organization led a successful repeal of Miami's sexual orientation-based nondiscrimination law, garnering nearly 70 percent of the vote. The following year, similar actions overturned nondiscrimination laws in St. Paul, Minnesota, Wichita, Kansas, and Eugene, Oregon.[20]

Similar initiatives also occurred at the state level. In 1992, Oregon's ballot featured Measure 9. Although it failed at the ballot box, had it passed it would have prohibited Oregon governments from promoting, encouraging, or facilitating homosexuality. The "No on 9" campaign established for LGBT groups what became a model for the systematic use of voter identification. Specifically, it focused on those most likely to vote ("chronic voters") within a narrowly focused set of "specific precincts or counties that were known as being Democratic, or more liberal."[21] This Oregon campaign led the National Gay and Lesbian Task Force (NGLTF) to develop a "Fight the Right" campaign kit that focused on how to get gay men and lesbians registered to vote.[22] This toolkit had broad applicability, often being filtered through statewide groups such as Michigan Equality. However, at times it was purposefully ignored. In 1999, a Ferndale, Michigan, activist organization, Keep Our Human Rights, consciously resisted national and statewide advice in their local electoral campaign. Similarly, direct action groups, like Lesbian Avengers with its Civil Rights Organizing Project (LACROP), criticized the Oregon model for being too mainstream and trying to minimize the visibility of lesbians and gay men. As an alternative tactic, LACROP tried to mobilize the LGBT community through actions such as a "Happy Homosexual" rally outside an anti-LGBT church in the week before an Idaho election.[23]

At the same time that the LGBT movement was experiencing electoral success in Oregon, it was experiencing statewide failures elsewhere. In Colorado, voters approved Amendment 2 in 1992, sanctioning legalized discrimination of lesbian, gay, and bisexual individuals. "LGBs reacted to Amendment 2 with deep distress and anger but they also used the election as a catalyst for personal empowerment and political activism."[24] They were "galvanized" and "became political" and the movement witnessed the "postelection presence of a statewide political infrastructure."[25]

At the national level, 1992 was a pivotal year in the relationship between the LGBT movement and electoral politics. "Clinton's election was unquestionably a historic event in gay politics, in which, as recently as a decade earlier, support of gay rights was considered political suicide for most candidates, and certainly for one seeking the presidency."[26] Bill Clinton, as did other leading contenders in the Democratic primary, reached out to LGBT voters. As his party's nominee, Clinton was rewarded electorally with 72 percent of the LGBT vote, according to exit polls. This solidified a long running connection between LGBT voters and Democratic presidential candidates. Exit polls document Democratic candidates' vote share in subsequent elections: 66 percent in 1996, 71 percent in 2000, 77 percent in 2004, 70 percent in 2008, and 76 percent in 2012.[27]

Some of this connection between the LGBT movement and Democratic presidential candidates can be traced to decisions made during the 1980s by Presidents Ronald Reagan and George H.W. Bush. Despite the enormous toll that the HIV/AIDS crisis took on the LGBT community, President Reagan did not mention AIDS until 1987 when he spoke to the Third International AIDS Conference in Washington, D.C.. This was six years after the Centers for Disease Control first reported on an AIDS death. He also did little to support AIDS research or to prohibit discrimination against people living with HIV/AIDS. Furthermore, he restrained his surgeon general from publicly addressing AIDS until his second term. While President Bush signed the Ryan White Comprehensive AIDS Resource Emergency (CARE) Act in 1990, he did not fund it at the level that its congressional supporters wanted. Also, Bush appointed Earvin "Magic" Johnson, a famous ex-professional basketball player who revealed his HIV positive status in 1991, to the National Commission on AIDS. However, Mr. Johnson resigned when Bush underfinanced the Commission. On the other hand, President Clinton supported full funding of the CARE Act and used his Department of Justice to pursue discriminatory actions against those living with HIV/AIDS. It should be noted that while President George W. Bush eliminated the White House AIDS office, in 2003 he proposed the Emergency Plan for AIDS Relief, tripling the amount of money going to international AIDS relief efforts.[28]

As Paschall notes elsewhere in this volume, in terms of transgender people, there is evidence of a connection between them and the national Democratic Party, but similar evidence does not exist with the national Republican Party. More specifically, openly transgender candidates have served as delegates to Democratic presidential nominating conventions since 2000, and platform planks have addressed gender identity since 2008. At the Republican national conventions, there have been no openly transgender delegates and no platform language addressing issues related to transgender people.

The electoral support of Democratic presidential candidates combined with the largely hostile record of Republican presidents should not be construed as complete identification of LGBT voters with the Democratic Party. As Hertzog notes, although there is "pronounced aversion to identification with the Republican party," "party identification with the Democrats remains relatively weak."[29] Gallup daily tracking surveys of LGBT people that concluded in September 2012 revealed that 44 percent identified as Democrats, 43 percent as Independents, and 13 percent as Republicans. (This contrasted with 32%, 39%, and 30% among the general population.)[30] This does not suggest that LGBT Republicans do not try to alter the status quo. The Log Cabin Republicans is a party organization representing LGBT Republicans and their allies. The group champions awareness and acceptance of LGBT issues at national, state, and local levels of government. For instance, "in Texas, the Log Cabin Republicans have fought state party officials to gain acceptance within the Republican Party and win recognition for gay assistance in the election of moderate Republicans."[31]

DISENGAGING AND ENGAGING LGBT VOTERS

Questions remain as to whether LGBT individuals are helped or hindered by various electoral arrangements at the local level. For example, when one compares local jurisdictions that feature at-large elections versus those jurisdictions that feature district elections, evidence suggests that LGBT people are not helped at the local level by district elections.[32] There are several factors that could account for this. For instance, the overall percentage of LGBT people within the overall population is not large, but it could be large in any given electoral district. Well known LGBT enclaves such as Chelsea in New York City, Dupont Circle in Washington, D.C., and West Hollywood in Los Angeles illustrate the point; they are recognized because of their distinctiveness. In the vast majority of US cities, it is virtually impossible that one could construct a so-called majority-minority district in which LGBT people are a majority of a district's constituents. In terms of congressional districts, the ability to construct a majority-minority district, given the approximately 700,000 people who constitute a U.S. House district, is rather fanciful. In fact, the congressional district with the largest percentage of LGB voters is the Eighth Congressional district in San Francisco, California, with an estimated 16.6 percent of LGBs in the adult population.[33]

Another element of the electoral process that can be used to disenfranchise LGBT people is voter identification requirements, which especially affect transgender people who face a "unique obstacle." In the November 2012 elections, it was estimated that 25,232 voting-eligible transgender voters across nine "strict photo ID states" had no updated identification, which likely created "substantial barriers to voting and possible disenfranchisement."[34] This came about because states toughened their voter ID laws after passage of the 2002 Help America Vote Act. "Requirements for updating state-issued IDs vary widely by state and can be difficult and costly" and those who have transitioned may not have updated their ID.[35] While obtaining or updating a U.S. passport may be more viable than updating one's state ID, doing so is a costly option. The voter identification issue significantly affects transgender people of color, with low incomes, with disabilities, those who are young, and those who are students. To exacerbate this situation, just a few days before the 2012 election it was revealed that "a right-wing, Tea Party organization called 'True the Vote' (was) training their volunteer poll watchers to target transgender voters." The organization produced and distributed a training manual that featured a "transphobic image" and claimed that "transgender people are fraudulent voters and should be denied the right to vote."[36]

One factor that enhances LGBT voting and therefore can mitigate the disenfranchising factors previously discussed is the selection of appropriate messaging on an electoral issue. For example, in 1978, California voters rejected the anti-LGBT Proposition 6. The defeat was attributed in part to a successful campaign centered on a theme of "Come out! Come out! Wherever you are." This brought personal narratives into the electoral campaign, as opposed to focus group-tested messages generated by national organizations that often do not resonate at the local level with LGBT voters and their allies.[37]

Another countervailing influence to tactics that disenfranchise LGBT voters is the effort to build voting coalitions, which cut across racial, class, and gender divides. Shared issues are identified and addressed, including comprehensive medical care, HIV/AIDS, hate crimes, the Employment Nondiscrimination Act, youth issues, and educational initiatives regarding differences among people.[38]

THE IMPACT ON ELECTORAL OUTCOMES

Have LGBT voters ever been critical to an electoral outcome; has the LGBT movement ever been critical to an electoral outcome? These may seem to be the same question worded differently; however, they refer to different cross-sections of the electorate, because the movement includes not only LGBT voters but also LGBT allies and coalition partners. Due to factors related to data availability, the following discussion refers primarily to those who identify as lesbian or gay, or in some cases, bisexual people.

Perhaps the most commonly cited national election in which the influence of gay men and lesbians was most pronounced was Bill Clinton's inaugural victory in 1992. Lesbians and gay men contributed $2.5 million to Clinton's campaign and supported him with 72 percent of the vote.[39] During that same year, lesbians and gay men were instrumental in ensuring the reelection of openly gay members of Congress.[40]

What engendered this support? As a candidate, Clinton reached out to the lesbian and gay community in order to create a winning coalition and also increase his campaign contributions. Clinton and his surrogates met with gay leaders and attended fundraisers. The prominent activist David Mixner linked the campaign to wealthy members of the community, and the campaign helped fund get-out-the-vote (GOTV) drives in gay neighborhoods. The end result of these various activities was the belief among many that Clinton was "embracing the gay community at the New York convention."[41]

As discussed earlier, gay and lesbian voters helped defeat a statewide anti-LGBT rights initiative in Oregon. Opponents of gay rights may have unwittingly created a context in which gay voters helped decide the outcome. When these anti-LGBT rights groups expanded the scope of conflict to place an initiative on the ballot, "the campaigns can also politicize gays and lesbians so they become more politically active."[42] Further evidence of the impact of Oregon's gay and lesbian community is the fact that the number of openly gay legislators in the state legislature went from zero before the ballot initiative to four in 1994, more than in any other state.[43]

Also at the local level, lesbian and gay voters have been credited with impacting electoral outcomes. A 1993 national-level survey queried local officials in 251 communities—half of them with a nondiscrimination law and half without such a law—about the role of gay voters. Nearly 1/3 (31%) of the officials in communities with such laws attributed the passage of the law to the mobilization of gay and lesbian voters.[44]

In October 2006, the Williams Institute estimated the degree to which LGB voters would influence the following month's midterm elections. The analysis suggested that LGB voters could have a disproportionate impact in competitive House races with Republican incumbents and in Senate races with Democratic incumbents. The analysis followed one conducted the previous year by the same organization in which the Institute estimated the number of LGB adults living in each congressional district. Estimates suggested that seven districts nationwide featured LGB populations in excess of 50,000 residents. Six of the seven districts were on the coasts, but one of them was in Atlanta, GA.[45] Typically these 50,000+ residents represented between 10 and 15 percent of a district's adult population.[46]

Regardless of the level of government one considers, lesbian and gay candidates' electoral success cannot be attributed solely to lesbian and gay voters' support. "Rarely sponsored by business, privilege, or wealth, openly lesbian and gay candidates have won on popular platforms combining the concerns of racial minorities, feminists, tenants, the elderly, neighborhood activists, labor union members, environmentalists, and, of course, gay people themselves."[47]

POLITICAL PARTIES AND LGBT VOTERS

Though a plurality of LGBT voters identify with the Democratic Party, it is important to understand why this association came to be, and also to realize that there are significant percentages of LGBT voters who identify with the Republican Party, a third party, or who identify as Independents. But why does a plurality of LGBT individuals identify as Democrats? Fetner suggests that events in the 1980s helped solidify the association between LGBT people and the Democratic Party, at the same time that the religious right became closely entwined with the Republican Party. "The religious right's rise to power within the GOP pushed explicitly anti-gay stances firmly into Republican Party politics."[48] This important point illustrates that the connection of LGBT voters with the Democratic Party may be based primarily on repulsion from the Republican Party as much as it is based on attraction to the Democratic Party. An interview with Cheryl Jacques, a former Human Rights Campaign (HRC) director, illustrates this point. "I think Democratic principles are . . . more encouraging for the future of equality of gay and lesbian people . . . (it is) no surprise that organizations like HRC are going to overwhelmingly endorse and give money to Democrats. My only caveat is that it's not that we necessarily had a choice."[49] Jacques added that in the 1980s, Democratic politicians were not rushing to support the lesbian and gay movement, and also "there was ambivalence of the lesbian and gay community toward national-level movement efforts."[50]

By the 1990s, Democratic Party presidential candidates made a concerted effort to reach out to LGBT voters. In 1992, "all five leading Democratic contenders actively courted the gay vote" and "endorsed a repeal of the ban on homosexuals in the military," as did Independent candidate Ross Perot.[51] The 1992 Democratic convention in New York City was "a celebration of (lesbians' and gays') arrival at the heart of political power," as evidenced by the presence of 133 delegates as well as openly gay speakers Roberta Achtenberg and Bob Hattoy, who was living with AIDS.[52] Hattoy told the assembled delegates: "We must vote this year as if our lives depended on it. Mine does. Yours could."[53] During the same convention season, President George H.W. Bush promised evangelical leaders that he opposed to gay rights. Also at the Republican Party's convention in Houston, Texas, delegates held placards reading *"Family rights forever, gay rights never"* while Patrick Buchanan labeled the Clinton/Gore ticket as "the most pro-lesbian and pro-gay ticket in history."[54] "The Republican platform opposed all federal, state, or local gay rights legislation and supported the ban on homosexuals in the armed forces."[55]

This did not result, however, in complete success for the LGBT movement. Although President Clinton appointed several gay men and lesbians to executive offices and consulted with lesbian and gay groups, "the Clinton era produced a number of broken promises and unforeseen challenges."[56] Consequently, many resisted the pull of the Democratic Party for both ideological and strategic reasons. For example, Rich Tafel, spoke of the Log Cabin Republicans when he wrote that "the ultimate contribution of Log Cabin (Republicans) may be to expose the dangers of stereotypes and remind both Republicans and gay activists that all of us are complex individuals, and America is a better place when it embraces true diversity, instead of pigeonholing people."[57] Urvashi Vaid also argued that lesbians and gay men "must be open to third-party candidates" so that gay and lesbian interests are not subsumed in a candidate's interests.[58]

POLITICAL AND SOCIAL VALUES ASSOCIATED WITH LGBT VOTERS

Several scholars make the point that supposedly shared values are difficult to identify, and this applies to the social and political values held by LGBT voters. No one made the point more forcefully than Sherrill, reminding us that LGBs are not typically socialized by other LGBs at home, in the workplace, or in schools; instead they are most likely raised by heterosexual parents, educated by heterosexual teachers, and work alongside heterosexual colleagues. As such, Sherrill argued, there is no shared political consciousness among LGB voters. "People who are randomly distributed about a nation, with multiple and conflicting cross-pressures, are not likely to formulate a highly structured and coherent agenda . . . a more sophisticated agenda would require a level of collective identity among gay people not found anywhere in the world."[59]

However, there exists evidence that the LGBT political movement has resulted in some shared issue stances, even in the absence of a larger shared consciousness. For example, "urbanism, and the social diversity that accompanies it, have been linked to innovative policies affecting gays."[60] The existence of said policies is due in part to lesbian and gay enclaves that "were somewhat insulated and protected from the larger culture and, in time, developed the critical mass necessary for political organization."[61] Quite often, these "innovative policies" have taken the form of antidiscrimination ordinances and policies adopted by various cities and counties throughout the United States.[62]

Over the years, opposition to the religious right has also encouraged gay men and lesbians to coalesce around certain issues and a common electoral strategy. For example, in the late 1980s and early 1990s, lesbian and gay activists turned away from "quiet activities and institution building" to street-level activism and direct democracy at the state and local levels.[63] The battle between the religious right and the gay and lesbian movement resulted in increased public awareness of gay and lesbian issues, improved cultural representation of gays and lesbians, and "political discourse and public debate about lesbian and gay rights has become more commonplace."[64]

Finally, HIV/AIDS spurred many gay men and lesbians to become politically active. Additionally, the radicalism of many AIDS activists, such as those involved in the group Queer Nation, helped bring bisexual and transgender people into the larger LGBT movement. Queer Nation (QN) was a radical activist group founded by former members of ACT UP (AIDS Coalition to Unleash Power). QN's founders believed that ACT UP's focus on equal rights and fair treatment for LGBTs was too assimilationist, that ACT UP was too focused on politics, its organizational structure was overly hierarchical and not sufficiently inclusive. QN, and other similarly radical groups, took the opposite tack. As liberationists instead of assimilationists, they focused on cultural targets instead of political ones, and their organizational structure was nonhierarchical. Most significantly, the radical groups were inclusive of bisexual and transgender people, and they pushed "the envelope of what was considered a normal or acceptable protest activity."[65]

The battle between assimilationists and liberationists does not mark the only point of distinction within the LGBT community regarding social and political values. At times a clear distinction arises between gay men and lesbians. Urvashi Vaid, in her seminal work *Virtual Equality,* argued that "lesbians are, as a whole, more politically progressive than gay men. Our skepticism about government, family, and patriarchy draws many of us to grassroots political action and to the democratic participation and individual control that direct action fosters."[66]

LGBT GROUPS AND THEIR IMPACT ON VOTING

One cannot begin to fully understand the voting behavior of LGBT individuals without exploring the role of both pro-LGBT and anti-LGBT rights groups. While the role of pro-LGBT rights groups can be inferred reasonably well, the role of anti-LGBT rights groups may be less intuitive. However, responses to the religious right and a key referendum in Boulder, Colorado, in 1974, caused national and statewide LGBT organizations to create a social movement infrastructure which has developed and nurtured tactics to fight anti-LGBT ballot measures. These include training programs, GOTV efforts, fundraising donor pools, disciplined messaging developed through focus groups and polling, and voter identification developed through door-to-door canvassing and phone banking.[67]

One particularly important LGBT group formed in 1969 in New York City: the Gay Activists Alliance (GAA), in part due to a "thought that meaningful reform would occur only if lesbians and gays organized politically and exercised their political muscle to force positive legislative change. Their involvement in electoral politics set the stage for a strategy that has come to dominate the contemporary mainstream lesbian and gay rights movements."[68] The GAA lasted only for about five years, but its work was absorbed by national-level organizations, such as NGLTF (formed in 1973), HRC (formed in 1980), and the Gay and Lesbian Victory Fund (founded in 1991).

Much of the interesting action concerning LGBT voters occurs at the state and local levels. As Rimmerman writes, "(W)e should not be surprised that the state and local levels are the locus of considerable progressive organizing," in part due to the large number of "gay-hostile" pieces of legislation being passed in state assemblies and town councils.[69] One statewide organization that long ago was credited for signaling a new direction for the LGBT movement is Basic Rights Oregon (BRO). In terms of voter outreach, BRO illustrated progressive leadership with its Voter File Project (VFP), a coalition of gay and lesbian, labor, environmental, and pro-choice groups that pooled their voters' lists and utilized a steering committee to decide which candidates and referenda to support or oppose. As a result of BRO's broad agenda of political, social, and cultural change, it developed the Fair Workplace Project in 1995, which worked with corporations to help them develop nondiscriminatory personnel policies. BRO also helped defeat the Oregon Citizens' Alliance's 'Student Protection Act,' which would have made it possible to fire openly lesbian and gay teachers, ban counseling programs, ban objectionable books and audio/visual materials, and curtail HIV/AIDS education.[70]

It is important to realize that electoral success for LGBT voters does not necessarily require a large LGBT population, a fact illustrated in Kalamazoo, Michigan, when a 2001 anti-LGBT legal-restrictive charter amendment was defeated despite the local LGBT community's fairly small size. The successful strategy for pro-LGBT movement activists incorporated a GOTV effort concentrated on three key Kalamazoo neighborhoods.[71] As discussed, another important factor determining success is coalitional politics. Passage of antibias legislation has been "dependent on gays having allies and developing political coalitions with additional groups. These supportive interests often included human rights organizations, especially the American Civil Liberties Union, local human relations boards or commissions, liberal church groups, African-American civil rights advocates, liberal women's groups, university or student organizations, the Democratic Party, and environmental groups."[72]

David Rayside wrote that a focus on electoral politics as a way to bring about changes desired by the LGBT movement leaders and voters is distinctive in the United States. His comparative analysis of LGBT politics in the United States, Canada, and Britain led him to assert that "(t)he American gay/lesbian movement . . . has attached more importance to entering electoral contests than movements in other countries."[73]

Most of this section has concerned the larger movement, but to what extent are LGBT groups' interests shared. Transgender voters have argued that their interests are not adequately represented by the leading LGBT organizations. As such, trans-specific organizations such as Trans United for Obama formed in 2012 to engage in electoral activities, including "door-knocking, data entry, engaging in grassroots fundraising, registering voters and getting the message out that President Obama" had contributed to a long list of accomplishments for transgender Americans.[74] Also, the National Center for Transgender Equality (NCTE) takes an even larger focus, educating and empowering transgender people on a variety of transgender-specific factors that affect their voting behavior, including but not limited to policies related to identification requirements and discrimination.[75]

THE FUTURE INFLUENCE AND BEHAVIOR OF LGBT VOTERS

A decade-long focus on marriage equality by many of the most prominent LGBT organizations and activists has resulted in many recent successes. As of 2014, 17 states plus the District of Columbia provide for marriage equality. This success masks the underside of the story. The United States is now home to what some recognize as "two distinct gay Americas."[76] One gay America exists in major cities and on the nation's coasts. The other gay America lives in the states of the Rocky Mountains and in the South. In these areas of the United States, LGBT citizens enjoy very few legal protections against discrimination.

In the years ahead, especially where marriage equality exists, we can expect the focus of the LGBT political community to shift away from marriage equality and toward efforts to enhance nondiscrimination ordinances in housing and employment, for legislation allowing gay parents to adopt, for immigration reform that keeps LGBT families together, and for family and partnership recognition of transgender people. Electoral strategies devoted to these issues will be guided by well-known national-level organizations such as HRC, the GLVF, and the ACLU, as well as lesser-known state-level organizations such as the Gill Foundation, based in Denver, Colorado. For example, the GLVF focuses on states with no openly LGBT elected officials on any level, like Mississippi and Idaho, as well as states like Michigan, which have no openly LGBT officeholders in their state legislatures.

Not only will the focus shift with respect to the political issues, but it will also shift in terms of coalitional partners. In terms of political parties, on the coasts and in the nation's major cities, a partnership with the Democratic Party has sufficed in terms of an electoral strategy. Such is not the case in the southern and Rocky Mountain states; instead, LGBT activists will reach out to sympathetic leaders of state- and local-level Republican Party organizations in order to achieve electoral and/or legislative success. In these same states, outreach to clergy and African-American civil rights organizations will be needed. Perhaps most importantly, a partnership with important corporations will be a key ingredient going forward. A model is found in Colorado, where the Gill Foundation helped fund "educational initiatives and liberal nonprofit groups, splitting social conservatives from the state's business establishment and working to elect pro-gay rights lawmakers."[77]

All of the above is not to suggest that the issue of marriage equality is going to be erased from the political landscape. In states where bans exist, LGBT activists and their allies are strategizing about when and how to go about reversing the bans. Ohio is a case in point. While both Equality Ohio and FreedomOhio support efforts regarding marriage equality in the state, they disagree over the best timing for a constitutional amendment to reverse the ban. Equality Ohio, along with national-level partner organizations such as HRC and Freedom to Marry, favors waiting until 2016, partly to allow more time for voter education but also to take advantage of a larger, and supposedly more liberal, electorate that will vote in the 2016 presidential election. Leaders of FreedomOhio, a group with fewer connections to national-level marriage equality organizations, argue that the 2014 midterm election is the right time. Although they were granted the go-ahead by the Ohio Ballot Board to gather signatures to place the constitutional amendment on the November 2014 ballot, they failed to get the required number of signatures. Regardless of this setback, FreedomOhio's central argument is important to understand. Group leaders argue that its superior understanding of Ohioans and Ohio's political environment trumps the understanding of those with a more national perspective. Given that a majority of states currently have same-sex marriage bans in place, it is reasonable to expect that debates such as the one occurring in Ohio in 2014 will take place in these other states in the future. As Stone noted, this gives cause for concern: "Ballot measure campaigns can potentially harm social movements by increasing movement infighting or dissent."[78] It is clear that significant and surprising gains occurred for the LGBT movement in a relatively short time period, thanks in large part to LGBT voters and their allies. What is currently unclear is how quickly gains, such as in marriage equality, will broaden to include all states, and how they will deepen to include other issues valued by LGBT people.

NOTES

1. Bisexual Resource Center, "About Us: Mission."
2. "A Survey of LGBT Americans," Pew Research Center.
3. Mottet and Tanis, "Opening the Door to the Inclusion of Transgender People."
4. "A Survey of LGBT Americans," Pew Research Center.
5. Hertzog, *Lavender Vote*, 2.
6. Button, Rienzo, and Wald, *Private Lives, Public Conflicts*, 74.
7. Hunt, *Historical Dictionary of the Gay Liberation Movement*, 13.
8. Haider-Markel, "Creating Change—Holding the Line," 248.
9. D'Emilio, *Sexual Politics, Sexual Communities*, 233.
10. Ibid., 244.
11. Ibid., *Sexual Communities*, 247.
12. Vaid, *Virtual Equality*, 62.
13. Marotta, *The Politics of Homosexuality*.
14. D'Emilio, *Sexual Politics, Sexual Communities*.
15. Phelan, *Sexual Strangers*, 117.

16. Ibid.
17. Stone, *Gay Rights at the Ballot Box*, 173.
18. Hunt, *Historical Dictionary of the Gay Liberation Movement*, 25.
19. Haider-Markel, "Creating Change—Holding the Line," 249.
20. Bronski, *A Queer History of the United States*, 220.
21. Stone, *Gay Rights at the Ballot Box*, 69.
22. Ibid., 78.
23. Ibid.
24. Russell, *Voted Out*, ix.
25. Ibid., 226 and 266.
26. Button, Rienzo, and Wald, *Private Lives, Public Conflicts*, 74.
27. Gates and Newport, "LGBT Americans Skew Democratic"; Gates, "LGBT Vote 2012."
28. Rimmerman, *The Lesbian and Gay Movements*.
29. Hertzog, *Lavender Vote*, 80.
30. Gates and Newport, "LGBT Americans Skew Democratic."
31. Haider-Markel, "Lesbian and Gay Politics in the States," 293.
32. Segura, "Institutions Matter," 220–241.
33. Gates, "Same-Sex Couples and the Gay, Lesbian, Bisexual Population."
34. Herman, "The Potential Impact of Voter Identification Laws on Transgender Voters," 1.
35. Ibid., 3.
36. "Tea Party Group Targets Trans Voters," National Center for Transgender Equality.
37. Bronski, *A Queer History of the United States*, 220.
38. Rimmerman, *The Lesbian and Gay Movements*; Segura, "Institutions Matter," 220–241; Vaid, *Virtual Equality*.
39. Button, Rienzo, and Wald, *Private Lives, Public Conflicts*, 74.
40. Haider-Markel, "Creating Change—Holding the Line."
41. Vaid, *Virtual Equality*, 127.
42. Haider-Markel and Meier, "The Politics of Gay Rights," 346.
43. Ibid., 332–349.
44. Button, Rienzo, and Wald, *Private Lives, Public Conflicts*.
45. Gates, "The Gay, Lesbian, and Bisexual Vote in 2006," 1.
46. Gates, "Same-sex Couples and the Gay, Lesbian, Bisexual Population," 2.
47. Adam, *The Rise of a Gay and Lesbian Movement*, 140.
48. Fetner, *How the Religious Right Shaped Lesbian and Gay Activism*, 76.
49. Ibid., 77.
50. Ibid.
51. Button, Rienzo, and Wald, *Private Lives, Public Conflicts*, 73.
52. Gallagher and Bull, *Perfect Enemies*, 77.
53. Ibid., 86.
54. Ibid., 88.
55. Hertzog, *Lavender Vote*, 5.
56. Fetner, *How the Religious Right Shaped Lesbian and Gay Activism*, 78.
57. Tafel, "Caught Between Worlds," 115–130.
58. Vaid, *Virtual Equality*, 129.
59. Sherrill, "The Political Power of Lesbians, Gays, and Bisexuals," 469–473.

60. Button, Rienzo, and Wald, "The Politics of Gay Rights at the Local and State Level," 280.
61. Ibid.
62. Wald, Button, and Rienzo, "The Politics of Gay Rights in American Communities," 1153.
63. Fetner, *How the Religious Right Shaped Lesbian and Gay Activism*, 84.
64. Ibid., 129.
65. Ibid., 88.
66. Vaid, *Virtual Equality*, 104–105.
67. Stone, *Gay Rights at the Ballot Box*, xix-xx.
68. Rimmerman, *From Identity to Politics*, 26.
69. Rimmerman, *Lesbian and Gay Movements*, 182.
70. Ibid., 182–183.
71. Stone, *Gay Rights at the Ballot Box*.
72. Button, Rienzo, and Wald, "The Politics of Gay Rights at the Local and State Level," 281–282.
73. David Rayside, *On the Fringe*, 288.
74. "Trans United for Obama," *Trans United for Obama*, Accessed 1 May 2014, http://www.transunitedforobama.org/.
75. "Voting While Trans," National Center for Transgender Equality.
76. Confessore and Peters, "Gay Rights Push Shifts Its Focus South and West."
77. Ibid.
78. Stone, *Gay Rights at the Ballot Box*, xxvii.

REFERENCES

Adam, Barry D. *The Rise of a Gay and Lesbian Movement*. New York: Twayne Publishers, 1995.
Bisexual Resource Center. "About Us: Mission." Accessed 28 April, 2014, http://www.biresource.net/aboutus.shtml.
Bronski, Michael. *A Queer History of the United States*. Boston, MA: Beacon Press, 2011.
Button, James W., Barbara A. Rienzo, and Kenneth D. Wald. "The Politics of Gay Rights at the Local and State Level." *The Politics of Gay Rights*. Ed. Craig A. Rimmerman, Kenneth D. Wald, and Clyde Wilcox. Chicago: The University of Chicago Press, 2000. 269–289.
Button, James W., Barbara A. Rienzo, and Kenneth D. Wald. *Private Lives, Public Conflicts: Battles over Gay Rights in American Communities*. Washington, D.C.: CQ Press, 1997.
Confessore, Nicholas, and Jeremy W. Peters. "Gay Rights Push Shifts Its Focus South and West." *New York Times* 27 April 2014.
D'Emilio, John. *Sexual Politics, Sexual Communities*. Chicago: The University of Chicago Press, 1983.
Gallagher, John, and Chris Bull. *Perfect Enemies: The Battle between the Religious Right and the Gay Movement*. Lanham, MD: Madison Books, 2001.

Gates, Gary J. "The Gay, Lesbian, and Bisexual Vote in 2006." The Williams Institute. October 2006. http://williamsinstitute.law.ucla.edu/wp-content/uploads/Gates-GLB-Vote-Oct-2006.pdf.

Gates, Gary J. "LGBT Vote 2012." The Williams Institute. November 2012. http://williamsinstitute.law.ucla.edu/research/census-lgbt-demographics-studies/lgbt-vote-2012/.

Gates, Gary J. "Same-Sex Couples and the Gay, Lesbian, Bisexual Population: New Estimates from the American Community Survey." The Williams Institute. October 2006. http://williamsinstitute.law.ucla.edu/wp-content/uploads/Gates-Same-Sex-Couples-GLB-Pop-ACS-Oct-2006.pdf.

Gates, Gary J., and Frank Newport. "LGBT Americans Skew Democratic, Largely Support Obama." *Gallup*. 18 October 2012. http://www.gallup.com/poll/158102/lgbt-americans-skew-democratic-largely-support-obama.aspx.

Haider-Markel, Donald P. "Creating Change—Holding the Line: Agenda Setting on Lesbian and Gay Issues at the National Level." *Gays and Lesbians in the Democratic Process: Public Policy, Public Opinion, and Political Representation*. Ed. Ellen D. B. Riggle and Barry L. Tadlock. New York: Columbia University Press, 1999. 242–268.

Haider-Markel, Donald P. "Lesbian and Gay Politics in the States: Interest Groups, Electoral Politics, and Policy." *The Politics of Gay Rights*. Ed. Craig A. Rimmerman, Kenneth D. Wald, and Clyde Wilcox. Chicago: The University of Chicago Press, 2000. 290–346.

Haider-Markel, Donald P., and Kenneth J. Meier. "The Politics of Gay Rights: Expanding the Scope of Conflict." *Journal of Politics* 58.2 (1996): 332–349.

Herman, Jody L. "The Potential Impact of Voter Identification Laws on Transgender Voters." The Williams Institute. April 2012. http://williamsinstitute.law.ucla.edu/research/transgender-issues/the-potential-impact-of-voter-identification-laws-on-transgender-voters/.

Hertzog, Mark. *The Lavender Vote: Lesbians, Gay Men, and Bisexuals in American Electoral Politics*. New York: New York University Press, 1996.

Hunt, Ronald J. *Historical Dictionary of the Gay Liberation Movement: Gay Men and the Quest for Social Justice*. Lanham, MD: Scarecrow Press, 1999.

Marotta, Toby. *The Politics of Homosexuality*. Boston: Houghton Mifflin, 1981.

Mottet, Lisa, and Justin Tanis. "Opening the Door to the Inclusion of Transgender People." National Center for Transgender Equality and National Gay and Lesbian Task Force. 2008. http://transequality.org/issues/resources/opening-door-inclusion-transgender-people.

Phelan, Shane. *Sexual Strangers: Gays, Lesbians, and Dilemmas of Citizenship*. Philadelphia: Temple University Press, 2001.

Rayside, David. *On the Fringe: Gays and Lesbians in Politics*. Ithaca, NY: Cornell University Press, 1998.

Rimmerman, Craig A. *From Identity to Politics: The Lesbian and Gay Movements in the United States*. Philadelphia: Temple University Press, 2002.

Rimmerman, Craig A. *The Lesbian and Gay Movements: Assimilation or Liberation?* Boulder, CO: Westview Press, 2007.

Russell, Glenda M. *Voted Out: The Psychological Consequences of Anti-Gay Politics*. New York: New York University Press, 2000.

Segura, Gary M. "Institutions Matter: Local Electoral Laws, Gay and Lesbian Representation, and Coalition Building across Minority Communities." *Gays and Lesbians in the Democratic Process: Public Policy, Public Opinion, and Political Representation*. Ed. Ellen D. B. Riggle and Barry L. Tadlock. New York: Columbia University Press, 1999, 220-241.

Sherrill, Kenneth. "The Political Power of Lesbians, Gays, and Bisexuals." *PS: Political Science and Politics* 29.3 (1996): 469–473.

Stone, Amy L. *Gay Rights at the Ballot Box*. Minneapolis: University of Minnesota Press, 2012.

"A Survey of LGBT Americans." Pew Research Center. Last Modified 13 June 2013, http://www.pewsocialtrends.org/2013/06/13/a-survey-of-lgbt-americans/.

Tafel, Richard. "Caught between Worlds: Gay Republicans Step Out, and into the Political Fray." *Creating Change: Sexuality, Public Policy, and Civil Rights*. Ed. John D'Emilio, William B. Turner, and Urvashi Vaid. New York: St. Martin's Press, 2000. 115–130.

"Tea Party Group Targets Trans Voters." *National Center for Transgender Equality*. Accessed 24 April 2014, http://transgenderequality.wordpress.com/2012/11/04/tea-party-group-targets-trans-voters/.

"Trans United for Obama." *Trans United for Obama*. Accessed 1 May 2014, http://www.transunitedforobama.org/.

Vaid, Urvashi. *Virtual Equality: The Mainstreaming of Gay and Lesbian Liberation*. New York: Anchor Books, 1995.

"Voting While Trans: Preparing for Voter ID Laws." National Center for Transgender Equality. Last modified 2014. http://transequality.org/issues/resources/voting-while-trans-preparing-voter-id-laws.

Wald, Kenneth D., James W. Button, and Barbara A. Rienzo. "The Politics of Gay Rights in American Communities: Explaining Antidiscrimination Ordinances and Policies." *American Journal of Political Science* 40.4 (1996): 1152–1178.

Chapter 18

From Freedom to Equality: Marriage and the Shifted Priorities of Lesbians, Gay Men, Bisexuals, and Transgender People

Andrew R. Flores and Kenneth Sherrill

Lesbians, gay men, and bisexuals did not place a high priority on same-sex marriage as the twentieth century ended. At that time, the highest priorities in the movement's policy agenda were placed on issues regarding discrimination in employment and housing and on issues related to HIV/AIDS.[1] The lesbian, gay, bisexual, and transgender (LGBT) rights movement has had different cycles of social movement strategies,[2] and the development of the LGBT social movement ultimately resulted in the creation of national organizations governing the policy agenda of the movement. However, a fuller understanding of the LGBT policy agenda requires an appreciation of the actions of organizations opposed to the advancement of LGBT rights. The opposition played an important role in defining the next steps of the LGBT rights movement, often relying on direct democracy to shape the LGBT rights agenda.[3] These actions constantly obligated the movement to be reactive to its opponents rather than pursue its own agenda. Issues on the policy agenda have only matured and evolved when groups in opposition to one another have kept those issues as fundamental differences.[4] What has shifted over time is fixing marriage equality as the central issue upon which the LGBT rights movement and its opposition differ.

THE ROAD TO MARRIAGE: A BRIEF HISTORY

The movement sought to reframe the discourse about homosexuality away from one of sickness, perversion, immorality, and threats to national security and toward accepting or at least tolerating LGBT people. Under the leadership of the Mattachine Society with cofounders Harry Hay and Frank Kameny, Kameny's famous "Gay Is Good" demonstration and the LGBT rights picket of the White House were clearly reflective of these pursuits. The Religious Right responded to these efforts toward incremental progress by using referenda such as Dade County's successful repeal of a local nondiscrimination ordinance in 1977 and the 1978 Briggs Initiative, a California proposition allowing the removal of LGBs from teaching positions. These referenda and initiative campaigns often used language depicting LGBT people as threats to children, families, and "traditional values."

Amy Stone argued that the Religious Right played a major role in defining what the policy agenda for the LGBT rights movement looks like.[5] The Religious Right's initial strategy was to use the initiative to repeal policies that were initially passed at the municipal level.[6] At other times, the backlash happened at the state level, and their strategy persisted even after the United States Supreme Court in *Romer v. Evans* (1996) struck down an initiative amending Colorado's constitution that prevented any governmental protections for sexual minorities.[7] A major effect of these initiatives was to place advocates of equality for LGBT people on the defensive. Rather than developing and advocating for a positive agenda for LGBT rights, movement leaders were compelled to devote time, money, and energy to resist efforts to deny these rights and to respond to rhetoric that demonized gay people. Those within the LGBT movement learned to strategize and persuade voters to support their rights or, more accurately, to persuade average people to reject efforts to deny equal rights to LGBT people. At the end of the twentieth century, it appeared that LGBTs were victorious on some fronts; they were winning municipal initiatives on sexual orientation employment and housing discrimination. However, the opposition modified its tactics, and centered on opposing same-sex marriage rather than continue to focus on nondiscrimination ordinances.[8] While the LGBT rights movement sought to identify issues that facilitated finding political allies, states continued to pass referenda limiting the right to marriage equality. After congressional enactment of hate crimes legislation and the repeal of Don't Ask/Don't Tell, positions on same-sex marriage became a clear indicator of support for marriage equality, and the issue dominated the discourse about LGBT rights with numerous members of Congress, and ultimately, President Barack Obama announcing support for marriage equality.

Same-sex marriage emerged on the nation's agenda without much initiative by the mainstream LGBT rights organizations in 1994 when the Hawaii State Supreme Court issued a ruling that potentially legalized same-sex marriage. This sparked passage of the Defense of Marriage Act of 1996 (DOMA). With little apparent control over the litigation by most of the major national movement organizations, victories by gay-rights advocates in state-level cases in Vermont in 1999 and Massachusetts in 2003 showed that same-sex marriage could be an issue that would continue to be contested in the judicial process.[9] The movement's leading organizations continued to invest their resources elsewhere.[10] Prior to the emergence of same-sex marriage as a major issue, ongoing organizational efforts centered on passing anti-discrimination and hate crimes protection policies, which had majority support of the public, while marriage equality did not.

Marriage equality's dramatic advance was a result of two things beyond the control of major national movement organizations. One was individual men and women who went to court to assert their rights, as litigation fosters broader agenda setting in social movements.[11] The other was the intense reaction to the lawsuits by the Religious Right and the Republican Party, which started with the passage of DOMA and continued with similar statewide bans in 1990s and 2000s. Marriage equality was not an issue that major national LGBT organizations' leaders wanted at the top of their agendas in the 1990s.

The legal battle over same-sex marriage was thrust upon LGBT organizations, and it was a fight for which they were not prepared. Instead, LGBT organizations continued debating whether same-sex marriage should remain their major issue.[12]

In this chapter, we discuss changes among national samples of LGBT Americans in terms of how same-sex marriage moved from being a fringe issue to one of major importance to the political lives of LGBT people by comparing a 2012 sample of LGBT likely voters with a 2003 sample used by Patrick Egan and Kenneth Sherrill to document the political opinions and priorities of LGBT Americans.[13] The results suggest that since 2003, same-sex marriage has become a mobilizing force for most LGBTs and, given the victories on the issue in 2012 in Maine, Minnesota, Maryland, and Washington, is likely to continue to remain one.

SHIFTING PRIORITIES OF A NEW GENERATION?

At a time when a majority of Americans lived in states that did not prohibit employment discrimination on the basis of sexual orientation and in the year when the Supreme Court finally struck down sodomy statutes, it would seem to be hard to persuade average LGBT people that marriage equality should be their highest priority.

Same-sex marriage has generally had support among LGBT people. The earliest available evidence supporting marriage equality comes from a 1972 survey of the leadership and rank and file membership of New York's Gay Activists Alliance.[14] In this survey, 84.9 percent of the organization's leadership agreed with the statement that "two people who live together but are not legally married should be able to file a joint tax return," as did 78.9 percent of those who attended GAA's Saturday night dances. However, the consensus about the issue does not mean it was necessarily the highest policy priority. In the same 1972 survey, the intensity of support for federal marriage benefits was not great. Of the nine items these LGBT people evaluated, filing a joint tax return was second-to-last regarding importance.

In their 2005 article, Egan and Sherrill presented data indicating that same-sex marriage was a youth-focused issue. Older LGBTs did not consider it to be an important policy area for the LGBT movement to pursue. Egan and Sherrill framed the LGBT rights movement as a conflict between two pursuits: liberty and equality. They framed the earlier movement activities as primarily focused on liberty, that is, the freedom to be left alone, the freedom to meet one another in public places, the freedom to have sexual relations, the freedom to walk down the street free of fear, while they framed the contemporary movement, with an increased emphasis on same-sex marriage, as strikingly about equality. This shift in the frame, to Egan and Sherrill, was a shift of LGBT's generations.

Contrary to Egan and Sherrill, Stone argued the shifting priorities may not be placed in younger generations as much as in the changing priorities of the movement's elite. She contended that a sea change occurred in the movement when Proposition 8 failed in California. The movement's leadership realized that winning same-sex marriage was something it must pursue, but did not really understand how to talk to people about the issue.[15] The California ballot initiative became the most expensive ballot initiative to that date. After Proposition 8, the movement's leadership decided that marriage equality should become the movement's defining issue.

The relationship between leaders and followers in social and political movements is a complex one that evolves over time as movements mature from early protest activity to the stage of institutionalization as interest groups. The LGBT movement may be considered an example of the classic "iron law of oligarchy."[16] According to the theory, organizations in their youth have a bottom-up process of decision-making, while their development inevitably results in top-down processes. In the early days of movement activism, movement priorities are more democratically established in a ground-up fashion by activists. Once movements transform into organizations, leadership is more top-down and organizations seek to shape the views and priorities of the rank-and-file. Organizations go from having membership meetings to having executive directors and boards of directors. The locus of decision-making and the process of establishing priorities are transformed. Pundits have amply documented the changing priorities of leaders and movement organizations. We use systematic social science to examine whether—and how—rank-and-file attitudes have changed. Sadly, our data do not enable us to answer the question of whether these changes represent a democratic process in which shifts in public opinion affect the priorities of movement organizations or whether we are observing an echo-chamber effect in which communications by leaders shape the views of average citizens.[17]

We note how this evolution in the everyday attitudes of rank-and-file LGBT people mirrors the evolving emphasis of LGBT movement organizations. While we cannot attribute causality and cannot say how much of the shift is led by rank-and-file members nor how much of it reflects opinion leadership by the organizations, we also cannot avoid seeing the two phenomena as interrelated. Movement organizations have become increasingly institutionalized and structurally similar to more mature, organized interest groups over the same period. One would expect rank-and-file views to become more responsive to cues sent by organizational leadership as movement organizations mature.

DATA

To examine changes in LGBT political opinion and behavior on the issue of same-sex marriage, we replicated the 2005 Egan and Sherrill analysis in order to provide comparable data. Egan and Sherrill analyzed data from a poll conducted by Harris Interactive in December 2003 with a sample of 748 LGBTs. We also used data from a Harris Interactive poll, one conducted in August 2012, prior to the general election; this poll had a sample of 1,190 LGBTs. Harris Interactive has been sampling LGBT people for decades, and they have advanced strategies in generating samples that are representative samples of LGBT Americans.[18] Whenever a comparable analysis can be conducted, it is. We reanalyzed the data Egan and Sherrill used in order to draw comparisons between their analysis and our own.

We must make one caveat about the sampling frame in the 2012 survey. The survey targeted LGBTs who indicated that they intended to vote in the upcoming election. Likely voters in mass politics tend to be more affluent, more educated, and more involved in their community.[19] However, we believe this does not make the comparisons uninformative of an ongoing discussion about mass attitude change among LGBTs. In fact, it is those participatory LGBTs who are most likely to exercise their roles as agents of social change.[20] Our reanalysis of the data used by Egan and Sherrill was only of LGBTs who were likely voters, in order to provide appropriate comparisons between LGBT likely voters in 2003 and 2012.

ANALYSIS AND RESULTS

One indicator of how important same-sex marriage may be to LGBTs is their knowledge about the issue. In 2003, 33 percent of LGBTs were incapable of identifying whether it was legal in any state to marry someone of the same sex. However, in 2012, this number fell to 17 percent. A vast majority, 63 percent of respondents, knew the legal status of same-sex marriage in 2003, and this increased to 83 percent in 2012. Political science research has shown that ballot initiatives tend to increase people's political knowledge.[21] In 2003, ballot initiatives on same-sex marriage were not as widespread as they were during the 2004 presidential election and had not attained much nationwide attention. By August 2012, 39 state initiatives had occurred and same-sex marriages had been legalized in six states and the District of Columbia, with the addition of eleven states as of 2014. In addition, there no doubt was an increase in media coverage of same-sex marriage, making it easier for LGBTs to get current information. As Figure 18.1 reveals, more LGBTs have correct knowledge about the legality of same-sex marriage since 2003, and this increase is statistically significant.

Figure 18.1
Political Knowledge about Same-Sex Marriage Policy in the States

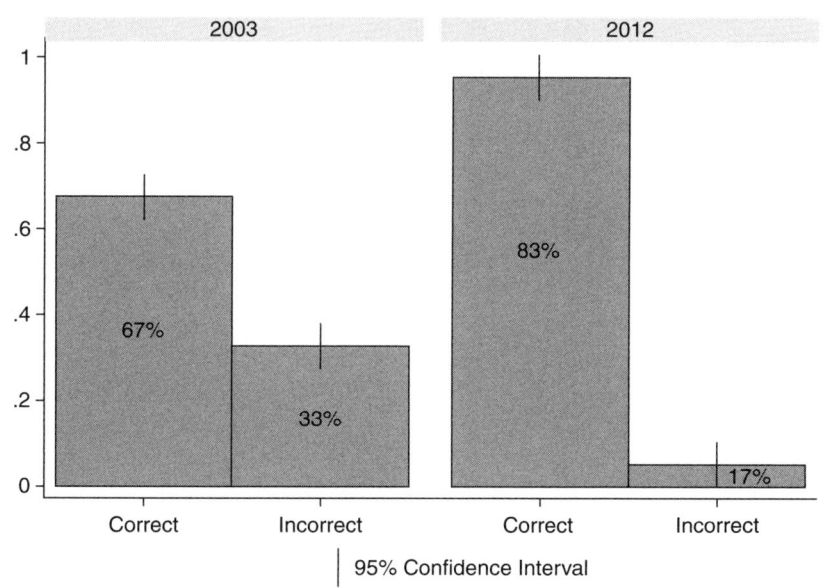

Source: Harris Interactive Poll, December 2003; Harris Interactive Poll, November 2012.

The question in 2012 may have been more likely to induce incorrect responses, as some respondents did reside in states where same-sex marriage was legal. When the question was asked in 2003, same-sex marriage was not legal in any state. However, the data indicate that in 2012, only 17 percent of LGBT respondents incorrectly identified whether the state they resided in performed same-sex marriages. LGBTs, in general, are much more knowledgeable about the issue in 2012 than they were in 2003. However LGBTs learned about the legality of same-sex marriage, the results of the 2012 survey indicated that LGBTs were much more knowledgeable than they were in 2003.

Simply knowing the current state of policy indicates that LGBTs are receiving better information but not whether they view the issue of same-sex marriage as important. As Table 18.1 demonstrates, LGBTs

Table 18.1
Policy Priorities of LGBTs by Age Cohort and Year

Age Cohort				
Ranking	1940 & Earlier	1940–1960	1961–1980	1981–1995
2003				
1	Workplace discrimination	Workplace discrimination	Workplace discrimination	Workplace discrimination
2	Hate crimes	Hate crimes	Hate crimes	Women's health research
3	Securing federal benefits	AIDS funding	AIDS funding	Hate crimes
4	AIDS funding	Securing federal benefits	Securing federal benefits	Same-sex marriage
5	Women's health research	Same-sex marriage	Same-sex marriage	AIDS funding

Source: Harris Interactive Poll, December 2003. n = 663.

2012				
1	Hate crimes	Hate crimes	Same-sex marriage	Same-sex marriage
2	Workplace discrimination	Workplace discrimination	Hate crimes	Hate crimes
3	Protect out active service*	Same-sex marriage	Workplace discrimination	Workplace discrimination
4	Protect LGBT youth	Protect out active service*	Protect LGBT youth	Adoption rights
5	Same-sex marriage	Protect LGBT youth	Protect out active service*	Protect LGBT youth

*protect the ability of LGBT military personnel to serve openly.
Source: Harris Interactive Poll, November 2012. n = 1,190.

of younger generations indicated that they viewed same-sex marriage as an important issue though not nearly as important as workplace discrimination. The results from 2003 indicated that same-sex marriage was largely a peripheral issue. In 2003, the issue was not listed among the most important issues by the oldest cohort (those born before 1940), and the second-oldest cohort (those born 1940 to 1960) ranks same-sex marriage last. These results contrast with the findings from the 2012 study. Analyzing the same age cohorts, the two youngest cohorts identified same-sex marriage as the highest priority issue. LGBTs in the second-oldest age cohort identified same-sex marriage as the third most important issue, and the oldest cohort also ranked the issue as important, though less important than other issues. These results indicated that the LGBT respondents did not support the legalization of same-sex marriage in 2003 to the degree that they did in 2012. In short, there were other priorities in 2003. Every age cohort thought that workplace discrimination was the most important issue to pursue. Older LGBT people tended to rank same-sex marriage as not as high a priority as other cohorts, but the issue did rank highly in 2012 though not in 2003.

We now assess how the priorities have changed when LGBTs are grouped by characteristics other than age. Particularly, we examined the impact of race, gender, and partisanship among LGBT people. Our general finding is that regardless of what groups we assess, LGBTs were much more likely to name same-sex marriage as the most important issue in 2012.

The priorities of LGBTs who identified as African American and those who did not are provided in Table 18.2. In 2003, 11 percent of the sample

Table 18.2
Policy Priorities of LGBTs, by Black Identification and Year

Race				
	2003		2012	
Ranking	African American	Not African American	African American	Not African American
1	AIDS funding	Workplace discrimination	Same-sex marriage	Same-sex marriage
2	Hate crimes	Hate crimes	Hate crimes	Workplace discrimination
3	Workplace discrimination	Adoption	AIDS funding	Hate crimes
4	Women's health research	Securing federal benefits	Workplace discrimination	Protect out active service*
5	Securing federal benefits	AIDS funding	Protect LGBT youth	Protect LGBT youth

*protect the ability of LGBT military personnel to serve openly.
Source: Harris Interactive Poll, December 2003; Harris Interactive Poll, November 2012.

identified as black while in 2012, 8.8 percent did. Noticeably, African Americans in both samples were more likely than the other respondents to name AIDS funding as a policy priority. Given the historical significance and prevalence of HIV/AIDS in communities of color, the prioritization placed on AIDS funding likely stems from an increased familiarity with the disease and a heightened awareness of insufficient action to provide prevention, treatment, and cure for it. Also noticeable is the rise of same-sex marriage as the most prevalent issue in 2012, regardless of race. While black LGBTs had a multitude of differing policy preferences in 2012, both black LGBTs and non-black LGBTs agreed that same-sex marriage was the top priority.

When we look at how priorities differed by gender, we found that the priority placed on same-sex marriage underwent a substantial shift. In 2003, same-sex marriage did not place among the top five priorities for gay, bisexual, and/or transgender (GBT) men and it placed fifth among lesbian, bisexual, and/or transgender (LBT) women. By 2013, it was the highest priority for both groups. We observed in 2003 that GBT men placed a higher priority on AIDS funding and federal benefits while LBT women placed a higher priority on women's health research and same-sex marriage. Just as LGBT men and women generally had consensus on the top priorities in 2003, LGBT men and women largely agreed that same-sex marriage, hate crimes, and workplace discrimination were the top priorities of the LGBT community in 2013 (see Table 18.3).

Table 18.3
Policy Priorities of LGBTs, by Gender and Year

Gender

	2003		2012	
Ranking	Male	Female	Male	Female
1	Workplace discrimination	Workplace discrimination	Same-sex marriage	Same-sex marriage
2	Hate crimes	Hate crimes	Workplace discrimination	Hate crimes
3	AIDS funding	Adoption	Hate crimes	Workplace discrimination
4	Adoption	Women's health research	Protect out active service*	Adoption
5	Securing federal benefits	Same-sex marriage	Protect LGBT youth	Protect out active service*

*protect the ability of LGBT military personnel to serve openly.
Source: Harris Interactive Poll, December 2003; Harris Interactive Poll, November 2012.

LGB people have long been supporters of the Democratic Party,[22] but there also are LGBTs who are not Democrats. LGBTs who are not Democrats might have different priorities for the LGBT agenda. We found that, for the most part, there was little partisan difference about the priorities of the LGBT community. In 2003, 63.6 percent of the sample identified as Democrats, 10.8 percent identified as Republicans, and 25.6 percent did not identify with one of the two major parties. In 2012 the sample found different proportions of Republicans (22.2%) and Independents (11.6%), but about the same percentage of Democrats (66.2%). The results in Table 18.4 indicate that in 2003, same-sex marriage was one of the top five issues only for Independents. The highest priority among all partisans in 2003 was workplace discrimination, followed by hate crimes, and then by adoption and AIDS funding. In 2012, same-sex marriage rose to the top among Democrats and Republicans, while Independents ranked it as the second-most important issue. LGBTs, regardless of their partisanship, generally agreed about what the priorities of LGBT community ought to be.

We find that there were substantially different patterns affecting opinions favoring same-sex marriage between 2003 and 2012. In 2003, the

Table 18.4
Policy Priorities of LGBTs, by Partisanship by Year

2003

Ranking	Democrats	Independents	Republicans
1	Workplace discrimination	Workplace discrimination	Workplace discrimination
2	Hate crimes	Hate crimes	Hate crimes
3	Adoption	Adoption	AIDS funding
4	Securing federal benefits	AIDS funding	Adoption
5	AIDS funding	Same-sex marriage	Securing federal benefits

2012

Ranking	Democrats	Independents	Republicans
1	Same-sex marriage	Hate crimes	Same-sex marriage
2	Workplace discrimination	Same-sex marriage	Hate crimes
3	Hate crimes	Workplace discrimination	Workplace discrimination
4	Protect out active service*	Adoption	Protect LGBT youth
5	Protect LGBT youth	Protect out active service*	Protect out active service*

*protect the ability of LGBT military personnel to serve openly.
Source: Harris Interactive Poll, December 2003; Harris Interactive Poll, November 2012.

question measuring support for marriage equality was slightly unconventional: "If you were in a committed relationship, would you personally want to obtain a marriage license?" Personally engaging in the act of marriage may be different from supporting the right of other people to get married. For our purposes, we treated those who would personally want to get married to be those who would favor marriage equality in general. In 2012, the question measuring support was, "Please indicate how strongly you support or oppose legalizing same-sex marriage." This is a more standard approach to asking about opinions on the issue. Though it would be ideal to have the same question, there are still inferences to be drawn by making comparisons of factors that led to support or lack of support over the years.

The findings in Table 18.5 are the results from probit regressions analyzing the effect of demographic characteristics of LGBTs on support for same-sex marriage. We found that in 2003, there was a positive relationship between the likelihood of favoring same-sex marriage and whether respondents were married or living with a partner. We also observed a lower likelihood of support among African Americans, Republicans, conservatives, those who identify as gay or lesbian (relative to bisexual or transgender identified people), college graduates, and older LGBTs. However, in 2012, we observed higher likelihoods of supporting same-sex marriage among those who identified as lesbian or gay and among college graduates. An insignificant relationship was observed for LGBTs who were married or living with a partner. Negative relationships were observed for those who were Republicans, and for those who identified as conservative, African American, or older.

Table 18.5
Correlates of Same-Sex Marriage Support among LGBTs

Variable	Effect in 2003	Effect in 2012
Married or Living with Partner	0.56***	−0.23
Republican	−0.58**	−0.67*
Conservative	−0.25	−0.63***
Gay or Lesbian	−0.16	0.37*
College Graduate	−0.28*	0.47**
African American	−0.45*	−0.58*
Age	−0.02***	−0.02*
N	663	1,190
Pseudo-R^2	0.11	0.18

Source: Harris Interactive Poll, December 2003; Harris Interactive Poll, November 2012.

Note: Cell entries are probit coefficients, dependent variable is opinion on same-sex marriage. All observations are weighted.

Probit coefficients are statistically significant at *$p < 0.05$, **$p < 0.01$, ***$p < 0.001$ (two-tailed)

Though we still observed a negative effect of age in 2012, the effect of age was substantively different between the two years, as the effect was much smaller for LGBTs in 2012 than it was for LGBTs in 2003. This reflected changes in the positions of LGBTs on the issue of same-sex marriage. Generational replacement alone would not predict these effects to decay as rapidly, so the changing effects are also attributable to changing minds among LGBTs. We provide the predicted probability of supporting same-sex marriage by age from the youngest respondent to the oldest respondent in both 2003 and 2012 in Figure 18.2. We also plotted the 95 percent confidence intervals to indicate the measure of uncertainty in the estimated probability of support. What is notable about Figure 18.2 is that we observed substantive differences by age in 2003. Then, the oldest individual is neither more nor less likely to support same-sex marriage, that is, the equivalent of a coin flip, but the oldest individual was significantly less likely to support same-sex marriage than the youngest individual. For 2012, we did not find a statistically significant difference between the oldest and youngest LGBT ($p = 0.055$). The oldest respondent in 2012 was significantly more likely to support same-sex marriage than oppose it, as the predicted probability is above 50 percent. The magnitude of the effect is also much weaker, showing that age was a weaker determinant of support for same-sex marriage in 2012. Since these polls are almost a decade apart, comparing 18-year-olds in 2003 to 28-year-olds in 2012 and so on, demonstrates the significant changes that have occurred over the 10-year period.

Figure 18.2
Predicting Same-Sex Marriage Support by Age

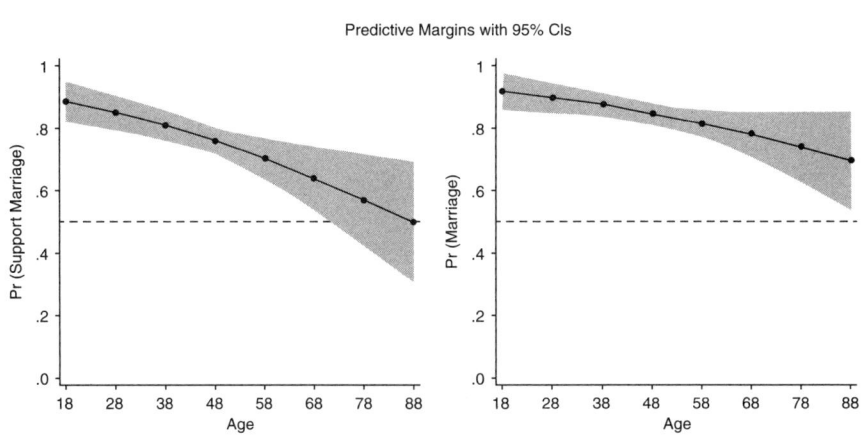

Source: Harris Interactive Poll, December 2003; Harris Interactive Poll, November 2012.

We also predicted the probability of support for same-sex marriage for each of the other variables. We plotted the effect of the demographic characteristics for both time points in Figure 18.3, and we provide 95 percent confidence intervals about those predictions. In 2003, LGBTs who were in committed relationships are 18 percent more likely to support same-sex marriage, college graduates were 10 percent less likely, and the oldest respondent was 44 percent less likely to support same-sex marriage than the youngest respondent.

In 2012, we found that partisanship and ideology were consequential to LGBT attitudes toward same-sex marriage, with Republicans 12 percent less likely to support same-sex marriage when compared to Democrats and Independents. Conservatives are 30 percent less likely to support same-sex marriage when compared to moderates and liberals. Thus, just as the partisan and ideological divide over marriage equality increased over our ten-year period,[23] *similar divisions* emerged among LGBT people over the issue of marriage equality. Identifying as gay or lesbian, (as opposed to bisexual and/or transgender), was associated with a 7 percent increase in support for same-sex marriage. College graduates in 2012 were 9 percent more likely to support same-sex marriage. Black LGBTs were 10 percent less likely to support same-sex marriage.

Figure 18.3
Predicting Same-Sex Marriage Support Min-to-Max Effects

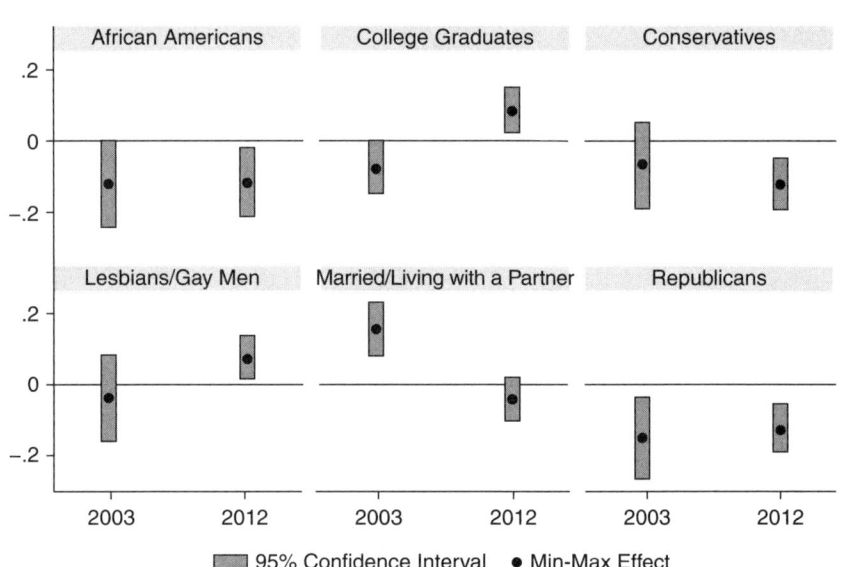

Source: Harris Interactive Poll, December 2003; Harris Interactive Poll, November 2012.

Figure 18.3 also shows the magnitude of change over the course of the decade. Of the significant changes that were observed, the greatest were for college graduates and those who were married or living with a partner. College graduates were significantly less likely to support same-sex marriage in 2003, but, in 2012, this effect reversed. Those who were married or living with a partner were more likely to support same-sex marriage in 2003 but were no more likely to do so in 2012. The changes in the decade may not be just about how these groups have changed as much as how these groups have changed relative to the average LGBT person. Although the average LGBT person has changed on the issue of same-sex marriage, we found some contrasts. For example, it was not surprising that LGBTs who were married or were in a committed relationship favored same-sex marriage relative to those who were not. While in 2003, LGB support for marriage equality was somewhat tinged by the self-interest of people in committed relationships.[24] While some of the differences may be attributable to question wording, we preferred to think that by 2012, marriage equality had evolved into being as aspiration for almost all categories of LGBT people. Support for same-sex marriage increased among all LGBTs (77% favor in 2003 and 85% in 2012), the distinctiveness of those in committed relationships diminished, making them no more or less likely to support same-sex marriage than other LGBTs.

DISCUSSION

E. E. Schattschneider wrote in *The Semisovereign People* that only so many conflicts can make it onto the national stage, and many issues are essentially tabled for discussion:

> There are billions of potential conflicts in any modern society, but *only a few become significant*. The reduction of the number of conflicts is an essential part of politics. Politics deals with the domination and subordination of conflicts. A democratic society is able to survive because it manages conflict by establishing priorities among a multitude of potential conflicts.[25]

Without having a place at the table, an issue has a limited lifespan, and it becomes impossible to engage with the mass public to change opinions or to change policy.[26] An issue not placed on the agenda may be relegated to a world of nondecision rather than become the subject of serious political debate.[27] Such agenda-setting processes occur on the national stage and also within interest groups and social movements.[28] The partisan cleavage over same-sex marriage has widened over the years, with the Democratic Party taking an official stance in favor of same-sex marriage in its 2012 national platform,[29] and the Republican Party remaining formally opposed to same-sex marriage. Since the 2012 election, some Republican leaders have sought to downplay the issue. Nevertheless, partisan division remains.

The decision-makers in the LGBT rights movement are not immune to, or uninvolved in, this process. One of the reasons why same-sex marriage maintains its national prominence is the consensus among the LGBT elites that it is an issue worth pursuing. The movement's history on this issue indicates that there have been substantial differences about what the movement should prioritize, and there have even been public disagreements about the movement's priorities.

Issues stay on the agenda because both leaders and average people think about them, have knowledge about these issues, and prioritize them. We find clear distinctions among rank-and-file LGBTs with regard to their knowledge, priorities, and thoughts on the issue of same-sex marriage between 2003 and 2012. These changes reflect both the evolving political lives of everyday LGBT people and the impact of the major movement organizations' opinion leadership. No doubt, there is a complex interaction between the two. Agenda setting is a function of both leaders and followers in political and social movements. The changing priorities away from frames about freedom and toward frames about equality in the movement for LGBT civil rights provide evidence of this process. Rather than finding discontinuities among rank-and-file LGBTs, we observe consensus. Same-sex marriage may not have been the top priority and may not remain the top priority among LGBT people, but as the current momentum or mobilization of bias is focused keenly on marriage equality, we find LGBTs know more about, prioritize, and support marriage equality.

ACKNOWLEDGMENTS

We are deeply indebted to Bob Witeck, who has made this entire project possible, and to his colleagues, Scott Swenson and Fred Lameck, who pored over the design of the survey. We are especially grateful to the individuals and organizations that provided us with these data and invited us into their project: David Goldstein, David Krane, Helen Lee, and Manny Flores at Harris Interactive; and Lisa Sherman, Michelle Auguste, Marc Legonard, Jason Shumaker, and Charles Runnette at Logo TV. A previous version of this paper was presented at the InsPIRES Conference on Marriage Equality at Stanford University, October 11–12, 2013.

NOTES

1. Haider-Markel, "Creating Change," 242–268.
2. See D'Emilio, "Cycles of Change," 31–53.
3. Stone, *Gay Rights at the Ballot Box*.
4. Schattschneider, *Semisovereign People*.

5. We refer to the *Religious Right* to describe social conservative Christians historically associated with notable conservative leaders: Pat Robertson, Jerry Fallwell, and Anita Bryant (also termed the *Christian Right* in other studies). See Green and Guth, "Christian Right in the Republican Party," 150–165; Green, Rozeel, and Wilcox, *Christian Right in American Politics*.

6. Gossett, "Dillon's Rule and Gay Rights," 62–88.

7. Donovan, Wenzel, and Bowler, "Direct Democracy and Gay Rights Initiatives after Romer," 161–192.

8. Fetner, *How the Religious Right Shaped Lesbian and Gay Rights Activism*; Stone, *Gay Rights at the Ballot Box*.

9. D'Emilio, "Will the Courts Set Us Free?" 39–64.

10. Leachman, "From Protest to Perry," 1667–1751.

11. Ibid.

12. Beyond Marriage Coalition, "Statement of Purpose."

13. Egan and Sherrill, "Marriage and the Shifting Priorities."

14. Sherrill, "Leaders in the Gay Activist Movement"; Sherrill, "Youth of The Movement," 269–296.

15. Stone, *Gay Rights at the Ballot Box*.

16. Michels, *Political Parties*.

17. Key, *Responsible Electorate*.

18. Krane, Witeck, and Combs, "Surveying among Gays and Lesbians."

19. Wolfinger and Rosentone, *Who Votes?*; Verba, Schlozman, and Brady, *Voice and Equality*.

20. Flores and Sherrill, "Consciousness, Identity, and Political Participation"; Arendt, *Human Condition*.

21. Smith and Tolbert, *Educated by Initiative*.

22. Exit polls have not collected data on transgender people, so we restrict our language referencing exit polls to LGB people.

23. Baunach, "Decomposing Trends in Attitudes toward Gay Marriage," 346–363; Baunach, "Changing Same-Sex Marriage Attitudes," 364–378.

24. Schaffner and Senic, "Rights or Benefits?" 123–132.

25. Schattschneider, *Semisovereign People*, 64.

26. Carmines and Stimson, *Issue Evolution*; Baumgartner and Jones, *Agendas and Instability in American Politics*.

27. Bachrach and Baratz, "Two Faces of Power," 947–952.

28. Strolovich, *Affirmative Advocacy*.

29. The Democratic National Committee, *Moving America Forward*.

REFERENCES

Arendt, Hannah. *The Human Condition*. Chicago: University of Chicago Press, 1958.

Bachrach, Peter, and Morton S. Baratz. "Two Faces of Power." *American Political Science Review* 56.4 (1962): 947–952.

Baumgartner, Frank R., and Bryan D. Jones. *Agendas and Instability in American Politics*. Chicago: University of Chicago Press, 1993.

Baunach, Dawn Michelle. "Decomposing Trends in Attitudes toward Gay Marriage, 1988–2006." *Social Science Quarterly* 92.2 (2011): 346–363.

Baunach, Dawn Michelle. "Changing Same-Sex Marriage Attitudes in American from 1988 through 2010." *Public Opinion Quarterly* 76.2 (2012): 364–378.

Beyond Marriage Coalition. "Beyond Same-Sex Marriage: A New Strategic Vision for All Our Families & Relationships." *BeyondMarriage.org* 6 July 2006. Accessed 15 July 2015. http://www.beyondmarriage.org/BeyondMarriage.pdf.

Carmines, Edward G., and James A. Stimson. *Issue Evolution: Race and the Transformation of American Politics*. Princeton: Princeton University Press, 1989.

D'Emilio, John. "Cycles of Change, Questions of Strategy: The Gay and Lesbians Movement after Fifty Years." *The Politics of Gay Rights*. Ed. Craig A. Rimmerman, Kenneth D. Wald, and Clyde Wilcox. Chicago, IL: University of Chicago Press, 2000. 31–53.

D'Emilio, John. "Will the Courts Set Us Free? Reflections on the Campaign for Same-Sex Marriage." *The Politics of Same-Sex Marriage*. Ed. Craig A. Rimmerman and Clyde Wilcox. Chicago, IL: University of Chicago Press, 2007. 39–64.

The Democratic National Committee. *Moving America Forward: 2012 Democratic National Platform*. Accessed 9 July 2013. http://assets.dstatic.org/dnc-platform/2012-National-Platform.pdf.

Donovan, Todd, Jim Wenzel, and Shaun Bowler. "Direct Democracy and Gay Rights Initiatives after Romer." *The Politics of Gay Rights*. Ed. Craig A. Rimmerman, Kenneth D. Wald, and Clyde Wilcox. Chicago, IL: University of Chicago Press, 2000. 161–192.

Egan, Patrick J., and Kenneth Sherrill. "Marriage and the Shifting Priorities of a New Generation of Lesbians and Gays." *PS: Political Science and Politics* (April 2005). DOI: 10.1017/S1049096505056350.

Fetner, Tina. *How the Religious Right Shaped Lesbian and Gay Rights Activism. Gay Rights at the Ballot Box*. Ed. Amy Stone. Minneapolis: University of Minnesota Press, 2008.

Flores, Andrew R., and Kenneth Sherrill. "Consciousness, Identity, and Political Participation: The LGBT Voter in the 2012 Election." Presented at the Annual Meeting of Midwest Political Science Association. Chicago, IL: 2013.

Gossett, Charles W. "Dillon's Rule and Gay Rights: State Control over Local Efforts to Protect the Rights of Lesbians and Gay Men." *Gays and Lesbians in the Democratic Process: Public Policy, Public Opinion, and Political Representation*. Ed. Ellen D. B. Riggle and Barry L. Tadlock. New York, NY: Columbia University Press, 1999. 62–88.

Green, John C., and James L. Guth, "The Christian Right in the Republican Party: The Case of Pat Robertson's Supporters." *Journal of Politics* 50.1 (1988): 150–165.

Green, John C., Mark J. Rozell, and Clyde Wilcox, eds. *The Christian Right in American Politics: Marching to the Millennium*. Washington, D.C.: Georgetown University Press, 2003.

Haider-Markel, Donald P. "Creating Change—Holding the Line: Agenda Setting on Lesbian and Gay Issues at the National Level." *Gays and Lesbians in the Democratic Process: Public Policy, Public Opinion, and Political Representation*. Ed. Ellen D. B. Riggle and Barry L. Tadlock. New York, NY: Columbia University Press, 1999. 242–268.

Key, V. O., Jr. *The Responsible Electorate*. Cambridge: Harvard University Press, 1966.

Krane, David, Bob Witeck, and Wes Combs. "Surveying among Gays and Lesbians: Harris Interactive's Techniques to Achieve Representative Data." *Harris Interactive*. Accessed 5 April 2013. http://www.harrisinteractive.com/vault/HI_CORP_PAPER_SurveyingGayLesbian.pdf.

Leachman, Gwendolyn M. "From Protest to Perry: How Litigation Shaped the LGBT Movement's Agenda." *UC Davis Law Review* 47 (2014): 1667–1751.

Michels, Robert. *Political Parties: A Sociological Study of the Tendencies of Modern Democracy*. New York: Hearst's International Library Co., 1915.

Schaffner, Brian, and Nenad Senic. "Rights or Benefits? Explaining the Sexual Identity Gap in American Political Behavior." *Political Research Quarterly* 59.1 (2006): 123–132.

Schattschneider, E. E. *The Semisovereign People: A Realist's View of Democracy in America*. Chicago: Holt, Rinehart and Winston, 1960.

Sherrill, Kenneth. "Leaders in the Gay Activist Movement: The Problem of Finding the Followers." Presented at the Annual Meeting of the American Political Science Association. New Orleans, LA: 1973.

Sherrill, Kenneth. "The Youth of the Movement," *Gays and Lesbians in the Democratic Process: Public Policy, Public Opinion, and Political Representation*. Ed. Ellen D. B. Riggle and Barry L. Tadlock. New York, NY: Columbia University Press, 1999. 269–296.

Smith, Daniel A., and Caroline J. Tolbert. *Educated by Initiative: The Effects of Direct Democracy on Citizens and Political Organizations in the American States*. Ann Arbor: University of Michigan Press, 2004.

Stone, Amy. *Gay Rights at the Ballot Box*. Minneapolis: University of Minnesota Press, 2012.

Strolovich, Dara. *Affirmative Advocacy: Race, Class, and Gender in Interest Group Politics*. Chicago: University of Chicago Press, 2010.

Verba, Sidney, Kay Lehman Schlozman, and Henry E. Brady. *Voice and Equality: Civic Voluntarism in American Politics*. Boston: Harvard University Press, 1995.

Wolfinger, Raymond E., and Steven J. Rosentone. *Who Votes*? New Haven: Yale University Press, 1980.

Chapter 19

Transgender Voters

Patrick A. Paschall[1]

Transgender people face many social and political barriers to full and meaningful participation in the political process, which often have the effect of excluding countless transgender people from involvement in elections. Although limited data exist on the political and voting behavior of transgender people, general research on the transgender population has universally found that transgender people experience extremely high levels of discrimination in all aspects of American society, leading to disparities in health, housing, employment, access to public accommodations, educational outcomes, and police targeting, among others. These disparate outcomes increase barriers, both structural and social, for transgender people, resulting in disenfranchisement in and lack of access to the political process. The transgender community represents an increasingly important constituency whose political influence is on the rise despite being historically stymied by barriers to full and equal participation in all facets of American life.

Some insight into the political and voting behavior of transgender people can be gained by examining how the political parties interact with transgender people, how transgender people self-report their levels of political engagement, and how openly transgender candidates participate in the political process. While the political activity by and treatment of transgender people in the context of political and policy issues does not give full insight into the motivations of transgender people in the voting booth, it can help understand where transgender people feel more comfortable engaging in politics. Analyzing how transgender people engage with the major political parties will help cast light on how the experiences of transgender people influence decisions about which political parties or issues transgender people are more likely to support.

In addition to learning what motivates transgender people to vote for a candidate, party, or issue, it is important to recognize the structural and social barriers that transgender people face in accessing polling places on Election Day. Discrimination in all facets of society has a significant impact on political engagement by transgender people. From employment discrimination and police bias to identity documents and social misunderstanding of transgender people, transgender people are often unable to access the basic mechanisms required to register for and access the franchise. Increasing state requirements that voters show photo identification, higher homelessness among the transgender population, disproportionate incarceration rates, and lower incomes all have a direct impact on whether transgender people can meet basic qualifications to vote.

This chapter examines how transgender people engage in the political systems in the United States, including analysis of barriers to voting that transgender people face, ways transgender people interact with major political parties, and participation in the political process by transgender political candidates. The chapter begins with an introductory discussion about transgender people and the basic data, and lack thereof, on the transgender population, then provides a brief history of organized political engagement by the transgender community, discusses how political parties engage on transgender inclusion in party activities, and concludes with a discussion about the many structural and social barriers that keep transgender people from participating in the political process.

INTRODUCTION TO TRANSGENDER PEOPLE AND ISSUES

Transgender is "[a]n umbrella term for people whose gender identity, expression or behavior is different from those typically associated with their assigned sex at birth, including but not limited to transsexuals, cross-dressers, androgynous people, genderqueers, and gender non-conforming people. . . . 'Trans' is shorthand for 'transgender.'"[2] Society often conflates sexual orientation and gender identity, and knowing the difference is necessary to understanding how transgender people navigate the world. While lesbian, gay, bisexual, and transgender (LGBT) people share aspects of a cultural identity and similar experiences of discrimination, sexual orientation and gender identity refer to two different aspects of a person's identity. Sexual orientation refers to an individual's sexual attractions, such as whether a person is attracted to men, women, or people of all genders. Everybody has a sexual orientation—some people may identify as straight (or heterosexual), gay or lesbian, bisexual, pansexual, asexual, or other sexual orientations. *Gender identity* refers to a person's internal sense of their own gender as a man, woman, or genderqueer. Like sexual orientation, every person has a gender identity. For most people, their internal sense of their own gender identity as a woman or man is consistent with their sex assigned at birth, female or male. For example, most people who were assigned male at birth self-identify as a man, and most people who were assigned female at birth self-identify as a woman.

For transgender people, however, their internal sense of their own gender identity is different than their sex assigned at birth. For example, a person whose sex at birth was female but who internally identifies as a man is a transgender man, and a person whose sex at birth was male but who internally identifies as a woman is a transgender woman. Transgender people, like everybody else, also have a sexual orientation. For example, a transgender woman who is attracted to other women may identify as lesbian, and a transgender woman attracted to both men and women may identify as bisexual. Gender identity is the lens through which the majority of this chapter discusses issues that affect transgender people.

Little Data Exist on the Transgender Community

Virtually no research exists on the political and voting behavior of transgender people, making it incredibly difficult to identify whether transgender voters are more likely to support liberal or conservative candidates, more likely to identify with one political party or another, or even to predict whether transgender people turn out to vote in higher or lower numbers than the general public. Indeed, little quantifiable data exists about transgender people at all. Researchers estimate that the transgender population is about 0.3 percent of the general population or just under 700,000 transgender adults in the United States, however estimates have ranged as low as 0.1 percent and as high as 3 percent of the general population.[3] Most estimates on the transgender population fall squarely in the range of 0.25 percent to 1 percent of the total population.[4]

There are a variety of challenges to collecting data on the transgender population. Transgender people have a long history of experiencing intense discrimination in American and European society, reducing their likelihood of voluntarily identifying as transgender on surveys. Other concerns are methodological: how do surveys sufficiently ask whether a person is transgender when many people do not fully understand who transgender people are or what being transgender means? Questions must be developed in a way that adequately identifies transgender people on surveys without returning inaccurate survey results by confusing the general population. Despite these challenges, research on the transgender population is increasing. Some small federal surveys in the health context, especially around disease prevention and risk behavior analysis, have included transgender-identity questions.[5] Moreover, the federal government is in the process of developing and testing gender identity questions for the country's largest health survey, the National Health Interview Survey.[6] Until some of these larger surveys produce effective quantitative data, widespread research on the transgender community is likely to remain extremely limited.

While research on the lesbian, gay, and bisexual (LGB) community is significantly further along than research on the transgender community, many surveys fail to differentiate between LGB respondents and transgender respondents when creating LGBT-identity questions. This is especially true in the context of political polling, such as exit polls and public opinion polls. From the early 1990s, such polls have asked sexual orientation identity questions, some only asking for lesbian/gay identity and excluding bisexual identity; however, no known political exit polling has specifically asked about and reported transgender identity data,[7] resulting in very little data in the public domain that specifically identify the trends and behaviors of transgender people in the United States.

In recent years, political surveys have begun to ask about sexual orientation and gender identity, but report the data as one large LGBT group rather than disaggregating lesbian, gay, bisexual, and transgender respondents.[8] With one notable exception that will be discussed in detail below, even when a survey specifically asks a transgender identity question, the small sample size of transgender respondents makes it difficult to ascertain statistically significant data about the respondents. In those instances, like the 2012 Pew Research Center and Harris Interactive polls that focused on LGBT voters, the number of transgender respondents was so small that transspecific data were not reported at all.[9]

One of the only existing publicly reported data sources on the political and voting behavior of transgender people is found in the National Gay and Lesbian Task Force Policy Institute's Black Pride Survey 2000.[10] This survey studied black LGBT people attending Black Pride celebrations across the country and reported data on the relatively low number of transgender-identified respondents to various political behavior questions. The researchers note that survey results may be influenced by the fact that the audience is made of black LGBT people attending Black Pride events who may be a pool of individuals more prone to political activity than other black LGBT people. The Black Prides Survey found that black transgender people had a high level of political participation. Over 55 percent of black transgender people reported being registered as Democrats, while only 6 percent of black transgender people reported being registered Republicans. An additional 7 percent reported being registered as Independents. In general, black transgender respondents were more engaged in the political process than their black lesbian, gay, and bisexual counterparts. The survey revealed that "[f]or example, transgender individuals who reported engaging in a form of protest also indicated higher levels of being arrested, joining an organization, participating in a march or rally, contacting a white GLBT organization, and being part of a protest meeting." The top three political behaviors transgender people reported participating in were voting in the 1996 presidential election (53%), voting in a local election (45%), and participating in a march or rally (45%). Interestingly, black transgender people had lower participation rates than their black LGB counterparts in all activities except one, with black transgender people reporting participating in a march or rally at 1.5 times the rate of black LGB men and women. In terms of issues that are important to black transgender people, the Black Prides Survey found that transgender people identified HIV/AIDS, drugs, and job discrimination as the three most important issues facing all black people as well as the three most important issues facing LGBT black people. Black transgender people also rated HIV/AIDS as the top issue facing all Black people, identifying HIV/AIDS as a top issue for all black people at higher rates than either LGB men or women. This should be unsurprising given that the National Transgender Discrimination Survey reports that one-in-four black transgender people are HIV positive.

The low number of transgender respondents combined with the facts that the survey focused solely on black LGBT people and survey responses were solicited at community activism events indicates that the Black Prides Survey is likely not representative of the entire transgender population. As such, while the Black Prides Survey provides important insight into how a segment of the transgender population participates in political activities, participation rates among black transgender people cannot be assumed to be true for the entire transgender population.

In addition to the Black Prides Survey, one additional data point regarding political participation by transgender people emerged from the National Transgender Discrimination Survey (NTDS).[11] That survey found that 92.5 percent of transgender U.S. citizens are registered to vote, compared to only 71 percent of the general population. Higher voter registration rates among transgender people may indicate higher likelihood of participation in the political process. Without more research, political scientists cannot accurately predict how high or low voter turnout is among the transgender community, whether transgender people generally support conservative or liberal candidates or campaigns, or the rates at which transgender people lack access to the voting booth due to cultural and political barriers that affect transgender people.

High Levels of Transgender Discrimination Place Significant Barriers to Political Participation

The limited data that do exist on the transgender population indicate that transgender people experience intense levels of discrimination in all facets of society, and those disparate outcomes effectively erect barriers that may lead to lower voter participation. The National Transgender Discrimination Survey conducted by the National Gay and Lesbian Task Force and the National Center for Transgender Equality is the only comprehensive survey of the experiences of transgender people and establishes the only reliable data point for discrimination that transgender people face in a variety of arenas. These findings suggest that transgender people experience catastrophic levels of discrimination in employment, education, housing, access to identity documents, public accommodations, and abuse by police and prison officials. These forms of discrimination have a significant impact on access to the voting booth for transgender people in a variety of direct and indirect ways.

In the employment context, 90 percent of transgender and gender nonconforming people report experiencing mistreatment, harassment, or discrimination on the job or taking actions to hide their identity to avoid employment discrimination. Additionally, 47 percent experienced an adverse job outcome such as being fired, not hired, or denied a promotion because of their gender identity. Transgender people are unemployed at double the rate of the general population, with black transgender people experiencing four times the unemployment rate of the general population. Adverse employment outcomes are linked to voter participation, as studies show that unemployed and underemployed individuals are far less likely to be registered to vote or participate in the political process.[12]

Additionally, transgender people experience high levels of housing discrimination. Nineteen percent of transgender people reported being refused a home or apartment, and 11 percent reported being evicted because of their gender identity or expression. One-fifth of transgender people reported experiencing homelessness at some point in their lifetime. Lacking a fixed address, moving around frequently, or being homeless make an individual unlikely to be registered to vote in the place they currently live, unaware of polling locations, or even unaware they have the right to vote in elections.

For transgender people, disproportionate rates of homelessness and housing discrimination likely have a significant negative impact on voter registration and turnout rates.[13] Transgender people are four times more likely to have a household income of less than $10,000 per year compared to the general population. Lower-income households are strongly linked to lower voter turnout.[14] For example, in the 2008 presidential election wealthy voters turned out at nearly twice the rate as low-income voters.[15] Data from the 2012 presidential election indicated similar trends of significantly lower voter turnout among lower-income earners than higher-income earners.[16]

Over half (52%) of transgender people reported being verbally harassed or disrespected in a place of public accommodation, such as hotels, restaurants, buses, airports, or government agencies. For some transgender people, experiences of discrimination or having heard about others' experiences of discrimination when accessing government agencies may lead the voter to fear attempting to access the polling place. This is especially true when 19 percent reported being denied equal treatment, 20 percent reported being harassed or disrespected, and 1 percent reported experiencing physical assault while accessing a government agency or official. Polling places often have a police presence, and transgender people reported unbelievably high rates of discrimination by police officers: 27 percent reported being harassed or disrespected by a police officer and 4 percent reported being physically assaulted by a police officer. With such high rates of discrimination from government officials and police officers, transgender people may intentionally avoid accessing government agencies and polling places out of fear of discrimination.

While there are a dearth of data on transgender people's experiences and participation in the political process, the limited data that do exist indicate that transgender people may experience significant levels of discrimination, which may deter them from political participation for a variety of reasons associated with discrimination. It also may be true, however, that transgender people access the voting booth at equal or higher numbers to the general population as a result of high resiliency rates. The National Transgender Discrimination Survey indicates that despite the high levels of violence and discrimination that transgender people experience, transgender people often find ways to overcome those barriers where possible. For example, more than three-quarters of respondents were able to receive access to transition-related hormone therapy despite major structural barriers to obtaining health care, including 19 percent of transgender people reported being refused access to a physician and half of respondents reported having to teach their doctor about transgender health. Moreover, transgender people were far more likely than the general population to persevere and seek educational opportunities while aged 25–44 years, even though rates of bullying, harassment, and violence in schools were extremely high.

These statistics are a sampling of the areas in which transgender people experience high levels of discrimination that directly impact access to the voting booth. Transgender people may avoid the polling place because of a lifetime of experience associated with harassment and violence at the hands of government officials, lack of adequate identity documents (more on that later in the chapter), low income, lack of a fixed address, or a whole host of other factors. Alternatively, high resiliency rates suggest an increased likelihood for transgender people to overcome the barriers they face and find ways to participate in the political process. The fact that no reliable data regarding voter turnout or voting behavior exist leaves political scientists unable to conclude how, why, and when transgender people participate in the political process.

POLITICAL ENGAGEMENT BY AND ABOUT TRANSGENDER PEOPLE

The two major political parties in the United States have generally taken no position on policy matters as they affect transgender people in their national platforms until recent years due in large part to the historically limited but recently increasing social awareness of who transgender people are and policy issues that affect them. Transgender people and issues are increasingly prevalent in the national political conversation since the early 2000s. Despite this fact, the way that the two major parties have reacted to the increased participation and political conversation around transgender people sheds light on how the parties view the role of transgender people in American society and potentially influences how transgender people participate in the parties. This section will give a brief overview of transgender political activism, followed by how the major political parties have addressed transgender people and issues in their platforms, policies, and appointments.

A Brief History of Transgender Political Activism

While transgender people have a long history of involvement in political activism and social change dating well before the famous Stonewall Inn riots of 1969, the national political conversation about transgender people really began in the late 1990s and early 2000s. Local laws explicitly prohibiting discrimination on the basis of gender identity date to the 1970s, when some cities and counties included gender identity protections in the definitions of sex or sexual orientation protections.[17] In 1993, Minnesota was the first state to pass a statewide law banning discrimination on the basis of gender identity—its Human Rights Act.[18] Since then, over 150 cities and counties, plus 18 states and the District of Columbia, have passed laws explicitly prohibiting discrimination on the basis of gender identity in areas such as housing, health care, public accommodations, employment, credit, and others.[19] Nationally, the patchwork of state, county and local nondiscrimination laws means that 47 percent of the nation's population currently lives in a jurisdiction with laws that explicitly ban discrimination on the basis of gender identity.

The vast majority of these policy changes came since 2000, in large part due to the rise of political advocacy organizations focusing on transgender rights issues. The National Transgender Advocacy Coalition, formed in 1999 by a group of experienced lobbyists who identify as transgender, lobbied Congress for laws to protect transgender people from discrimination. In 2001, an organization now called Equal Justice Works funded two projects that would, for the first time, have full-time staff at national LGBT advocacy organizations whose focus was to work on transgender rights issues. One funded fellowship opened a new project called the "Transgender Law Project" at the National Center for Lesbian Rights in San Francisco. In 2002, the project received funding to become its own, independent organization, called Transgender Law Center, whose mission is to "to change law, policy, and attitudes so that all people can live safely, authentically, and free from discrimination regardless of their gender identity or expression." The other project Equal Justice Works funded in 2001 was the Transgender Civil Rights Project at the National Gay and Lesbian Task Force's Washington, D.C. office. This project focuses on policy change at the federal, state, and local level to ensure full inclusion of transgender people in laws and policies. In 2003 the National Center for Transgender Equality opened its doors in Washington, D.C., and is a national social justice organization devoted to ending discrimination and violence against transgender people through education and advocacy on national issues of importance to transgender people. In 2008, Transgender Legal Defense and Education Fund became the first impact litigation organization dedicated to ending discrimination based on gender identity.

In addition to these four organizations that have full-time staff dedicated to transgender legal and policy issues, two transgender-specific membership organizations with unpaid staff have also emerged. The Transgender American Veterans Association was created in 2003 by transgender veterans, and the Transgender People of Color Coalition was formed in 2010 by transgender activists that felt existing resources dedicated to transgender policy issues should be more inclusive of transgender people of color. Until 2012, the national-level organizations working to engage policy makers on issues that affect transgender people were all non-partisan political advocacy organizations, many of which refused to endorse any candidates for office regardless of party. In the 2012 election cycle, the first partisan transgender issues group was formed to support the reelection of President Barack Obama. Trans United for Obama described itself as "a national volunteer effort to activate transgender people, their supporters, allies, families and friends to re-elect President Obama."

The rise of organizations that are dedicated to or have staff focused on transgender law and policy issues have significantly influenced the political discourse around transgender people. Before these organizations emerged, there was no serious conversation about federal level nondiscrimination protections that explicitly included gender identity as a protected class. Today, two federal laws explicitly add protections on the basis of gender identity—the Matthew Shepard and James Byrd, Jr. Hate Crimes Prevention Act of 2009 and the Violence Against Women Reauthorization Act of 2013—dozens of federal regulations add gender identity protections, and politicians as high as the vice president of the United States consider transgender equality to be "the civil rights issue of our time."[20]

Political Parties and Transgender People

Although virtually no data exist on the political affiliations of transgender people, some information can be gleaned by examining the ways political parties treat issues that affect transgender people, how visible within each party transgender people and issues are, and with which party openly transgender candidates for office affiliate themselves. In general, openly transgender people publicly affiliate themselves with the Democratic party more than the Republican party, and openly transgender candidates for office are generally registered Democrats.

For the national Democratic Party, inclusion of transgender people and issues in party activities dates to the 2000 Convention, and has increasingly incorporated issues that affect transgender people. According to the advocacy group Trans United for Obama, "[i]n 2000, Jane Fee of Minnesota was the first transgender delegate to the Democratic National Convention. In 2004, Georgia, New Jersey, New York, Pennsylvania, and Texas sent transgender people in their delegation to Boston. In 2008, . . . at the Denver National Convention. . . . Arizona, Indiana, Massachusetts, New Jersey, New York, Oregon and Texas sent delegates. . . . [I]n 2012, we have our largest and most diverse contingent of openly transgender delegates."[21] Indeed, 14 openly transgender delegates were recognized at the 2012 Democratic National Convention, and the trend seems to indicate that the 2016 Democratic National Convention will recognize even more openly transgender delegates. The Democratic Party platform first included explicit reference to transgender people in the 2008 platform in which the party vowed to fight discrimination on the basis of, among other classes, gender identity. In 2009, the Democratic National Committee (DNC) added gender identity as a protected class under the DNC's nondiscrimination policy. In 2010, Democratic president Barack Obama became the first president to appoint openly transgender people to political positions within the federal government.[22] To date, Obama has appointed four openly transgender people to political appointment positions within the administration. In 2012, the Democratic Party platform added references to policy positions regarding transgender people with a general statement that discrimination on the basis of gender identity should be prohibited and support for a transgender-inclusive Employment Non-Discrimination Act.

Through the 2012 presidential election, the national Republican Party platform lacked any explicit reference to transgender people or to protections on the basis of gender identity. In some states, the Party's platform includes specific references to opposing efforts to recognize transgender people as a protected class in anti-discrimination policies. For example, the South Carolina Republican Party Platform indicates a policy stance that "one's gender is fixed at birth and that no citizen should be entitled to special treatment or accorded any special benefits not accorded to others of the same birth gender regardless of how they have altered their anatomy or appearance." Accordingly, the South Carolina Republican Party "oppose[s] efforts to blur or disregard the uniqueness of male and female genders," and "oppose[s] federal, state, county, or municipal laws, regulations or ordinances that require a person to be granted special rights or protections based on his or her 'perceived' gender identity."[23] There are no documented cases of openly transgender delegates attending the Republican National Convention or any state Republican Party convention. Moreover, there are no documented cases of openly transgender political appointees in the federal government or in any state government under a Republican chief executive.

Transgender Political Candidates

The stark contrast with regard to gender identity-related policy positions and prominence of transgender people in the two major political parties may explain why the overwhelming majority of transgender people who run for partisan political office identify with the Democratic Party. Perhaps unsurprisingly, very few openly transgender people have sought political office in the United States at all. Less than 20 documented cases of openly transgender people running for office exist in the United States, and all except one of the openly transgender candidates ran during or after the 2004 election cycle. Running for political office as an openly transgender candidate has proven personally trying. Many openly transgender political candidates have received significant criticism, their campaigns often more about their identity as a transgender person than anything else.

Althea Garrison, a transgender woman who had run for many political offices in the 1980s, became the first known transgender person elected to office in 1992 by winning a seat in the Massachusetts State House, and served one term. Garrison did not publicly disclose her identity as a transgender person, but after her victory, a news outlet ran a story outing her as a transgender person, which had a detrimental effect on her future candidacy. Virtually every news story about Garrison referenced her gender identity, often using derogatory terms about her in the articles. Political analysts agree that disclosing her gender identity doomed her political career.

Besides Althea Garrison, there were no openly transgender candidates for statewide political office until 2004, when Amanda Simpson became the first openly transgender person to win a primary and receive a party endorsement for a race for state House. Simpson's campaign was unsuccessful. Twenty years after Althea Garrison's election, in 2012, another transgender person was elected to a state House when Stacie Laughton of New Hampshire won a seat in the state's House of Representatives, and she continues as the highest-level openly transgender person elected to office.

The first known *openly* transgender person to win any election was Michelle Bruce, who won a city council seat in Riverdale, Georgia, in 2003. Running for reelection in 2007, two of her challengers brought a lawsuit against her for misleading voters and engaging in election fraud for running as a transgender candidate. The case made its way to the Georgia Supreme Court, which unanimously held that no election law was violated and that there was no evidence of fraud, misconduct, or illegal action on Michelle Bruce's part.[24] As it made its way through the courts, the election continued. Some believe that the lawsuit cast a cloud over Michelle Bruce's candidacy, causing her to lose, even though the charges were ultimately ruled unfounded.

In 2005, Rapid City, South Dakota Council Member Marla Marissa began her gender transition while serving on City Council. During that process, she applied to have her name changed in local court. A political opponent, who lost to her in the most recent election, opposed her name change and petitioned the judge to deny it on the grounds that voters had elected an "alderman" not an "alderwoman." The judge ultimately granted the name change. Murphy did not run for reelection citing fear after political opponents threatened to target her for recall, she received numerous threats, and she was protested by ultra-conservative, religiously affiliated groups. She decided to run for election again in 2011, and was unsuccessful after every news story about her election focused on her 2005 gender transition and subsequent threats.

Regardless of political affiliation, transgender people seem to face deep criticism when running for office because of their gender identity. The criticism openly transgender candidates have faced, as well as fear of potential criticism, may have a significant deterrent effect on transgender people seeking political office. With examples of transgender candidates sued for voter fraud and opponents using one's transgender identity as a campaign issue, it is unsurprising that very few openly transgender candidates run for political office.

The overwhelming majority of the transgender candidates for political office are Democrats. Of the documented cases of openly transgender candidates seeking office, only three ran as Republicans. Althea Garrison ran for office as a Democrat, Republican, and Independent, but she was the Republican nominee the year she won her Massachusetts House seat. Donna Milo is a Republican who ran unsuccessful campaigns for Congress in 2010 and Miami Commissioner in 2011. Finally, Chrissy Nakonsky unsuccessfully ran for the Republican nomination for a seat in the Minnesota legislature in 2008. While these factors do not conclusively indicate how transgender people engage with political parties, the level of involvement by the parties with transgender people, combined with the way that openly transgender candidates affiliate themselves with parties, seems to indicate a likelihood that transgender people will identify with and support the Democratic party at higher rates than the Republican party. Despite a propensity for transgender people to affiliate themselves with liberal candidates and issues, it would be unfair to state conclusively that transgender people overwhelmingly support Democrats in elections. Aside from the lack of quantifiable data, examples from other marginalized communities indicate that there are likely a significant percentage of transgender people who are conservative or affiliate themselves with the Republican Party. Despite disproportionate inclusion in Democratic Party policies, Republican-affiliated LGBT advocacy groups exist and polls indicate that as many as one in five LGBT Americans identify as Republicans.[25] Transgender voters come from a wide variety of backgrounds and political views, and should not be seen as monolithic. While further data may reveal trends among transgender people, there currently are not enough data to make broad proscriptions about the transgender community's political affiliations.

BARRIERS TO VOTING FOR TRANSGENDER PEOPLE

While there are limited data on the political behavior of transgender people, the significant barriers to the franchise likely have a significant impact on the ability of transgender people to participate in the political process. Discrimination in various sectors of society have the effect of making seemingly simple acts like registering to vote and showing identification to poll workers very difficult for a large proportion of transgender people. Increased voter scrutiny based on fear of voter fraud and current administrative barriers that increase the burdens on transgender people who attempt to vote, along with the heightened discrimination transgender people experience throughout society, make it likely that transgender people attempt to vote at lower rates than the general population. This section focuses on the various administrative barriers to participation in the political process that transgender people experience, from homelessness to incarceration to accessing identity documents. Many of these barriers effectively disenfranchise large numbers of transgender people across the country, limiting their very ability to vote.

Administrative Barriers

As a result of significant disparities in access to housing and employment, law enforcement, and discrimination at the hands of government employees, many transgender people face significant barriers to accessing the voting booth. Seemingly unrelated disparities such as higher rates of incarceration and homelessness likely eclipse the opportunity for some transgender people to register, actually access the polling place on Election Day, or be accepted as an eligible voter when they do arrive at the polling place.

Transgender people are four times more likely to live in extreme poverty than the general population, according to the National Transgender Discrimination Survey. This fact alone makes transgender people more likely to experience difficulty registering to vote due to transportation costs associated with physically accessing the necessary government offices to register to vote. While many states offer voter registration at a state's Department of Motor Vehicles, transgender people are disproportionately less likely to seek a driver's license or own a vehicle because of lower incomes. Related to higher rates of extreme poverty, transgender people are far more likely than the general population to experience housing discrimination. Two percent of respondents to the National Transgender Discrimination Survey reported being currently homeless, which is double the rate of the general population. Studies indicate that the homeless population is extremely unlikely to vote, or even be registered to vote.[26] Eleven percent of eligible voters nationwide do not have proper photo identification and the percentage is unquestionably higher among people experiencing homelessness.[27] Voter registration rates among the homeless population may be a result of policies designed to prevent voter fraud, but that have a disproportionate impact on the homeless population. In most states, voters unable to prove they are eligible to vote in a district may cast a provisional ballot. Often times, provisional ballots require voters to take a second step, namely appearing before an election panel to certify that their statements were accurate. These additional steps erect barriers to full and equal participation in the political process, especially for homeless voters who are unlikely to produce sufficient evidence that they live in the designated district. Where transgender people are twice as likely as the general population to be homeless, lack of access for homeless people has a significant impact on transgender voters.

Transgender people are also disproportionately targeted by law enforcement. Seven percent of transgender respondents to the NTDS reported being arrested or held in a cell strictly due to police bias based on the respondent's gender identity or expression. For transgender people of color, incarceration rates were significantly higher—41 percent of black transgender people and 21 percent of Latino/a transgender people reported being arrested and jailed because of gender identity bias. Outside the context of bias-based incarceration, transgender people report exceedingly high incarceration rates. For example, 16 percent of transgender people reported being incarcerated for any reason, compared to far lower rates among the general population.[28] As with bias-based incarceration, rates of imprisonment among transgender people of color is significantly higher than the general population. Black transgender people report being jailed for any reason at 47 percent, followed by 30 percent for American Indian transgender people and 25 percent for Latino/a transgender people.

The number of transgender people convicted of felonies is unknown, but if the available data are any indication, the rate of felony conviction for transgender people is likely high as a result of bias-based police practices. All but two states currently have some form of voting restriction for people convicted of felonies, varying in degrees from denying voting while serving a prison sentence to permanent disenfranchisement.[29] Eleven states continue to permanently disenfranchise people convicted of a felony for the remainder of their lifetime. With the prevalence of disenfranchisement among those convicted of a felony, which are disproportionately people of color, misinformation about whether formerly incarcerated individuals are eligible to vote is rampant. Higher rates of incarceration and targeting by law enforcement among the transgender community likely has a significant impact on voter access and turnout, both because formerly incarcerated transgender people may be unaware of their eligibility to participate in the political process and because poll workers lack complete understanding of the requirements for those who have been incarcerated.

Misinformation about how to properly process transgender voters may also be actively advertised in an attempt to dissuade transgender voters from having full access to the franchise. In the 2012 general election, an organization called True The Vote, a nonprofit organization concerned about voter fraud, included explicit messaging to its members targeting transgender voters for disenfranchisement by arguing that transgender voters were attempting to commit voter fraud if their gender expression is inconsistent with the gender marker shown on the voter's identification.[30] The advertisement included cartoon images of a hairy man wearing a dress with the message "Prevent voter fraud!" displayed across the top. This is the first documented case of any organization explicitly targeting transgender people for additional scrutiny when attempting to vote. This message, along with messages expressing concern about voter fraud and advocating for strict photo ID requirements, may have the effect of confusing voters and poll workers about the requirements associated with processing transgender voters. Many transgender voters may choose not to vote at all because the name they use or the way they appear is inconsistent with the name, photo, or gender marker on their identity documents.

Transgender people's experiences of discrimination by government officials and police, and when accessing public accommodations may also deter transgender people from voting. For example, 52 percent of transgender people reported being verbally harassed or disrespected in a place of public accommodation, such as hotels, restaurants, government agencies, or public transportation. That includes the 19 percent of respondents that reported being denied equal treatment by a government agency or official, 27 percent who reported police harassment, and 11 percent who had been denied equal treatment or harassed by judges or court officials. For those concerned about being harassed by government officials, police, or court officials, their concern is exacerbated at the polling place because officials representing all three entities are present. Aside from the humiliation of being verbally harassed, disrespected, or denied equal treatment in public accommodations, transgender people report high rates of physical assault while accessing public accommodations as well. One percent report being physically assaulted by a government agency or official, an additional 1 percent report being physically assaulted by a judge or court official, and 4 percent report being physically assaulted by police. For many transgender people, simply accessing certain amenities in society brings challenges and fear of discrimination or assault. With the rise of photo identification requirements and the barriers that exist to accessing updated identity documents for transgender people, misinformation and fear of discrimination likely has the impact of deterring voters from even attempting to access a polling place.

Voter ID Requirements

Perhaps the most significant barrier to voting for transgender people is the voter identification requirement. While photo identification is only required in a handful of states, Americans commonly believe that photo identification is required to vote. Recent efforts in many states to impose strict identification requirements for voters, including some states that will not allow a voter to cast a ballot without photo identification, effectively disenfranchise thousands of transgender voters who lack access to updated photo identification. The Williams Institute estimated that strict photo ID requirements may have disenfranchised over 25,000 transgender voters in just nine states during the 2012 election cycle.[31] Even in states that do not have strict photo identification requirements, high rates of transgender people lacking access to updated identity documents makes accessing the voting booth difficult for many. The National Transgender Discrimination Survey reports that only 21 percent of transgender people have been able to update all of the identity documents and records with their new name and gender. Indeed, a full one-third of respondents had been unable to update any of the identity documents or records. Less than 60 percent of respondents reported updating their driver's license or state ID, less than half reported updating a Social Security record, and about one-quarter reported updating their passport.

Access to updated identification is often contingent upon medical interventions that can be expensive, even for those with health insurance coverage. Most health insurance plans exclude from coverage any care related to gender transition, meaning that transgender people are often left without transition-related health care or required to find a way to pay for it out of pocket. Because of high rates of un- and underemployment, which leads to high rates of poverty among the transgender community, accessing transition-related medical care is often impossible. Yet access to transition-related surgery significantly increases the likelihood that a person will be able to obtain updated identification. National Transgender Discrimination Survey respondents reported that 81 percent of those that had some type of surgery were able to update their driver's license, compared to only 37 percent of those that hadn't had any surgery. Each state sets its own policies and legal requirements for an individual to change one's name and gender marker on state-issued identification, and in many states there are different standards for different documents.[32] A state may have different requirements for how an individual updates one's name or gender marker on a driver's license or birth certificate, which may be different from the federal government's standards for updating a Social Security record or passport. The confusing web of differential requirements for updating different documents leaves transgender people often lost in trying to update identity documents. In addition, many transgender people assume that they must have had surgical interventions in order to update identity documents, whether or not the policy actually includes such a requirement. Misinformation among front-line staff is also a concern for transgender people. Many front-line staffers inaccurately believe that a policy requires proof that a person has undergone surgical intervention before being allowed to update an identity document and therefore impose additional burdens beyond those required by state law or regulation. For many people, even the fear of being asked to prove that they have undergone surgical intervention can deter them from trying to update their identity documents.

For many transgender people, lack of accurate identification presents significant barriers. Transgender people are often able to update one or two identity documents but not all of them. This may be because a transgender person has not had surgical interventions and are therefore ineligible to update their gender marker on certain documents, like a Social Security record or, in many states, a birth certificate, but have been able to secure identity documents of other types with lower documentation requirements, such as passports or driver's licenses. This leaves many transgender people with multiple forms of identification, each with a different name and/or gender marker. Transgender people are often encouraged to bring both types of ID with them to the polling place so that they can have some ID that will match the voter registration record, and can prove to the poll workers that they are the person listed on the voter registration record. When presenting an ID during the ordinary course of life that didn't match their gender identity or expression, 40 percent of transgender people reported being harassed, and 3 percent reported being attacked or assaulted. Additionally, 15 percent reported being asked to leave the establishment. With the rise of concerns about voter fraud and organizations targeting transgender people for additional scrutiny at the polls, transgender people may be afraid to even attempt to vote.

A first step in updating identity documents is often to seek a legal name change. This process alone can be daunting because, while a person has a legal right to change one's name for any reason, often there are significant costs and stresses associated with changing one's name. For many, the processes associated with legally changing one's name are so complicated that the person must hire an attorney to do the paperwork for them, which can be economically impossible for low-income transgender people. For those feeling confident enough to attempt the process without an attorney, there are often court filing fees and requirements to publish name change announcements in local newspapers. Moreover, many jurisdictions require individuals to appear before a judge and answer questions about the name change. In some jurisdictions, judges refuse to grant the name change to transgender people even though there is no legal basis to deny the application. For transgender people that have been victims of police harassment or harassment by a government or court official, the last step of appearing before a judge may impose significant psychological burdens. The process is often more difficult for changing one's gender marker on identity documents. While individuals have a legal right to change their name for any reason, many jurisdictions impose strict requirements for changing a gender marker, and in some jurisdictions changing a gender marker on records like birth certificates is impossible.

There are many ways that incongruent identity documents or having outdated identity documents can present serious problems at the polling place for transgender voters. For transgender people who have been able to obtain an updated name and/or gender marker on identity documents, they must then update their name and gender marker on a long list of documents. As is true of any time people change their name, they will have to update their name with banks, credit cards, educational institutions, employers, government agencies such as the Social Security Administration and the Internal Revenue Service, and others. It is easy to forget to update voter registration or to forget whether a person updated their name on their voter registration record before Election Day. A voter may appear at the polling place with an updated identity document and present that name to poll workers as their registered voting name. If they have updated their voter registration file and have updated identity documents, voters should not experience any additional scrutiny at the polling place, although data indicate that transgender people are often subject to additional scrutiny in circumstances that require them to show identification, regardless of whether it is justified. If they have not updated their voter registration record, voters may find that their previous legal name continues to be listed on the voter registration record. Since the voter has updated some but not all forms of identification, the voter can then show one of the not-yet-updated forms of identification to the poll worker. This will surely subject the voter to additional scrutiny as their physical presentation and the name they first gave to the poll worker appear inconsistent with the information listed on the voter registration record. With increasing emphasis on concerns about voter fraud from a variety of sectors in society, transgender voters may be denied access to the polls or be required to cast a provisional ballot.

Transgender people face roadblocks to political participation in a variety of ways that are not directly designed to impact the ability of transgender people to vote. Unfortunately, the very ability to access the franchise is limited for many transgender people by factors associated with income, employment, housing, police profiling, incarceration, and in perhaps the most significant way, identity documents. These obstacles, combined with increasing scrutiny of voters out of fear of voter fraud, have erected barriers that close access to the voting booth for transgender people. Even where these barriers do not actually exist, their prevalence across the country and lack of accurate information for many transgender people has effectively deterred transgender voters from even attempting to participate in the political process.

CONCLUSION

For a variety of reasons, transgender people seem to be less likely to engage in the political process, but when transgender people do participate in the political process they seem to be significantly more likely to support liberal causes or Democratic politicians. Due to a lack of data, the political and voting behavior of transgender people cannot be truly known at this time. Researchers lack any reliable data on turnout rates, political ideology, or virtually any other measure of political engagement. Despite this lack of data, one thing is clear: transgender people and issues that affect transgender people are gaining increasing attention in the mainstream political discussion and are largely supported by Democrats. As the political engagement of transgender people increases and more data are collected on this understudied population, the influence of transgender people as a voting block will play an increasingly significant role in how political parties address social issues that affect transgender people. Despite the increased attention paid to political issues that affect transgender people and the increased participation within political parties by transgender people, many transgender people are effectively barred from participation in the political process due to a variety of administrative barriers that have a disproportionate impact on transgender people. In order for political scientists to fully understand what drives the political motives of transgender people and for policy makers to fully understand the barriers that exist for transgender political participation, a significant amount of research in this area is sorely needed.

NOTES

1. Patrick A. Paschall is a senior policy counsel at the National Gay and Lesbian Task Force and City Council member in Hyattsville, Maryland. The author would like to thank the National Gay and Lesbian Task Force, and Task Force Holley Law Fellows Kaley Lentini and Arielle Schwartz for their in-depth research assistance.
2. National Center for Transgender Equality, "Transgender Terminology."
3. Gates, *How Many People Are Lesbian, Gay, Bisexual, and Transgender*?
4. National Center for Transgender Equality, "Understanding Transgender."
5. Camacho, *Top Health Issues for LGBT Populations Information.*
6. American Psychological Association, "Data on LGBT Populations to be Collected in Major Federal Health Survey."
7. Hertzog, *Lavender Vote.*
8. Gates and Newport "Special Report: 3.4 percent of U.S. Adults."
9. Pew Research Center, *Survey of LGBT Americans.*
10. Battle et al., *Say It Loud I'm Black.*
11. Grant et al., *Injustice at Every Turn.*
12. Burden and Wichowsky, *Unemployment and Voter Turnout.*
13. Walters et al., *Voting Rights.*
14. Demos, "Voter Turnout by Income, 2008 US Presidential Election."
15. Hunt, "Stacked Deck."
16. *NonprofitVote, America Goes to the Polls.*
17. National Gay and Lesbian Task Force, *Scope of Explicitly Transgender-Inclusive Anti-Discrimination Laws.*
18. Hunt, *State-by-State Examination of Nondiscrimination Laws and Policies.*
19. National Gay and Lesbian Task Force, *Jurisdictions with Explicitly Transgender-Inclusive Nondiscrimination Laws.*
20. Bendery, "Joe Biden: Transgender Discrimination."
21. Meet the Delegates! (n.d.). Accessed from Trans United for Obama website: http://www.transunitedforobama.org/delegates.html
22. LGBT for Obama, *President Obama's Accomplishments for Transgender Americans.*
23. SCGOP, *Platform of the South Carolina Republican Party.*
24. *Fuller v. Thomas*, 284 Ga. 397, 667 S.E.2d 587 (2008).
25. Gallup, "LGBT Americans Skew Democratic, Largely Support Obama."
26. Walters et al., *Voting Rights.*
27. *Letter to Attorney General Holder*, National Coalition for the Homeless.
28. The National Transgender Discrimination Survey reports that "A 2003 report of the Department of Justice shows that 2.7% of the general American population is imprisoned at some point in life. However, the Department of Justice report does not include jails, so the general population rate for being held in jail or prison should be higher than the simple prison rate." NTDS at 163.

29. State Felon Voting Laws.
30. "Tea Party Group Targets Trans Voters," National Center for Transgender Equality.
31. Herman, "Potential Impact."
32. Mottet, "Modernizing State Vital Statistics Statutes."

REFERENCES

America Goes to the Polls: Voter Participation Gaps in the 2012 Presidential Election. n.d. http://www.nonprofitvote.org/documents/2013/09/america-goes-to-the-polls-2012-voter-participation-gaps-in-the-2012-presidential-election.pdf.

Battle, J. et al. *Say It Loud I'm Black and I'm Proud: Black Pride Survey.* 2000. http://www.thetaskforce.org/downloads/reports/reports/SayItLoudBlackAndProud.pdf.

Bendery, J. "Joe Biden: Transgender Discrimination Is 'The Civil Rights Issue of Our Time." 31 October 2012. http://www.huffingtonpost.com/2012/10/30/joe-biden-transgender-rights_n_2047275.html.

Burden, B. C., and A. Wichowsky. *Unemployment and Voter Turnout.* 2012. http://users.polisci.wisc.edu/behavior/Papers/Burden&Wichowsky2012.pdf.

Camacho, A. *Top Health Issues for LGBT Populations Information & Resource Kit.* 2012. http://store.samhsa.gov/shin/content/SMA12-4684/SMA12-4684.pdf.

Data on LGBT populations to be collected in major federal health survey. July 2011. https://www.apa.org/science/about/psa/2011/07/data-populations.aspx.

Fuller v. Thomas, 284 Ga. 397, 667 S.E.2d 587 (2008).

Gates, G. J. *How Many People Are Lesbian, Gay, Bisexual, and Transgender?* April 2011. http://williamsinstitute.law.ucla.edu/wp-content/uploads/Gates-How-Many-People-LGBT-Apr-2011.pdf.

Gates, G. J., and F. Newport. "Special Report: 3.4% of U.S. Adults Identify as LGBT." 18 October 2012. http://www.gallup.com/poll/158066/special-report-adults-identify-lgbt.aspx.

Grant, J. M. et al. *Injustice at Every Turn: A Report of the National Transgender Discrimination Survey.* http://endtransdiscrimination.org/PDFs/NTDS_Report.pdf (NTDS). (The Report cited a voter registration rate of 89% among the entire transgender population but the raw data found that the voter registration rate among U.S. citizens was 92.5%).

Herman, J. L. "The Potential Impact of Voter Identification Laws on Transgender Voters." April 2012. http://williamsinstitute.law.ucla.edu/research/transgender-issues/the-potential-impact-of-voter-identification-laws-on-transgender-voters/#sthash.AmmISUGx.dpuf; http://williamsinstitute.law.ucla.edu/research/transgender-issues/the-potential-impact-of-voter-identification-laws-on-transgender-voters/.

Hertzog, M. *The Lavender Vote: Lesbians, Gay Men, and Bisexuals in American Electoral Politics.* New York: New York University Press, 1996.

HHS acts on Institute of Medicine recommendation.

Hunt, J. *A State-by-State Examination of Nondiscrimination Laws and Policies: State Stacked Deck: How the Dominance of Politics by the Affluent & Business*

Undermines Economic Mobility in America. June 2012. http://www.demos.org/stacked-deck-how-dominance-politics-affluent-business-undermines-economic-mobility-america.

Inaugural Gallup findings based on more than 120,000 interviews.

Jurisdictions with Explicitly Transgender-Inclusive Nondiscrimination Laws. June 2012. http://www.thetaskforce.org/downloads/reports/fact_sheets/all_jurisdictions_w_pop_6_12.pdf.

Letter to Attorney General Holder. "National Coalition for the Homeless." 17 August 2011. http://nationalhomeless.org/projects/vote/NCH_Holder Letter_Aug11.pdf.

"LGBT Americans Skew Democratic, Largely Support Obama: Conservative LGBT Individuals Tend to Be Older, White, and More Religious. 18 October 2012. http://www.gallup.com/poll/158102/lgbt-americans-skew-democratic-largely-support-obama.aspx.

"Meet the Delegates!" n.d. http://www.transunitedforobama.org/delegates.html.

Mottet, L. A. "Modernizing State Vital Statistics Statutes and Policies to Ensure Accurate Gender Markers on Birth Certificates: A Good Government Approach to Recognizing the Lives of Transgender People." *Michigan Journal of Gender & Law* 19.2 (2013).

National Center for Transgender Equality. "Transgender Terminology." May 2009. http://transequality.org/Resources/NCTE_TransTerminology.pdf.

National Center for Transgender Equality. "Understanding Transgender: Frequently Asked Questions about Transgender People." May 2009. http://transequality.org/Resources/NCTE_UnderstandingTrans.pdf (NCTE estimates ¼ to 1% of the total population identify as transsexual, which represents a subset of all people that fall under the umbrella term "transgender").

Nondiscrimination Policies Fill the Void but Federal Protections Are Still Needed. http://www.americanprogress.org/issues/2012/06/pdf/state_non discrimination.pdf.

Pew Research Center. *A Survey of LGBT Americans: Attitudes, Experiences and Values in Changing Times.* 13 June 2013. http://www.pewsocialtrends.org/files/2013/06/SDT_LGBT-Americans_06-2013.pdf.

"The Platform of the South Carolina Republican Party as Adopted by the 2012 South Carolina Republican Party State Convention." 2012. http://www.scgop.com/wp-content/uploads/2012/06/SCGOP-Platform-Adopted-2012.pdf.

President Obama's Accomplishments for Transgender Americans. n.d. http://www.transunitedforobama.org/uploads/1/1/2/9/11297030/trans_accomplishments.pdf.

Scope of Explicitly Transgender-Inclusive Anti-Discrimination Laws. n.d. http://www.thetaskforce.org/downloads/reports/fact_sheets/TI_antidisc_laws_7_08. pdf.

State Felon Voting Laws. 12 February 2014. http://felonvoting.procon.org/view.resource.php?resourceID=000286.

"Tea Party Group Targets Trans Voters" [Blog post]. n.d. http://transgende requality.wordpress.com/2012/11/04/tea-party-group-targets-trans-voters/.

"Voter Turnout by Income, 2008 US Presidential Election." n.d. http://www.demos.org/data-byte/voter-turnout-income-2008-us-presidential-election.

Walters, J. et al., eds. *Voting Rights: Registration Manual You Don't Need a Home to Vote.* August 2012. http://nationalhomeless.org/projects/vote/Manual_2012.pdf.

Conclusion

Minority Voters—Present and Future

Over 33 chapters, we presented readers with a thorough analysis of minority voting blocs' participation in U.S. elections. Here, we summarize the findings and place the information in a more general, theoretical context from which we attempt to predict minority voters' influence, collectively, on future U.S. elections.

WHAT IS A MINORITY GROUP AND WHY SHOULD THEY BE STUDIED?

A fundamental assumption we and our authors make when discussing minority voters is that the reader understands the concept of minority group. But for those who were confused or uncertain about how minority group is defined, we employed a definition originally developed by Ralph Linton.[1] The dominant group in a society ascribes a group a lower societal status because the minority groups' members exhibit one or more physical or behavioral characteristics that are different from the dominant groups' characteristics. The dominant group imposes the designation to affirm its power over the other groups in the society. For example, all people are *Homo sapiens*, which makes all people the same; however, if a society's dominant group has white skin, and if white people identify people with a skin color other than white as different, then white people are ascribing (or defining) people with different skin colors to a minority group and, very likely, to a lower social status. Note that the dominant group need not constitute a numerical majority within the society, but it does determine what characteristics differentiate members of the society from the dominant group, thereby assuring its dominant position. An excellent example is South Africa, where the white minority's Apartheid policies subjugated a much larger black population.

In the United States, the dominant group historically was white, Christian, heterosexual men, which begins to explain how U.S. society came to identify women, non-Christian, nonwhite people, and people whose sexual orientation is not heterosexual, as minorities. Though ascription to a minority status does not assure that a minority group will experience discrimination, either de jure or de facto,[2] the correlation between minority status and discriminatory treatment is high.

As discussed in the introduction, we undertook this study of minority voters to understand their patterns of political participation, especially their voting behavior. But why should anyone be interested in how minority members vote? There are two excellent reasons. First, all social scientists are fascinated by distinct and unique groups within a society or culture in order to understand the group's members' thoughts and actions, or stated differently, there is intrinsic interest and value in studying minority groups. In the natural sciences, this is considered basic research and is widely accepted and valued. Second, and more relevant to our project, we seek to understand and predict the voting behavior of minority groups in order to produce generalizations that may lead to a theory of minority voting behavior. The increasing numbers of minority voters and their impact on the 2008 and 2012 presidential elections strongly suggest that minority voters are, and will continue to be, a significant force in future local, state, and national elections.

Indeed, William H. Frey[3] uncovered four trends in his study of immigration's effects on America's racial composition using 2010 U.S. Census data that confirm their growing political influence. First, Latino, Hispanic, Asian, and multiracial populations are expanding dramatically because of immigration, minority groups' higher birth rates, and increasing numbers of interracial marriage.

Second, whites are aging faster and their birth rates are declining more steeply than immigrants, who are younger and have higher fertility rates. Third, the slow expansion of the black middle class and the reverse migration of blacks to the South, for example, North Carolina and Georgia, suggest that Southern states may not be as reliably Republican as they have been since 1980. And fourth, by mid-21st century, there will be no single racial group that is a majority of the U.S. population.

MINORITIES IN THE UNITED STATES: A BRIEF OVERVIEW

E Pluribus Unum—out of many, one—is the unofficial motto of the United States that appears on currency and the Seal of the United States.

Though originally intended as a way of expressing the unity of the 13 sovereign and different colonies, the phrase evolved to capture the image of the United States as a melting pot, a country that absorbs people of all races, colors, and creeds, and assimilates them into the nation's identity. In the nation's earliest days, the vast majority of the population was white and of European origin. There were Native Americans, of course, and blacks, but the former were never considered citizens and the latter were slaves, and therefore, ineligible for citizenship. There is a certain irony with the motto, then, when one considers that not long after the Declaration of Independence was announced, and certainly by the time of the adoption of the Constitution of 1787, a dominant group, namely white, Protestant men of some financial means, emerged and ascribed those who were not like them to be minorities and imposed limits on their behavior, particularly their political participation.[4] As an obvious example, the franchise in nearly every state was extended only to white, male, property owners who were 21 years or older. In a few states, only Christians, but not Catholics, could vote. Freed blacks, women, and Native Americans were conspicuously excluded from the franchise, and in some states, were also legally barred from certain occupations, property ownership, and the like.

The nation endured a Civil War to free the slaves and give blacks full citizenship and rights, while women finally achieved the franchise in 1920 with the Nineteenth Amendment. But waves of new immigrants arrived during the 19th and 20th Centuries, initially bringing mostly Europeans, who were predominantly white, but also people of color from Latin and South America and Asia. As their numbers swelled and immigrants became voting citizens, the states adapted their voting rules to exclude the newcomers, but eventually, the white, non-native-born Americans received the vote. Not until the 1965 Voting Rights Act and its subsequent amendments were citizens of color guaranteed the right to vote, though having the right and actually exercising the right were not the same. Minority groups, as our authors argue, continue to fight for full access to the polls and equal status as citizens.

Unaddressed in the discussion thus far are those minority groups who lived in America before the colonists arrived (Native Americans), were born in the United States but made citizens under a treaty's terms (Mexican Americans in 1848), were born in the United States territory of Puerto Rico, or who by virtue of their sexual identity (lesbian, gay, bisexual, and transgender Americans) experienced discrimination. These groups span the nation's history, and demonstrate again that a dominant group can impose its will on others in a society or political system and exclude them. As the chapters on each group reveal, each group's members struggled to be recognized and to achieve equal political rights with the dominant group. In a number of cases, their struggles continue.

THREE COMMON THEMES

As we considered the essays in their entirety, three themes emerged. First, all the minority groups faced discrimination at the hands of the dominant group, whether social, political, or in most cases, both, and the experience of discrimination deeply affected the groups' members. Native Americans, women, African Americans and other people of color, non-Christians, and nonheterosexuals suffered discriminatory practices at the hands of the dominant white, male majority. Initially, most minority groups accepted their lower status, however grudgingly, but eventually challenged the establishment and demanded equality under the law and in practice. Depending on the group, the struggle for equality took years, a few decades or many decades before achieving some success.

The second theme is that most minority group members favor liberal social and political policies, and tend to view government, especially the federal government, as a positive force in their lives. As of 2014, they are more likely to support the Affordable Care and Patient Protection Act of 2010 (otherwise known as Obamacare), social welfare programs, federal regulations of financial institutions, which some translate as opposition to America's capitalist system, reproductive rights, raising taxes, and affirmative action.[5] This theme holds true for native-born minorities and foreign-born minorities.

A corollary to this theme is that the Democratic Party's liberal positions make it more likely to attract more minority voters than the Republican Party's policy positions. More will be said of this in the following section.

Many minority group members who are citizens are either not registered to vote or, if registered, do not vote regularly. This theme is particularly apparent for members of several large minority groups, such as Mexican Americans, Latinos, and many of the Asian American groups. The authors note this behavior and the repercussions for their respective group's current and future political influence. The implications of the choice not to participate in elections are profound, as candidates and their parties are accurately aware of which constituent groups vote and how reliable their voters are. When any group, but particularly minority groups, fail to exercise their vote, the group is much less likely to have its important issues addressed by the government, regardless of the level of the government.

IMPLICATIONS FOR THE DEMOCRATIC AND REPUBLICAN PARTIES AND FUTURE ELECTIONS

The 2008 and 2012 presidential elections placed in stark relief the critical significance of minority voting blocs for future presidential candidates as they strategize to reach 270 Electoral College votes. Both Obama victories would not have been possible had he not carried states like California, Iowa, North Carolina, Florida, and Colorado in 2008 and the same states minus North Carolina in 2012, which have high concentrations of minority voters. As noted earlier, the Census Bureau predicts that by mid-21st century (approximately 2042), the U.S. population will not have a majority racial group; however, as the growth of several minority populations is concentrated in a few states, such as Texas, Arizona, and Nevada, their potential to dominate electorally will be felt as early as 2025. Eventually, all electoral candidates will need to be ready and able to address minority voting blocs' important issues. How the parties' candidates, and the parties as organizations, respond to the challenge remains to be seen. What follows is an analysis of the practical options for each party, beginning with the Democrats.

The Democratic Party appears to benefit most from the increasing numbers of minority voters, given the general preference of a majority of minority group members for liberal social and economic policies and government action to protect their rights. Such was clearly the case in the 2008 and 2012 presidential elections, and many political commentators anticipated a near future in which Democrats continued to hold the White House, while Republicans maintained control of the Congress, with a more distant future in which the Democrats ruled over both branches. Such visions were based on the idea that Obama had forged a new coalition of voting consistencies from the remnants of the old New Deal coalition, one that could be sustained over decades, just as FDR's had.

During his four terms as president, Franklin D. Roosevelt assembled the New Deal coalition, named after FDR's policy agenda, and at its peak, it contained the following groups (all of which were minorities, except for the South—the former Confederate States): the South, union workers, Catholics, Jews, ethnic minorities/foreign-born immigrants, farmers, and blacks. Each group, with the possible exception of the South,[6] experienced social and/or political discrimination by the dominant group, and sought relief from government. When individual state governments proved unwilling or unable to offer assistance, Roosevelt's Progressive philosophy, which he infused in the Democratic Party's platform and implemented as far as he could while in office, transformed his party. Democrats were viewed as defenders of the underdogs, the less fortunate, the "little people," and their coalition successfully elected presidents and members of Congress in both houses over nearly 50 years.

Ronald Reagan's election in 1980 marked the New Deal coalition's end, and the Democratic Party struggled to assemble another winning alliance of disparate groups. Obama's coalition is constructed of the following minority groups: women, particularly younger, single and those who lead a single-parent household; blacks; and other people of color, especially foreign-born citizens, Jews, Muslims, union workers (now more white collar than blue collar), and members of the LGBT community. Though together their total number does not equal a numerical majority of the American electorate, these groups have twice played a significant role in electing a president because they are concentrated in electorally rich states. Obama did, however, need to attract white, male voters as well, particularly in Northern states.

Should the Democrats feel secure that this new coalition will indeed guarantee continued success at the polls? The 2014 mid-term elections undermined any confidence that Democrats may have had in the ability of the coalition to deliver victory. Though Obama's unpopularity at the time clearly contributed to the Democrat's loss of control of the Senate and a large loss of House seats, low turnout by the coalition's elements also played a significant role. As noted earlier among the themes, minority voters tend not to register or vote in large numbers; the 2014 elections exhibited the risk of building an electoral coalition on a shaky foundation. For the Democrats to make their coalition's members' participation more predictable, the Party must continue to engage in voter education and mobilization drives. It must also continue to advance a platform that calls for immigration reform that makes citizenship a possibility for at least some of the illegal immigrants now in the United States, because the *legal* minority citizens, who are related to the illegals, view this as an important issue when they vote. Obama's executive action on the matter in 2014 was a step in this direction.

The discussion thus far has focused exclusively on presidential elections, but Democrats have also done very well in states and communities where minorities are concentrated. The chapters on Muslim Americans in the Detroit metropolitan area, Asian Americans in the San Francisco Bay area, and Native Americans in Washington provide examples. As minorities spread to new communities, such as North Carolina, and increase their numbers and voter registration rates where they currently reside, for example, Texas and Nevada, the Democratic Party can expect to improve its competitiveness and increase its strength.

With so many minority voters apparently predisposed to support Democratic candidates, what steps should the Republican Party take to win over these citizens? Divisions within the Republicans' ranks as of 2014 between "Establishment Republicans" and "Tea Party Republicans" make the task difficult but not impossible.

Establishment Republicans understand the challenges that confront their party as they attempt to appeal to minorities, especially native- and foreign-born immigrants. Their congressional leaders are amenable to immigration reform that offers some opportunity for citizenship for illegals, as well as adapting some policy positions to accommodate the specific needs of immigrant citizens, especially as they relate to improving the nation's economic climate. In the 2014 elections, the Party recruited candidates for federal and state offices who were able to speak to the issues important to immigrant citizens and win their votes, such as Greg Abbott who won the Texas gubernatorial election in 2014.

For many of the minority groups studied in this book, the authors found that group members ranked issues such as jobs and the economy, health care, national security, as important as white voters. Therefore, if Establishment Republicans modified their positions on these issues slightly to appeal to minority voters while also engaging in voter education programs, they improve their chances of winning minority support. It is when the GOP emphasizes its opposition to immigration reform in what appears as a race-baiting manner or when it criticizes minority communities as sources of gangs and criminal activity, as presidential candidate Donald Trump did in June 2015, it alienates minority voters and drives them to the Democratic Party.[7] Republicans must practice greater racial, ethnic, gender, and religious sensitivity if they hope to convince minority voters that their Party is genuinely interested in them.

Another strategy open to Establishment Republicans is to push hard in states where the population is aging and white, and where minorities make up a smaller percentage of the total population, like Pennsylvania, and attract Democratic voters who have become disillusioned with their Party's positions on immigration reform or Obamacare. This may be a much more perilous strategy, however, as it may marginalize the Party with future immigrant voters in those states as they migrate to replace the aging, whites who will eventually die.

The Tea Party wing of the Republican Party is more problematic. It consistently opposes any immigration reform as "amnesty" for illegal immigrants, and its fiscal conservatism and antigovernment positions make it much less attractive to nearly all the minority groups discussed in this book. Among its more extreme positions is limiting the number of *legal* immigrants entering the United States as soon as possible by changing the immigration quotas by statute.[8] It is difficult to imagine that Tea Party Republicans will ever change their positions, but instead expect minority voters in time to come to accept their values and positions. We believe this is unrealistic.

Ultimately, until the Republican Party can resolve its internal differences, it will find it difficult to make consistent and coherent appeals to minority voters, whether women, blacks, or other people of color. If the Tea Party wing eventually dissolves or is outmaneuvered in primaries by the Establishment wing during the 2016 election cycle, Republicans may be able to position themselves to make greater inroads with minority voters in 2016 and beyond. As a complementary strategy at the state level where the Party controls state legislatures and governorships, Republicans sponsored, and in most instances passed, voting rule changes that make it more difficult for some minorities, especially people of color or those who are transgender, to vote by requiring photo identification and shortening the available days and times when ballots may be cast. Such obstacles work, but may prove costly in the long run, as those affected minority group voters will remember who created the barriers when they finally reach the polls.

It is eminently clear to us that minority voting blocs are important elements within America's electorate in 2014, and as their numbers grow, their significance and influence will expand proportionately in the future. We hope that this book gave the reader insight to people who compose the minority voting blocs reviewed here—the issues that motivate them to participate in our democracy—and how their participation in America's civic life enlivens and enriches us all.

NOTES

1. Linton, *Study of Man*.
2. *De jure*—"by law" discrimination that occurs with the authority of the state/government. *De facto*—discrimination that occurs by custom or norms within a society unsupported by statutes or law.
3. Frey, *Diversity Explosion*.
4. For a critical review of U.S. history from the people's perspective, see Zinn, *People's History of the United States*.
5. Hawley, "Liberalizing Immigration Will Liberalize the U.S."
6. It may be argued by residents of the former Confederacy that they suffered discrimination at the hands of the North during Reconstruction.
7. Donald Burns, Pushing Someone Rich, Offers Himself.
8. See the Eagle Forum, *How Mass (Legal) Immigration Dooms a Conservative Republican Party*.

REFERENCES

Burns, Alexander. (2015) "Donald Trump, Pushing Someone Rich, Offers Himself." Referenced on line July 20, 2015. http://www.nytimes.com/2015/06/17/us/politics/donald-trump-runs-for-president-this-time-for-real-he-says.html?_r=0

Eagle Forum. *How Mass (Legal) Immigration Dooms a Conservative Republican Party*. Washington, DC: The Eagle Forum, 2014.

Frey, William H. *Diversity Explosion: How New Racial Demographics Are Remaking America*. Washington, DC: The Brookings Institution, 2015.

Hawley, George. "Liberalizing Immigration Will Liberalize the U.S." *Real Clear Policy*. 2013. 16 December 2014. http://www.realclearpolicy.com/articles/2013/10/24/liberalizing_immigration_will_liberalize_the_us.html.

Linton, Ralph. *Study of Man*. New York: Appleton-Century-Crofts, Inc, 1936.

Zinn, Howard. *People's History of the United States*. New York: Harper & Row, 1980.

About the Editors and Contributors

THOMAS J. BALDINO is a professor of political science at Wilkes University. His teaching and research interests include legislative politics, parties and elections, and Pennsylvania government and politics. He was a faculty associate to the Legislative Office of Research Liaison of the PA House of Representatives and currently serves as the associate editor of *Commonwealth*, the journal of the Pennsylvania Political Science Association. With Kyle L. Kreider, he has published *Of the People, By the People, For the People: A Documentary Record of Voting Rights and Electoral Reform* (2010) and *U.S. Election Campaigns: A Documentary and Reference Guide* (2011). He is currently at work on *Pennsylvania Government and Politics: Unlocking the Keystone State* with Paula Holoviak to be published in the fall of 2016.

KYLE L. KREIDER is an associate professor of political science at Wilkes University. His teaching and research interests include the Supreme Court, civil rights and civil liberties, and courts' use of social science. He has coauthored two books with Thomas Baldino, *Of the People, By the People, For the People: A Documentary Record of Voting Rights and Electoral Reform* (2010) and *U.S. Election Campaigns: A Documentary and Reference Guide* (2011). In addition to teaching and research responsibilities, Dr. Kreider also serves as Wilkes University's coordinating pre-law advisor.

SAMUEL J. ABRAMS is a political scientist with interests in political behavior and culture. He is professor of politics and social science at Sarah Lawrence College and is a research fellow at the Hoover Institution at

Stanford University. His current research interests involve the understanding of "red/blue divide" in the United States and mapping Jewish community political and electoral behavior. He is also at work on a number of projects exploring ideology and partisanship. Sam was recently named as one of the United States' "40 under 40" professors, and though he lives in New York City, he still roots for the Red Sox!

MAYA BERRY is executive director of the Arab American Institute, a nonprofit, nonpartisan, national leadership organization created in 1985 to nurture and encourage the direct participation of Arab Americans in political and civic life in the United States. With a passion for issues that concern Arab Americans and U.S.-Arab relations, Berry previously served as the legislative director for House Minority Whip David E. Bonior (D-MI) and started her career in public service working for ACCESS, the nation's oldest and largest Arab American human services nonprofit.

PEGGY SPITZER CHRISTOFF is a lecturer in the Department of Asian and Asian American Studies at Stony Brook University. She received her doctorate in international relations from the American University in Washington, D.C. Her publications include *Tracking the Yellow Peril: The INS and Chinese Immigrants in the Midwest* and "Key Statistics on Voting Behavior among Asian Americans" for the East-West Center's *Asia Matters for America* project.

STEVEN M. COHEN is research professor of Jewish social policy at HUC-JIR, and director of the Berman Jewish Policy Archive at NYU Wagner. In 1992 he made aliyah and taught at The Hebrew University, having previously taught at Queens College, Yale, and Jewish Theological Seminary of America. His books include *The Jew Within* (with Arnold Eisen) and *Two Worlds of Judaism: The Israeli and American Experience* (with Charles Liebman). He received an honorary doctorate from the Spertus Institute of Jewish Studies, the Marshall Sklare Award, and a National Jewish Book Award. He serves as president of the Association for the Social Scientific Study of Jewry.

ANDREW R. FLORES is director of Public Opinion Project at the Williams Institute, UCLA School of Law. His recently completed dissertation project at the University of California at Riverside examines how varying social and political environments condition the political attitudes and behaviors of the mass public and of LGBT people. His current and ongoing research projects build upon his previous work on LGBT politics.

JOAQUIN JAY GONZALEZ III, PhD, is Mayor George Christopher Professor of Government and Russell T. Sharpe Professor of Business at the

Ageno School of Business at Golden Gate University. For close to a decade, Dr. Gonzalez served as commissioner for immigrant rights with the City and County of San Francisco. He has published extensively, has served as a consultant for many governmental and nongovernmental organizations, and is a media commentator on Philippine politics and immigration issues.

JEANETTE YIH HARVIE received her PhD in political science from the University of California, Santa Barbara, in 2014. Her major research interests are in U.S. identity politics. Specifically, her dissertation addressed the theoretical link between acts of military service and concepts of citizenship for Asian American veterans and service members.

DEEPA IYER is the former executive director of South Asian Americans Leading Together, a national nonprofit organization dedicated to addressing issues affecting South Asian communities through a social justice lens. She is the Activist-in-Residence at the University of Maryland's Asian American Studies Program (2014–2015). Deepa's essays on immigration, civil rights, and post-9/11 America have been featured in a variety of publications including *The Nation*, *The New York Times*, and *USA Today*. She is working on a book about multiracial America to be published by The New Press.

BRUCE E. JOHANSEN is Jacob J. Isaacson Professor of Communication and Native American Studies at the University of Nebraska at Omaha, where he has been teaching and writing since 1982. He has authored 39 books, the most recent being *Up from the Ashes: Nation-Building at Muckleshoot* (2014). He writes frequently about environmental subjects, including *The Encyclopedia of Global Warming Science and Technology* (2 vols., 2009), *Global Warming in the 21st century* (3 vols., 2006), *The Global Warming Desk Reference* (2001), *The Dirty Dozen: Toxic Chemicals and the Earth's Future* (2003), and *Indigenous Peoples and Environmental Issues* (2004), a 200,000-word encyclopedia of indigenous peoples' struggles with corporations with a worldwide scope. He also writes as a journalist in several national forums, including *The Washington Post* and *The Progressive*. He is coeditor of the *Encyclopedia of American Indian History*, (4 vols., ABC-CLIO, 2007), as well as the *Handbook of Contemporary Native American Issues* (2 vols., Praeger, 2007). His *Eco-Hustle! Global Warming, Greenwashing, and Sustainability* was published in April 2015.

JAMES S. LAI is an associate professor who holds a joint appointment with the Ethnic Studies Program and the Department of Political Science at Santa Clara University. His teaching and research interests and specialties include U.S. racial and ethnic politics, U.S. immigration, Asian American politics, urban politics, community studies, and California state and local politics. In 2011, Dr. Lai published his book *Asian American Political Action: Suburban Transformations* (Lynne Rienner Publishers), which examines the demographic shifts and the rise of Asian American political incorporation in small- to medium-size suburbs throughout the continental United States. Dr. Lai has commentated in state, national, and international media such as National Public Radio's "California Report" and "Forum," the *San Jose Mercury News*, the *San Francisco Chronicle*, *China Daily News*, *World Journal*, the *New York Times*, and CNN.

DR. LOAN K. LE is the president and CEO of the Institute for Good Government and Inclusion, a domestic public policy think tank conducting research and education into four domains of interest: (1) the rule of law, (2) respect for persons, (3) transparency in government, and (4) democratic inclusion. She previously served as director of research at UC Berkeley's Center for Latino Policy Research and as visiting assistant professor at UCLA in the Department of Political Science and in the Department of Asian American Studies.

PEI-TE LIEN is professor of political science and of Asian American studies and feminist studies at the University of California, Santa Barbara. Her primary research interest is the political participation and representation of Asian and other nonwhite Americans. She is author of *The Making of Asian America through Political Participation* (2001), lead author of *The Politics of Asian Americans: Diversity and Community* (2004), and coeditor of *The Transnational Politics of Asian Americans* (2009).

GLENN D. MAGPANTAY, Esq., is the director of the democracy program at the Asian American Legal Defense and Education Fund (AALDEF). He has represented Asian American voters in several voting rights lawsuits and briefs to the U.S. Supreme Court. He oversees AALDEF's Asian American Election Protection efforts and multilingual exit poll in 15 states. He attended New England School of Law and graduated cum laude after being admitted as an affirmative action beneficiary.

YOON M. LEE, PhD, graduated from the Seoul National University, Seoul Methodist Theological Seminary, South Korea, and earned MA and PhD degrees in sociology from Loyola University Chicago. He briefly taught courses on race and ethnicity and research methodology at the School of Social Work of the Loyola University Chicago for the 1997–1998 academic year. He has served as the chief editor of the *Korea Times of Chicago* since 1972, and is actively involved in the city's Korean community. He is affiliated with the Hansa Institute of Chicago, a nonprofit research organization, which he founded in 2005. He retired from the Illinois Department of Human Rights after 15 years of service as the chief of research, planning and development in 2007. He wrote reports including *Home Mortgage Lending Patterns in the Chicago MSA, Sexual Harassment in Illinois,* and *Hate Crimes involving Asian Americans.* He authored the book *Seventy Years' History: 1923–1993, The First Korean United Methodist Church of Chicago* in 1995.

PATRICK A. PASCHALL is a senior policy counsel at the National LGBTQ Task Force where he advances policy priorities in federal agencies and at the White House, and provides technical assistance to national, state, and local partners on policies benefiting the lives of lesbian, gay, bisexual, and transgender people. Patrick is a member and union delegate for Service Employees International Union, Local 1199, and was also elected in 2013 to the City Council in Hyattsville, Maryland.

JURIS PUPCENOKS, PhD, is an assistant professor of political science at Marist College, Poughkeepsie, NY. A specialist in international relations and comparative politics, Dr. Pupcenoks received his MA and PhD degrees at the University of Delaware. He previously taught at the University of Delaware and Washington College, MD. He has conducted field research in Muslim communities in the United Kingdom, Italy, and the United States, and published in journals including *Nationalism and Ethnic Politics, Middle East Journal,* and *Journal of Muslim Minority Affairs.* His research has been supported by grants and awards from the International Studies Association, University of Delaware, and Marist College. Currently, his main research focus is on completing a book manuscript analyzing reactive conflict spillover to migrant communities.

JENNIFER L. ROBINSON serves as the director for the Center for Public Policy & Administration at the University of Utah. She has done extensive research on elections, political participation, and governance. She coauthored *Native Vote: American Indians, the Voting Rights Act, and the Right to Vote* and was coeditor of *Rise of the West in Presidential Elections.* Working with her team at the Center, she has supervised dozens of applied research projects to improve governance at the local, state, and national levels. In 2014, she was appointed by Governor Herbert to the Women in the Economy Commission and also serves as a member of the Salt Lake Chamber's Capitol Club and cochairs the University of Utah's Veterans Day Committee.

FARID SENZAI is an assistant professor of political science at Santa Clara University where he teaches courses on U.S. foreign policy and Middle East politics. He is also a fellow at the Institute for Social Policy and Understanding in Washington D.C. Dr. Senzai was previously a research associate at the Brookings Institution and a research analyst at the Council on

Foreign Relations. He served as a consultant for Oxford Analytica and the World Bank. Dr. Senzai is on the board of advisers at The Pew Forum on Religion and Public Life. He coauthored *Educating the Muslims of America* (Oxford University Press, 2009). His most recent book is *Political Islam in the Age of Democratization* (Palgrave Macmillan, 2013). Dr. Senzai received his MA in international affairs from Columbia University and PhD in politics and international relations from Oxford University.

KENNETH SHERRILL is professor emeritus of political science at Hunter College, CUNY, specializing in public opinion, political participation, voting, and elections as well as LGBT politics. He has been studying the political behavior of LGBT people since 1972. Long active in electoral politics, he became New York's first openly gay elected official in 1977.

IRA M. SHESKIN, PhD, is professor and chair of the Geography Department and the director of the Jewish Demography Project of the Sue and Leonard Miller Center for Contemporary Judaic Studies, both at the University of Miami. Dr. Sheskin has completed 43 major Jewish community studies for Jewish federations throughout the country. He has also been a consultant to numerous synagogues, Jewish day schools, Jewish elderly housing, Jewish agencies, and Jewish community centers throughout the country. Dr. Sheskin was a member of the committee that completed both the 1990 and 2000–2001 National Jewish Population Surveys. His publications include *Survey Research for Geographers*, *How Jewish Communities Differ*, and *Comparisons of Jewish Communities: A Compendium of Tables and Bar Charts*. He is the editor of the *American Jewish Year Book* and is the author of numerous articles on Jewish demography, including the annual article on Jewish demography, which appears in the *American Jewish Year Book* and at http://www.jewishdatabank.org.

PHI HONG SU is a PhD candidate in the Department of Sociology at UCLA. Her research interests include international migration and politics, with a particular focus on resocialization after regime change.

BARRY L. TADLOCK is an associate professor of political science at Ohio University. He is the coeditor, with Ellen D. B. Riggle, of *Gays and Lesbians in the Political Process: Public Policy, Public Opinion, and Political Representation* (Columbia University Press, 1999). He has authored and coauthored numerous book chapters concerning various LGBT issues, the most recent of which can be found in *Transgender Rights and Politics: Groups, Issue Framing, & Policy Adoption* (Jami K. Taylor & Donald P. Haider-Markel, editors, University of Michigan Press, 2014). Other research interests include the impact of 1990s-era welfare reforms and congressional elections, with publications in journals including the *Legislative Studies Quarterly*, *Journal of Children and Poverty*, *American Review of Politics*, *Politics and Policy*, *Affilia: Journal of Women and Social Work*, and *Public Administration Quarterly*.

RICHARD C. WITMER, PhD, is an associate professor of political science at Creighton University, Omaha, Nebraska. His research and teaching focuses on American Indian politics, policy, and law as well as American politics. His work has appeared in numerous journals including the *Journal of Politics*, *Political Research Quarterly*, *PS: Political Science and Politics*, and *Social Science Quarterly*. He is coauthor of *Forced Federalism: Contemporary Challenges to Indigenous Nationhood* (University of Oklahoma Press, 2011).

Index

Note: Page numbers in *italics* followed by *f* indicate figures and by *t* indicate tables.

Abrams, Samuel J., 95, 439–40
ACT UP, 381
Adair, James, 28
Affordable Care Act and Patient Protection Act (2010, Obamacare): Filipino Americans and, 280; Native Americans and, 48; "Opinions of Asian Americans and Pacific Islanders: Affordable Care Act" (NAAS), 364; support of by minorities, 434
African American Muslims, 157–59, 161–65, 170, 180, 190
African Americans: Asian Americans' solidarity with, 227–28; Black Prides Survey (National Gay and Lesbian Task Force Policy Institute, 2000)/LGBT people, 411–12
Alamin, Jamil Abdullah (H. Rap Brown), 161
Allen, George, 242
American-Arab Anti-Discrimination Committee, 141
American Civil Liberties Union, 141
American Community Survey (ACS), annual Filipino American and Asian American annual income demographics, 269

American Indian Movement, 33
American Indian voters, history of voting rights, 3–25; background, 3–4; citizenship for, 5–10; Civil Rights Act (1866), 5–6; Fourteenth and Fifteenth Amendments and *Elk v. Wilkins*, 6–8, 13; Indian Citizenship Act (1924), 3, 7–8; literacy tests/states with, 9, *11t*, 13; Marshall Trilogy (*Johnson v. M'Intosh, Cherokee Nation v. Georgia, Worcester v. Georgia*), 4–5; methods to prevent Indians from voting, 8–10; multimember districts, challenges to, 13–16; states prohibiting voting rights, 8–9; Trade and Intercourse Acts (1790–1834), 4; U.S. Constitution references to legal status of American Indians, 3–4; Voting Rights Act (1965) and Supreme Court rulings, 3, 10–17; Voting Rights Act (1965) impact on American Indians, 18–19. *See also* American Indian voting issues; Native American voters, sovereignty and treaty rights

American Indian voting issues, 41–57; 2012 Native Vote, 47–48; acts, 47–48; background/examples/landscape, 41–42; bills lobbied on by California tribes (2000–2004), *50t*; Carlson, Kirsten Matoy on, 49–51; conclusion, 54–55; Corntassel, Jeff and Richard Witmer survey, 46, *47t*; demographics, 43, 44–46, *47t*; federal government and, 43–44; gaming, 43, *50t*, 51–54; Gorton, Slade (Washington state) and, 41–42; Heitkamp, Heidi (North Dakota) and, 42, 54; Indian Self-Determination and Educational Assistance Act (1975)/self-determination, 44; issue diversity, 42–44; in state legislatures, 48–54, *50t*; Stubben, Jerry survey, 45–46, *47t*; treaty-based rights, 43. *See also* American Indian voters, history of voting rights; Native American voters, sovereignty and treaty rights

American Jewish Committee's (AJC) annual survey of American Jewish Public Opinion, 62–63

American Jewish Year Book (2000), 68, 70

American Muslim Taskforce on Civil Rights and Elections, 166

American National Election Study (2008), 63

American Recovery and Reinvestment Act, 280

American Samoa, historical context, 252–53. *See also* Pacific Islander (Native Hawaiian and Pacific Islander, NHPI) voters

Androgynous people, 409

Arab American Institute, 141

The Arab American News, 142

Arab American Political Action Committee, 141

Arab American voters, 127–54; 2000 presidential election, 133–34; 2004 presidential election, 135; 2008 presidential election, 136–38; 2012 presidential election, 132, 138–39; demographics/countries from/states residing in, 127–29, *130f*, 142–43; disenfranchisement/voter intimidation, 135–43; emotional ties to family's country of origin, *144f*; ethnic pride and issues, 132; immigration waves (three), 127–29; importance of U.S. policy in Middle East in determining congressional votes, *146f*; importance of U.S. policy in Middle East in determining presidential votes, *145f*; issues, 143–47, *143f–46f*; language barrier, 134–35; Michigan, 133, 136, 137, 149; Minnesota, 148; New Jersey, 149; party identification, 132–33, *133f*; political participation, 131; post-9/11, 129, 135–36, 164–68, 170–71, 179; profiling of, 140–43; Texas, 147; Virginia, 149; Washington state, 148. *See also* Muslim American political incorporation and mobilization; Muslim Americans in Detroit

Arab and Muslim American voters. *See* Arab American voters; Muslim American political incorporation and mobilization; Muslim Americans in Detroit

Arizona Indian Voter's Convention, 41

Asian American annual income demographics (ACS), 269

Asian American Justice Center, 251

Asian American Legal Defense and Education Fund (AALDEF), "Asian American Vote in 2012," 364–65

Asian American Legal Defense and Education Fund (AALDEF) exit polls, 206; South Asian Americans, 238–39. *See also* Asian American voting rights

Asian Americans in the San Francisco Bay Area, 304–25; Bay Area as the epicenter of Asian American political incorporation, 307–11; Board of Supervisors (BOS), 308, 311–16; conclusion, 321–22; counties in the Bay Area, 307; Democratic County Central Committee (DCCC), 311–12; demographics in the Bay Area and Los Angeles, 305; ethnic diversity of the Bay Asian and Pacific Islander population (2010), 310–12, *310t*; ethnoburbs of Silicon Valley—political incorporation in Cupertino, Santa Clara County, 316–19; Filipino American organizations in the Bay Area, *277t*; intersection 1. race and geopolitical space, 313–14; intersection 2. identity and ideology, 314–15; Lee, Ed, (first Asian American elected San Francisco mayor, 2011), 311–12, 315–16; new challenges to the South Bay Asian American coalition, 320–21; Santa Clara County cities by race (2010), *317t*

"Asian American Vote in 2012" (AALDEF), 364–65

Asian American voters/voting rights, 205–37; 2010 and 2012 vote, 305–7; Asian American Legal Defense and Education Fund (AALDEF), 206; Asian American voter—trending toward the Democratic Party, 305–7; background of political behavior and participation and the Asian American Legal Defense and Education Fund (AALDEF) exit polls, 219–20; congressional elections (Senate and House of Representatives), 224, *225t–26t*, 226–27; demographics by U.S. states, 305; demographics of Asians in American suburbs, 304; election day discrimination, 206–8; English proficiency by language group, *220f*; exit poll results, November 6, 2012 (AALDEF), *210t–11t*; general demographics/growing segment of the electorate, 220–21; Hamtramck, Michigan voting violations (1999) and, 240–41; history of exclusion/court cases, 205–6; Language Assistance Provisions of the Voting Rights Act (Section 203), 208–9, *212t*, 214, 214–18; multilingual exit poll, November 2012: language minority groups, *213–14t*; multilingual exit poll, November 2012 (AALDEF), *209f*; NAAS surveys voting, 306–7; "Opinions of Asian Americans and Pacific Islanders: Affordable Care Act" (NAAS), 364; party enrollment by ethnicity, *221f*; political campaigns, 207–8; poll sites on election day, 206–7; poll workers' disparaging remarks, 206–7; presidential elections, *222f*, *223f*, 221–24; solidarity with Blacks and Latinos, 227–28; summary and conclusion, 228–29. *See also* Headings under specific groups (in Table of Contents)

Baldino, Thomas J., 439
Behind the Mule: Race and Class in African American Politics (Dawson), 156, 163, 164
"Behind the Numbers, Post-Election Survey of Asian American and Pacific Islander Voters in 2012" (NAAS), 364
Berry, Maya, 127, 440
Bingo: Native Americans and, 51–52
Bisexual, defining, 371–72, 374. *See also* Lesbian, gay, bisexual, and transgender (LGBT) voters
Black Prides Survey (National Gay and Lesbian Task Force Policy Institute, 2000), 411–12
Boldt fishing-rights decision, 30, 35
Briggs Initiative (1978), 391

Bruce, Michelle, 419
Bryant, Anita, 374
Bureau of Indian Affairs, 28
Bush, George H.W., HIV/AIDS and, 376, 380
Bush, George W., 31, 34; Arab Americans and, 133–34, 135, 141–42, 163, 188
Byrd, James, Jr., 417

California v. Cabazon Band of Mission Indians, 52
Cantwell, Maria, 41
Carlson, Kirsten Matoy, 49–51
Carter, Jimmy, 131
Chae Chan Ping v. United States, 205
Cherokee Nation v. Georgia, 4–5
Chez, Joseph, 8–9
Chinese Americans. *See* East Asian American voters
Chinese Exclusion Act (1882), 284, 287
Chinese Exclusion Repeal Act (1943), 288
Christoff, Peggy Spitzer, 247, 440
Citizenship: for American Indians, 5–10
Civil Liberties Advisory Panel, 142
Civil Rights Act (1866): American Indian voters rights and, 5–6
Clinton, Bill: LGBT community and, 375, 376, 378
Clinton, Hillary: Indian (South Asia) Americans and, 243
Cohen, Steven M., 95, 440
Colonialism: American Indians and, 29–30
Computer-Assisted Passenger Screening (CAPS) system, 140, 142
Congress of Arab American Organizations, 187
Conyers, John, 149
Cooksey, John, 242
Corntassel, Jeff and Richard Witmer American Indian survey, 46, *47t*
Council on American Islamic Relations (CAIR), 163, 167–68
Crevecouer, Hector Saint John de, 27

Cross-dressers, 372, 409
Cupertino, Santa Clara County. *See* Asian Americans in the San Francisco Bay Area
Current Population Survey (2004): Taiwanese American naturalization rate, 291; Vietnamese American Voters, 350

Daughters of Bilitis (for lesbians), 373
Dawes Act (1887, General Allotment Act), 7
Dawson, Michael, "linked fate" in *Behind the Mule: Race and Class in African American Politics*, 156, 163, 164
Defense of Marriage Act (DOMA, 1996), 392
DellaPergola, Jewish survey, 68
Democratic Party, minority voters and implications for future elections, 434–38. *See also* Headings under specific minorities; Jewish American Voters
DeSipio, L., 155
DesiVote (Hindi ballots), 244
Detroit: *See* Muslim Americans in Detroit
Dingell, John, 149
Disenfranchisement. *See* Headings under specific minorities
Don't Ask/Don't Tell, 391
Dow v. United States, 206

East Asian American voters, 283–303; background, 283–84; Chinese Exclusion Act (1882), 284, 287; conclusion and outlook for, 298–300; demographics/ immigration from China, Japan, Korea, and Taiwan, 284, *285t*, 286–87; historical barriers to voting, 287–89; patterns of contemporary voting participation, 291–93, *292t*; patterns of historical voting behavior, 289–91; policy issues and ballot preferences, 296–298, *296t–98t*; political party

affiliation/partisanship, 293–95, *294t–95t*; voting and registration in November 2004 elections, *292t*
Egan, Patrick, 392, 394–95
Elk, John, 6–7, 29
Elk v. Wilkins, 6–7
Ellison, Keith, 148, 190, 242
Employment Nondiscrimination Act, 378
"Establishment Republicans," 436–37
"Ethnic community hypothesis," 342
Ethnoburbs. *See* Asian Americans in the San Francisco Bay Area

Fifteenth Amendment, Indian voting rights and, 7–8
FilAm voters. *See* Filipino American (FilAm) voting
Filipino American (FilAm) voters, 264–82; Affordable Care Act and the American Recovery and Investment Act, 280; annual income demographics (American Community Survey), 269; conclusion, 280–81; demographics (Census Bureau), 264, *265t*; discussion/analysis of the Filipino bloc's affiliation with one or more parties over time, 273–77; Filipino American election winners, *274t*; Filipino American WWII veterans marching for G.I. benefits, *279f*, 280; history of FilAm immigration and incorporation, 269–73; issues, 277–80, *278t*, *279f*; organization types in San Francisco Bay Area, *277t*; party identification, *276t*; Rescission Acts, 279–80; top 10 U.S. states with Filipino populations (Census Bureau), *266t*; in U.S. and major California counties, 268–69, *268t*; U.S. state department visa bulletin for February 2014, *278t*
First American Education Project (FAEP), 33, 35
Flores, Andrew R., 390, 440
Fourteenth Amendment: Indian voting rights and, 6–8, 13

Franklin, Benjamin, 28–29
FreedomOhio, 385
Frey, William H., four trends in study of immigration, 432

Gaming, Native American, 43, *50t*, 51–54
Garcia, F. C., *Pursuing Power: Latinos and the Political System*, 155
Garrison, Althea, 418–19
Gay Activists Alliance, 382
"Gay Is Good" (Kameny), 391
Gender identity, 410
Gender non-conforming people, 409
Genderqueers, 372, 409
General Allotment Act (1887, Dawes Act), 7
Georgia v. Ashcroft, 17
Gonzalez, Joaquin Jay, III, 264, 440–41
Gore, Al, 34; Arab American voters, 133–34, 142
Gorton, Slade: Amphitheatre (Washington State) debate, 34–36; reelection loss, 41–42
"Great White Father," 31–32
Ground Zero Mosque (Park 51), 170–71
Group consciousness, 342
Guam and the Northern Marianas, historical context, 251, 253–55. *See also* Pacific Islander (Native Hawaiian and Pacific Islander, NHPI) voters

Harrison v. Laveen, 9
Harvie, Jeanette Yih, 283, 441
Hate crimes legislation, 391
Hate Crimes Prevention Act (2009), 417
Hawaii, historical context, 251–52. *See also* Pacific Islander (Native Hawaiian and Pacific Islander, NHPI) voters
Hay, Harry, 391
Heitkamp, Heidi, 42, 54
Helping Expedite and Advance Responsible Tribal Home Ownership Act (2012, HEARTH Act), 48

Hispanic voting over time, *64f*
HIV/AIDS, 376, 381, 383, 390, 412
Hizb al-Tahrir and Khalifornia, 161
"Homeland pull" effect, Korean Americans and, 329, 338, 341–42
Human Rights Act (MN, 1993), 415

Immigration Act (1952), 288
Immigration and Naturalization Act (1965), 240
Indian Citizenship Act (1924), 3, 7–8
Indian Gaming Regulatory Act (1988), 51–53
Indian Health Service, 48
Indian Reorganization Act (1934), 28
Indian Self-Determination and Educational Assistance Act (1975), 44
In re Mozumdar, 240
Islamophobia, 164–65
Iyer, Deepa, 236, 441

Japanese Americans. *See* East Asian American voters
Jefferson, Thomas, 29
Jewish American voters, 61–94; American Jewish Committee's (AJC) annual survey of American Jewish Public Opinion, 62–63; *American Jewish Year Book* (2000), 68, 70; changes in Jewish population in the U.S. by census region and census division (1971–2014), 66–68, *67t*, 70; compared to Hispanic voters, 64, *64f*; conservative percentage by demography and religiosity, *81t*, 82–83, *83t*; data sources (summary), 62–63; DellaPergola, 68; demographics of Jewish and other ethnic voters, 61–64, *64f*; immigration from the former Soviet Union (FSU), 70, 86; Jewish Community Center (JCC) members, 79, 80; Jewish community studies sponsored by local Jewish federations, 62; Jewish culture and, 84, 88; Jewish Federations of North America (JFNA), 62; Jewish population in the U.S. by state (2014), *65t–66t*; Jewish population in top 20 Metropolitan Statistical Areas (MSAs, 2014), 68, *69t*; liberal percentage by demography and religiosity, 80–82, *81t*, *83t*; National Jewish Population Survey (NJPS), 62, 68, 72; Orthodox Jews, 75–77, *76t*, 86; part 1. reasons Jews play a significant role in American politics: geography and demography, 63–71, *64f*, *65t–66t*, *67t*, *69t*; part 2. political parties and political ideology of, 71–83, *73t*, *75f*, *76t*, *78f*, *81t*, *83t*; part 3. reasons most Jews continue to vote Democratic, 83–87; percentage of Democratic by demography and religiosity, 77–79; Pew Research Center Survey of Jewish Americans, 62; political party community comparisons, 72–74, *73t*; problems with national polls, 63; Republican voters, 74–77, *75f*, *76t*, *78f*, 79–80; self-identified partisanship (1972–2008), 74, *75f*; summary and conclusions, 87–88; synagogue members, 79, 80; telephone surveys, 61; *tikkun olam* and *tzedakah*, 84; views on Israel and, 86–87; voting Democratic in 2012, 86–87; Workmen's Circle/Arbeter Ring 2012 American Jews' Political Values Survey, 87. *See also* Jewish liberalism
Jewish Federations of North America (JFNA), 62
Jewish liberalism, 95–123; background, 95–98; conclusion, 122; ideology/attitudes/issues, 97, 103–7, *106f*, *107f*, 110–11, *111f*, *112f*; income and, *118t*, 119; intermarriage, 119, 120, *121t*, 122; liberal leanings across the board, 113–14, *115t*; notable points in 2012 survey, 104–5; Orthodox

exceptionalism, 111–12, *111f*, *112f*, 114, *115t*, 116, 122; partisanship and behavior, 98, 100–103, *99f–103f*; Pew Research Center Survey of Jewish Americans (2013), 62, 112–16, *115t*, *117t*, *118t*, 119, 120, *121t*; political variables by age, four groups, non-Orthodox only, *117t*; political variables by denomination, *115t*; slightly mounting liberalism among the youth, 116, *117t*, 119. *See also* Jewish American voters

Johansen, Bruce E., 26, 441

Johnson, Andrew, 5

Johnson, Tim, 33

Johnson v. M'Intosh, 4

Kameny, Frank, "Gay Is Good," 391

King, Peter, 138, 169

Korean American voters, 326–48; 2012 election voters, 334, *334t*; assimilation theory and, 326; conflicts, group consciousness, and voting, 342–43; delayed naturalization problem, 329; demographics/background, 326–28, *328t–31t*, 333–34, *334t*, 336–37, 340; dependent variable = electoral behavior, 327; eligible voters by state, *330t*; English proficiency and, 329, *331t*, 335, *336f*; future of voting behavior and power, 340–41, 343–44; Gordon's seven stages of assimilation model (used in this study), 327; growth of, 328–29, *329t*; immigration and population, *328t*; influence to the election outcome, 336–37; intra-networks and delay of civic identity, 341; Korean American organizations and, 332–33; Korean homeland issues and civic identity, 329, 338, 341–42; liberal issues and Democratic Party preference, 337–38, *337f*, *338t*; mobilization by political parties, 333; party affiliation/preferences, 339–41, *339t*; patterns of voting behavior by, 333–34; perceived discrimination as problem and voting, *343t*; political mobilization theory and, 326–27; problems encountered by, 331–32; removing language barriers (Voting Rights Act, Section 203), 332; socioeconomic resources and, 326–27, 335; studies of electoral behavior (U.S. Census and Pew Research 2012 Asian American Survey), 327–28; voter registration, *329t*, 334. *See also* East Asian American voters

Kreider, Kyle L., 439

LaHood, Ray, 140

Lai, James S., 304, 441–42

Language Assistance Provisions of the Voting Rights Act (Section 203), 208–9, 212, 214–18

Language barriers. *See* Headings under specific minorities

Latinos, Asian Americans' solidarity with, 227–28

Lee, Ed (San Francisco's first Asian American mayor, 2011), 311–12, 315–16

Lee, Sheila Jackson, 147

Lee, Yoon M., 326, 442–43

Le, Loan K., 349, 442

LEP. *See* Limited English proficient

Lesbian Avengers Civil Rights Organizing Project, 375

Lesbian, gay, bisexual, and transgender (LGBT) voters, 371–89; background/definitions/descriptions, 372–73; black LGBT voters (Black Prides Survey), 411–12; Colorado and, 375, 384; demographics, 372; disengaging and engaging, 377–78; enclaves, 377; forming a social movement and gaining access into the electoral arena, 373–74; future influence and behavior

of, 384–85; impact on electoral outcomes, 378–79; LGBT groups and their impact on voting, 382–84; at the local, state, and national levels, 374–77; Ohio and, 385; Oregon and, 375, 379, 383; political and social values associated with, 381–82; political parties and, 379–80; Stonewall raid, 373; voter identification requirements, 377; voting coalitions/shared issues of, 378. *See also* Same-sex marriage; Transgender voters
Liberalism, Jewish. *See* Jewish liberalism
Lien, Pei-te, 283, 442
Limited English proficient (LEP), 241
"Linked fate" (Dawson), 156, 163, 164
Linton, Ralph: defining minority groups, 431
Literacy tests: American Indians and, 9; ban on, 13
Lobbying, American Indians and, 36–37, 49, *50t*
Log Cabin Republicans, 376–77, 380
Luce-Celler Act (1946), 240
Lyons, Oren, 30–31

Magpantay, Glenn D., 205, 442
Majority-minority districts, LGBTs and, 377
Marissa, Marla, 419
Marriage equality. *See* Same-sex marriage
Marshall, John, 29
Marshall Trilogy (*Johnson v. M'Intosh, Cherokee Nation v. Georgia, Worcester v. Georgia*), 4–5
MAS Freedom Foundation, 166
Mattachine Society (for gay men), 373
McCain, John: Arab American vote and, 136–37; Muslims and, 243; South Asian American vote and, 244
McDermott, Jim, 148
McGovern, George, 131
Michigan, Arab Americans in, 149. *See also* Muslim Americans in Detroit

Milo, Donna, 419
Minnesota, Arab Americans in, 148
Minority voters—present and future (conclusion), 431–38; 1. discrimination theme, 434; 2. favor liberal social and political policies theme, 434; 3. choosing not to vote theme, 434; defining/studying, 431–32; four trends (Frey), 432; historical background, 432–33; implications for the Democratic and Republican Parties and future elections, 434–38; New Deal coalition, 435; Obama's coalition, 435–36
Mobile v. Bolden, 13, 14
Moran, Jim, 149
Morgan, Lewis Henry, 28
MSA. *See* Muslim Student Association
Multimember districts, challenges to, 13–16
Murkowski, Lisa, 54
Muslim American political incorporation and mobilization, 155–78; 2000 presidential election, 163–64; African American Muslims, 157–59, 161–65, 170, 180, 190; assimilationists, *160f*, 161; background, 155–57; conclusion, 170–71; Council on American Islamic Relations (CAIR), 163, 167–68; dearth of research on, 156; demographics, 159, 161–62, 165–67; differences between African American and immigrant American Muslims, 157–59; Ground Zero Mosque (Park 51), 170–71; historical integration of American Muslims, 157–59; integrationists, *160f*, 161–62; Islamophobia, 164–65; isolationists, 160–61, *160f*; "linked fate" (Dawson) and, 156; mosque as a catalyst for, 168–70; organizations/institutions, 162–63, 166–67; political incorporation/level of engagement, 159–62, *160f*;

post-9/11, 129, 135–36, 164–68, 170–71, 179; pre-9/11, 162–64; Salafi Muslims, 160–61; Zogby International's Muslim Americans in the Public Square (MAPS) project, 156–57, 165–66, 167. *See also* Arab American voters; Muslim Americans in Detroit

Muslim American Public Opinion Survey (MAPOS), 165, 169, 181, 182–86

Muslim Americans in Detroit, 179–201; acts of political participation by age, *184f*; acts of political participation by educational attainment, *185f*; acts of political participation by gender, *185f*; acts of political participation by generation, *186f*; background/immigrant and African American Muslims, 179–81; challenges to participation, 194–95; community, advocacy, and research organizations (building), 191; community outreach and interfaith efforts, 192–93; conclusion, 196–97; congressional districts (CDs), 189–90; Dearborn (suburb), 180, 187–90; demographics/surveys/MAPOS survey/MAPS survey, 181–84, *182f–86f*, 186, 187; evolution of types of participation, 186–93; immigrants from Greater Syria, 181; impact of participation, 195–96; Islamic teachings/compatibility with participation in politics, *183f*; issues of concern, 193–94; Muslim Student Associations (MSAs), 186–87; political organizations (building), 190–91; racial composition of Muslims in Michigan, *182t*; voting and running for office, 188–90. *See also* Arab American voters; Muslim American political incorporation and mobilization

Muslim Americans in the Public Square (MAPS). *See* Zogby International's Muslim Americans in the Public Square (MAPS) project

Muslim American voters. *See* Arab American voters; Muslim American political incorporation and mobilization; Muslim Americans in Detroit

Muslim Student Associations (MSAs), 162, 186–87

Naff, Alixa, 128
Nakonsky, Chrissy, 419–20
National Asian American Survey (NAAS), 239, 251, 289, 293, 350; "Behind the Numbers: Post-Election Survey of Asian American and Pacific Islander Voters in 2012," 364; "Opinions of Asian Americans and Pacific Islanders: Affordable Care Act," 364; "Public Opinion of a Growing Electorate: Asian Americans and Pacific Islanders in 2012," 255
National Center for Lesbian Rights in San Francisco, "Transgender Law Project," 416
National Center for Transgender Equality, 383–84
National Congress of American Indians, 27, 37, 37–38
National Gay and Lesbian Task Force: "Fight the Right" campaign, 375; Transgender Civil Rights Project, 416
National Gay and Lesbian Task Force Policy Institute's Black Pride Survey (2000), 411–12
National Indian Gaming Commission, 51
National Jewish Population Survey (NJPS), 62, 68
National Security Entry/Exit Registration System (NSEERS), 239–40
National Transgender Advocacy Coalition, 416

National Transgender Discrimination Survey (NTDS), 412, 421–22

Native American voters. *See* American Indian voters, history of voting rights; American Indian voting issues; Native American voters, sovereignty and treaty rights

Native American voters, sovereignty and treaty rights, 26–40; background, 26–27; clan mothers, 28; common context of colonialism, 29–30; confederacies, 27–28; Democratic Party and, 32–33; demographics, 33; Elk, John, 29–30; future of native political participation, 36–38; Gorton, Slade (senator) Amphitheatre debate and (Washington state), 34–36; historical precedents, 27–29; influence by state, 27; lobbying, 36–37; Obama, Barack and, 32; political participation and treaty rights, 30–33; Shannon County, South Dakota (Pine Ridge Reservation), 33–34; small numbers, large impact, 33–34

Native Hawaiian and Pacific Islander, NHPI voters. *See* Pacific Islander (Native Hawaiian and Pacific Islander, NHPI) voters

Native Vote (2012). *See* American Indian voting issues

New Jersey, Arab Americans in, 149

Nixon, Richard, 33

North Dakota, Democrat Heitkamp's win in, 42

Northern Marianas. *See* Guam and the Northern Marianas

Northwest Austin Municipal Utility District v. Holder, 17

Obama, Barack: Affordable Care Act and the American Recovery and Reinvestment, 280; Arab vote and, 132, 136–38, 164, 166, 167, 188–89; East Asian American vote and, 283; Jewish vote and, 86; marriage equality and, 392; Native American vote and, 32; Obama's coalition, 434–35, 435–36; South Asians Americans and, 243, 244; Trans United for Obama, 416

Obamacare. *See* Affordable Care Act and Patient Protection Act (2010)

"Obsession, Radical Islam's War against the West" (Islamophobic film), 137

"Opinions of Asian Americans and Pacific Islanders: Affordable Care Act" (NAAS), 364

Orthodox Jews, 75–77, 76*t*, 86, 111–12, 111*f*, 112*f*, 114, 115*t*, 116, 122

Ozawa v. United States, 205, 287–88

Pacific Islander (Native Hawaiian and Pacific Islander, NHPI) voters, 247–63; 2012 presidential election turnout, 251; American Samoa (historical context), 252–53; categorizing/group identities/ethnic groups recognized by the Census Bureau, 247; conclusion about voter engagement, 258–60; demographics by the Census Bureau, 247–48, 261*t*–62*t*; English-language proficiency, 250, 250*f*; Guam and the Northern Marianas (historical context), 251, 253–55; Hawaii (historical context), 251–52; issues, 255–56, 257*f*; key factors that affect the level of political participation, 249–51; "Opinions of Asian Americans and Pacific Islanders: Affordable Care Act" (NAAS), 364; in the San Francisco Bay Area, *310t*

Paine, Thomas, 29

Palin, Sara, 137

Partisanship. *See* Headings under specific minorities

Party identification/affiliation/partisanship. *See* Headings under specific minorities

Paschall, Patrick A., 372, 376, 408, 443

Pascrell, Bill, 138, 149

PATRIOT Act, 138, 140, 164, 166, 239
Pew Research 2012 Asian American Survey, 327. *See also* Korean American voters
Pew Research Center Survey of Jewish Americans (2013), 62, 112–16, *115t*, *117t*, *118t*, 119, 120, *121t*
Pew Research Center Surveys of Arab Americans, 156, 166–67
Pilot National Asian American Political Survey, 293
Pine Ridge Indian Reservation (SD), 33–34
Profiling: of Arab Americans, 140–43
"Public Opinion of a Growing Electorate: Asian Americans and Pacific Islanders in 2012" (NAAS), 255
Pupcenoks, Juris, 179, 443
Pursuing Power: Latinos and the Political System (Garcia), 155

Queer Nation, 381–82

Reagan, Ronald: 1980 election marked the end of the New Deal coalition, 435; HIV/AIDS and, 376
Religion, the mosque as a catalyst for political mobilization, 168–70
Religious Right, LGBT rights movement and, 391
Reno v. Bossier Parish, 17
Republican Party, minority voters and implications for future elections, 434–40. *See also* Headings under specific minorities
Rescission Acts, 279–80
Rice, Susan, 149
Robinson, Jennifer L., 3, 443
Romer v. Evans, 391
Romney, Mitt: Arab vote and, 132, 138
Roosevelt, Franklin D., New Deal coalition, 435
Rothman, Steve, 138
Ryan White Comprehensive AIDS Resource Emergency (CARE) Act (1990), 376

Salafi Muslims, 160–61
Sali, Bill, 242, 243
Same-sex marriage, 390–407; acknowledgments, 404; analysis and results for study, 395–403, *395f*, *396t–400t*, *401f–2f*; correlates of same-sex marriage support among LGBTs, *400t*; data/samples for study (Egan and Sherrill), 392, 394–95; Defense of Marriage Act (DOMA, 1996), 392; discussion, 403–4; historical background/court cases and legislation, 390–92; policy priorities of LGBTs by age cohort and year, *396t*; policy priorities of LGBTs by black identification and year, *397t*; policy priorities of LGBTs by gender and year, *398t*; policy priorities of LGBTs by partisanship by year, *399t*; political knowledge about same-sex marriage policy, *395f*; predicting same-sex marriage support by age, *401f*; predicting same-sex marriage support min-to-max effects, *402f*; shifting priorities of a new generation, 392–94. *See also* Lesbian, gay, bisexual, and transgender (LGBT) voters; Transgender voters
San Francisco Bay Area. *See* Asian Americans in the San Francisco Bay Area
Santa Clara County. *See* Asian Americans in the San Francisco Bay Area
Save Our Children Network, 374
Schattschneider, E.E., *The Semisovereign People*, 403
Seminole Tribe of Florida v. Florida, 53
The Semisovereign People (Schattschneider), 403
Senzai, Farid, 155, 179, 443–44
September 11, 2001 terrorist attacks: post-9/11 and South Asian Americans, 240, 241–42; post-9/11 Arab American voters and, 129, 135–36, 164–68, 170–71, 179; pre-9/11 Arab American voters and, 162–64

Sex assigned at birth, 409–10
Sexual orientations, 409–10
Shalala, Donna, 131
Shannon County, South Dakota (Pine Ridge Reservation), 33–34
Shelby County v. Holder, 12, 17
Shepard, Matthew, 417
Sherrill, Kenneth, 390, 392, 394–95, 444
Sheskin, Ira M., 61, 444
Simpson, Amanda, 418–19
South Asian Americans Leading Together, 244
South Asian American voters, 236–47; Asian American Legal Defense and Education Fund (AALDEF)'s exit polls, 238–39; background, 236–37; barriers to voting/court cases/legislation, 240–44; changes in population of voting age (2000–2010), 238t; changes in South Asian population (2000–2010), 237t; courting the new electorate/future for, 244–45; Democrat leaning, 239; demographics/identifying, 237–38, 237t–38t; first-time voters on rise, 238–39; Hamtramck, Michigan voting violations (1999) and, 240–41; language access and Section 203 of the Voting Rights Act, 241; National Asian American Survey (NAAS), 239; voter choice, 239–40; voting problems, 240–41; xenophobic political rhetoric, 241–44
South Carolina v. Katzenback, 12
Stone, Amy, 391, 393
Stonewall gay bar raid, 373
Stubben, Jerry American Indian survey, 45–46, 47t
Suburbs. *See* Asian Americans in the San Francisco Bay Area
Su, Phi Hong, 349, 444
Syrian refugees, 128, 149

Tablighi Jamaat Muslim group, 160
Tadlock, Barry L., 371, 444–45
Taiwanese Americans. *See* East Asian American voters
"Tea Party Republicans," 436–37
Tester, John, 54
Texas, Arab Americans in, 147
Thornburg v. Gingles, 15
Thune, John, 33
Tikkun olam (Hebrew for "repairing the world"), 84
Trade and Intercourse Acts (1790–1834), 4
Transgender American Veterans Association, 416
Transgender Civil Rights Project (National Gay and Lesbian Task Force), 416
"Transgender Law Project" (National Center for Lesbian Rights in San Francisco), 416
Transgender Legal Defense and Education Fund, 416
Transgender People of Color Coalition, 416
Transgender voters, 408–30; administrative barriers to voting, 420–23; black LGBT voters (Black Prides Survey, 2000), 411–12; conclusion, 426–27; definitions and terms, 371–72, 374, 376, 409–10; discrimination issues resulting in disenfranchisement and demographics of discrimination, 408–9, 413–15; historical background of transgender political activism/legislation/policy changes, 415–17; lack of data on the transgender community, 410–12; National Transgender Discrimination Survey (NTDS), 412; organizations for, 416–17; political parties and, 417–18; transgender political candidates, 418–20; voter identification and, 377; voter ID requirements, 423–26. *See also* Lesbian, gay, bisexual, and transgender (LGBT) voters; Same-sex marriage
"Transphobic image," 378
Transsexuals, 372, 409
Trans United for Obama, 416
Treaty rights. *See* Native American voters, sovereignty and treaty rights

Tribal Law and Order Act (2010, TLOA), 42, 48
Two-spirit, First Nations term for homosexuals, 372
Tzedakah (Hebrew for "justice"), 84

United States Census, 327. *See also* Korean American voters
United States v. Thind, 205–6
United States v. Washington, 30
United States v. Wong Kim Ark, 206, 288
U.S. v. Bhagat Singh Thind, 240

Vaid, Urvashi, *Virtual Equality*, 380, 382
Vietnamese American voters, 349–68; background, 349–50; bivariate statistics—demographic characteristics by nativity and waves of immigration, 357, *358t*; bivariate statistics—political incorporation outcomes by waves and generation, 357, 359, *359t*; data sets used for study (CPS and NAAS), 350; discussion/conclusion/issue trends/future research, 362–67, *363t*; elections of politicians Tran, Vo, and Cao, 349; exit and reception contexts, 351–53; hypothesis, 356–57; model 1. citizenship, 350, 360, *361t*; model 2. registration, 350, 360–62, *361t*; model 3. voting, 350, *361t*, 361–62; multivariate statistics—predictors of political incorporation outcomes, 360–62, *361t*; native-born, *358t–59t*, *361t*, *363t*; participation stages (citizenship, registration, turnout), 350; political incorporation, 350–51; pre-1975 immigrants, 353, *358t–59t*, *363t*; stereotypes of immigrants, 349; wave 1. asylum and post hoc legislation (1975–1979), 354, *358t–59t*, *363t*; wave 2. standardization and orderly departure (1980–1994), 354–55, *358t–59t*, *361t*, *363t*; wave 3. after ODP (1995–present), 355–56, *358t–59t*, *361t*, *363t*; waves, background/defining, 353
Violence Against Women Act, 42, 47
Violence Against Women Reauthorization Act (2013), 417
Virginia, Arab Americans in, 149
Virtual Equality (Vaid), 380, 382
Vote dilution, 14–15
Voter intimidation/disenfranchisement. *See* Headings under specific minorities
Voter News Service (VNS), 219
Voting and Registration Supplement to the Current Population Survey, 350
Voting Rights Act (1965), 3; amendments to, 13–17; permanent and temporary provisions of, 17; sections important to American Indian voting rights, 11–12, 15, 17. *See also* American Indian voters, history of voting rights
Voting Rights Act, Language Assistance Provisions of the Voting Rights Act (Section 203), 16, 135, 208–9, 212, 214–18, 241, 332

Washington State, Arab Americans in, 148
White v. Regester, 12–14
Williams Institute, 379
Witmer, Richard C., 41, 445
Worcester v. Georgia, 5
Workmen's Circle/Arbeter Ring 2012 American Jews' Political Values Survey, 87

Xenophobic political rhetoric, South Asian Americans and, 241–44

Zimmer v. McKeithen, 13, 14
Zogby International's Muslim Americans in the Public Square (MAPS) project, 156–57, 165–66, 167, 187